Dictionary of Literary Biography • Volume Fourteen

British Novelists
Since 1960

Part 1: A-G

Dictionary of Literary Biography

1: *The American Renaissance in New England*, edited by Joel Myerson (1978)

2: *American Novelists Since World War II*, edited by Jeffrey Helterman and Richard Layman (1978)

3: *Antebellum Writers in New York and the South*, edited by Joel Myerson (1979)

4: *American Writers in Paris, 1920-1939*, edited by Karen Lane Rood (1980)

5: *American Poets Since World War II*, 2 volumes, edited by Donald J. Greiner (1980)

6: *American Novelists Since World War II*, Second Series, edited by James E. Kibler, Jr. (1980)

7: *Twentieth-Century American Dramatists*, 2 volumes, edited by John MacNicholas (1981)

8: *Twentieth-Century American Science-Fiction Writers*, 2 volumes, edited by David Cowart and Thomas L. Wymer (1981)

9: *American Novelists, 1910-1945*, 3 volumes, edited by James J. Martine (1981)

10: *Modern British Dramatists, 1900-1945*, 2 volumes, edited by Stanley Weintraub (1982)

11: *American Humorists, 1800-1950*, 2 volumes, edited by Stanley Trachtenberg (1982)

12: *American Realists and Naturalists*, edited by Donald Pizer and Earl N. Harbert (1982)

13: *British Dramatists Since World War II*, 2 volumes, edited by Stanley Weintraub (1982)

14: *British Novelists Since 1960*, 2 volumes, edited by Jay L. Halio (1983)

Yearbook: 1980, edited by Karen L. Rood, Jean W. Ross, and Richard Ziegfeld (1981)

Yearbook: 1981, edited by Karen L. Rood, Jean W. Ross, and Richard Ziegfeld (1982)

Documentary Series, volume 1, edited by Margaret A. Van Antwerp (1982)

Documentary Series, volume 2, edited by Margaret A. Van Antwerp (1982)

Documentary Series, volume 3, edited by Mary Bruccoli (1983)

Dictionary of Literary Biography • Volume Fourteen

British Novelists Since 1960

Part 1: A-G

Edited by Jay L. Halio
University of Delaware

Foreword by Malcolm Bradbury

A Bruccoli Clark Book
Gale Research Company • Book Tower • Detroit, Michigan 48226
1983

Manufactured by Braun-Brumfield, Inc.
Ann Arbor, Michigan
Printed in the United States of America

Library of Congress Cataloging in Publication Data

Main entry under title:

British novelists since 1960.

   (Dictionary of literary biography; v. 14)
   "A Bruccoli Clark book."
   Contents: pt. 1. A-G
   1. English fiction—20th century—Bio-bibliography.
2. Novelists, English—20th century—Biography—Dictionaries.
I. Halio, Jay L. II. Series.
PR881.B73   823'.914'09 [B]   82-2977
ISBN 0-8103-0927-0 (pt. 1)   AACR2

For June

Contents

Contents

Foreword

Despite the funeral sermons that have been constantly pronounced over its death, the novel has probably never been more various, more interesting, more inventive, or more international in its sources and its scopes than today. It can count among its best stylistic citizens Günter Grass and Peter Handke, Italo Calvino and Max Frisch, Saul Bellow, Bernard Malamud and Norman Mailer, Samuel Beckett and John Fowles, Thomas Pynchon, John Hawkes and Robert Coover, Doris Lessing, Muriel Spark and Iris Murdoch, Alain Robbe-Grillet, Claude Simon and Nathalie Sarraute, Jorge Luis Borges, Marquez and Cortazar, V. S. Naipaul and Patrick White, and many, many more. Anyone who seeks a definition of its primary characteristics must therefore wander over a wide range of stylistic assumptions, a wide range of countries and continents, and a massive intermixture of generations. Our "style" now stretches from, say, the fictionalist and fabulatory worlds of Italo Calvino, through John Barth's modernizations of the narrative stock bequeathed to us by old acts of narration, to Donald Barthelme's narrative fragments, scraps of story running away into their own incompleteness; from Raymond Queneau's parodies, which turn writing into an endless multiplication of texts, through Angus Wilson's high mimicry, to John Fowles's pastiche of nineteenth-century realism practiced by a writer who articulates himself as the stylistic contemporary of Roland Barthes; from William Burroughs's cut-up, fold-in method of composition, through the intense psychofantasies of John Hawkes, to the exposed modern consciousness of Norman Mailer's psychohistorical fiction; from the hard text of Peter Handke to the softer subjective confession of Sylvia Plath or the decomposed male cry of Philip Roth. It is a scene of enormous variety and formal promiscuity, and to venture into it as a critic is to enter a world of contention and confusion from which no easy deductions may be drawn.

Nonetheless, if this is a vigorous creative age, it is also a vigorous critical one, and the critics try. There are perhaps two main ways of trying to look at the various scene and define its character and characteristics. One is to take the strong-minded view that fiction at the end of the twentieth century is indeed marked by a discernible tendency, a dominant style, one which has been constituted from the hesitations of our philosophy, the displacement of the human subject from the text, the severance of the signifier from the signified. Certainly the late twentieth-century novel has questioned and redefined itself, and with effort we may see the intellectual direction behind all this and aspire to an adequate definition. The traditional lineage and character of the novel have been doubted, and the realisms of the nineteenth century have suffered serious challenge; so, too, have the experiments of the early twentieth century, which themselves radicalized the novel and questioned its realism. We have found a name for this earlier questioning, which is Modernism; it might therefore be appropriate to characterize the contemporary experiment as Postmodernism. As for its character itself, we might define that from certain primary experimental tendencies—the *noveau roman* in France, the "metafiction" of a significant number of American novelists of the 1960s and 1970s, the "magical realism" of certain Latin American authors, and so on. A relevant way into the new style might then be to see behind it a history, a larger *episteme*, in which language itself has become displaced, in which a new nominalism prevails, in which the old referentiality of the novel, and its possible substitutes in structures of coherent form, have alike collapsed. We may see a movement toward a provisional text, generated not by attentiveness to "character," formal design, or elicited codes of value or sympathy, but by the rhythm of composition itself, authenticating the lexical performance, in which the alliance of writer and reader, pen and page, an "about" and a "not-about," becomes the manipulable matter of fiction. So there is a new text, post-realist and postmodernist; and a new critic, probably poststructuralist, who understands it.

The other view of the contemporary novel is rather more open, and to my taste preferable. It supposes that the novel has always been a plural form, and has long functioned across the spectrum from realism and referentiality to self-questioning and fictionalist awareness. It sees these elements as in constant change, and under historical pressures, but it recognizes the infinite variousness of the possible outcomes. It sees the power of Modernism in twentieth-century writing, but also observes much writing that was modern without being modernist. In our own times, it recognizes certain clear directions, but some toward the fracturing of traditional forms and narrative practices, some toward their recreation and reconstitution. It might take as an appropriate image André Malraux's evocation of the *musée imaginaire* in which we live; for we live indeed in a polyglot time when, thanks to modern mechanical methods of storage, transmission, and translation, thanks to the weakening of nationalism and the breaking of strong cultural frontiers, most of the styles of past and present seem available to us simultaneously. Our age might then be seen as one of extraordinary stylistic profusion, a time of stylistic melting pot in which some styles and forms seem to be the derivatives of national tradition, others come from far distant cultures, some come from our perplexing relation to the past, some from our own urgent presentness. In this case it would be harder to distinguish one line or type of experiment as *the* central line, and critical eclecticism rather than critical certainty would be the best approach to contemporary writing.

But if there is evidence of great creative vitality and invention in the novel now, then where in it does the contemporary British novel stand? Certainly it does not seem to stand very high in terms of critical attention. Indeed for most critics contemporary English fiction still appears to mean that crucial period from about the turn of the century to 1941, when both James Joyce and Virginia Woolf died, the period of the late James, of Conrad, Lawrence, Ford Madox Ford, Wyndham Lewis, James Joyce, Katherine Mansfield, and Virginia Woolf. This indeed is the period of Modernism, the period in which the once densely narrative, insistently realist, firmly chronological and historiographical species called the novel transformed itself into a new art of consciousness and form in a period of remarkable innovation and internationalism. It is a period in which the British novel retained an international significance in the onward development of the form, but the period since its decline or disappearance has been a vague one. It is indeed commonplace now to assume that the innovative impetus passed elsewhere, into French fiction, American fiction, Latin-American fiction, while at the same time the British novel, like the British empire, retreated, backward into the tradition, toward the spirit of nineteenth-century fiction, toward a liter-

ary provinciality. To many eyes, its works seem not to have paralleled those of major writers in other countries, and though there are notable talents—Iris Murdoch, William Golding, Doris Lessing, Anthony Burgess, Angus Wilson, John Fowles, and others—the sense of the weakening and withdrawal of British fiction has been widely felt and has become, indeed, a critical cliche.

This, certainly, has been the drift of most of such criticism as has been devoted to the subject. One of the few general studies of the postwar British novel, by R. Rabinowitz, has the title *The Reaction Against Experiment in the English Novel, 1950-1960* (1967), and indeed documents a mood of withdrawal from Modernism among British novelists; Bernard Bergonzi, in *The Situation of the Novel* (1970), declares the contemporary British novel "no longer novel." There is sufficient truth in these views of an English novel disposed to turn toward the novel's nineteenth- or eighteenth-century sources, to deal with local or national subjects, to maintain a social curiosity and a sense of the dominant reality of the exterior world, to be a characterization of at least one part of the impulse behind postwar British writing. At the same time, however, the fuller and more up-to-date story has been little documented. Few British critics have concerned themselves with the contemporary novel; most, indeed, teach in universities where contemporary literature is very rarely taught, and where the attitude to writers is often close to that said to have been felt by the U. S. Cavalry toward Indians: the only good one is a dead one. Most British fictional reputations are in fact no longer made in Britain at all, but elsewhere, in Europe or in the United States. The result is an absence of intellectual and aesthetic debate surrounding British fiction which may well be associated with its questionable condition: "The most discouraging thing about writing novels, I should think, for a young novelist in this country," said novelist David Storey in an interview explaining his preference for writing plays, "is the fact that they have no importance, I mean they have no intellectual currency."

The gloom, then, spreads to the writers themselves. Thus, in a symposium on "The State of Fiction" organized in the (alas) final issue of the literary magazine the *New Review*, a variety of novelists indicated their aesthetic and also their commercial doubts about the current state of the novel in Britain, and many found the larger excitements in fiction elsewhere. More directly a recent issue of the Cambridge-based magazine *Granta* was devoted gloomily to "The End of the English Novel." For the apparent malaise, many reasons have been offered: the conservatism of British publishers, the parallel conservatism and also the brevity of the British reviewers, the high cost of books, the domination of library borrowing, the insufficiency of bookshops, the indifference of readers toward new fiction, the lack of adequate financial support for British writers, and the powerful claims exerted by alternative media—a vital theater, a vigorous television drama—drawing new talents into other forms. The conditions for the writing of serious fiction in Britain have never been ideal, but in a time of inflation, publishing commercialism, and a generally poor economy they have become less so. Yet the gloom seems to me to conceal a scene far more various and interesting than is often assumed, just as the critical emphasis on the conservatism of British fiction obscures a scene far more inventive than is often assumed.

The result is that in my view the postwar British novel has had a period of under-observed vitality and change, unrecognized in the standard histories. The maps drawn in the 1950s of the postwar novel still seem to be doing sterling service, despite the fact that British fiction has changed radically since then, and they were provisional at the time. The aim of my comments is therefore to try to draw new ones—no less provisional in their way, as is proper with contemporary writing, but looking at the scene rather more expansively than most of the known records seem to do. I write as someone who has himself been producing fiction over, more or less, the period from the 1950s which I wish to observe, a period of very considerable change in fiction which I sense in experience and which I hope these views will lay a little more open, just as the rest of this book will cover the broad range of talents at work and explore their very various characteristics, qualities and concerns. My view is that, just as most contemporary fictional experiment has come from the inner debates of national lineages as well as from a new formal mood, so such a debate and a re-exploration of the novel have gone on within the British tradition. One national fictional tradition never quite meshes with another; apparently similar fictional experiment does not in fact arise in different countries from like premises. But there has been a cycle of change in British fiction not unrelated to that elsewhere, among older novelists who have sustained their careers at a level of complexity and formal awareness, and among younger writers still just coming to notice.

Most histories of the contemporary novel start with World War II, for a simple reason; in most fictional traditions, as in the historical world beyond, the war was a fundamental watershed, destroying the structure of many European nations, altering the map of global power, shifting the ideological direction of the century, changing all its forms of expression. Old social, industrial, and economic structures crumbled, old cultural frontiers altered and old alliances broke, old faiths and ideological commitments were rescinded and new ones begun. The war ushered in a new era of anxiety that was dominated by holocaust and atomic and political fear. It divided the changed world between two principles—of Communist collectivism and capitalist individualism—which developed into a global conflict between two new superpowers. The liberal values that had been summoned to justify the fight against Fascism now seemed under threat again, and they encountered a world that now seemed historically bloodied in new ways: by revelations about genocide, by fears of global annihilation. The sense of historical transition was felt in most countries and expressed in most arts; Britain was no exception. The nation emerged from the war undefeated, a victor, but nonetheless depleted; its imperial role was waning, the economy was drained and close to collapse, and the social system of the 1930s, and the social ideologies that arose from it, now seemed deeply in question. Indeed Britain was, as the war ended, passing through a quiet but nonetheless real social revolution, a shifting of social power and political values marked by the coming of the new Welfare State and the election in 1945 of a Labour government committed to change. Intellectual doubts and guilts raged; as in the United States, the postwar period saw the uncertain reemergence of a new, anxious, self-critical liberalism, guilty about its own revolutionary allegiances during the 1930s, conscious of a rising new threat from totalitarianism as Russia secured its westward boundaries through dominating the eastern European countries, conscious of the continuing threat to democracy. Yet it was a liberalism challenged in its rational hopes and its political expectations, marked as much by its own doubt as by any certainties about the possibilities afforded by the postwar future.

It thus found itself at some distance from the Modernism of the earlier part of the century, as well as from the social and political realisms of the 1930s. The Modernist era indeed seemed over, its closure marked by the deaths of Virginia Woolf and James Joyce in 1941, and critics began to search for the evidence of a new literary generation who would express the changed spirit of the times. A number of important writers from the 1920s and 1930s continued to write, including Ivy Compton-Burnett, Evelyn Waugh, Aldous Huxley, Graham Greene, Christopher Isherwood, C. P. Snow, Anthony Powell, and George Orwell, and some had considerable influence on their successors when they came. Some of these writers, like Orwell and Waugh, displayed a distinct change in fictional direction before the anxious new postwar world; others, like Greene and Isherwood, continued to explore the sense of historical disorder, moral indirection, and existential exposure they had already perceived; still others, like Ivy Compton-Burnett, maintained a stylish refusal to change fictional subject and manner; yet others, like Forster and Orwell, had a direct influence on the new anxious liberal mood—a mood that linked with the "new liberalism" of the United States and with the existential and absurdist tendencies in France. But if Modernism seemed to lapse, there were some writers from the 1930s who provided an experimental continuity. One was Samuel Beckett, who could hardly be claimed as a British writer, since he was an Irishman living in Paris and now writing in French. Yet he displayed the continuity on from Joyce, and the trilogy on which he worked between 1947 and 1950, appearing in English as *Molloy* (1951), *Malone Dies* (1952) and *The Unnamable* (1953), represented an extraordinary fusion of reflexive fictional skepticism and postexistentialist absurdism, and it was to have a continuing if oblique influence on many younger English writers. In 1947 appeared one of the most extraordinary of postwar British novels, Malcolm Lowry's *Under the Volcano*, a work of internationalist experimental ambitions. Lowry had published before the war, and *Under the Volcano*, set before it, seemed at the time largely a parable of the historical collapse of Europe under Nazism; this and the fact that Lowry was living in Canada perhaps made British readers slow to see it as the remarkable expressionist work it is.

Yet, as in other countries, the dominant mood of the young writers who now began to emerge in significant numbers during the late 1940s and early 1950s, when many of the leading reputations of today began, was indeed one of withdrawal from Modernist experiment and toward an engagement with the historical and the social world. Virginia Woolf had, before the war, expressed in her essay "The Leaning Tower" her own feeling that fiction should consciously reconcern itself with social and political issues. This seemed to be the direction pointed by Angus Wilson, who came startlingly into notice with two striking volumes of satirical short

stories, *The Wrong Set* (1949) and *Such Darling Dodos* (1950), stories about a postwar world in which a once dominant bourgeoisie found itself displaced by a new, liberal social change. But the voice of Wilson's liberalism is complex and ambiguous: the new world of bureaucracy and managers, of the new England placed on top of the old, was to become the basis of strain and ambiguity in his work as it developed to novel size in *Hemlock and After* (1952), about the problems of the liberal-creative conscience in such a world, and to large, socially panoramic novels like *Anglo-Saxon Attitudes* (1956), much influenced by the novels of Charles Dickens, on whom Wilson wrote a brilliant book. Wilson's revival of the Victorian sources of the novel was matched by William Cooper's return to the middle ground of fiction in *Scenes from Provincial Life* (1950), which takes its title from George Eliot and which deliberately deals with the provincial, commonplace and ordinary world in a dangerous historical time, the months before the outbreak of World War II, avoiding the conventional upper-middle-class and metropolitan subjects of much British fiction. It began a sequence of novels which were set in British provincial life and were written from lower-middle-class or working-class viewpoints, reflecting the social change that had been reshaping British life over the years following the war.

To this extent, the reaction against Modernism was complicated by social factors; it was also a revolt against "Bloomsbury," the upper-middle-class metropolitan intelligentsia who had seemed to date to dominate English writing, and of whom Virginia Woolf was held to be representative. There was a return to nativism and provincialism both as a subject matter and as a source of value—a return accompanied by a rejection of elaborate artistic pretensions and an insistence on the realistic function of the novel and its place as a social form. "We had our own reasons for being impatient," Cooper was later to explain. "We meant to write a different kind of novel from that of the Thirties and we saw that the Thirties novel, the Experimental Novel, had got to be brushed out of the way before we could get a proper hearing." And indeed *Scenes from Provincial Life* helped set the tone for a sequence of novels which were to explore class and classlessness, the anxious separation of self from society, the need for purposive realism. In John Wain's *Hurry on Down* (1953), Kingsley Amis's *Lucky Jim* (1954), Iris Murdoch's *Under the Net* (1954), John Braine's *Room at the Top* (1957), Alan Sillitoe's *Saturday Night and Sunday Morning* (1958) and David Storey's *This*

Sporting Life (1960) the critics read the signs of a new movement of fiction, the fiction of the "Angry Young Men," a tendency of dissenting realism where the heroes are frequently "outsider" figures ostensibly at odds with the prevailing social system, though frequently they adapt to its claims in the end, for they are precisely the claims of ordinariness and commonsense empiricism on which these novels depend. Hence the books tend to move, with whatever doubts or ironies, toward civilization and acceptance of moral duty, of marriage and social promotion, of empirical satisfactions. Discontent was real but modest, as is indicated in the title of Kingsley Amis's *I Like It Here* (1958), for "here" is England and the book has a note of provincial retraction from "abroad," from expatriate experimentalism and foreign influence. And as Wilson explicitly amends the Dickensian tradition, and Cooper the Eliot tradition, so Amis acknowledges and amends the tradition of comic realism in eighteenth-century British fiction exemplified in Henry Fielding. In their realism and liberalism, their concern with manners and morals, these books do (either implicitly or explicitly) acknowledge the renewability of the great tradition of fiction and the capability of mimetic forms. The postwar renewal of fiction seemed to lie in the recovery of sources and pretexts deep in the national tradition, and Modernism appeared now to have been a temporary disturbance or dislocation which could be set aside or used on occasion.

During the 1950s it seemed that this return to realism and the tradition was to be the direction of the British novel. Yet the dominance of this trend was to be greatly exaggerated. For the decade saw the appearance of other works which suggested alternative directions for the novel and offered quite other emphases. With *Lord of the Flies* (1954) William Golding offered a major work in the line of what Robert Scholes has called "fabulation"; Lawrence Durrell's *Alexandria Quartet* (*Justine*, 1957; *Balthazar*, 1958; *Mountolive*, 1958; *Clea*, 1960), a complex sequence of mirror novels narrated by multiple voices reflecting and refracting the Freudian intersections of the story, is a work of experimental fantasy. What is more, the term "angry young men," a reviewer's convenience, baggaged together a group of new writers of apparently naturalist inclination many of whom quickly broke from the frame in which their first works were perceived. Angus Wilson, David Storey, Muriel Spark, Anthony Burgess, and Doris Lessing were all to prove, as their work developed, very doubtful realists. In some cases they were from the start: Iris Murdoch was certainly not angry and certainly not a man, and her first novel, *Under the Net* (read as an "angry" book because its hero is a detached drifter, an "outsider") is in fact a philosophical-surrealist text dedicated to Raymond Queneau, influenced by Beckett and Sartre, and alluding in its title to Wittgenstein. The recovery of a liberal realism was an important feature of British writing of the 1950s; indeed it parallels the development of the existential-realist novel in France, in writers like Sartre and Camus, and the Jewish moral realism of American writers like Bellow and Malamud. It refocused the debate of British fiction and it had important implications for a whole generation of novelists whose work was to develop through it but often away from it. But a recovery of liberal realism was never the only tendency, and many of the best writers were to oscillate between it and the claims of a more reflexive and fantastic view of the novel.

This has been apparent in the subsequent development of the best of these writers. Some stayed within the confines of comic realism or a social naturalism; in any event, these have proved the least interesting. But far more important have been those writers whose works have moved away from the mood of empiricism and provincialism that was part of the equation. A significant example is Angus Wilson, whose later work turned firmly against the forms with which his earlier work had been associated. The fantastic and the grotesque had always been part of his writing; his later work has transformed his subject. Thus *No Laughing Matter* (1967) is a radical pastiche of his earlier work, taking the form of the Galsworthyan bourgeois novel, the panoramic novel of class, history and family, but undercutting its structure through telling the story not from a firm base of realism but through imitating and parodying the discourse of other writers; the book's dominant image is that of the distorting system of mirrors in which, in the opening scene, members of the central family see themselves as mirrors which multiply, distort, parody, and challenge identity. *As If by Magic* (1973) parodies the provincialism of 1950s fiction and moves on to become an international, indeed a global, novel largely set in the Third World. Anthony Burgess's work moved from the relative realism of his early works toward the complex lexical and musical codes of works like *MF* (1971) and the ebullient mixture of pastiche and moral anxiety of *Earthly Powers* (1980). Doris Lessing's work began in moral and political realism, but this realism dissolves into the complex anxieties and the multiple texts of *The Golden Notebook* (1962), a remarkable novel which attempts to display the means by which we displace realities into the instructive formal falsehoods of art, seeking to constitute a new reality; the path has led her forward into the science-fantasy of her most recent work.

Thus the realistic, liberal revival of the 1950s now must seem the starting point for a generation of writers the best of whom have taken the British novel off into a variety of experimental directions, fictionalist or fantastic, directions which have challenged and reconstituted the mimetic constituents of fiction while not dismissing its realistic sources entirely. Iris Murdoch was indeed never a conventional realist; but she has written seriously of the need for realism in the novel, celebrating the great Russian writers, and above all Tolstoy, for whom a sense of life's contingency prevents the novel's ever becoming a crystalline and self-functioning formal object. Yet her own work has strong formal desires and a powerful aspect of fantasy; more recently it has become a speculative theater in which the mystery of art's making has been explored, its platonic displacements considered, the role of the artist and the imagination exactingly explored, and late novels like *The Sea, The Sea* (1978) turn on the late Shakespearean analogy to reflect on art's deceit and its power. Similar transitions have shaped the writing of Muriel Spark, whose work has always explored the fictional ironies. Her first novel, *The Comforters* (1957), was already a piece of fictionalist self-questioning, a Catholic novel in which the analogy between God and the novelist is explored, and one character persistently objects to her presence within the author's text and plot. The theme becomes sharpest in her work of the late 1960s and early 1970s, notably *The Public Image* (1968), *The Driver's Seat* (1970), and *Not to Disturb* (1971), texts of very precise economy, short, often present-tense, tightly plotted, end-directed, with a powerful authorial presence but an obsessed inner speculation about the rights of an author over her invention, so that characters may quarrel with the novelist over who possesses the driver's seat. Her text, laying its causalities bare, becomes a hard presence; there is a profitable analogy with the *nouveau roman*, save that Spark has an implicitly religious-absurdist view of the world. In much of this writing, the discourse of social and moral realism becomes a text to be reexamined, tested in many of its essential presumptions, so that we ask again what a book is, what a plot, what an ending, what a character. And that retextualizing of realism becomes a dominant theme in the rising experimental inquiry that runs through the best British fiction of the 1960s.

This rising mood of experiment and textual inquiry clearly has analogies with developments in the novel which were taking place elsewhere. The French *nouveau roman* began to be discussed from about 1953; the fictionalist inquiry in the American novel developed during the 1950s under the influence, particularly, of Nabokov and Borges, and extended and intensified during the 1960s and 1970s. Each tradition emphasized some features of contemporary fictional possibility over others, and each was deeply shaped by the national tradition in which it arose. The French *nouveau roman* was greatly conditioned by the belief that the French novel has changed little since Flaubert, and certain of its developments, in the work of Nathalie Sarraute and Claude Simon, for example, would not seem entirely novel to a writer trained in the tradition of Joyce, Gertrude Stein, or Virginia Woolf. Modern American writing owes much to the way American novelists earlier in the century adopted naturalism and turned it into a sociological, biological and psychological exploration, and then penetrated this with Modernism; the naturalist imprint still lies behind much of the postmodernist work of writers like Pynchon. The English novel was largely stabilized in the nineteenth century through a commitment to liberal realism attentive to the double historiography of personal moral mobility and historical growth; much of this commitment persisted through British modernism and, as the fiction of the 1950s showed, was capable of renewal. It was this tradition that began to be questioned and challenged by writers like Wilson, Lessing, Spark, Murdoch, Burgess and others as their work developed. In part this challenge might be read as a matter of personal development, but it also coincided with a climate of change; the developments of British fiction in the 1960s relate to, but are not identical with, those in other fictional traditions in the decade. They show a new attitude toward the constituents of a fiction; a new obsession with the status of a text, or the nature of a plot, or the substance of a character, or the sense of an ending. But what they amend is the social and moral consensus of fiction in the 1950s, and many of the humanistic and mimetic elements of that fiction remain as powers.

This is perhaps best exemplified in the work of one of the best novelists to emerge during the 1960s, John Fowles. Fowles's first book, *The Collector*, appeared in 1963; his second, *The Magus*, about the forgery and power of art, came out in 1965, with a revised edition in 1977. The first two display a fascination with the pursuit of the enigmatic symbol and the problem of the relation between the historical and the formal world; this is what is condensed in his next novel, *The French Lieutenant's Woman* (1969), a key book of the 1960s. It is a novel which takes the text of realist and narratively powerful Victorian fiction and plays across it the narrative doubts of an author who locates himself as a contemporary of Robbe-Grillet and Roland Barthes; the result is a superb pastiche of Victorian fiction, telling one of the age's archetypal fables and using the manners and types of Victorian narrative, which also intrudes upon itself, ushering in its own modern author as forger and as intellectual. The plot itself deals with historical evolution, and part of that evolution itself suggests the powers which generate fictional change and a modern notation in the novel. The book first moves toward a realist or liberal ending where the social order is restored, then retracts it, and moves toward two more endings in which an existential world-view opens up through the independence of the central female character, bringing the book to two more endings, set in the decadent spaces of an artist's studio, where the characters have the opportunity to emerge as modern figures, free of the narrative authority of the author. The final two endings, left open to the reader, in fact emphasize not so much the fictionality of the text as the emergence of the characters into imaginative independence; in this sense the book ends on a note of existentialist humanism rather than of pure textuality.

Fowles's endeavor to set his characters "free" indeed bears some resemblance to similar attempts by other contemporary British writers. Muriel Spark thus insists on the ordinances of *her* text, but occasionally offers her characters the rights of struggle and even of grace, the freedom to choose not the ending but the way to it. Iris Murdoch, for all the patterned rituals of her novels, seeks a novel form that will be "a fit house for free characters to live in." And one distinguishing feature of many of the more experimental fictions of the 1960s is the desire to recover for the novel a humanist authenticity—a realm of moral, political or social truth which permits an element of realism to remain. Fowles's ambiguous text—poised somewhere between realism and antirealism, between serious engagement in the novel's narrative momentum and a parodic detachment from it, between a strong sense of narrative authority and a sense of its onerous and counterfeit nature—seems somewhere near the middle ground of the more interesting British fiction of the 1960s. The tone was rather a questioning than a total disavowal of realism: Lessing's *Golden Notebook* is thus an exploration of the difficulties of

attaining to any structure of truth, but not a disavowal of reality. The young novelist B. S. Johnson, whose tragically early death cut off a remarkable career, beginning with *Travelling People* (1963), in which he explicitly confessed an experimental debt to the work of Laurence Sterne, went on in his later novels to use elaborate techniques exploiting the book-as-object (novels in boxes, holes in the page) to defeat the lie of fiction. His books show an intense anxiety about the relationship between autobiographical and personal truth and fiction's play, a concern that reached its finest balance in *See the Old Lady Decently* (1975), the first volume of a trilogy that his death left incomplete.

The 1960s indeed also saw some experimental texts which insisted most emphatically on their own textuality, some of these very explicitly influenced by the *nouveau roman* in France; there is thus the notable work of Ann Quin (*Berg*, 1964), Christine Brooke-Rose (*Out*, 1964, and *Between*, 1968), and Gabriel Josipovici (*The Inventory*, 1968). But more commonly the experimental methods were used to reach toward a new realism. Thus Alan Burns in *Babel* (1969) uses—as he noted in Giles Gordon's anthology *Beyond the Words* (1975)—"the cut-up method," but with a clear intention to explore "the network of manipulations that envelopes the citizens and makes them unaware accomplices in the theft of their liberty," the end being to produce a documentary immediacy. Similarly David Lodge's novel *The British Museum Is Falling Down* (1965) marvelously parodies the literary texts of others, but against a realistic base that insists on the referential world to which fiction alludes. In this process the laws of realism are challenged but not overthrown; hence these are not quite the "metatexts" that have been found in contemporary French and American writing. Rather they are experimental mediations between the liberal realist novel and new forms, works in which fictional invention and fantasy are released on new levels.

I am suggesting the growing presence during the 1960s of a new reflexive spirit, a new speculation about the constituents of fiction and the status of its form, which has altered the direction of postwar British writing, and which has changed the mood of the novel perhaps most notably by releasing in younger British writers a greater sense of fictional freedom and a greater inclination toward fantasy. Its effects have shown remarkably in the more open mood of the British novel of the 1970s, a period hard to draw into focus not solely because many of its important authors are still young but because the directions taken are very broad. A vastly more imaginative use of historical material showed itself in the notable novels of J. G. Farrell, who, in *Troubles* (1970), *The Siege of Krishnapur* (1973) and *The Singapore Grip* (1978) created a trilogy of enormous power relating historical detail to an intense symbolism. John Berger's *G* (1972) is likewise an extraordinary historical recreation, using a modernized version of the Don Juan legend, of the early twentieth-century European world, which reaches out toward fantasy. In the novels of Beryl Bainbridge, like *The Dressmaker* (1973) and *Injury Time* (1977), an apparently real world is minimalized and then drawn into grotesquerie. Fantasy has merged with realism from the other direction: writers like Michael Moorcock and J. G. Ballard, whose work began in science fiction, have brought characteristic invention into play with more familiar worlds in works like Moorcock's *The Condition of Muzak* (1977) or Ballard's *High-Rise* (1975). The classic dissolutions of fantasy, the breakings of identity, the surprises of unfamiliarity, the losses of signification, the admission of unconscious forces, have increasingly become the material of British fiction, playing against the traditional definiteness of realistic writing.

And this seems to be the broad direction of the writers who have continued to change the climate of British fiction during the decade of the 1970s: writers like Angela Carter, Emma Tennant, Elaine Feinstein, Robert Nye, Martin Amis, Ian McEwan and Clive Sinclair. In Amis and McEwan the landscape of modern society and sexual relationships turn into grotesquerie; in the recent stories of Angela Carter, the laws of traditional fairy story are reemployed to admit psychic feminist myth (*The Bloody Chamber*, 1979). D. M. Thomas's *The White Hotel* (1981) extraordinarily reconverts a Freudian psychotherapy (Freud is a central figure in the book) into a deep twentieth-century historical fable, using the language of letters, poetry, myth and fantasy. Where, in the 1950s, it seemed possible to characterize a dominant tendency in British fiction, and in that tendency to find a return to tradition and to nationality, the task is vastly harder today. The tradition has grown free and various; many of the best writers we associate with British fiction are—like Ruth Prawer Jhabvala (*Heat and Dust*, 1975), Anita Desai (*Clear Light of Day*, 1980), or Salman Rushdie (*Midnight's Children*, 1981)—British neither by birth nor subject. A good deal of this writing is clearly deeply influenced by contemporary international tendencies and contains among its bulk much that is genuinely experimental. Though critics may despair at the state of the novel, and writers at the critics and the insufficiencies of the market, I can only observe—as one whose business it has been recently to read some seventy new British novels submitted for the Booker-McConnell Fiction prize—a vigor and talent among younger British writers which points less to the end of the British novel than to a new period of expansion and possibility. In the end the task of the novelist is to free us from our previous critical convictions and fictions; there seems to me to be today a British fictional scene that is doing just that.

—*Malcolm Bradbury*

Preface

Although most critics still attribute supremacy in fiction to American, Continental, and some Latin American writers, the novel in Britain is not dead, despite various obituaries that have been written. Since 1960, in fact, a remarkable flourishing has occurred that has seen the rise of many new writers, a significant number of them women, whose achievements are becoming recognized within Great Britain and, more gradually, outside of it. While causes for this flourishing, especially in view of the increasingly adverse economic circumstances for publishing, are difficult to ascertain, some things are clear: British writers have a great deal to say, and they are finding a greater diversity of ways to say it. The novel of manners, long the standard form of the novel in Britain, is now being successfully challenged by other forms of fiction, some of them highly experimental. British writers have learned much not only from the innovations of James Joyce and Virginia Woolf and their followers; they have also benefited from their European and American contemporaries, without at the same time losing their particular insular qualities. The British novel is still British, but it is not a diminished thing, as some have thought.

The writers included in these volumes cover a wide range of interests and approaches to the novel. The aim has been to include as many representative writers as possible whose work began to appear roughly around 1960, and who have attracted serious critical attention. Inevitably, there is some overlap with other volumes of the *Dictionary of Literary Biography*, since many of the writers included here have written in other modes, such as poetry and drama. The age spread is also wide, as a number of writers who, according to their birth dates, may belong to the period preceding this one, did not begin writing or publishing their work until later in their lives; hence, they are more closely associated with the last two or three decades than with the decades just after World War II. And a few who did publish earlier may not have gained recognition until afterward. Readers should thus consider these volumes a continuation of, and in some ways a supplement to, the immediately preceding

volume, *British Novelists, 1930-1959*. Where omissions have occurred, these will be filled eventually through the publication of the *DLB Yearbook*.

Every attempt has been made to present as much pertinent biographical material as possible in each of the essays in these volumes, although living writers naturally guard their privacy, some more fiercely than others. At the same time, the critical analysis of their work has tended to be comprehensive, with observations on other genres where analysis of them has been relevant to the primary focus on the novel. Bibliographies have not always been complete where a certain amount of the writer's work has been in distantly related publications; the rubric "Selected Books" has therefore been used to signal this fact. Both British and American publication dates, places, and publishers have been included in the lists of primary materials which head each essay. Secondary materials, where appropriate, including the writer's other published work, performances of plays, films, etc., are cited at the end of the essay. Typically, an entry begins with a statement of the writer's claim to serious critical consideration and ends with an assessment of his or her major accomplishment and an indication, usually, of work in progress or expected. Since living writers have a tendency to continue writing even as their biographies are being prepared, some of the entries included here will soon be overtaken by new achievements, and in some instances this has already occurred. Rather than apologize, I suggest congratulations are in order as the situation offers further evidence of the fertility of the imagination and the vigor of the novel in Great Britain today.

The foreword and the appendix to part two are designed to give the reader a general overview of the novel in the decades beginning in 1960. They contain references to many, though not all, of the writers included here as well as to a few in the preceding volume, with whom there are certain affinities or with whom contrasts and comparisons may prove illuminating. A bibliography of books and articles for further reading concludes this work.

J. H.

Permissions

The following people and institutions generously permitted the reproduction of photographs and other illustrative materials: John Topham Picture Library, pp. 5, 39, 289, 296, 303, 349, 357; Jerry Bauer, pp. 15, 235, 244; Stuart Cooper, p. 19; Mark Gerson, pp. 23, 33, 70, 109, 124, 132, 138, 159, 220, 224, 231, 264, 270, 298; Fay Goodwin, pp. 31, 51, 78, 86, 118, 209, 257, 363; Whittaker, p. 58; Ian Townsley, p. 75; Jean Mohr, p. 91; Emil Christensen, p. 115; Werner Borman Archive, p. 151; Euan Duff, p. 276; Jacob Sutton, p. 309; Jennifer Beestow, p. 346.

Acknowledgments

This book was produced by BC Research.

Karen L. Rood is the senior editor for the *Dictionary of Literary Biography* series. Sally Johns was the in-house editor.

The production staff included Mary L. Betts, Joseph Caldwell, Patricia Coate, Angela Dixon, Lynn Felder, Joyce Fowler, Robert H. Griffin, Patricia Hicks, Nancy L. Houghton, Sharon K. Kirkland, Cynthia D. Lybrand, Shirley A. Ross, Walter W. Ross, Joycelyn R. Smith, Robin A. Sumner, Cheryl A. Swartzentruber, Carol J. Wilson, and Lynne C. Zeigler. Anne Dixon did the library research with the assistance of the following librarians at the Thomas Cooper Library of the University of South Carolina: Michael Freeman, Dwight Gardner, Michael Havener, David Lincove, Donna Nance, Harriet Oglesbee, Jean Rhyne, Paula Swope, Jane Thesing, Ellen Tillett, Gary Treadway, and Beth Woodard. Special thanks are due to the British Library; the Camden County Libraries of London; the University of London Library; the Hugh M. Morris Library, University of Delaware; Ellen Dunlap and the staff of the Humanities Research Center at the University of Texas; Anne-Marie Ehrlich; Georgia L. Lambert; Mary O'Toole; and Keith Walters. Photographic copy work for this volume was done by Colorsep Graphics of Columbia, South Carolina, and Pat Crawford of Imagery, Columbia, South Carolina.

Dictionary of Literary Biography • Volume Fourteen

British Novelists
Since 1960

Part 1: A-G

Dictionary of Literary Biography

Brian W. Aldiss
(18 August 1925-   )

Colin Greenland
North East London Polytechnic

BOOKS: *The Brightfount Diaries* (London: Faber & Faber, 1955);

Space, Time and Nathaniel (London: Faber & Faber, 1957);

Non-Stop (London: Faber & Faber, 1958); revised as *Starship* (New York: Criterion, 1959);

Equator (London: Digit, 1958); republished as *Vanguard from Alpha* (New York: Ace, 1959);

The Canopy of Time (London: Faber & Faber, 1959); revised as *Galaxies Like Grains of Sand* (New York: New American Library, 1960; London: Panther, 1979);

No Time Like Tomorrow (New York: New American Library, 1959);

Bow Down to Nul (New York: Ace, 1960); republished as *The Interpreter* (London: Digit, 1961);

The Male Response (New York: Beacon, 1961; London: Dobson, 1963);

The Primal Urge (New York: Ballantine, 1961; London: Sphere, 1967);

Hothouse (London: Faber & Faber, 1962); republished as *The Long Afternoon of Earth* (New York: New American Library, 1962);

The Airs of Earth (London: Faber & Faber, 1963); revised as *Starswarm* (New York: New American Library, 1964; London: Panther, 1979);

The Dark Light Years (London: Faber & Faber, 1964; New York: New American Library, 1964);

Greybeard (New York: Harcourt, Brace & World, 1964; London: Faber & Faber, 1964);

Best Science Fiction Stories of Brian W. Aldiss (London: Faber & Faber, 1965); republished as *Who Can Replace a Man?* (New York: Harcourt, Brace & World, 1966);

Earthworks (London: Faber & Faber, 1965; Garden City: Doubleday, 1966);

Cities and Stones: A Traveller's Jugoslavia (London: Faber & Faber, 1966);

The Saliva Tree and Other Strange Growths (London: Faber & Faber, 1966; Boston: Gregg, 1981);

An Age (London: Faber & Faber, 1967); republished as *Cryptozoic!* (Garden City: Doubleday, 1968);

Report on Probability A (London: Faber & Faber, 1968; Garden City: Doubleday, 1969);

Barefoot in the Head: A European Fantasia (London: Faber & Faber, 1969; Garden City: Doubleday, 1970);

Intangibles Inc. and Other Stories (London: Faber & Faber, 1969); revised as *Neanderthal Planet* (New York: Avon, 1969);

The Hand-Reared Boy (London: Weidenfeld & Nicolson, 1970; New York: McCall, 1970);

The Shape of Further Things: Speculations on Change (London: Faber & Faber, 1970; Garden City: Doubleday, 1971);

The Moment of Eclipse (London: Faber & Faber, 1970; Garden City: Doubleday, 1972);

A Soldier Erect (London: Weidenfeld & Nicolson, 1971; New York: Coward, McCann & Geoghegan, 1971);

The Book of Brian Aldiss (New York: DAW, 1972); republished as *Comic Inferno* (London: New English Library, 1973);

Billion Year Spree: The History of Science Fiction (London: Weidenfeld & Nicolson, 1973; Garden City: Doubleday, 1973);

Frankenstein Unbound (London: Cape, 1973; New York: Random House, 1974);

The Eighty-minute Hour (Garden City: Doubleday, 1974; London: Cape, 1974);

Science Fiction Art (London: New English Library, 1975; New York: Bounty, 1975);

The Malacia Tapestry (London: Cape, 1976; New York: Harper & Row, 1977);

Brothers of the Head (London: Pierrot, 1977; New York: Pierrot/Two Continents, 1977);

Last Orders and Other Stories (London: Cape, 1977);

Enemies of the System: A Tale of Homo Uniformis (London: Cape, 1978; New York: Harper & Row, 1978);

A Rude Awakening (London: Weidenfeld & Nicolson, 1978; New York: Random House, 1979);

New Arrivals, Old Encounters (London: Cape, 1979; New York: Harper & Row, 1979);

This World and Nearer Ones: Essays Exploring the Familiar (London: Weidenfeld & Nicolson, 1979; Kent, Ohio: Kent State University Press, 1981);

Life in the West (London: Weidenfeld & Nicolson, 1980);

Moreau's Other Island (London: Cape, 1980); republished as *An Island Called Moreau* (New York: Simon & Schuster, 1981);

Helliconia Spring (London: Cape, 1982; New York: Atheneum, 1982).

Brian Aldiss writes with zest and aplomb, embracing polarities and contradictions that have fractured other careers. Equally at home writing the most extravagant science fiction and the most earthy social comedy, as comfortable with short stories as novels of any length, a keen critic and historian, no less adept at radical technical experiments than at traditional, lapidary prose, and apparently able to deliver any of these at any stage, Aldiss defies handy categorization. He has said of his diverse career: "Writers mainly fall into two groups; either they are forest clearers or explorers. Some like to tidy the world and reduce it to a clear and understandable diagram. Others prefer to wander in the wilderness, rejoicing in it for its own sake. I like the wilderness. I have tried to put down a few human ambiguities without attempting to clear them away."

With all his accomplishments, Aldiss has a number of failings. Many readers point to his dialogue as unnatural, often inadequately differentiated from the narrator's voice. Similarly, his characterizations can be awkward, though there are strong examples to the contrary in *The Malacia Tapestry* (1976), *Life in the West* (1980), and his novels about the character Horatio Stubbs. Some readers have found Aldiss's diversity a weakness rather than a strength, but the consistent breadth, as well as length, of his career has been a prominent factor in establishing his prestige as a writer.

Brian Wilson Aldiss was born 18 August 1925, the son of Stanley and Elizabeth May Wilson Aldiss. He and his sister Betty were brought up in East Dereham, Norfolk, over the premises of H. H. Aldiss and Sons, a prosperous draper's and outfitter's business belonging to his grandfather. Aldiss's memories are of a happy childhood in a close, loving family in a typical small English town, disrupted too soon when he was sent off to St. Peter's Court Preparatory school at the age of eight. The disruption does not seem to have been too traumatic for his later life, though he has the usual recollections of the institutionalized tyrannies of the British public school. At every stage of his career his work has shown the benefits of a broad education, particularly in literature. In 1938 his father left the shop and moved his household to Gorleston-on-Sea, Norfolk, where Aldiss discovered American pulp magazines, labeled "Yank Mags," offered for sale in Woolworth's. They were his introduction to science fiction as a commercial genre, but there was already other imaginative fiction on his shelves to give it a context. By developing a taste for both the extravagant romance of the pulps and the scientific and social speculations of H. G. Wells and Aldous Huxley, Aldiss attained in his thinking a dynamic interaction of imagination and intellect which he has sustained throughout his life. Similarly he has kept his science-fiction writings free from the literary apartheid, enjoyed by the fans and perpetuated by publishers, that has made science fiction a genre too often bound by tradition, despite its apparent preoccupation with novelty.

Of his education at Framlingham College,

burning, palaces being blown up. . . .

"Some of me never came back from the Far East. It's a place where Life and Death stand in naked confrontation at every street corner. . . ." He returned to England three and a half years later, "a sort of exile, not knowing how to deal with English girls or English coinage; that feeling of exile has never left me." Exile is one of many recurring themes or conditions in Aldiss's fiction, which also employs the luxuriant, oppressive scenery of the tropical and equatorial jungle.

Aldiss left the army in 1947. Glad of the opportunity to escape a future in his grandfather's shop or his uncle's firm of architects, he went to live in Oxford, in and around which he has lived ever since. In 1949 he married Olive Mary Fortescue; their son, Clive, was born in 1955, and their daughter, Caroline Wendy, was born four years later. At the time of his marriage he was working as an assistant in bookshops, an employment which stimulated his catholic literary appetite. He read eighteenth-century authors such as Samuel Johnson, Henry Fielding, and Laurence Sterne. In 1947 he submitted his first story to John W. Campbell's *Astounding Science-Fiction*, and he offered a second two years later, but neither was accepted. He spent three years during this period writing his first novel, "Shouting Down a Cliff," which remains unpublished. Aldiss describes it as "Dickens with a dash of Proust and Kafka for piquancy." He also recalls writing a long poem in blank verse about World War III, called "The Flight Across the Asiatic Surface," doubtless influenced by his father, who had composed a similar poem about World War I. Aldiss's first professional sale was a short story, "T," to Peter Hamilton's *Nebula Science Fiction* in 1953, but owing to difficulties and delays in production, "T" was not published until November 1956.

In the meantime Aldiss had begun a determined campaign of writing and was submitting material to all available science-fiction magazines, but his first published story, "A Book in Time," which appeared in the *Bookseller* in February 1954, was not science fiction. The editor, Edmond Segrave, then asked if Aldiss could supply an article that would "turn a representative bookshop assistant inside out," a request which produced "On Being an Assistant" for the April issue. When Aldiss offered to follow this piece with the fictitious journal of an assistant in the book trade, Segrave replied, "A bookshop diary is the very thing I've been looking for." "The Brightfount Diaries," published under the pseudonym Peter Pica, ran for two years

Suffolk, and West Buckland School, Devon, Aldiss recalls that he was "distinguished only for wit and subversion," though he did play on the school rugby team. On leaving school in 1943, Aldiss volunteered for the army before he could be conscripted. Reading matter in his kit bag included science-fiction pulp magazines and *The Golden Treasury*, Francis Turner Palgraves's popular anthology of sixteenth-through mid-nineteenth-century poetry. His experiences serving in Burma, Sumatra, India, Hong Kong and Singapore were vital to his imagination. As he reflected later, "The war took me from the sheltered terrors of the bourgeoisie out into the big world, where many of my beliefs melted like chocolate among the forests of the Far East. I saw dead men piled up and turning black in the sun, forests in the *Bookseller* and proved remarkably popular. Charles Monteith invited Aldiss to collect the articles into book form for Faber & Faber, and he responded eagerly. He recalls that as many as six other publishers made the same request. At the same time he was amused to receive a letter from the manager of a bookshop in Australia offering him a job: Peter Pica, he wrote, sounded like just the sort of assistant he was looking for. Aldiss replied that he hardly resembled his pseudonym, an unattached youngster living in a bedsitter, but rather had a family to maintain. Faber & Faber published *The Brightfount Diaries* under Aldiss's name in November 1955, and the book met with some success.

In December 1954, Aldiss's short story "Not for an Age" had won a competition in the *Observer* for fiction set in the year 2500. In the same newspaper's humorous short-story competition the following Christmas his "Tradesman's Exit" tied for first place. In 1957 Faber & Faber published *Space, Time and Nathaniel*, a collection of the science-fiction stories he had published to date plus two new pieces, "The Shubshub Race" and "Supercity." That same year Aldiss took over the post of literary editor of the *Oxford Mail*, for which he had been reviewing books of all kinds since 1954, and he committed himself to a full-time literary career.

His first novel, *Non-Stop*, appeared in 1958. Years after the failure of an interstellar expedition, the descendants of the original crew are in orbit around the Earth, but cut off from all communication with it. Their culture, organized tribally and motivated by superstition and fear, is in decline. Among the jungles of the overgrown hydroponic system they do not realize that they are living inside a spaceship, a revelation which is delayed for the reader too, except in the United States, where an editor for Criterion Books decided to spoil the mystery by retitling the novel *Starship*, at the same time making some unauthorized excisions from the text. (Aldiss's work continued to attract editorial interference for many years, and is still habitually altered by some publishers who feel that his sales will be increased by a change of title.) Aldiss refers to *Non-Stop* as a crucial novel, not just because it was his first one published, but because in it he dealt with themes and images which have remained central to his work: the Sumatran jungle as well as themes of isolation and seclusion.

The characters of *Non-Stop* are trapped by their circumstances. Aldiss not only emphasizes the constraints of history upon the individual, but also sees the process of history, in his own life as in all others, as an exile, a series of departures. At the same time, he celebrates the liberating imagination and his own escape, in his life from the small-town restrictions of his childhood, and in his work from the generic prescriptions of science fiction. *Non-Stop* is a direct reply to "Universe" and "Common Sense" (1941), Robert A. Heinlein's stories about the lost starship *Vanguard*. Heinlein uses the confined crew to demonstrate that human societies "naturally" evolve into a brave, intelligent, muscular ruling class and a subservient, unenterprising rabble. Opposing him, Aldiss argues that seclusion in space would be more likely to expose human frailties than to incubate heroes.

Aldiss's policy was to try to make science fiction more humane, more sensitive than it had commonly been to the emotional and moral implications of its material. That the time had come for such a move was demonstrated when he was voted Most Promising New Author at the World Science Fiction Convention of 1958 and made president of the British Science Fiction Association two years later.

For his second short-story collection, published in 1959, Aldiss wrote brief introductions designed to locate all the contents within a single history of the future, calling the book *The Canopy of Time*. He thought the links "tenuous," but they are fuller and hence more successful in the American version of the book, a slightly different selection, published in 1960 as *Galaxies Like Grains of Sand*. Both versions contain what is still Aldiss's most popular story, "Who Can Replace a Man?," about the extinction of the human race and the survival of automata. Equipped with various levels of artificial intelligence, the machines begin to organize themselves into a caste system and power structure, but on discovering an abject human survivor, all revert at once to servitude. Though man clearly delights Aldiss, this story represents a sentimental affirmation of man's superiority unusual for him, and one which he has never made again so simply. In 1974 he said, "In my writing I've never been in the reassurance business. Yet my most-reprinted story by far is a short called WHO CAN REPLACE A MAN? about robot intelligences; its theme is reassuring: man remains master. This must be a great public need for discussion and reassurance on such matters."

Equator, Aldiss's second novel, was published in 1958 (and in the United States the following year, as *Vanguard from Alpha*). Set in Padang, it takes the form of a thriller in which Tyne Leslie, a secret agent, discovers evidence that the humanoid Roskians, who have established a colony on Earth, are planning to invade the planet. His next three novels all received their first publications in the United States. The first of them, *Bow Down to Nul* (1960), republished as *The Interpreter* (1961) in Britain, is another thriller. Gary Towler, interpreter between the human race and the Nuls, its alien rulers, has to try to break through the limitations of his office to make a deposition on behalf of mankind to a visiting Nul inspector. In both *Equator* and *Bow Down to Nul* Aldiss exploits the incompatibility of alien languages, making conventional plot mechanisms of misunderstanding, concealment, and surprise carry an investigation into the moral complexities of communication. Power consists in the proper deployment of information, but information cannot always be efficiently delivered or received. Aldiss marks the happy ending of each book with a significant incident of nonverbal communication. For example, in *Equator* Leslie is attracted to Benda Ittai, a Roskian woman:

> Frustratedly, he turned to Benda Ittai. Here at least was someone worth trying to comprehend.
> He felt like spending a life at it. . . .
> She smiled at him. It was a very comprehensible smile.

And in *Bow Down to Nul*:

> Towler . . . began to laugh, partly from the irony of it, partly from sheer lightheartedness. There was no word for how he felt, either in his own tongue or in Partussian. . . .
> In the bright sunlight, it was as if everyone was suddenly laughing.

Both sexual attraction and laughter animate his next two novels, *The Male Response* (1961) and *The Primal Urge* (1961). In these lightweight moral comedies, British restraint and embarrassment are forced into public confrontation with the power of sex, represented in the first by the carefree sensuality of tribal Africans, in the second by Freudian libido. Aldiss has said on many occasions that his early literary inclinations were strong toward other forms than science fiction. He might have founded his career on poetry or social comedy, but felt daunted by the achievements of contemporary poets and satirists. His continual choice of sexual themes and subjects shows again his impatience with formal prohibitions, especially within science fiction, where sex was still taboo in the early 1960s. At the same time it may be that he had a private cause for sexual concern in the failure of his mar-

riage. He and his first wife separated in July 1960, and she took the children to live in the Isle of Wight. In 1960 Aldiss began his secondary career as an editor of anthologies, with the first of three very popular anthologies for Penguin Books, whose line of science-fiction novels he also supervised. Later, with his friend Harry Harrison, another science fiction author, he was to edit a series of *Best Science Fiction* annuals for Berkley in America and Sphere in England.

His most important fiction of 1961 appeared as short stories describing a far-future Earth overrun by vegetation, published in the *Magazine of Fantasy and Science Fiction*. In 1962 they were published as a single book: *Hothouse* in Great Britain and *The Long Afternoon of Earth* in the United States, where the editor for Signet Books at New American Library was afraid that the original title might cause it to disappear among books on horticulture. *Hothouse*, which won the Hugo Award for Best Short Fiction in 1962, again shows Aldiss trying to find a way from the short story to the novel form, more successfully than in *The Canopy of Time*, though the original breaks between the sections are still visible. The result is a rich fantasy much enhanced by Aldiss's invented vocabulary for the teeming flora which have evolved to usurp the conditions and functions of the dwindling fauna. The remaining humans, dwarfish and green, struggle for survival against thinpins, jittermops, and fuzzypuzzles. Gigantic vegetable "traversers" spin webs to the moon, which, with the Earth, is stopped in its orbit. A morel fungus mutated into a free-living brain delivers a sermon on the unity of life in all forms and prophesies the "devolution" of these forms back down the scale of specialization to the primordial cell. Like other quasi-scientific rationalizations scattered through the text, this one hardly fits the facts in the story, but it gives a good indication of Aldiss's cosmic liberalism, his powerful compassion for conditions other than the known, developed at length through all his work. *Hothouse* is structurally similar to *Non-Stop*: another story of degenerate humanity trapped in hostile circumstances dynamically depicted as the mysterious and implacable fecundity of the jungle. It is remarkable, however, that Gren, one of the doomed humans, chooses to stay and die in the jungle rather than to venture into space with his companions.

In two weeks during January 1962 Aldiss wrote 46,000 words defying the orthodoxy of fiction in general and of science fiction in particular: an antinovel called "A Garden with Figures." Under the influence of *nouveaux romanciers* Michel Butor and Alain Robbe-Grillet, and especially the latter's work with Alain Resnais on the film *Last Year in Marienbad*, Aldiss contrived a mechanically descriptive style which confounds the imagination while pointing toward the assumed neutrality of the cinecamera. An inscrutable story of three servants who, dismissed after some unspecific crime, linger to spy on their mistress and her estate, its themes are once again exile, seclusion, and the limits of perception. Everything is observed; nothing is certain. "A Garden with Figures" remained unpublished until March 1967, when it appeared rewritten in *New Worlds* as "Report on Probability A."

The Airs of Earth, published in 1963, is a collection that displays the breadth and variety of enterprise of Aldiss's short fiction. In his introduction he warns various readers and reviewers against the assumption that science fiction is (or should be) a single, definable mode of writing created by rules and conforming to unities, and also against the belief that science fiction cannot be criticized by "ordinary literate standards." The collection, he says, includes only one piece of "proper sf," a puzzle of parasitology called "The Game of God." Other stories range from the mordant antimilitary satire "How to be a Soldier" through near-future political extrapolations ("A Basis for Negotiation" and "The International Smile"), to the strange and tantalizing "Shards," which uses a surreal stream of consciousness to express the conditions of two bizarre transplant patients.

The Dark Light Years (1964), Aldiss's next novel, continues the exploration of perception and communicability through the story of an alien encounter, one of the traditional devices of "proper sf." Traditional the device may be, but this book provoked further anxiety among publishers, for the aliens are most incomprehensible to man not because they are bovine and bicephalic, but because they combine the most exalted intellectual sophistication with a fondness for their own feces. Their human examiners have difficulty crediting the utods with intelligence, let alone civilization, for civilization, as Aldiss observes, "is the distance that man has placed between himself and his own excreta." His American publishers tried to increase that distance by altering the word "shit" to "manure" throughout. It is now more obvious than it could have been at the time that *The Dark Light Years* was not merely an amusing diversion but actually a milestone in Aldiss's career, a declaration of his belief that science fiction should be a challenging, contentious mode, opposed to ingrained assumptions, conventions, and platitudes. It should go be-

yond the limits of genre fiction, which provides formulas of reassurance, this way into seriousness and that into absurdism; it should disturb readers while it delights them. *The Dark Light Years* is a passionate denunciation of what C. S. Lewis called "human-racism," occasioned by its author's reading of two books for review in the *Oxford Mail*: *Man and Dolphin* by John Lilly and *Madkind* by Charles Berg. Aldiss was dismayed to read Lilly's account of his early experiments to ascertain the intelligence of dolphins by surgical methods, including the planting of electrodes in dolphin brains. Turning from *Man and Dolphin* to Berg's book, a work of antipsychiatry setting out to demonstrate that there is no real difference between the behavior of the sane and that of those they elect to call mad, Aldiss could only agree. His response was *The Dark Light Years*, written straight out in a month of anger. Its blackness is also comic, however. Aldiss's humor, though rarely subtle or elusive, is difficult to define. A kind of vigorous irony that combines resonant wordplay with high moral acuity, it remains the strongest mark on his work of his early readings in eighteenth-century literature.

Never one to do the predictable, Aldiss next produced *Greybeard* (1964), a beautiful elegiac novel of the English countryside. His model for the prose in this book is Thomas Hardy, rather than Michel Butor or Samuel Johnson. Set in and around a future Oxford, it tells of humanity made sterile by radioactive fallout from careless missile testing. As man dies out, the aging survivors cohere in tattered tribes, while the rest of nature flourishes untamed. In alternating chapters Aldiss tells the present adventures and the life history of Algy Timberlane and his impulsive journey downriver in search of hope, tantalized by persistent rumors that there are children still living in the woods. *Greybeard* is one of the most singular and compelling visions of a new feudalism after the holocaust. The comparison with Hardy, which has been mentioned by critics as well as the author himself, is not fortuitous. *Greybeard* relates the end of the industrial age as Hardy recorded its beginning; as Hardy was concerned with the social repression of natural impulses, so Aldiss adds that a thoughtless and self-centered society can pollute or bomb nature out of court—and itself out of existence. Moreover, while *Greybeard* is another tale of human beings trapped and dying in dense forests, this vegetable empire is of man's own making, however hostile to his own survival. Characters and landscape are morally and emotionally interlocked: another parallel with Hardy.

In January 1964 Aldiss finished an expansion

of "Skeleton Crew," a short story published the previous month in *Science Fantasy*, into a new short novel called *Earthworks*, to be published the following year. It is a bleak story of the world stripped by human greed and folly, its races divided into nomadic scavengers and harshly regimented societies, all motivated by hunger. Aldiss contrives some peculiar and powerful scenes on an Earth at once overpopulated and desolate, and a new, bold symbolism of life and death, sickness and rebirth. This symbolism cuts obliquely through the narrative, operating differently at different levels: sometimes structural and implicit, sometimes imposed on his experience by the narrator's diseased imagination, desperate and hallucinating. With the collapse of Europe and America, the only hope of recovery for humanity lies with the President of Africa and his power to unite the nations under him—the tropics once again serving Aldiss as a symbolic region of fertility. Ironically, also in January 1964, *The Male Response*, Aldiss's comedy of black sexuality, was banned by the South African Publications Control Board.

In March Aldiss, accompanied by Margaret

Cover for 1962 Science Fantasy

Manson, his collaborator and future wife, set off to tour Yugoslavia in a Land Rover, having secured a commission from Faber and Faber to write a travel book about the region, which eventually appeared as *Cities and Stones: A Traveller's Jugoslavia* in November 1966. A conscientiously informative account, this book also conveys, perhaps unintentionally, much of the inevitable discomfort and distaste associated with living cheaply in a foreign country, always on the move; Aldiss's eternal theme of exile surfaces once again. He returned to England in time to take his place as Guest of Honor at the Twenty-third World Science Fiction Convention, held in London in August 1965, and the *Magazine of Fantasy and Science Fiction* for September featured his novella *The Saliva Tree*. Set in the "last years of the nineteenth century," it tells of the arrival of a "space machine" on an East Anglian farm. The crops, livestock, and people all suddenly begin to thrive before it becomes apparent to the protagonist, Gregory Rolles, that they are being fattened to feed invisible alien invaders. The story is a deliberate act of homage to H. G. Wells, taking themes and incidents from his fiction and including some felicitous imitations of his style. Rolles conducts a correspondence with Wells on matters scientific and socialist, and the story ends, after the departure of the aliens, with the innkeeper telling Rolles that Wells has arrived in the village and wishes to hear about what has been going on. *The Saliva Tree* also represents a fictional return for Aldiss to the Norfolk of his earliest youth, where he visited farms with his father. The Science Fiction Writers of America gave it their Nebula Award for best novella of the year, and it opened his next volume of stories. *The Saliva Tree and Other Strange Growths*, published in March 1966.

Among the "growths" are "A Pleasure Shared," a horror story based on the crimes of John Christie, and "The Day of the Doomed King" and "Paternal Care," two stories set (and written) in Yugoslavia. The last story in the collection, "The Girl and the Robot with Flowers," is a chapter of semifictionalized autobiography in which the author bemoans his professional preoccupation with robots and vacuum and "centuries of misery" while his life, this one afternoon, is actually full of cats and sunlight and his love for Marion, who challenges him to make a science-fiction story with all those things in it. The story of the challenge becomes, of course, the story she demands, with the author's abandoned story of robots contained perfectly inside it: a Borgesian nesting of references whose implications unfold even wider. "The Girl and the

Robot with Flowers" is Aldiss's most categorical statement of his principal objection to the science-fiction genre, phrased elsewhere as "Too much hardware, too great a lack of respect for human software!" It also presents a remarkable act of self-observation, for it records Aldiss's state of mind in the summer of 1965 when he finally became free to marry Margaret Manson, which he did in December of that year.

"The Girl and the Robot with Flowers" voices Aldiss's hope that his fiction will become less depressive and more joyful from now on. There is a corresponding sense of confidence and self-reliance in his letters at this stage. "From now on, I write only to delight only myself," he told Joan Harrison in March 1965. "Anything I'm not 100% interested in—out. I've over-reached myself enough." A year later he wrote to Charles Platt: "I have always discovered many compartments in myself, all of which need an airing occasionally." *Cryptozoic!* (1968), the first novel of the new period, though it airs a good number of Aldiss's ideas and talents, is not much more cheerful than *Earthworks*. (*Cryptozoic!* is the original and current title: Aldiss changed it to *An Age* for the first British edition, published in 1967, but changed it back later.) Edward Bush, a kinetic sculptor, is highly proficient at the art of mind traveling, a kind of time travel using a drug and a set of mental preparations rather than a machine. In fact, Bush spends more time wandering aimlessly through the past than he does on his work—as does a large proportion of the population of England. The country is bankrupt and falling under a totalitarian dictatorship. Bush is forced to serve as a mind-traveling secret policeman, trailing "disaffected elements" through the past. After hideous experiences in Yorkshire during the Depression and farcical scenes at Buckingham Palace in 1851, he is persuaded to return to his own epoch and help to overthrow the Fascists, but a military coup intervenes, and Bush ends up incarcerated in a mental institution, his mind trapped in a hallucinatory realm between past and present.

There is much that is unsatisfactory about *Cryptozoic!* The pathos and the absurdities fit uncomfortably beside the secret agent shoot-outs and the chronicling of Bush's improbable neuroses. At the crux of the novel Aldiss sets the revelation that time actually flows backward, not forward. This apocalyptic proposition is intended to have a redemptive effect: that is, things do not ultimately fall apart, but merge. However, Aldiss (not being in the reassurance business) also wishes to pass judgment on Bush for his selfish indolence. Since the concept

of guilt predicates a straightforward time scheme in which action (or inaction) is followed by consequences, the two main points of the book tend to disqualify each other. Writing to James Blish in October 1966, Aldiss said that he had completed "an ambitious novel called CRYPTOZOIC, but I failed in the ambitions, so that one will just get marketed and there's an end to it."

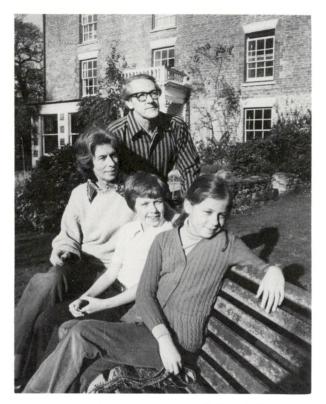

Brian and Margaret Aldiss with their children

Ambition was the character of all his activity in this period. December 1966 saw him campaigning for an Arts Council grant for Michael Moorcock's magazine *New Worlds*, threatened with closure by the collapse of its distributors. Under Moorcock's editorship, a number of writers such as J. G. Ballard, Thomas M. Disch, and John Sladek were working to break down the conservative conventions of science fiction and redeploy its themes and images. Aldiss found the intentions and the company congenial and stimulating. Government finance for a science-fiction magazine was unheard of, but he elicited support from J. B. Priestley, Kenneth Allsop, Roy Fuller, and Marghanita Laski, and the grant was awarded in January 1967. To ensure continuity of publication while new arrangements were being made, Aldiss donated material for two interim issues. *New Worlds* for March 1967 carried "Report on Probability A," a revised version of his antinovel, "A Garden With Figures," written five years previously. Faber and Faber had been unenthusiastic about it then, but in the experimental ambience of the later 1960s they proved more adventurous and published a full version, compiled from the unpublished novel and the short-story revision, in 1968. As a study of the uncertainties of purpose, of time, and of art, *Report on Probability A* is far more successful than *Cryptozoic!*, and it established Aldiss as an author who valued the freedom to experiment above the security to be won by catering to an audience's expectations.

The first child of Aldiss's second marriage was born in August 1967 and christened Timothy Nicholas. This was also the year in which Aldiss became acquainted with the work of Anna Kavan—the adopted name of Helen Woods Edmonds, novelist, short-story writer, and assistant editor of Cyril Connolly's literary magazine *Horizon*. The principal subject of all her fiction is the divided mind of the dreamer, the schizophrenic, and the heroin addict. Her last work, *Ice* (1967), the story of a desperate quest at the onset of a new ice age, made a deep and lasting impression on Aldiss, as did his meeting with the author in May of the following year, only seven months before her death. In December 1967, he was elected chairman of the Oxford branch of the Conservation Society, a strong concern of his, as his many fictional warnings about pollution demonstrate. His work for conservation is evidence of his belief in the values of stability and security, in contrast to his commitment to experiment, renewal, and the autonomy of the imagination. His experiments with fiction continued in a series of stories published in *New Worlds* and its companion magazine, *SF Impulse*, between 1967 and 1969, when the complete sequence, extensively rewritten, was published as *Barefoot in the Head: A European Fantasia*. Tackling many popular issues of the time, it is the story of a displaced Yugoslavian and his travels through a Europe devastated by hallucinogenic bombs. He takes the name Colin Charteris (borrowing the last name from the author of the "Saint" books, which he admires) and comes to England where he is adopted as the rock'n'roll messiah by a band of young nomads. Charteris develops a doctrine of alternative realities and multiple time streams from the teachings of Russian mystic George Gurdjieff and his disciple, P. D. Ouspenski. He leads what he believes to be a crusade of liberation, but his creed promotes only selfishness and chaos: though the psychedelic fall-out has left everyone more isolated than ever before, at the mercy of their own distorted senses, Charteris is advocating less social responsibility, not more.

To present the disintegrating systems and prolific ambiguities of a psychedelic world, Aldiss used a complex and impacted style that fully exploited his skill at wordplay and lexical innovation. The text dissolves into verse, incorporates poems, songs, and word pictures, blurring the boundaries between modes of writing as Aldiss had consistently overruled the distinctions between the genres of fiction. Words collide and mingle: *suburbanal*; *perplextives*; *cyanightmarine*. Many readers, especially the science-fiction writer and critic James Blish, invoked the obvious comparison with Joyce's *Finnegans Wake*, but Aldiss replied that the style was generated by the subject rather than borrowed from outside, wisely asserting independence but not freedom: "I never set Joyce up as a model, but you know if you write that sort of thing, then JOYCE is *there*, just as Picasso is *there* if you paint a picture of a goat, or Shakespeare if you write English. I never did finish the *Wake*. And life's too shored to embark on it now." *Barefoot in the Head*, written during the throes of the hippie revolution, is a phenomenally accurate account of the failure of flower power to bear fruit. Its evocation of essentially inexpressible qualities of psychedelic experience is remarkable from an author who has never sampled a hallucinogen. Over and above these achievements it remains Aldiss's boldest statement on the dilemma of the individual in history, and the need for love and social involvement to transcend the restrictions of solipsism.

In November 1968 Aldiss was again honored by the British Science Fiction Association, who voted him Britain's Most Popular Science Fiction Writer. At this time, however, he had completed the first volume of a continuing series which has been one of his most popular literary ventures, and one which has brought him the most professional satisfaction—a series which has no science-fiction element at all. The ambitious aspect of *The Hand-Reared Boy*, the first of the Horatio Stubbs stories, was entirely different from that of *Report on Probability A* and *Barefoot in the Head*: quite simply, Aldiss wanted to write about the developing sexuality of a young Englishman, a story intended to be comic, and serious, and honest, but in tone quite unlike that of pornographic confessions and memoirs. The audacity of such a venture, even in the "permissive" decade, can be illustrated by the fact that when *The Hand-Reared Boy*, which deals extensively with juvenile erotic sensibilities, was finally accepted by Weidenfeld and Nicolson in October 1968, it had already been rejected by fifteen other publishers. Philip Roth's *Portnoy's Complaint* (1969) was still an outrageous novelty; Aldiss recalls the "sinking feeling" he had when he first heard of it, while *The Hand-Reared Boy* was actually in the press. Many British publishers, though priding themselves on their liberal attitude toward books about sex, could not accept one about masturbation, however funny, accurate, and rich in observation of the British middle class of the 1930s; nor did the publishers think the British public would accept such a book. Many reviewers agreed. In fact, however, *The Hand-Reared Boy* was on the best-seller lists within a week of its publication in January 1970. It is a remarkable success in every way, written in a tone of irrepressible cheerfulness, though poignant too in the last half, which tells of an adolescent's hopeless love affair with a strange, schizophrenic public-school matron, Sister Virginia Traven. It avoids lewdness on the one hand and mawkishness on the other, tempering coarseness with eloquence: by writing it as the autobiography of Horatio Stubbs, Aldiss was able to narrate the book in a heartier version of his own voice and give it substance with many of his own reminiscences.

An urge to autobiography also stimulated his nonfiction book of this period. *The Shape of Further Things* (1970) starts with an account of a conversation about dreams, which took place on the night of 8 January 1969. The book covers a month, sometimes in the form of a journal, sometimes as a subjective history of science fiction. It includes speculations for a computerized future, a chapter on H. G. Wells, one on aggression, and reflections on dreams, art, and the function of imagination in the human mind, with an inventory of the contents of Aldiss's own highly individual imagination. He attributes the form, free-ranging in time and space while always emphatically personal, to archaeologist and poet Jacquetta Hawkes. (*A Land*, Hawkes's 1951 romantic meditation on the genesis of the British Isles, is a very singular book, but one which is itself descended, through Thomas De Quincey, from the essays of Francis Bacon and Sir Thomas Browne. No doubt Laurence Sterne is in the genealogy too.) *The Shape of Further Things* did not sell at all well, but it has produced more letters from readers than anything else Aldiss has written. For many it represents the essential Aldiss, the characteristic mind at large, unencumbered by the necessities of story telling. Though its compass is nominally confined to the thoughts and occurrences during January 1969,

the book was published with an introduction and a postscript to bring it up to date with the birth of Charlotte May Aldiss in March and the first moon landing in July of that year.

In addition to *The Hand-Reared Boy* and *The Shape of Further Things*, 1970 saw the publication of *The Moment of Eclipse*, given a British Science Fiction Association award in 1972 and generally regarded as Aldiss's best collection of short fiction. It is certainly one which shows him at his most erudite and versatile. The title story, based on "Poem at a Lunar Eclipse" by Thomas Hardy, is an elegant description of an incident of corruption and obsession that recalls Edgar Allan Poe. For "Orgy of the Living and the Dying," "The Village Swindler," and ". . . And the Stagnation of the Heart," Aldiss returns to India, whose arid landscape has always proved fertile to his imagination. "Working in the Spaceship Yards" is perhaps his funniest story ever, and "Swastika!," an interview with Adolf Hitler, is his most pungently sustained act of irony.

A sequel to *The Hand-Reared Boy* was completed in April 1970. Originally called "The Old Five-Fingered Widow," it was published in 1971 as *A Soldier Erect*. Once again the reviewers were disgusted and the public delighted, and the book became a best-seller. *The Hand-Reared Boy* had closed with a memory of Sister Virginia Traven "in the double jungle: the real jungle of London and the equally real one that she had built in her own mind." *A Soldier Erect* takes Horatio Stubbs into the real jungle of India and Burma with the Second Royal Mendip Borderers: it was the first time Aldiss had worked directly from his own wartime experiences, vital as they had been to him. Stubbs's all-consuming lust for sex becomes a campaign against alienation, a heated affirmation of self in the face of exile and sudden death, a metaphor for survival. Inevitably this novel recalls *Non-Stop*, *Hothouse*, and *Greybeard*, stories of people struggling for meaning in the hostile or indifferent jungles of their isolation.

Early in 1971 Aldiss wrote four connected short stories to develop a locale first glimpsed in "The Day We Embarked for Cythera. . . ," a story collected in *The Moment of Eclipse*. The short-story title refers to Antoine Watteau's painting "L'Embarcation pour Cythère"; the milieu, which Aldiss describes as "peaceful, picturesque, rather shoddy around the edges," is the fantasy city-state of Malacia, where change is forbidden. The stories were first published in 1973, in the twelfth volume of Damon Knight's anthology series *Orbit*, but not until 1976 were they published in their final form, the novel *The Malacia Tapestry*.

In the meantime Aldiss was writing an extravaganza called *The Eighty-minute Hour* (1974), a comic "space opera" laden with parodic versions of the cliches of science fiction and of the related fantasy genre known as "sword and sorcery," and populated by characters with names like Monty Zoomer and Devlin Carnate. Many reviewers felt that the book was too self-indulgent to be successful, but it remains a diverting science-fiction pastiche by a man well-versed in the vagaries of his favorite fiction. It is easy to see *The Eighty-minute Hour* as a necessary overflow from the four years of research which he was presently writing up as *Billion Year Spree: The History of Science Fiction* (1973).

In 1972, DAW Books published a mixed collection of short stories under the portentous title *The Book of Brian Aldiss* (retitled *Comic Inferno* for its English publication in 1973). Among stories originally published as far apart as 1957 and 1973, probably the most striking is one from 1969, "The Soft Predicament." It deals sensitively if simplistically with the divided nature of mankind, of the human brain, and of consciousness itself, by means of a story about dream research, one of Aldiss's chief interests of the period. By June 1972, two and a half years of writing had brought *Billion Year Spree* to its completion. Aldiss made use of his long and extensive familiarity with science fiction to write an admirably comprehensive history which makes a strong case for setting Mary Shelley's *Frankenstein* (1818) at the beginning of the genre and helps answer the problem of the relation between science fiction and earlier forms of fantastic, satirical, and utopian fiction. Aldiss, remembering how he himself had discovered science fiction as a boy, also stresses the double tradition of the genre: the literary influence of H. G. Wells and the commercial influence of the American pulp magazines. It was originally intended that the critic Philip Strick should contribute his knowledge of contemporary science fiction to the later chapters of the book, but this plan fell through at the beginning of 1972. *Billion Year Spree* succeeds both as a reference book for the science-fiction specialist and as an introduction to the field for the general reader. It illuminates the background of much of Aldiss's own fiction, most notably *The Eighty-minute Hour* and *Frankenstein Unbound* (1973) which he began writing in the autumn of 1972 after another trip to Yugoslavia, this one commissioned by the *Daily Telegraph Magazine*.

Frankenstein Unbound makes serious use of a convention responsible for sensational effects in *The Eighty-minute Hour*: the "timeslip," which leaves different parts of the world isolated in different periods of history. The narrator, a Texan named Joseph Bodenland, is slipped from 2020 A.D. back 200 years, to a Switzerland inhabited not only by Mary and Percy Bysshe Shelley, Lord Byron, and Doctor John Polidori, but also by Victor Frankenstein and the monster he has brought to life. Aldiss was displeased when an American editor complained, with some justice, that the cultural dislocation of the narrator is insufficiently realized. Nevertheless, the importance of the book lies in its reanimation of the modern theses of Mary Shelley's novel: the nature and moral responsibility of scientific endeavor and, by analogy, of artistic creation, as well as the tyranny of human technology. The character of the monster displaces the crude cinema versions that have usurped the name of Frankenstein and proves no less metaphysically inclined than the original.

Another rejoinder to an admired early science-fiction classic occupied Aldiss in 1973 and early 1974. *Moreau's Other Island* (1980) brings up to date the issues of Wells's *The Island of Doctor Moreau* (1896), which Aldiss considers "one of the most striking science fiction novels ever written." In *Moreau's Other Island*, set 100 years after the publication of Wells's novel, Aldiss supposes that Dr. Moreau really existed. His self-appointed successor, Mortimer Dart, lives on the island and uses the descendants of Moreau's experimental beast-people as slave labor in his attempt to create a new species equipped to survive World War III, which is just beginning. Dart himself is a thalidomide victim, and his research is a secret project funded by the U.S. Department of State. The novel is a stringent investigation of what Dart calls "the relativity of flesh" and the limits of humanity. Nevertheless, Aldiss felt dissatisfied with *Moreau's Other Island*, thinking it inadequate as a continuation of Wells's original book, and it remained unpublished for six years.

In 1973 he also began working on a new form of short fiction, imagistic rather than narrative, which he called "enigmas." These are often surreal and bear titles like "The Eternal Theme of Exile" and "The Daffodil Returns the Smile"; they overlap with other stories from the same period which are set on the "Zodiacal Planets," artificial space habitats where the human impulse toward baroque variegation flourishes. An important influence on all these stories, in several of which she appears as a character, is Anna Kavan. To a correspondent who observed that there are also strong traces of Kavan in the portrait of Mary Shelley in *Frankenstein Un-*

Dust jacket for Aldiss's reanimation of Mary Shelley's monster

bound, Aldiss wrote, "I knew her so little that she is able to embody for me various ideas I have about artistic integrity, failure, success, huntedness, frustrated sexuality, etc. etc.—rather a mess, as you can see, but 'numinous' all the same. You would be surprised if you knew how the idea of Anna haunts me."

Aldiss's next published novel, perhaps his greatest, if one may be singled out from the copious variety, was *The Malacia Tapestry* (1976), written between 1974 and 1975 from short stories of 1971. Malacia is a utopia in aspic, for which Aldiss combined artistic, legendary, historical, and geographical material from widely different origins. The principal model is a Shakespearean city of Europe, though there are elements of Byzantium, Babylon, and Imperial Rome too. A vital element comes from the mysterious and magical engravings by the eighteenth-century Venetian painter Giambattista Tiepolo which are included as illustrations. The central character is Perian de Chirolo, a selfish, charming, improvident young actor. Between his poverty and his ambition, courting a noblewoman and distinguishing himself heroically in a dinosaur hunt with her family, he sees life at every level and comes unwillingly to awareness of the political and sexual corruption and inequalities in Malacian soci-

ety, on which his existence is little more than parasitic. These themes are treated with both vigor and sensitivity. Projected sequels of revolution and invasion in Malacia, presaged by subterranean rumblings in this first volume, have not been written yet.

In June 1974 Aldiss was Guest of Honor at a science-fiction convention in Stockholm, and in April 1975 at the American Lunacon. In May he was working with Harry Harrison on *Hell's Cartographers* (1975), a collection of autobiographical essays by six science-fiction writers, including both editors. Another project inspired in the course of writing *Billion Year Spree* was a profusely illustrated account of the art of illustration in science-fiction magazines, published in large format as *Science Fiction Art* in October 1975. In this year Aldiss's papers were deposited on loan in Oxford's Bodleian Library, and the library held an exhibition of items from this collection in October and November, only its second exhibition of the papers of a living author.

Brothers of the Head is another illustrated novel, though as different as could be from *The Malacia Tapestry*. It is a grim dossier of the careers of two brothers, Siamese twins with a dormant third head, who leave their desolate Norfolk birthplace and become rock stars. Introduced by their sister and including contributions from the twins' solicitor, manager, and doctor, and a study of their lyrics, *Brothers of the Head* is an interesting attempt to tell Tom and Barry's story from several viewpoints; another is provided by the stark and edgy illustrations by Ian Pollock. The technique enables Aldiss to imitate much of the complexity of life, especially when the narrators contradict each other, revealing their own interests and values. He also takes the opportunity for side glances at various bleak aspects of contemporary culture, though he set the book, as if by habit, some ten years in the future. This staunch realism is unfortunately undercut by inconsistent characterization and by the twins' songs, which are far too literary to have been written by the punks Aldiss is trying to describe. *Brothers of the Head* was published in 1977, the year in which Aldiss was chairman of the Society of Authors and in which he won the first James Blish Memorial Award for Science Fiction Criticism. *Last Orders and Other Stories*, also published that year, includes five of his "enigmas"; another dream research story, "Journey to the Heartland," rather reminiscent of John Fowles; and a story from 1973, "The Expensive Delicate Ship," which itself originated in a dream.

Enemies of the System (1978), subtitled *A Tale of Homo Uniformis*, is the story of a group of the elite from a future Earth under totalitarian communism. One of their privileges is to spend holidays on the planet Lysenka II, whose first colonists have degenerated into savagery and even evolved into different animal forms. When their vehicle breaks down and strands them in the wilderness, some of the characters accept the natural order of the planet, while others, more doctrinaire, resist it, even at the cost of their own comfort and chances of survival. The ones who adapt best are denounced, upon rescue, for transgressing the teachings of the party, one might almost say for "thoughtcrime." The book is a curiously unadventurous one for Aldiss, conforming closely to dystopian totalitarian models in previous science fiction, closest of all to George Orwell's *1984* in its depiction of characters from a routinely repressed society. One of them, Millia Sygiek, even has a golden reminiscence of proles toiling in a peach orchard. Aldiss says that the story was written as a polemic reply to writers from Communist countries who claim that Western authors never envisage Communist utopias, though *Enemies of the System* seems more to support their contention than to invalidate it. He wrote it originally as a novella and had it published as a book in its own right in 1978 only at the suggestion of the publisher Jonathan Cape; it does not benefit from the extra

attention this promotion has earned it.

Though Aldiss at the time considered *A Rude Awakening* (1978), the third Horatio Stubbs novel, one of his best, it did not sell as well as the first two. Set in Sumatra in 1946, it tells how both amorous and military engagements continued in full spate after the general end of hostilities. Waiting for demobilization, Stubbs becomes entangled with two Chinese women and witnesses more of the corruptions encouraged by war—Fascist inhumanities among his own army—as bad in their own way as the vicious and violent deaths still happening on all sides. After the fury of combat in *A Soldier Erect*, a kind of enervated sickness pervades Medan, imperiling Stubbs's increasingly desperate sex life and sense of comedy. Where the previous volume was concerned with the loss of innocence, Stubbs's "rude awakening" is to a world which has lost its stability and much of its logic—losses all the more jarring for being gradually appreciated against a background of official peace. Aldiss has plans for a fourth volume, "Time of Discharge."

In 1978, at the end of his term as chairman of the Society of Authors, Aldiss became chairman of

Brian W. Aldiss

28.ix.81

DRACULA

Author: Bram Stoker
First Book Publication: 1897
Type of work: novel
Time: Present day
Locale: Transylvania and England (mainly Whitby and London)

Space

One of the most famous and frightening of all fantasy novels,
Count Dracula, has risen from the pages of Bram Stoker's ~~novel~~ to become
known throughout the world. Cunningly constructed, the book
still gives off a heady aroma of Victorian ~~decay~~ *Corruption*, while its vampire
villain,

Space *INSERT HERE p.1A*

Although the name of Dracula is ~~as familiar~~ almost as
much a household word as, say, Freud's, most people know of the vampire
Count *only* at secondhand. The novel, however, is ~~considerably~~ more ~~potent~~
powerful than most of its derivations. It is *intellectually* ~~cunningly~~ constructed, and
has ~~great~~ *considerable* narrative ~~power~~ *strength*, incorporating ~~a terrifyingly large~~ number of grisly scenes,
which, despite ~~a strong~~ doses of melodrama, *and are* operate on more than one
level.

Bram Stoker was ~~unmistakeably~~ Irish, born in Dublin in 1847, ~~and~~
In *Dracula*, by far his best novel, we are reminded of ~~another~~ *his* near-
contemporary, another Dubliner, Sheridan LeFanu. Although LeFanu is
the better writer, *Dracula* has many LeFanuesque attributes, such as ~~its~~
able construction, ingenuity of plot, and ~~an inclination towards~~ *a relish for* the
supernatural. It owes a debt to LeFanu's superb vampire short story, "Car-
milla".
Stoker was an invalid throughout his childhood, *compensating with*
~~a state~~ *His elder brother (Sir) Thornley Stoker, became a famous Dublin surgeon;* of hyperactivity when ~~an~~ adult. Like LeFanu, ~~he went to attended~~
THORNLEY/ Stoker attended Trinity College, Dublin and, after a spell in the ~~civil~~ civil service,
became associated with the great actor, *Henry Irving.* ~~Henry Irving. Irving made~~
Stoker ~~actor-manager~~ of the Lyceum, a position he held until Irving's
~~death in 1905~~ (Irving became lessee and manager of the Lyceum in 1878).
In 1878, the year that ~~his~~ Irving took over the Lyceum, *Theatre in London;* Stoker ~~held this~~
accepted & held the exacting position *of manager. He arranged* ~~arranging~~ all Irving's tours and many *other* commitments,
faithful lieutenant until Irving died in Bradford after a performance ~~of Tennyson's Becket~~,
in 1905. During this long period, the large, amiable, red-haired Irishman
travelled the world with Irving and
produced a number of ephemeral novels; *of these novels,* only *Dracula* remains among the *literary*
Un-Dead. Stoker himself died in 1912.

One of *Henry* Irving's most memorable performances was ~~as~~ a weird and
chilling *impersonation* ~~performance~~ of Mephistopheles ~~of~~ *in* a version of *Faust* (1885-87);
~~and it may be that in this characterisation Stoker found inspiration for~~
~~his immortal character, Dracula.~~ Irving's Mephistopheles lives on in
the theatrical character of Stoker's Count.

[Left margin handwritten note:] Stoker's uncommunicative biographer, Ludham, tells us that Stoker married Florence Balcombe in that eventful year of 1878; she bore him one son, Noel.

[Right margin handwritten note:] but ran in the family, as it were.

Revised typescript for a recent essay on Dracula

their Cultural Exchanges Committee. He was also a member of the Arts Council Literature Panel from 1978 to 1980. In 1979 he produced a collection, *New Arrivals, Old Encounters*, not linked by commentary as *Starswarm* was, but connected through a system of speculations about the relationship of mind to universe, and communication between the two. "Non-Isotropic" equates the Big Bang with the Logos of Genesis by locating God at a subatomic level, omnipresent, rippling through the universe (which consists of the ripples): "We ourselves, our bodies, are composed of the consciousness of God in a phase transition." "Song of the Silencer" suggests that the human brain is not a receiver but a filter, cutting out some of the total godhead-signal to give us room for independence of thought and action. Unusually for Aldiss, this volume reprints two stories already collected (in *Comic Inferno*): "Amen and Out" and "The Soft Predicament." *This World and Nearer Ones*, a miscellany subtitled *Essays Exploring the Familiar*, was published at the same time. The topics, "familiar" to Aldiss readers but extraordinarily diverse from any other viewpoint, include the literature of drug taking, science fiction in television and the cinema, the paintings of G. F. Watts, the writings of Josef Nesvadba and Jules Verne, and observations on California, Russia, and Sumatra, which Aldiss revisited in 1978 after writing *A Rude Awakening*.

Life in the West, a novel set in 1977 and 1978, was published in Britain in 1980. A commentary on cultural and political tension between Russia and the West, it is focused on Thomas Squire, a celebrated critic attending an international conference on contemporary popular culture during a crisis in his marriage. Squire is one of Aldiss's most complex and successful characters: an impoverished aristocrat and media pundit with a record of secret service in British Intelligence. Aldiss shows Squire's activities from outside, in their cultural context, as well as from inside, while Squire himself applies his critical technique to all his memories and experience, providing a highly suspect biological and spiritual rationalization for his hatred of communism, condemnation of his wife's adultery, and justification of his own. The text is liberally dotted with Aldiss's habitual fascinations: Yugoslavia, *Frankenstein*, Singapore, Tiepolo, Gurdjieff, Norfolk. It even includes a capsule lecture on science fiction. Given the book's strong pro-Western theme, it is surprising that it has not found a publisher in America.

In 1979 Aldiss commenced preparation for his first commissioned work, a huge trilogy set on the planet Helliconia. This will continue to occupy him into 1984; but whatever constraints it imposes on his immediate future, it has only encouraged his expansive imagination. His working material includes a globe and geophysical map, with extensive documentation of languages, inhabitants, climate, and astronomy. The first volume, *Helliconia Spring*, was published in February 1982 by Cape and Atheneum and rose at once to the best-seller list. Readers who may have felt a decline in the substance of Aldiss's science fiction over the last few years have welcomed it as a major reestablishment. In the meanwhile Aldiss has been Guest of Honor at the Singapore Book Fair in 1980, and in 1981 (with John Barth) at the Second Conference on the Fantastic in the Arts, Boca Raton, Florida.

Though Aldiss is the sort of writer who has never allowed even his most attentive readers to guess what he will produce next, he has rarely had to cope with the struggle with uncooperative publishers that afflicts many science-fiction writers; nor has he ever been obliged to turn out inferior work for commercial interest. This is not to say his career has been luxurious or easy, but its challenges have on the whole been aesthetic rather than economic ones. The liberty of his imagination and style both within and beyond the boundaries of the genre is surely related to that liberty from artistic compromise. He occupies a position of great respect and affection in the science-fiction community and continues to represent the acceptable face of science fiction to those literati who still cannot bring themselves to acknowledge the genre. His works have been abundantly translated, and he is as welcome in Scandinavia or Australia (and recently even in China) as in England, though his writing as a whole has quite an English tone and many national preoccupations. It declares a mind that is generous, erudite, and energetic—a rare combination—and represents the triumph of an intelligent, wholehearted imagination over conservatism, divisiveness, and aimlessness in contemporary ficiton.

Other:

Farewell, Fantastic Venus!: A History of the Planet Venus in Fact and Fiction, edited by Aldiss and Harry Harrison (London: Macdonald, 1968); abridged as *All About Venus* (New York: Dell, 1968);

Hell's Cartographers: Some Personal Histories of Science Fiction Writers, edited by Aldiss and Harrison

(London: Weidenfeld & Nicolson, 1975; New York: Harper & Row, 1975).

Bibliography:
Margaret Aldiss, *Item Eighty-Three: Brian W. Aldiss—a Bibliography 1954-1972* (Oxford: SF Horizons, 1972).

References:
Colin Greenland, "The Times Themselves Talk Nonsense: Language in *Barefoot in the Head*," *Foundation: The Review of Science Fiction* (September 1979): 32-41;

Fredric Jameson, "Generic Discontinuities in SF: Brian Aldiss' *Starship*," *Science-Fiction Studies*, 1 (Fall 1973): 57-68;
Richard Mathews, *Aldiss Unbound: The Science Fiction of Brian W. Aldiss* (San Bernardino, Cal.: Borgo Press, 1977);
Charles Platt, Interview, in *Who Writes Science Fiction?* (Manchester, U.K.: Savoy, 1980); republished as *Dream Makers* (New York: Berkley, 1980), pp. 297-309.

Papers:
The Bodleian Library, Oxford, has a collection of Aldiss's papers.

Keith Alldritt
(10 December 1935-   )

Malcolm Page
Simon Fraser University

BOOKS: *The Making of George Orwell: An Essay in Literary History* (London: Edward Arnold, 1969; New York: St. Martin's, 1969);
The Visual Imagination of D. H. Lawrence (London: Edward Arnold, 1971; Evanston, Ill.: Northwestern University Press, 1971);
The Good Pit Man: A Novel (London: Deutsch, 1976);
The Lover Next Door (London: Deutsch, 1977; New York: St. Martin's, 1978);
Eliot's "Four Quartets": Poetry as Chamber Music (London & Totowa, N.J.: Woburn Press, 1978);
Elgar on the Journey to Hanley (London: Deutsch, 1979; New York: St. Martin's, 1979).

Keith Alldritt had three novels published between 1976 and 1979, starting a sequence intended, according to the dust jackets, to "deal with the course of Midlands society." All three are rooted in exact description, not only of places around Wolverhampton in the West Midlands but also of such details as the way meals are served and what is eaten. The first, *The Good Pit Man: A Novel* (1976), is set in the present, while the second, *The Lover Next Door* (1977), more ambitiously is set primarily in the years of World War II and seen through the eyes of a small boy. The third, *Elgar on the Journey to Hanley* (1979), goes back to the end of the nineteenth century to give a friend's view of composer Edward

Elgar. Each novel was welcomed by reviewers on publication and initial hardback printings sold out in Great Britain, though Alldritt is so far known only to a small circle of readers.

Alldritt was born in Wolverhampton in 1935 to Alan James and Elsie Tongue Alldritt; his experiences as a young child in wartime England are reflected in *The Lover Next Door*. He attended Wolverhampton Grammar School from 1946 to 1954, then went up to St. Catherine's College, Cambridge, in 1954. He read French and German, as well as doing some work in English, attending F. R. Leavis's seminars in criticism at Downing College. Receiving his B.A. in 1957, he began work at Cambridge on a thesis on D. H. Lawrence and Nietzsche. He abandoned this, however, to take a post as Lektor at the University of Vienna, Austria, for 1958-1959, after which he taught for two terms at a new comprehensive school at Willenhall, Staffordshire. He then became an assistant professor at the University of Illinois, Urbana, until 1963, when he moved to the University of British Columbia in Vancouver, where he remains. Though he has lived mostly out of England for more than twenty years, he frequently visits his native country and defines himself as an Anglo-Canadian with the emphasis on "Anglo." He married in 1960 and had a son. Divorced, he remarried in the mid-1970s and has a daughter born in 1976 and a son born in 1981. He has held a Canada Council Fellowship and been elected to the Royal Society of Literature.

After his books of criticism dealing with George Orwell and D. H. Lawrence were published, Alldritt turned to fiction. He likes to write at least three mornings a week, though the bulk of his writing is done in the summers when he is free of teaching responsibilities. As he grows more experienced, he finds increasing rewriting is necessary, for he has become more conscious of technique and perhaps, in his words, also "more fastidious and quirky." He is deeply engaged with the West Midlands, west of Wolverhampton, his childhood home. The area was, he says, "the base of much of the heavy-industry technology which made Britain a world force until 1945." Further, the region was "a dynamo of Western thought for the hundred years from 1780 to 1880." Hence, he has planned a group of twelve novels, linked by their setting in the Midlands (or, in the fourth, by people who come from the Midlands).

The main character of Alldritt's first novel, *The Good Pit Man*, is Ray Wilcock, a middle-aged miner ("pit man") turned ambulance driver. He also teaches driving to Vera Marshall, the fiftyish wife of a successful businessman and local councillor. The relationship suddenly erupts into an affair, though the exact attraction is never clear (some idea derived from D. H. Lawrence that working-class males are more vital seems implicit). Then on a Sunday drive they are seen together by women from their village, and the scandalized reaction occupies the amusing chapter five. Ray's wife, Annie, is told of the affair, and she orders Ray out of the house. His problem is solved by Vera, who buys him an old trailer and finds a picturesque quarry nearby for him to keep it in. Through the summer Vera drives out to the trailer three times a week. She has conveniently passed her driving test; Ray is conveniently on night shift; and Tom, Vera's husband, is conveniently either absent or too busy to notice. Then Tom reveals that he knows of the affair, but chooses not to care, especially as he is unexpectedly about to move them to London. Though the move is delayed, Vera and Ray's parting at the end of the novel is harmonious. By this time, too, Ray has come to enjoy living alone, in rural peace.

The novel attends closely to place: Vera shops in Wolverhampton; the lovers visit Hardwick Hall; and they drive down the M6 motorway to buy the trailer in Wednesbury. Alldritt attends painstakingly to accents and ways of speaking ("Ah cor stop an' talk to ye today. Ah've gorra catch the twelve

o'clock buz"). Alldritt's writing could aid some future social historian: "Vera laid out the cutlery and the heavy cups and saucers and plates that she had bought at Harrods on her last visit to London. She placed woollen napkins of a warm green colour by each plate. Then she made the tea, removed the food from the big shiny frying pan and they were ready to eat." Place is described carefully: "They drove down to the A5 and turned left. Vera liked the Watling Street even if it was often congested and sometimes dangerous. She liked the ring of history it had and liked to imagine how it looked before all the ribbon development and factories and service stations had existed."

Robert Nye in the *Guardian* found the novel derivative, observing that "the local colour is spread on overmuch in Lawrentian style, with thick impasto, and there were moments and whole scenes where I felt that Mr. Alldritt's imagination was still going to school to his masters." *The Good Pit Man* was generally praised for the accuracy and intelligence with which the main characters are depicted, as well as their region and the values of their community. Nye praised the book as "an honest and interesting

Keith Alldritt

debut," and Lorna Sage described it in the *Observer* as "convincing and unpretentious" and "a likeable, alert book."

The Lover Next Door describes through the eyes of a small boy next-door neighbors in Wolverhampton during World War II. Frank is a bright boy at elementary school, his father is overseas in the army, and his simple, well-meaning mother is often on night shift at the local factory. When she is out at night, young Frank is sent next door to sleep at the Biddles'. They are the fat, moody Old Girl, rarely stirring from her armchair, and her two daughters in their forties, Doris and Cath. Listening and observing, fascinated, while playing the board game snakes and ladders with the sisters, Frank pieces together his child's view of the household, becoming a kind of shock absorber between mother and daughters.

Doris is visited during the war years in turn by three admirers. First comes the faded elderly Mr. Gogarty, who on one memorable occasion takes Frank along to a show at the Hippodrome. Soon after, ordered out of the house by the Old Girl, Mr. Gogarty dies of a heart attack. Doris's next friend is Teddy Eynon, a draftsman working on Defiant fighters, who is soon helping Frank build a model plane. After quarreling with Cath and the Old Girl, Teddy risks calling Doris his "very best friend," then is never seen at the house again. Her third friend is Pietro, an Italian prisoner of war allowed much freedom around the town. He comes often to tea, takes on the gardening, and builds a wooden arbor. The Old Girl, however, takes a rare walk down the garden and discovers him kissing Doris—and he, too, never returns to the house.

Cath now suddenly marries a widower named Cedric, who is thought to be a sweeper at the locomotive works, though he claims to be building engines. One Sunday Cath drives the Old Girl and Frank out to the big country house where the Old Girl used to work and a third daughter is buried. Cedric disgraces himself by smoking beside the grave and thereafter is banned from the house by the Old Girl. Frank, by now age nine or ten, has "gained precocious insight into what deep involvement with others might mean—and cost," as Anne Redmon said in the *Sunday Times*. Frank has formed, too, in the words of the novel's epigraph from essayist John Ruskin, "his first ideas of female tenderness and beauty."

A few short scenes conclude the tale. When Frank's father returns after the war, they move to a better house and rarely see the Biddles again. Doris and Cath both decline after the Old Girl dies and later, having left the city, Frank learns of Cath's death. Years later he makes a final visit to Doris so that she can give him papers, books, and toys still in the house—among them a speech written by Cath and lists of Italian words written out by Pietro.

Redmon faulted the novel's structure—"an awkward beginning and loose ending dissipate the life and warmth he has evoked"—but otherwise reviewers welcomed Alldritt's talents. Nye in the *Guardian* recognized the accuracy of the picture of the war years, with the details of powdered eggs and National Savings stamps, rationing and air raids. Adolf Wood in the *Times Literary Supplement* found Alldritt had "the gift of the drab—he conveys, with really impressive skill, in prose deliberately drained of colour, the meagre substance of his characters' lives and the seedy flavour of their environment." Redmon admired his "passive gift of letting life occur in his characters. Before you know it, you're hooked into caring what happens to them inside their heads—not for what events might impose on them." Peter Ackroyd in the *Spectator* saw the novel as concerned with memory and its unreliability: "The novel is not so much *about* [the Biddles], as about the idea of remembering them." The real theme is "that reality is only powerful when it is seen nostalgically. Frank can enter the adult world, but only at the price of leaving the novel and its fantasy world."

Alldritt's third novel, *Elgar on the Journey to Hanley*, focuses on Dora Penny, a young woman who becomes a friend of Edward Elgar, the English composer. The first fifty-six pages describe in great detail Elgar and his wife, Alice, spending a half day with the Penny family in Wolverhampton, when Elgar is on his way from his home in Malvern to Hanley. The date is 1896, with Elgar in his early forties. Dora is about twenty, musical, pretty, unconventional in thought but in practice obedient to her stern father, the Rector. Elgar is at once taken with young Dora and impulsively leads her off to watch a soccer game.

The rest of the novel describes the relationship between Elgar and Dora during the next ten years. Alice Elgar at times issues invitations to make it possible for the pair to be together, flying kites and climbing the North Hill at Malvern. Since the Rector refuses Dora her train fare, she takes to cycling the forty miles to Malvern for stays with the Elgars, audacious for a woman in these early days of bicycles. She attends Elgar's concerts and becomes a part of his circle of friends there. Then comes the "moment she would remember as the supreme instant of her life": he composes "Dorabella" about

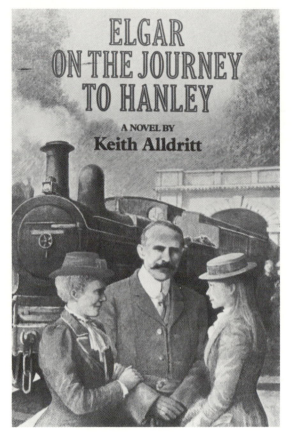

Dust jacket for Alldritt's third novel on "the course of Midlands society"

her, to become a part of his "Enigma Variations." "She felt, at that instant, a whirl of pride, pleasure and almost shame that he should have written something so beautiful about her." A potentially sexual moment occurs soon after when they are out in the country together, but then Elgar thinks of his wife, and both he and Dora fall asleep. As time passes, Elgar moves to Hereford (no longer within cycling distance), is knighted, and forms a grander circle of friends. In 1909 Dora finally realizes that whatever affection he once felt for her has been transferred to another woman.

Toward the end of the book, Alldritt slips in a few hints of what actually happened later, Dora's eventual apathetic acquiescence to a dull marriage in her middle age, and then Elgar's cutting her in the street. He even directs the reader forward to the present: "She stood on the very spot where some three-quarters of a century later and in a different building another band of musicians from this borough sang to their groupies and their fellow townspeople." Alldritt also alludes to a future book when Dora crossed the path of "the young American poet who was to become famous for his dedica-

tion to the art of the troubadours. . . . This poet was, of course, to become a noted polygamist."

This novel studies the ways in which eighty years ago a man could have a friendship with an attractive single woman half his age and examines the curious role of his wife. But the man is Elgar—moody, unpredictable, apparently insensitive to the girl's feelings, and outwardly an unappealing social climber. He is a man known now by his music, and Alldritt writes well but sparingly of his compositions, or rather of the way Dora perceives them. One consequence of reading the novel will be to make many people listen to the "Enigma Variations" (and not only to Number 10). The novel can be seen more broadly as presenting the way a man of great talent looks to the ordinary people around him. Finally, this is less a document about Elgar than about a shrewd study of a friendship and of facets of the West Midlands at the end of the nineteenth century.

Alldritt worked for six years on Elgar's biography and personality: Andre Deutsch, his publisher, stressed the need for accuracy to avoid any possibility of a libel case. Though the *Elgarian* complained that the novel was unfair to Lady Elgar, others assured Alldritt that his picture was correct. Alldritt has said that his aim was to present Elgar as a man of the 1890s, of the world of Oscar Wilde and the young W. B. Yeats. He sought to understand Elgar rather than to hero-worship and to show what it was like trying to be a composer in that somewhat unfavorable time and place.

Critics praised *Elgar on the Journey to Hanley*. Nye wrote in the *Guardian*: "If I say that Alldritt has succeeded in capturing in prose some of the erotic ecstasy and guilt which you find in Elgar's own supreme musical achievement, the cello concerto, then you will have some notion of the flavour of his novel." Hermione Lee in the *Observer* found the book "unostentatious, . . . a nostalgic and carefully detailed picture of provincial life," delicately studying "the awkward, unaccountable feelings between the girl and the composer, and of his wife's diplomatic and humiliating role as emotional procuress and protectress."

Alldritt has completed two more novels and is working on the sixth in his twelve-book Midlands cycle. "From Sea to Shining Sea," the fourth, is set in the 1960s in Vancouver's West End (where Alldritt has lived for nearly all of his years in the city), picturing immigrants to Canada, what he calls "the Canadian matrix." The fifth, "Progress and Privilege," is set in Lichfield, Staffordshire. It focuses on the intellectual and scientific enquiries of

Joseph Priestley and Erasmus Darwin and their Lunar Society, and thus on the course of English thought between the American and French Revolutions. This eighteenth-century novel is likely to be the earliest chronologically of his sequence, though Alldritt has toyed with a novel about the Dark Ages and the legendary Offa, who built a dyke between England and Wales. The sixth, "Rose of the Staffordshire Knot," which draws on Alldritt's experi-

ences of Cambridge and teaching school, advances from the 1950s to the 1970s.

Each novel by Keith Alldritt appears deceptively slight, almost totally successful within limited ambitions. Further, each of the published works is an improvement on its predecessor. His total achievement, however, is one to be judged only in the future when the complete vision of the twelve novels is available.

A. Alvarez
(5 August 1929-   )

Sibyl L. Severance
Pennsylvania State University

BOOKS: [Poems] (Oxford: Fantasy Press, 1952);
Stewards of Excellence (New York: Scribners, 1958); republished as *The Shaping Spirit* (London: Chatto & Windus, 1958);
The End of It (N.p.: Privately printed, 1958);
The School of Donne (London: Chatto & Windus, 1961; New York: Pantheon, 1962);
Under Pressure (Harmondsworth & Baltimore: Penguin, 1965);
Beyond All This Fiddle (New York: Random House, 1968; London: Penguin, 1968);
Lost (London: Turret Books, 1968);
Twelve Poems (London: The Review, 1968);
Apparition (St. Lucia, Queensland: University of Queensland Press, 1971);
The Savage God (London: Weidenfeld & Nicolson, 1971; New York: Random House, 1972);
Samuel Beckett (New York: Viking, 1973); republished as *Beckett* (London: Fontana, 1973);
Hers (London: Weidenfeld & Nicolson, 1974; New York: Random House, 1975);
Autumn to Autumn and Selected Poems 1953-1976 (London: Macmillan, 1978);
Hunt (New York: Simon & Schuster, 1978; London: Macmillan, 1978);
Life After Marriage: Love in an Age of Divorce (New York: Simon & Schuster, 1982; London: Macmillan, 1982).

A. Alvarez writes of people under pressure. His two novels, *Hers* (1974) and *Hunt* (1978), rigorously explore the tensions of private experience. Apparent in this fiction as well as in his criticism and

his poetry is Alvarez's belief that the artist must face "the full range" of experience "with his full intelligence." In his insistence upon seeing the whole individual, Alvarez stands as a modern Metaphysical, himself a follower of "the school of Donne."

Alfred Alvarez was born in London in 1929 into a family of Anglo-Sephardic background whose ancestors had lived in England since the seventeenth century. His parents were Bertie and Katie Levy Alvarez. As a child he was surrounded by the comfortable security of an upper-middle-class world. The family's wealth came from a businessman grandfather; its cultural life centered on music, which gave him his first awareness of the inner rhythm of sound. Yet in the midst of the security provided by tradition, wealth, and culture were the pressures of a stormy childhood, the memory of a time when both his parents "halfheartedly put their heads in the gas oven," a memory that helped focus his thoughts on suicide in *The Savage God* (1971).

When deciding upon a preparatory school, he was guided by an intense "ten-minute" interest in becoming a scientist and therefore attended Oundle, a Northhamptonshire school noted for its rugby as well as its science. Rugby turned out to be the more absorbing activity for Alvarez. Of most lasting influence at Oundle, however, was an English master's introduction of John Donne by way of the lyric "Witchcraft by a Picture." Leaving Oundle in 1948 at nineteen, Alvarez was frustrated over his failure to secure a scholarship to Oxford and spent a year teaching French in a preparatory school before entering Corpus Christi College, Oxford.

After he entered Oxford, one of Alvarez's particularly significant activities was his founding of the Critical Society. Members of the society were responding to the excitement generated by the writing of I. A. Richards and William Empson. The group hoped that the stringent critical analysis encouraged by New Criticism would revitalize poetry at Oxford, which they believed had become enervated. Although active in the Critical Society's program, Alvarez avoided an intense involvement in university literary politics, determinedly adhering to the conviction which was to surface again and again in his work: individual fate is a personal matter to be resolved privately—to be removed, if possible, from a clamorous public shaping.

After receiving a first from Oxford and spending an extra year there on a Senior Research Scholarship, Alvarez began a writing career dominated by literary criticism, at least until 1966, and marked by periods of teaching at American universities. Alvarez believes his experience at Princeton as a visiting fellow in 1953-1954 was noteworthy in two ways: first, in the development of his "passionate love affair with America" (where he found it

easier to be Jewish than he had in England), and second, in the opportunity to become acquainted with R. P. Blackmur, who made him a protege. Later Blackmur was instrumental in securing for Alvarez a Rockefeller Foundation Fellowship (1955-1956) and the Christian Gauss Seminar at Princeton, which he gave in 1957 and 1958. In addition to these honors, Alvarez received a D. H. Lawrence Fellowship in 1958. Through this financial assistance, he spent periods in the years from 1955 to 1958 in New Mexico, at Harvard, back in London, and then at Princeton, writing and teaching. His first two books, both works of literary criticism, were the result. It was also during this time, in 1956, that he married his first wife, Ursula Barr.

His earliest full-length book, entitled *Stewards of Excellence* (1958) in the United States and *The Shaping Spirit* in England, drew upon his literary studies on both sides of the Atlantic, setting forth Alvarez's conviction that modernism influenced American poetry only, that British poetry in the twentieth century was chiefly concerned with extending "what has always been there in the most vital of our tradition." In this first book Alvarez noted the shaping presence of John Donne, the example of what to him was most invigorating in the English poetical tradition. That he should next write *The School of Donne* (1961) was almost inevitable; he had begun work for his Ph.D. at Oxford by studying the Metaphysicals; additionally, since his study at Oundle, he had felt the vivid presence of Donne in his own poetry and in the literature of his country. The Christian Gauss Seminars at Princeton proved the place to develop his ideas on Donne.

While Alvarez was writing these first books of literary criticism, he was also serving as the poetry critic and editor for the London *Observer*, a position he held from 1956 to 1966. Additional critical work included what he calls his disastrous theatrical reviews for the *New Statesman* written when he was drama editor from 1958 to 1960, a period he has referred to as "the two unhappiest years of my life." At this time he was also writing for such periodicals as *Saturday Review*, *Commentary*, *New York Review of Books*, the *Kenyon Review*, the *Partisan Review*, and, later, the *Spectator*. In his critical articles he was most excited about the poetry of Ted Hughes and Thomas Gunn in England, Robert Lowell and John Berryman in America, and, later, Sylvia Plath. In writing of these authors, he believed that he, too, was a shaping spirit as he offered ways this unfamiliar poetry could be read.

By age thirty Alvarez had completed his stint as drama critic, had written two books of literary

criticism, and was teaching at Brandeis University as a visiting full professor. Although the next year, 1961, was to bring him the Vachel Lindsay prize from *Poetry* magazine, he withheld his own poetry from publication in England, not wanting to create a seeming conflict between his creative work and his responsibilities as a poetry editor. Nineteen sixty-one was a year of personal crisis: Alvarez attempted suicide and was divorced. In the fall, trying to re-focus his life, he traveled to Europe on a BBC commission. He has characterized this and the next few years in the early 1960s as "a chaotic, difficult time." Engaged in questioning his own values, he found a renewed interest in the reactions of other artists to pressure. *Under Pressure* (1965) recorded his observations of writers under societal stresses. His interviews with poets in eastern European countries, such as Czechoslovakia, Poland, Hungary, and Yugoslavia, furnished the material which was the basis of his comparison of authors in eastern Europe and the United States. He characterized the book as a "kind of intellectual travelogue," concerned with the "present sense of trouble," which Alvarez found pervading both countries and artists.

Alvarez believed that eastern European writers, although in varying circumstances, possessed an iron in their souls which enabled them to persevere in their art. Of the authors he met, he came to especially admire the Polish poet Zbigniew Herbert and his work. On the other hand, what emerged in his examination of the artist in America was the difficulty of living in that democracy during the Kennedy years, the "seductiveness of the United States in its combination of three ambiguous virtues: loneliness, energy, and independence." Most striking for Alvarez was the pressing sense of isolation and responsibility of the American artist, who felt he must create "his whole world—his moral order, his style and his tradition—for himself and from scratch."

Throughout the years from 1961 to 1966, Alvarez was traveling, observing how artists worked and lived, evaluating their art, writing, and maturing, so that by 1966 he was ready to devote himself more fully to his own writing. From five years of questioning his commitments came the realization that if he were to be a "real" writer, he must write his own books; not to do so was ultimately "an evasion of responsibility." By 1966 Alvarez was eager for new directions in his career and in his personal life. In that year he stopped reviewing poetry for the *Observer* and married his second wife, Anne Adams.

His new resolve to write was furthered by the suggestions of Tony Godwin, an editor at Penguin, who in 1962 had published the popular anthology *The New Poetry*. Alvarez had selected and introduced the poems for this volume, commenting that the book might be subtitled, "Beyond the Gentility Principle." When Godwin read Alvarez's essay "Beyond All This Fiddle" in the *Times Literary Supplement* in 1967, he suggested that Alvarez gather his essays into a collection, which was published the following year as *Beyond All This Fiddle*. That *Beyond All This Fiddle* was to be the *nunc dimittis* for Alvarez's full-time career as a critic is suggested by its epigraph from Marianne Moore's "Poetry": "I, too, dislike it: there are things that / are important beyond all this fiddle." Nevertheless, the book is a tribute to the various sounds of all that fiddling and a fine example of the range of Alvarez's wit and concerns, as he moves from poetry to an essay on Sigmund Freud to climbing the cliffs of Shiprock. Of special importance is the title essay praising the Extremist style of poetry as "the most courageous response" to the precarious world of the artist where "internal confusion transmuted into new kinds of artistic order becomes the only possible form of coherence."

What most involved Alvarez during the late 1950s and the 1960s is apparent in his own poetry, also published in 1968 in *Lost*. Its epigraph from Donne—"To chuse, is to do: but to be no part of any body, is to be nothing"—had appeared earlier as a quote in *The School of Donne* and discloses Alvarez's preoccupation with an insistent energy opposing an enervating fear of isolation and nothingness. This opposition has simultaneously impelled and overshadowed much of Alvarez's work and life. *Lost* mourns two disappearances—the natural world of "lucid, moving air, the swaying elms" and love, since now the alienated lovers stay in "grey untender rooms / Sleeping the nights apart in the same bed." The speaker in "The Survivor" passes "life like a traveller who taps / The earth and cries, 'Dear mother, let me in.'" Endings and beginnings merge in a common negation and protest. Repeatedly and paradoxically, presence denotes absence, as in "Back," which recounts the flatness of an unfamiliar world which the speaker returns to after his attempted suicide: "They took the tube from my arm / And plugged the strange world back in place."

Lost exemplifies the writer's use of his own skin "as wallpaper," that act of Berryman's which has become a part of Alvarez's poetics. Nowhere is Alvarez's painful transmutation of private experience into art more clear than in *The Savage God*, a study of artists' suicides or attempted suicides. When Tony Godwin secured the advance which gave time for the book, Alvarez planned on two years for its completion, but this time stretched into four years, to 1971. While he writes poetry quickly, Alvarez's prose is rewritten and rewritten, sometimes as many as eight times, before he is satisfied that it is right. Alvarez says of *The Savage God* that his whole point was "to write a genuinely existential piece of criticism about people, about myself, but it was also about art and discipline." This book contains Alvarez's most extended statement on the Extremist poets and their lives. He sees such poets as Lowell, Berryman, Plath, and Hughes "committed to psychic exploration out along that friable edge that divides the tolerable from the intolerable." The mastery of their art rises from equal commitments "to lucidity, precision and a certain vigilant directness of expression." The reasons why such explorations can end in suicide, the explanation of this terrible waste, and the history of the act, especially in Western culture, are the subjects of the book.

While the work studies the artist and his suicide in relation to determining social and cultural forces, the book's primary emphasis is on the course of the individual artist's experience, as is manifested in the two most moving sections of the work, the beginning chapter on Plath and the concluding one on Alvarez himself. Throughout the work, Alvarez empathetically examines the mysterious transformation of private pain into art. That this dark mix of creativity and destructiveness is lucid and compelling for the public is reflected by the sales figures of 35,000 hardback copies in the United States. Such financial success finally offered Alvarez the opportunity to write his novels, although before the appearance of *Hers* and *Hunt, Apparition* (1971) and *Samuel Beckett* (1973) were published.

Apparition, including previously published poems, was illustrated by Charles Blackman's gouaches, which seemed to Alvarez "to express perfectly everything I was fumbling towards." Alvarez's introduction compares Blackman with himself, finding both "articulate, quick in our reaction to things, more than a touch aggressive and not prone to reverence." Similarities extend to their work where "both of us were preoccupied . . . more with our inner lives than with strictly aesthetic criteria. . . . We took artistic discipline and control for granted and were using them to pursue quarries more elusive and personal."

A respite from pursuing the personal was the writing of *Samuel Beckett*, a return to literary criticism and a vivid demonstration of the directness and acuity which had distinguished his earlier criticism. Alvarez decided that "had Duns Scotus been alive and well and writing novels in the twentieth century, he might have written *Watt*." His sensitive judgments of Beckett illuminate the book. In summarizing the effect of *How It Is* (1964; published first in French as *Comment c'est*, 1961), Alvarez deftly discloses the essence of Beckett as artist: "Even at its most disintegrated, when the shattered syntax is scarcely that of the gasp, there is a kind of clenched lucidity about Beckett's writing that somehow justifies one's efforts."

In his first novel, *Hers*, Alvarez's own efforts were directed toward writing about a woman in her early thirties, Julie Stone, who is so possessed by self that she is only "hers," in spite of her marriage, her children, and her lover, Sam Green. Today Alvarez believes that her husband, Charles, a Renaissance scholar who is well past fifty, is the more interesting character. In spite of great apparent dissimilarities, both the Stones exhibit similar central characteristics and have parallel experiences. Both have detachment from others rather than compassion or a full humanity. Both are essentially passive, moved by outside forces, waiting to be crushed. For the delicate Julie, Charles's obsessive lovemaking resembles a landslide. Charles is physically threatened and emotionally shattered by the Outcasts, a gang of four motorcyclists. In addition, his humanity is threatened by an outpouring of quotations that is his automatic response to every situation. Sam, a graduate student in literature, says about Charles: "His whole life is just a series of footnotes to other people's texts."

In other parallels both Charles and Julie are fettered by their betrayals of fathers and origins. Charles has left behind the Midlands town of Derby, rejecting its working-class certainties for the shifting, dubious knowledge of his academic life, but he is dogged by his belief that he has been false to his fathers—his father by birth and his spiritual father and teacher, Mr. Rotherham. After a fumbled attempt at suicide from an overdose of alcohol and sleeping tablets, he can pray only to "Our Father, Who art in the library." Yet Charles retrieves a measure of humanity when he returns to Derby with his young children; he turns toward the direct friendliness of Arthur Clegg, the lorry driver who rescued him from the Outcasts. In his recognition of his past and of the worth of other lives beyond his footnotes, he is freed to work again but with a new dignity, as he thinks of a letter of Freud: "Let us love one another and work." He accepts that for him the "slogging away" must be all.

Julie, too, in flesh and spirit denies her father, most overtly when she goes to the Iserthal Clinic in

Germany and immerses herself in its prescribed routines. Here she embraces the young ex-Nazi drug addict Kurt Wolheim and deliberately elevates the evil her minister father had rejected. Before returning to Germany, she had longed for Europe and its Black Forest "like the Congo. All that darkness. No wonder they believed in evil." After an abortion at the clinic, she acknowledges her absorption of evil: "the core of darkness at her center would remain, the black jewel for which she had waited so long."

The novel's third major character, Sam Green, offers a respite of energy through his passion for Julie, his impulsive rejection of the university pedantry and anti-Semitism, and his finding of challenges and freedom in rock climbing. His disdain for an intellectual life defined by footnotes and his exhilaration over rock climbing parallel Alvarez's own young manhood.

Alvarez sees the book as being "very much on private life," about the reluctance in England "to let private life into the equation." Yet the book is also about the way public expectations and events determine that equation. The social violence rising from war, gangs, prejudice, and false intellectual values wrenches private experience or negates human will. That Alvarez is intent on seriously exploring how the individual can live his life is evident. But although he believes that the "worlds of the novel generate their own energy," such generation falters in *Hers*. Writing in the *New York Times*, Paul Delaney found the work to have "a sour but delicate taste." Admiring the novel's "moral strenuousness," he regretted that in the sexual conflicts of the book "there is so little reason for the reader to care which fighter can claim to have won." The reviews were generally in agreement that the purpose of the book was noble but its fulfillment was flawed.

In preparing to write his second novel, *Hunt*, Alvarez heeded these criticisms, which were made more telling by the evaluation of his friend, novelist Dan Jacobson, who told Alvarez that *Hers* had "none of Alvarez's vitality in it." Alvarez resolved that his next novel, "a sort of a thriller," would contain some of the things which interested him. Seeking to evade the gloominess he found in *Hers*, Alvarez enlivened *Hunt* with humor, especially in the conversations and with intense accounts of that "marvelous art form," poker. Additionally, Conrad Hunt, the protagonist, has "a certain personal liveliness" and energy which are directed toward doing one thing really well. He is obsessed with achieving one realized painting, one genius hand of poker.

Nevertheless, much of his life eludes ordering; to Alvarez he is a "kind of fall guy." Conrad stumbles into an absurd world of spies and peril, yet he insistently confirms his human identity by following his own curiosity, hunches, and will. His acts may be ineffectual and dangerous; he may be frightened, but he insists on his right to question, to respond, to decide to be. His contemporary rearrangement of Descartes' conviction, "I hurt, therefore I am," affirms his identity. Against Inspector Davies's assurance that "you don't have any choice," Conrad continues to choose. The change in passivity from *Hers* to *Hunt* is signaled by the allegorical names of the characters: Alvarez has replaced the Stones with Hunt, thus supplanting an object with an act.

The principal setting of the novel is Hampstead and its Heath, a location familiar from the Sylvia Plath essay in *The Savage God*. (Alvarez's own home lies a block and a half from the Heath.) Conrad is in his mid-thirties, involved in a purposeless marriage and tediously working as an assistant sales manager. On the Heath while walking his dog late at night, Conrad discovers the unconscious body of a young woman, Olivia. Phoning the police from a kiosk in the early dawn, he refuses to give his name but is noticed by a postman. When trying to tell his wife of his discovery, he is frustrated by her sleepy refusal to understand and is thus isolated in his knowledge.

Later in the day he travels to an exclusive Knightsbridge shop, whose label was in Olivia's shawl, and, in his search for clues about the woman, encounters the police, who later arrest him. Conrad discovers during his imprisonment that the source of his vulnerability is his innocence. A Kafkaesque breakdown in reason occurs, which continues after his release from prison. He realizes his wife has a lover. His gambler friend, Abe, tells him that no longer does a sharp separation exist between the CIA and the Mafia: "It's a crumbling world we live in." Conrad's conviction that it is "better to play out the hand" which has been dealt brings him to visit Olivia in the hospital and to begin an affair with her. Olivia's loyalties are tangled since she has a fiance, a government official named Tim, and another lover, Elizabeth Staff. The latter arranges the passage of classified information secured from Tim to mysterious sources in Eastern Europe. Olivia acts as the carrier. At the novel's close, Conrad accompanies Olivia on one last information drop. She now works as a double agent for Abe and the CIA. Conrad's

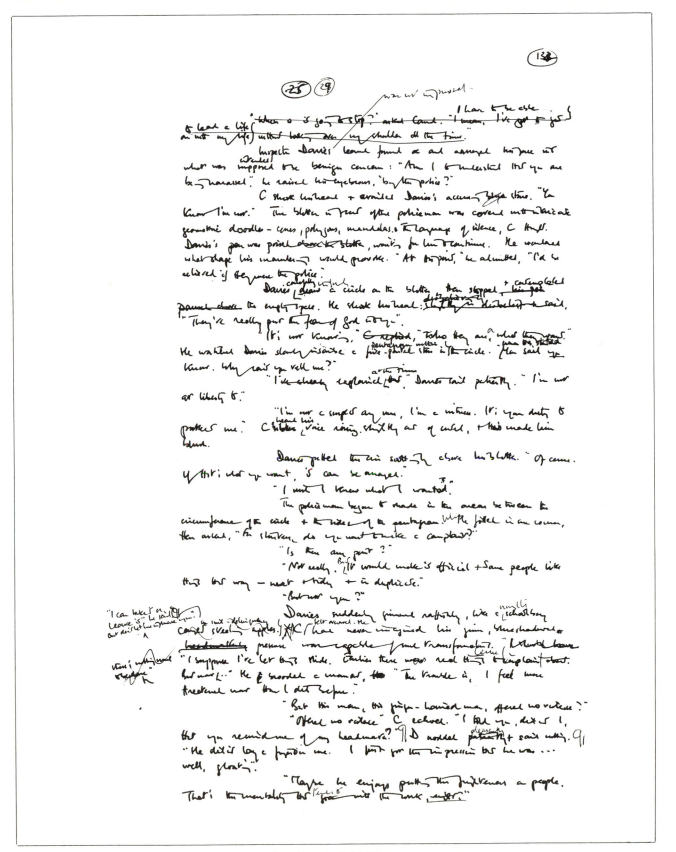

Working draft for Hunt

final act is to run into the darkness of the Heath, to run without a specific goal in mind beyond his act of running.

Here again Alvarez examines individual experience pressed and twisted by exterior forces. Hunt is an existentialist, firm in his sense of his own existence and in his persistent *no*'s, whether to his own mediocrity or to government authority, yet his life also shows the presence of inevitable tedium, the relentless reduction of possibility. Alvarez's novel resembles the work of his friend John Le Carré and Graham Greene in its crisp mastery of suspense and in the moral questioning which haunts the turns of his plot. Alvarez has reacted to the comparison with Greene by noting that during the writing of *Hunt* he took care not to read Greene because of the contagion of Greene's style. Critics, in evaluating the book, noted the resemblance to Greene but were generally more positive in their praise of the second novel than the first, as in the review by Stuart Sutherland in the *Times Literary Supplement*: "Alvarez achieves his effects with more economy and precision than Greene himself." The novel is characterized as "fast-moving and compulsive" as well as "a splendid entertainment."

The same year *Hunt* was published, Alvarez published a book of selected poems, *Autumn to Autumn*, which is particularly distinguished by the title sequence, covering the year from September 1974 to September 1975. In the autumn of 1974, after not writing poetry for ten or twelve years, Alvarez began again, writing seven poems in the course of the next year. Later he realized that they formed a sequence, which he considers the best he has written.

Alvarez's latest work, *Life After Marriage* (1982), extends his prose exploration of the interweaving of the public and private in a study of the public problem of divorce as it affects the individuals involved. The method of the book has been to use his facility in talking with people to discover from their stories what divorce has done to their lives.

While Alvarez's development has been away from the literary criticism of his early years as a writer, he has never completely abandoned it. For example, he gave the Hopwood Lecture at the University of Michigan in the spring of 1980 and there renewed his examination of Extremist art in his address, "The Myth of the Artist." And his more recent works of poetry, fiction, and nonfiction have shown his persistent emphasis on the whole man. Distinguished by its fidelity to that man's private experience, Alvarez's work has found favor among critics and readers alike. His work moves energetically and eloquently as he addresses what is of worth in our books and our lives.

Screenplay:
The Anarchist, 1969.

Other:
The New Poetry, edited with an introduction by Alvarez (Harmondsworth, U.K.: Penguin, 1962; enlarged, 1966);
Penguin Modern Poets 18, includes poems by Alvarez, Roy Fuller, and Anthony Thwaite (Harmondsworth, U.K.: Penguin, 1970).

Interview:
Ian Hamilton, "Good-by to All That," *New Review*, 4 (March 1978): 11-18.

Martin Amis

(25 August 1949-   )

Marla Levy
University of Delaware

BOOKS: *The Rachel Papers* (London: Cape, 1973; New York: Knopf, 1974);

Dead Babies (London: Cape, 1975; New York: Knopf, 1976);

Success (London: Cape, 1978);

Other People (London: Cape, 1981; New York: Viking, 1981).

"Wit and talent and mordant perception . . . Martin Amis is surely by far the most interesting of the new English writers," proclaims Dennis Potter on the dust jacket of Amis's latest novel *Other People* (1981), and certainly Amis is one of the most talked about figures on the London literary scene today. At the age of thirty-two he has already written four popular novels along with a succession of journalistic pieces. According to novelist Francis King, Amis "is going to leave the novel, however marginally, different from how he found it."

Martin Amis was born in Oxford, England, the son of well-known author Kingsley Amis and Hilary Bardwell Amis. Martin attended schools in Britain, Spain, and the United States as he was growing up. In all, he was enrolled in more than thirteen schools and then a series of "crammers" in London and Brighton to prepare for university entrance examinations. He gained a formal first in English at Exeter College, Oxford. After leaving Oxford, Amis began working on the editorial staff of the *London Times Literary Supplement*. At age twenty-four he won the Somerset Maugham Award for his first novel, *The Rachel Papers* (1973). Amis wrote numerous articles and gained the prestigious literary editorship of the *New Statesman*. During the 1970s he wrote two other novels, *Dead Babies* (1975) and *Success* (1978), and he also wrote three screenplays. However, only one, *Saturn 3*, has actually been produced. His latest novel, *Other People*, was published in March 1981.

Currently, Amis works as a staff writer and reviewer for the *London Observer*. Much of his work involves traveling to the United States to do research on aspects of American life for feature essays that appeal to the British sense of humor. Norman Mailer and born-again Christianity have been among his latest subjects. Amis lives in a small flat near Queensway in the Kensington section of London, and much of his fiction centers on this area. The influx of foreigners and London's increasing cosmopolitanism, especially in the Queensway area, are commented on gloomily by Amis's characters, who reveal the alienation and rootlessness felt by many Londoners.

In his novels, Amis writes humorously about the sorry state of the human condition. He has a curious way of extracting laughs at the expense of human baseness and poverty; even the pathetic appears funny when he describes it. He writes about the breakdown in communication between people and their brutality toward each other. Several images appear consistently throughout Amis's fiction, such as the dirtiness and loneliness of London streets. Baldness, obesity, and other unsettling physical shortcomings, along with the neuroses they can produce, are explored by Amis. Yet, however unappealing these images are, they are funny and appear worthy of consideration.

A recurrent theme in Amis's fiction is the boredom and insincerity of sex. In his novels, women are often described as annoying beings useful only for their sexual potential. Several critics refer to Amis as sexist, and some even go so far as to accuse him of misogyny. Passages such as this one from *Success* are typical: "What's happening to girls these days? It's their nerves which really drive me mad. When did they start thinking they had to be nervous all the time? Post-coital tears disgust me and the dreadful things they say. They keep trying to understand you; they keep wanting to talk about proper things; they keep trying to be people. For all their many charms they just aren't very interesting." However, Amis believes that his books are basically satires and that any apparent sexism is a parody of the egotistical male disposition. People in general are abusing the sexual relationship, and thus no one wins. Among women writers Amis admires George Eliot and Jane Austen, who were adept at coolly perceiving the inconsistencies in men. Amis admits that the writer in him always remains critical and detached in everything he does. He satirizes life, which includes women and sex.

Amis told *Cosmopolitan* in a 1978 interview:

"Looked at seriously, of course, my books are ghastly but the point is they are satire. I don't see myself as a prophet; I'm not writing social comment. My books are playful literature. I'm after laughs." Amis denied any autobiographical influences in his novels: "Because there is a narrator element to the books, people assume that it is the true me expressing attitudes but it simply isn't so. That is too glib an interpretation." During this same interview, when asked if he would write more serious, meaningful literature, he replied: "I don't believe literature ever changes people or alters the way society is going. Do you know any books which have? What it does is to throw out ideas and to stimulate and entertain." He has little sympathy for didactic literature.

Amis is not concerned with the battle between good and evil or with rewarding good characters and punishing evil ones. In a 27 March 1981 interview with *Time Out* he said, "The idea that the novelist punishes bad characters and rewards good ones doesn't bear up any more. Of course the nastiness is an element in my stuff. I write about that because it's more interesting. Everyone's more interested in the bad news. Only one writer has ever written convincingly about happiness and that's Tolstoy. Nobody else seems to be able to make it swing on the page."

Amis considers ideas to be the novelist's downfall. He is more interested in style and the many different ways of expressing human emotions and actions. Sanity is also one of his prime concerns. He says, "I'm more interested in rival versions of sanity—one person saying to another, 'My sanity is saner than yours.'"

In his novels Amis considers through his characters the people one might see on any street or in any underground station. He may describe the legless busker playing a harmonica in the Holland Park tube station or the young man obviously insecure about his height or lack of it. Amis says, "I'm more obsessed by down-and-outs and the griefs of ordinary people than in life at the top end of the scale. It's not the novelist's business to worry about social causations. All he must be alive to is the effects they have." His literary hero is Vladimir Nabokov, yet he admires his father's writing as well. The fiction he is currently working on follows a direction similar to his father's. When asked how helpful it has been to have an established author for a father, Amis replied, "I suppose having the name which strikes a chord with publishers is helpful, but I'm arrogant enough to think I would have made it on

my own. I believe my father thinks so too."

Amis's first novel, *The Rachel Papers*, has been called a celebration of adolescence. Although the book spans the events of one evening, far more is encompassed by means of flashbacks and memories. It is the eve of Charles Highway's twentieth birthday. In what he feels is an appropriate observance of this occasion, he reflects upon his first real love affair. An intelligent, sensitive, and enterprising young man, Charles is an avid writer who has filled several pads and notebooks with words about his former girl friend, Rachel Noyes. Through references to these notes and other memories, Charles, the first-person narrator, unfolds an entertaining and witty account about growing up.

Martin Amis

Charles has lived all his life in Oxford with his family, a life more or less governed by a laissez faire attitude. His father, Gordon Highway, is a trim man who has a series of young mistresses, while Charles's aging mother looks after the house and the children, pretending ignorance of her husband's philandering. Charles disapproves of his father's exploits and cultivates a hatred for him. Throughout the novel he writes a letter to his father voicing his disapproval. The letter turns into a speech, yet at the end of the book Charles drops it in the wastebasket. Charles has learned quite a bit about life and relationships after spending a year in London. He realizes his expectations of his father may have been unrealistic. When Charles moves to London to study with tutors for the Oxford examinations, he is excited about leaving stifling Oxford for the big city, and especially looks forward to seeing Rachel, whom he has met at a London party. After much perseverance, he begins a romance with her, and they have a gratifying time exploring each other physically and emotionally. Although he enjoys this new experience and the material it offers, Charles notices that all of his privacy is disappearing, that despite the joyous and necessary experience of first love, a part of himself that he is not yet ready to relinquish is slipping away. He takes the Oxford examinations and is accepted. Not long after, he writes a letter to Rachel in London ending their relationship. It is at this point that Charles realizes he does not hate his father. Charles has learned much from both his experiences and his writing about them.

Dead Babies, a "wickedly clever black comedy of manners," shows Amis's usual humor and satire but with an especially decadent setting and bizarre violence. A group of six young people sharing a large house outside London (Appleseed Rectory) take part in a shocking, drug-filled weekend. Although the novel spans only the period from Friday morning to Sunday, Amis again uses flashbacks extensively to develop in depth each of his six characters, all of whom are somehow affiliated with the University of London.

Quentin Villiers is good-looking, intelligent, and suave. He is editor of the university newspaper but expends little effort in the job, using the paper mainly as a vehicle for his own stylish yet fraudulent journalism. To many, he seems always to do the right thing, but his true character when finally uncovered is surprising. Celia Evanston, his wife, is a demure, mousey, good-hearted person. She has led an upper-class, sheltered, somewhat lonely life. Now that she has met Quentin, however, she is happy and fulfilled. Andy Adorno is a robust, energetic fellow who fancies himself quite sexy. Although rather insensitive, he is not rotten to the core. Diana Barry, his girl friend, is elegant and almost untouchable. Terribly selfish and self-centered, she has had an upper-class, pampered, and somewhat isolated upbringing. Looking for a

close relationship with Andy, she is destined to disappointment; she is also jealous of Quentin and Celia's sex life.

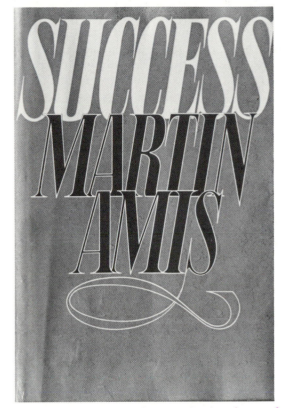

Dust jacket for Amis's third novel, an examination of success from two perspectives

Giles Coldstream is a very rich but ineffectual young man whose domineering mother has caused him serious psychological problems (she used to climb into bed with him and still calls him Baby Giles). He also suffers neurotic fears concerning his teeth. Too wrapped up in himself to be close to the others at Appleseed Rectory, he does nevertheless provide them with a constant supply of liquor. Perhaps the most sensitive and compassionate person in the group is the despised and ugly dwarf, Keith Whitehead, who, because of an inherited gland problem, is doomed to obesity. Pimple-faced and prematurely balding as well, his appearance has caused strangers to scream when they see him. Once institutionalized for severe depression, he now tolerates his physical appearance, while the others at the rectory veer between abusing and accepting him.

On Friday of the weekend, three Americans—Marvel, Skip, and Roxeanne—visit the rectory and spark the wild events. The first night is taken up with bed hopping and various successful and unsuccessful couplings after an evening of drugs and other entertainments. On Saturday, Giles's mother visits, everyone drinks a great deal, and Keith is physically abused. Marvel and Skip force Keith into violent sex acts and give him an overdose of drugs, tying him to a tree to prevent him from falling asleep. Marvel gives the others a strange drug that makes them regress and become depressed. Throughout the weekend a mysterious intruder leaving notes signed "Johnny" plays a number of nasty practical jokes on everyone.

The novel builds to a climax of violence and death, as Quentin reveals himself as Johnny and murders his wife, Marvel, and Diana; Giles dies in the hospital from drinking and drugs; Skip goes berserk, killing himself, Andy, and Roxeanne while driving his car. As Keith returns to Appleseed Rectory with the news of Giles's death, Quentin is lying in wait for him. The book ends here leaving the reader with the expectation of Keith's death as well. These incidents caused many people, including Amis's stepmother, to find the novel repulsive or horrifying, but it was nevertheless widely reviewed and praised. The paperback edition, however, was published under a different title, *Dark Secrets*, as the original one was considered too morbid to have any popular appeal.

While *Success* shows much of the dark humor of *Dead Babies*, it also competes with *The Rachel Papers* for sheer hilarity. Written in first person with foster brothers Terence (Terry) and Gregory narrating alternate chapters, the novel demonstrates how amusingly the same events can vary when described by two different people. Principally concerned with success, as the title indicates, the brothers reveal during the course of a year's monthly entries in their diaries a gradual shift in stature. Elegant, handsome Gregory, a success with the ladies, gradually emerges as vain and self-deceiving, a failure not only in his once-posh job, but in everything else as well. By contrast, Terry, who lives with him and stands in awe of his sexual prowess and upper-class breeding, becomes increasingly confident and successful, despite the handicaps of an unprepossessing physical appearance and an unprivileged upbringing that has been marred by family violence.

Still experimenting with form and content in his fourth novel, *Other People*, Amis writes what he subtitles ambiguously *A Mystery Story*. In fact, nearly everything in the novel is ambiguous; Amis expects the reader to determine what is good and what is evil. For example, is the protagonist, a young

woman who takes the name "Mary Lamb," a victim of total amnesia who awakens in a hospital and proceeds to discover what contemporary existence is all about; or is she the infamous Amy Hide who has died and is now in limbo or in hell? The people Mary meets and lives with at various times after escaping from institutions certainly seem likely candidates for damnation: Sharon, who is a promiscuous alcoholic; Trev, who shows Mary sex and violence; Alan, who eventually commits suicide; and others. Keeping an eye on Mary is John Prince, supposedly a police detective, who keeps feeding her information about Amy Hide. Prince may be either the "Prince of Darkness" or the intrusive third-person narrator. Is hell here "other people," as in Sartre's *No Exit* (although another source for the novel is Jorge Luis Borges's story, "Funes the Memorious")? Whatever the answers, Amis has succeeded in writing an extraordinary book that has stimulated interest, controversy, and considerable speculation among both critics and readers.

Amis is currently working on a fifth novel, "a realistic book, with lots of comic exaggeration, Dickensian names, and so on." However, he does not regard himself as an experimentalist like Gabriel Josipovici or Giles Gordon. He remarked in the *New Review* symposium on fiction (Summer 1978): "A new tradition can only evolve out of an old one; it cannot be induced. If I try very hard, I can imagine a novel that is as tricksy, as alienated and as writerly as those of, say, Robbe-Grillet, while also providing the staid satisfactions of pace, plot and humour with which we associate, say, Jane Austen. In a way, I imagine that this is what I myself am trying to do—but I wouldn't expect anyone to be encouraged or discouraged by that melancholy fact."

Interviews:
"The Two Amises," *Listener*, 15 August 1974, pp. 219-220;
Angela Neustatter, "Amis and Connolly—The Best-Seller Boys," *Cosmopolitan*, 185 (August 1978): 71-72;
Ian Hamilton, "The Company He Keeps," *Sunday Times* (London), 8 March 1981, p. 43;
Richard Rayner, "The Style Is the Man," *Time Out* (27 March 1981): 20-21.

Reference:
Claude Rawson, "The Behaviour of Reviewers and their Response to Martin Amis's novel, *Other People*," *London Review of Books* (7-20 May 1981): 19-22.

Paul Bailey
(16 February 1937-   )

Thomas J. Cousineau
Washington College

BOOKS: *At the Jerusalem* (London: Cape, 1967; New
    York: Atheneum, 1967);
Trespasses (London: Cape, 1970; New York: Harper
    & Row, 1970);
A Distant Likeness (London: Cape, 1973);
Peter Smart's Confessions (London: Cape, 1977);
Old Soldiers (London: Cape, 1980).

Paul Bailey's career as a novelist began when a
friend suggested that he turn away from writing
plays, which had brought him little satisfaction. He
sent the first seventy pages of a manuscript to publisher Jonathan Cape, where he found warm encouragement. The completed novel, *At the Jerusalem*
(1967), won the Somerset Maugham Travel Award
and an Arts Council of Great Britain Award (1968)
as the best first novel published between 1965 and
1967. Since then, he has had five novels published,
as well as many reviews and articles. Other awards
have included the E. M. Forster Award, presented
by the National Institute of Arts and Letters (1974),
a Bicentennial fellowship (1976), and the George
Orwell Memorial Prize (1978) for his essay "The
Limitations of Despair," published in the *Listener*.
He is widely regarded as one of the best among the
younger generation of novelists in Great Britain. In
a review of Bailey's latest novel, *Old Soldiers* (1980),
C. P. Snow regrets that, while Bailey has established
his reputation as a "writer's writer," he has not yet
gained a wider public. Snow comments, "He is very
good indeed, which may be an understatement."

While his work has gained him several American admirers, Bailey has not been published in the
United States since 1970. He believes that his novels
are considered "too English and, I suppose, too
short." Writing for the *Guardian*, Alex Hamilton
similarly suggests that the relative neglect of Bailey's
work can be explained by the predilection of "reviewers in papers like the *New York Times* for 'mam-
moth' novels." Bailey's current work in progress, a
novel entitled "Gabriel's World," is both long and at
least partly set in America. Perhaps this combination will at last earn him the wide readership which
his work merits.

Bailey was born in London, to a working-class
family, on 16 February 1937. His father, Arthur
Oswald Bailey, a garbage collector, had married
once before and had already raised his first children
to adulthood. He died when Bailey was eleven years
old; during the long school holidays, while his
mother (Helen Burgess Bailey) worked, Bailey was
cared for by an elderly couple whom he recalls with
deep affection. Both the death of his father and the
companionship of elderly people later became important elements of his fictional world.

Paul Bailey

His introduction to literature seems to have
begun with his father's reading to him from Dickens. His fondness for books earned him the titles of
"The Professor" and "Bleeding Macbeth" from his
childhood friends. His relation to the theater began
when, as an aspiring actor in an all-boys' grammar
school, he played several female roles, including
Sarah, Duchess of Marlborough. It was not until his

last year at school that he played a male part, the King in "*Henry IV* (Part I)—my only nondrag role."

He was awarded a scholarship to study acting at the Central School of Speech and Drama in London. The first career did not, however, lead to the success which he had expected. Eventually, he was to give it up: "I was spending all my time sitting in scouts halls in West London, rehearsing bad parts in bad television plays." During this time he also wrote several plays which he has subsequently destroyed. A surviving one was published in a 1974 issue of the magazine *Plays and Players*. He took a job at Harrods, a London department store, where he discovered "that there are people who have to purge their system by being rude to shop assistants." A clerk by day, at night he was preparing his new career as a novelist.

Bailey discusses his homosexuality, a theme which appears with varying degrees of importance in most of his novels, in the British newspaper *Gay News*. His "coming out," which occurred in the course of a review for the *New Statesman*, was motivated in part by his agreement with Angus Wilson that "anyone who is in the public eye in anyway should make a statement." The first homosexual work he ever read was Andre Gide's *Corydon* (1924), which had been given to him by a school friend. Years later, he left it behind at home, "in the hope that my mother would find it and read it and be more understanding about it."

In 1976, he was awarded a Bicentennial fellowship which allowed him to travel to North Dakota State University as a visiting professor. Asked by his chairman to teach a course on homosexuality in modern literature, he was struck by the lack of materials of sufficient literary quality. Exceptions included Constantine P. Cavafy's poems, Joe Ackerley's *My Father and Myself* (1969), and James Baldwin's *Giovanni's Room* (1956). He found himself obliged to rely on some second-rate material, including "that terrible thing, Gore Vidal's *The City and the Pillar* (1948)."

Bailey was amused to discover that in North Dakota homosexuality is not legally condemned because, as people explained to him, "we don't believe it exists around here." Less amusing was his experience as a panelist at a conference entitled "Forum on Homosexuality" held in Fargo, North Dakota. After the conference, alone in his hotel room, he was terrified of what might happen to him. Earlier in the day, during a radio talk show, a caller had asked, "When did we last hang one of those freaks?"

His first novel, *At the Jerusalem*, was inspired by a visit to a home for the mentally ill which he made

in the company of an acting troupe. It begins with the arrival of Mrs. Gadny at a rest home (the Jerusalem). In part one is seen her resolute unwillingness to adapt to the changed circumstances which her new life imposes. Bailey conveys vividly the sense of indignity she feels at being required to sleep on a soft bed and at being examined by a female doctor. She is befriended by Mrs. Capes, who insists that they share snapshots of their families. Mrs. Capes's photographs are of her son, "a beautiful boy," who was frequently beaten by his father. The boy, who later became a homosexual, committed suicide at age thirty-five.

Mrs. Gadny tears up photographs of her dead husband and daughter; memories of their life together are constantly on her mind and she has no need of pictures to evoke their presence. Her immersion in the past is further evidenced by her correspondence with Mrs. Barber, a neighbor with whom she was warm friends for twenty years, but who has been dead for two years now. As one would expect, the management of the Jerusalem looks with increasing disfavor on Mrs. Gadny's lack of sociability. By the end of part one she has been transferred to a private room, having earned for herself the nickname of "Dotty Faith."

In part two, the circumstances which led Mrs. Gadny to the Jerusalem are revealed. She had at first gone to live with her stepson Henry and daughter-in-law Thelma. Thelma's mother, Marjorie Nutley, serves as a foil for Mrs. Gadny. She and her husband had prepared for their retirement by buying a home, which they call "The Haven." During one of their conversations, Mrs. Gadny ruefully reflects that she had been respected by eminent people, loved by a good husband, "and here she was, listening to Mrs. Nutley, a woman with blue hair." Thelma, who disconcerts Mrs. Gadny by referring to her living room as a "lounge," finally decides that her mother-in-law must leave. She complains that Mrs. Gadny has become ghostlike, staring into space, hardly ever engaging in conversation, and preferring her grandson Michael because he is a sullen child.

In part three, which ends with Mrs. Gadny's exclusion from the Jerusalem, the reader learns that she had also felt excluded from the affections of her beloved husband. She recalls that once while making love and again later, when he was dying, he called her "Doll," mistaking her for his first wife, Dolores, whom he found more appealing sexually. A memory of her husband also occurs at the end of the novel when she is being taken to an asylum following a nervous breakdown. She tells her stepson, who is accompanying her, about Mrs. Capes's son's never having forgiven his father for beating him. Her stepson recalls forgiving his own father for similar behavior.

At the Jerusalem is probably Bailey's most conventional novel. When first published, it recalled to critics the virtues of traditional fiction at a time when experimental techniques were in vogue. It was surprising as well, according to Peter Lewis, to discover a first novel by a young man who wrote so sympathetically about the lives of old people.

Ralph Hicks, the narrator and main character of *Trespasses* (1970), also experiences a breakdown which leads to his being committed to an asylum. His narrative is in the form of fragments ranging in length from one sentence to several pages and bearing such recurrent titles as "Her," "Us," "Here," and "Before." This technique permits Ralph to focus sharply on particular, isolated moments of his experience and to suggest both the apparent randomness and the underlying emotional logic of his thoughts. The major event of his adult life is the suicide of his wife, Elspeth. His responsibility for her death is suggested by the suicide note in which she tells him, "I would rather be dead than live with your contempt." His failure as a husband seems to be linked to aspects of his own family life. His father had lost interest in his mother soon after their marriage and had turned to an affair which was profoundly humiliating to her. The son was himself left with a feeling of abandonment after his father's death, which occurred when he was only eleven years old.

Bernard Proctor, a homosexual friend of Ralph's late wife, has a similar history. His father had "lived off" his mother for years, leaving her for an actress when Bernard was ten. Later, Bernard has a homosexual relationship which is ended by his lover's death in World War II. The importance which is given to the presentation of Bernard's life (he does not influence the main action of the novel, but his biography occupies fifteen pages in the text) might be explained by the hypothesis that he and Ralph represent alternative outcomes of similar childhood experiences. Bernard is led to humiliating sexual encounters, Ralph to a failed marriage and a breakdown.

The last section of the novel reveals that Ralph's narrative has been undertaken with a serious purpose in mind. He hopes that the exploration of his past will awaken in him that sense of a strong personal identity which has until now eluded him. Throughout the novel he is shown as being incapable of love. The reader understands toward the end the connection between his emotional coldness and his lack of a sense of himself as a person. He sees himself easily as "Mr. Hicks" and as "Mummy's Ralphie," but only with great difficulty as "Me." His autobiography records his growing awareness of his uniqueness: "I am Ralph Hicks, I am Mummy's Ralphie. I am not Bernard Proctor, I am not my mother, I am not my wife." The novel ends with a brief paragraph entitled "Man" in which he expresses the hope that this designation will one day apply to himself: "My name is Ralph Hicks and I hope I will become a man. It is a beginning."

Trespasses is a more experimental work than *At Jerusalem* and may well be Bailey's finest novel. His rendering of characters' speech patterns is exact and moving. His fragmentary presentation of plot achieves an intense cumulative effect, without ever seeming arbitrary. His "autobiographies" of Bernard Proctor and Ralph's mother demonstrate his uncanny ability to represent the emotional lives of very different types of characters. His recurrent use of certain words and phrases invests the novel's essential realism with hypnotic and poetic effects. Ralph's use of language as a means toward self-discovery is powerfully dramatized.

A Distant Likeness, published in 1973, also presents a character who must deal with a catastrophic development in his life. Frank White has been deserted by his wife, Pamela, because they have been unable to conceive a child. She is now expecting a baby by another man. The narrative is a stream-of-consciousness recording of Frank's memories of various episodes of his life. He works as a police inspector and is presently involved with the case of a wife murderer named Belsey. The novel begins with Frank awakening in the morning, praying "to the God he no longer believed in for an end to his pain." He is the end result of a process of cultural estrangement which began with his father, a Neapolitan immigrant who, ashamed of his origins, adopted the name White and boasted "I am English like roast beef."

The London which he knows as a police inspector is a modern-day inferno; having rejected the "superstitious" religiosity of his ancestors, he is forced to confront the city's sordidness without the aid of a consoling vision. At one point in the novel, Frank's estrangement from his Mediterranean origins is explicitly connected to a dominant trait of his personality: his ambivalence toward the code of conventional morality. Piers, a homosexual with whom he has had a one-night stand, describes him as a "randy Puritan," and, expressing surprise at Frank's Italian heritage, suggests that his soul is badly in need of "the Mediterranean sunlight." His puritanism finds an outlet in his work on his memoirs, in which he defends the honor of his profession against a decadent society. His lasciviousness surfaces in his encounters with Piers and with prostitutes with whom, ironically, he uses his position as a police inspector to gain free services. Toward the end of the novel, Frank gives Belsey a knife and urges him to kill himself; the similarities between Frank and Belsey, the "distant likeness," suggest that the desire for self-destruction is his underlying motive. If that is the case, then he meets with partial success. Belsey tries to murder his warder; Frank is arrested as an accomplice and taken to jail.

Some critics found the stream-of-consciousness technique employed in *A Distant Likeness* confusing and irritating. It is probably less effective than the more explicitly controlled technique of *Trespasses*. One feels at times that a rather large technical effort is being used to create a rather slight aesthetic effect. On the other hand, Jonathan Raban found in it echoes of T. S. Eliot's *The Waste Land*, though without Eliot's Christianity, and Peter Lewis commented favorably on the novel's "hyper-concentration of linguistic effect."

Bailey's first three novels ended with the main character facing some terminal situation: an insane asylum or jail. *Peter Smart's Confessions* (1977) begins with its main character waking up in the intensive care ward of a hospital; he has failed, once again, to commit suicide. He imagines that he is in heaven, and that the nurses are wingless angels. The rest of the novel deals with various incidents in Peter Smart's life. The chief event of his childhood was the death of his father, which left him the victim of an unbearable mother. He remembers his "mother's blight" making him long to be seized by a "fatal illness." He thinks of his father's death as the cause of irreparable pain: "My father vanished for good. I put away childish things. The world darkened, and so did I."

The account of his adult years focuses on his experience as an actor and on the important emotional relationships of life. He wins "rave reviews" for his performance as Reynaldo in an avant-garde production of *Hamlet* in which congenital syphilis is the alleged cause of Hamlet's moodiness. The later decline of his career leads him to the verge of suicide. He decides to jump from a bridge but finds himself rescuing another would-be suicide instead. They become lovers and, after discovering her pregnancy, decide to marry. Their son, Stephen, is raised mostly by Peter, who struggles to compensate for his wife's indifference to motherhood. Toward the end of his narrative, Peter describes a reunion with Wolfram, a homosexual lover from years before, now grown bald and fat. He leaves his wife and soon after has a nervous breakdown.

The novel ends with an afterword by Neville, a close friend of Peter. Peter has died of cancer, leaving Neville instructions to destroy his memoirs. Neville reveals that Peter's last attempted suicide was precipitated by the sight of his son, "head shaved; face decorated with streaks of white paint; dressed in a saffron robe and sandals—selling *Back to the Godhead* in Oxford Street." Peter had abandoned acting and turned to social work. He had also fallen in love "with a tattooed thief named Freddy." Visitors to his sickbed included the author of a ballet "inspired by the death of the dancer Barry Capes," the homosexual son of the Mrs. Capes who appeared in *At the Jerusalem*.

Alex Hamilton, writing for the *Guardian*, describes *Peter Smart's Confessions* as Bailey's funniest novel and notes that many of the more ludicrous events are based on Bailey's actual experiences. While parts of the novel are indeed humorous, the humor seems to reside more in isolated set pieces—the bizarre production of *Hamlet*, for

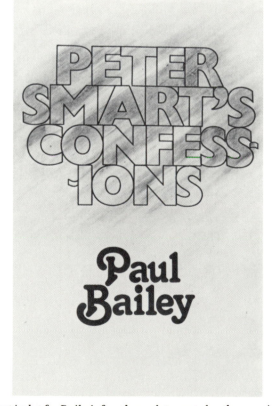

Dust jacket for Bailey's fourth novel, presented as the memoir of a neurotic actor turned social worker

example—than in any underlying novelistic conception.

Bailey's most recent novel, *Old Soldiers* (1980), begins with the arrival of Victor Harker in London after a fifty-year absence. He has come from Newcastle where he has recently buried his much-beloved wife, Stella. He can no longer live at home because every object and detail of his life there has become emblematic of her absence. Victor's recollections of Stella evoke the one satisfying adult relationship to be found in all of Bailey's work. Victor's happiness as an adult seems to have resulted from his determination to avoid his father Billy's example. Unlike those sons who, in earlier novels, suffer from the father's premature disappearance, Victor consciously willed his separation from his father: "Billy had been the swamp across which he had built his fortress over the years. . . . He had wanted to be anyone but Billy. Had he been like Billy, he would not have known love." He was also fortunate in meeting Stella, who saw immediately "the cause of his dustiness" and freed him, through her love, from the prison which he had created for himself.

Victor returns to various landmarks associated with childhood in the East End of London. While visiting St. Paul's Cathedral, he is approached by another elderly man who introduces himself as Harold Standish. They dine together at Standish's invitation. Both men are survivors of World War I and both have vivid memories of the Battle of the Somme. The man who calls himself Standish visits a public lavatory and reappears in the disguise of a tramp named Tommy. Later, he transforms himself into a "still unrecognized" poet named Julian, who makes speeches at Speakers Corner. Toward the end of the novel he has a heart attack after visiting a prostitute and commits suicide by jumping into the Thames.

While Victor and his acquaintance, whose real name is Eric Talbot, are very different characters, they do have one thing in common: their behavior is profoundly shaped by the experience of death. Victor has returned to London to escape the memory of the death of his wife. His tour of the city focuses on cemeteries and tombs. Talbot's disguises are part of a bizarre effort to escape from himself and the inevitability of his own death. We learn at the end of the novel that he deserted his regiment at the Battle of the Somme and has spent his life trying to hide from the feelings of guilt provoked by his cowardice. After revealing his true identity to Victor, he commits suicide, as had his father before him. The novel ends with the abrupt announce-

ment that "The ashes of Victor Harker were scattered, like Stella's, among squalling seabirds." He has had a happy marriage but has left no heritage; his only son, born prematurely during the last war, died three days later.

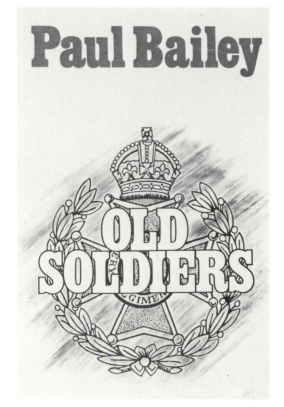

Dust jacket for Bailey's 1980 novel, about an elderly man's return to London after a fifty-year absence

Writing for the *Times Literary Supplement*, Peter Lewis describes *Old Soldiers* as Bailey's "most satisfying" novel since *At the Jerusalem*. Reviewing the same novel, Auberon Waugh gives Bailey "A gold medal with congratulatory First Class Honors." C. P. Snow regards *Old Soldiers* as "a beautiful example of his work." Clearly, the talent which was so widely acclaimed with the publication of *At the Jerusalem* has continued to receive the serious and enthusiastic attention of British readers.

Unlike the three intervening novels, *Old Soldiers* shares with *At the Jerusalem* a focus on elderly characters. Its techniques seem also to represent a return to the traditional form of Bailey's first novel. Its one weakness might be, as in *Peter Smart's Confessions*, a tendency to indulge in wit for its own sake, without due consideration for the novel's tone. This would, however, be only a minor flaw in a novel which conveys, as do the best moments in all of his novels, the impression that Bailey is a writer who possesses a remarkable sensitivity to human relations and an exceptional gift for rendering the inner lives of his characters.

In reviewing all five of his novels, one is struck by the recurrent appearance of an underlying pattern. In each novel the stability of the main character's life is undermined by some painful circumstance: death of a loved one, desertion, and suicide are the chief examples. It frequently happens as well that the catastrophe is provoked at least in part by the main character's personal inadequacies. Further, these present difficulties are usually related to some determining situation in the character's earlier life; with Bailey's young male characters, a troubled relationship with the father is indicated in every case. These fathers fail, either through death or abandonment, to exercise adequately their paternal function; their sons later experience difficulties as husbands and fathers.

Regardless of age or sex, Bailey's characters are generally isolated from normal human relationships. Mrs. Gadny's husband and daughter are dead, and she is estranged from her stepson and his wife. In the later novels the main characters are stranded between generations. Ralph Hicks remembers his father as a shadowy figure and his mother as an oppressive presence; his marriage leads ultimately to his wife's suicide. Similarly, Peter Smart's childhood is marked by the absence of his father, and his adult life by the contempt of his son. Frank White, like his father before him, has isolated himself from his origins; he has been unable to father a child. Victor Harker, who repudiates his father and enjoys a successful marriage, is left childless by the death of his son.

Bailey expects to return to his current novel, "Gabriel's World," after completing a book about a notorious London brothel, entitled "An English Madam: The Life and Work of Cynthia Payne." He has been commissioned to write the official biography of novelist Henry Green and has also produced BBC documentaries on Jean Rhys and Isak Dinesen. He visited the United States in the fall of 1981 to gather materials for a documentary on writers of the South.

Beryl Bainbridge

(21 November 1933-   )

Barbara C. Millard
La Salle College

BOOKS: *A Weekend with Claud* (London: New Authors, 1967);
Another Part of the Wood (London: Hutchinson, 1968; revised edition, London: Duckworth, 1979; New York: Braziller, 1980);
Harriet Said (London: Duckworth, 1972; New York: Braziller, 1973);
The Dressmaker (London: Duckworth, 1973); republished as *The Secret Glass* (New York: Braziller, 1974);
The Bottle Factory Outing (London: Duckworth, 1974; New York: Braziller, 1975);
Sweet William (London: Duckworth, 1975; New York: Braziller, 1976);
A Quiet Life (London: Duckworth, 1976; New York: Braziller, 1977);
Injury Time (London: Duckworth, 1977; New York: Braziller, 1977);
Young Adolf (London: Duckworth, 1978; New York: Braziller, 1979);
Winter Garden (London: Duckworth, 1980).

Having published ten novels in thirteen years, primarily to "tell her story," Beryl Bainbridge has good reason to view her literary career with satisfaction. An unassuming and deferential person, Bainbridge is a spartan writer whose wit, humor, and originality have won her a loyal, ever-growing audience in England and abroad. Bainbridge initially achieved recognition as a writer of macabre thrillers. More recently, however, her "little" novels have received more serious critical attention for their economical, elegant craft and for their oddly angled, shockingly funny portraits of harried, lower-middle-class people caught in a world that, according to one of them, is "menacing and full of alarms."

On 21 November 1933, in Liverpool, England, Beryl Margaret Bainbridge was born to Winifred Baines and Richard Bainbridge. When she was six months old, she moved with her parents and six-year-old brother to a small, semidetached house in Thornby, on the seacoast about twelve miles from Liverpool. Her later "obsession" to write about her family life developed within the tense household atmosphere created by her mother's preoccupation with class distinction and by her father's manic temper. Bainbridge describes her father as a morose man who loved poetry and radio, a "Willy Loman" salesman who told stories of his past exploits in diamonds, shipping, real estate, cotton, and of his eventual bankruptcy. Hating the present, he taught his daughter the fascination of the past. Before his death, Bainbridge says, she came to love her father; after his death, when she was twenty-three, she learned of his bankruptcy and has endeavored since to understand the point of view of the emotionally volatile man who "paid the bills from a little tin box kept on the table." She attributes her early interest in writing to the stories of Dickens (especially the "awful bits about prisons

Beryl Bainbridge

and slums" read to her by her father), to the pencils and exercise books provided by her mother, and to the family album of snapshots which inspired her "to take verbal photographs of my life and my family." Despite her mother's objections, Bainbridge loved to visit her paternal aunts in their working-class Liverpool neighborhood. That house with its Victorian furniture combined with the Dickensian "bits" to provide a pervasive atmosphere of portent which Bainbridge strives to evoke in her novels.

At eleven, Bainbridge wrote a book derived from parts of Dickens's works and Stevenson's *Treasure Island*. She also wrote love letters to her mother, a difficult, clever woman who taught Beryl simultaneously that men were privileged creatures and that she, the mother, was "totally superior to any man." Adoring her mother, the child defended her during marital squabbles by jumping on her father's back and bringing him to the ground. The climate of strain and anxiety was one which Bainbridge says she has duplicated over and over in her writing and has finally exorcised: "Fortunately I did it late enough. If I had done it twenty years ago, I wouldn't have been neurotic for twenty years and so I wouldn't have written." She is amazed now by comments that her vision of life in the novels is peculiar. Maintaining that "It's all true," she describes her childhood as having been spent with people who were disappointed: who married the wrong person, who failed in business, who had been manipulated by others. Clinging to her middle-class respectability and conventionalism, Mrs. Bainbridge eventually discouraged her daughter from her interest in reading and writing. Bainbridge took to roaming the dunes, going to movies "at least twice a week," and playing the joker to relieve the pressure at home. Of her wanderings, says the woman who now stays within the house as much as possible, "I had no fear of danger. My parents thought I was a little bit touched."

Her father wanted her to be a journalist or a doctor, and Beryl was sent to the Merchant Taylor's School at Great Crosby. But Mrs. Bainbridge was a stage mother, and Beryl enjoyed a theatrical career which began with her tap-dancing at six and included instruction at the Arts Educational Schools, Ltd., at Tring. By ten, she was on the radio, and by fifteen, in the theater. At fifteen, also, she ran away to London to escape the "rows" at home. She had returned home to work in a repertory company in Liverpool, however, when, at sixteen, she met and fell in love with her future husband, artist Austin Davies. Sensing the hopelessness of the affair,

Bainbridge ran away to London again and continued an acting career which would last until 1972 and included work in Windsor, Salisbury, Dundee, Liverpool, and London theaters, in television, and in radio. Her whirlwind activity notwithstanding, Bainbridge's relationship with Davies continued. In an attempt to avoid what she foresaw as a problematic marriage, she went to Scotland where she could become a Catholic before the age of twenty-one without parental consent. Neither her deliberate conversion, which she thought would discourage Davies, nor her own misgivings prevented the match. On 24 April 1954, she married him and "forgot about being a Catholic after that." Although, by her own account, she was totally undomesticated in the early years of her marriage, she sought a domestic anchor and wanted children. In 1956 while expecting her first child, Aaron Paul, she began to write seriously in the back room as her husband painted in the front room.

Her first novel, *Harriet Said* (1972), was completed in 1958 as she realized her marriage was over. Although *Harriet Said* was not published until later, after two subsequent novels, this first composition defined the formula for her fiction. Taking her cue from Dickens, she was and is convinced of the necessity for a strong narrative line. She derived the plot for *Harriet Said* from a news story about two girls in Australia who had murdered their mother. Noting the Freudian undertones in her selection of this plot, Bainbridge comments, "I think now it's very odd to pick such a plot, and maybe I didn't do the genuine plot in *Harriet Said* because I was too frightened to write about a girl who hit her mother over the head." Taking only the detail of two girls involved in a murder, then, Bainbridge drew from details of her own childhood friendship with a girl like Harriet, a clever art student who introduced Bainbridge to such writers as Virginia Woolf. Supposedly a tale of "corrupt childhood," *Harriet Said* is narrated in the first person by a plump, frizzy-haired, anonymous thirteen-year-old girl who is completely dominated by the charming, cunning fourteen-year-old Harriet. The novel's suspenseful structural design is one Bainbridge would use again in *The Dressmaker* (1973). The opening pages catapult the reader into the girls' breakneck escape from what will eventually be revealed as the scene of the crime. The rest of the novel is a flashback to the events preceding the opening scene, so that the final chapter necessitates rereading the first.

At first the girls' summer exploits seem typically adolescent: sneaking out to meet each other at

Dust jacket for Bainbridge's first novel, derived from an Australian news story about matricide

night; roaming the dunes at all hours with boys, if possible; garnering "experience" to record in their secret diary; spying on the "tzar," Mr. Biggs, and his fat, contemptible wife. The innocence of these intrigues becomes questionable when the masochistic Mr. Biggs becomes implicated in the girls' plot to seduce and punish him. As their activities intensify, the girls treat each other with greater circumspection; they begin to compete with each other. Sinister and morally ambiguous scenes at a county fair, in a graveyard, by a tadpole pool culminate, first, in the sad copulation of the narrator and Mr. Biggs (an "uncomplicated ritual" after all) and, second, in the murder of Mrs. Biggs, hit over the head by the narrator at the urging of Harriet. The implication that Mr. Biggs will bear the blame for this violence is clear, but the issue of the girls' relative guilt or innocence, evil or naivete, is not. Bainbridge's tight, spare prose and narrative directness leave all judgment to the reader, while she presents images (like the pinned specimen butterfly) that challenge any easy determination of the narrator's relationship with either Harriet or Mr. Biggs. Although this novel has the incisiveness of her later work, its humor is grim rather than witty. When Bainbridge submitted the manuscript to publishers in 1959, she received outraged response, including the comment that the book was "too indecent and unpleasant even for these lax days." *Harriet Said* was not published until 1972, after her next two novels had been published. Its release at that time caused some sensation and established her reputation as a writer of bizarre tales. Although there were some accusations of worthlessness, most reviewers respected the narrative panache and psychological truth beyond the sensational plot.

Meanwhile Beryl Bainbridge's second child, Johanna Harriet, had been born shortly before her divorce in 1959. With her two children she remained in Liverpool, "having a very hectic life," painting, and acting. She began *A Weekend with Claud* in Liverpool and finished it in London where she moved because Davies wanted the children closer to him. By this time a third child, Ruth Emmanuella, had been born. In 1967, three years after its completion, the novel was published by New Authors Ltd., a subsidiary of Hutchinson, formed expressly to assist hitherto unpublished authors. In this, the only experimental novel she has written, Bainbridge uses the photographic-image motif to structure the work. A photograph Claud finds in an antique desk leads to the three stream-of-consciousness narratives which describe a weekend he spent a year ago with the waifish Maggie and her entourage. In a style strongly suggestive of Faulkner, Bainbridge presents the stories of Maggie; her boarder, "Victorian" Norman; and her bag-lady friend, Shebah. Claud's is the fourth reminiscence. An undisguised "photograph" of the author, with her "beaked nose" and untidy hair, Maggie and her untidy life provide the focal point for all the narratives and motivate the mysterious but not fatal shooting of the sagacious Shebah. The difficult-to-follow story line deals with Maggie's attempts to define her relationships with several men: Claud, Victorian Norman, Billie (the "wild Colonial Boy" who may have left her pregnant), and Edward, her present lover who does not marry her. As the narrators define her problems and disappointments, they convey their own pain, hostility, and inevitable isolation. In Claud, Bainbridge presents the first of her predatory men. He is tigerlike in his ruthless wooing and possession of women, and he creates what will become a familiar tension between the vulnerable female and the exploitative male. The novel lacks the author's characteristic crispness; its

fuzzy prose is rescued only by the pointed imagery which projects an exact vision of the despair and folly of love and lovemaking. The book received a few good notices, but Bainbridge was disappointed with it when it finally appeared in print. Its narrative style she dismisses now as "impossible . . . it just goes on and on," and considers it a failed attempt, and her only one, at experimentation.

She continued to write, however, and Hutchinson published *Another Part of the Wood* in 1968. Bainbridge has rewritten the novel since and had the new version published in 1979. She describes the first book as hastily written, a reaction to the breakup of her marriage and an attempt to impress her former husband. Her revision is primarily stylistic and retains the plot which focuses on the cruel, self-centered Joseph, a recently divorced, sometime father. Joseph takes his mistress; his son, Roland; a disturbed "case-study," Kidney; and some friends to a cabin in the country for a holiday. The father's perfectionism and insensitivity prove fatal to Roland in both versions, however much the revision mitigates what Bainbridge admits is the personal anger of the earlier version. Although her publishers encouraged her to continue writing, she became dissatisfied with the "drivel" of her attempts and thought she might not write again. She took her children to a farm in Lancashire but returned to London after a year, to her present Camden Town Victorian-era house. During this interlude, Bainbridge took a job as a cellar-worker in a wine-bottling factory near her home, an experience which inspired one of her best novels, *The Bottle Factory Outing* (1974). This employment was followed by clerical work at Duckworth Publishers where she met her future editor and most constructive critic, Anna Hycraft. Hycraft had read Bainbridge's two books and asked for other manuscripts. She was enthusiastic about *Harriet Said* and, after its publication and positive critical reputation, suggested that Bainbridge continue writing about her childhood experiences.

Consequently, Bainbridge chose her paternal aunts and their small house in Liverpool as her subject in *The Dressmaker*, which she wrote in her kitchen in eight weeks. Published in 1973 and titled *The Secret Glass* in the American edition, *The Dressmaker* depicts the cramped, impoverished lives of working-class Liverpudlians during the darker days of 1944. The psychological realism of the novel goes beyond reminiscence and proves Bainbridge a master of detail and atmosphere. At seventeen, the protagonist, Rita, lives within the stifling climate of her aunts' care. The image of Rita in bed, bundled for warmth between her two swaddled aunts, embodies all the claustrophobic horror of her existence. As in *Harriet Said*, the first chapter is the epilogue to the main action and immediately establishes the tone of emotional repression which was the cause of the violence in the flashback plot. Nellie, the stolid dressmaker, is the caretaker of the family, presiding over their deaths and protecting her dead mother's furniture. With her tape measure as a stole and her mouth full of pins, Nellie sits down to her Singer "like the great organ at the Palladiam cinema before the war." Disregarding her niece's anguish, she evokes the definitive morality and caution of another era.

Rita's dreary existence is offset somewhat by her once married younger aunt, the fifty-year-old "girl," Margo, who alternately sympathizes and competes with Rita in the niece's desperate pursuit of an illiterate Yank. In this drab setting the boorish G. I., Ira, is an exotic addition and source of hope for Rita, but a threat to Nellie's notions of propriety. Deluding herself as to Ira's sleazy character, Rita tries to improve him, only to lose him to Margo who "knows instantly what sort of man he is." When Nellie discovers Margo and Ira scratching the top of her mother's table in the storage room, the result is gothic comedy. Nellie stabs Ira in the neck ("She is that annoyed") and he tumbles down the steps and cracks his head on an umbrella stand, pilfered pearls spilling from his pocket. Like the proverbial pearls cast before swine, Bainbridge's talents, some critics felt, were wasted on this sensational denouement. Many, however, found the entire novel painstakingly authentic and brilliantly shaped. She was compared to Poe as striking exactly the right note. Her wit is wicked here: Margo and Nellie wrap up the body because they do not want "young Rita tripping over him." As she sews his shroud, the dressmaker utters an ironic understatement of this wartime period: "We haven't had much of a life. . . . I don't see why we should pay for him." The novel, nominated for the Booker Prize, expanded Bainbridge's English readership and began to develop her audience in America.

In 1974, Bainbridge produced the novel that some consider one of her best, *The Bottle Factory Outing*. Writing intensively—sometimes all night—for six months, Bainbridge established the procedure she still uses to produce a novel each year. *The Bottle Factory Outing* is a social comedy in the grotesque mode which exhibits the elaborate plotting and attention to detail that have become hallmarks of her writing: "I revise constantly. I never go on to the next paragraph until I've got that paragraph right. I write about fourteen pages to every page of finished copy." Drawing from her own spirited time with primarily Italian immigrant workers in the bottle factory, Bainbridge again focuses on a pair of women, one (Freda) large and romantic, the other (Brenda) timid, deferential, and ascetic. The photograph on the dust jacket of the British edition is a tongue-in-cheek illustration by Austin Davies of Bainbridge as Brenda, her friend who inspired the character as Freda, and Bainbridge's publisher and accountant as Italians—all grouped for the outing. The tangled relationship of the two Englishwomen provides the powerful core of the story, while the plot involves the robust Freda's organization of the outing. All the events in the novel—beginning with the funeral across the street from the women's flat—move relentlessly toward Freda's death in Windsor Park. Workdays consist of various romantic intrigues and tippling. While Freda pursues Vittorio, the owner's nephew, he in turn schemes to marry the manager's niece. Meanwhile, Rossi, the manager, corners Brenda at every opportunity, until Brenda, unnerved, urges Freda to confront him. The outing is Freda's grand plot to realize her fantasy and seduce Vittorio. However, the tone of the picnic turns sinister almost immediately: the transportation is mysteriously cancelled, couples quarrel, various characters disappear into the woods, and picnic games become brutal. It is Brenda, whom death has supposedly stalked in the form of a crazed, pistol-toting ex-mother-in-law, who discovers Freda's corpse in the woods. The catastrophe is only the beginning of Freda's strange voyage in Brenda's care, as survivor and victim change roles. Brenda, compliant and fearful, escorts her friend's purple-cloaked body past the indolent gaze of the shabby animals in the safari park, takes time for tea, and presides over the candlelight wake in the factory. For Brenda, demoralized by her own deference, the mystery of Freda's murder is less important than the problem of disposing of her in a manner least troublesome to the management. So Freda is put out to sea, pickled in a brandy cask. In depicting the wry tension between the two women, Bainbridge uses a motif of theatricality—elaborate pretenses, role and costume changes, and rehearsals. Brenda ruefully observes that she is inadequate in a part more suited to Freda, who "would have beat her breast and shrieked her lamentation." Such a motif aptly conveys Bainbridge's central theme, the conflict between self-knowledge and self-deception, between the person and the role, between reality and fantasy.

J. Raban in *Encounter* called the novel "near to perfect" with its "perfect pitch," but voiced a repeated objection regarding Bainbridge's narrow focus and detached narrative style: "There is finally and nigglingly something about it which is as self-enclosed and remote as a monastic cell." Yet other responses praised the novel's expansive characterization, vibrant atmosphere, and exquisite comedy. Universally acknowledged to be both original and unsettling, *The Bottle Factory Outing* generated the controversy which continues regarding the sympathy or callousness of Bainbridge's tone toward her disconnected characters and their cultural confusion. Nevertheless, the novel gained a more serious reputation for the author as more than a writer of horror stories. It was nominated for the Booker Prize and won the Guardian Fiction Award in 1974.

In *Sweet William*, published the following year, Bainbridge continues her exploration of the human tendency toward self-deception and self-parody. A less menacing story than *The Bottle Factory Outing*, *Sweet William* depicts the crazy world created by people who mistake all about them. How much error is perversity and how much the fated human condition is one question Bainbridge's novels, beginning with *Sweet William*, continue to ask. In a *tour de force* of compelling characterization, Bainbridge ensnares the reader in the trap of William's performance, as experienced and narrated by the vulnerable protagonist, Ann Walton. Playwright and satyr, baby and cad, William charms Ann and reader alike. Like Ann, the reader detects his insincerity and destructive solipsism and finds them fascinating. When she meets William, Ann is engaged to the overbearing Gerald, a lesser cad who, despite Ann's visiting mother in the next room, insists on a sexual romp the night before his departure to a job in America. Mrs. Walton exhibits the selfish petulance and righteous nastiness of several Bainbridge mothers who adhere to the old social rules but resent doing so. Daughters of such mothers can never win, and Ann does not: her fiance is all wrong, her behavior is despicable, her rejection of middle-class respectability portends disaster. Thus chastened and alone, Ann is easily seduced by William's impassioned imperatives. The affair incubates for weeks in her womblike pink bedroom, and then Ann's life becomes completely absorbed by William. She stops eating when they run out of food. She quits her job and drops her friends; she signs the letter breaking the engagement to Gerald, which William composes but never mails. William never loses momentum: he seduces Ann's cousin and her landlady; he moves his wardrobe in and out; he comes and goes, but

mostly goes, on his bicycle, "rear light glowing like a small red star." Nothing can undeceive Ann, not William's vulgar flamboyancy, not his lies, not his wives (former and current), not even his play "The Truth Is a Lie." In view of the many "compartments" in his life, Ann must give up her illusions, so she settles for a new apartment in Regency Park and a new pram in the hall. William, recognizing that the pregnant Ann's "capacity for deception was as great as his own," shifts his attention to a new companion, Chuck, while monitoring Ann's pregnancy. Ann's baby proves to be the final deception, however, its eyes being Gerald-brown rather than William-blue. The novel asserts that possessiveness and selfishness are invariably intermingled with love, whether between parents and children or between lovers. William and Ann are the kind of people who, in their need for both romance and acceptance, look to their lovers to become surrogate parents. Like the images of mummy wrappings and snail casings, her narrative unfolds swiftly and surely.

Sweet William was a commercial success and has since been filmed for television. Appreciation for this brighter, more open book was mixed with regret for the missing suspense and sinister plot. In an ambivalent review of Bainbridge's work, Frank Kermode admires her "fantastic talent" and notes that she has managed to escape "the rather stifling conditions of normal contemporary competence," but finds *Sweet William*, "though very effective . . . a shade less impressive than the earlier work." From a later vantage point, however, the novel indicates Bainbridge's development of surer techniques and deeper characterization.

At this time, since her mother had died (while she was writing *The Bottle Factory Outing*), Bainbridge decided to write her admittedly autobiographical novel, *A Quiet Life*. Published in 1976, the novel is still her favorite. Although veined with the comic details of family eccentricities, this is generally a somber, perhaps tragic story of the precariousness of love in a family deadlocked by its own emotional, psychological, and economic strife. Bainbridge's first male narrator is an older brother, Alan, who meets his sister, Madge, to divide a slim inheritance after their mother's death. In a flashback narrative, he recalls a period of family tension in a village near Southport just after World War II and before the father's death. At the end of the novel it is clear that Alan has remembered only what he could bear and has transformed or forgotten what he could not. The truth of families is ambiguous. Which child is best loved? Which more privileged? Which parent is the more culpable and destructive? Which child is the peacemaker? Which the troublemaker? These questions emerge through a series of vignettes: a prickly visit from grandparents, the courting of frigid Janet Leyland, the father-son ritual of buying a new suit, Parents Day at school, a family walk on the beach, the constant quarrels about household tasks and money. Alan is at first conciliatory and tolerant of injustices, but his attempts to ride the emotional waves become more futile. Home is "worse than bombs in the blitz." As Alan becomes caught in a web of repression, he loses his own chance at independence and duplicates the very traits he despises in his parents. Aware of the folly and danger of their cramped lives, he cramps his own; yearning for stability and correctness, he trades his soul for "a quiet life." Madge, on the other hand, escapes this fate, but only at the price of respectability and, perhaps, maturity.

The climactic scene of the father's death exemplifies Bainbridge's skill at defining theme through black comedy. In a gesture of futility and defiance, the father, raging in his A.R.P. uniform, burns a chair of sentimental value to his wife and chops down a tree. In a similar gesture Alan confronts his father with the revelation that his mother is not secretly meeting a lover but reading romantic novels at the train station every night because "she can't stand being in the same room" with him. Does the father suffer a heart attack as the result of his frenzied activity or Alan's venom—or both? Within such moral ambiguity, he dies smirking because he left mud on the carpet. While her husband is dying, his wife's primary concern is in finding a clean pillow slip before the doctor arrives. Alan's traumatic experience within the bosom of the family has at its center the painful uncertainty of parental approval or rejection and suggests an analogue to fate: one neither deserves nor is even able to anticipate the box on the ears which inevitably comes. Bainbridge seems to suggest that one must choose to live either like the young Alan, on the edge and in fear, or, like the mature Alan, with morbid detachment.

A Quiet Life is generally estimated to be Bainbridge's best novel thus far and has been called "the quintessential family novel." Admiring Bainbridge's ability to tell so dramatic a story through a semiarticulate character, Julia O'Faolain comments that the novel itself is quiet, relying on incident and motif: "Such devices help Bainbridge catch the essential selves of her lower-middle-class people, while respecting their reticence."

Satisfied with this last exploration of her own past, Bainbridge moved up to the present in her next novel, *Injury Time* (1977). This book, which the author says she enjoyed writing most of all, was to have been "definitive on middle-age love affairs, but ended up absurd." Using multiple points of view, Bainbridge returns to the problems people have distinguishing reality from their own invented scenarios. Binny at forty is unmarried, has three children (one of whom is a difficult teenager), gets

Dust jacket for Bainbridge's novel on middle-age love affairs that "ended up absurd"

hot flashes, and cries often. But she convinces her married lover, the tired Edward, that they should give a respectable dinner party for his friends. Edward would rather prune his roses, but he extends an invitation to a casual business associate rumored to have a "woman of the world" for a wife. Portents of disaster stalk Binny as she prepares for this social ritual. The streets and stores harbor menace: rude line-jumpers, violent youth, abandoned prams, and a covert bank robbery. Like so many Bainbridge women, Binny has lost control of her life. Her children confound her; her untidy house thwarts the Hoover; the dessert falls behind the refrigerator; and other neighborhood women, just as hapless, wail off the balcony across the street, copulate behind her dust bins, and drunkenly crash her dinner party. It is hardly surprising that the fleeing bank robbers decide to take Binny's dinner party hostage. Even the thieves are victims of their own ineptness.

Bainbridge is amazed at the charge that her plots are incredible. She insists that the improbable events described in her novels are based on her own actual experiences. (Ironically, as those improbable situations have become more probable in today's society, Bainbridge's work is recognized for closing the gap between art and the real thing.) Edith Milton has observed: "She mocks at the same time our lives' drab imitation of fiction, and our fictions' bright imitation of life." The characters in *Injury Time* are so adept at their daily illusions that the real violence, brutality, and rape perpetrated by the criminals strike them as second-rate drama. For Binny, a "voyeur of murder, arson and war," the real scene is often unconvincing. "I keep thinking I'm watching television," she says. "There doesn't seem to be much difference." The novel's title refers to its central image likening middle age to the second half of a football game which "long since decided . . . was drawing to a close." The scarred and weary players only wait for the final whistle. In Binny's case the rules of the game have never worked, and the final whistle signals her kidnapping by the fleeing robbers. "I always knew it would be me," she resignedly declares at the novel's end. The review of the book in the *Times Literary Supplement* aptly expressed the kind of response this unconventional novel inspired. Calling *Injury Time* a "first-class minor novel," both convincing and unimaginable, Michael Irwin declared, "The idiosyncrasy of mode can be both entertaining and instructive. For the reader it is a pleasure to come to terms with so sharp an eye and so original an imagination." There was also some sentiment that Bainbridge had gone too far this time and had actually parodied her own work. Also called into question were the rather abrupt ending and "punishment" of the characters. Such criticism notwithstanding, Bainbridge received the Whitbread Literary Award for the novel in 1977. In 1978, she became a Fellow of the Royal Society of Literature.

Having written steadily for six years, producing a novel a year, Bainbridge experienced a writing block after *Injury Time*. She agreed with those who thought it time she attempted a work of greater scope; she could no longer write about her life and childhood. Fearing she might never be able to write again, she went to Israel with a group of British writers. There, a visit to Yad Vashem evoked

memories of an adolescent preoccupation with the Holocaust, which she describes in an afterword to the 1979 American edition of *Young Adolf* (published in London in 1978). Upon her return to England, she read *The Life and Death of Adolph Hitler* (1973) by Michael Robert Payne and noted that Hitler's half brother, Alois, arrived in Liverpool in 1910. On a subsequent visit to New York, Bainbridge saw the entry in the diary of Bridget Hitler, Alois's wife, which indicated that in 1912, Adolf Hitler, carrying false papers and fleeing a military draft, visited his relatives in England. Although the claim that Adolf Hitler visited England at any time has been called into doubt, Bainbridge continued to research Hitler's life and began writing *Young Adolf*. The Liverpool setting she knew well, but the similarities she imagined between her father's manic personality (he was born the same year as Hitler) and that of "young Adolf" presented her with problems. Her protagonist became "more rounded and lovable, and I had to start all over again." The character she eventually created is not very attractive but still vulnerable and human. The interest of the book, however, depends in large measure on the reader's awareness of the later, real career of its main character. Bainbridge hardly misses an opportunity to exploit this dramatic irony and salts the novel with clever suggestions for Hitler's later modus operandi. Uneasy with her brother-in-law but pitying his destitution, Bridget makes him a shirt from a piece of mildewed brown cloth and instructs him to comb his hair over his forehead to conceal a scar. A Jewish man befriends him and includes him in an intrigue to hide poor children from welfare authorities, thus teaching him the thrill of clandestine plotting. When the plotters are routed without any struggle, Adolf notes the power of a few hard men when the majority fear violence. As a bellboy in the Adelphi Hotel, he becomes convinced that a uniform and a grand hotel setting are worthy of him. Low comedy takes on a prophetic chill as the twenty-three-year-old draft dodger jumps onto a Christmas dinner table and delivers a drunken manifesto, complete with Fascist salute, inspired by the song "The Boy I Love Is Up in the Gallery." As he tumbles from the table and rolls under it in a stupor, a bewildered guest asks, "Is he going to be a priest then?"

Although the book was generally well received, Bainbridge believes that *Young Adolf* has been underrated. American response was more critical of the conceit of the book, found to be an "exercise," and less appreciative of its wit. In the context of Bainbridge's other novels and their themes regarding victimization, one critic sees young Adolf as struggling with his self-deception and powerlessness "in a world that despises him." The characterization of the nervous, Bainbridgean female, Bridget Hitler, is skillfully done, and the author is at her best with proliferating detail in the novel. However, Bainbridge indulges in stereotypes and grotesques with such characters as Dr. Meyer, Dr. Kephalus, and hairy Mary O'Leary, while her portrait of the fanatic as a young man sometimes suggests Chaplinesque caricature. Confusion exists as to what language characters are supposed to be speaking, German or English; Adolf's English runs from poor to Oxbridge perfect.

Young Adolf also seems to mark a turning point in Bainbridge's career, as she has since become more involved in writing film and television scripts based on her novels. *A Quiet Life* appeared on British television, and both *Harriet Said* and *The Bottle Factory Outing* are going into production as "theatrical features." Offshoots of *Young Adolf* include collaboration with Phillip Seville on a two-part play for the BBC entitled *The Journal of Bridget Hitler*, and a series of lectures which Bainbridge has given throughout Britain. These activities kept her from beginning any new fiction for a time, but she did rewrite the earlier work *Another Part of the Wood* in 1979. Believing that the original novel deserved "rescue," she began by cutting eighty pages of text. A comparison of the rewrite with the original serves to illustrate Bainbridge's development as a stylist. While the plot structure is the same as in the 1968 edition, the writing of the 1979 version is sharper and more subtle. Some episodes are expanded with pertinent detail while others are cut severely. The result is a more precise if understated version of Roland's literal and allusive journey to the dark tower. Like so many of Bainbridge's other characters, those who gather for a camping holiday in this novel strive for human community and fail at love. As if to the Ark, they come, led by Joseph to the Welsh woods in two's: two couples, two children, two hosts. The characters cluster and regroup; still all remain isolated, spectators to each other. They try to do the right thing: Dotty patiently endures Joseph's stings; Joseph tries to "improve" the troubled boy, Kidney; Balfour, a shy tool fitter, does social work; Lionel dotes on his shrewish wife; and the taciturn owner of the property, George, is preoccupied with conservation and the suffering of the Jews. But the novel is a devastating portrayal of the destructiveness of modern solipsism, and the idyll turns into tragedy with the death of Joseph's child Roland.

For all of Bainbridge's revision, Joseph remains the worst of her bullies. Narcissistic and unfeeling, he meticulously analyzes his own dreams, a practice about which the hapless Dotty observes: "It didn't seem to help him much to know what they meant. Sometimes she felt it would be more valuable to him if he wrote down what he did in his waking hours." In a setting of phallic images, the men are generally impotent. Joseph refuses to sleep with his mistress and resists all her efforts to mitigate his egotistical gestures; Lionel makes love to his wife by reciting Thomas Moore's poem "Lalla Rookh": "Golden dreams, are you coming back again?" The landscape of Bainbridge's perverse pastoral is mined with omens: swollen rabbits hang from trees, sheep tremble, wasps' nests wait underfoot, chemical toilets fail, and trees burst into flame. Small wonder the characters who raise their arms and hearts to the sky end up sheltering their heads. Transforming reality into fiction, as Lionel does with his coin story and Roland does with the tower visit, is an attempt at survival, but these illusions ultimately destroy what they would protect. Lionel loses his coin to the wasps, and Roland takes an overdose of those pills which he believes will make him more attractive to his neglectful father. Bainbridge's final irony is in keeping with the theme. No one realizes the child is dying because he appears to be so peaceful, and, anyway, the Monopoly game is more important.

The question of moral blame, like that raised in *A Quiet Life*, is not easily resolved. Like the sudden outbreak of fire in the woods or the death of Lear's daughter in Kidney's version of the story, "nothing is entirely accidental or entirely planned." Bainbridge's thematic comment in this work casts the accidents of her previous novels in relief. Because no one can foresee with accuracy the feelings generated by another, the chaos resulting from human frustration could "escalate to such a point that what preceded it achieved a degree of order." Only George's friend, Balfour, understands the nature of the center which no longer holds. The core, he realizes, is loyalty if not pride "in your own flesh and blood . . . there wasn't anything else." The others had "cut themselves free from that sort of thing, gone out on a limb. They didn't really feel they belonged to anyone any more." One would like to think that the death of a little child would lead some of the characters toward a communion. But Bainbridge's ironic use of Biblical allusion—to Joseph's coat of many colors, the Mount of Olives, and Moses, among others—suggests that betrayal of the fundamental bonds will continue. Upon hearing the story of Abraham and Isaac, Roland was confident: "My dad would never sacrifice me. He doesn't believe in God." At the end, the witness, Balfour, receives no revelation, no truths, can feel no emotion. Roland's death would only result in another "dispersal into landscape, a journey to another part of the wood." But if one becomes numb to life, Bainbridge offers, art still remains. Balfour may, in telling the story, feel something. This revised version of the story, it is generally agreed, is a much more expert one, and Bainbridge appears to have rewritten so as to reflect the thematic emphasis and complexity of her later novels. As in Bainbridge's other novels, physical details become pointers to fate and take on moral meaning. Small accidents have large consequences. One reviewer notes the Pinteresque menace in the establishment of so intimate a relationship between the ordinary and the horrible. In her analysis of the two versions, Patricia Beer finds the later book less explanatory but "more truly outspoken." Like Beer, other critics welcomed the 1979 text as a noteworthy addition to Bainbridge's mature work, citing its technical skill and its thematic significance as another portrait of the failure of love. While calling attention to the novel's expert sense of timing and the brilliant use of juxtaposition in the rewrite, Julia O'Faolain concludes:

"Summaries do her no justice. Her genius is for a tapestry of ephemera."

Bainbridge's latest novel, *Winter Garden* (1980), has all of the deadly striking power of her earliest work while delivering the usual high comedy. According to the author, the novel's central character is the Edward of *Injury Time*, quite recovered from his fall from the getaway car and renamed Ashburner. Bainbridge drew many of the details of the novel from her own visit to the U.S.S.R. as part of a cultural exchange tour. Consequently, *Winter Garden* chronicles Ashburner's tour of Russia with a small group of artists. Now a married Admiralty lawyer, Ashburner tells his wife that he is off to Scotland for a fishing trip and duly takes his rods and waders. Actually, he joins his artist paramour for what he hopes will be a romantic interlude, but, as in so many other Bainbridge novels, romantic expectation runs amuck in the perverse landscape of reality. The holiday has hardly begun when the mistress, Nina, and Ashburner's suitcase mysteriously disappear. Further complications arise when Douglas Ashburner is doubly mistaken for both Nina's husband, a famous brain surgeon, and a fellow traveler named Bernard Douglas, an artist given to wandering off to do his own secretive drawings. Thus

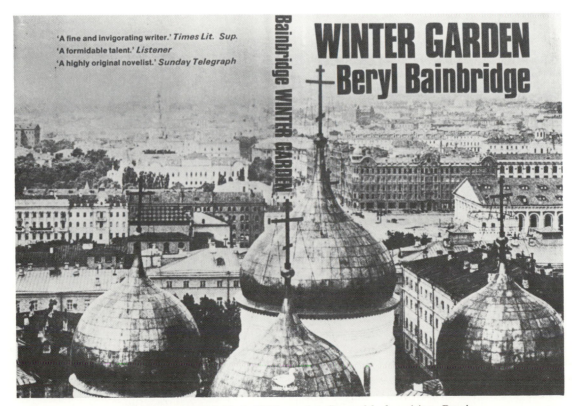

Dust jacket for Bainbridge's 1980 novel, influenced by her visit to Russia

Ashburner moves in a surrealistic Russian terrain of political shrines, cavernous restaurants, and immense cemeteries, trying to survive intrigue, hallucination, alcoholic binges, and his own paranoia.

Once again, Bainbridge probes the irony in scenarios which individuals and states can invent for their purposes. The English delegation is driven in the official car "to a palace to take tea with a metal worker," but Ashburner, in his fraudulent identity as a brain surgeon, is whisked away to a hospital to observe an operation. In an observation booth above the operating theater, Ashburner—frozen by the sound of the drill over the intercom—watches, horrified by the technicolored spectacle of gouging and plugging. Once he discovers the television screens in his little booth, however, he can watch the operation on the screens quite calmly. Similarly, whenever his fears—for the missing Nina, of the K.G.B., about the discovery of his affair—threaten to disrupt the group, Ashburner is tranquilized by translations of reality: vodka, bogus phone calls from Nina, more vodka, a substitute in his bed, and his own hallucinations. These visions cause the other travelers to dismiss him as totally "whacked," but they bring Ashburner closer to the truth of the winter garden. Finally, driven by his vision of Nina, Ashburner ducks the transportation provided to the airport and dashes to the fated rendezvous. When the authorities at this address find certain suspicious drawings of Russian installations in Ashburner's fishing-rod case, the reader is not surprised, and neither is Ashburner.

The central image of the "winter garden" begins with a little terrace in Chelsea, where Ashburner's wife skips rope on summer nights, and expands to include the sunless stretch of Soviet society, and finally, the chilling design of life itself. Confounded by a plot in which everything has conspired to this ending, Ashburner contemplates his wife's smiling face in a photograph and comments succinctly on the novel's theme: "Even a man who is sensible and composed, he thought, must pale before life's contradictions." Although there has been some reservation about the flow of events in the novel in general, and the ending in particular, critical commentary suggests that the setting is the perfect vehicle for the author's theme of human bafflement and that the central metaphor, the winter garden, is as dark and ambiguous as the grave it evokes. Citing the "blandness and delicacy" with which Bainbridge's writing "excoriates the mind," Anne Ducheme says that the novel "opens and enters quite new and freezing latitudes, where even comedy fails to comfort."

Bainbridge is committed to recording her own experience, "because then you know where you are in your bones." Recently, she has said that, because she is finished with writing about the distant past, she can no longer write of "love, sacrifice, or morality. I have no convictions about such things." Regretting that she did not live within the certainty of Victorian mores, she says she would like to write a book for her grown children which would chart the contemporary wilderness of mature adult life, especially the rearing of adolescents. Death, too, interests her as a future subject. Whatever direction her writing takes, Bainbridge has secured an audience for her novels and an impressive literary reputation. Critics have tried to compare her to Franz Kafka, Harold Pinter, Iris Murdock, Henry Green, and Flannery O'Connor, but Bainbridge's work defies comparison, and she wants to keep it that way. Although admiring writers like D. H. Lawrence, William Faulkner, and Graham Greene, she tries not to read much fiction. Trained to mimic and having a photographic memory, she fears her predisposition for imitation. That she has learned to write by doing accounts perhaps for both her inventiveness and her ingenuousness in discussing her own work. "I love the syntax of sentences," she says, "the technique of writing, of plotting." She revises each sentence for cadence because rhythm is important to her. Disliking any excesses of style, she strives for discipline and clarity in her own.

As to future writing, she responds slyly to criticism that her novels are too "thin": "I've got to stop writing 158 pages and try to write 168." Actually Bainbridge's poised style has had a positive impact on contemporary British fiction. In view of what John Barth has identified as a "used-up" or exhausted narrative mode in contemporary fiction, the vigor of Bainbridge's lithe, imaginative novels compensates for the "minor mode" she has chosen. As James Price once observed, the "big Truth" may not be there, but the "little ones slip through." Some critics have recoiled from what they consider to be the author's cold detachment from her characters and her refusal to confront evil. Bainbridge protests that her novels' tones derive from the plots she "pinches from the newspaper": "The macabre element is a structural thing. But as I only choose accident or death plots, it appears horrifying." She chooses sensational material because she believes the modern attitude toward most experience is blase. She is equally candid about drawing so many details from her personal life, a practice which necessitates a certain objectivity in the creative act. Professing a philosophical agnosticism, she insists that she has sympathy for all her characters and that all have their own dignity. Her photographic images have been much admired for presenting sharply defined figures in relief to the grainy texture of life. Others view her detachment as subtlety and justly remark her use of detail, motif, and the ironic juxtaposition of events. Appreciation for her work has expanded from interest in her plotting and technique to acknowledgment of her expertise in psychological portraiture. One is hard put to fix Bainbridge's literary reputation, however, because opinion varies greatly as to her seriousness as a writer. Some critics still regard her work as primarily entertaining, however skillful. And one cannot relegate her to a single mode; her novels have been variously characterized as tragic, comic, mannerist, absurd, gothic, grotesque, naturalistic, and satiric. She has been called both the "Oscar Wilde of the 1970's" and *the* novelist of lower-middle-class manners. The Bainbridgean female, alternately silly and wise, loving and self-absorbed, rebellious and conformist, deluded and perceptive—but always accommodating and vulnerable—has been interpreted as the image of a befuddled and helpless postwar England, and finally, as the image of modern humanity perplexed in the extreme. Her men and women are in the same modern fix—having escaped the old repressive rules of Victorian middle-class respectability, they yet seek normality but end up adrift in a sea of too many choices. Criticized early in her career for her "dark view" of a violent world, Bainbridge is now credited with having identified, accurately, moral and cultural confusion as the contemporary malaise. Yet her characters have remained resilient, and the books have retained their good humor.

Although Bainbridge is commercially successful in Britain and enjoys an international reputation, she has not quite caught on in the United States. It may only be a matter of time, however, since each successive book receives greater critical attention. James Brockway describes her growing appeal: "Miss Bainbridge would be the last novelist in London to be portentous or to appear for one moment to be coming along with a message and writing a series of novels on a Grand Theme. Yet the more I read her the more I suspect that the grip her work has taken on us . . . is not merely due to her being an exquisite entertainer . . . but also to the powerful subconscious appeal of her subject matter: our parlous postwar condition." Writing with cunning and compassion about the weak and the inept, Beryl Bainbridge has emerged as one of the most original and dependable of contemporary

British novelists. So far, her novels have received very little attention from academic literary circles, and a serious study of her work remains to be done.

Television Scripts:
Tiptoe Through the Tulips, 1976;
The Warrior's Return, 1977;
It's Lovely Day Tomorrow, 1977;
Sweet William, BBC, 1979;
A Quiet Life, BBC, 1980;
The Journal of Bridget Hitler, by Bainbridge and Phillip Seville, BBC, 1980.

Periodical Publications:
FICTION:
"Eric on the Agenda," in *Bananas*, edited by Emma Tennant (London: Quartet Books, 1977), pp. 176-184;
"Everything's in Books," *Spectator*, 241 (30 December 1978): 32-33.
NONFICTION:
"Departures: The Loss of Liverpool," *Listener*, 90 (29 November 1973): 729-730;
"Bringing Hitler to Liverpool," *Times Literary Supplement*, 3 November 1978, p. 1276;
"Beryl Bainridge, Novelist, Painted a Drama That Happened to Herself," *Sunday Times Magazine*, 17 February 1980, p. 33.

Interviews:
Barbara A. Bannon, "PW Interviews: Beryl Bainbridge," *Publishers Weekly*, 209 (15 March 1976): 5-6;
Paul S. Nathan, "Violator of Privacy," *Publishers Weekly*, 215 (9 April 1979): 34;
"Beryl Bainbridge Replies to a Review of *Young Adolf*," *New York Times*, 18 May 1979, p. 26.

References:
Patricia Beer, "*Another Part of the Wood*," *Times Literary Supplement*, 29 February 1980, p. 246;
James Brockway, "Penalty Areas," *Books and Bookmen* (December 1977): 51-52;
Margo Jefferson, "Violence Under Glass," *Newsweek*, 90 (12 August 1974): 75-76;
Diane Johnson, "*Young Adolf*," *Times Literary Supplement*, 1 December 1978, p. 1385;
Edith Milton, "*Injury Time*," *The New Republic* (25 March 1978): 27-28;
Julia O'Faolain, "Getting Away with Murder," *New York Times Book Review*, 20 March 1977, p. 6;
J. Pickerin, "Drabble, Byatt, Dunn and Bainbridge: Their Lives and Their Books," *Albion*, 11 (1979): 197.

J. G. Ballard

(15 November 1930-   )

John Fletcher
University of East Anglia

SELECTED BOOKS: *Billennium* (New York: Berkley, 1962);

The Wind from Nowhere (New York: Berkley, 1962; Harmondsworth, U.K.: Penguin, 1967);

The Voices of Time and Other Stories (New York: Berkley, 1962);

The Drowned World (New York: Berkley, 1962; London: Gollancz, 1963);

The Four-Dimensional Nightmare (London: Gollancz, 1963);

Passport To Eternity (New York: Berkley, 1963);

The Burning World (New York: Berkley, 1964); expanded as *The Drought* (London: Cape, 1965);

The Terminal Beach (London: Gollancz, 1964); revised as *Terminal Beach* (New York: Berkley, 1964);

The Crystal World (New York: Farrar, Straus & Giroux, 1966; London: Cape, 1966);

The Impossible Man and Other Stories (New York: Berkley, 1966);

By Day Fantastic Birds Flew Through the Petrified Forest. . . . (Brighton: Esographics for Firebird Visions, 1967);

The Day of Forever (London: Panther, 1967); republished with deletions and additions (London: Panther, 1971);

The Disaster Area (London: Cape, 1967);

The Overloaded Man (London: Panther, 1967);

The Atrocity Exhibition (London: Cape, 1970); republished as *Love and Napalm: Export U.S.A.* (New York: Grove Press, 1972);

Chronopolis and Other Stories (New York: Putnam's, 1971);

Vermilion Sands (New York: Berkley, 1971; London: Cape, 1973);

Crash (New York: Farrar, Straus & Giroux, 1973; London: Cape, 1973);

Concrete Island (New York: Farrar, Straus & Giroux, 1974; London: Cape, 1974);

High-Rise (London: Cape, 1975; New York: Holt, Rinehart & Winston, 1977);

Low-Flying Aircraft and Other Stories (London: Cape, 1976);

The Best of J. G. Ballard (London: Futura, 1977);

The Unlimited Dream Company (London: Cape, 1979; New York: Holt, Rinehart & Winston, 1979);

The Venus Hunters (St. Albans, U.K.: Granada, 1980);

Hello America (London: Cape, 1981).

J. G. Ballard is more than just a science fiction or futurist fantasy merchant; he is one of the most significant of those British novelists who have established themselves since 1960.

Ballard is an ambitious author who has often stressed that the kind of fiction he writes is the authentic literature of the twentieth century, the only fiction which responds imaginatively to the transforming nature of science and technology. He believes that the present, rather than the future, is now the period of greatest moral urgency for the writer, and that science fiction becomes the mainstream—rather than a cult literature of dubious respectability—if, like his, it concerns itself with what he calls the inner space, as opposed to the outer space of the traditional, gadget-preoccupied science fiction. He made the same point more extensively in a recent interview:

> I began writing in the mid-Fifties. Enormous changes were going on in England at that time, largely brought about by science and technology—the beginnings of television, package holidays, mass merchandising, the first supermarkets. A new landscape was being created. The so-called mainstream novel wasn't really looking at the present day. The only form of fiction which was trying to make head or tail of what was going on in our world was science-fiction.
>
> It had been too concerned with the future, right from its origins. I wanted a science-fiction of the present day. I am interested in the technology of the present of this world. I am not interested in imaginary alien planets. I am certain you know that the only alien planet is Earth. It is this world that is the strange one. All the extra-terrestrials we need are walking around in these streets.

Ballard is also something of a paradox. In America where his books are published in paperback by Berkley, he has never had much success in the science fiction market, though his reputation in Great

Britain has grown so that he is now published by one of the most discriminating fiction publishers, Jonathan Cape. He has done well in France, where his particular blend of erotic fantasy and surrealistic imagery seems less unfamiliar than it does in the English-speaking world.

With nine major novels and many short stories to his credit, Ballard has been unjustly neglected by critics and academics. As a stylist and innovator Ballard invites comparison with French author Alain Robbe-Grillet, though Ballard has not yet been taken nearly as seriously in Great Britain or the United States as Robbe-Grillet is taken by his countrymen. For that reason Ballard lacks Robbe-Grillet's sense of an assured readership, of a guaranteed maturity of response; and it is symptomatic that where there are several monographs on Robbe-Grillet in print, there is only one on Ballard which has had little impact. But the opinion is changing, and with the emergence of younger novelists like Ian McEwan and Christopher Priest, who write in a mode of heightened realism or imaginative fantasy, Ballard's work is becoming better understood and thus more highly appreciated.

James Graham Ballard was born in Shanghai, China, of British parents (his father was a businessman), and as an adolescent during World War II he was interned in a Japanese civilian prison camp until the camp was liberated by the American army. He has said that China had an enormous influence on him, and indeed one can see that the novel *High-Rise* (1975), about a huge apartment block overwhelmed by barbarism, may owe the distant origins of its conception to reminiscence like the following, which Ballard shared with an interviewer in 1980:

> I didn't leave China until after the war, at the age of 16, and it had an enormous influence. I mean the landscape around Shanghai, paddy fields in the summer, the mouth of the Yangtze—on the one hand, extremely modern with apartment blocks and office blocks everywhere, American cars in the streets, and on the other hand these huge sheets of water. There were fusions and peculiar inversions—particularly those that came during the war when Shanghai was suddenly a city of half-empty apartment blocks, of abandoned factories, of empty airfields.

Ballard studied medicine as an undergraduate at King's College, Cambridge, but left after two years without a degree. Then followed a period of

odd jobs until he joined the Royal Air Force for his military service and went to Canada as a pilot. He married Helen Mary Matthews in 1953, and they had three children; her death in 1964 had a deeply disturbing effect on him and on his writing, which he appeared to abandon for about a year afterward. But following this interruption the writing, first begun in the mid-1950s, resumed and took a new direction.

J. G. Ballard

Indeed, the three novels published before 1964 all concern worlds which punish man for tampering with them. In *The Wind from Nowhere* (1962) Shaftesbury Avenue and Holborn in London are turned into a "city of hell" when they are ripped to pieces by freak high-velocity winds, and a similar ecological disaster, resulting from the melting of the polar ice caps, afflicts the people of *The Drowned World* (1962). In *The Drought* (1965) radioactive waste has prevented evaporation of the sea, making rain a thing of the past. The sun beats down on the parched earth and on the parching spirit of man. Out of the dead land—Ballard echoes T. S. Eliot's *The Waste Land* deliberately—a cruel new breed of men emerges and water, replacing money as the effective currency, becomes the source of a bleak new evil. (*The Drought* was an expanded version of the book that first appeared in America in 1964 under the title *The Burning World*.)

As Frederick Bowers has written, Ballard's novels of this early period are concerned thematically with "the delicate natural equipoise upon which our existence depends, the ease with which the balance may be upset, and the consequences of the resulting imbalance." Certainly a novel like *The Drowned World*, in which "the earth's protective ionosphere is penetrated as a result of solar storms and the world turned into a vast equatorial swamp in which man returns to the autistic world of the womb," bears this out. Nevertheless, as Bowers points out, these novels go far beyond environmentalist propaganda of the Rachel Carson variety. They are concerned with the wider issue of man's desperate place in the universe. This reminds Bowers of T. S. Eliot:

> The first three novels probe areas which directly relate to particular preoccupations in the Prufrock poems and *The Waste Land*, while *The Crystal World* has the same concern as the *Four Quartets* in its search for "the still point of a turning world." Such a comparison, made in terms of image and thematic concerns, might be expected to diminish Ballard, but it doesn't; nor should one conclude that Ballard's energy is dependent on Eliot; it is rather that both derive their strength from their underlying concern about man in his universe.

The Crystal World (1966) shows a change of direction in Ballard's fiction. Absent is the apocalyptic note so stridently and chillingly sounded in the first three books, and a note of mysticism comes forward. The frosted, jewel-encrusted world which he enters in the company of a former lover is seen by the narrator as a kind of lost paradise suddenly regained in which his old "ideas of time and mortality" are permanently undermined, and which leads to what he considers the "illumination" of his life in that the rest of the world appears like "some half-abandoned purgatory." The note is different from the doom-laden warnings of the earlier books.

If his first three novels represent one phase in Ballard's career as a novelist—a phase preoccupied with ecological nemesis—and *The Crystal World* another—one concerned with a paradise regained—then *Crash* (1973) inaugurated a third

which includes *Concrete Island* (1974) and *High-Rise*. Critics recognized Ballard's considerable gifts even when they found fault with his stylistic impressionism. The *Times Literary Supplement* noted the "originality and power" of his vision and began to refer to him as "one of the most sensitive and enigmatic novelists of the present day." In this third phase Ballard began to focus on the technological breakdown of the contemporary world. He had tested the water with his stories collected in *The Atrocity Exhibition* (1970). Although he personally had nothing to do with a reading of his story, "The Assassination Weapon," at the Lambda Theatre in London in 1968, he did mount a sculpture exhibition entitled "Crashed Cars" at the New Arts Laboratory Gallery, London, in April 1969. This exhibition illustrated a scene from *The Atrocity Exhibition* and was also intended as a test before he embarked on *Crash*.

Crash represented a departure for Ballard, a turning away from tales about ecological disasters or mutations to an unsentimental scrutiny of the dehumanized eroticism and the brutality that he feels are inseparable from the new technologies. Lest Ballard's gaze upon these things be considered prurient, we should bear in mind David Pringle's comment: "the implied author of Ballard's fiction is a wry figure with a slight smile and melancholy eyes; he rarely laughs." There is also the uncanny fact that, quoting Pringle again, "one constantly gets the feeling that Ballard was *there first*: his stories have illuminated, with tremendous insight and a truly prophetic relevance, the public moral concerns of our age." As Ballard put it in a 1969 interview, "the trouble with Marxism is that it is a social philosophy for the poor—what we need now is a social philosophy for the rich."

Exploration of that philosophy began in *Crash*. All the junk and trash of consumerism, of which perhaps the airport duty-free liquor store is the paradigm, are set against the dehumanized eroticism and brutality of the new technology. The theme of this particular novel is "the perverse eroticism of the car-crash" and it is orchestrated at obsessive and perhaps unnecessary length (although the published version is considerably shorter than the typescript Ballard originally submitted to his publishers). The inescapable moral question in *Crash* is the extent to which Ballard is sensationalizing and sentimentalizing his material. Ballard undoubtedly sees himself as a satirist of contemporary sicknesses, but his readers may feel that he lacks the consistent moral stance and the sharp intelligence required of a modern George Orwell. Even if the moral issue is

THE ULTIMATE CITY ①

All winter, as he worked on the
sailplane, Halloway had never been
certain what drove him on to build
his grotesque aircraft, with its ungainly
wings and humpback fuselage. Even
now, in the final seconds before his
first flight, he was still unsure why
he was perched on the cliff
above the inlet waters of the sound,
into which he would
plunge. The tapered wings
shivered in the cold air, as if trying
to rip open the cockpit and eject
him onto the beach below.

It had taken Halloway and his
helpers — the ten-year-olds who formed
an enthusiastic claque and coolie-gang —
to drag the sailplane from
the barn behind his

Manuscript for "The Ultimate City," collected in Low-Flying Aircraft and Other Stories

set aside, there is the problem of a distinct monotonous quality to the writing. Yet, while lacking narrative substance, the novel possesses, in its dark surrealism and obsessive intensity, an almost hallucinatory cumulative effect.

Concrete Island is shorter than *Crash* and does have narrative substance. This develops clearly and logically out of the opening sentences:

> Soon after three o'clock on the afternoon of April 22nd 1973, a 35-year-old architect named Robert Maitland was driving down the high-speed exit lane of the Westway interchange in central London. Six hundred yards from the junction with the newly built spur of the M4 motorway, when the Jaguar had already passed the 70 m.p.h. speed limit, a blow-out collapsed the front near-side tyre. The exploding air reflected from the concrete parapet seemed to detonate inside Robert Maitland's skull. During the few seconds before his crash he clutched at the whiplashing spokes of the steering wheel, dazed by the impact of the chromium window pillar against his head. The car veered from side to side across the empty traffic lanes, jerking his hands like a puppet's. The shredding tyre laid a black diagonal stroke across the white marker lines that followed the long curve of the motorway embankment. Out of control, the car burst through the palisade of pinewood trestles that formed a temporary barrier along the edge of the road. Leaving the hard shoulder, the car plunged down the grass slope of the embankment. Thirty yards ahead, it came to a halt against the rusting chassis of an overturned taxi.

Maitland, badly injured, discovers that he shares the waste area within the motorway intersection—a sort of grotesque desert island effectively cut off from the rest of the world—with a tramp and a prostitute, and finds that he can survive on garbage dumped regularly over the perimeter fence by truckers serving the restaurant trade. (This notion of superfluity leading to waste is an increasingly prominent motif in Ballard's fiction.) Maitland establishes an ambiguous relationship with both of his fellow-inhabitants, but eventually the tramp Proctor is killed and the prostitute Jane leaves. Still badly injured from the accident, Maitland is clearly going to stay where he is and make no serious attempt to escape the island; it is as if he has successfully displaced the other inhabitants and can take over their dismal territory.

Like Ballard's other books this one has its strengths and weaknesses. The psychology of the characters is perfunctory: little explanation is given

for their behavior, and thematically Maitland's complex attitude toward his Robinson Crusoe situation is never fully worked out. While Ballard's attitude toward sex is brutally unromantic, there is an almost hallucinatory vividness in some of his images, such as the moment when Maitland takes off his torn dinner jacket and squeezes the sodden fabric in his bruised hands: "the muddy water ran away between his fingers," Ballard writes, "as if he were washing out a child's football gear." This line brilliantly highlights the horror of Maitland's situation in a simile which arrestingly juxtaposes the homely and banal with the perfectly nightmarish. The reviewer for the *Times Literary Supplement* found the novel "most intelligent and interesting. . . . The skill with which Mr. Ballard manages, in the most uncontrived way, to have Maitland compulsively regress to self-discovery is itself considerable; that in doing so he reveals undertones of savagery and desolation beneath a metaphor of apparent neutrality is a tribute to him as our foremost iconographer of landscape."

High-Rise "makes the point that the high-rise building is not so much a machine for living as a brutal playground full of essentially solitary children," as Pringle says. It bears out, in the dimension of imaginative fiction, a fact noted by leading art-historian Robert Hughes in his essay "Architecture and the Utopian Dream." Hughes is here discussing Le Corbusier's only attempt at building high-rise mass housing in France, the famous *Unité d'habitation* at Marseilles, and ponders on the ironic discrepancy between the architect's vision of the good life and the reality with which residents of the building have to contend: "Today the pool is cracked, the gymnasium closed (some optimist tried to turn it into a disco, which naturally failed), and the track littered with broken concrete and tangles of rusty scaffolding. . . . In its decrepitude, it . . . has a heroic sadness approaching that of a Greek temple." Like the hapless tenants of the *Unité d'habitation*, the people who live in Ballard's elegant forty-story tower block are "living in a future that ha[s] already taken place." The class structure of contemporary British society is reproduced in miniature among Ballard's residents. Characteristic of his somewhat simplistic view that man himself is the worst predator that mankind has to fear, Ballard describes the affluent inhabitants of the building hell-bent on an orgy of self-destruction in which, for example, cocktail parties degenerate into marauding attacks on "enemy" floors above or below, and the once luxurious amenities become an arena for technological mayhem. The society of the high rise collapses into barbarism as the inhabitants, driven by primal urges which are never properly explained, recreate a world ruled by the brutally simple law of the jungle: to survive one must prey on others and keep out of the way of those who would prey upon oneself.

As always, the writing is cool and the observation exact, and like an Alfred Hitchcock movie, it works so long as the reader is held captive by suspense, but it tends to crumble when certain prosaic questions are asked, such as why the police were not on hand to prevent the worst excesses committed by the residents. There is occasionally, too, a certain arch cynicism, as in the following aside: "She had accepted him as she would any marauding hunter. First she would try to kill him, but failing this give him food and her body, breast-feed him back to a state of childishness and even, perhaps, feel affection for him. Then, the moment he was asleep, cut his throat. The synopsis of the ideal marriage." On the other hand, there is no gainsaying the skill with which Ballard sets up the contrast between normality and horror, from the opening sentence "as he sat on his balcony eating the dog. . ." to the last.

The story is told in flashback. After the brief shock opening in which an evidently well-educated man, Dr. Laing, is shown squatting like a modern troglodyte beside a fire of telephone directories over which he has roasted the hindquarters of his Alsatian, the narrative moves back three months in time when normality still reigned in the high rise. The narrative then gradually brings the reader up to date, and the last chapter picks up where the first paragraph left off. The novel closes with Dr. Laing looking out at another high rise 400 yards away, and watching its lights fail as a prelude to its own descent into barbarism, "Laing watched them contentedly, ready to welcome them to their new world." One of the remarkable insights of this book is that people can adapt to savagery and even, in a perverse way, come to prefer it to civilized conduct.

In his review of *High-Rise*, John Sutherland in the *Times Literary Supplement* referred to Brian Aldiss's comment that Ballard had not resolved the problem of "writing a novel without having the characters pursue any purposeful course of action." In a mixed review of praise and blame (typical of many reviews of Ballard's fiction), Sutherland went on to say, "As usual, Mr. Ballard contrives to unsettle and tease the reader."

It is also characteristic of Ballard that he should set his terrifying stories in surroundings with which he is extremely familiar: he lives in Shepperton, not far from London's Heathrow Airport, in a residential area famous for its film studios. This is the setting for his next novel, *The Unlimited Dream Company* (1979). The familiar settings contribute to Ballard's irony as they make the stories more disturbing by emphasizing that the reality of the environment in which they take place is the present.

The Unlimited Dream Company together with Ballard's most recent novel, *Hello America* (1981), form a fourth phase in his development as a writer, one that blends fantasy and humor in ways that his earlier work would hardly lead one to expect. Thus he is a writer who consistently resists stereotyping. What has remained constant, as critic David Punter rightly reminds us, is his "almost manic fertility of idea and form" along with a hallucinatory portrayal of "the claustrophobia of excessive information and the corresponding breakdown of selective retrieval systems," in which war has become the "new barbarity, all the worse for the high level of hidden organization at which it operates." Nor has the technique varied in essentials: a Ballard story vibrates to a higher key as the suspense is progressively tightened, a particularly frightening device which can be seen in nearly everything Ballard has written.

The Unlimited Dream Company is then, like all the other novels, strong on imagination and intensity of vision, but weak on narrative interest, characterization, and dialogue. It shares with *Crash* an almost adolescent obsession with semen, particularly when produced by masturbation, but is a little more lighthearted about it than *Crash* was. The main character finds himself transformed into a buck and proceeds to mount every doe in sight; even in human form he feels an indiscriminate randiness not only for women but also for children and even trees.

The story is the most surrealistic which Ballard has composed to date. An aircraft cleaner at London Airport steals a light aircraft which catches fire and crashes into the Thames at Shepperton. He is drowned, but somehow survives and proceeds to haunt the good burghers of Shepperton with his dreams so that the whole community becomes an "unlimited dream company." He carries on his chest bruises which he assumes were caused by whatever lifesaving action was necessary after he was rescued. But at the end he encounters his own corpse, and the two struggle together desperately for life. "I realised then," the narrator says, "whose mouth and hands I had tried to find since my arrival in this small town. The bruises were the scars of my own body clinging to me in terror as I tore myself free from that dying self and escaped from the drowned aircraft." He manages to calm his alter ego and absorbs him into himself, and then he is free to celebrate in the air the wedding feast with his bride, Dr. Miriam, with whom he has been in love since he crashed in Shepperton near her clinic. He becomes temporarily parted from her, but is confident, in the closing paragraph of the novel, that he and she will eventually be reunited for eternity:

> There I would rest, certain now that one day Miriam would come for me. Then we would set off, with the inhabitants of all the other towns in the valley of the Thames, and in the world beyond. This time we would merge with the trees and the flowers, with the dust and the stones, with the whole of the mineral world, happily dissolving ourselves in the sea of light that formed the universe, itself reborn from the souls of the living who have happily returned themselves to its heart. Already I saw us rising into the air, fathers, mothers and their children, our ascending flights swaying across the surface of the earth, benign tornadoes hanging from the canopy of the universe, celebrating the last marriage of the animate and inanimate, of the living and the dead.

This ending is extraordinarily and uncharac-teristically lyrical for Ballard, and represents a sunnier, more optimistic vein in his writing. It compensates for the childish pornographic fantasies and willful paradoxes which fill much of the book. *The Unlimited Dream Company* more than gestures toward a serious meditation upon the reality of death and upon the nature of divinity. (The protagonist sees himself as a pagan god, or at least as one in communion with unseen powers.) Though he does not succeed in his meditation, it is unusual in contemporary British fiction for the attempt even to be made, and Ballard deserves credit for trying to inject an awareness of the surreal and an aspiration toward myth into a form which is often content with a tired realism.

Ballard's latest novel, *Hello America*, is described by the publishers:

> Frank Sinatra, Charles Manson and forty-six Presidents of the United States play their part in J. G. Ballard's tribute to American dreams past and future: idealistic, liberating dreams; elitist, messianically acquisitive dreams; fantastic technological dreams that are often trivial and sometimes deadly. The drama is played out, as one has come to expect from Ballard, in a landscape of haunting vividness.

Dust jacket for Ballard's "tribute to American dreams past and future"

The book, which Galen Strawson praised for "provid[ing] a wealth of images," pursues the vein of surreal humor which surfaced in *The Unlimited Dream Company* and which was conspicuously lacking both in the apocalyptic novels of Ballard's first phase and the nightmarish visions of his middle period; so it also shows him at his apocalyptic best:

> The end came quickly. In 1999 General Motors declared itself bankrupt and went into liquidation. A few months later it was followed by Ford, Chrysler, Exxon, Mobil and Texaco. For the first time in over a hundred years no motorcars were manufactured in the United States. In his Millennial Address to Congress in the year 2000, President Brown recited a poignant Zen tantra and then made the momentous announcement that henceforth the operation of private gasoline-driven vehicles would be illegal. Despite this emergency decree, there was a widespread sense that once again the government of the United States had been overtaken by events. Traffic had long ceased to flow along the great turnpikes and interstate highways of America. Waist-high weeds flourished in the cracked concrete of the California freeways, millions of abandoned cars rusted on flattened tyres in the garages and parking lots of the nation.

Ballard's achievements in areas other than the novel merit attention, particularly his accomplishments as a short story writer. Like most science fiction authors, he began by using the shorter form and has published several collections of stories. In this medium he has won the high regard of Anthony Burgess, among others. As David Pringle points out in his monograph, Ballard is not a writer to be judged by his novels alone: "He is very much at home in shorter lengths, and his talents are often displayed to the full within the compass of, say, 10,000 words. Ballard tends to compression; at one extreme this leads to the remarkable density of the *Atrocity Exhibiton* pieces (few of which are more than three or four thousand words long)." As Pringle notes, both *The Drowned World* and *The Crystal World* began as magazine novellas, and Ballard has commented in his notes to *The Best of J. G. Ballard* (1977) that some of his early stories, like "The Sound-Sweep" and "The Voices of Time" were over-compressed novels, while some of his recent novels are really extended short stories. Of the stories in *Low-Flying Aircraft* (1976), Michael Irwin has said: "He taps our memories of disused railway-stations or airstrips, dumped cars, derelict cinemas or factories. The world he creates seems credible because it has already begun to exist." Five of the stories in the volume, or three-fourths of the book, are "works of real imaginative force, dreamlike, vivid, unpredictable in their effect." And as always there are the memorable landscapes, of which Ballard is the undisputed master in contemporary fiction. Of an earlier collection of stories, *Vermilion Sands* (1971), a reviewer said that the stylistic effects of his landscapes were comparable to those of the painter Dali insofar as they showed "a mixture of appalling clarity and the exotic." From nearly every point of view, Ballard's achievements as a writer are solid and the advances of his most recent fiction indicate that he is likely to rise in literary stature.

Reference:

David Pringle, *Earth Is The Alien Planet: J. G. Ballard's Four-Dimensional Nightmare* (San Bernardino, Cal.: Borgo, 1979).

John Banville

(8 December 1945-   )

George O'Brien
Vassar College

BOOKS: *Long Lankin* (London: Secker & Warburg, 1970);

Nightspawn (London: Secker & Warburg, 1971; New York: W. W. Norton, 1971);

Birchwood (London: Secker & Warburg, 1973; New York: W. W. Norton, 1973);

Doctor Copernicus (London: Secker & Warburg, 1976; New York: W. W. Norton, 1976);

Kepler (London: Secker & Warburg, 1981);

The Newton Letter (London: Secker & Warburg, 1982).

John Banville is the most interesting and resourceful Irish novelist of his generation. A writer who has let his published work do most of his talking for him, he has done more than most of his contemporaries to challenge accepted ideas of what might constitute a tradition of Irish fiction, and has by his example moved aesthetic concerns much closer to the preeminence usually given to history and social preoccupations in Irish fiction.

Banville was born in Wexford, the county seat of Ireland's most southeasterly county. He was educated locally at the Christian Brothers primary school and St. Peter's College, the main diocesan secondary school. He did not attend university. He presently lives with his wife in the Dublin suburb of Howth and works as a copy editor for the *Irish Press*, a national daily. His artistic output has been confined almost exclusively to the novel, of which he has written five to date. The last two may be considered members of a series devoted to the great astronomers, the overall concept of which has been clearly influenced by Arthur Koestler's study, *The Sleepwalkers: A History of Man's Changing Vision of the Universe* (1959). Besides his achievement in the novel, Banville has written a small amount of short fiction, though it is less compelling than his longer works. He has also contributed some reviews to *Hibernia*, an Irish journal of arts and politics. His work has received public recognition in Ireland, including the Allied Irish Banks prize for *Birchwood* in 1973 and the Irish Arts Council Macauley Fellowship in the same year. In 1976 he was given the Irish-American Foundation Literary Award. Despite his success, Banville is a self-effacing, intensely private man, with a public demeanor which makes a welcome change from the "broth-of-a-boy" rambunctious school of Irish writers. He reads his work in public without dramatic emphasis and in a clear, unemotional tone. In appearance he is unassuming, clerkish, a little withdrawn.

John Banville

Long Lankin (1970), Banville's first book, consists of a sequence of stories and a novella. The opening story is based on the English ballad from which the book takes its name. The ballad deals with love and murder, and the story establishes a mood of emotional bleakness which is shared by various characters who are either witnesses to or implicated in the murder.

The scene of the rest of the book is contemporary Dublin, and the theme is the mores of nouveau riche suburban life. Banville sketches sexual relations of various kinds, including incest (which he was to feature again in the two novels which immediately followed *Long Lankin*). The tone and atmosphere of these interrelated stories resemble those found in the earlier films of Michelangelo Antonioni. They convey—with a tact, delicacy, and undertone of obsession remarkable for a writer as young as Banville was then—a sense of yearning and confusion, a mystique of love, which is intended to be the fallout, so to speak, of the sin in the novella. The author's means are too elliptical to be entirely successful. His daring, however, commands respect. In addition, this work raises interesting implications for the romance as a viable modern genre, and these Banville has continued surreptitiously to explore in his later works.

The stories range over familiar territory—childhood memories, courtship rituals among young adults, a Saturday night on the town. Banville's point, however, is not that of the naturalistic writer or the comedian of manners. His primary interest is not in his material as such, but in the way the material may be perceived and the emotional aura which surrounds it.

Critical response was, on the whole, generous. The *New Statesman*'s reviewer hailed the book as "a ray of hope for the future of fiction. . . . Mr. Banville displays an amazing sophistication." While the *Spectator* reviewer thought ". . . although the idea has promise . . . the writing is fatally bogus," the *Times Literary Supplement* critic reported that "The overriding seriousness of the book does lead, at times, to an uncharacteristic self-indulgence. . . . But the book is more often truthful and perceptive; and for a writer in his early twenties, is an impressive first appearance." The most judicious appraisal was that of the noted Irish poet Derek Mahon in the *Listener*: "When he escapes from the muted, unemphatic rendering of landscape from which so much Irish fiction suffers, and avoids the temptation of fantasy, John Banville reveals himself as a writer of strength and promise."

One of the characters we encounter in perplexed and amoral suburban Dublin is a writer named Ben White, who becomes the narrator of Banville's second work of fiction, *Nightspawn* (1971). Ostensibly a thriller involving White in the events leading up to the installation of the Colonels' junta in Greece in 1967, this novel is more crucially concerned with the interplay of myth and contemporary history in a way that totally recasts and makes more substantial the intellectual and artistic preoc-

cupations of *Long Lankin*. Events in the workaday world of White's island environment follow no pattern. Plot becomes counterplot without the benefit of logic, structure, or justification. White, who might well (as a writer) be expected to have a flair for plot, is swept along by a tide of contingency, which ultimately shows itself to have a direct bearing on the fate of a contemporary European democracy. The narrator cannot control his destiny. The various subversives and interlopers who are agents of that destiny can control neither it nor themselves. Circumstances assume various unpredictable shapes, depending on who is looking at them and interpreting them. Historical time is a flux, to which (judging by White's experience, which geographically is based on Banville's own 1966-1967 residence in Greece) one has no alternative but to give oneself.

The story describes Ben White's involvement with two different groups of somewhat surreal characters. One group consists of Erik, an internationally known journalist, who is a drunkard; Erik's Greek friend, Andreas, a cripple; and Colonel Aristotle Sesosteris. These three represent the supposedly real world of social concerns, historical events, and chronological time. In contrast, the other group consists of characters who belong to the realm of myth and archetype. These characters are Julian Kyd; his child bride, hermaphroditic Helena; and Helena's brother, the epicene Hyacinth. White has a variety of sexual encounters with all three. As a writer, White is seduced by the Kyd world of psyche and symbol, while at the same time he cannot completely inhabit it due to the fortuitous plotting of external circumstances. *Nightspawn* concludes that its narrator is in no position to choose between one version of the world and another: it ends on a note of defensive inconclusiveness.

Critical response was mixed. "*Nightspawn* is a nightmare, alternatively brilliant and tiresome, defying logic and chronology the way that nightmares do. Any attempt to summarise its plot seems doomed to failure," said the *New Statesman* reviewer, but went on: "The style is scintillating. The language has a musical intensity, something that you listen to rather than read—an exuberant love of the *sounds* of language." In the United States the *Saturday Review* writer reported that *Nightspawn* "is full of tricks, a literary sleight of hand, which often seemed to be little more than ends in themselves. Still, for readers who enjoy fireworks displays, here is a dandy exhibition." The conclusion of the *Times Literary Supplement* reviewer was that "There are times when . . . the author seems about to develop some complexity which has its origin in real, difficult human situations. These moments are few, though, and very short-lived."

If Ben White proved unable to place one model of being above another, his creator shows himself to be under no such disability in *Birchwood* (1973). Here the protagonist, Gabriel Godkin, is able to jettison his background and heritage as a son of a decaying Irish Big House and take to the highways and byways of his native land.

The story of *Birchwood* contains the usual ingredients of Banvillean baroque: incest, social dissolution, entropy. The first part of the novel describes the decay of the Godkin family through the eyes of its son and heir, Gabriel. Godkin senior is evasive and menacing. Other members of the family drink themselves into dementia, and Gabriel's grandmother is consumed by an act of auto-da-fe. In part two, Gabriel presents his sojourn with Prospero's circus. He plays no active part in either the practical or the exotic aspects of circus life. He seems to be just borne along in the wake of it, passively delighting in its freedom, though the land through which they travel is in a state of famine. Part three finds Gabriel returning home to Birchwood, where he confronts his incestuously begotten half brother, Michael. The issue between them is possession of the family home, and Gabriel is victorious, though to what specific end is not clear, as Gabriel admits: "There is no form, no order, only echoes and coincidences, sleight of hand, dark laughter. I accept it."

Gabriel's rejection of his inheritance is not a conscious act of rebellion. It is simply, or more incontrovertibly, the case that house, lineage, family, property, and the human (as distinct from the social) obligations that accompany them are temperamentally unappealing to him. There is nothing he can do about his nature apart from express it as best he can. In that sense he is at once a more discreet and more dramatically effective representation of Banville's attitude to his culture. Rather than emphasize a struggle with tradition, Gabriel simply obviates it and in its place installs the circus and its freely acknowledged figments, not to mention its innocence and camaraderie.

The time that Gabriel spends on the road with the troupe of travelers enables him to confront his heritage in its last vestiges of grotesque dissolution. Confront it he must, however, in order to inhabit fully the freedom of his nature. The sin of his being born into an incompetent and dessicated human condition must be expunged. In place of the historically relativized state of the Godkin family we are invited to see the absolute freedom of Gabriel's self-deliverance.

Perhaps the Irish dimension of *Birchwood* blinded critics to its achievement, but it is the least well reviewed of Banville's novels. The *New York Times Book Review* dismissed it as "A jump, evidently, on to a fashionable fantasy bandwagon (or rather circus wagon)." Martin Amis in the *New Statesman* declared: "Mr. Banville has plenty of talent and style but he will get nowhere with this kind of hero, the opinionated sensualist forever spellbound by the difference between himself and everyone else."

Birchwood is Banville's most provocative novel to date, and the one which is sufficiently close to concerns in Irish literary culture to have difficulty in being a critique (in the form of a parable) or a rejection (in the form of a black comedy). It has the interesting feature, too, of being a historical novel which overrides history, and artistic departure which has not seemed available for the vast majority of Irish writers since the inception of a modern Irish literature. Moreover, in having evolved a means of dealing with historical and cultural resonances as if their impact could only be felt if they were confined to a subtext, Banville has discovered a means of broadening his thematic range, the results of which may be seen in his most satisfactory novel so far, *Doctor Copernicus* (1976).

On one level *Doctor Copernicus* may be regarded as a fine historical novel. A vivid reconstruction of the life of Copernicus, it contains cunning details and telling vignettes of life in his times. Satisfactory as these tableaux are from an artistic standpoint, there is something objectionable about them when viewed moralistically. The life depicted is disease-ridden, squalid, war-torn—in a word, the chaos of history is depicted as being more rampant than ever. And like all the other characters, Copernicus is infected with this chaos. The difference in his case is not that he confronts the chaos, but that he attempts both to endure it physically and to supplant it psychically. The latter operation, presented graphically in all its unlikelihood, mania, and agonizing inchoateness, is what triumphs. Stargazing is what changes the world. In his characterization of Copernicus, Banville has succeeded in consolidating the values of Gabriel Godkin's position while at the same time eliminating the more egregious features of that character's subjectivism. *Doctor Copernicus* is Banville's most intense and elaborate novel yet.

It is also his most favorably received novel. In England, the *Times* reviewer thought *Doctor Copernicus* "exciting, beautifully written and astonishingly redolent of the late mediaeval world." The *Times Literary Supplement* writer declared: "*Doctor Copernicus* is good enough as a historical primer; as a novel it is better than most." Even an otherwise grudging *New Statesman* notice acknowledged that the historical background is presented "with some informed vigour, especially the sense of cosmic claustrophobia which agonised Copernicus into the idea of a heliocentric universe." In the United States all the limited number of reviews agreed with the *Library Journal*'s verdict: "In this historical novel, Banville meets every serious expectation of the genre."

Kepler (1981) continues in the same vein as *Doctor Copernicus*. The emphasis is on the protagonist's pathetic humanity, his puny accomplishments in the sphere of human relationships, his derision of historical figures, his alienation from the temper of his times. The larger frame of reference which contemporary events might provide exists in *Kepler* merely as a skeleton, an unavailable area of relevance. Kepler is depicted as an embarrassed, fretful, irascible, impoverished genius. But his genius enables him to transcend the pettiness of human frailty, a saving grace which is not vouchsafed to the other characters in the novel. The reader is at a loss to know how they, thus deprived,

survive the death of infants, the brutality of the law, and the arbitrary whims of circumstance—which is all most of them know of life. The novel concentrates on the years of Kepler's success, from his being an underling to the Imperial astronomer Tycho Brahe to his appointment to the same post under the Emperor Rudolph and the aftermath of that unfortunate ruler's reign.

Thematically, *Kepler* is to a considerable extent a repetition of *Doctor Copernicus*. It is written with the same flair, the same delicate and passionate penchant for a telling phrase and rapid narrative development. *Kepler* is, however, Banville's most accessible novel—it might well be thought obvious and transparent in comparison to his earlier books. It has been uniformly well received, with most British reviewers echoing the *Times Literary Supplement*: "It is Mr. Banville's achievement to charge each of Kepler's discoveries with the sublimity and the poetry that they held for the astronomer himself."

The same preoccupation is present in Banville's most recent novel, *The Newton Letter* (1982). As the narrator remarks: "It wasn't the exotic I was after, but the *ordinary*, that strangest and most elusive of enigmas." This novel's focus is not scientific, however (at least not directly), but literary. Whereas the drama of the earlier works in the sequence con-

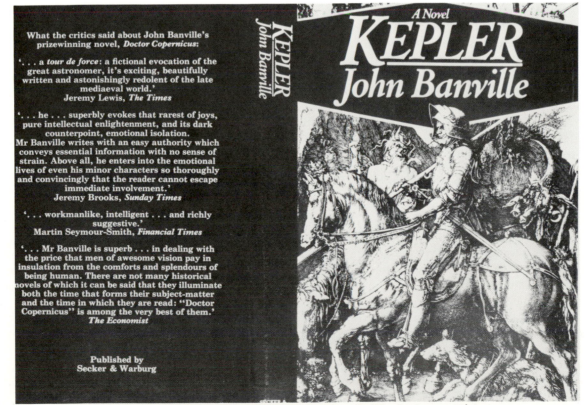

Dust jacket for Banville's 1981 novel, based on the life of Johannes Kepler

fronts struggles to achieve, in this book it is vitiated by a contemplation of aftermath. Newton is pictured in Cambridge in 1693 thus: "He does not know what to do, what to think." The narrator's approach to Newton rejects biographical reconstruction; instead it faces the hollowness which explanation distractingly disguises. "Shall I say I've lost my faith in the primacy of the text?," the narrator asks rhetorically, adding, as though to explain, "Real people keep getting in the way now, objects, landscapes even." By virtue of such preoccupations *The Newton Letter* looks back to *Nightspawn* and nods in self-conscious acknowledgment to its postmodernist mentors.

Banville's output has a range and unity remarkable in a writer who is still at the outset of his career. There are signs in his most recent work that the influences of such modern masters as Vladimir Nabokov, Jorge Luis Borges, and Italo Calvino have now been fully assimilated and are being put to their proper use, though for now it is probably more appropriate to think of Banville's work as exemplifying an idiosyncratic mode of critical realism rather than the antirealism of his predecessors. His writing style is marked by an increasingly impressive degree of narrative fluency, and he is gradually ridding it of the self-conscious mannerisms which marked his early work. He is not a dull wordsmith; rather, he practices a quiet flamboyance—the paradox being a tribute to the manner in which he achieves some of his most striking effects. His work has also grown more exciting to read, thanks to the increasingly fastidious sense of timing it displays, itself the outcome of the broad time span of his later novels.

It is difficult to assess accurately his impact on his own generation, partly because he has resolutely resisted the role of spokesman on the part of one mode of writing or another. Nevertheless, judging by the most recent work in Irish fiction, it would appear that a number of the most promising Irish writers of the present generation are taking his example to heart. What that example amounts to may be judged by the following statement from John Banville himself: "You take something and you give it an intensity which in its own life in the world it doesn't have. Say you describe something very, very well. You really catch it. The thing has a kind of surprised sense. A chair is standing there looking at you saying 'goodness, I never realized that about myself.' It's the thing that keeps you writing. Or a person. You get them so perfectly and so vividly that they exist with an intensity which they didn't have in real life. That is what Art is for." Statements such as that, and novels like those of John Banville, are giving new, unexpected life to Irish fiction.

Interviews:

"Novelists on the Novel. Ronan Sheehan talks to John Banville and Francis Stuart," *Crane Bag*, 3 (1979): 76-84;

Rüdiger Imhoff, " 'My Readers, That Small Band, Deserve a Rest,' An Interview with John Banville," *Irish University Review*, 11 (Spring 1981): 5-12.

References:

Seamus Deane, "Be Assured I Am Inventing: The Fiction of John Banville," in *The Irish Novel in Our Time*, edited by Patrick Rafroidi and Maurice Harmon (Lille, France: Presses Universitaires de France, 1976), pp. 329-338.

Irish University Review, 11 (Spring 1981), special Banville issue.

A. L. Barker

(13 April 1918-   )

Kim D. Heine
Pennsylvania Institute of Technology

BOOKS: *Innocents: Variations on a Theme* (New York: Scribners, 1948);

Apology for a Hero (New York: Scribners, 1950; London: Hogarth Press, 1950);

Novelette with Other Stories (New York: Scribners, 1951; London: Hogarth Press, 1951);

The Joy-Ride and After (London: Hogarth Press, 1963; New York: Scribners, 1964);

Lost Upon the Roundabouts (London: Hogarth Press, 1964);

A Case Examined (London: Hogarth Press, 1965);

The Middling: Chapters in the Life of Ellie Toms (London: Hogarth Press, 1967);

John Brown's Body (London: Hogarth Press, 1969);

Femina Real (London: Hogarth Press, 1971);

A Source of Embarrassment (London: Hogarth Press, 1974);

A Heavy Feather (London: Hogarth Press, 1978).

In 1946, shortly after her stories began to appear in British periodicals, A. L. Barker was offered (but declined) the British Atlantic Award in Literature. The following year, *Innocents*, her first collection of short stories, won her the first Somerset Maugham Award. Subsequently, Barker has written plays, poetry, several short-story collections, and five full-length novels, and she has contributed to several periodical publications. She wrote the screenplay for *Pringle*, a play based on one of her stories, and several other stories have been adapted for broadcast on BBC. In 1962, Barker received the Cheltenham Festival Award and in 1970 was given the Arts Council Award for her continued contributions to literature. Barker does not reveal herself in her work. Although most of her fiction is firmly set in her familiar English surroundings, her alienated, insular characters, improbable conflicts, and surrealistic episodes seem removed from her personal experience. Barker's tense, unemotional style, while it lends her work precision and control, sets a tone of authorial detachment.

Audrey Lillian Barker was born in St. Paul's Cray, Kent, England, where she began writing at the age of nine. She left school at sixteen and worked in a London office. Later, she moved to a literary agent's office and then to the Amalgamated Press, into a position she describes as "a very assistant very junior subeditor." During World War II, she spent six months in the Land Army and over three years with the National Fire Service. After the war she joined the staff at the BBC. Characteristically, Barker is reticent about herself, saying only that she has led "a well-grooved, mundane life."

The themes of Barker's work are the isolation of the human personality, the impossibility of communication, and the ambivalence of love. Throughout her fiction, Barker explores the world of social and psychological outcasts: the ill, the poor, the lonely. Her subjects do not represent deviations from the norm as much as intensified examples of the unfortunate or the misunderstood. They are people who have sat out their lives in constant disappointment, who have formed the habit of self-delusion. In Barker's stories the strong protagonists are selfish and cruel, and the weak are self-pitying victims. Yet her ironic detachment renders her work not oppressive but strangely comic. Through caricature and understatement, Barker infuses her work with humor. She has a penchant for horror and the macabre, which ironically lightens the tone by lifting the weight of unrelieved realism.

Barker's first book, *Innocents: Variations on a Theme* (1948), is a collection of eight short stories, each dealing with one person's crisis. Barker examines the complex relationships between oppressors and their victims. Innocence in these stories is synonymous with inexperience, and the conflicts arise out of the character's first contact with tragedy and evil. In most of the stories the protagonists are children, but Barker reveals that youth is not necessarily naive and guileless. Two of her "innocents" are the adult victims of malicious children. The critics were nearly unanimous in their praise of this award-winning collection. Barker was commended for her ability to write convincingly from a child's point of view, as well as for her literary craftsmanship. Several critics anticipated the appearance of her first novel, believing that her talents

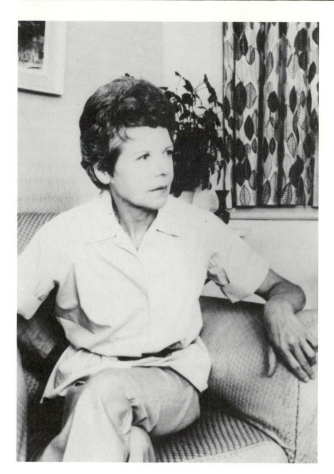

A. L. Barker

would best be revealed in an extended form.

That first novel, *Apology for a Hero* (1950), came as something of a disappointment. The novel's hero is Charles Candy, a middle-aged clerk who, after working twenty years in a London office, receives an inheritance that enables him to gratify his taste for leisure and travel. Candy goes to Italy to become the adventurous man he has fashioned in his daydreams. While in Italy he meets, woos, and marries Wynne Delaat, a "small, clear, and sufficient" woman who is not of his dream world, but rather reflects his attraction to the mundane, practical side of life. Candy says he loves her "because she could give him himself." He is happy and comfortable in his marriage to Wynne until her sister, Perry, an amoral, gypsylike figure, comes to stay with them. Perry distrusts Candy's ordered life and offends his sense of decorum; he envies her independence and uninhibited manner. When Wynne suddenly dies, Candy is drawn into Perry's unconventional world and a series of unlikely events, including a mysterious ocean voyage during which he falls overboard and drowns.

Throughout *Apology for a Hero* Barker reveals Candy's restive nature. He wants security and domestic calm, but he is attracted to uncertainty and intrigue. Although this conflict is universal, the reader finds it difficult to sympathize with Candy, whose search for himself seems artificial and external. Barker's narration remains separate from the action, distancing the reader from the characters, and treating the protagonist with faint derision. Though *Apology for a Hero* was praised for the authenticity of its setting, it was generally criticized for its unconvincing characterizations. As critic Charles Rolo points out in his review for the *New York Times*, Barker's first novel did "not show a mastery of the larger form."

In her third work, *Novelette with Other Stories* (1951), Barker returned to the shorter form. *Novelette*, like *Innocents*, examines the social outcast to explore the themes of man's isolation and cruelty. But the stories in *Novelette* extend beyond the merely unusual and approach the supernatural. In several of the eleven stories the characters are victims not only of their own nature and social position; the action of the stories binds the characters to suffer consequences which seem disproportionately harsh.

In "The Freak," for example, a young woman loses her self-confidence because of a chance remark made by an older relative. In another story, "Romney," a family is haunted by the memory of its young favorite, who has been dead for over a year. Although Barker's stories never embrace the supernatural, they suggest or border it. In "Jane Dore, Dear Childe," a priest reminisces on a case of witchcraft. "Domini" tells of a rejected child who is angered by her mother's promiscuity and neglect. The child is urged by a friend to set fire to her mother's clothing, a symbol of the woman's behavior. The mother and a lover burn in the fire, and the reader learns that the girl's companion, Domini, is actually a projection of her own consciousness.

In the title story and only sustained piece, "Novelette," Barker abandons the supernatural and improbable. "Novelette" chronicles a brief wartime encounter between a young working-class soldier and the wife of a village draper. The heroine, Luise Mallory, not unlike Madame Bovary, is married to a dull man and has an affair with William Felice, who has been sent to the Mallorys to convalesce from his war wounds. Although the domestic drama of "Novelette" is sometimes convincing, this longer work is not as powerful as the other stories.

Barker's next work, *The Joy-Ride and After*, did not appear until 1963. It is comprised of three loosely connected stories, "The Joy-Ride," "The Narrow Boat," and "A Likely Story." As in *Novelette*, the opening story is a novel-length work. "The Joy-Ride" centers on a London slum teenager, Joe Munn, who works in a garage and fantasizes about driving his employer's fast car. One night at the prompting of his cousin, Esther, with whom he has a love-hate relationship, the two of them take a ride in the "borrowed" car. Their joyride ends in a hit-and-run accident in which Joe believes he has killed a woman. The second story relates the strange, nightmarish experience of Alice Oram, the victim of the accident in "Joy-Ride." Alice, suffering from amnesia, becomes the ward and prisoner of a vulgar, slightly deranged boatman who taunts and ridicules but does not otherwise harm her. The final

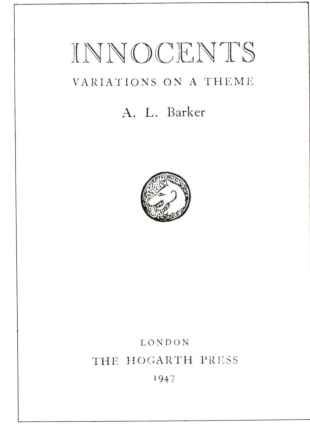

INNOCENTS

VARIATIONS ON A THEME

A. L. Barker

LONDON
THE HOGARTH PRESS
1947

Title page for Barker's first book, a collection of short stories about the "relationships between oppressors and their victims"

story returns to Esther, now married to an amiable man, who is exposed as an incurable liar when she distorts the events of her joyride with Joe.

The Joy-Ride and After reveals the pain and disappointment of people unable to adjust to their circumstances and the realities of life. The stories are hallucinatory and surreal; the sharply detailed environment contrasts with the confusion of the

characters. The book was greeted with mixed reviews. Some critics who, as before, praised her story telling and setting, believed it "fulfilled the promise of earlier works," while others criticized the unbelievable characters and the tenuous connection between the stories.

In 1964 Barker had *Lost Upon the Roundabouts* published; this collection of ten short stories further explores the ideas contained in *Innocents*. The central characters in this collection are parasites, dependent on other people for their own identities. As in her earlier stories, Barker sees man as isolated and tragic. Most of the stories deal with an attempt at a relationship, but ultimately the people are incompatible and must practice deception to conceal from themselves and others the fact that they have been "lost upon the roundabouts."

This strong collection contains two excellent stories, "Miss Eagle" and "View in a Long Mirror." In the first story, Alice Eagle, an unmarried woman of fifty who has devoted herself to her mother, finally attempts to become the Miss Eagle of her daydreams, only to find that it is too late. Her mother's death does not free Alice from the narrow, confined world in which she has spent her life. Instead, it brings the realization that she no longer has the strength to escape it; at the end of the story, she settles comfortably in the refuge of her mother's rocking chair. In "View in a Long Mirror," Delie Rivers, an aging understudy for a famous actress, experiences her only triumph by surviving the actress, the great Magdala. When a visitor comments on the lifelong likeness between them, Delie points out, "I fancy there's a lot to choose between us now." Although this collection contains many of the themes and motifs of Barker's earlier work, there is a sense of closure and resolution in these stories. The characters come to an acceptance or understanding of themselves which separates them from the characters in her earlier works.

In 1965 Barker's second full-length novel appeared. *A Case Examined* explores the self-deceptions of Rose Antrobus, the chairwoman of a charity committee with the power to allocate money to either a destitute family or a church improvement fund. Rose is a middle-aged housewife who has always insulated herself against suffering. She opposes giving the money to the needy family because she cannot accept the vulgar, violent world they represent. She believes despair and pain are created by the self or result directly from improper behavior. Through a series of conflicts in which she is forced to glimpse the truth, and a reunion with an old friend who has undeservedly suffered, Rose loses her smugness and gains self-knowledge. Although she eventually comes to the right decision about the money, she retains her narrow values and remains an unsympathetic character throughout.

A Case Examined is well written. Much of the dialogue between Rose and her friend Solange is convincing and revealing, but the basic conflict of the novel seems unworthy of such extended and weighty treatment. As one critic pointed out, reading *A Case Examined* has the "strangeness of watching ants at some minutely herculean task." The novel is most powerful when the reader is distanced from the characters by a quietly comic view in which Rose and the problems of charity become caricatures.

Barker's third novel, *The Middling: Chapters in the Life of Ellie Toms*, was published in 1967. *The Middling* plots the decline of its narrator, Ellie Toms, from youth and idealism to drunken middle age. The novel is structured into five episodes or "chapters" of Ellie's life. In the first episode Ellie as a child is raped by an old colonel who is a trusted family confidant. She then relates the story of her brief affair with an older man whose homosexual ex-roommate comes in to nurse her through a miscarriage. Little is revealed about Ellie between her late teens and middle age. The reader may see her failed relationships with men as a result of her childhood trauma; yet it is he and not Ellie who draws this conclusion. Later, when Ellie is working as a hack writer for a children's comic publication, the reader watches her idealism turn to disillusionment. These episodes, however, do not prepare the reader for the final chapter in which Ellie, now married to a pleasant man, her children grown, is a pathetic alcoholic.

The separate chapters are related only because Ellie Toms is the protagonist in each. Themes are not carried over from one episode to the next; the other characters in each are gratuitously dispensed with at the end of a chapter. Ellie's failure seems rooted in her own flawed temperament: she is a dreamer whose dreams are never realized. But this does not fully explain her disintegration or make her a convincing character. The reader is not provided with enough information to find Ellie believable or sympathetic. Reviews of *The Middling*, like those of the early novels, praised Barker's style and her eye for background and detail but expressed dissatisfaction with the novel as a whole. One of the book's strengths is the deft characterization of minor figures such as Ellie's mother, who thinks food cures all ills. In spite of its strengths,

however, the novel lacks the unity and clarity which distinguish her short stories.

Two years after *The Middling* appeared, Barker's fourth novel, *John Brown's Body*, was published; it combines many of the elements of her earlier work. The isolation of the characters in this novel, as in many of her short stories, causes them to suspect and mistreat others. Using the skeletal framework of the mystery novel, Barker explores the theme of self-deception which is at the heart of the work. In *John Brown's Body* Marise, the child bride of middle-aged Jack Tomelty, lives in fantasies to escape her mundane life. Marise notices that her neighbor Ralph Shilling resembles John Brown, a fugitive double murderer. She soon deceives herself and several others into believing that Shilling is John Brown. After a series of unusual events—Marise lures Shilling into attempting to abduct her—the characters, including the introverted Shilling, are forced to realize their misperceptions and distortions of reality.

The critics were divided in their assessment of *John Brown's Body*. The novel was praised for its unified and consistent narrative. Barker's style and use of detail remain solid, but some critics disparaged her reliance on the conventions of mystery and her fascination with the abnormal.

Woman is the focus of *Femina Real* (1971), a set of tersely written portraits which view women at various ages and in many circumstances. Barker reveals the underlying strength of women in situations of apparent vulnerability. But the overall view of women is not favorable: their revenge is balanced against their suffering. In one story, a sick, frail woman dominates those around her through weakness. In another story, a ten-year-old crippled girl achieves revenge by turning the tables on the man holding her prisoner. As in *John Brown's Body* and the stories in *Novelette*, some of these portraits include elements of mystery and the macabre.

Femina Real was generally regarded as one of Barker's stronger collections. Although her harsh view of women sometimes caused critics to maintain that she has a jaundiced view of her own sex, her narrative is clear and her observations are accurate. Most of the characters in *Femina Real* are convincing examples of recognizable types.

Barker's most recent work, *A Source of Embarrassment* (1974), contains many of the same themes, character types, strengths, and weaknesses of her earlier works. In *A Source of Embarrassment*, a cheerful narrator reveals a world in which the unusual is usual. Confusion is the norm; incest, the seduction

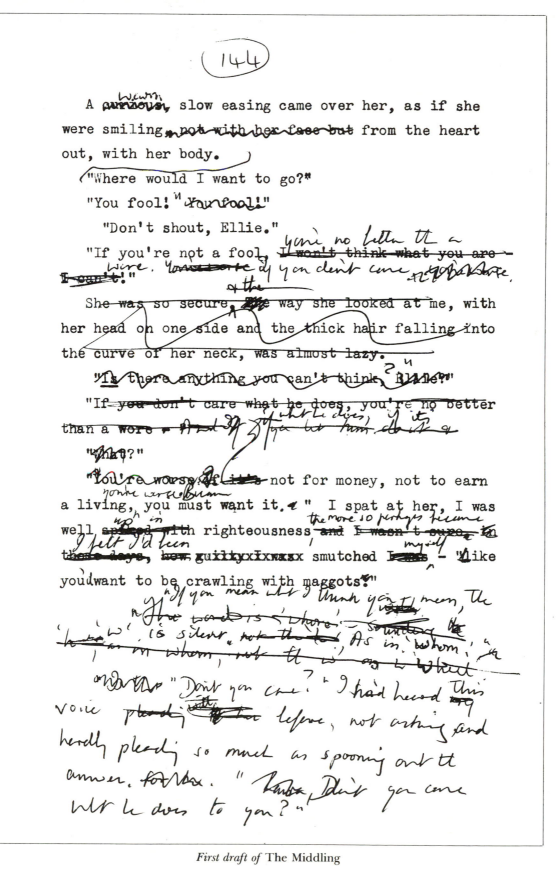

First draft of The Middling

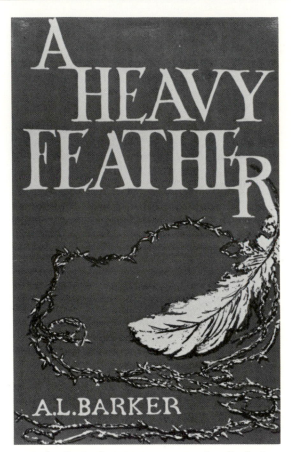

Dust jacket for Barker's most recent novel, a finely drawn narrative of a woman's progress through life

of teenagers, and belief in faith healers seem commonplace. The novel focuses largely on a family whose members are all dissatisfied for various reasons. The protagonist, Edith, supposedly has a brain tumor and only three months to live, but whether her illness is real or imagined is purposely left unclear to both characters and reader. Her husband, who is interested in another woman, would like to have the matter settled. Their sixteen-year-old daughter, Corinne, has sexual fantasies about her brother, Robert. Midway through the novel the secondary characters fade without warning, and Edith eventually finds a faith healer who cures her. As in most of Barker's work, the characters in *A Source of Embarrassment* make clumsy attempts at relationships which generally fail. The book was praised for its lucid style and sharp detail; it was also criticized for its premature dismissal of characters and the unlikeliness of events. The strength of the novel is the detached humor of the narrator. Although the events are only superficially comic, the narrator's stance reveals an amused tolerance of human weakness.

Although the themes of her work vary only slightly, Barker is always a good storyteller. She has the satirist's ability to select detail and delineate character while handling her material lightly and skillfully. Though she sometimes fails to maintain realism, her ability to fuse character and incident lends a consistent tone to each work. Although the majority of critics seem biased against her choice of subjects and the apparent lack of unity in her extended works, a number of admirers appreciate her ability to treat the absurd and the grotesque comically.

Clearly Barker has not fully mastered the novel form. Though her two most recent novels illustrate her ability to approach the novel as an extended narrative rather than a compilation of loosely connected episodes, her choice of subject matter and her aloof treatment of characters continue to limit her development as a novelist. Though since her first publication critics have expected Barker to write a great novel, she continues to display her talent most effectively in the short story.

Screenplay:
Pringle, BBC, 1958.

Stan Barstow

(*28 June 1928- *)

Elizabeth Allen

SELECTED BOOKS: *A Kind of Loving* (London: M. Joseph, 1960; Garden City: Doubleday, 1961);

The Desperadoes (London: M. Joseph, 1961); revised as *The Human Element* (London: Longmans, 1969);

Ask Me Tomorrow [novel] (London: M. Joseph, 1962);

Joby (London: M. Joseph, 1964);

The Watchers on the Shore (London: M. Joseph, 1966; Garden City: Doubleday, 1967);

Ask Me Tomorrow [play], by Barstow and Alfred Bradley (London & New York: French, 1966);

A Raging Calm (London: M. Joseph, 1968); republished as *The Hidden Part* (New York: Coward-McCann, 1969);

A Season with Eros (London: M. Joseph, 1971);

Stringer's Last Stand, by Barstow and Bradley (London: French, 1972);

The Right True End (London: M. Joseph, 1976);

A Brother's Tale (London: M. Joseph, 1980).

Stan Barstow achieved fame as one of a group of novelists from northern England with working-class backgrounds who began to attract critical attention in the late 1950s and the 1960s. Like others in that group (John Braine, Alan Sillitoe, and Keith Waterhouse), Barstow has diversified into other media, most notably television plays and dramatizations, but unlike a number of his northern contemporaries, who have moved to London and the southeast of England, he has continued to live in the north and to draw on the industrial towns for his materials.

Barstow was born in 1928 in the village of Horbury in Yorkshire, the only child of Wilfred Barstow, a coal miner, and his wife, Elsie; his upbringing was not one to encourage literary pretensions. He has said: "My circumstances and background didn't seem a very helpful breeding ground. . . . There were no writers in the family (there were, in fact, few real readers)." Having passed the necessary examination he attended the high school in the nearby town of Ossett but had no academic leanings, and in 1944 he left school to work in the drawing office of an engineering firm in the same town. Only then did he feel the urge to write: "It was the total frustration of my working life which led me to write: I had no alternative outlet."

The experience of Wilf Cotton in *Ask Me Tomorrow* (1962) may illuminate Barstow's situation. Among Wilf's peers at school—even the more intelligent—there is little ambition and imagination about life's possibilities. "The highest most of them looked was to a teaching position in a local school, with short hours and long holidays. For the rest there was the vague idea of some job without physical labour." Wilf takes one of these nonmanual positions, working as a wages clerk at the colliery where his father and brother are miners. "For Wilf . . . the restlessness was not long in making itself felt. . . . What nagged more and more was a dissatisfaction with his life as a whole, which grew with a dawning awareness of a world and values outside the village and the knowledge that the opportunity given him . . . he had largely wasted." As in the case of his author, Wilf's dissatisfaction and restlessness find a creative outlet in writing, although Wilf appears less aware than Barstow of the problems facing an aspiring author in that place at that time. Barstow says of his own experience: "The important thing, the thing that can't be over-emphasised, is the extreme isolation of myself and of other regional and working class writers in the mid-fifties. We had the temerity to think we could write but no teachers and no models." This was before regional and working-class settings gained the vogue they later achieved through the success of Barstow—together with Braine, Waterhouse, Sillitoe, and David Storey—as a novelist, and through the popularity of television plays and series with such backgrounds.

Barstow began to try his hand as a writer but continued to earn his living in the engineering firm. In 1951 he married Constance Mary Kershaw and they later had two children, Neil (born in 1954) and Gillian (born in 1957). Barstow, lacking any sense of what was possible, began writing what he imagined to be commercial stories, inspired by his belief that "many of the stories that I read in magazines weren't very good and that with a bit of application I ought to be able to do as well." These stories were not successful in either sense: "I found that writing insincerely rarely works and realised that what I ought to be writing about was the kind of working class life that I knew from my own experience." An important influence at this time was the work of H. E. Bates, in particular his short stories, which provided a positive model. Yet although Barstow was now more decided about the need to write from his own working-class experience, "It quickly became apparent to me that very few people wanted to know about this kind of life. I sold only four short stories in the first nine years of my writing life." But the conviction that he had found his authentic voice paid off. As Gordon Taylor in *A Brother's Tale* (1980) tells the painter Ted, "If you find your own real way of looking at things you'll also find the audience that takes pleasure in the way you paint." Other working-class regional novelists were beginning to find an audience, and in 1960 with *A Kind of Loving* Barstow found his.

Critics were eager to praise Barstow's skill: according to the *Punch* reviewer, "It is not often that a first novel gives me the feeling that its author is a natural writer who must have been born with some of the tricks of the trade." Critics also lauded his application of this skill to a world newly discovered by contemporary literature. The reviewer in the *Sunday Times* said, "Like D. H. Lawrence Mr. Barstow is a miner's son, but Lawrence's genius swept him inevitably and rapidly out of this world: Mr. Barstow has no need to waste any of his talent, his intellectual energy, on escaping from a world rich, lively with possible change, and scarcely scratched yet by its born writers."

Set, like most of Barstow's novels, in Cressley, an unattractive industrial town in West Yorkshire, *A Kind of Loving* is the story of Vic Brown and his relationship with Ingrid Rothwell as they move through romantic, tender infatuation, growing physical obsession and attendant emotional numbness, to a marriage forced by pregnancy. Because of their relative poverty they live with Ingrid's parents, where Mrs. Rothwell's dislike of Vic, her snobbery, and her intellectual poverty increase the strains on the couple's fragile relationship. Vic, goaded beyond patience, leaves, but, encouraged by the strictures of his admired sister, resolves on a further attempt to "make a go of it." The ending presents little joy, but rather the peace of resignation. Vic envies the relationship of his sister, Chris, and her husband, but is determined to do the best he can.

"And, who knows, one day it might happen like Chris said: we might find a kind of loving to carry us through. I hope so, because it's for a long, long time." The ending of the novel, refusing either sentimental reconciliations or dramatic partings, has a low-key, painful honesty. Barstow later tampered with this effective resolution, however, by reactivating Vic and Ingrid as personae for two further novels.

Stan Barstow

A Kind of Loving demonstrates the strengths of a novel written from intimate knowledge of a particular society; it is full of small details which are part of the novel's fabric, not grafted on as local color: Vic's pleasure in cleaning shoes, the smell of ironing filling the house, the problems of getting out of bed on a winter morning in a house without central heating. There is, too, an exact ear for dialogue: the bantering between Vic and his workmates, the strained conversation between Vic and Ingrid, Vic's mother's continuous criticism born more of habit than conviction.

The use of such a milieu as a setting for the central characters was relatively new in 1960, but it was not social novelty alone which gave the book its success. Another strength is the sense of conviction of Vic's changing feelings toward Ingrid, the depiction of him as a young man far from ideal but capable of suffering and enlarging his understanding. The portrait of Mrs. Rothwell verges on caricature, but for Vic and Ingrid one retains sympathy and understanding.

The novel was a Book Society choice, and a notable British film was subsequently made from it: in 1961 this success allowed Barstow to leave the engineering company, where he was now a sales executive, and become a full-time writer. Meanwhile, a collection of short stories, *The Desperadoes* (a number of which had previously been broadcast by the BBC), was published in 1961. The reviews were again favorable: "The dialogue positively leaps out from the page," said Anthony Burgess. The inevitable comparison with D. H. Lawrence was made: "[the stories] have that very rare compassion and pity that distinguishes the really good writer from the merely able. Some of these stories are right up in the same class as D. H. Lawrence," noted the *Guardian* reviewer. The social settings are like those of *A Kind of Loving*, a world of narrow social morality

and close family ties. Barstow understands the important ways in which material conditions affect responses: when Jack Lister in "One Wednesday Afternoon" hears that his wife has been seriously injured in an industrial accident, he travels to the hospital by bus; there is no question of taking a taxi.

In 1969 a selection of stories from *The Desperadoes* was published in a special edition for use in schools, with questions and notes on each story, this time under the title *The Human Element*. Barstow contributed a special essay to this edition, in which he commented that the short-story writer "must . . . leave the reader with a sense of completeness at the end. . . . This instinctive feeling for saying not too much or too little, but just enough, that is the mark of the real short story writer." It is arguable whether in these stories the balance is always achieved. In several the moral is drawn too explicitly, leaving little to inference or imagination. However, the collection provides a nice blend of humor, compassion, and the bizarre, with the title story giving an interesting account of a young man's motives for social aggression: "You've got to have a bit of

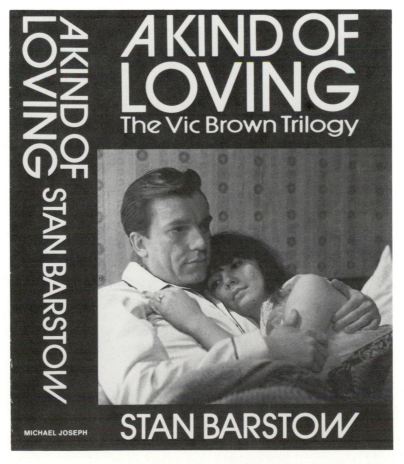

Dust jacket for Barstow's first novel

fun. . . . You spend all day workin' to fill somebody else's pocket with brass, and everybody allus on to you. . . . Sometimes you feel you can't rest until you've smashed summat."

When some critics and readers complained that the author's lack of overt disapproval of these desperadoes implied endorsement of their attitudes and behavior, Barstow replied: "I think the answer of most writers to such a charge would be that it is not their job to judge their characters, only to tell about them and leave the rest to the reader." This idea seems oddly disingenuous from an author aware of his responsibilities in creating characters and situations rather than recounting what already exists, who usually sets his characters within certain moral frameworks overtly endorsed or rejected by characters who appear to enjoy the author's approval.

Such a character is Wilf Cotton, the coal miner's son and aspiring writer in *Ask Me Tomorrow*, whose dissatisfaction with the conditions of his life and work echoes Barstow's own. Wilf leaves home to concentrate on writing his first novel. Eschewing the romantic discomfort of starvation in a garret, he takes a mentally undemanding job by day and the comfort of his landlady's bed at night. Wilf's struggles and ultimate conviction in his vocation as a writer are the main theme in the novel, and his discussions with the novel's other central character, Marguerite Fisher, suggest Barstow's own views. When Wilf distinguishes between the "caterers" who "work to satisfy a ready made market" and the "creators" who "work to make their own market," one remembers Barstow's comments about his early efforts to write commercially and his rejection of the caterer's approach. It is Marguerite who speaks up for the rights of the provinces and the working class to recognition: "What you're trying to do is to put down on paper a kind of life that hasn't had its fair due in fiction."

Wilf, too, expresses belief in the kind of novel that he (as well as Barstow) is writing, and the reader can infer from Wilf's assertions Barstow's sense of what is important in fiction. Of his just finished novel Wilf says: "It was good because it was real and true . . . his [Wilf's] was an authentic world, his people harsh and dour, without the comic idiosyncrasies designed to appeal to the illusions of people who never travelled north of the Trent." In none of Barstow's other novels is there such detailed discussion of the processes of writing, of "the need to express the throb and quiver of life on the page." However, Wilf appears briefly in *The Watchers on the Shore* (1966), where he comments on the regional novel from a vantage point several years later: "People won't take north country working class stuff for its novelty value any more. It's got to be good in its own right."

As the reviewer in the *Times Literary Supplement* noted, the creation of Wilf shows Barstow's developing ability to handle an evolving character. There is a weakness in the novel's moral structure, however, in that we are offered no wider perspective on the ideas and attitudes advanced by Wilf. In his attitudes to and relationships with women, he has much in common with Vic Brown of the later novels and Gordon Taylor in *A Brother's Tale*. Each is ready to love a sympathetic young woman, who need not be a virgin but who gives the impression of sexual moderation. At the same time each evinces distrust and contempt for women seen as sexually voracious teases—June in *Ask Me Tomorrow*, Miriam in *The Right True End* (1976), Eunice in *A Brother's Tale*. Both Wilf and Gordon are able to accept sexual release with older, large-breasted, nurturing women who offer no threat. Wilf at least recognizes the ambivalence of men who require that women enjoy sex but at the same time distrust that enjoyment: "You looked for uninhibited sexuality and suspected it when you found it of being mere licence." Yet Wilf, in protecting his brother, acts with an instinctive hard morality against June Betley: "You can't crucify a girl because she posed for a pin-up picture once," he says to her husband, but adds that the fact of her having done so has to cast doubt on her present virtue.

Marguerite asserts that most Englishwomen regard sex as "something not quite nice," a threat to the stability of marriage and the family unit. This belief in a tension between unbridled sexuality and married love is perhaps what underlies the hostility of certain of the male characters toward those women whose behavior suggests that they may prefer sex to stability, thus threatening accepted stereotypes and the security of society.

Ask Me Tomorrow did not have the public impact of *A Kind of Loving* but won some approving critical notice. While thinking little of Barstow's ability to fashion plots, the *Times Literary Supplement* reviewer stated: "Mr. Barstow can do most of the essential things. He can write a vivid scene and give it tension . . . a book full of promise and life."

The novel which followed, *Joby* (1964), is different in style and subject matter from all Barstow's other novels. The experiences of the eleven-year-old boy in the months just before World War II possibly suggest Barstow's memories of that period. Again, the detail is vivid, with the descriptions of the

The Pity of it All   STAN BARSTOW   3.

Now she was telling Nancy that she'd had a reply from a guest house in Bournemouth, whose address a friend had given her, and they could have accommodation for the last two weeks in August. Nancy's mother thought the south coast would be a pleasant change, but if Nancy wanted to go elsewhere with a friend it would be no trouble for her and Nancy's father to take little June with them. But no, there was nowhere else that Nancy wanted to go.

Afterwards, Nancy found she could remember that moment in the vivid clarity, though its components were all familiar ones she had seen and heard many times before. There was the attitude of her mother's body, as she held the vacuum cleaner while she wound the flex on to the hooks; the sudden rush of water in the automatic washer as it performed its last rinse; the sunlight on the step outside the scullery door. The voices of the children were no longer close

"Just have a look out at June, will you," she said as she opened the washer and passed clothes over into the drying compartment. "They've gone quiet."

And then a minute or so must have passed, but it seemed like no time at all before Nancy's mother was calling from the end of the passage: "June! June, where are you? Ey, you two, bring June back here. Don't you know how busy that road is? No, keep hold of her! Don't let her —!" And Nancy was out and running across the flagstones and into the street, as though she knew before she heard that awful screech of tyres and saw the car slewed round and the little legs in the blue-and-white Marks & Spencer socks, washed just once, and the stupid, stupid older girls who had led her into it, standing, petrified, wordless, and she herself making no sound — not yet — while her mother set up an endless ~~chanting~~ moaning chant beside her: "Oh, oh, oh, oh, oh ———"

✳

Manuscript for The Pity of It All, *1965 television script*

"two-penny rushes" (the cheap cinema matinees where the children crowd in for the Flash Gordon serial and throw pellets during the advertisements), the holiday clubs where one saves through the year ("They would be splashing the lot on one glorious week away from washing and cleaning and cooking"), and the hospital where children cannot be admitted as visitors. Again, there is the accurate dialogue, the pointless repetitious conversations of the adults which verge on bickering but do not quite descend to it, the status-conscious conversations of the children. The story is told from Joby's viewpoint, although it is not limited to his vocabulary; in a funny yet touching incident he is embarrassed over the nature of the operation for which his mother is in the hospital. He understands that the operation concerns her breasts but knows only the word "tit," which certainly cannot be applied to his mother.

The mother's absence and the father's desire for his rather simple cousin Mona threaten the security of Joby's home, but these crises in his life are dealt with without mawkishness, and Joby develops a sense of his parents as being more than extensions of himself and as people to whom he has responsibility. His shoplifting forays have seemed simply a way of scoring points "in the running battle between (children) and the world of grownups" but, when they are discovered and he sees their effect on his mother, he begins to see them as wrong.

Reviews of *Joby* were polite rather than enthusiastic. "An honest agreeable book," said the *Times Literary Supplement* reviewer; "All the same it is something of a disappointment. It is careful and sympathetic but a little thin." Frederick Bowers in *Contemporary Novelists* points out the thematic link between this novel and *A Kind of Loving*, finding in both "The presentation of a workaday human love not only as the best one can hope for but also as an essential condition of life." In the late 1970s *Joby* began to be widely read in British schools.

In Barstow's next novel, *The Watchers on the Shore*, however, Vic Brown, who had tried in *A Kind of Loving* to settle for workaday human love, is unable to accept what he sees as too little: "The thought that comes to me time and time again: Is this all?" His wife Ingrid is seen here (and in the final book of the trilogy) as an intellectual constraint on Vic: "Common in the mind, in the way she never searches for anything herself but just sits back and lets it all wash over her." One can find many echoes of D. H. Lawrence, here and elsewhere in Barstow, of women who, to protect the stability of their homes, emasculate their menfolk sexually and intellectually.

Vic leaves Cressley for a job near London, while Ingrid remains with her now widowed and sick mother. There is no actual break between them, but Vic is determined to explore possibilities outside the society he knows. By the end of the second novel in the trilogy, in his love for the actress Donna, he has found justification for his belief that relationships between men and women can offer more than he has found with Ingrid. This discovery makes it inevitable that he leave Ingrid, though there can be no happy ending; for Donna, pregnant (by another man, he believes), has abandoned him, and the novel ends with Vic's recognition of the sadness of a situation which leaves Ingrid "small and scared and lonely in that flat and me, small and scared and lonely here."

Ten years later Barstow chose to continue and complete the story of Vic, Ingrid, and Donna in *The Right True End*. The final novel in the trilogy begins with the acrimonious divorce proceedings and then jumps ten years to find Vic an established business executive, Ingrid remarried, and Donna about to make a comeback in both Vic's life and her acting career. Both sequels to *A Kind of Loving* have the problems of all sequels: to what extent can the author rely on readers being familiar with earlier events, to what extent should these be repeated? The flashback to conversations in *A Kind of Loving* is not a successful device, and neither of the sequels has the solidity and emotional conviction of the first novel. Sympathy for Vic's yearning for a true relationship, for his refusal to comply with family pressures, is undercut by his acceptance of the business world in which he moves, with its dirty jokes and macho ethics working against the possibility of good man-woman relationships. In many ways he is an interesting portrait of a mid-1970s man who can accept new social mores in certain areas of his life—young women with none of Ingrid's guilt and a new competence with contraception—but who does not question the status quo in the old northern family world, whose ethics require his sister Christine to give up any thought of emigration in order to care for her parents: "It's women's work and Chris will have to cope, as she expects to, as I suppose it was written into her future that she would one day." On such matters as education and apartheid he holds orthodox liberal views, but these do not extend to personal relationships. This characterization could be seen as a complex critical analysis of certain contemporary attitudes, but there is no sense that the author invites criticism of Vic; rather, it appears that the sympathy called forth by his genuine and generous love for Donna endorses his attitudes.

A Raging Calm has two main stories, both love relationships, but these are strongly linked and complemented by other relationships of parent and child, friend and friend, political colleagues and

Stan Barstow

The ending of Vic Brown's story was considered by several reviewers to be weak. In the *Sunday Times* David Pryce-Jones commented: "Sentimentality and realism go here hand in hand." Sue Limb wrote: "Isn't Romantic Reconciliation with a lost love who happens to be an actress rather a sentimental and unlikely cop-out for tough old Vic Brown?" While saying this ignores the softness at the center of the tough talking that characterizes Vic throughout the trilogy, the accusations of sentimentality have good foundation.

In *The Watchers on the Shore* and *The Right True End*, political comment is fleeting, merely background detail or an index of character. The novel that appeared between these two offers a more complex analysis, where political convictions are presented as the bedrock of character, where there is a serious effort to marry beliefs and behavior. *A Raging Calm* (1968) is in a strong tradition of regional novels with a wide cast of characters and a mixture of public and private concerns.

opponents. The long affair between Alderman Simpkins and Norma Moffat is a fulfillment of the "kind of loving" that Vic had sought with Ingrid, while the relationship between the schoolteacher Philip Hart and Simpkins's secretary, Andrea Warner, offers that sense of absolute love which is the grail of Vic's quest. There is a strong sense of balances, with both love and responsibilities acknowledged, and no easy answers are offered.

As in earlier novels, the setting is a northern industrial town. Barstow has said that he considers himself to be "non-metropolitan oriented," and this setting (as well as northern scenes in the Vic Brown novels) has an interest and conviction that is absent in the London base of *The Right True End*. Philip and Andrea may watch trendy French films, and Norma's son Nick may find himself desired by both a man and a woman, but it is still a world where homes have no telephones and where one does not linger in cold winter bedrooms.

The political beliefs—the socialism of Nick

and Philip, the cautious, kind pragmatism of Tom Simpkins—are integrated into the fabric of their lives and discussions, and the occasional piece of overt analysis, as in Nick's irritation at his mother's outmoded (as he sees it) view of authority, is in character and interesting.

Critical reaction to the novel was good. The quality of feeling was praised by the *Tribune* reviewer: "This is the core of his power as a writer; he cares about people. It needs more than narrative skill to manage this; it takes imaginative warmth and a rare balance of sensibilities." The *Guardian* critic observed that "deeply felt and skilfully told the novel will certainly enhance Mr. Barstow's already high reputation."

A Season with Eros (1971) was a second collection of short stories, some of which had been broadcast by the BBC, while others had been published in periodicals as diverse as *Penthouse* and the *Guardian*. Two of the stories, "Love and Music" and "A Bit of a Commotion," tend to the over-neat, insistently ironic conclusion, but, while there is the same mixture of black humor and compassion as in the earlier collection, these stories call for a greater variety of response.

In the title story, Ruffo marries the sensual Maureen and enjoys a brief season of sexual ecstasy until Maureen's mother convinces her of the excesses of her sexy underwear and unbridled behavior, and the realities of pregnancy and rationed sex are asserted. The story is both funny and thought provoking; while seeing the horror of the prudery which denies the demands of Eros, one sees too the selfishness and unreality of Ruffo's demands. Quite simply, his desires and those of Maureen are irreconcilable: "He had thought he was moulding her, but now in a flash of intuition he perceived his fate as a function of the phases of *her* life."

Several of the stories speak for the value of affection over reason and respectability—although there is a worrisome tendency to make women the cleaners of hearth and language, the disapprovers and life-deniers, another echo of Lawrence. One story, "Holroyd's Last Stand," in which the wife and daughters of an elderly miner who is having a final fling trick him into bringing his other woman to Sunday tea, is an oddity in the casual cruelty of its humor; the women may be realistic, but their defense of home and morality is shown to lack all conscience and affection: the mother "spends a very interesting time discussing with her daughters new ways of making his life miserable." A different story is "Estuary"; here Barstow parallels the great tides

of the estuary to the sexual needs of a woman. It is an obvious metaphor but is an effective way of focusing the reader's response and a new technique for Barstow.

The collection contains two more lengthy stories, "Madge" and "The Assailants," the former with a strong story line but an over-contrived moral, the latter providing some of the complexities and difficult resolutions of the novels. The final story, "This Day, Then Tomorrow," has a special interest in that Ruth, whose first novel is accepted for publication, is in many ways an amalgam of Wilf and Marguerite in *Ask Me Tomorrow*; her belief in her creation and her sense of concerned responsibility toward it are those of Wilf while her emotional history is in part that of Marguerite.

Much of Barstow's work during the 1970s was for television, radio, and the theater. Two of his plays, written with Alfred Bradley, were published, *Ask Me Tomorrow* (1966), an adaptation of his second novel, and *Stringer's Last Stand* (1972). His most successful work, however, was probably done for television, in particular his adaptation of Winifred Holtby's Yorkshire novel *South Riding* and the serialization of *A Raging Calm*. In 1974 the Writers' Guild of Great Britain awarded him the prize for the Best British Dramatisation, and the following year he won the Royal Television Society Writer's Award.

A Brother's Tale, Barstow's most recent novel to date, appeared in 1980. The brothers of the title are Gordon and Bonny Taylor; Gordon is a school teacher with small success as a writer, Bonny an inspired football star who has cracked under the pressure of expectation and fame. Bonny takes refuge with his brother and his sister-in-law, Eileen, but the nature of his presence is such that it attracts disaster, both in ways directly attributable to him and in ways which he cannot control. Not only does his presence destroy his brother's marriage and cause the usually equable Gordon to abuse colleagues and become involved in barroom brawls, it also causes dead birds to fall down chimneys and a neighbor to kill her wife-battering husband. The sense of disaster and violence not far from the surface of ordinary lives is present in a number of Barstow's novels, but here this sense of threat is more central. Where there is social analysis of any of the characters, it tends to be simplistic: "She was a potential battered wife who found a battering husband." The novel's strength is its depiction of a recurring violence whose nature is unexplored and perhaps unknowable, but whose persistence raises wider questions about the existence of cruelty and evil. There is an interesting discussion between Gordon and a fellow teacher about the dangers of "creative writing" for the unpracticed, about the need to understand how to make patterns of one's experience which protect one by controlling and giving significance to that experience. But is art enough to control those problems that the novel raises? Problems that cannot be tackled by the expedients of decency and quiet affection alone, they are more intractable than those of earlier novels. Their scale is suggested by the religious overtones of the novel's final question: "What was to become of us, the three of us? How were we to be saved?"

The particular and strongly realized settings of Barstow's novels are a great strength, but the novels' claims to wider validity are weakened when not enough questions are asked about the assumptions which underlie the lives of even the more "liberated" characters. Their world view may be as valid as any other, but it is not absolute, and at times it needs a wider perspective. The real virtue of the novels, as most critics have pointed out, is their genuine sympathy for the characters; there is little that is judgmental and much that is moving. Barstow has never, except in some of the short stories, implied that human relationships are easy to formulate or to experience; the new questions raised in *A Brother's Tale* may point to further developments. Barstow says that he feels himself to be at a "watershed and ruminating about trying something new." Fundamentally, however, he holds to the view that one should avoid the lure of trendiness, of novelty for its own sake: "As writers we should just do the best we can."

Plays:

Ask Me Tomorrow, by Barstow and Alfred Bradley, Sheffield, Yorkshire, 1964;

A Kind of Loving, by Barstow and Bradley, Sheffield, Yorkshire, 1965;

An Enemy of the People, adapted from Ibsen's play, Harrogate, Yorkshire, 1969;

Listen for the Trains, Love, music by Alec Glasgow, Sheffield, Yorkshire, 1970;

Stringer's Last Stand, by Barstow and Bradley, York, 1971.

Television Scripts:

The Human Element, 1964;

The Pity of it All, 1965;

A World Inside, documentary by Barstow and John Gibson, 1966;

Mind You, I Live Here, documentary by Barstow and Gibson, 1971;

A Raging Calm, 1974;

South Riding, adapted from Winifred Holtby's novel, 1974;

Joby, 1975;

The Cost of Loving, 1977;

Travellers, 1978;

A Kind of Loving, 1982.

Radio Scripts:

The Desperadoes, 1965;

We Could Always Fit a Sidecar, 1974.

Nina Bawden
(19 January 1925-   )

Gerda Seaman
California State University, Chico

SELECTED BOOKS: *Who Calls the Tune* (London: Collins, 1953); republished as *Eyes of Green* (New York: Morrow, 1953);

The Odd Flamingo (London: Collins, 1954);

Change Here for Babylon (London: Collins, 1955);

The Solitary Child (London: Collins, 1956);

Devil by the Sea (London: Collins, 1957; Philadelphia: Lippincott, 1959);

Just Like a Lady (London: Longmans, Green, 1960); republished as *Glass Slippers Always Pinch* (Philadelphia: Lippincott, 1960);

In Honour Bound (London: Longmans, Green, 1961);

Tortoise by Candlelight (London: Longmans, Green, 1963; New York: Harper, 1963);

Under the Skin (London: Longmans, Green, 1964; New York: Harper, 1964);

A Little Love, A Little Learning (London: Longmans,

Green, 1966; New York: Harper, 1966);

A Woman of My Age (London: Longmans, Green, 1967; New York: Harper, 1967);

The Grain of Truth (London: Longmans, Green, 1968; New York: Harper, 1968);

The Runaway Summer (London: Gollancz, 1969; Philadelphia: Lippincott, 1969);

The Birds on the Trees (Harlow: Longman, 1970; New York: Harper, 1970);

Squib (London: Gollancz, 1971; Philadelphia: Lippincott, 1971);

Anna Apparent (London: Longman, 1972; New York: Harper, 1972);

Carrie's War (London: Gollancz, 1973; Philadelphia: Lippincott, 1973);

George Beneath a Paper Moon (London: Allen Lane, 1974; New York: Harper, 1974);

Afternoon of a Good Woman (London: Macmillan, 1976; New York: Harper, 1976);

Familiar Passions (London: Macmillan, 1979; New York: Morrow, 1979);

Walking Naked (London: Macmillan, 1981; New York: St. Martin's Press, 1981);

Kept in the Dark (London: Gollancz, 1982; New York: Latrop, Lee, & Shephard, 1982).

Nina Bawden is perhaps best known for her incisive satirical inquiry into the family relationships of the educated middle class. Less well-known is the fact that she began her career as a writer of two elegantly plotted murder stories, and then worked her way through several other varieties of the novel, including the gothic romance, the Bildungsroman, and the horror story. Since these early talented formal explorations, she has moved toward the psychological investigation of modern middle-class existence. With an urbane irony and often surprising violence, she exposes the uneasy alliances which keep chaos at bay and provides a circumstantial account of the domesticated brutality at the heart of modern life.

Bawden was born in London in 1925. She spent her childhood there until the outbreak of World War II when she was evacuated and lived in a South Wales mining village and in a farmhouse in Shropshire. At this time she lived with various mining families during the school year, and learned, during her summers on the farm, to drive a tractor, care for farm animals, and organize a group of Italian prisoners of war who were sent out to work on the farms.

Following graduation from grammar school, Bawden was awarded a scholarship to Somerville College in Oxford where she studied politics,

philosophy and economics. She graduated in 1946, took an M.A. in 1951, and in 1960, following the publication of several novels, attended the Salzburg Seminar in American Studies.

Upon her graduation Nina Mabey married H. W. Bawden. She has two sons from this marriage, which ended in divorce. She married her present husband, Austen Kark, now Controller of the BBC's World Service, in 1954. They have a daughter.

Bawden tells us she was writing at an early age. "I wrote plays for my toy theatre and an epic poem in blank verse." This writing seems to have functioned in several ways for her: as a stay against the confusions of experience, and as almost palpable protection. In a recent interview she said, "Writing helps to explain things." And in her latest novel, *Walking Naked*, the main character (a novelist herself) expands this notion: writers, she says, "are compulsive rearrangers, obsessional shapers of patterns," but she insists that this is only "to make the truth clearer." In the same novel the protagonist also speaks of the comforts of writing: "I can always make myself brave with words, drawing them on like a comforting garment against the cold weather." She admits that her own "love of pattern" has sometimes led to flaws in her novels, though it has also been a source of great strength. To read her work is to encounter a writer of great integrity whose search for truth in style and content has not invariably been successful, but whose insights and technical skills have noticeably developed with each successive novel.

Bawden states that her ambition, initially, was to write like Graham Greene, and indeed her early novels are thrillers with a nice edge of menace. *Eyes of Green* (1953), published in London as *Who Calls the Tune*, is a carefully plotted thriller for which the *New Statesman* praised her as having the cunning of Agatha Christie, though other critics were less kind about her construction of character.

Her next novel, *The Odd Flamingo* (1954), presents us with a respected and brilliant headmaster who is accused of seduction and murder. The search for the killer is conducted by a lawyer friend of the headmaster's—a sort of Watson character with the very suitable name of Will Hunt. Hunt's slavish admiration for his arrogant friend makes him a rather confused investigator, but he is not an uninteresting one. It is the setting here which is the least convincing element of the novel. The writer does not seem at home with the scenes of the London underworld to which she introduces her characters. Bawden has described her interest in the crime story as a frame within which she could comment on character: it provided "the bizarre complexity of motive behind simple actions" and enabled her to explore "the difference between what people say and what they actually mean."

Change Here for Babylon (1955) is introduced as a story of "murder and retribution among people caught in a situation they are unable to control or understand." It would perhaps be more accurate to say that the protagonists are caught in the defects of their own characters. The story opens with an execution—the execution of Geoffrey Hunter. Hunter's wife, Emily, is having an affair with the novel's self-absorbed "hero," Tom Harrington, and Hunter is none too pleased about it. In fact, he turns out to be a totally manipulative upper-class scoundrel who assumes that the world owes him status and privilege even if he has to kill for them. He is, however, out-manipulated by Harrington, whose

grubby infidelity fades into relative insignificance beside Hunter's more robust crimes. Hunter is an evil version of Johnny Prothero whose antiquated virtues are examined in a later novel.

Bawden's next novel, *The Solitary Child* (1956), is almost straight gothic romance. Harriet, the heroine, marries James Random, who has been tried and acquitted of murdering his first wife. Even her best friends warn her against the marriage, but Harriet not only moves back to the ancestral farmhouse; she also ignorantly cherishes Maggie, her husband's psychopathic daughter, who is the real cause of the disasters in the neighborhood. The heroine's lack of self-esteem is well drawn, but on the whole, both characters and plot lack conviction.

Devil by the Sea (1957) begins a new phase for Bawden. In its opening lines she demonstrates the elegant satiric touch for which she has become famous: "The first time the children saw the Devil, he was sitting next to them in the second row of chairs in the bandstand. He was biting his nails." This Devil turns out to be a dim-witted and crazed derelict who murders an objectionable child called Poppet, and is recognized as the murderer by Hilary, the ten-year-old heroine of the novel. Hilary's equivocal relationship with her father and her mother leads to her inability to explain her predicament and so find protection within the world of adults. In the end, though her father comes to understand her, he dies before he can help, and it is another child, her friend Wally, who tells the police she has gone off with the murderer and thus saves her.

What Hilary learns is what novelist Bawden is still concerned with in her most recent work: that there is a world which is childhood's end, a world where "other people are not to be relied upon . . . promises can be broken; loyalty abandoned." Bawden puts it only slightly differently in *Walking Naked* (1981): "We all know (or believe secretly) that when we were children we were happy and trusting and hopeful and good and that we would still be all these pleasant things if sometime, somewhere, somehow, we had not been betrayed." Children, for Bawden, seem to live in a prelapsarian moral world. Their betrayal into maturity has consequences which are explored in her adult characters.

In 1960, with *Just Like a Lady*, Bawden began the writing of what she has called her "social comedies with modern themes and settings." Her gift is strongly satiric, but it is not the classical satiric view which decries "modern" failure while referring us directly or indirectly to some accepted standard. She is an ironist who shows via irony only the absence of standards of morality from the adult world. She offers no standard for contrast.

Though leaning toward satire, the novels have a strong, almost classical, comic element. This is particularly noticeable in two witty reversals of the classic comic recognition scene: George, the hero of *George Beneath a Paper Moon* (1974), learns that his passion is not incestuous when he recognizes that his daughter is *not* his daughter; and Mary Mudd of *Familiar Passions* (1979) finds an inherited taste for dissembling and her own "healthy vein of coarseness" when she discovers that her adoptive father is indeed her real father.

John McCormick in *Contemporary Novelists* describes *Just Like a Lady* as "an English adventure in *bovarysme* which carries freshness, conviction, and the power of psychological truth." The heroine, Lucy, is an orphan brought up by relatives in near squalor. She expects much from life and finds little: a pompous husband and a tepid lover. This novel was retitled *Glass Slippers Always Pinch* when published in the United States. Life for Lucy turns out to be no fairy tale.

In 1961 *In Honour Bound* was published. It is the story of an upper class hero whose antique virtues do not fit the England in which he must live after the excitement of being a flyer in World War II. Johnny Prothero is courageous and charming but totally untrained (both intellectually and emotionally) to earn his living. His wife, Mary, whose origins are lower middle class, admires him, but also sees that the world for him can only remain "a decent place as long as one is buttressed with money." The war had lengthened the "period of his illusion so that by the time it ended the facts of life were distorted beyond his power of correction." Johnny's assumptions about honor are jolted, but he has nothing with which to replace them. His business partner betrays him; his wife is unfaithful to him; and his final act, a dramatic suicide, is a useless gesture toward the heroic ideal, totally out of place in the modern world.

Two years later *Tortoise by Candlelight* offers us a child's perspective once more. Emmie, the fourteen-year-old heroine, is totally committed to her responsibility for the members of her family: "the things that drain the spirit out of people, illness and pain and hope deferred, had not touched her yet." But Emmie's commitment is also her shield. She draws her family around her like a cloak, protecting her younger brother from the consequences of his pilfering, and reminding her older sister, Alice, that her sensuality may prove to be at odds with her ambition to be a nurse. Emmie must fight the consequences of time and adult weakness, both physical and moral.

The characters of this novel are beautifully drawn. Certain incidents stand out for the reader: Alice strapping up her breasts with sticking plaster for want of a decent bra; and Emmie, humiliated by her encounter with a neighbor's jealous wife, diving frantically in the gravel pit. Emmie succeeds finally, at the expense of an unconvincing and gratuitously violent ending, but along the way there are splendid insights into the ambiguous tensions which work on the sensitive adolescent.

In 1962, following what she refers to as "the failure" of a novel for adults, Bawden's husband suggested that she might write a book for children. Since then, eleven of her children's novels have been published, many to high literary acclaim. Most of these have been dramatized on British television, and U.S. viewers were fortunate enough to see *Carrie's War* on public television. Critic and author Mary Stolz said of *The Runaway Summer*: "she should be as much valued by children as she is by her adult audience."

When asked about the relationship between her children's and her adult novels, Bawden pointed to *Squib* (1971), which deals with one child's concern for another—a frequent theme. Squib, the focus of the book, is not its hero. He is a battered child whom the heroine, Kate Pollack, is able to rescue with the help of her friends. After she had written about Squib, Bawden said she was puzzled as to how such a child would turn out when he grew up. She found that, having written this children's book, she wished to explore the character further. This she did in *Anna Apparent* (1972), a more recent adult novel, though she changed the battered boy child into a girl.

The *London Observer* described *Under the Skin* (1964) as a novel which "deals perceptively with the problems of an intelligent young couple who befriend a charming Negro student and discover that neither 'prejudice' nor 'enlightenment' are as straightforward as they had thought, and that goodwill is not enough." John Grant has visited Africa and met Jay Nbola. When Nbola comes to study at the London School of Economics, Grant and his wife invite him to stay in their home. But small family hatreds are enlarged by the Grants' anxiety to appear liberal and decent, and the suffering inflicted on their guest drives him out of their home. One admires this novel because Bawden offers no easy answers, and indeed there is no real resolution. The novel ends with the Grants about to embark on an African visit; we are left with the uneasy suspicion that the Grants may learn their real lesson in Africa.

Like *Tortoise by Candlelight, A Little Love, A Little Learning* (1966) is the story of a young girl growing into adulthood. The story is told in retrospect by Katey, who looks back on the twelfth year of her life. Katey lives with her mother, her stepfather, and two sisters in a small parochial English town. There she and her sister Joanna learn that actions have consequences which reach out far beyond their own intentions. Katey discovers that the "strength of personal virtues" will not always serve to protect good men like her stepfather. She finds that to put one's trust in them is "an old-fashioned and innocent delusion that people wiser in the world had discarded." And yet it is Katey's repetition of the kind words her stepfather says about her real father that saves the family from emotional disaster, and so, in a sense, virtue triumphs. The strength of this novel lies in the exploration of the children's need to test the limits of their parents' affection. As the *Christian Science Monitor* describes it, Bawden "depicts human weakness accurately, never remorselessly."

Bawden's protagonists are mainly female, but

Nina Bawden in mid-1970s

she does not regard feminism as an immediately important issue. When asked about her attitude toward feminism and women's issues generally, she responded by mentioning what she called her "women's lib novel" and by quoting an anecdote attributed to George Macaulay Trevelyan, the Cambridge historian: "When he was told that attendance at Chapel was rising, he said he thought they had settled *that* argument years ago." Few feminists of any stripe would agree either with her description of *A Woman of My Age* as a "women's lib novel," or with her conclusion that the "argument" about women's problems was settled years ago. The novel is about the difficulties and inequities of marriage. It is in many ways a very fine study of an ignorant, idealistic girl who makes herself a bed she is bound to be uncomfortable in. Elizabeth marries because she is pregnant and stays married because she has no real alternatives. She has a husband who is ashamed of his social origins, but chooses to create his own hierarchy by referring to people as having first or second class minds. Elizabeth can feel nothing for this man, perhaps because she is constantly obsessed by what she ought to feel; her "ought" is here defined according to conventional public middle-class expectations. A chorus rings in Elizabeth's head: *"Elizabeth is such a nice person, she puts herself out for the most boring people."* When she gives up her work for the Labour Party, work which gives her at least a limited sense of power, she does so because she wants to feel that she is doing the "right thing." But she knows that her husband's new kindness and solicitude are of the sort one might show to "a caged bird."

We watch the protagonists and their marriage during a crucial few days of their North African holiday. Bawden's artistry is manifested here particularly in the brilliance of her juxtaposition of scenes. The present is linked and opposed to the past in such a way that the characters are illuminated in action. The ending is beautifully foreshadowed in an early incident in the novel. Elizabeth is watching several men recapture a horse which has escaped: "It was as if he hadn't really wanted freedom, only to assert his right to be free if he chose."

Bawden says that she particularly enjoyed writing *The Grain of Truth* (1968). It is not an entirely successful novel, but it is her first real experiment with a variety of narrative points of view. The novel is perhaps somewhat too schematic in its deliberate alternation of perspectives. It opens and closes with Emma's fearful and manipulative cry for help, "Someone listen to me."

Every case different, never the same set of circumstances, the same set of features, and yet what one remembers are the similarities. People steal from supermarkets assorted ragbags of articles - three packets raisins, two tins scouring powder, three 100 watt light bulbs, one tin boot polish, a half bottle of gin.

They say 'I don't remember doing it'. They have all suffered losses. Their husbands have left them. Their children are getting divorced, have failed their examinations. For women - the menopause.

A husband gives evidence on behalf of his wife. Shined face, shaking hand, as he takes the oath. How long married? 35 years. How many children? The wife weeps. The man recites family troubles. The defending counsel leads gently. 'I believe your son was ill at the time'. The husband weeps, a sad, dignified labourer, hands clasping the edge of the witness box. Our son is dead now.

'Human law — what a farce!'

Page from notebook for Afternoon of a Good Woman

8

seems very narrow.

Shoplifters, for example. Women, my age, steal from supermarkets
assorted ragbags of articles. Three packets mixed nuts, two
tins scouring powder, a bottle of lemonade, black boot-polish,
a pound of beef sausages, a dozen light-bulbs, a pair of nylon
tights not their size. Caught, they say much the same things.
They 'can't remember what happened.' They 'don't know what
came over them.' They usually have enough money on them in
their worn purses, are willing / eager / to pay. They have
recently suffered from depression/ the menopause / some
domestic unhappiness. Husbands, taking the day off work,
speak on their behalf with lined, concerned faces. They have
been married twenty / twenty-five / thirty years. Have two /
three/ five children. Nothing like this has ever happened
before. The wife often weeps at this point, the court usher
takes her a glass of water and the magistrates look away
while she drinks it: her situation, so unbelievably terrible
to her, is embarrassingly common to them. Only rarely does
some small thing make a case of this kind memorable, turn
the court-room into a theatre. A husband stumbles as he
speaks of a 'family tragedy.' Defending counsel leads gently.
'I believe one of your children was ill at the time this
incident happened?' The husband weeps; old, shaking, veined

21

Page from final typescript for Afternoon of a Good Woman

Emma, like Hilary of *Devil by the Sea*, and like many children described in psychiatric literature, fears she has killed someone. This fear has complex psychological functions. It is first a source and justification for self-hatred. Emma thinks of herself as so wicked she is not worth loving, but with part of her mind she is also aware that it wasn't "anything I had done, but what I knew I was capable of doing." (A woman's potential for evil, or even the possibility of an impure motive, is a source of masochistic self-doubt for many of Bawden's heroines.) But this same fear also functions to control and manipulate Henry, Emma's husband. Her best friend, Holly, points out that Emma, like her mother, believes "unhappiness gives you a moral advantage." But Holly also ultimately prevents her from taking this advantage. When Emma insists on going to the police with a confession of guilt in her father-in-law's death, Holly lies to save her by insisting that she, Holly, was present at the moment of death, and that this disclosure by Emma can only be the figment of a distressed mind.

It is Emma's husband, Henry, who uncovers "the grain of truth" that feeds Emma's fear. As readers we are persuaded that we have been given an understanding of Emma's character, and even perhaps that Emma will learn to come to terms with her problem. But we remain unconvinced that Henry is capable of this psychological insight. As the plot builds he is portrayed, like many of Bawden's men, as basically self-deceiving. Such men vary from the kindly to the brutally inept. Rarely do they appear capable of much insight into their own predicaments, much less into the psychological intricacies of their wives.

When asked about her rather absent and passive male characters, Bawden conceded that perhaps her own experience of a frequently absent marine engineer father might have contributed to these portraits. But she is rarely as hard on these men as she is on her women characters, reserving her sharpest ironies for domineering mothers like Emma's or their insecure, approval-seeking daughters.

The Birds on the Trees (1970) was described by Sheila Mitchell on BBC radio as "one of the best novels I have read about the family situation as we have it nowadays." It is the story of Toby, a sensitive, charming drop-out. On drugs, he has a psychotic episode and later gets a girl pregnant. Bawden treats this apparently banal 1960s material with the delicacy of a gifted miniaturist. No element of the story is out of place, and the interweaving of perspectives rehearsed in *The Grain of Truth* is perfectly controlled here. One of her admirers has linked it to the works of Guy de Maupassant, but it is far less sardonic. This is perhaps her most compassionate work. Middle class parents can identify with these adults and have a sense that they are, if not absolved, at least understood. One suspects that children like Toby and his brother and sister would also be well pleased with their portraits.

Anna Apparent is Bawden's exploration of the consequences of a battered childhood. Annie May is rescued from brutal foster care by an egotistical and vain woman for whom this child represents an opportunity to play a new role. Crystal Golightly has recently been abandoned by her husband, and her outrage and sense of failure are alleviated by this chance to exercise benevolent dictatorial powers: "She was marvellous with the child; no less so because that was how she saw her behavior. To act in a way that would be seen to be admirable had become the main spring of her life." Annie survives this upbringing to become "Crystal's good girl," going so far as to marry Crystal's real son, Giles, a man whose emotional parasitism is only slightly more perverse and sophisticated than his mother's. Annie becomes Anna, the model wife and mother. Only her nightmares suggest that this Anna also wants "to smash something." Although Anna is in some senses a special case, she is Bawden's first clear portrayal of a woman who discovers that she needs to define *herself*. Her sense of herself in which "the others" were real, and she was "only the stage on which they moved," had led her to a monstrous explosion of rage and the death of an innocent stranger.

George, the travel-agent hero of *George Beneath a Paper Moon* (1974), is from a different, more delightfully comic world. Somehow reality only comes secondhand to George. He interprets his life through the anecdotes of his friends and acquaintances, and occasionally even via parable. Thus it is not surprising that he grows rich on the creation of fantasy for others, though he thinks of it with "missionary innocence" as the fulfillment of their need for "romance and excitement, beauty and truth." It takes Turkish intrigue and an earthquake to get George to appreciate that life is not a fairy tale, but by a glorious irony, George gets his own fairy-tale ending.

In 1968 Bawden was appointed a Justice of the Peace in Surrey. She was nominated by her local Labour Party and served for eight years. *Afternoon of a Good Woman* (1976) with its heroine, Penelope, is

Dust jacket for Bawden's novel based on her experiences as a justice of the peace

one outcome of this experience. Penelope, like her creator, is a Justice of the Peace. Unlike her mythological namesake, she is not one to sit at home weaving and unraveling her tapestry. She has decided to leave her husband for a lover who needs her more, and as she sits in judgment on the bench, she sits in judgment on her own past and present. Part of what she discovers is her own unconscious affinity for weakness; with this insight she comes to acknowledge that she might prefer to respond to strength. The reader applauds her final decision to leave both men.

The book's epigraph by Leo Tolstoy is apt: "Human law—what a farce." The skillful interweaving of the life and situation of the accused with that of the accuser creates a tapestry in which life and law are both revealed in their true colors.

Familiar Passions (1979), Bawden's next work, starts from an almost directly opposed plot premise. This time the heroine's husband has decided to leave *her*. On their thirteenth wedding anniversary he takes her to an expensive dinner and then breaks the news to her. Bridie Starr, whose very name is her husband's creation, goes back to being Mary Mudd. But she cannot accept herself as Mary Mudd either, since she is an adopted child. She therefore decides to discover who she is by seeking out her real mother and father. Genealogy here is less important than Bridie/Mary's discovery that she must learn to define herself. She finds her natural mother, who is willing to give her information about her antecedents, but unwilling to provide emotional support. With a splendid lack of sentimentality she tells Bridie (who has, after all, two perfectly adequate adoptive parents): "I think this has been the most interesting conversation we are ever likely to have." And so Bridie is forced to learn for herself that her nature includes an aptitude and a taste for intrigue and deception, and that being "good" as defined for her by others (including an angelic adoptive mother) is not a necessary corollary of being a woman. As Bawden herself puts it, "Having to be good twists people; you're so afraid you won't be loved."

Walking Naked (1981), Bawden's most recent novel, received rather mixed reviews. It so irritated one usually enthusiastic London reviewer that he headed his piece: "If only nasty Laura had kept her clothes on. . . ." Bawden attributes this lack of sympathy in part to her heroine's unforgivable act: she sends the two children of her first marriage to her ex-husband and his new wife, assuming that they will prefer living there. But far more radical incidents and assumptions appear in this novel, and though they are not mentioned by reviewers, they may well cause unease in the establishment. This is at least partly a novel about a woman who makes a choice between a deeply affectionate, at least partly erotic friendship with a woman, and marriage with her second husband. This heroine, Laura, is not a "good girl," and the chaos and brutality which haunt the periphery of most of our lives are expressed in the novel by her fears that "the house will fall down." In content this book is the development and culmination of Bawden's previous themes; in technique it does not achieve the unity and elegance of some of her earlier novels.

In writing her novel about a novelist, Bawden suggests a number of parallels between the artist and the woman. Artists, like women, are manipulators; like women they are to be feared because everything is grist to their mills; the element of self-display so necessary to the artist is, however, seen from the outside as self-regarding and dishonest. This is an interesting parallel which suggests something about both artists and women, but is not successfully integrated into the fabric of the novel.

In 1970 Nina Bawden was made a Fellow of the Royal Society of Literature. Her clear-eyed satiric studies of men, women, and children have always probed the hypocritical motive and the mechanical response. Most recently they have also offered us honest alternatives.

David Benedictus
(16 September 1938-   )

T. Winnifrith
University of Warwick

SELECTED BOOKS: *The Fourth of June* (London: Blond, 1962; New York: Dutton, 1962);

You're A Big Boy Now (London: Blond, 1963; New York: Dutton, 1964);

This Animal is Mischievous (London: Blond, 1965; New York: New American Library, 1966);

Hump (London: Blond, 1967);

The Guru and the Golf Club (London: Blond, 1969);

A World of Windows (London: Weidenfeld & Nicolson, 1971);

Junk: A Guide to Bargain Hunting (London: Macmillan, 1976);

The Rabbi's Wife (London: Blond & Briggs, 1976; New York: Evans, 1976);

A Twentieth Century Man (London: Blond & Briggs, 1978).

David Henry Benedictus was born in London at the height of the Munich crisis, the son of Henry Jules and Kathleen Constance Ricardo Benedictus. He was educated at Britain's most socially exclusive school, Eton, and then at Oxford's most intellectually exclusive college, Balliol, where in 1959 he obtained a second class degree in English Language and Literature. He also spent a short time at the University of Iowa, but it is Eton which is satirized in *The Fourth of June* (1962). The timing of Benedictus's first novel was admirable, as it coincided with a wave of satire directed against the Macmillan government, full of old Etonians and racked by sexual scandals. In the next fifteen years Benedictus produced seven more novels, some plays, and a book on antiques—as well as working for television, for the Royal Shakespeare Company, and running his own antique stall. This hectic existence perhaps explains why some of the later novels are so chaotic. In his latest *The Rabbi's Wife* (1976) and *A Twentieth Century*

Man (1978), Benedictus appears to have matured, and here, instead of showing the rottenness behind apparent respectability, he concentrates on showing how fundamental decency is inevitably warped by public events in the last thirty years.

The Fourth of June was denounced by the headmaster of Eton as pornographic and untrue. It is difficult at first to see the justification for the former charge. Some voyeurism by a visiting bishop, the seduction of a housemaster by the mother of one of his refractory pupils, and some mild heterosexual and homosexual interest by the senior boys that is scarcely translated into activity seem comparatively tame by today's standards, and the language used to describe these peccadilloes is suitably decorous. We have to remember that the behavior of the bishop and the housemaster would even now be considered reprehensible, even though the behavior of the boys seems curiously repressed. Whatever the truth of the charges leveled against Etonian boys, masters, and bishops— and the headmaster can scarcely be blamed for denying them—the charge of pornography, peculiar though it may seem in these enlightened days, does have a certain amount of justification in that the supposedly lurid scenes of sexual license have little to do with the main plot of the novel and seem to be added to provide gratuitous excitement.

The central character of the novel is Scarfe, the son of an East Anglian chicken farmer, who is sent to Eton as an experiment by his local authority who pays the fees. There were such boys at Eton; but there is no evidence to support or refute the suggestion that they were so badly ignored, patronized, and bullied as Scarfe is. Encouraged by a visiting bishop, who is in fact more interested in the chaplain's daughter as she undresses, Scarfe forms

David Benedictus

a friendship with Phillips, a more conventional Etonian with sensitive literary tastes. Phillips is, however, made a prefect; in Etonian terms this is oddly (almost ironically, in view of the prevailing philistinism) known as being elected to the library. Scarfe tries to visit Phillips in his room. This is against the rules, and Scarfe is savagely beaten three times by Defries (the head prefect, or house captain) while the other members of the library (the sinister Morgan and Pemberton, the dashing Berwick, and Phillips himself) watch. The first beating is interrupted by Mrs. Molarkey, a domestic servant who is dismissed for her interference. The second beating is interrupted when Scarfe runs away, but the third takes its full course of nine strokes, and Scarfe retires to the sanatorium, temporarily paralyzed. The doctor complains to the housemaster, Manningham, who expels Defries and exonerates Phillips, who is made House Captain. Pemberton, Morgan, and Berwick are allowed to stay in the school on probation, largely as a result of the fury of Pem-

berton's mother and an amorous assault by Berwick's mother on Manningham. The fate of these boys is decided on the Fourth of June, Eton's major day of celebration, accompanied by fireworks, processions of boats, and the ritual saturnalia of the English upper classes, described in great but hardly loving detail. The episode when visiting royalty enter a tent tactfully marked "Toilets" only to have the tent collapse on top of them is meant to deflate the pomp of the English aristocracy.

While the tent is collapsing and Manningham is desperately trying to deal with Lady Pemberton and Alethea Berwick, the boys who are most involved in the story are otherwise engaged. Scarfe travels home to his parents. Phillips and Berwick have a more interesting time, the former being engaged in gauche but brutal assaults on the virtue of Jill, a girl he has met during the holidays, and the latter being engaged in resisting the advances of his mother's hairdresser's sister, whom his mother has kindly but mistakenly invited to the Fourth of June celebration. We are meant, perhaps too obviously, to see the contrast between the apparently idealistic Phillips's coarseness and the apparently sophisticated Berwick's innocence, but this contrast is insufficiently developed. In a topsy-turvy world such a contrast is perhaps more important than royalty underneath the toilet tent or Manningham succumbing to Alethea Berwick's advances, although it is Manningham who emerges as the central character of the second half of the novel. Like many satirists, from Juvenal onward, Benedictus can be accused of incoherence and of being so busy attacking everything that he ends up offering no positive values; he can also be accused of exaggeration and improbability. Those who have no knowledge of Eton will find the world Benedictus describes unbelievable; even those with some first-hand acquaintance with Eton find Scarfe's punishment excessive, Manningham's conduct improbable, Morgan's and Pemberton's characters unpleasant. An attack on snobbery is not helped by snobbish contempt of people like Scarfe. The undercutting of Phillips's idealism is sad. Nevertheless, *The Fourth of June* is full of promise and extraordinary verbal felicity, as shown in the phrase comparing the aristocracy to monkeys climbing up their family trees. The novel was an instant commercial success, although the *Times* reviewer loftily maintained that Benedictus was wrong in assuming that the naive is the only alternative to the corrupt.

Benedictus's next novel, *You're A Big Boy Now* (1963), contains less of the topical interest and few of the virtues of its predecessor. It is the story of

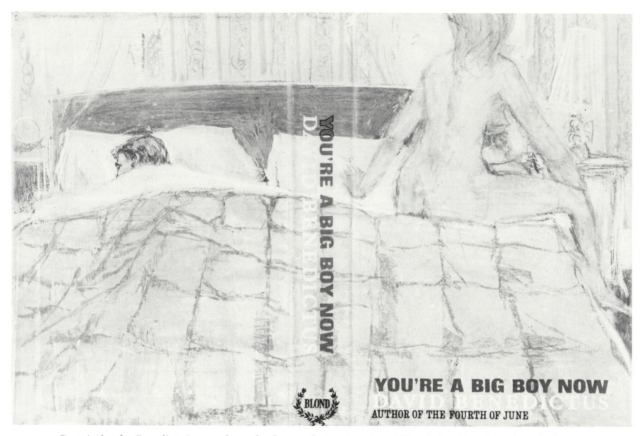

Dust jacket for Benedictus's second novel, about a shop assistant and his relationship with a beautiful actress

Bernard Chanticleer, a callow shop assistant, who is first taken up and then cruelly abandoned by a beautiful young actress, Beatrice Darling. An attempt is made to explore Bernard's insecurity, fostered by the coy lies of his lower-middle-class upbringing, and in this sense Bernard is an improvement on Scarfe, but Beatrice is a wholly unconvincing character, although we hear a great deal about her childhood when she is ravished by Professor Kurt Doughty. In this book the verbal fluency of *The Fourth of June* hinders rather than helps: Benedictus cannot resist a playful remark on anything that takes his fancy, as when he tastelessly compares the face-lifting of Oxford colleges with the face-lifts of the American tourists who visit them.

Benedictus's third novel, *This Animal is Mischievous* (1965), is an incoherent account of a brother and his sister, Georgie (the brother, who narrates, is never named). Their involvement with a black man, Tiger, leads to a nightmarish racial struggle and a mysterious Fascist conspiracy. The climax of the story occurs on Mount Parnassus where Georgie is killed, the Fascists are defeated, and everything returns to normal; Benedictus's

political awareness and his fears of fascism are themes developed better in his later books. This novel is part thriller, part farce, and sometimes neither, and the *Times* reviewer found it irritating, with ill-thought-out allegory and symbolism taking the place of viable action.

Hump (1967) and *The Guru and the Golf Club* (1969) received little critical attention. In these novels Benedictus's interest in outsiders takes an absurd form with the stories of a hunchback creating havoc in a theater and an Indian fakir overturning the values of a suburban community. Benedictus is clearly out to assault established values, but the form he chooses is so unusual that it is virtually meaningless.

Hump and *The Guru and the Golf Club* were published during the years of student unrest in Great Britain and America. *A World of Windows* (1971) reveals something of the pressures of these years. The protagonist, Mike, works at the BBC, and, married to an ordinary wife, Joy, he seems to have a comfortable bourgeois existence. But Mike becomes obsessed with looking from an attic at his neighbors in the house opposite, and he neglects his job and his family until he eventually goes mad and kills his daughter. The narrative sequence has to be pieced together from a series of flashbacks by both Mike and Joy, interspersed with some reflections from Mike's present prison cell. As in previous novels, suburban normality (as portrayed by Joy) and decent liberalism (as portrayed by the family on whom Mike spies) are cruelly treated and shown to be no match for Mike's paranoia. Like Benedictus's other novels, *A World of Windows* suffers from a lack of central focus, and we do not know whether Mike's breakdown is a result of his working for television (vaguely suggested by the window sym-

also published *The Rabbi's Wife*, although it would seem to have been written much earlier, since it is dedicated both to the Jewish athletes who died at the Munich Olympics and to the Palestinian refugees, and it ends with the Yom Kippur war of 1973. *The Rabbi's Wife* reestablishes Benedictus's claim to be considered a serious novelist. The novel tells how Susannah, married to a British rabbi, Jamie, and living in Blackheath, is kidnapped by Palestinian terrorists on Yom Kippur, 1972, while she is celebrating the festival with several children. A rescue attempt is bungled by the British authorities. Some children die, some are rescued, but Susannah is

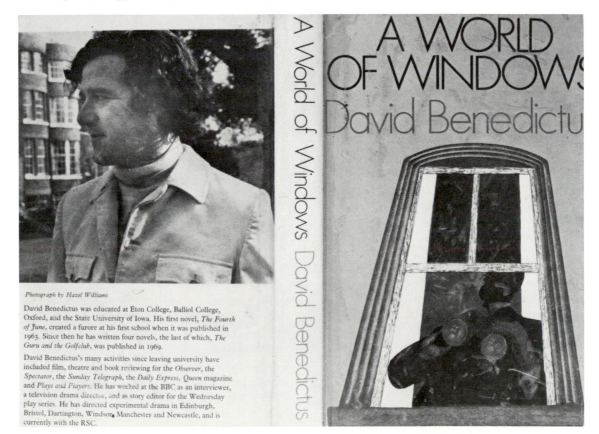

Photograph by Hazel Williams

David Benedictus was educated at Eton College, Balliol College, Oxford, and the State University of Iowa. His first novel, *The Fourth of June*, created a furore at his first school when it was published in 1963. Since then he has written four novels, the last of which, *The Guru and the Golfclub*, was published in 1969.

David Benedictus's many activities since leaving university have included film, theatre and book reviewing for the *Observer*, the *Spectator*, the *Sunday Telegraph*, the *Daily Express*, *Queen* magazine and *Plays and Players*. He has worked at the BBC as an interviewer, a television drama director, and as story editor for the Wednesday play series. He has directed experimental drama in Edinburgh, Bristol, Dartington, Windsor, Manchester and Newcastle, and is currently with the RSC.

Dust jacket for Benedictus's 1971 novel, about a middle-class man gone mad

bol) and his ruthless exposure of the sordid truth, or of his obsession with childhood and his sister, Claire. The mixture of past and present is confusing, and there is the same irritating tendency to digress into useless jokes.

For five years after *A World of Windows* Benedictus did not produce another novel. During this time he married actress Yvonne Antrobus, set up an antique stall in Twickenham, and wrote an excellent if slightly facetious account of the antique market, appropriately entitled *Junk*, which was published by Macmillan in 1976. In the same year Benedictus

hustled off to the Middle East. Her captors maltreat her, rape her, and then—after she has become pregnant—photograph her in a compromising position with one of her captors. This photograph causes difficulties for Jamie and for some of the children who survived the attack. Just before she is due to give birth, Susannah is rescued by Israeli gunmen, takes refuge with Sir Bertram Kidlington, the British ambassador in Beirut, and is eventually reunited with Jamie. He has not prospered in her absence, having been accused of homosexuality by Susannah's mother, and having made an unsuccessful attempt both to murder and rape the female Palestinian terrorist who helped abduct his wife.

Dedicated to both Jews and Palestinians, *The Rabbi's Wife* shows far more compassion than earlier novels. At the age of 38 in 1976, Benedictus would seem to have lost his sympathy with the student generation of 1968, if he had ever truly had it. The dilemma of both Jamie and Susannah is handled with sympathy instead of cruelty. Sir Bertram Kidlington, who would seem an easy task for facetious satire, acts kindly, wisely, and sensibly. Jethro and Ruth, two of the children who escape the raid, end up with fates worse than death, the former in a mind-expanding commune in Camberwell, the latter posing for photographs wearing a school blazer and nothing else; but their sad fate is a comment on the present age of meaningless violence. The *Sunday Times* reviewer noted that in this novel Benedictus had changed and grown up, and that without losing his capacity to entertain he had struck a moving note of human concern.

A Twentieth Century Man (1978) is mainly concerned with events after World War II, although the main character, Alan Redbone, an unsuccessful conservative member of Parliament, is such an old-fashioned character that the title is appropriately ironic. The novel consists of Redbone's 1977 predicaments, which are certainly not old-fashioned, and of flashbacks to events in the war and his subsequent political career. Unlike previous novels, the interplay between past and present is neatly if a little obviously handled; thus Redbone is hit at a party in 1977, and we are reminded of how he ingloriously acquired his war wound in 1945. In 1977 Redbone's wife, Selma, is an alcoholic; his mistress, Claire, from whom he demands unusual sexual satisfaction, is unsatisfactory; his son Mark is arrested for drug taking; he himself is being subjected to unreasonable pressure to misuse his position as a member of Parliament; and he attends a disgusting party given by the vice squad. All this is a far cry from the naive but idealistic Alan Redbone who visits Belsen in 1945 and marries Selma, an inmate there. And yet, though Alan's success in being elected to Parliament is a result of his father's influence, and his failure to gain ministerial office is a result of his own mistakes in consistently choosing the wrong side, we feel that he is a man of essential decency destroyed, as is his wife, by the corrupt world in which he lives, but to which he has not really contributed. Alan's ultimate political failure is signaled when the leader of his party via her private secretary intimates to him not very delicately that it would be better if he left the House of Commons. He gains—perhaps too late—some moral success when he follows Selma (who has burnt their house down) on a pointless but symbolically significant pilgrimage to Belsen. The *Daily Telegraph* reviewer saw an honorable purpose behind this novel, but did not find the work convincing.

A Twentieth Century Man contains a few of Benedictus's irritating tricks. Was it necessary to make Redbone submit to flagellation from Claire, or to make the vice squad party so horrible, or to introduce, in Redbone's depressing canvassing of his constituents, a man who exposes himself? History has played a small part in some of the other novels, but here Eden, Macmillan, and Mrs. Thatcher play an important part, and the way in which they successively dash Redbone's hopes is described with crude, cruel, and devastating journalistic accuracy. Benedictus does not really have time to investigate the malaise affecting British politics, but he does have time to appreciate the predicament of Alan and his wife. Benedictus remains in 1982, as he was in 1962, a novelist of promise, and readers must hope that with increasing maturity his skill with words and his insight into problems will not be dissipated by a wish to shock, amuse, or merely titillate.

John Berger

(5 November 1926-   )

G. M. Hyde
University of East Anglia

BOOKS: *A Painter of Our Time* (London: Secker & Warburg, 1958; New York: Simon & Schuster, 1959);

Permanent Red: Essays in Seeing (London: Methuen, 1960);

The Foot of Clive (London: Methuen, 1962);

Corker's Freedom (London: Methuen, 1964);

The Success and Failure of Picasso (Harmondsworth, U.K. & Baltimore: Penguin, 1965);

A Fortunate Man: The Story of a Country Doctor, photographs by Jean Mohr, text by Berger (London: Lane, 1967; New York: Holt, Rinehart & Winston, 1967);

Art and Revolution: Ernst Neizvestny and the Role of the Artist in the USSR (London: Weidenfeld & Nicolson, 1969);

The Moment of Cubism and Other Essays (London: Weidenfeld & Nicolson, 1969; New York: Pantheon Books, 1969);

The Look of Things: Selected Essays and Articles (London: Penguin, 1971; New York: Viking, 1974);

Ways of Seeing (Harmondsworth, U.K.: Penguin, 1972; New York: Viking, 1973);

G (London: Weidenfeld & Nicolson, 1972; New York: Viking, 1972);

A Seventh Man: A Book of Images and Words About the Experience of Migrant Workers in Europe, photographs by Mohr, text by Berger (Harmondsworth, U.K. & Baltimore: Penguin, 1975);

Pig Earth (London: Writers & Readers Publishing Cooperative, 1979; New York: Pantheon, 1979);

About Looking (London: Writers & Readers Publishing Cooperative, Ltd., 1980; New York: Pantheon, 1980).

John Berger

John Berger was born on 5 November 1926 in London, son of S. J. D. Berger and Miriam Branson Berger. Twice married and the father of three children, he now lives in the French Jura. Berger has not confined himself as a writer to any single genre or type of writing, but has produced innovative work in fiction, art criticism, social criticism, and "books of images and words" (the subtitle of the 1975 documentary *A Seventh Man*, produced in collaboration with Jean Mohr, the Swiss photographer). These set out to break down generic boundaries in order to synthesize creative and critical functions. In all his work the "unconditional modality of the visual image" (to borrow Yuri Lotman's phrase) is used to question what David Caute has called the "privileged anonymity" of the author.

He began his working life teaching painting and drawing and having his work exhibited at several London galleries (including the Wildenstein, the Redfern, and the Leicester). He wrote at the same time for *Tribune*, and from 1951 on a regular basis for the *New Statesman*, where he was for ten years a regular art critic, enjoying the support of editor Kingsley Martin. From material published between 1954 and 1959 he assembled his first book of art criticism bearing the symptomatic title *Permanent Red* (1960). In its republication (1979) Berger speaks of his feeling, on rereading it nineteen years later, that at the time he wrote it he was "trapped" by the need to express all his feelings and thoughts in "art-critical terms." The sense of enclosure fostered by the Cold War was, he says, the reason for the "puritanism" of many of his judgments; he also points out that (Kingsley Martin excepted) editorial pressure to conform made composition difficult. We know from Robert Hewison's book *In Anger* that Berger's unfashionable championship of realist painting in the early 1950s, especially his exhibition at the Whitechapel Gallery in 1952 of realist work under the title *Looking Forward*, aroused much animosity from, among others, Sir Herbert Read and Patrick Heron, another art critic working for the *New Statesman*. The recurring theme of *Permanent Red*, "the disastrous relation between art and property," underlies much of Berger's work. Critics seized on what they called Berger's habit of judging from fixed premises without indicating what they are. Equally annoying to many was his eschewal of the given historical categories of art criticism in favor of an existential engagement with the historical moment of the artist and the work of art.

Berger's effort to humanize bloodless categories leads him to a kind of fictionalizing of the moment of creation and the process of decoding, and even before these essays were collected he had written his first novel, *A Painter of Our Time* (1958), which explores many of his interests: the relationship between the work of art and the life-experience of the artist, the meaning of artistic "abstraction," the relating of subjectivity to social praxis, and the function of the painter in a consumer society. Janos Lavin, the fictional painter-hero, a Hungarian emigre, unites these themes. His work is perhaps modeled on that of Fernand Léger, who learned how to "discover the spirit, the ethics, the attitude of mind" needed to make use of modern technical achievements (Berger wrote at length on Léger and technology in *Marxism Today* in 1963). The choice of the artist/exile as protagonist focuses the issue of artistic commitment; and the narrative technique—the narrator in the abandoned studio searches in Lavin's diary for clues to his disappearance—juxtaposes document with fiction in such a way as to dissolve their boundaries. The decoding of the journal (this constitutes the plot) is effectively related to the composition and "reading" of the paintings which form the "real" life of the artist.

Between 1952 and 1958 (as he tells us in an essay collected in *The Look of Things: Selected Essays and Articles*, 1971, drawn from *New Society* as well as the *Statesman*), Berger was close to the Hungarian sculptor Peter Peri, who was living in poverty in Camden. He had, says Berger, the face of a ghetto dweller who carried "a microcosm in a sack," the turmoil of central European culture which he hardly expected the English to understand. "Something of the meaning of being such an exile I tried to put into my novel," says Berger, and he adds that he discussed the novel with Peri, who was "enthusiastic about the idea of my writing it." Some traits of Lavin are therefore drawn from Peri, others from the Hungarian art historian Frederick Antal, "who, more than any other man, taught me how to write about art. . . . What Lavin and Antal share is the depth of their experience of exile." But Berger adds that Lavin is not a portrait of Peri.

A Painter of Our Time was hostilely reviewed in *Encounter* and elsewhere, and parts of it are awkward and ill contrived, but Berger's intense existential concern with the complex perspectives upon the world which art creates illuminates Lavin's journal. The condition of exile, though not romanticized, and represented as bought at a very high price, is seen to be a necessary condition for artistic freedom in certain kinds of society. Lavin is free to be unimpressed by high society art patrons; he is free to ignore both middle-class values and their alternative, the life-style of the coterie. His passionate defense of art against the plausible ethics of ownership is memorable. In this way Berger counters objections to "formalism" which the Left continues to bring against him. Lavin echoes Berger's ideas and methods in both political and artistic matters. Reflecting upon art and politics, for instance, Lavin finds an example of the dialectical process in the technique of cross-hatching, where the intersecting lines form a new diamond shape not inherent in either. The compositional principle of journal plus commentary, perhaps owing something to Jean Paul Sartre, is the embodiment of this dialectic. Thus the novel incorporates a critique of fictionality, a critique which Berger was to take much

Dust jacket for Berger's fictional depiction of an artist in the modern world

further in his later ventures into cultural criticism and reportage. It is also interesting to note that before (one presumes) he had read the German literary theorist Walter Benjamin, whose work was at this time more or less unknown to English readers, Berger was using the Benjaminesque method of identifying intuitive, unmediated relationships between forms of thought (or creative processes) and historical processes, via the painterly image. History is thus a kind of unconscious which the work of art, like the Freudian dream-work, both reveals and conceals. Hence the vivid elliptical shifts between object and concept, fact and metaphor, that are to remain typical of Berger.

At the end of this first novel Berger's hero disappears as if he has been "taken up to heaven in a chariot." His disappearance and return to Hungary (in the year of the uprising which radically changed the course of Hungarian political life) are also symptomatic of a deepening conviction on Berger's part about the task of the artist and the processes of artistic creation in the modern world. This conviction may perhaps be stated most effectively in relation to Berger's treatment of Pablo Picasso, the modern "artist as hero," in *The Success and Failure of*

Picasso (1965). Berger in effect sets out to strip away the ideological accretions that have made it difficult to "see" Picasso: he demythologizes the "man of genius" (the commodity value that painters have acquired in an age that grants them no effective place in society). There is, Berger believes, a "dualism at the very heart of the bourgeois attitude to art. On the one hand, the glory and mystery of genius; on the other hand, the work of art as a saleable commodity." Picasso himself believed in "genius as a state of being": Berger interprets this belief in terms of the class structure of Spain, Spanish anarchism, and the facts of Picasso's childhood, while managing to avoid any crudely Marxist or Freudian generalizations. Thus what Berger calls the "discontinuity" of Picasso's life and work, often related to his perennial youthfulness, is seen as an ambiguous phenomenon inextricably linked to a failure to develop.

Only after establishing these imaginative structures in Picasso's work does Berger turn his attention to the subject matter of his paintings (the sympathy with the outcast in his early work, for example) and to the short-lived "promise of the modern world" which Cubism contained. Berger attaches particular significance to the failure (or radical inability) of Cubists (Picasso among them) to respond to the age of "essential politics" inaugurated by World War I. It is at this point that "the legend of Picasso as a magician now begins." The increasing subjectivity of Picasso's art—even in the 1930s, and notably after 1940—is contrasted with the public dimension of Léger's. Berger finds that in certain key works Picasso becomes solipsistic by virtue of the fact that "there is nothing *to resist him*: neither the subject, nor his awareness of reality as understood by others." Thus Picasso ended his career as a "national monument," doyen of the West and (as a Communist) exploited by propaganda in the East. Berger somewhat extravagantly uses Aimé Césaire, the Martinique poet whose work he translated in 1969, to suggest how Picasso might have avoided such stereotyping by engaging with the culture of the Third World.

Just as Berger's critique of Picasso demystifies the "artist as hero," so his second novel, *The Foot of Clive* (published in 1962, when D. J. Enright commented in the *New Statesman* on its "derivative technique" but also its "smell of humanity"), abolished both hero and plot in order to concentrate on what Lavin called the "diamonds" that form in the cross-hatchings. Berger studies the life of an institution (a hospital) in relation to the institutionalized life of those who temporarily inhabit or compose it, the patients. The patient is one who is acted upon, and whose mind is peculiarly in touch with his body: he is a representative of complex forms of mediation between subjectivity and structure, humanly exposed. Thus what each individual is for himself is "cross-hatched" with commentary that is more like the probing of the camera (which Benjamin has compared to the surgeon's knife) than the naturalizing consistency of the narrator. Moreover, characters narrate themselves and each other, interacting with a directness that is only everyday life writ large, weaving together their pasts and their futures from within their peculiarly vulnerable present. This microcosmic society, engaged in writing its own history, is intruded upon at the end of part one by a new patient, Jack House the murderer; and part two ("The Screens") and part three ("The Execution") unfold against the background of this ominous presence. House embodies the fear of the unknown and the presence of death, "screened off" from the "normal" world, more difficult to relate to and contain, even, than the world of nature which is constantly evoked in what Enright called the novel's "curious kind of bestiary." House's presence crystallizes the latent

violence in the men: they both need him (he stands for Law and Judgment) and anathematize him. Part four, "The Survivors," dissolves the precarious synthesis of Clive Ward back into professional objectivity, with the doctors treating the patients as case histories, Robin reading of House's execution, and the little community opening up to the outside world with Robin's discharge. We reflect upon the kinds of "freedoms" encountered in Clive Ward's uncensored intimacies, and the ways in which they relate to the possibility of freedom in the "real" world.

In his next novel, *Corker's Freedom* (1964), Berger, by contrast with his method in *The Foot of Clive*, creates a central hero, the manager of a small employment agency: but here again, though the method could be called more traditional, and the writing is extraordinarily assured and exact, the basic components of the fiction—hero, plot, and setting—are all seen as problematic. Berger himself describes *Corker's Freedom* as "partly a film scenario and partly a historical document," and this is consistent with his wish that "my books transcend the categories into which they are generally forced." Berger does not give us a portrait of his hero; he claims in his essay "The Changing View of the Man in the Portrait" (reprinted in *The Look of Things*) that the portrait will eventually be replaced by a kind of multimedia memento set. In *Corker's Freedom* Berger confronts the problem of representing an individual with limited faculties of self-knowledge and still more restricted powers of self-expression, but whose need for the "freedom" of a richer social milieu and more positive field of personal and social action is very urgent. The small employment exchange which Corker runs becomes the focus of a critique of a culture which values individuals only for their earning potential (though to state it in these terms is to impose a tendentiousness which the novel is wholly free of). The narrator, assisting Corker by telling the reader what Corker thinks and what he knows (as distinct from what he is able only to *say*), breaks open narrative convention in order to offer Corker the freedom of which he dreams. This freedom is symbolized for the "hero" by his romantic nostalgia for far-away places, especially Vienna, the city which for Corker represents the (impossible) cultural ideal which will guarantee his "freedom." Especially original and effective is the episode of the slide show given to the local church social club, in which Corker shows the holiday slides which signify freedom while two petty crooks are burgling his office. The melodramatic climax of the novel is consistent with its "cinematic" organization,

Corker ending up as a small-time con man and spokesman for a shabby Pan-European political organization.

The mixed-media effects of *Corker's Freedom*, reflecting Berger's interest in film and television and his work for Granada and for BBC's *Monitor* (arts program), are extended in his two major photo-documentary volumes, *A Fortunate Man* (1967) and *A Seventh Man* (1975), produced in collaboration with Swiss photographer Jean Mohr. The earlier of these is a documentary record of the work of a doctor in a poor rural community in the north of England; but the doctor himself serves to focus questions that pass beyond immediate, "vocational" ones. The book creates a landscape, "no longer only geographic but also biographical and personal," in which the doctor works, which he acts upon, and which acts upon him. Initially, he sees himself in the guise of a Conradian Master Mariner, the man with special skills and a special responsibility, but later as one who enters "dialectically" into relationships with patients, with an ironic sense of his limitations. The community, as Berger himself points out in a footnote, suffers as a whole from the "Corker" problem: "They are deprived of the means of translating what they know into thoughts which they can think." Illness discloses needs and even faculties that lie hidden behind the "common sense" of the group, that common sense which Berger challengingly describes as "the home-made ideology of those who have been kept ignorant." The doctor becomes the "lost possibility of understanding and relating to the outside world." This role makes him keenly aware of his inadequacy; but (or because of this) he is able, unlike the teacher, to "introduce the possibility of a hitherto unseen pleasure or satisfaction without extrapolating the idea of a fundamentally different way of life": such an idea would not be available to his patients, reduced as they are by circumstances to a "spiritual minimum." The questions with which Berger concludes, as to the "social value of a pain eased, a life saved," seem hyperbolical, and as he admits can be answered only "by the creation of a more human society." But his other photo-documentary, *A Seventh Man* (winner of the Prize for Best Reportage, Union of Journalists & Writers, Paris, 1975), shows that there may be a different way of asking the questions, one which points to an answer in other than generalized humanistic terms.

Between these two books lie two crucial events for Berger: the political and cultural struggles of 1968, and (related at the deepest level) the publication also in 1968 of Hannah Arendt's selection of essays by Walter Benjamin, *Illuminations*. *A Seventh Man*, produced in collaboration with Jean Mohr, is "about" the fate of migrant workers (in Germany as in Britain one out of seven manual workers is an immigrant). But equally, as the title poem "The Seventh" by Attila Jozsef indicates, it is about the absent other, the individual who exceeds the total of his functions or roles in the world, and yet is constituted by these functions and roles. Photography is not only a component of the book, but a part of its form, its manner of existing: the photograph carried by the migrant "defines an absence," the family in which he no longer fills a place, though he hopes to do so again one day; but the photograph *we* see makes present what is absent.

This contradiction hangs over all the photographs in the text (the migrant returns to his village with photographs of naked women but "will not say who they are"; the man being led illegally over the frontier gives half his torn photograph to the guide, who will use it to claim payment from the migrant's family). It is, as Benjamin remarks in discussing Marcel Proust, a "matter of chance whether an individual forms an image of himself, whether he can take hold of his experience"; and the migrant stands for all who sell their labor and mortgage their present to an unsure future. "His migration is like an event in a dream dreamt by another"; the frontier he crosses demands the severance of organic ties with family and community and entrance into the community of the immortals. Migrants are immortal because they are "continually interchangeable. They are not born, they are not brought up: they do not age: they do not get tired: they do not die." By means of such metaphoric shifts Berger defamiliarizes their predicament and illuminates the contradiction between the individual and society.

In the American film journal *Jump Cut* (in a review of the New York Critics Prize-winning script which Berger wrote for Alain Tanner's film *Jonah Who Will Be 25 in the Year 2000*), Linda Greene, John Hess, and Robin Lakes take Berger to task (as many on the left have done) for not focusing sharply enough on the processes of exploitation in capitalist society: yet nothing could be more vivid than his analysis of the way that the "valuable economic resource—human labour" is transferred from poor countries, which need it desperately and cannot use it, to rich countries, which exploit it in every sense of the word. The predicament of the migrant is universalized but not generalized as Berger shifts (in the way characteristic of his later style) between metaphor and metonymy. The concept of "time and motion," for instance, is correlated with the "interrupted gestures" which Benjamin finds characteristic of Bertolt Brecht's alienation effect, while at the same time crystallizing around the sharp-edged frozen images of Mohr's photographs, and the strategic use of stark statistics, to evoke acute societal and personal deprivation. The description of the migrant working in the tunnel under Geneva becomes a chilling metaphor of life "under" capitalism: the image bears out the truth of Berger's claim that "the migrant is not on the margin of modern experience; he is absolutely central to it." Berger won the George Orwell Memorial Prize in 1977, partly for *A Seventh Man*.

This is not to suggest that Berger's political attitudes are doctrinaire. The study of the work of the Soviet artist Ernst Neizvestny, *Art and Revolution* (1969), had already stated a position that Berger was to develop: that the role of criticism is "intervention" and not "competitive claims" for the importance of one's subject. Cooperating with Jean Mohr, Berger documents the function of the artist in a socialist society where men are "inclined to think" that their "destiny is larger than [their] interests." Berger demonstrates that Russian art has at all times had a complex political dimension, never more so than in the early years of this century. The "intense spiritual energy" of Russian art appreciation was, he says, blocked by the "sterile academicism" of socialist realism. This academic system forced Neizvestny to become a "petty criminal" (in the matter of obtaining his materials on the black market, for instance). But in devising a means for expressing "man's contradictory, extensive nature," he becomes "the epic, public artist" (this line of reasoning, as Berger himself admits, is by no means self-evident). Berger's characteristic summarizing formula is "man is stronger than most of his parts, and may one day become stronger than any of them." Thus Neizvestny expresses endurance, courage, life out of and against death. Berger's argument is backed up by reference to the role of the Soviet Union (and implicitly the Soviet artist) in combating imperialist distortions of humanity: it is a rather lame conclusion, not altogether consistent with the facts, and it does not persuade one to overlook the faults in Neizvestny's work which no one has described better than Berger himself.

It was this "humanist" impasse that Benjamin's work helped Berger out of. *Ways of Seeing* (1972), the essentially collaborative television venture subsequently published as an influential book, pays detailed tribute to Benjamin, and especially to his essay "The Work of Art in the Age of Mechanical Reproduction." The subject of Berger's project is the ubiquity of images: it was conceived in part as a riposte to Sir Kenneth Clark's imposing *Civilisation* series. Mechanical reproduction makes the art of the past "available" in forms and circumstances unknown to its producers: this historical "gap" becomes a constituent element of the meaning of the image, so that as the "aura" of the "original" fades, a new kind of value discloses itself. This consists in the awareness of something like Wolfgang Iser's concept, in literary analysis, of the "implied reader": a set of attributes, attitudes, formal relations, strategies of representation, formed within the cultural significance acquired by a given work as part of the network of relations existing between painter, subject, tradition, and viewer/buyer/patron.

Thus Berger concerns himself with the image of women, and especially women's sexuality, in painting and advertising; with the painting as commodity and as confirmation of the power of accumulated wealth; with a society and culture obsessed by property; with the use of publicity in preempting the future and substituting illusory choices for real choices. *Ways of Seeing* is a contribution to the cultural criticism long practiced in England within a more pedagogical tradition (associated perhaps with F. R. Leavis or Raymond Williams) but it breaks new ground in its confident appropriation of the media; it seems as if the camera is doing the work, and the author can discard the prophetic mantle of omniscience and authority which has draped such cultural critics since Thomas Carlyle. The disclosure of the power of the image is two-edged. While we are invited to take a fresh look at a demystified culture, we are also being given an insight into the potential freedom that the ubiquity of the image contains. The foregrounding of the device is consistent with Benjamin's analysis of the functions of the camera: it is also central to the method of Berger's fourth novel, *G*, which won the *Guardian* Fiction Prize (1972), the Booker Prize for Fiction (1972) and the James Tait Black Memorial Prize (1973) amid controversy.

"The painter maintains in his work a natural distance from reality, the cameraman penetrates deeply into its web . . . multiple fragments assembled under a new law. . . . The camera introduces us to unconscious optics as does psychoanalysis to unconscious impulses." These quotations from Benjamin's "The Work of Art in the Age of Mechanical Reproduction" may serve to illuminate *G*. Whereas the author formerly emulated the painter, he now emulates the cameraman. Perhaps his hero is the camera itself, penetrating, analyzing, breaking down, rendering visible hidden gestures as the psychiatrist discloses hidden desires. G himself is more a set of hypotheses or angles of vision than a character; he is the point of intersection of subjectivity and history. As the illegitimate offspring of high bourgeois society, he embodies its contradictions, flouts its taboos, and initiates its decline in the anarchy of war. His exploitation of women (he is Don Giovanni as well as Garibaldi) is simply the disclosure of the truth about the prevailing ethic of his society: he demystifies in this as in other things and thus offers freedom while embodying constraint. He lays claim to an identity, like Giovanni and Garibaldi, but the narrative makes him less than a hero by accounting for him in terms of a historical process which (especially insofar as it allows women to free themselves) renders him obsolete (as the new technology is rendering obsolete the old bourgeois ethic). The fragmented narrative, composed in terms of Cubist "fields of force" rather than as a linear continuum, multiplies contradictions between personal (subjective) and historical systems of interpretation: at a number of points the author intervenes only to tell the reader that he has no privileged access to knowledge or to any interpretative schema, or even at one point to counter a

"voice" which accuses him of excessive theorizing. The insurgent crowds of Milan, the exploited Africans of Beatrice's past, the crowds that follow the aviator Chavez, with whom G is temporarily identified, the people of Trieste on the eve of war are as central to the action of the novel as G or the women imprisoned by men (here Berger quotes his own *Ways of Seeing*).

G is a diffuse and calculatedly unresolved work. *Pig Earth* (1979) by contrast—Berger's most recent fiction and the first section of a projected trilogy, "Into Their Labours"—is strongly attached in time and place to Berger's adopted home in rural France. The community evoked in the novel has a strong oral tradition and culture: its coordinates of time and space are as immediate as a row of melons and as extensive as the maquis and the war (the section entitled "The Three Lives of Lucie Cabrol"). The narrator is only one more storyteller, helping (like the others, but from a somewhat privileged distance) to maintain the identity of the community. Berger unobtrusively appropriates the idiom of one or another of the great storytellers of his adopted culture: Émile Zola is here, as are Guy de Maupassant and Alphonse Daudet. But *Pig Earth* remains very contemporary. The epic "The Three Lives of

Dust jacket for the first novel of the "Into Their Labours" trilogy

Lucie Cabrol," for example, demonstrates exactly what Berger means when he speaks of peasants as survivors and why survival matters also to those who are not peasants. (The estranged narrator here is the migrant, the one who leaves the community, comes back to tell the tale, but is excluded from the experience of the *Toussaint*, the festival of the dead evoked as in a dream which embodies the essential significance of overworked terms like community and tradition.) This power of survival is the exact inverse of the immortality of the migrant in *A Seventh Man*. If this implies a kind of conservatism, "It is a conservatism not of power but of meaning. It represents a depository of meaning. . . ." In this way, the peasant experience is seen to be peculiarly relevant to the modern world which envisages its destruction. "The peasant suspicion of 'progress' . . . is not altogether misplaced or groundless." With the annihilation of the "survivors," Berger suggests, we may lose not only a complex way of relating to nature and to animals (a major theme of this book and documented elsewhere by Berger): the destruction of the world's peasantries could be "a final act of historical elimination."

Little of lasting significance has been written about Berger, though his work has attracted reviews of more than usual passion and coherence. This is no accident: more than any other significant novelist of our time, Berger sees his work as contributing to a continuing dialectic rather than as aspiring to classic status. As a novelist of ideas who is continually engaging with problems of literary realism, he perhaps stands outside of the mainstream of contemporary English fiction. The lasting value of his work consists precisely in the intellectual restlessness which makes it necessary for him to cross the frontiers between established cultural and social institutions in his pursuit of a synthetic critique of contemporary civilization.

Screenplays:
Marcel Frishman, 1958;
A City at Chandigarh, 1968;
The Salamander, 1971;
The Middle of the World, 1974;
Jonah Who Will Be 25 in the Year 2000, 1975.

Translations:
Bertolt Brecht, *Poems on the Theatre*, translated by Berger and Anya Bostock (London: Scorpion Press, 1961);
Brecht, *Helene Weigel, Actress*, translated by Berger and Bostock (Leipzig: VEB Edition, 1961);
Aimé Césaire, *Return to My Native Land*, translated by Berger and Bostock (Harmondsworth, U.K. & Baltimore: Penguin Books, 1969).

References:
David Caute, "What we might be and what we are: The art of John Berger," in *Collisions* (London: Quartet Books, 1974), pp. 135-146;
Peter Fuller, *Seeing Berger: A Revaluation of Ways of Seeing* (London: Writers & Readers Publishing Cooperative, 1980);
Robert Hewison, *In Anger* (London: Weidenfeld & Nicolson, 1981).

Caroline Blackwood
(16 July 1931-   )

Priscilla Martin
University of East Anglia

BOOKS: *For All That I Found There* (London: Duckworth, 1973; New York: Braziller, 1974);
The Stepdaughter (London: Duckworth, 1976; New York: Scribners, 1977);
Great Granny Webster (London: Duckworth, 1977; New York: Scribners, 1977);
Darling, You Shouldn't Have Gone to So Much Trouble, by Blackwood and Anna Haycraft (London: Cape, 1980);

The Fate of Mary Rose (London: Cape, 1981; New York: Summit, 1981).

Caroline Blackwood has published a collection of stories and journalistic pieces, three short novels, and a cookbook. With this relatively small output she has earned a high and growing reputation in England. Her novels have won almost unanimous praise from the critics, along with some wry expressions of discomfiture. Her first book, *For All That I Found There* (1973), provoked a chorus of shudders at her pessimism and misanthropy. The review in the *Times Literary Supplement* was headed "Hopeless Cases" and asserted: "reading them consecutively one can only repeat, how near the precipice this time?" Francis King in the *Sunday Telegraph* characterized the "constant theme" of the stories as "destructiveness." Gabriele Annan in the *Listener* described it as "the unbearable," remarking that "she does not seem to like human beings at all." Reviewing Blackwood's latest novel in the light of her whole

Caroline Blackwood

career, Peter Kemp in the *Listener* began: "Wounds appall and fascinate Caroline Blackwood: her imagination can hardly tear itself away from them." Her material is anguish, dementia, and despair—injuries of all kinds, insanity, rape, murder, internecine marriages, a disastrous face-lift, suicidal isolation. Her distinctive power is to direct an unflinching gaze at the intolerable and convey it in elegant, witty, and dispassionate prose.

Caroline Blackwood was born 16 July 1931, the daughter of the Marquis and Marchioness of Dufferin and Ava, an Irish peerage. Her full name is Lady Caroline Hamilton-Temple-Blackwood. On her father's side she is descended from the dramatist Richard Brinsley Sheridan; on her mother's side she is a Guinness. She grew up in the beautiful, crumbling, leaky ancestral mansion, Clandeboye, in County Down, the basis for the white elephant of a stately home in *Great Granny Webster* (1977). Despite her adult memories of the tedium of Northern Ireland and her dismissal of the *Great Granny Webster* estate as "so emotionally and financially draining that, as was obvious to any outsider, it should long ago have been sold," she recalls Clandeboye as a magical place to be a child.

Blackwood's secondary education was at an English boarding school and, although she owns a house in Dublin, she has not lived in Northern Ireland since she was seventeen. She seems to share some of the detachment of the Anglo-Irish nobility which she describes in *Great Granny Webster*. The narrator's grandfather has been educated in England, has sent his children to English schools, reads only English newspapers, and looks forward perpetually to the visits from England of his more loyal and stoic friends. Trapped in Ireland he "lived in Dunmartin Hall as if it was an English island and he was a man who had been shipwrecked." Blackwood also writes of the province and its doomed, dotty inhabitants in *For All That I Found There*. This collection is organized under three headings, "Fiction," "Fact," and "Ulster." (Does she find the land too boring for fiction, too bizarre for fact?) The pieces in the Ulster section are autobiographical. They include an account of the young Caroline's wartime experience of being the only girl at a Protestant boys' school, where she therefore invited, along with the new boys and the neighboring Catholic children, the terroristic attentions of the school bully. In "Memories of Ulster" she recalls how the Northern Ireland of her youth seemed the archetypal place where nothing would ever happen; she wonders if the troubles in Northern Ireland are in part the inhabitants' rebellion against their "internment" in the province. Internment, in all its guises, was to be a potent theme in her later work.

In her early twenties Blackwood married painter Lucian Freud; his portrait of her, reproduced on the dust jacket of *The Stepdaughter* (1976), shows a girl of remarkable childlike beauty with steady gaze and a vulnerable mouth. This marriage ended in divorce. In her late twenties she married American composer Israel Citkovitz, with whom she lived in New York and had three daughters; this marriage also did not last. In 1970 poet Robert

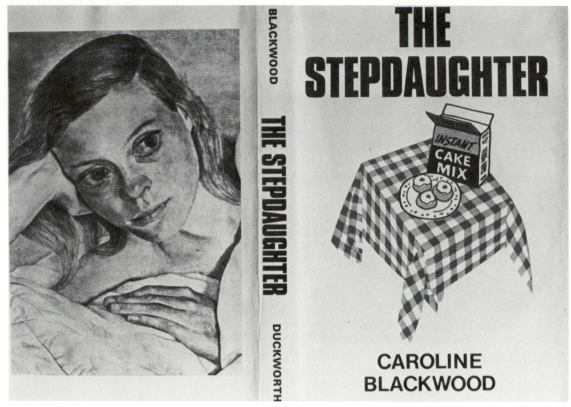

Dust jacket for Blackwood's first novel, illustrated with a 1952 portrait of her by Lucian Freud

Lowell, then married to his second wife Elizabeth Hardwick, arrived in England to take up a visiting academic post. He and Blackwood had met four years before in New York. In *The Dolphin* (1973) Lowell wrote of their love affair, his breakdown and hospital confinement, the movement of his relationship with Elizabeth Hardwick toward divorce. In one poem of this volume the beautiful Caroline, with her "Alice-in-Wonderland straight gold hair, / fair-featured, curve and bone," appears as a mermaid, only half human, symbolic of both love and art. The section entitled "Marriage" celebrates their union and the birth of their son, Robert Sheridan, in 1971. In the next year, after his divorce from Elizabeth Hardwick, Lowell and Blackwood were formally married. For the rest of his life Lowell continued to teach one semester a year at Harvard, so that their time was divided between the United States, Lowell's English country house, Milgate, in Kent, and their London home in Redcliffe Square, Earls Court.

Blackwood's marriage to Lowell coincides with an apparent development in creativity. She had previously published only journalism, some of which was collected in her first book, *For All That I Found There*. As well as the pieces on Ulster, there are "Fact" and "Fiction" sections, categories which are not sharply demarcated in Blackwood's imagination. The fiction shines with a documentary clarity, the facts are surreal in their extravagance. The stories are cool vignettes of human vanity, lovelessness, and cruelty; most of them deal, directly or obliquely, with the failures of marriage. One was selected by several reviewers as emblematic of the author: the account of a woman recovering from a face-lift operation which has left her unable to weep or to close her eyes. The fact section contains some hilarious, sardonic, rearguard appraisals of the beatniks, an evening with the women's movement, and a visit to a progressive school in Harlem. One piece seems centrally characteristic and is continually recalled in reviews of her later work: an agonizing account of a hospital "Burns Unit," in which one of Blackwood's daughters was a patient.

The Stepdaughter, her first novel, was undertaken at her publisher's suggestion; she doubts she would have written it otherwise. Like all her novels, *The Stepdaughter* can be seen as a modern variation on an established form. It is a miniature epistolary novel whose arena is, like Samuel Richardson's, the conscience of a threatened and isolated woman. But, unlike Richardson's Pamela and Clarissa,

Blackwood's K has lost her moral and social moorings. The novel is nudged toward modernism by its reference to Kafka's hero and by its brevity; it is 100 pages long. "People don't really read long books," says Blackwood, and her novel indicates that perhaps their attention span for other human beings is similarly limited. K has been abandoned by her husband in a luxurious penthouse apartment in New York with her small child, her obese and withdrawn stepdaughter, and her maltreated French au pair girl. She scarcely speaks to this suffering and neglected trio, but instead writes letters into the void to an imaginary confidant. In these K distills her resentment, jealousy and—most of all—self-hatred. She dislikes herself as much as she loathes her hideous and silent stepdaughter, symbol of her blighted marriage and her husband's escape.

K is interned: in her apartment, where she also imprisons the other inmates; in the straitened circumstances of her life; in her own foul and apparently immutable personality. But K is not completely the prisoner of her own nature. When she finally talks with her stepdaughter, Renata proves to have her own knowledge and perspective to contribute. In the last pages of the book K experiences a change of heart, but it is too late. Ignorant that her stepmother is now prepared to love her, Renata runs away into another freezing and dangerous world outside. The novel ends: "Will only write again if I have good news." Blackwood says that she cannot begin a story until she knows exactly how it will end; her characters certainly look like hostages of inevitability.

The Stepdaughter was extremely favorably received. It was hailed by the *Guardian* reviewer as a "small epic of modern neurosis" and was cited by several newspaper writers in the "Critics' Choice" columns at the end of the year. It was a finalist for the S.E. Arts Literature Prize and was awarded the 1976 David Higham Prize for the best first novel of the year.

Great Granny Webster, published in 1977, was Blackwood's next novel. A condensed family chronicle, it encapsulates the history of four generations in less than 100 pages. It ends with the funeral of the dour great-grandmother, whose energies have been devoted since 1894 to the merest and most joyless survival. The novel moves through a series of pictures rather than events: the great-granddaughter's miserable stay with the grim old lady whose life is restricted to her straight-backed chair and a daily ride in a closed car; ravishing and hedonistic Aunt Lavinia's account of her suicide

attempt; the grandparents in their rotting Irish mansion; the grandmother's insanity "in the prison of her marriage"; the macabre comedy of the funeral. The form suggests that detailed annals of the family would be redundant. These vignettes tell everything about the characters, frozen in their inheritance. Great-Granny sits for decades, rigid in her excruciating chair; she will remain fixed thus in the narrator's memory. Aunt Lavinia will successfully commit suicide when the amusements pall.

Dust jacket for Blackwood's "minutely crafted, intensely unsettling study of three emotionally isolated people, bound in a parody of family life"

The same meal is served for lunch and dinner by the helpless cooks in the uncontrollable stately home. The roof will leak forever. Everyone is imprisoned. Out of this bleakly deterministic vision, Blackwood creates an elegant and unforgettable comedy. *Great Granny Webster* received favorable response from the critics. A typical comment is that of the *Sunday Telegraph* reviewer: "Her world is small and her treatment witty but her vision is drawn from outer darkness." The novel was nominated for the 1977 Booker Prize For Fiction.

By 1977 Blackwood's marriage to Lowell had developed problems. He returned to New York and in September died of a heart attack in a taxicab. This loss was followed by other bereavements: the death of Blackwood's second husband, Israel Citkovitz, and the accidental death of her eldest daughter, who had become a drug addict.

Perhaps these tragic events contributed to the darkest and most violent of her fictions. Blackwood's third novel, *The Fate of Mary Rose* (1981), teases the reader by its resemblance to a conventional thriller. It is narrated by Rowan Anderson, a historian, whose unloved wife (Cressida) and daughter (Mary Rose) live in Beckham, a charming and historic village, which he occasionally visits. A child from the neighboring housing project is raped and murdered on a night of which Rowan—who can only get through weekends with his family by drinking continuously—remembers nothing. This mystery form encloses questions as disturbing as the identity of the murderer. Cressida, the obsessively pure wife, attempts to create in Beckham a perfect environment for Mary Rose, whose name recalls the sugary retarded innocence of the enchanted child-wife in J. M. Barrie's play of the same name. But the crime and the reactions to it reveal that the serpent also lives in this Eden of commuterland. The detached and rational historian proves to have little understanding of causality, the logic by which his unloved child is unlovable. Puzzled by her drabness, the father does not see that his own lack of interest produces it. He is working on a study of a woman engineer but makes no effort to empathize with the women in his own life. The rape inflames the antagonism between the sexes: the deranged Cressida is the most extreme example of women's punitive fear and hatred of men. Mary Rose is de-stroyed by her mother's paranoia and her father's indifference, as much a victim as the murdered girl. Finally Rowan, like the narrator of *The Stepdaughter*, experiences a change of heart that comes too late to save the child.

The novel was warmly received by the critics, who were equally impressed by its poise and its power to disturb. Shelley Cox wrote in *Library Journal*: "a minutely crafted, intensely unsettling study of three emotionally isolated people, bound in a parody of family life . . . Blackwood expertly plays on the tensions between surface normality and inner emptiness, skilfully exposing the underside of 'normal' family relations." Patricia Craig in the *Times Literary Supplement* observed: "Caroline Blackwood joins that small group of distinguished women novelists . . . whose task is to comment obliquely on the dangers and infirmities of contemporary life."

In addition to her novels, Blackwood has (with Anna Haycraft) compiled a cookbook called *Darling, You Shouldn't Have Gone to So Much Trouble* (1980). In rebellion against the traditional, elaborate cooking fashionable in the 1960s, the editors offer shortcut, sophisticated recipes confided to them by various friends and celebrities; the book is aimed at the busy career woman who wants to talk and drink as well as cook. After her three fictional exposures of family life, one reviewer expressed misgivings at the thought of Blackwood in the kitchen; another wrote a vehement purist denunciation of corner cutting and instant potatoes. The result was high sales and several reprintings.

Caroline Blackwood is presently working on what she calls an unorthodox biography of the Duchess of Windsor. With her children she shares a house made into separate flats in Redcliffe Square, London; she occupies the upper story, where she is able to work on her novels and other literary pursuits.

Dirk Bogarde
(28 March 1921-   )

Frank Crotzer
University of Delaware

BOOKS: *A Postillion Struck by Lightning* (London: Chatto & Windus, 1977; New York: Holt, Rinehart & Winston, 1977);
Snakes and Ladders (London: Chatto & Windus, 1978; New York: Holt, Rinehart & Winston, 1979);
A Gentle Occupation (London: Chatto & Windus, 1980; New York: Knopf, 1980);
Voices in the Garden (London: Chatto & Windus, 1981; New York: Knopf, 1981).

Talent and creative energy find many forms of expression, especially in the arts. Dirk Bogarde has demonstrated an abundance of both, first as an art student, then as an actor on the stage and in films. With some sixty film credits in a little over thirty years, Bogarde is one of Britain's most versatile and popular actors. His long and successful film career has not, however, exhausted his creative energy; his talents have found a new medium of expression, writing. Following his two autobiographical books, *A Postillion Struck by Lightning* (1977) and *Snakes and Ladders* (1978), Bogarde's first novel, *A Gentle Occupation*, was published in the spring of 1980. His second novel, *Voices in the Garden*, appeared in September 1981. Both novels have received mixed, but generally favorable, reviews that praise Bogarde's characterization.

Derek Jules Gaspard Ulric Niven Van den Bogaerde (the author's full name) was born on 28 March 1921 in the London borough of Hampstead. His father, Ulric Jules Van den Bogaerde, was, for many years, art editor of the London *Times*. Margaret Niven Van den Bogaerde, the author's mother, was an actress before her marriage, and her father, Forrest Niven, was an actor and a painter. The elder Van den Bogaerde, of Dutch and English descent, came from a family which Bogarde describes in *A Postillion Struck By Lightning* as "an ancient, Catholic family which traced its origins, I am told, to Anne of Cleves." He says the family was "gently noble at its start" and explains that the name Van den Bogaerde means "of the Orchards." Bogarde's mother was of Scottish and Spanish an-

Dirk Bogarde

cestry. A sister, Elizabeth, and a brother, Gareth, both younger, complete the family.

Bogarde's early life was spent in Hampstead and in the Sussex countryside. *A Postillion Struck By Lightning* describes young Bogarde's time at the family's cottage in Sussex as a happy, carefree existence spent wandering the countryside with his sister, fishing and playing games. The time in Hampstead, associated with schoolwork, was less happy. Bogarde excelled in creative subjects, such as drawing and crafts, and in botany; math, cricket, and football were less appealing and successful for the youngster. He says in *A Postillion Struck By Lightning*: "I hated all three. Mathematics, Cricket and, above all, Football. I found them totally illogical pursuits." In 1934 Bogarde was sent to Glasgow to live with an aunt and uncle and to attend a new, more rigorous school. He returned to Hampstead three years later and entered Chelsea Polytechnic School (now the Chelsea School of Art) as an art student. He was admitted six months before reaching the required admission age of seventeen because the superintendent felt he showed promise.

Dust jacket for Bogarde's first book, a widely acclaimed autobiography

Bogarde's father wanted him to attend art school and hoped that his son might one day succeed him at the *Times*, but the young Bogarde had decided long before that he wanted to be an actor. As a child he had acted out parts from the books he read, and he had designed original plays in which his sister and his friends could act with him. Bogarde's father discouraged his son's aspirations for an acting career, feeling that it was a career with no future; Bogarde's mother sympathized with his love of acting. During his summer break from Chelsea, Bogarde acted in local repertory companies in Sussex, where he performed well, often playing characters older than himself. He convinced his father to let him try acting in London for a year to see if he could support himself in his chosen vocation. Thus ended Bogarde's life as an art student.

Bogarde applied his artistic training to scene design and scene painting and was able to get jobs in that capacity at London theaters in which he eventually got acting roles. He performed at the Q Theatre and the Amersham Rep, among others, until his call-up for World War II. He gained valuable experience and proved to his father that he could earn a living as an actor. He also met three people who would be important in his later life: Peter Ustinov, a fellow novice actor who would become a close friend; Basil Dearden, who would later direct him in several films; and Anthony Forwood, who became his agent for a while, his friend, and his advisor on his acting career.

Bogarde's acting career was disrupted by World War II. In 1940, shortly after his nineteenth birthday, he entered the British army and served for five and a half years. He began as an enlisted man headed for the Royal Corps of Signals, but he became an officer and served as an aide de camp to two different commanding officers and in Photographic Intelligence Interpretation. His army experience led him from Europe to India to Indonesia. (The locations of service and experiences of Captain Ben Rooke in *A Gentle Occupation* closely parallel those of Bogarde, who was discharged with the rank of major.)

Bogarde admits that his acting career before the war was aided by the fact that many experienced actors had entered the service before him, a situation which made it easier for inexperienced actors to get roles. The situation after the war was reversed; the number of experienced actors seeking work far exceeded the number of roles available. Since the war had interrupted his acting career, Bogarde gave it up and accepted a post as a teacher at a preparatory school. Having to wait a year before his teaching job began, he returned to London and to the stage to support himself in the interim. His agent before the war, Tony Forwood, had himself become an actor, leaving Bogarde without an agent, and Bogarde found himself one of the multitude seeking parts.

Under these conditions, talent was not enough to be successful. Bogarde's return to the stage and his eventual movie stardom, as he describes them in *Snakes and Ladders*, seem like a series of fortunate accidents. In one case, he found himself in a theater full of aspiring actors, all trying for several parts in a

Dust jacket for Bogarde's first novel, based on his army experiences during World War II

one-act children's play. Bogarde got the lead part in the play when the director literally tripped over his feet while walking up and down the aisles. In another instance he was the fortunate victim of mistaken identity. When he went to audition for a part in a BBC production, a woman casting a play in the same building thought he was there to read for her play and did not discover her mistake until after Bogarde had read the part. He left the audition in embarrassment, but shortly afterward learned that he had gotten the role.

Power Without Glory opened on 25 February 1947 at the New Lindsay Theatre with Bogarde in the role of Cliff. The play was a great success, and Bogarde won good reviews. Noel Coward attended the production and spoke to the cast afterward; his final admonition was "and never, ever, go near the cinema." As *Power Without Glory* continued its successful run, director Ian Dalrymple saw Bogarde perform and offered him a part in *Esther Waters*. Bogarde was originally signed for a supporting role

in the film, but got the male lead when Stewart Granger withdrew. *Power Without Glory* had convinced Bogarde again that he was an actor, and he resigned his teaching post before ever assuming it. After *Esther Waters*, he signed a seven-year contract with Rank, and despite Noel Coward's advice, became a film actor.

Bogarde was to be steadily employed for the next few years; by the end of 1953 he had done fifteen films in which he played a variety of roles. He also became popular and was listed among the top ten British box-office favorites. In 1954 two films appeared which were important for Bogarde's career for different reasons. In the first, a light comedy called *Doctor in the House*, he portrayed a young intern, Dr. Simon Sparrow—a role he repeated in three sequels: *Doctor at Sea* (1956), *Doctor at Large* (1957), and *Doctor in Distress* (1963). The other important film was *The Sleeping Tiger*, in which Bogarde acted for the first time under the direction of Joseph Losey. Losey was to direct him later in one of his best-known and most highly acclaimed roles, as Barrett in *The Servant*, whose screenplay, based on a Robin Maugham novella, was written by Harold Pinter. Losey, whom Bogarde respected highly because he "stretched his resources," also directed him in *King and Country*, *Modesty Blaise*, and *Accident*.

After fourteen years with the Rank organization, Bogarde obtained a release from his contract in 1961. The years with Rank had brought him steady work, popularity, and financial security. He had been able to develop his skills as an actor, but he desired more challenging roles than those which Rank was supplying. Among the roles that Bogarde chose in the 1960s were those of Franz Liszt in *Song Without End* and Melville Farr in *Victim*. To play Liszt, he spent more than 100 hours learning to finger the piano music (which was played by Jorge Bolet). In *Victim*, Bogarde played a successful barrister with repressed homosexual desires who lays his career and his marriage on the line to stop a pair of blackmailers preying on homosexuals. The film pointed out the damaging effects of the law which made homosexuality a crime, a law which was referred to as "the blackmailer's charter." This controversial film was rated X in Britain and was confined to art theaters in the United States. Bogarde received critical praise not only for his performance in the film, but also for his courage in taking the part.

In 1963 Bogarde starred with Judy Garland in *I Could Go On Singing*. He had met Garland a couple of years before the film, and a close friendship had developed. In *Snakes and Ladders* Bogarde says: "If the film was a critical success, it was a public disaster, crumbling away like a piece of old lace." He suggests that the title, which was changed from "The Lonely Stage" during production, may have led the audience to expect "a straight Garland musical" and that Garland fans may have been upset by her playing a character "so close to the truth of herself." (The film deals with the types of problems that plagued Garland's career.)

The 1970s brought two important films, among others, for Bogarde. The first was *Death in Venice*, directed by Luchino Visconti, who had also directed him in *The Damned*. He played Von Aschenbach in Visconti's version of the Thomas Mann classic. Both the role and the director were demanding, and Bogarde spent many hours in uncomfortable makeup. The other film was *The Night Porter*, which remains one of his best-known films.

Bogarde has won numerous awards in his career, including being named Best Actor by the British Motion Picture Academy of Arts and Sciences on two occasions, for *The Servant* in 1964, and for *Darling* in 1965. His role in *The Servant* also led him to finish second to his longtime friend Rex Harrison in the balloting for the New York Film Critic's Award. In addition to his varied film roles, Bogarde has also continued to appear on the stage. Among his roles have been Orpheus in *Point of Departure* and Alberto in *Summertime*. He rarely appears on British television, but has made several appearances on American television, including a performance in a 1966 NBC production of Noel Coward's *Blithe Spirit*.

Bogarde has always preferred a quiet, private offstage life to the glamorous, public lives of some actors. He has resided primarily in country homes; for the past twelve years he has lived in a seventeenth-century French farmhouse near Nice. One of his favorite hobbies is gardening; he has twelve acres of gardens and olive groves and produces his own olive oil. He still makes films occasionally, but he is highly selective of his roles, telling *New York Times* interviewer Susan Heller Anderson, "I'm only interested now in directors." Bogarde has never been married.

Bogarde's interest in writing dates back to his childhood when he wrote plays and skits. He has also written poetry much of his life. Two of his poems, based on his experiences in the army, were published during the war: "Man in the Bush" in the *Times Literary Supplement* in 1941, and "Steel Cathedrals" in *Poetry Review* in 1943. These poems are also anthologized in *The Terrible Rain*, a collection of war poems edited by Brian Gardner.

Bogarde's first two books are autobiographies. *A Postillion Struck By Lightning* covers the period from his childhood to his call-up for World War II. *Snakes and Ladders* begins with an account of some of his military experiences and extends through the filming of *Death in Venice* in 1971. Both books proceed in a chronological order, with flashbacks or recollections interspersed throughout. They are the candid memories and reflections of a man who has led a life of interesting and varied experiences both on and off the stage or motion picture set. Bogarde is currently working on a third volume to bring his autobiography up to the present, as well as another book on his childhood. His autobiographies do not tell much about his World War II experiences; instead, he chose to focus on the war in his first novel. Explaining this decision in a *New York Times* interview, he says: "Second-hand wars are a bore. But the novel is about my war—I was there."

Captain Ben Rooke is there in *A Gentle Occupation*. "There" is a fictitious island in the Dutch colonies of the Far East. The British are serving in a police or caretaker capacity on the island while its inhabitants recover from the recent Japanese occupation and while the Dutch officials try to reorganize. Rooke is sent to the island from India, to serve until he is discharged from the army. The British officers and the Dutch civilians are busy trying to restore order and civilization to the major city of the island while in the jungle Marxist nationalist guerillas plan attacks against the British, who are to them the symbols and Dutch proxies of European imperialism.

The focus of the novel, however, is the British officers and the civilians involved with them. Bogarde shows characters caught in a changing world and in difficult, unfamiliar circumstances, with particular attention to how such conditions affect human relationships. The British commander, General Cutts, is involved with Miss Foto, a woman with a dubious background. Another officer, Major Pullen, is in love with a Dutch woman whose husband is missing in action at the beginning of the novel, but is found alive and is returned home physically and mentally injured near the end of it. Rooke falls in love with a half-Dutch, half-Indonesian girl who does not wish to return to England with him for fear of bigotry against her mixed blood. These and other relationships must endure the confusion and uncertainties of the situation.

The novel deals with many themes: manhood, moral values, politics, the atrocities of war, and the class system. Characterization is probably the strongest aspect of Bogarde's writing in this novel, owing to his background in drama. Many of the characters are stereotypes, but most of them have individuality as well. General Cutts, for instance, is the typical career army officer, but Bogarde provides him with problems and feelings, which makes him more than a stock character. This blend of the character type with individual traits makes the characters real and compelling.

The plots and subplots of the novel fit together, but as Robert Kiely observes in the *New York Times Book Review*, Bogarde fails "to provide not merely a conventional hero but a single consciousness of depth or sensitivity through which events are perceived and interpreted." Rooke sometimes performs this function, but he is not present in every scene; scenes switch from one set of characters to another, as in a movie, and sometimes the transitions are not smooth. Bogarde also includes flashbacks, usually involving Rooke, much like those in his autobiographies. The transitions between these flashbacks and the present of the novel are also rough on occasion.

Despite technical flaws, Bogarde shows several strengths as a novelist. His dialogue is usually good and natural, and his senses of scene, action, plot, and characterization are impressive. His training as an actor enables him to get inside his characters and to express a broad range of human emotions. He is also able to blend well the serious with the comic. All of these strengths are apparent in his second novel, *Voices in the Garden*.

Bogarde describes *Voices in the Garden* as "a story about today, set here in France, and about the way we all pretend a great part of our lives in order to 'get through.'" He adds that it "will show that however old we may become, we're not born with wrinkles and thinning hair." These ideas are developed in the novel as a disparate group of people are brought together at the villa of Sir Charles and Lady "Cuckoo" Peverill in southern France. Practically all the characters are pretending in one way or another. Sir Charles, for instance, pretends to smoke cigarettes, even brushing imaginary ashes from his trousers and insisting that he must cut down on his smoking. Lady Peverill plays the socialite and hostess to hide the frustrations of her life and, as is revealed at the end of the novel, the fact that she is dying of leukemia. Leni Minx, the female half of the young couple who enter the Peverills' life, creates an entire personality and history to hide her true identity as Luise von Lamsfeld, a German countess. Umberto Grottorosso, the Italian film director who serves as a quasi-villain in the novel,

struggles to maintain a "macho" image to mask his latent homosexuality and his sadistic tendencies.

The novel opens with the return of Lady Peverill from England, where she has learned of her terminal disease. She attempts suicide by filling her pockets with stones and wading into the sea, but is rescued by Marcus Pollock, the nineteen-year-old son of broken-down English actors, who is on a holiday and is unknowingly trespassing on the Peverills' private beach. Marcus pretends along with Lady Peverill that she has simply slipped into the water, and as thanks for rescuing her he is invited to stay at the villa. He is joined shortly by his girl friend, Leni, and a conflict develops when Leni sees that Marcus is becoming accustomed to the luxury that she is fighting to escape.

The other major conflict for Marcus centers on his amazing resemblance to L'Aiglon, the son of Napoleon Bonaparte. L'Aiglon is Sir Charles's subject of expertise as a historian and the subject of Grottorosso's latest film. Grottorosso, the nephew of the Peverills' friend, Minerva, is on his way to the villa to seek technical advice from Sir Charles. Marcus's resemblance to L'Aiglon is noticed at once by Sir Charles and later by Grottorosso, who is unhappy with the young man he is already training for the part. The producer invites Marcus to his yacht to discuss a part as a double for his star, but in the meantime, Grottorosso intentionally wounds his star in their fencing practice so that he can have Marcus as his L'Aiglon. Marcus, however, sees Grottorosso for what he is and declines the part, telling Grottorosso what a sick person he is.

The novel ends with the arrival of Marcus's "uncle" Desmond (actually a friend of Marcus's mother), who is also his employer. Marcus is to return to England and take over the business from Desmond, who is going to marry and retire. Before the group at the villa is separated, however, some of the characters' pretenses are cast off. Leni finally admits her true identity to Marcus, and Lady Peverill learns to accept her impending death.

This theme of pretending in *Voices in the Garden* challenges Bogarde's greatest strength as a novelist: his characterizations. In this novel Bogarde must create not only his actual characters, but also the characters that they create for themselves. He achieves an interesting blend of reality and fantasy in creating these double characters. This reliance by Bogarde on his ability to characterize holds the reader to *Voices in the Garden*.

The point can be strongly made that Bogarde's career as an actor has had important effects on his novels. The structure of both novels is very much like that of a film, with close attention to the locus of the action, the division of action into scenes, and the emphasis on character and dialogue. In a more general sense, however, Bogarde's novel writing is a natural progression from his acting career. As an examination of his career in film shows, and as he has stated in his autobiographical writings, Bogarde has sought and chosen, as his career progressed, roles and directors to challenge his creativity. He has sought opportunities not to just "play" roles or characters, but to create them. In his novels, Bogarde is finding an even more challenging situation: he is not only working in a new medium, but he is having to create many characters, not just one.

Dirk Bogarde began his career as a novelist late in life, but this fact allows him to draw on his wealth of experiences. His novels will have to be of high quality and quantity to approach the achievements of his brilliant career as an actor. His writing may well be overshadowed by his acting, but judging from the creative energy, dedication, and hard work that he has put into his film and stage careers, it is likely that he will produce some fine novels.

Malcolm Bradbury

(7 September 1932-   )

Melvin J. Friedman
University of Wisconsin–Milwaukee

SELECTED BOOKS: *Eating People Is Wrong* (London: Secker & Warburg, 1959; New York: Knopf, 1960);

All Dressed Up and Nowhere to Go (London: Max Parrish, 1962);

Evelyn Waugh (Edinburgh: Oliver & Boyd, 1964);

Stepping Westward (London: Secker & Warburg, 1965; Boston: Houghton Mifflin, 1966);

Two Poets, by Bradbury and Allan Rodway (Nottingham: Byron Press, 1966);

What Is a Novel? (London: Edward Arnold, 1969);

The Social Context of Modern English Literature (Oxford: Blackwell, 1971; New York: Schocken Books, 1971);

Possibilities: Essays on the State of the Novel (London & New York: Oxford University Press, 1973);

The History Man (London: Secker & Warburg, 1975; Boston: Houghton Mifflin, 1976);

Who Do You Think You Are? Stories and Parodies (London: Secker & Warburg, 1976).

Malcolm Bradbury is part of a new breed of British academic who is as seriously involved in novel writing as he is in literary criticism and theory. His university teaching seems to reinforce his writing (both fictional and critical) at every turn; he never strays far from campus life in his fiction—his three novels and many of his stories have academic settings—and his criticism appears securely linked to his role as classroom lecturer. As much at ease abroad as he is in his native England, he negotiates the literary and cultural terrain of America and France with the enviable assurance of the insider. This cosmopolitanism is as evident in his novels as in his nonfiction. Bradbury is a direct literary descendant of Tobias Smollett, Henry Fielding, and Laurence Sterne in the eighteenth century; of Jane Austen in the nineteenth; of Evelyn Waugh and E. M. Forster in the modernist period; and of Kingsley Amis, Angus Wilson, Iris Murdoch, and Muriel Spark among older contemporaries. And he is never far from the expatriate sensibilities of Henry James and Vladimir Nabokov.

Malcolm Stanley Bradbury, the son of Arthur and Doris Ethel Marshall Bradbury, was born in Sheffield, England, and educated at West Bridgford Grammar School in Nottingham—D. H. Lawrence country. Although Lawrence seems not to have had an appreciable influence on Bradbury's work, his name appears frequently in Bradbury's fiction and criticism. Thus the principal characters of Bradbury's latest novel, *The History Man* (1975), Howard and Barbara Kirk, are referred to in their graduate school days as "the Lawrence and Frieda of backstreet Leeds." (Bradbury seems also proud of the fact that his earliest stories were published in the *Nottinghamshire Guardian* where Lawrence's first story also appeared.) This working-class Midlands background, with an occasional nod to Yorkshire, is a dominant presence in his work. His characters usually rise above humble origins by taking First Class Honours degrees and/or by writing celebrated books, then settle into university appointments.

Bradbury took his degrees at a variety of redbrick universities, Leicester, London, and Manchester (where he earned his Ph.D. with a thesis entitled "American Literary Expatriates in Europe: 1815 to 1950"). Following the completion of his M.A. in English literature at Queen Mary College, University of London, he spent a year at Indiana University (1955-1956) on an English Speaking Union Graduate Teaching Fellowship. He managed a year at Yale on a British Association of American Studies Junior Fellowship (1958-1959) and did postdoctoral study at Harvard on an American Council of Learned Societies Fellowship (1965-1966). Bradbury was a brilliant student whose First Class Honours degree set the pace for his graduate and teaching career; his study in England, carried out at a remove from Oxford and Cambridge, was confined to redbrick universities; he spent three extended periods on prestigious American campuses, during his pre- and postdoctoral years. He speaks of these matters in an after-

Malcolm Bradbury

word he wrote for a 1978 republication of his first novel, *Eating People Is Wrong* (1959):

> When I left Leicester, I did not, in fact, go into management, or schoolteaching; nor did I go into writing, though I almost went into copywriting. I gained a fortunate first, was offered a research scholarship, and spent much of the rest of the 'fifties as an habitual post-graduate student, working in the British Museum, and then, a bit later, in the static electricity of the libraries of the United States—a very characteristic career, it now seems, since this was the great era of the fellowship and the graduate assistantship and the English voyage in search of American redemption.

Bradbury's teaching career took him to Hull for two years (1959-1961) and Birmingham for four (1961-1965) before he settled permanently at the University of East Anglia—where he ascended the academic ladder with astonishing rapidity, being named Professor of American Studies in 1970 at the youthful age (by British standards) of thirty-eight. During his years at East Anglia he has managed more than his share of university stints elsewhere: visiting professorships at Zurich and the University of California, Davis; a visiting fellowship to All Souls College, Oxford; British Council- and USIS-sponsored lectureships all over Europe and America. Bradbury's movements across the international academic scene make him one of the best traveled literature professors of his generation.

He started his writing career with a novel, *Eating People Is Wrong*, published in 1959. He speaks in the 1978 afterword of this time as being "a rather hectic and decisive point in my life; the book, my first novel, came out, I married, and I took up my first university teaching post, all in the space of a few days." Reviewers, in their haste to place the book in a suitable tradition, thought of Kingsley Amis's *Lucky Jim* (1954) and other literary offspring of the 1950s—dramatically christened "The Angry Decade" by Kenneth Allsop the year before *Eating People Is Wrong* appeared. Bradbury, who has always been uneasy about false labeling by critics ("reviewers' convenience"), insists in the same afterword that he wrote the novel "from the innocent, fascinated standpoint of the student, in fact the first-generation student, for whom universities were both a novelty and a social opportunity." Given this information, the character he would seem more nearly to resemble in the novel is the rough-hewn, bumbling, ingenuous student Louis Bates, rather than the professor Stuart Treece. Although, looking back, Bradbury is aware of the irony that he later became a literature professor like Treece, the similarities end at that point. The bachelor Treece, with his awkward flirtations and his "far from Lawrentian vision," little resembles the self-assured Malcolm Bradbury who has settled into a career as professor-novelist-literary critic, has been married to the same woman for twenty-three years, and is the father of two sons. One can say also that Treece is neither a Jim Dixon nor a Professor Welch; Amis's characters do not share with Treece that abiding concern with "what the right things were." The resemblances, then, with *Lucky Jim* are largely a matter of surfaces and textures.

Eating People Is Wrong is set in "a small university in the provinces." "The good and liberal" Treece heads an undistinguished English department; his liberalism seems to force on him an unending series of responsibilities toward his junior colleagues and his students. Foreign students' parties seem especially burdensome yet are an essential aspect of the professorial role he has sharply defined for himself. Treece is clearly the Jamesian central intelligence, and he seems gently to coerce the action and to offer it its compositional center. He is a Lambert Strether under quite different circumstances and has as his Maria Gostrey a student named Emma Fielding—whom he manages, awkwardly and unskillfully, to take to bed. (Henry James would not have permitted such intimacies, but might have been amused at the way Treece goes about his "seduction.")

Treece, who generally arranges and even orchestrates things, finds himself at one point the unwilling host of a novelist, Carey Willoughby, who had once used an unflattering anecdote about Treece in one of his novels. Willoughby proves to have all the panache and irreverence of the "angry young men" of the 1950s. Critics place him in the company of Kingsley Amis and John Wain, but Willoughby brashly asserts "that he had got on to it all first, and the others were just taking advantage." His behavior during "Poetry Weekend," which he was expected to grace with his presence, is characterized by his delivering a lecture elaborately cribbed from Edmund Wilson's *The Wound and the Bow*; by his insulting his hosts, especially Treece, at every turn; and by his stealing a complete Proust from a local bookshop. Bradbury, publishing his novel at the end of the "angry decade," was not writing another *Lucky Jim* (1954) or *Hurry on Down* (1953), but was signaling the end of the kind of hero

celebrated by Amis and Wain in their pages. Willoughby is a Jim Dixon or a Charles Lumley in caricatured recipe; his boorishness and lack of caring far exceed theirs.

Eating People Is Wrong, after engaging in broad comedy, ends on a sour note—the attempted suicide of Louis Bates which results in his being placed in a mental hospital. Treece and Emma conclude the novel by discussing their responsibilities. Treece has the final say: "Guilty's all you can feel. I suppose all you can say for us is, at least we can feel guilty."

Bradbury, in the 1978 afterword, describes the book as being "a sad comedy, perhaps even a tragicomedy." He also speaks of the "two poles" open to the novelist: "one of experimental self-questioning, the other of a realistic reporting of the social and material world." He admits that in *Eating People Is Wrong* he opted for the second, as did most of his English contemporaries in the years following the end of World War II. His first novel is part of that reaction against the generation of James Joyce,

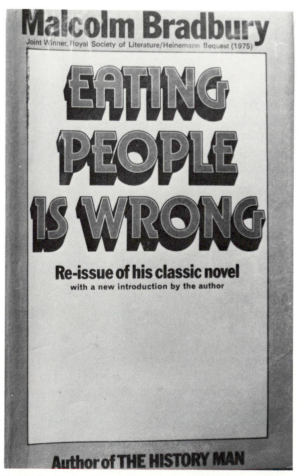

Dust jacket for Bradbury's first novel, which he later called "a sad comedy, perhaps even a tragicomedy"

Marcel Proust, and Virginia Woolf which Rubin Rabinovitz (without mentioning Bradbury) characterizes in his book *The Reaction Against Experiment in the English Novel, 1950-1960* (1967). Bradbury seems to find storytelling very congenial: quite the opposite of the distaste expressed by Flaubert in a famous letter to Louise Colet: "I have to write a narrative; and that is something I find very tiresome."

Stepping Westward (1965) is no more experimental than *Eating People Is Wrong* and seems to advance Bradbury's penchant for "realistic reporting." Critic Martin Green sees it as part of "a distinct genre of modern British fiction" in which "the central character, who represents the novelist, comes to the U.S.A., responds reluctantly to its various challenges and invitations, gradually makes up his mind for it as opposed to England, but (usually) returns home nevertheless, feeling unable to meet those challenges adequately."

The central character in *Stepping Westward* is the British novelist James Walker, who is invited to spend a year as a Creative Writing Fellow at Benedict Arnold University, located in the town of Party which "lies in the American heartland somewhere near the point where the various wests collide— where the middle west meets the far west and the south-west the north-west." Walker has the advance billing of being an "Angry Young Man," but he resembles the type far less than does Carey Willoughby. "But far from seeming, now, angry, Walker looked excessively phlegmatic," is the reaction of his host, Bernard Froelich, on first meeting him.

After a prologue, which sets the scene of Benedict Arnold University with all its academic chicanery, we abruptly move to the humble Nottingham "top-floor flat" Walker shares with his wife and daughter. Across the way from where Walker teaches part-time "was the now emptied University College where Lawrence had gone; he could see it from the window as he debated on the disease-imagery of *Women in Love*." Leaving wife and daughter behind, Walker willingly exchanges D. H. Lawrence country for the groves of American academe. (Bradbury did something of the same early in his career and repeated the process in a series of later transatlantic academic jaunts.) The Atlantic crossing and a brief stay in New York occupy most of book one. Aboard ship Walker meets two passengers who return to haunt the later narrative: Julie Snowflake, a Hillesley college student, and Dr. Jochum, an emigre professor who lost his job at Hillesley only to turn up at Benedict Arnold.

(Jochum bears a certain similarity to Vladimir Nabokov who, incidentally, taught at Wellesley College shortly after he arrived in America. Julie Snowflake once likens Jochum to the main character in Nabokov's 1957 novel *Pnin*, and when Julie and Walker go on an elaborate trek to California and Mexico late in the novel, they seem to be reproducing something of the extravagant journey of Humbert Humbert and Lolita.)

Walker arrives at Benedict Arnold, with Bernard Froelich waiting for him at the railroad depot, at the beginning of book two. The university is described to him as being "slightly paradoxical in that it's both a private and a state university." Bradbury may have mingled here his memories of Yale and Indiana. The novel at this point joins the extensive literature devoted to academic life, to which Bradbury contributed earlier with *Eating People Is Wrong* and later with *The History Man* and some of the stories in *Who Do You Think You Are?* (1976). The important difference is that *Stepping Westward* concerns an American rather than a British university, and the satire seems broader and perhaps more outrageous than in his academic fiction set in England. Stuart Treece, Louis Bates, and Emma Fielding arouse our compassion; Bernard Froelich and his colleagues at Benedict Arnold are an unseemly, self-aggrandizing group who prove to be uniformly distasteful. Walker is no more than a pawn in Froelich's ambitious schemes and is little more than a showpiece, a disappointingly inelegant and shabby one at that, for the remainder of the faculty and university administration. Unlike Carey Willoughby, Walker is a victim rather than a victimizer. He suffers through the tedium, boorishness, and nastiness of the American academic scene for several months; takes the *Lolita*-like western trip with Julie Snowflake; and returns six months earlier than expected to his wife and daughter in Nottingham. The epilogue intentionally mirrors the prologue, with subtle and ironic differences. Froelich has now been elevated to the chairmanship of the English department and urges, in a complete volte-face, that the writing fellowship funds, which had been responsible for Walker's brief flirtation with the American academic scene, be used to launch a literary quarterly. Froelich accounts to himself for Walker's failure and his own success in these terms: "Walker was subjective pessimism and he was objective history, a turning wheel. . . . he had tried to be mentor, to show Walker that to live in the ethically flabby belief that the world is good and innocent and that all men can be assimilated and loved without hurt was wrong, that deeper connections

A

18.

TWO _____

Three days later, on the Monday morning, Howard Kirk wakes up in an
unhappy temper. Surfacing out of unconsciousness and into being, he finds
the space in the bed beside him empty; Barbara is already up. He groans,
and smoothes his hair down, and looks out of the window: a heavy rain is
pouring down, washing dreariness over the damaged houses. He gets out of
bed and pads along the landing to the bathroom, to sculpt round the elegance
of his Zapata moustache. He plugs his razor into the two little holes
beneath the bleak round globe of the light. His face comes up in the mirror;
in the cool urban sheen of morning he inspects the Condition of Man. It is
unpromising; in the streaky glass, finger-marked by children, k the beaky
face, all manifest discontent, wearing its moustache like a glower, stares
back at him. He touches and presses the flesh into position and rides the
razor over it. A sense of irritated unfulfillment runs through him and he
recalls that last night he and Barbara had not made love. A depression always
on the edge of his mind settles deeper. `Beside the bathroom window, the rain
washes over the uneven guttering and thumps down onto the gaunt glass of
the Victorian conservatory beneath; no flowers grow there, and it is d deposit
for children's toys. The razor buzzes and downstairs the children yamp in

The first and eighth drafts of a segment from The History Man

H

III

In the morning Howard woke up in green and white striped pyjamas
to unmitigated daylight, a busy teaching ppogramme, and the detritus
of his party. He inspected the contents of his head; a residue
of pleasure, guilt and migraine was suspended there from last night.
He opened his eyes and inspected the bed; it was his own. He
turned and inspected his companion: it was Barbara. He opened his
eyes wide and inspected the room; it was smoke-filled, ashy, abrasive, with dirtied plates on the chairs, wine glasses on the window-
sill, ashtrays littering the floor, a smaller, nastier room than the
one he recalled sitting in last night, squatting on the floor, while
his head grew vivid with consciousness. The translucent things had
turned solid again and sat squatly in their thinginess. An old
velvet dress hanging askew behind the door, cracked apart by its
open long zip. The scratched, boughmade chest of drawers, with one
handle missing and two that needed mending. Rain pattered outside.
He turned his head and inspected the Habitat alarm clock on the side
table: iixs the time, it said, was VII to VIII.

had to be made." Froelich's cynicism *appears* to be triumphant.

In the decade following the publication of *Stepping Westward*, Bradbury went on to establish himself as one of England's most influential critics of the novel. His ambitious studies include *The Social Context of Modern English Literature* (1971) and *Possibilities: Essays on the State of the Novel* (1973). The fifth section of *Possibilities*, "Towards a Poetics of the Novel," offers what is perhaps Bradbury's most incisive statement about the alternatives available to the critic of fiction. He opposes what he calls the "neo-symbolist view" to the "realistic view" and asks for "a more inclusive typology." He ends with these reasoned and sober words:

> Thus, while we must regard novels as verbal constructs, which they inescapably are, we must see what is constructed not alone as a self-sustaining entity but a species of persuasion—the writer handling material for the reader to engage him properly in the world of this once-and-for-all work. And one point needs firm restatement: only if we have some such theory of structure, however empirical, are we likely to move near to a meaningful descriptive poetics of the novel.

All of Bradbury's writing on the novel—and there is a great deal of it—has a strong modernist ring. The basic texts for his critical theories are Henry James's prefaces, E. M. Forster's *Aspects of the Novel* (1927), E. K. Brown's *Rhythm in the Novel* (1950) and, later on, Ian Watt's *The Rise of the Novel* (1957), the second edition of Bernard Bergonzi's *The Situation of the Novel* (a 1979 study which briefly mentions Bradbury's fiction), and David Lodge's *Language of Fiction* (1966) and *The Novelist at the Crossroads* (a 1971 work which gently but firmly takes to task certain of Bradbury's theories of the novel). Although he acknowledges postmodernism, in both criticism and literature, he seems uncomfortable with its deconstructions and disruptions. The orderliness of modernism and the tidiness of its critics are very much to his liking. It is no accident, then, that among the many volumes Bradbury has edited in recent years is *Modernism: 1890-1930* (1976). Put together with the help of his colleague at East Anglia, James McFarlane, this massive contribution to the series Pelican Guides to European Literature is surely the most comprehensive treatment of the modernist period. The opening essay, "The Name and Nature of Modernism," which Bradbury coauthored with McFarlane, is a model of clarity and critical elegance. There are few brief treatments of the modern novel quite as fine as "The Introverted Novel," which Bradbury co-authored with another East Anglia colleague, John Fletcher. *Modernism*, in sum, represents one of the finest recent examples of literary collaboration.

By the time Bradbury had established himself as a novelist and critic, he was ready to detour in other directions. He comments on these alternatives in his intriguing monograph, *What Is a Novel?* (1969): "The modern novelist is probably therefore likely to feel the contemporary limitations as well as the advantages of his form, as a medium of expression, as an instrument for influence, and as a medium of success. In England, at least, he may find his career a shaky one. So he may well not write novels alone, but also television scripts and film scenarios, or poems and plays." This autobiographical insertion helps account for Bradbury's flirtations with radio, television, and the theater, usually in collaboration with someone else, like his wife Elizabeth, his friend David Lodge, or his colleague Christopher Bigsby. He even turned poet, in a collaborative gesture with Allan Rodway, to produce *Two Poets* (1966). His poetry is distinctive and suggestive; he writes, for example, a kind of ars poetica in "Toads and Gardens" (whose title and manner seem indebted to Marianne Moore), which begins with this stanza:

> Poems are a comment on experience
> And a comment on writing
> Grow like young girls who
> Running through the clear air, delighting

Indeed several of his poems have to do with the experience of writing.

The History Man, Bradbury's third novel, won the Heinemann/Royal Society of Literature Award. The ten-year "layoff" from novel writing seems to have helped sharpen the tools of his craft and alerted him, in an almost modernist way, to the demands of technique. In discussing what was then a novel-in-progress, he commented in *Contemporary Novelists*: "As for what I am now doing, I find myself increasingly obsessed with formal problems and, linked with that, a far greater ironic distance from my characters and any worlds I can give them to inhabit."

The History Man was cordially received on both sides of the Atlantic. Typical of the response was George Steiner's review in *The New Yorker*, which likened the novel to Henry James: "It has the same density of convention, the same alertness to the flick of intonation." Steiner rightly invokes at one point *The Awkward Age* (1899), James's most dialogue-ridden novel. *The History Man* thrives on dialogue; entire chapters are scenically rendered, almost like playlets (especially chapter seven). Another sign of the dramatic is the insistent use of the present tense.

Bradbury's techniques are admirably suited to this novel which chronicles a brief period in the lives of Howard and Barbara Kirk, who are "true citizens of the present." The setting is the University of Watermouth; the Kirks had moved there from Leeds in 1967 and are now, in 1972, firmly established as "a very well-known couple." The description of Watermouth's campus as being "massive, one of those dominant modern environments of multifunctionality that modern man creates" makes one think of Bradbury's own University of East Anglia—situated outside of Norwich on a vast plain dominated by multitiered white concrete buildings. *The History Man* has less plot, more pattern and design than the two earlier novels. A sense of history or "plot of history" seems to be a dominant structural presence. Bradbury comments on it in his contribution to *The Contemporary English Novel*: "The text is hard, presented in long paragraph blocks which immerse the agents and their speech."

The History Man starts with a party given by the Kirks at the beginning of the autumn term and ends with another one given by them at the end of the autumn term. In between is what George Steiner characterizes as "the autonomous spiralling of language." "The game of being is the game of words," Steiner explains. The academic society depicted by Bradbury is one of surfaces, of casual encounters, of emotionless liaisons. The seduction scenes never ring quite true as they tend to disappear in a flow of words. Anger, love, assertions of friendship, attempts at suicide—all get lost in verbal formulas. Henry James, Karl Marx, and William Blake are invoked at the most tender and delicate of moments, when their presences seem least appropriate. Tragedy threatens to break through, but language never permits it to. This is probably part of what Bradbury meant when he spoke in *Contemporary Novelists* of attaining "a far greater ironic distance from my characters" in *The History Man*.

Although *The History Man* is set on a university campus, it is not simply an academic novel in the way that *Eating People Is Wrong* and *Stepping Westward* are; it is a more anxious and skillfully textured work. Comedy, although present, does not come as easily, with the same broad strokes, as in Bradbury's first two novels; the author in fact has suggested that Goya stands hauntingly in the background of

The History Man. The supporting cast of characters, who attend the Kirks' parties and who engage in amorous and verbal exchanges with them, are a more interesting lot than those who surround

Malcolm Bradbury, 1975

Stuart Treece and James Walker. Flora Beniform, one of Howard's current lovers, who makes a habit of going to bed with men who have troubled marriages, seems to resemble Treece's sensual colleague, Viola Masefield, but Flora is more intriguingly fleshed out and humanized. Miss Callendar, the recently hired "Renaissance man" in the English department, who plays verbal games with Howard until he finds his way to her bed, is also worth caring about if only for her cleverness.

Bradbury gathered together many of his shorter pieces in *Who Do You Think You Are?*; the collection contains seven stories and eight parodies. Bradbury is really not at his best in the shorter form. Two of the stories reintroduce characters from the novels: Flora Beniform appears in the title story, and Stuart Treece and Louis Bates are the principal characters in "The Adult Education Class." A third story, "Composition," offers some oblique reminders of *Stepping Westward*. The parodies, which in their choice of subjects range across contemporary

English and American fiction, are all capably managed, with those devoted to Angus Wilson, Muriel Spark, and J. D. Salinger being especially memorable. Yet as a *pasticheur* he clearly is neither a Proust nor a Joyce.

With Bradbury in mid-career, not yet having reached his fiftieth birthday, it is difficult to make anything more than a tentative assessment. His eventual place in literary history should not be far removed from that of David Lodge, another of the new breed of professor-critic-novelist. The two have had their friendly quarrels in attempting to assert a poetics of the novel, but respect for the other's position is always in evidence. Bradbury's *Possibilities*, in fact, is dedicated in part "to my friend David Lodge," and *What Is a Novel?* contains on its acknowledgment page: "Above all to one colleague in particular, David Lodge, a very fine novelist and a very fine critic." Lodge comes closest to Bradbury as a novelist in his *Changing Places: A Tale of Two Campuses* (1975). This novel, which involves the exchange of a British and an American professor, offers alternating and parallel scenes which view each settling into his adopted university. It took Bradbury two novels, *Eating People Is Wrong* and *Stepping Westward*, to assess, in broad satirical terms, the British and American academic scenes; Lodge manages this assessment in one novel—but a novel which benefits crucially from a close reading of Bradbury's two. *The History Man*, which appeared the same year as *Changing Places*, should repay close reading even more. Steiner is probably right when he speaks of it as "one of the funniest, most intelligent novels to come out of England in a long time."

Other:

Forster: A Collection of Critical Essays, edited by Bradbury (Englewood Cliffs, N.J.: Prentice-Hall, 1966);

E. M. Forster: "A Passage to India," A Casebook, edited by Bradbury (London: Macmillan, 1970);

The American Novel and the Nineteen Twenties, edited by Bradbury and David Palmer (London: Edward Arnold, 1971);

The Penguin Companion to Literature 3: United States and Latin America, edited by Bradbury, Eric Mottram, and Jean Franco (Harmondsworth, U.K.: Penguin, 1971; New York: McGraw-Hill, 1971);

Modernism: 1890-1930, edited by Bradbury and James McFarlane, Pelican Guides to European Literature Series (Harmondsworth, U.K.: Penguin, 1976; Atlantic Highlands, N.J.: Humanities Press, 1978);

The Novel Today: Contemporary Writers on Modern Fiction, edited by Bradbury (London: Fontana, 1977; Totowa, N.J.: Rowman & Littlefield, 1977);

The Contemporary English Novel, edited by Bradbury and David Palmer (London: Edward Arnold, 1979).

References:

Bernard Bergonzi, "Fictions of History," in *The Contemporary English Novel*, edited by Bradbury and David Palmer (London: Edward Arnold, 1979), pp. 43-65;

Bergonzi, *The Situation of the Novel*, second edition, revised (London: Macmillan, 1979);

Martin Green, "Transatlantic Communications: Malcolm Bradbury's *Stepping Westward* (1966)," in *Old Lines, New Forces: Essays on the Contemporary British Novel, 1960-1970*, edited by Robert K. Morris (Rutherford, Madison, & Teaneck, N.J.: Fairleigh Dickinson University Press, 1976), pp. 53-66;

Ronald Hayman, *The Novel Today 1967-1975* (Essex: Longman Group Ltd., 1976);

David Lodge, *The Novelist at the Crossroads and Other Essays on Fiction and Criticism* (London: Routledge & Kegan Paul, 1971);

George Steiner, "Party Lines," *New Yorker*, 3 May 1976: 130-132;

Richard Todd, "An Interview with Malcolm Bradbury," *DQR: Dutch Quarterly Review of Anglo-American Letters*, 11, no. 3 (1981): 183-196;

Todd, "Malcolm Bradbury's *The History Man*: The Novelist as Reluctant Impresario," *DQR: Dutch Quarterly Review of Anglo-American Letters*, 11, no. 3 (1981): 162-182.

Papers:

Bradbury's manuscript collection is housed at the Nottingham Public Library.

Melvyn Bragg

(6 November 1939-   )

Peter Conradi
Kingston Polytechnic

SELECTED BOOKS: *For Want of a Nail* (London: Secker & Warburg, 1965; New York: Knopf, 1965);

The Second Inheritance (London: Secker & Warburg, 1966; New York: Dodd, Mead, 1967);

Without a City Wall (London: Secker & Warburg, 1968; New York: Knopf, 1969);

The Hired Man (London: Secker & Warburg, 1970; New York: Knopf, 1970);

A Place in England (London: Secker & Warburg, 1970; New York: Knopf, 1971);

The Nerve (London: Secker & Warburg, 1971);

Josh Lawton (London: Secker & Warburg, 1972; New York: Knopf, 1972);

The Silken Net (London: Secker & Warburg, 1974; New York: Knopf, 1974);

Speak for England (London: Secker & Warburg, 1976; New York: Knopf, 1976);

A Christmas Child (London: Secker & Warburg, 1976);

Autumn Manoeuvres (London: Secker & Warburg, 1978);

Kingdom Come (London: Secker & Warburg, 1980).

Melvyn Bragg, whose reputation as a novelist was established in the 1960s, has published eleven novels. In the 1970s his career as a Television Arts presenter also bloomed, and he has become a small-scale celebrity. The two careers have interacted oddly and not always fortunately.

Though he feels his writing cannot be easily categorized, Bragg is in some ways typical of a new grouping in the history of the English novel. After World War II this group comprised ambitious, provincial, lower-middle- or upper-working-class men (there were no women), often from the North, who benefited from the 1944 Butler Education Act which made provision for a grant system in higher education. This grouping, prefigured a generation earlier by C. P. Snow, included writers as diverse from one another as Alan Sillitoe, David Storey, Stan Barstow, Kingsley Amis, John Wain, John Braine, and Malcolm Bradbury. They championed the renascence of a provincial realism in the novel.

Modernism was seen as the art form of an aesthetic Bloomsbury-ite *Haute Bourgeoisie* which had held literary and intellectual hegemony for too long. Realism was the new program, and like nineteenth-century realism it was to be moderately reformist, making its peace with aesthetic crisis and its truce with nightmare and apocalypse. The fiction which resulted was meliorist in temper, deliberately modestly ambitious in its attitude to formal innovation, and it spoke for a whig individualism which in some ways continued the radicalism of the last century. Like that radicalism also, it was easily neutered. Nonconformist liberal humanism has traditionally been easily accommodated to the status quo in England. Just as the aesthetic radicalism of this group was essentially conservative (though the best writers—for example, Amis and Bradbury—have significantly and sometimes drastically altered their initial aesthetic positions), so it was often also socially and politically conservative. Bragg consorts oddly with the group in some respects. He is significantly younger than most. His career has been extravagantly dramatic: he rose from only child of a miner-turned-tenant publican in remote Cumbria to successful London television personality. His fiction has, with the exception of *The Nerve* (1971), been more than usually conservative. In both his public career as mediator and popularizer of minority cultures, and his private career as a novelist, he could be said to have stood for the defensible compromise.

Bragg was born at the beginning of World War II to working-class parents in North Cumbria, a part of England with strong literary associations, having been the cradle of English literary Romanticism. Wordsworth and Coleridge are associated with the Lakelands to the South, and Walter Scott with the Scottish Lowlands to the North. Wigton, his hometown, affectionately commemorated in his collection of interviews *Speak for England* (1976), is a town of about four or five thousand inhabitants, involved with both farming and industry. Bragg's mother worked in a biscuit factory, then in a local clothes-making factory which specialized in gentlemen's tailoring, earning a salary of slightly more than a dollar a week. His father worked successively as a miner in the pits, on the land as a farm laborer, in a big house as a bootblack, and as a fitter in the local cellophane factory; during World War II he mended damaged aircraft in a maintenance unit at the local airfield, though he wanted and eventually found a more active role abroad. When released from military service he tried going back to the factory, then worked as a bookie, before becoming tenant-landlord of a local pub.

Melvyn Bragg

The family moved from a one-up, one-down cottage in the center of Wigton to a much larger council house with the woman who had brought up Bragg's mother. At the center of the small town, well away from the war but with a number of its residents in active service, the house had its share of comings and goings.

The postwar period, Bragg thinks, was a favorable time for children to be brought up in England. The "de-mobbed" soldiers were determined to give children a good time and much entertainment was provided: youth clubs, choirs, car-

nivals, brass bands. Like other children Bragg took advantage of all of these activities, and he accurately reflects this postwar world in the second novel of his Tallentire trilogy, *A Place in England* (1970).

In 1950 Bragg won a scholarship to the local grammar school, Nelson Thomlinson, where he worked hard and enjoyed sports (particularly rugby). Later, he won a scholarship to Wadham College, Oxford, where he read modern history from 1959 to 1961.

Although he did not enjoy his first year there, he became acclimatized and made good use of the experience in his work. Wigton had been a good place to grow up: so enjoyable that everything which followed was "downhill all the way." This was, however, a time when it was becoming fashionable to be working-class and Northern, and he felt uncomfortable to be assured in his first year at Oxford by a public school headboy that he was "jolly lucky" to be "just working-class." The metropolis was then "having a bit on the side with the North—no promises, no commitments." The North had been the engine-house of English commerce, the first place to be exploited in the industrial revolution by the "softer" and "politer" South; the first to be abandoned and suffer during the Depression. Now, in the 1960s in Britain, an unofficial truce was declared. If the North had been and partly still was the exploited handmaiden to the necessities and luxuries of the South, the 1960s, Bragg felt, were a time in which the civilized conspiracy that all Englishmen were equal could, briefly, become a ruling myth—encouraged by the Beatles. "From the start of the sixties they turned the North into . . . a Klondyke of talent. The North became the flagship of U.K. Limited-Company Director H[arold] Wilson from Huddersfield . . . the greys and blacks of the factories seemed showered with psychedelic light and hope; the nuts and bolts of public morality were eased and squeezed to the beginning of real tolerance—and the four pied pipers from Merseyside led half the world a dance until the barricades went up in Paris, the napalm went down in Vietnam and it all turned out to have no more reality than Sergeant Pepper," Bragg later wrote.

After he left Oxford Bragg joined the BBC as a general trainee and gravitated to "Monitor," an arts program for which he wrote "The Debussy Film" directed by Ken Russell. His six years with the BBC were happy and productive and gave him a good grounding in the contemporary arts.

Although he knew that he wanted to excel, Bragg had been unusual for an ambitious scholarship boy in not knowing what career he wished to pursue. He had read massively and omnivorously, and one afternoon ventured to write a short story (which he has never published or shown to anyone). Over the succeeding years he wrote seven novels, none of which satisfied him, until he wrote *For Want of a Nail* (1965), his first published book to negotiate fully his Cumbrian background. In the *Times Literary Supplement* he recounted that until then the novel had seemed to him the fictional newsletter of the cultured middle classes. "There is a security of tenure lodged between the boards of a heavy hardback which is a contract between one property owner and another. . . . The working-class I saw in 'literature' . . . were servants, skivvies, caricatures, criminals, mutes, 'turns,' and almost invariably embarrassing after the first affectionate recognition."

For Want of a Nail is written as a Bildungsroman, charting Tom Graham's education and growth from childhood into young manhood. Tom wins scholarships to the local village school and finally to Oxford where, at the end, he is about to matriculate, leaving his Cumberland village family behind. It begins with a beautifully evoked hunt (a recurrent motif for Bragg; his part of Cumbria is John Peel country). Tom's grandfather, who commits the unforgivable solecism of shooting the fox and is beaten by a huntsman, becomes increasingly eccentric. As the book progresses Tom's ineffectual father, Edward, is interested only in betting and beer. His mother is young, handsome, and independent. Tom discovers a mystery about his paternity that is finally and painfully resolved. The book contains passages of lyrical beauty, and the imagined landscape of North Cumbria is a real and active presence.

"I have two opposed landscapes," Bragg noted in "Class and the Novel," an essay he wrote in 1971 for the *Times Literary Supplement*. "So far I have written out of one, out of the language and opportunities and discoveries and achievements of one about the other." The tension between these two worlds, and two kinds of conscience, often provides Bragg with the necessary narrative locomotion, as in his second novel.

In *The Second Inheritance* (1966), two families, one from each of Bragg's two opposed social landscapes, are neighbors along Hadrian's Wall, built by the Romans to keep the Scots out of England, and thus a potent symbol of the division between peoples. The Langleys, who own the land, are middle gentry and on the way down; the Fosters are rising yeomen. Young John Foster becomes involved with the weak Arthur Langley, each admiring the other's complementary qualities. Arthur's

jealous sister Pat divides them by engineering an affair with John. Like Bragg's first novel, the book has a fine and lyrical poetic economy.

Early reviewers tended to associate Bragg with D. H. Lawrence and Thomas Hardy. Both are in some sense regional novelists. Lawrence is seen as lying behind Bragg's capacity for sensuous immediacy, Hardy as funding the convention of tragic rural epic. Two other similarities might be noted. All three writers can be described as didactic Romantic novelists, operating out of that Romantic radical-conservative lineage which is concerned with eliciting or with elegizing tradition, community, organism, growth, wholeness, and continuity. Bragg's early novels typically employ plant imagery to suggest wholeness. The second point is that all three are uneven in achievement and capable of very bad writing.

Bragg's novels divide, after the first two, between those which purportedly document Cumbrian life, but are in fact clearly in the perennial tradition of courtly pastoral (here the writer invisibly refreshes himself, sinking his own complications in the artful simplicity of a lost Cumbrian past) and those in which the authorial presence is visible in a usually ill-focused proxy-character. In the first group, authenticity can be imagined from the inside, unimpeded, however sour or tragic the narrative mode; in the latter group, authenticity is struggled for and invoked and will not come. London features in this second category, and part of the point about London in Bragg's novels is that it frustrates one's attempt to discover coherence or authenticity. It may not always be Bragg's intention to show the search itself as inauthentic or in bad faith, though that is sometimes the effect.

After the success of his second novel Bragg left the BBC to freelance as a scriptwriter. He was living by an odd mixture of rules, partly puritan and partly hedonistic. His third novel, *Without a City Wall* (1968), takes Richard Godwin, a freelance writer working in London, to Cumbria where he hopes to revive his life. Like Bragg, who between 1968 and 1970 wrote three filmscripts, Godwin finances his retirement to Cumbria by his screenwriting, in a sense subserving the values he questions to retreat from them. He is the first of Bragg's heroes to be seen as through a double exposure on a film: as both deeply tainted—if not corrupt—and simultaneously quaintly honorable. He is the more honorable the more publicly he admits his corruption. For him "many words had gone . . . all except 'Goodness.' . . . And if what [goodness] evoked for him was to do with the past rather than the present, with retrogression rather than progression, with evasion rather than with confrontation, then he was to accept these accusations. . . . 'A good man': to be that would be something." Godwin wants to "see the weight of the life I live, to see what a day passing means." He meets and falls in love with Janice (daughter of two "good people") who has left the university to bear another man's child. His efforts toward virtuous wholeness are mocked by his cynical friend, David, for whom "Good is dead" and for whom success, snobbery, and the fickle loyalties of the London media world are everything. Godwin searches for a writing style "that would not be clogged with self-disgust or self-regard, nor be dissipated in nervous, nerveless stupidities."

The book shows a stubbornly innocent attitude to the problems of finding narrative grace, sometimes stumbling on it and sometimes missing altogether. It is the first of Bragg's novels to read partly as though it were written with careless haste and partly as if it were a painful attempt at "purple" lyricism. It has nonetheless real and considerable strengths, such as a well-conceived structure, and won for Bragg the 1969 John Llewelyn Rhys Memorial Prize.

The Hired Man (1970), winner of an English Centre of International P.E.N. "Silver Pen" Award in 1970, is among the most successfully shaped and achieved of Bragg's books. It is the first novel of his Tallentire family trilogy, inspired partly by Thomas Mann's *Buddenbrooks* (1901), partly by Bragg's desire to imagine his family history in fictional terms. Avoiding fruitless soul-searching London-Cumbrian dialectic, it dramatizes John Tallentire's life from 1898 until after World War I. As the novel opens, he is at a public "hiring"; eighteen and newly married, he is hoping to secure employment with a farmer. His grandfather gives him a piece of straw to stick in his mouth or under his hat as a sign that he is for hire. His proud refusal to put up this sign is indicative of the novel's concern with the changing attitudes toward work among working men during the first two decades of this century. In contrast to John, his brother Isaac fecklessly lives for sport, for the carnival world of horses, dogs, fighting-cocks, boxing, gambling, and raillery. The third brother, Seth, is involved with the emerging trade union movement. Their grandfather had lived in a world of clearly demarcated distinctions and deferences. The novel, which charts the various progresses of the grandsons, could have been diagrammatic; instead, it is finely compressed and yet full of acutely rendered detail. At the novel's end John has survived the collapse of his marriage, the collapse of the mine in which he had been working, the collapse of the values which, before World War I, had sustained him. He is once more for hire.

A Place in England continues the saga into the next generation. John's son, Joseph, after losing his job as a footman, confronts the 1930s and the Depression. "We've had poor work, lad, and we've had slave work. But that was better than no work," says John. Compressed like *The Hired Man*, the novel is further ranging in theme and manner. The characters aspire to control their destinies and succeed better than preceding generations; but they are still "blown like chaff, man: there's neither sense nor purpose in it." Joseph goes into the RAF and eventually becomes a pub landlord. Though John's empire has been labor, Joseph's is the pub. Joseph and his wife fall out and try to argue out their differences, as had John and his wife Emily before; but they lack a language in which to express their discontents. "This is what happens to you if you haven't been educated, see? I *feel* all these things, but I can't explain them," Joseph says.

Joseph's son, Douglas, who is Bragg's fictional persona, will acquire the articulacy with which he can as a writer explain, justify, and dignify his parents' lives. "He would find a Cumbrian name for his family and have a fictive self both appear in the book and write it so that he could both know 'everything'—as the old novelists did—and have a partial view as would be necessary." The books are to concern the history of "a family who do not consider themselves a family (unlike the Buddenbrooks or the Brangwens) and have always been strangers to history—even their own."

Douglas notes that his three-generation novel is to treat working people without condescension. He suggests to himself a pattern of "Epic—pre-grandfather; Heroic—grandfather; Silver—father; Decadent—self"; and after this he notes "too facile." The pattern of a fall nonetheless also inheres in this story ("One look at that old man [Douglas's grandfather] convinced Douglas who had fallen"); so does the contrary scheme of emancipation. Douglas's emancipation leaves him with a feeling of desperate emptiness which only the thought of writing can counter. The question of the value of Thurston, where Douglas grew up, recurs and is unresolved. Joseph and his sister discuss whether their youth was a period of good or of bad times and are undecided while Douglas elegizes the village world as follows: "Of course there was snobbery, bullying, meanness, hypocrisy, and despair in Thurston; that was to be expected in any community. What was moving was the warmth of feeling the place evoked. It was in some measure by talking of the town that they talked to each other—and warmth, especially, was transmitted through this knowledge of the people in the place."

In 1961 Bragg had married Lise Roche, a novelist of French origin who had been his contemporary at Oxford; they had one daughter. She had published one novel before her suicide in 1970. Her death is an event whose consequences directly resonate within Bragg's ensuing fiction. *The Nerve* is an account of a breakdown; *Josh Lawton* (1972) is the story of the destruction of innocence; and *The Silken Net* (1974) has a heroine partly based on Lise Roche.

An inflamed eye that Bragg once suffered was the inspiration for a short story that became *The Nerve*. The book's narrator-hero, Ted, has a nervous infection of the eye which causes him to weep uncontrollably. A novel about breakdown, this is the only "experimental" work Bragg has written, one that explores the consequences the subject matter of the book has on its form. Ted, who teaches at a technical school and does some reviewing, muses about the inescapable stereotypes which define both the Cumbrian world he has left behind and the Hampstead world to which he has gravitated. Northerners, formerly stereotyped as "Blunt, Thrifty and Common," are now required to be

"Bright and Abrasive and Original." Having lived in the South, Ted finds that he is expected at home to appear "Soft, Smooth and Southern," the more as he inhabits Hampstead which is "Intellectual, Arty and Smarty." This "spurious North-South dialectic," as he calls it, and the realities it masks, have entrapped him. He is provided with counterparts who dramatize his predicament: "the Tough," an anonymous, inarticulate, and violent ruffian jealously in love with the girl with whom Ted unsuccessfully experiments (sexually and in other ways); and the cynically successful Rod, with whom Ted was in school (kin to the earlier David of *Without a City Wall*) and whose voice and views Ted periodically impersonates. Ted is halfway between Rod and "the Tough" and experiences a "terrifying and violently exhausting" suspension of belief in his own identity, a situation reflected by Bragg's narrative. The disjunctions and fictive playfulness thus produced are uneasily contained in the novel. A passage is devoted to the narrator's problems in presenting his own incoherence coherently, in responsibly subduing his own chaos.

While discursiveness is praised in *The Nerve*, Bragg's next work, *Josh Lawton*, is arguably his least discursive and best organized. Its mode is a mythic realism akin to Herman Melville's *Billy Budd*. The

Dust jacket for Bragg's seventh novel

incredibly beautiful orphan Josh Lawton attracts the devotion of an ex-soldier, Cedric, who wants to train him as a runner; of the vicar, who may be the only character to love him without seeking to use him; and of the local Delilah, Maureen, who, after bearing him a daughter, leaves him for the more aggressive Blister. Blister, unlike Josh, is able to dominate her as she wishes. The resulting tragedy is handled with a skillful, moving, hard-won simplicity.

In 1970 Bragg had become a Fellow of the Royal Society of Literature. In 1975, to mark his fellowship, he gave the Wedmore Memorial lecture, which was laden with prophetic implications about his career. On "Thomas Hardy and *Jude the Obscure*" he suggests in the lecture a new reason for Hardy's abandonment of fiction after that work. Bragg eloquently suggests that it was in part Hardy's inability to confront fully his own sense of shame at having belonged to, then left and "betrayed," the class of small artisans, which rendered him, so far as the novel was concerned, voiceless. "The gap between the cosmopolitan life he led and the provincial life he fed on for his fiction was growing—and there are indications that each was endangered by the other."

In the early 1970s Bragg drifted back to BBC. After his first wife's death, he discovered that, like the youth in John Berryman's "Dream Songs," he had, on his own, "no inner resources." He remarried in 1973 and has one son by this marriage. He produced two series of Chekhov and Joyce short stories for BBC television with prestigious directors (Karel Reisz, Jonathan Miller, Ken Loach) and writers (David Storey, David Mercer). In 1973 he accepted an invitation to introduce a program called "Second House," a weekly mixed arts program of variable length. He came to realize, after the depressed solitude of the preceding years, how important it was for him to work with other people. He invented, directed, and was master of ceremonies of a BBC 1 book program called "Read All About It," which was successful and popular. It began an inadvertent process whereby Bragg changed from being a novelist who occasionally worked in broadcasting to being that curious contemporary phenomenon, a media personality and celebrity. It is hard not to read his account of Hardy's difficulties in the 1890s as a prophetic warning to himself. The process was accentuated when, in 1978, he left the BBC to run the much acclaimed "South Bank Show" for the independent commercial network, London Weekend Television. Leaving the BBC was in some ways like leaving Wigton a second time, since the BBC

has an absorbing community atmosphere. One advantage of the move was that the South Bank Show, unlike the program with which Bragg had formerly been involved, was not restricted to books but took on the whole range of the contemporary arts, including music (pop and classical), opera, film, and theater.

The success of these series has not so far had fortunate results for Bragg's fiction. He describes the change as having had his "cover" as an established figure on the literary landscape "blown." His books have lately been less well received by the reviewing establishment. Reviewers may have felt that as Bragg has frequent public exposure in front of the television cameras, other lesser-known writers might be more deserving candidates for exposure in the review columns. Bragg mounted an eloquent defense of the democratizing of the role of television in an article on Norman Mailer ("The American Author Norman Mailer" in the *New Review*, 1974). One critical point is that readerships are notoriously possessive and like to feel they own their author. The old audience for his books has been unhappy about sharing him with his new audience. Another point is that his best books have simply not come out of this period of high public exposure. *The Silken Net* and *Autumn Manoeuvres* (1978), the latter a somewhat factitious novel about politics and electioneering, are demonstrably less successful than *The Hired Man* and *Josh Lawton*.

The rare and unusual Rosemary Lewis in *The Silken Net* is, like other Bragg protagonists, caught between opposing worlds. She was born in France to a French bourgeoise, who came to a messy end in a one-night cheap hotel in Marseilles, and an English painter who died in World War I. She is thus brought up by English relatives in Cumbria but drawn to the South, though she never manages more than a day trip to Boulogne. Her affections, too, are unsettled and oscillate between her cousin Wilfrid, a cultured lecturer from a spacious London home, and the rougher native Cumbrian Edgar. *The Silken Net* is arguably Bragg's most rambling and ill-planned book. Wilfrid's career would have benefited from amplification, while the book as a whole would have profited from some savage pruning.

Speak for England, a collection of interviews with villagers from Bragg's native Wigton, was criticized by the *Spectator* reviewer for its uncertainties about its form. Bragg is alternately "irresponsibly absent" and "intrusively present" in the text. More seriously, Bragg's attitude toward the past, which his interviewees are recalling, is ill-considered. "He deplores the past as inequitable, squalid and oppressive and yet his subjects, who lived in it, are happy to sentimentalise it. Even his disapproval of the insanitary unjust early days of this century is betrayed by the epigraph . . . which suggests that Wigton is after all a dour and wintry version of Chesterton's Merrie England, a place of gruff simplicity and festive indigence." This ambiguity is sustained and developed by the portentous conclusion, in which the author rhetorically links the future of England with the memorialized past.

Kingdom Come (1980) completes the Tallentire trilogy and brings it up to the present. The self-made Douglas Tallentire is now a jet-setting television personality who suffers his good luck with fortitude and an occasional bout of self-disgust. He is a puritan guest at the worldly feast, who can neither purge nor forget his own self-regard, and who has both a sense of sin and a "hopeless hope of redemption." His mother tartly comments that he likes Cumbria and everybody in it "far better when he is away from it." He nonetheless yearns for it and ponders "metropolitan getting and spending; on the other hand, rural sitting and stewing: on the other hand, city—superficialities: on the other hand, country—pedantries: and vice versa: urban flash, rural blankness: ennui and accidie. . . . There is no other hand. They are the same." But they are not. Organic imagery surrounds Cumbria, while London is mechanical. Rural life has "superior authority," and the further away we are from our past, "the more eagerly we seize on the chances to revisit it." Douglas is divided between a physical wife and a mistress, as well as this familiar metaphysical pair. His problems are variously illuminated: by the "inviolable goodness" of his stay-at-home cousin Harry; by the competing cleverness of his one-time school friend Joe, who also has never left Thurston and who assures Douglas that "luck's earned"; by the tragedy of his childhood friend Alan's suicide, which Douglas is busy converting into art; by the sad career of his petty-adventurer cousin Lester; by the nonagenarian grandfather John (from *The Hired Man*) who is finally dying; and, finally, by the nasty and talented bisexual pop star Merlin Raven. Moreover, the meretricious and meritorious are presented as hard to distinguish. Thus Merlin Raven's much-heralded pop concert is shown on Christmas Eve; the producer of the television program about the concert significantly borrows an empty office on the floor normally given over to religion. Ancient theological certainties not only are no longer underwritten, but have yielded precedence to the world of pop. What the book struggles to replace them with is the thin and equally "flip" value of sincerity.

Perhaps to contend for the primacy of the audience today, whether in television or fiction (as Bragg does in his article on Mailer), is to opt for a middlebrow solution. It is debatable whether the perennially virtuous task in art is to celebrate "individualism" and strenuously to imagine the lives of people not oneself; it is sure that the forms through which history has permitted these imaginings to elicit their own shape have, at any rate, not remained constant.

To argue for "real values," which has been the classic concern of liberal humanism, in an increasingly collectivized age and with various corporate futures in view, means increasingly to argue for a pastoral form of art. Art is then used to soothe contemporary pain and panic. Such an art risks having it all ways, being anodyne and on equable terms with both God and Mammon. Bragg's later novels, like those of others writing in the vein of provincial realism, have not always avoided these dangers. Bragg admires that great Dandy writer Evelyn Waugh, and his own best writing, for all the obvious differences between them, belongs to the dandy-ish and reticent rather than to the relentlessly wistful attempt to marry plain thinking and high living (to reverse the old truism). He hopes now to have made his peace with the past. He still keeps a Cumbrian cottage, part of which is piously unmodernized, while the neighboring barn is, equally symbolically, stylishly up-to-date. His early books show what he is capable of writing. His admirers are bound to hope that he will recapture some of their peculiar and lasting quality.

Screenplays:

Isadora, by Bragg and Clive Exton, Universal, 1968;

Play Dirty, United Artists, 1970;

The Music Lovers, United Artists, 1970;

Jesus Christ Superstar, by Bragg and Norman Jerrison, Universal, 1973.

Television Plays:

Charity Begins at Home, BBC, 1970;

Zinotchka, BBC, 1972;

Clouds of Glory, ITV, 1978.

References:

Kenneth John Atchity, "Plot-Luck," *Kenyon Review*, 31 (1969): 675-684;

Roger Pybus, "The Fiction of Melvyn Bragg," *Stand* (Summer 1970): 68-74.

Christine Brooke-Rose
(1926-   )

Morton P. Levitt
Temple University

BOOKS: *Gold* (Aldington, Kent: Hand & Flower, 1955);

The Languages of Love (London: Secker & Warburg, 1957);

The Sycamore Tree (London: Secker & Warburg, 1958; New York: Norton, 1959);

A Grammar of Metaphor (London: Secker & Warburg, 1958);

The Dear Deceit (London: Secker & Warburg, 1960; Garden City: Doubleday, 1961);

The Middlemen: A Satire (London: Secker & Warburg, 1961);

Out (London: M. Joseph, 1964);

Such (London: M. Joseph, 1966);

Between (London: M. Joseph, 1968);

Go When You See the Green Man Walking (London: M. Joseph, 1970);

A ZBC of Ezra Pound (London: Faber & Faber, 1971; Berkeley: University of California, 1971);

Thru (London: Hamilton, 1975);

A Structural Analysis of Pound's Usura Canto (The Hague: Mouton, 1976).

Christine Brooke-Rose is typically described as a "European intellectual," one who is capable through her education and interests of bridging gaps between cultures—this at a time when English culture seems particularly hostile to foreign concerns. It is Brooke-Rose on whom the *Times* of London calls when it needs an essay on contemporary French writing for a special supplement on France. But her efforts to make accessible French critical thought and to integrate into her fiction innovations associated with the French "new novelists" are largely unknown to her countrymen. She is one of those literary outsiders whom the English can tolerate, even respect, and then simply ignore. (The "Great Tradition" of English realism—as defined by contemporary English novelists and critics alike—is so narrow as to preclude most foreigners [Conrad excepted] as well as all those concerned with "experimental" narrative technique that might be labeled as foreign: hence Joyce, Beckett, and even Woolf have been arbitrarily eliminated from consideration by most English critics and from evaluation by most English novelists.) Being an English literary "supra-national" in these days of the European Community is, ironically, a thankless occupation. But there is more to Brooke-Rose. She is also, as a novelist, a literary chameleon, able to adapt the literary modes of others—from early Iris Murdoch to late James Joyce—with a consistency of theme and a facility that is most unusual and most impressive: if she is not a major writer, she nonetheless points the way to what might have proved a fruitful path for English fiction in the period following World War II. Instead, her career as critic and novelist demonstrates further the sad insularity of postmodernist English literary culture.

Brooke-Rose was born in Geneva, child of an English father and a half-Swiss, half-American

Christine Brooke-Rose

124

mother, and raised in Brussels. Thus, although truly bilingual, she spoke French before English. She was educated in both Belgian and English schools, served as an intelligence officer in the British Women's Auxiliary Air Force during World War II, and read English philology at Somerville College, Oxford, receiving her B.A. in 1949, her M.A. in 1953, and then her Ph.D. from University College, London, in 1954. Her doctoral thesis, which she would later describe as "monumental and quite unpublishable," was a grammatical analysis of Old French and Middle English poetry, "comparing methods of expression in both at a time when French had considerably influenced the development of English." In a practical, immediate sense this led to her study of English poetic usage in *A Grammar of Metaphor* (1958); more indirectly, the interpenetration of language and its effects became a principal theme of her later fiction. Indeed, the mixed circumstance of her birth and education are reflected throughout her career as critic, novelist, and teacher.

From 1956 to 1968, Brooke-Rose worked as a free-lance reviewer and journalist in London. Since that time, she has taught English literature and literary theory at the experimental Vincennes campus of the University of Paris. Her literary and critical concerns have coexisted throughout, always with an emphasis on the need to communicate and the frequent failure to do so. *A Grammar of Metaphor* is a study of fifteen English poets, from Chaucer to Dylan Thomas, which examines the grammatical and syntactical influence of metaphors on the words to which they are connected. "Limited though a purely grammatical approach to metaphor may be," the author writes in response to the usage of New Criticism, "it seems to me necessary if only to restore the balance." This philological study is sensitive not just to the word but to the work as a whole. It demonstrates an aspect of poetic continuity that is not often found by more traditional methods. A similar responsiveness to poetic language may be found in Brooke-Rose's two books on Ezra Pound, that prime example of "polyglottism": *A Structural Analysis of Pound's Usura Canto* (1976), which endeavors to apply Roman Jakobson's structuralist approach to the controversial Canto 45, and *A ZBC of Ezra Pound* (1971), which suggests that the Cantos as a group are readable, as well as "funny, soothing, exhilirating, infuriating, tender beyond endurance, dogmatic beyond belief . . .—in short, totally human, alive and relevant."

In 1956, during the serious illness of her husband, the Polish writer and professor Jerzy Peter-kiewicz (whom she had married in 1953 while still at Oxford), Brooke-Rose, from "the worry of it," abandoned "my serious work . . . to write—with incredible speed—my first novel." Six years later, when she "fell desperately ill," her fiction changed radically, and she began to write, now with excruciating slowness, a new kind of fiction. "During my long illness, I found that I couldn't read novels, good or bad, about love-affairs, class-distinctions and one-upmanships, or portraits of society on any scale from parochial to professional: the sort of novel, in fact, that I had been writing." She speaks of reading scientific texts and of being attracted to their language. "Such phrases, of precise significance to the scientist, fired my imagination as poetic metaphors for what happens between people, and people are and always will be the stuff of the novel." Only her short stories approach this model, however. It would be simpler and perhaps more accurate to say that at this point Brooke-Rose stopped writing English Edwardian novels and began to write under the aegis of Joyce and his French successors.

Brooke-Rose's earlier fictional mode is best illustrated by *The Sycamore Tree* (1958), which seems almost to have been written by Iris Murdoch. Its philosophical concerns (a disquisition on the nature of reality), its intriguing and not fully believable characters (the Chelsea literary crowd), its exotic plot with its dependence on circumstance and violence, its frequently omniscient summing up and commentary, its social satire and ironic perspective make it seem a pastiche. Yet this is not a superficial endeavor. Brooke-Rose so absorbs Murdoch's style and intent (with minor echoes also of Virginia Woolf and Evelyn Waugh) and so ably blends Murdoch's model with her own experiences and concerns that *The Sycamore Tree* seems virtually a national literary product. Murdoch, after all, has continued to write such novels for more than a quarter of a century and has been much admired for them. *The Sycamore Tree* is a conventional English novel and was reviewed conventionally.

Brooke-Rose's true development as a novelist begins with *Out*. Published in 1964 and winner of the 1965 Society of Authors Travelling Prize, *Out* is modeled after Alain Robbe-Grillet's *La Jalousie* (1957). (In 1969 she won the Arts Council Translation Prize for rendering into English another of his novels, *Dans le Labyrinthe*.) Robbe-Grillet seems to employ the same scientific perspective to which Brooke-Rose was attracted during her illness; he was trained as a tropical agronomist—a fact which she must have known—and his language has the emotional flatness and geometrical precision of a scientific report. But her work is actually an inversion of his and her purpose diametrically different: she adopts his limited point of view and attenuated perspective in order to deny his now well-known theme that humanism is dead and metaphor outmoded because it implies human values. (He did not realize, she later wrote, because of his French insularity, that he was not the first to attack the pathetic fallacy, that Ruskin had done so much earlier.)

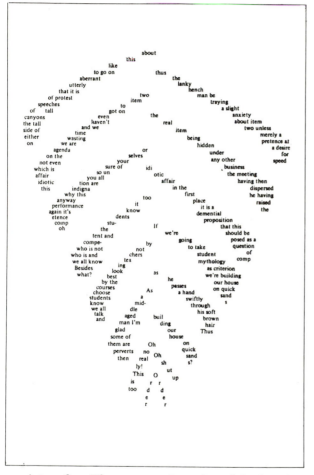

A page from Thru, *an experimental novel dominated by the example of James Joyce*

The action of *Out* is set in the future, in Africa, in the aftermath of nuclear war. Because radiation deprives its victims of color, color in this new society is a sign of health and hence of social significance. The pale white protagonist of *Out* is thus at the lowest level of plantation life; Robbe-Grillet's hero is the plantation master. The view in *La Jalousie* is from the plantation house out toward the regular rows of banana trees; the view here is reversed, from the plantation shacks toward the big house.

No workers are seen in Robbe-Grillet, no buildings which might house workers, no issues of politics, no sense of history or of human identity beyond the psychotic observer's immediate needs. The observer in *Out* is aware, however, both of social and historical change and of his own place in the process. His is a full human personality, affirming even in disease his humanness. As a viewer, he closely resembles Robbe-Grillet's jealous husband (the obsessively observed fly on his knee recalls the ubiquitous centipede of *La Jalousie*, and Mrs. Mgulu, mistress of the big house, reminds us of A. . . , seen so often by her husband at her dressing table). But Brooke-Rose's viewer is conscious throughout of what he observes, of its implications for him as a man ("Through all the false identities that we build, the love-making, the trauma-seeking, the alchemising of anecdote to legend, of episode to myth, what really happened to us?"); he only appears to be limited, like his original, to scientific language and events "of precise significance" to the observer.

In *Such* (1966), which shared the James Tait Black Memorial Prize for 1967, Brooke-Rose expands her involvement in scientific subjects, language, perceptions, as a means of confronting basic human concerns. The observer here is an astronomer called Lazarus, who dies while peering through his telescope. He is one who has looked at life as he has at the skies, coolly, unemotionally, from a distance. During the three minutes covered by this narrative—a time during which he is brought back to life by heart massage—he dredges through his past, as a scientist, with a dispassion that speaks to his entire career, not to the intensity of this moment. If he cannot judge himself or the mode of existence which he represents, he can at least enable us to make such judgments.

In Robbe-Grillet, again, that act of judging would be at best incidental, allowed but not made necessary by the author. Even so obviously symbolic a name as Lazarus would, in Robbe-Grillet, be a deception, designed to suggest possibilities of redemption or of failure but actually indicating neither. In Brooke-Rose's narrative, however, it is a functioning metaphor, part of the judgment to be made by the reader, part of her effort to combine the traditional moral concerns of the English novel with the new reality—and the new ways of seeing reality—of the nouveau roman. Thus, Brooke-Rose's novel points to William Golding's *Pincher Martin* (1956), with its similar subject and moral concern, and to Claude Mauriac's *La Marquise sortit à cinq heures* (1961), with its similar condensation of time and point of view. (Further parallels may be made to Bernard Malamud's 1967 story, "The Old People," for its comparable scientist hero, and to

Christine Brooke-Rose

Doris Lessing's 1971 novel, *Briefing for a Descent into Hell*, for its comparable situation.)

The language, structure, and theme of *Between* (1968) are inevitable developments from the preceding novels. Its very theme (as well as its structure) is language, and the problems of understanding which exist despite or because of language—even for one with a mastery of languages. The protagonist of *Between* is a professional translator, a member of a team which travels from conference to international conference, working among ever-changing languages and cities and topics. Her personal tale, sporadically revealed, is one of love, marriage, divorce, and children, of engagement and disengagement, of uncommunicated and perhaps uncommunicable feelings. It is told in New York, Paris, Athens, Istanbul, and

elsewhere, amidst words of peace and food and science and, finally, in Prague, of "a new and vital theme, The Writer and Communication"—or is it finally in Avignon and "The Role of the Writer in the Modern World"? "We live," thinks the translator-protagonist, "between ideas . . . on one level one hardly listens. On another one has to understand immediately." The translator works with ears and voice and "the distant brain way up." The emotions of her failing personal life and her near-desperate search for a stable home seem lost in this complex of overlapping tongues ("welgohome," says a Greek to a German), of undifferentiated cities and subjects entered often without transition, of repeated images whose meanings are never quite clear. The airplane flight on which the narrative opens and closes suggests that a principal source for the novel may be Michel Butor's *Réseau aérien* (1962). *Between* won no literary awards; it was already beyond the pale of acceptable influence and "experimentation," an English critical pejorative when applied to the modern novel. *Between* makes it clear that Brooke-Rose moves in regions outside the narrowly redefined "great tradition" of English fiction.

That sense of movement apparent in Brooke-Rose's titles is advanced still further in her next novel, *Thru* (1975). The example of Joyce, present in the background throughout the novels from *Out* to *Between*, dominates here at the center. The artist as trickster, punster, storyteller, visionary, manipulator of languages and literary forms, creator of personal and epic myths: this late Joycean model from *Finnegans Wake* (1939) is the starting point for *Thru*. *Thru* is also the most self-reflexive (because it deals, in the postmodernist mode, with its own creation) of all Brooke-Rose fictions; the narrative's concern with its construction is a logical outgrowth of her persistent interest in communication, in ways of seeing and ways of telling:

The show within the show
What?
of hands juggling
within a secret ballet of the I . . .

It is a work profoundly aware of—suspicious of and respectful of—literary tradition: ". . . unlearning a text within a text passed on from generation to generation of an increasing vastness that nevertheless dwindles to an elite initiated to a text no-one else will read. . . ." Much of the novel is more easily seen than described; the rear-view mirror of a car, a retro

Manuscript of "Queenie Fat and Thin," collected in Go When You See the Green Man Walking viseur, becomes the reactionary vizier who threatens to behead the artist:

```
                           Some tale-bearer
(O capital!                                    your
                           story or           your
                           life
           wot no          story?
              no           life
punishment)    So that
Hang it all
              no           life
                           story
           off with                            your
head       said the
chief      in-sultan to                        his
                           red red rose
           washed by
           once upon
           (some times)   purple passages
```

Often effective, always readable (if not always easily), *Thru* is a further effort of the author to bridge the gaps between cultures and peoples. So the car drives off, highly metaphorically,

across the bridge in the scintillating foreign city

Brooke-Rose had no illusions about her novel's reception in England; she sent it off in the certain knowledge, product of her life and her literary career, that "reaction against foreign influences always turns out to be parochial."

Living and working in France, Brooke-Rose is in a sense removed from the parochialism which has infected most contemporary English fiction. She does not believe that the modernist example must inevitably be repudiated as foreign to English experience. This openness has been her greatest strength as a novelist. It has also, however, been her principal weakness, for she has removed herself not only from national roots but also from a potential national audience. To the English, she will likely always be something of an exotic, acceptable as an "experimenter" if only because she is somehow foreign, and undeniably outside the tradition. Her attraction to us, at the same time, is that she has intelligently and courageously attempted to expand that tradition. She will likely continue to do so. But she will also likely remain an outsider, not benefiting appreciably from those remaining strengths of the English novel and not significantly amending its pervasive weaknesses.

Translations:

Juan Goytisolo, *Children of Chaos* (London: MacGibbon & Kee, 1959);

Alfred Sauvy, *Fertility and Survival: Population Problems from Malthus to Mao Tse Tung* (New York: Macmillan, 1960; London: Chatto & Windus, 1961);

Alain Robbe-Grillet, *In the Labyrinth* (London: Calder & Boyars, 1968).

Jeremy Brooks
(17 December 1926-   )

Georgia L. Lambert

BOOKS: *The Water Carnival* (London: Eyre & Spottiswoode, 1957);

Jampot Smith (London: Hutchinson, 1960; New York: St. Martin's Press, 1962);

Henry's War (London: Macmillan, 1962; New York: St. Martin's Press, 1963);

Smith, as Hero (London: Eyre & Spottiswoode, 1965);

The Magic Perambulator (London: Harrap, 1965; New York: Day, 1966).

It has been over fifteen years since Jeremy Brooks has had a novel published, yet he is a serious writer who tackles significant themes and has earned substantial critical praise. He treats the issues of pacifism, identity, and emotional commitment with insight and tenderness, and the consequences of his characters' choices, even when choosing not to choose, wend their way unobtrusively through his novels. Brooks himself drifted away from novel writing out of economic necessity. When faced with a growing family and literary reputation but pitifully small financial success, he opted for commissioned work, earning substantial sums for writing adaptations of plays and stories for stage and screen as well as original scripts.

He was born in Southampton, Hampshire, on 17 December 1926 to William Meikle and Patricia Jenner Brooks. Young Jeremy attended Brighton Grammar School in Sussex. His father, a civil servant, was transferred to Wales in 1940 at the onset of World War II; the family was evacuated along with him. Jeremy completed his schooling in Wales, then enlisted in the Royal Naval Volunteer Reserve in 1944, which sent him to Magdalen College, Oxford, in an effort, he says, to turn him into a "temporary gentleman." His naval service included over two years in the fifth minesweeping flotilla in the Mediterranean. Brooks's teenage years in Wales and his experiences in the Navy figure prominently in two of his novels, *Jampot Smith* (1960) and *Smith, as Hero* (1965).

He left the Navy with a rank of sublieutenant in 1947 and attended the Camberwell School of Art, London, from 1947-1949, where he majored in scenic design and met Eleanor Nevile, an art student, whom he married on 21 July 1950. From 1949-1950 he worked as a stage designer in Dartford, Kent at Scala Theatre, learning, he says, nearly every aspect of theater production (but doing very little stage designing). He had been writing poetry and keeping a journal and, in 1950, decided to turn to writing as a profession, obtaining a job as a feature writer with *Pictorial Press* in London. He and his wife settled into a boat on the Thames River near Richmond.

In 1952, disillusioned with journalism, Brooks joined Christy and Moore as a literary agent. He spent more than a year as a "reader," evaluating other people's work, until, in 1953, he and his wife sold their boat and moved to Lincolnshire, Eleanor's home, where Brooks wrote two novels (unpublished) and worked part-time as a waiter and bartender. Their first child, Josephine, was born in March 1953. In order to live more economically, Brooks decided to return to Wales. Isolated on the northwest coast in Gelli, Llanthfrothn, a few miles south of Snowdon, the Brooks family moved into a sixteenth-century cottage and, he says, "lived the ecological life" with their 600 chickens and a nearby trout stream. Brooks worked in a hotel during summer months and wrote during the off-season.

While in Wales Jeremy Brooks spent three months writing *The Water Carnival* (1957), his first published novel. Putting to practical use his summer employment at the hotel and his knowledge of houseboats on the Thames, Brooks wrote a light comedy containing farcical elements about a hotel and its inhabitants on an island in the Thames.

The story utilizes a first-person narrator, Cyril Dropmore, who is secretary to Auk-Wilson, the hotel proprietor, "a splendid old fraud" who uses the hotel "as bait to trap social and artistic lions." Cyril describes himself as "not really a person at all, but an amalgam of several persons," and the manipulative devices he resorts to in order to achieve his devious but never criminal ends are comically revealing of his character. Auk-Wilson has delegated so many of his responsibilities to his secretary that Dropmore can smugly state that Auk-Wilson "never dares, these days, to allow himself to be annoyed with me for long. Since, in a sense, I *am* Auk-Wilson more solidly than he is himself, he cannot risk losing touch with what little tangible reality his personality contains."

Jeremy Brooks at his Welsh home, circa 1956

The island is peopled with supposed artists, most of whom are fakes and eccentrics who do nothing but socialize all day long. One "real" artist, George Higgs, is persuaded to moor his boat at the island and subsequently loses his ability to create, thanks to an unhappy love affair with an actress and the goings-on of the island residents. The plot advances slowly as plans for a water carnival (a pageant depicting English life) commence, and a freeloading but likeable intruder ingratiates himself into Cyril's and George's lives and onto their houseboats. George is completely unable to paint and, deeply depressed and in his cups, tells Cyril that he believes in nothing, that "one is the child of one's time. . . . You've got to believe in something, at some period

of your life, or you'll never believe in anything. . . . I came of age in a vacuum. War's a great big noise, the only thing that can come after it is a great big silence. It's like a heavy body falling through the air—it creates a vacuum behind it. Who the hell can live sanely in a vacuum?"

The novel concludes with the water carnival somehow managing to be a success in spite of impending disaster and a half-expected twist ending. Although it contains some humorous caricatures of English "types," *The Water Carnival*'s characters fail to engender loyalty or sympathy, and the plotting is somewhat dull. The novel sold reasonably well for a first book, and it was widely reviewed: According to the *Times* (London), "Mr. Brooks is sophisticated, funny and something more, and what that something more is the novel reveals as it develops." On the day of publication, Brooks relates that he traveled by rail to London and, on the train, read an uncomplimentary review in the *Daily Telegraph*. Crushed, he couldn't bear to read the other newspapers he had purchased, which carried, as Brooks recalls, "smashing reviews."

The themes of identity and war and peace are further developed in *Jampot Smith*, published three years after *The Water Carnival*. It is a sensitive exploration of emotional commitment among a group of adolescents growing up in wartime Wales. Some factual details about Bernard Smith, the title character, are based on Brooks's own life, but he says it is not an autobiographical portrayal.

Brooks spent seven years, off and on, writing *Jampot Smith*. Its original length was 200,000 words; he submitted it to his friend and former co-worker John Smith of Christy and Moore, who advised him to shorten it. By now the father of two more children (Margaret, born in July 1954, and William, born in December 1955) and in need of money, he hastily wrote *The Water Carnival*, knowing that it was publishable, and returned to reworking *Jampot Smith* to a more manageable length while employed as "steward" for an industrial magnate, Sir George Binney. Between 1956 and 1958 he worked in London as a publisher's reader for Robert Hale, Eyre & Spottiswoode, Macmillan, and David Higham.

In 1958 the principal characters of *Jampot Smith* were introduced to the public in a short story, "I'll Fight You," published in *Winter's Tales 4*. By this time (1958-1960), Brooks was supplementing his income by writing reviews for the *Guardian* and serving as a play reader for BBC-TV (1959-1960) in London.

Jampot Smith was finally published in 1960. The story is set in Llandudno, Wales, a charming, peaceful town nestled between the mountains and the sea. Bernard Smith is the well-meaning, troubled youth who narrates the novel. Like Brooks's family, Smith's has been evacuated to Wales from London early in 1940. The "new boy" in grammar school, Bernard has only one friend, but soon develops a very strong relationship with another English youth, Epsom Jones, whose family is also evacuated to Wales; together they share wartime boyhood fantasies and escapades. Jones is a well-developed, articulate character whose maturation from a mischievous prankster to a serious-thinking conscientious objector is finely conveyed by Brooks and lamentingly, bewilderedly recorded by Bernard.

A focal point in the novel is Bernard's fifteenth birthday party. Until the party Bernard has played and conversed fairly easily with other boys, and has met Kathy, a sensitive girl who has a crush on him. His party is a classic depiction of teenage intuitions and embarrassments. Girls and boys are experimenting with each other, defining roles, playing kiss-in-the-dark games. Bernard earns the nickname of "Jampot" because he supposedly attracts girls like flies around a jampot; more accurately, however, as Epsom explains to Kathy's jealous boyfriend, Dewi Hughes, "I called him that simply because he's scared stiff of the women. . . ."

Bernard discovers that inaction in a relationship can be as detrimental as action in dealing with other people's emotions: "No matter how much I tried to avoid them, no matter with what care I abjured any action that could involve the emotions of others, the traps would still set themselves, and, when I was least expecting it, ensnare me in their webs of unplumbable feeling. To fall into the web, no action of mine was required . . . to exist at all, it seemed indeed, was positive action."

After school examinations Epsom is due to go in the Army. He begins to formulate pacifist theories and tells Bernard, who has never thought about such things, "Perhaps I wouldn't invite the Jerries into my house, but I ought to! To do that sort of thing needs a kind of courage stronger than any a soldier will ever need. And if I *did* find the courage, perhaps it would help other people to do the same. It's only another drop of water in the pool, but it all helps." After he is forced to train for combat, Epsom applies for conscientious objector status.

Bernard, in the meantime, gets involved with Kathy before he goes off to war. He is ecstatic, comfortable, seemingly committed: "I had no reservations about Kathy now; had allowed myself to

be borne away by the river which I had been afraid might drown me, and found it bearing me up. . . ." Yet their time together becomes too much for him, and when, as he is leaving for the Army, she instigates lovemaking, he rejects her. Although she is completely undone, he wants only to get away from this emotional confrontation.

Jeremy Brooks remains pleased with *Jampot Smith*, and says with satisfaction that he "got it right." The novel was received warmly by the critics. One reviewer said: ". . . this group of schoolchildren is so beautifully depicted in its loves and inhibitions, its intimacies and withdrawals, . . . its betrayals and regroupings, . . . that the reader can participate in this most awkward age without the embarrassments usual in stories of adolescence." *Jampot Smith* sold out its first edition of 5,000 copies and was published in a library edition and a paperback edition, as well as in the United States. It is his only novel which, Brooks says, he "can still read with pleasure."

"Christmas with Sir Henry" is a short story based mainly on Brooks's experiences while working with the industrial magnate. It was published by *Transatlantic Review* in 1961. In Brooks's next novel, *Henry's War*, published in 1962, emotional commitment and pacifism are again the dominant themes.

Jeremy Brooks

Brooks was living in London and employed as a drama critic for *New Statesman* from 1960-1961 and as a fiction critic for the *Sunday Times* from 1961-1962. Although under constant financial pressure, he produced a book which successfully blends light humor with the serious concerns of nuclear disarmament.

The story is a departure from first-person narrative. As it begins, the main character, Henry Hywel Hughes, an unintellectual Welshman living in London, is writing spy thriller adventure novels, eking out a living in blissful—if impoverished—independence. His best friend, Charlie Evans, is also a Welshman living in London. They have been school chums and have served together in the British Army. While stationed in Cyprus, Henry has shot a young man in battle and has realized that "for himself one killing was more than enough to live with for the rest of his life." Once out of the service, having begun to write, he meets Veronica, a "Ban the Bomb" activist who pursues him; he drifts into a relationship with her, but finds her zealous commitment to a cause and her assumption of his own commitment to both her and the "cause" annoying. He meets a refreshingly innocent young woman, Berty, who is homeless and he begins, to his consternation, to fall in love with her. He is delighted to extricate himself from these tangled relationships when, during a fictitious national crisis, the Reserve is called up and his friend Charlie asks him to desert with him to Wales. Charlie is an intellectual who has made a clear political choice to desert—he feels that Britain is wrong to crush the current uprising—but, says Henry, ". . . none of that means much to me." He goes along with Charlie out of a sense of camaraderie, a desire not to kill, bewilderment about his emotional attachment to Berty, and hostility to Veronica.

The relationship between Charlie and Henry is reminiscent of that between Epsom Jones and Bernard Smith. Once inseparable friends, they are alienated from each other by their beliefs. On the Welsh farm to which they flee, Henry devotes himself to finishing his novel, while Charlie (with Elwyn, the owner of the farm and an old school friend) studies the newspapers and the political implications of the national crisis, becoming less and less sure of his stance as a deserter. An amnesty period is declared, and Charlie, whose complex beliefs are changing, attempts to persuade Henry to surrender with him during the amnesty period. Henry's desire not to kill is, of course, unchanged. The rift between the friends grows as Henry, writing madly, becomes

"too deeply involved in his imaginary world to know that he [has] given offence in the real one."

Charlie decides to return to the Army on the final day of the amnesty period, but Henry refuses to fight and remains at Elwyn's Welsh farm. Berty, who is in love with Henry, follows him to Wales from London, and Henry, reenacting a courtship scene described to him by Elwyn's old father, is caught poaching a salmon. He fights the game warden and realizes the absurdity of his position: he, a pacifist, is forced to fight the establishment because the "law" (the game warden) threatens his "freedom as a person who refuses to fight." Henry turns himself in. In a postscript, the reader is informed via letters to Henry in prison that Veronica is proud of his action, and that Henry's publisher thinks the book he has finished at the Welsh farm is terrible. Elwyn writes morosely of Charlie's death from a sniper's bullet; and Berty, who has remained on the farm with Elwyn and his family awaiting Henry's return, describes Elwyn as "in a dreadful state," for he spends hours up in his children's room, not letting them in, playing a logical and deadly game enacting the political and military moves leading to nuclear war. Henry, in debt, imprisoned, and in love, will perhaps resume writing and emerge from prison true to his principles and unscathed.

Critics praised *Henry's War* and Brooks's handling of ironic humor and pathos: "he can juxtapose the two, as in life they are so often yoked ungainly together, and never threaten farce." Brooks's message regarding the possibility of nuclear disaster is as relevant today as ever.

Smith, as Hero, a sequel to *Jampot Smith*, was published in 1965. Working at that time as literary manager for the Royal Shakespeare Company, Brooks spent nearly three years writing his last novel to date. He uses third-person narrative and, in fact, introduces himself, J.C.M. Brooks, as a minor character who was a year behind Bernard Smith at school in Wales. Bernard is a midshipman on a minesweeper in the Mediterranean early in 1945. He is "both ignorant and innocent"; his two prime objectives are to lose his virginity and to become a hero. He is still exploring, searching for "a self-conception from which to operate," and this search for identity is the main theme of the story. Bernard adopts the role of "bored aesthete to whom the Navy and all its works were occasion only for a tolerant, wondering humour." In his desire to be thought of as "sophisticated," he encourages rumors which allege he has homosexual tendencies and boasts about his past sexual conquests of girls back home (conquests which are, of course, completely fictitious). His confused search for identity is effectively illustrated in these two contradictory "fictions."

Bernard becomes friends with Lt. Terence Tetteris, a young aristocrat who has had an odd relationship with his mother and who seems to be the eccentric ideal which Bernard is striving to emulate. Bernard's shady reputation catches up with him when he falls in love with an aristocratic young nurse who rejects him because of his alleged homosexuality. He is enraged at having "slanderous lies" spread about him, completely forgetting that he himself started them and has also been equally guilty of telling lies about other people's sexual conduct.

During the story, information about several old friends from *Jampot Smith* is casually imparted: Epsom Jones spent time in jail for refusing to fight during the war and is now a coal miner; Dewi Hughes, Bernard's rival for Kathy's affections and a main character in Brooks's short story "I'll Fight You," appears briefly as an intelligence officer who scornfully informs Bernard that Kathy had a nervous breakdown after Bernard's abrupt departure from Llandudno. Later, the character Brooks informs Bernard that Dewi was drowned in the Pacific a few days before the end of the war. Bernard, who had stolen Kathy's affections from Dewi and thus was indirectly responsible for Dewi's leaving university to join the Navy, denies that the story could be true and denies that Dewi was ever a friend of his. He cannot grasp or acknowledge the suffering of other people.

Bernard becomes a "hero" when a floating mine strikes his ship and he is sent by the captain to check for damages. The executive officer of the ship has been trapped inside the bomb-damaged room, which is rapidly filling with water. Bernard cannot free the unconscious officer, but he realizes that the area must be sealed off immediately to protect the rest of the ship. He coolly orders that the door be locked and sealed, abandoning the wounded officer. Although Bernard is commended for his quick thinking, it is unclear to him or to the reader whether the officer was dead or merely unconscious, and his "heroism" is tainted with the knowledge that *he* could have been the trapped man and the executive officer the hero, had the watch schedule been reversed—and if so, would the executive officer have abandoned *him*?

Bernard at last achieves his second goal, the loss of his virginity, when, in a fit of pique with

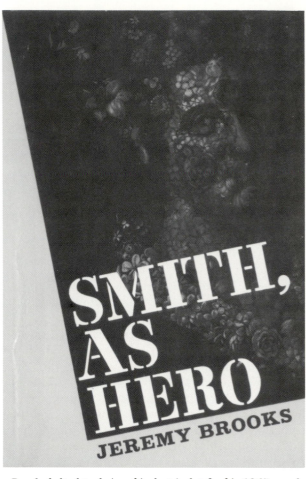

Brooks helped to design this dust jacket for his 1965 novel.

Tetteris and the nurse who has rejected him, he befriends an aging prostitute.

Bernard is forced to confront his emotions when he is ordered to board an illegal Jewish refugee ship which is in danger of sinking. Tetteris informs him that the Jews will be refused entry to Palestine, and Bernard comes face to face with human suffering. It is hard for him to fit this knowledge into his world, and when he is finally ashore he assuages his anger and guilt by fighting with a fellow officer and telling his friend Tetteris to shut up.

Critical reception of *Smith, as Hero* was good to excellent, and it is the only one of Brooks's novels to appear on the best-seller list. Considered too "English" to be marketed in the United States, the novel earned less than £1,300 and Brooks, who by this time had four children ranging in ages from one to eleven (Olivia having been born in September 1963), drifted into "commissioned" writing, abandoning his idea of a five-part novel series, "Try to be

Good," with Bernard Smith as the central character.

Inspired by his own growing family, Brooks tried his hand at a children's story, *The Magic Perambulator* (also published in 1965) which was illustrated by Robert Bartelt, an artist who lived near the Welsh cottage. The *Times Literary Supplement* reviewer described it as "a surprisingly good story about a rich Sultan's lonely little daughter who had everything that money could buy but no one of her own age to play with" and considered it too difficult for children under the age of nine to read alone, but "suitable for reading aloud."

Brooks's most recently published prose is a novella entitled "A Value," which he worked on for a year. Published in the April 1975 *New Review*, it concerns an aging, near blind poet, Hamish Macphee, who, frustrated by politicians' blindness (they "knew how far their molish tunnels had gone, and unlike others, appreciated how much they had weakened the fabric of the palace they were plundering . . ."), builds a metaphorical bomb to explode in Parliament.

Brooks effectively utilizes symbolism to convey his theme that a writer must be carefully read, must gain attention, to have his words heeded. The "bomb" is hidden in an old book which Macphee has lovingly and painstakingly filled with carefully juxtaposed quotations from world literature. He is sure the words will finally be of value when they "explode" on the floor of Parliament: "He had made this thing, not out of pride, not for self-glory, not to advance a cause or bully others into submission, but simply as a *proof*, the one and only incontrovertible proof of the simplest but most commonly ignored concept: that the Value of an object, artefact or event is not in its result but *as* a result." The bomb is constructed so that all that is needed to start its chain reaction is "a modest amount of time." Macphee throws the volume into the House of Commons chamber and falls; his last conscious thought: "The power of words!"

Since the mid-1960s Jeremy Brooks has used his creative energy in writing theatre and film scripts and feature articles and reviews. He has been a Literary Advisor for the Royal Shakespeare Company since 1969 and has adapted a number of Russian plays and stories for the English stage and screen. In addition, he has written and has had produced three original screenplays and three original stage plays, an original television play, and numerous documentary plays, shorts, talks, and features. He continues to write poetry and is currently on retainer to the *Sunday Times*.

In "An Artist's Story," a 1974 television play which Brooks adapted from the Anton Chekhov short story, he worked closely with David Jones, the director of the production. He enjoys being associated with Jones and has since adapted a number of other plays and stories for Jones's productions. For his English adaptation of Maxim Gorky's play, *Summerfolk*, in 1974, Brooks received an Obie Special Citation.

In adapting Russian plays, Brooks works closely with a translator, Kitty Hunter Blair. He is usually "working towards a particular production, and for a particular director," he says; production of the final work is completed in three to four stages, depending on the extent of collaboration with the director of the play. Stage one is the literal translation from the Russian of the author (Maxim Gorky, Anton Chekhov, Nikolai Gogol). Brooks's first draft is stage two, still "full of unsolved problems," he says, some of which solve themselves as the play develops, and others of which are dealt with by the translator or the director. Some, he says frankly, remain unsolved. Stage three is "a series of pitched battles in which the winner must always be the play. . . . Applied to an original work this would be a destructive process; applied to a translation it is illuminating, exciting—and immensely exhausting." Many pages are rewritten and checked again with the translator and the director before the script is sent for typing. During rehearsal period, stage four, Brooks polishes the dialogue after hearing it performed. He says his justification for adapting these plays is the poetry which an adaptor can instill in a work during stage two, "that period of dreamy identification with [the playwright] when the adaptor is under the illusion, briefly, that he is actually writing an original play, and allows himself little bursts of creativity which, if they survive stages three and four, are his justification for the whole enterprise. Apart from the cash."

During the late 1960s and early 1970s, Brooks wrote several original film scripts which have never been screened due to production or financing problems. Although he was paid for his writing efforts, he finds the situation "maddening." In the early 1970s his adaptation of "Enemies" by Gorky was televised in the United States, and he has had opportunities to work on American and Canadian film projects, but he prefers to live in Britain so has not pursued commercial film work.

Brooks spent six months in early 1981 adapting two plays for production on the English stage. The first, which was performed by the Royal

Shakespeare Company at Stratford-upon-Avon in April, is an adaptation of Alexander Ostrovsky's *The Forest*. It was written in 1871 by one of Russia's leading playwrights. His second adaptation of 1981 was of Aleksandr Solzhenitsyn's *The Love-Girl and the Innocent*, which opened at the Aldwych Theatre, London, in September.

Jeremy Brooks has two prose works near completion and many others in his notebooks, but is wary of rushing into print since his displeasure with *Smith, as Hero* after publication. He said he realized too late "just how many corners I had cut while writing it, how many problems had been shelved or hidden instead of solved, how many passages had a 'flip' style which had no place in a novel sequence intended, eventually, to deal with weighty matters. . . . What to do? One can't withdraw a published novel."

He is experimenting with narrative forms at present. "An American Au Pair," his current novel-in-progress, utilizes the technique of a girl writing letters home to her mother and father. "The Book of Churls," a semiautobiographical fantasy now being reworked, is presented in journal format with an omniscient machine which "beeps" when the journalist records a false value; footnotes which elaborate on the falsehood constitute the bulk of the book. Brooks is also contemplating an original play which would employ holograms to depict the theme of differences between generations, using the genre of science fiction. He continues to write poetry; it has been years, however, since he submitted any poetry for publication, although he recalls with some delight that early poems were his first published works.

Wales continues to attract Jeremy and Eleanor Brooks, and they escape from London to their Welsh cottage as often as possible. He enjoys photography and sculpting and takes an active interest in his wife's career as a sculptor and painter. (One of her recent exhibitions was "A Portrait of Mrs. Spinks," presented at the Biddick Farm Arts Centre.) Now that their children are nearly grown, Brooks believes that he will be financially able to devote more time to the novel, the genre he enjoys most, and which, he says, remains "the one in which I have unfulfilled ambitions."

Brooks is a serious, thought-provoking writer who has proved himself capable of depicting significant, sensitive themes in an entertaining format. He has diversified too much, perhaps, to be considered outstanding in any one realm of writing, but may yet return in triumph to the field of fiction.

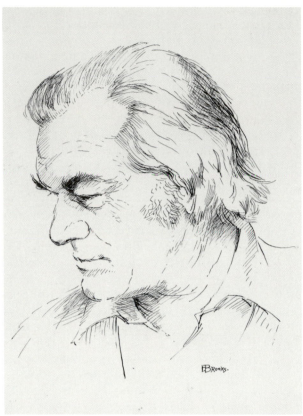

1981 drawing of Brooks, by his wife Eleanor

Plays:

The Government Inspector, adapted by Brooks and Edward O. Marsh from Nikolai Gogol's play, London, Aldwych Theatre, 19 January 1966;

Enemies, adapted by Brooks and Kitty Hunter Blair from Maxim Gorky's play, London, Aldwych Theatre, 22 July 1971;

The Lower Depths, adapted by Brooks and Blair from Gorky's play, London, Aldwych Theatre, 29 June 1972;

Summerfolk, adapted by Brooks and Blair from Gorky's play, London, Aldwych Theatre, 27 August 1974;

Comrades, adapted from August Strindberg's play, London, The Place, 19 October 1974;

The Forest, adapted by Brooks and Blair from Alexander Ostrovsky's play, Stratford-upon-Avon, The Other Place, 22 April 1981;

The Love-Girl and the Innocent, adapted by Brooks and Blair from Aleksandr Solzhenitsyn's play, London, Aldwych Theatre, 8 September 1981.

Screenplays:

Our Mother's House, by Brooks and Amanya Harari, MGM, 1967;

Work . . . Is a Four Letter Word, Universal, 1968.

Television Scripts:

Death Happens to Other People, BBC, Cardiff, 9 September 1966;

A Misfortune, adapted from Anton Chekhov's story, BBC, London, 20 January 1973;

On the High Road, adapted from Chekhov's play, BBC, London, 14 April 1973;

An Artist's Story, adapted from Chekhov's short-story, BBC, London, 2 February 1974.

Other:

"I'll Fight You," in *Winter's Tales 4* (London: Macmillan, 1958), pp. 38-71.

Periodical Publications:

"Christmas with Sir Henry," *Transatlantic Review* (Spring 1961): 70-94;

"Translating Gorky," *Theatre Quarterly*, 3 (January/March 1973): 24-27;

"A Value," *New Review* (April 1975): 37-48.

Brigid Brophy
(12 June 1929-   )

S. J. Newman
University of Liverpool

BOOKS: *The Crown Princess and Other Stories* (London: Collins, 1953; New York: Viking Press, 1953);

Hackenfeller's Ape (London: Hart Davis, 1953; New York: Random House, 1954);

The King of a Rainy Country (London: Secker & Warburg, 1956; New York: Knopf, 1957);

Black Ship to Hell (London: Secker & Warburg, 1962; New York: Harcourt, Brace & World, 1962);

Flesh (London: Secker & Warburg, 1962; Cleveland: World, 1963);

The Finishing Touch (London: Secker & Warburg, 1963);

The Snow Ball (London: Secker & Warburg, 1964);

Mozart the Dramatist: A New View of Mozart, His Operas and His Age (London: Faber & Faber, 1964; New York: Harcourt, Brace & World, 1964);

Don't Never Forget: Collected Views and Reviews (London: Cape, 1966; New York: Holt, Rinehart & Winston, 1967);

Fifty Works of English and American Literature We Could Do Without, by Brophy, Michael Levey, and Charles Osborne (London: Rapp & Carroll, 1967; New York: Stein & Day, 1968);

Religious Education in State Schools (London: Fabian Society, 1967);

Black and White: A Portrait of Aubrey Beardsley (London: Cape, 1968; New York: Stein & Day, 1969);

The Burglar (London: Cape, 1968; New York: Holt, Rinehart & Winston, 1968);

In Transit (London: Macdonald, 1969; New York: Putnam's, 1970);

The Longford Threat to Freedom (London: National Secular Society, 1972);

Prancing Novelist: A Defence of Fiction in the Form of a Critical Biography in Praise of Ronald Firbank (London: Macmillan, 1973; New York: Barnes & Noble, 1973);

The Adventures of God in His Search for the Black Girl (London: Macmillan, 1973; Boston: Little, Brown, 1974);

Beardsley and His World (London: Thames & Hudson, 1976; New York: Harmony, 1976);

Pussy Owl: Superbeast (London: BBC, 1976);

Palace Without Chairs (London: Hamish Hamilton, 1978; New York: Atheneum, 1978).

"Professors, psychologists, the frenzied do-gooders and the jangling drop-outs make divergent proclamations," wrote Donald Zec in the *Daily Mirror* in the autumn of 1968. "But all of them, the swingers and the Simon-pure, are agreed on one devastating fact: *Something odd is going on in the state of the universe*." One of the oddest, most brilliant, and most enduring of these 1960s symptoms was Brigid Brophy. Novelist, journalist, vegetarian, polymath, pundit and polemicist, she reflected and transmitted the style of the age. A thumbnail sketch in the *Observer* in 1975 summed her up as a " 'terrible child' of the mid-sixties: campaigned against marriage, Vietnam, factory farmers, religious education in schools, for Greek in schools, bisexuality, vegetarianism, *Fanny Hill* and Writers' Action Group." She wrote and spoke about all these as well as the Bomb, Mozart, Mickey Mouse, the Pill, Lucretius, the Rolls Royce, vivisection and Chelsea football club. She became notorious for her views on sex and for her pugnacious image. *Nova* described her as "the tigress, that crafty slasher"; the *Sunday Express* threatened to burn her as a witch. She confessed to having been expelled from Oxford for being drunk in chapel. She attacked Kingsley Amis and the English sense of humor. She ate a daffodil, stalk and all, in the Cafe Royal to proclaim her vegetarianism. When the Oxford University magazine *Isis* asked her for an article on Mrs. Beeton (the Victorian writer on cookery and household management) to celebrate its 1500th issue, she replied on a postcard: "The Freudian symbolism of Mrs. Beeton must lie chiefly in her name. One only hopes that she enjoyed being it." She described herself Irishly as the highbrow's lowbrow and her work

as a howl for tolerance. In a *Guardian* interview she called herself a most un-English writer: "I am really most interested in intensity. I cannot stand anything that is lukewarm." Journals of the 1960s are peppered with her remarks. "I prefer animals to people, which is why I married Michael." Norman Mailer's *The Prisoner of Sex* "is modelled on a dribble: long, and barely continuous." "I obdurately insist on believing that some men are my equals."

Witty herself, she has inspired wit in others. *Private Eye* lampooned her as Frigid Frophy, the *Evening Standard* called her "a female Brendan Behan," Geoffrey Grigson—who agreed with her that there were always too many stuffed classics around—"a queen wasp," and Anne Duchene "the finest pun-up girl we have." She was widely compared to Mary McCarthy, favorably by Irma Kurtz, unfavorably by Julian Symons, who said, "every nation gets the Mary McCarthy it deserves. And Britain is a poor nation." Admirers have contradicted the iconoclast image, calling her the arch-priestess of the permissive society, one of the rare and precious human beings who have done something positive, and a saint. Interviewers have been surprised to find a courteous and secluded hostess who claims that she becomes involved in controversies inadvertently, and protests her humility: "I have always assumed I have to think more intensely than other people simply to keep up with them." This apparent calm has unsettled some men. Anthony Quinton detected "a nervous, heavy-breathing desperation about Miss Brophy's endeavours to make herself out to be meek and rational that inhibits belief." More graphically, Zec reported that "the handsome statue in her room of a classical, unclothed gent was sawn off or shattered in its essentials." David Pryce-Jones commented, in a review of *Don't Never Forget* (1966), "Miss Brophy is two persons, two rivals, who wrestle for sole possession of her essays: the dandy and the heckler." These rivals assume different disguises at different stages of her career, but the war between them helps explain the poetic quality of her best work and the stridency of her worst.

Her background is as complicated as her character. The only child of Charis Grundy and John Brophy, she inherited a mixture of Irishness, social and religious nonconformity, cultural breadth and emotional energy. Her mother— brilliantly sketched in *Don't Never Forget*—was Chicago-born and Liverpool-bred, daughter of an architect who gave up his profession to become the Irvingite bishop (designated "Angel") of Liverpool. The Irvingites, now defunct, were a romantically

Brigid Brophy

apocalyptic sect founded in the early nineteenth century by Edward Irving, a Scottish preacher and friend of Thomas Carlyle. "In moments of depression," said Brigid Brophy recently, "I remind myself I am the granddaughter of an Angel." Charis Grundy served in France in the Women's Army Auxiliary Corps during World War I, read English at Liverpool University, was, according to her daughter, "one of the bravest Air Raid Wardens in London" during the blitz, and worked as headmistress, amateur hospital nurse, and prison visitor; in a *Guardian* interview Brigid Brophy described her as "a high-minded sinner."

John Brophy, a novelist, also read English at Liverpool following active service in World War I (having enlisted at the age of fourteen). Brigid Brophy calls him "an Irishman of at that time poetic temperament, luminous purity and Sinn Fein politics," and says his family hailed from "a small place just about in the middle of Ireland called Ballybrophy." John Brophy was born in Liverpool, which forms the background of two of his novels, *The Bitter End* (1928) and *Waterfront* (1934). He worked as an assistant in the Liverpool department store Lewis's, as a teacher in Egypt, and as chief copywriter to a London advertising agency before becoming a professional author. With Eric Partridge he compiled *Songs and Slang of the British Soldier 1914-1918* (1930), and during World War II he edited the English periodical *John O'London's Weekly*. After the war he had published three nonfiction books (which he modestly called "out-of-the-ordinary") and which are subtle and original studies in ontology, deserving to be better known: *The Human Face* (1945), *Body and Soul* (1948), and *The Mind's Eye* (1949). "My father," Brigid Brophy has said, "was one of those people who are totally open and completely mysterious."

In 1940 he wrote, "I have a daughter, ten years old, who excels me in everything, even in writing." Not surprisingly, Brigid Brophy has described herself as a hereditary writer. She began with poetic dramas, inspired by Shakespeare and Scott; she read Oscar Wilde, George Bernard Shaw and Ronald Firbank as a child, and *Finnegans Wake* at the age of nine. "My basic education," she writes, "consisted of the elements of the craft of prose, which I picked up from my father, and the principles of English and Latin syntax, which I learned painlessly from my mother, a teacher by both profession and inspiration." Her "idyllic childhood" and her schooling were interrupted by the war. "At eleven I was one of those wartime children who was to be sent to America for safety. My tickets were bought.

My bags were packed. And the night before I was to sail, it was decided I shouldn't go. It may have been the first decision I ever made. I was desperate not to go, because I thought it meant I was abandoning my parents to their death." Instead she was shifted from school to school—"which gave me an unrivalled view of the varieties of educational practice"—including St. Paul's Girls' School, a secretarial college, and an art school.

In 1947 she was awarded a Jubilee Scholarship at St. Hugh's College, Oxford, to read classics, but after four terms she was expelled. This "squalid little injustice," as she later called it, took place partly because she was rumored to have a sex life, partly because she arrived drunk in chapel to read the lesson, partly because she was thought to have exerted a disturbing influence on her fellow students. "I was disturbed by *them*," she said. "At the time I was sent down, I had been drunk for six weeks. And yet not one single person in authority at Oxford asked: 'Why are you so unhappy?' Not one. I couldn't, at nineteen, convince myself of my innocence against the weight of recognised authority that had rejected me as unfit to consort with my fellow-humans. I shall never describe, because I won't risk re-living, the distress I suffered."

After leaving Oxford she worked for several years as a shorthand typist in London, writing short stories in her spare time. These were collected and published in January 1953 as *The Crown Princess and Other Stories*. The volume was praised by a reviewer in the *Times Literary Supplement* who discerned "exceptional acuteness and penetrative power" and identified Brophy with "such tough and sharp American talents as those of Miss Mary McCarthy and Miss Eleanor Clark." The two most characteristic tales are the title story—which in its conflict between aristocratic and egalitarian impulses anticipates much of her later writing—and "Late Afternoon of a Faun," a Huxleyan fable about the disappearance of magic and superstition in Roman-occupied Greece (which Brigid Brophy wrote when she was thirteen, in a Latin lesson at school).

"In my twenty-fifth year," says Brophy, "I sat down to write a narrative poem and rose a fortnight later (a fortnight of which I have no memory) having written instead a brief novel called *Hackenfeller's Ape*, which is probably the best I shall ever write and which already displays at its most intense the violently romantic feeling in a precisely classical form to which most of my fiction aspires." *Hackenfeller's Ape* was published late in 1953 to wide praise. The gist of the story is that an absentminded professor of zoology, observing the mating ritual of a rare species of ape at the London Zoo, learns that the male is scheduled for use in a rocket experiment and decides to rescue him. With the help of a modern Moll Flanders he sets the ape free, but liberation causes more problems than imprisonment did. In an interview in *The Beast*, Brigid Brophy says she wrote the novel while living near the London Zoo. Deeply affected by pity and terror for what she saw there, she says, "I was trying to establish a parallel between shutting people up in prisons and shutting animals up in zoos." The novel seems to take off from a sentence in John Brophy's *The Human Face*: "Long hours have I spent in front of the big cages, watching the dark-haired creatures puzzling and pondering their big heads with the almost human faces in which it is not difficult to trace, as if in a slow-motion cinema film, the aching, painful, obstinate processes of elementary cognition." It is partly a study of the animal life of the mind, partly a satire on man—a mixture of intellectual fable, science fiction, and fantastic poem. Unlike Aldous Huxley or William Golding, Brophy does not solidly bond the properties of fable, fiction and poetry. This flaw weakens the novel, but it also allows an endearing gentleness to play through the more stringent implications of the story, and it leaves space for Brophy's first attempt at a type she draws expertly: the delicate, ineffectual male.

Hackenfeller's Ape was awarded the Cheltenham Literary Festival first prize for a first novel in 1954. In the same year Brigid Brophy married Michael Levey, then Assistant Keeper at the National Gallery, now Sir Michael Levey, Director of the National Gallery since 1973 and author of books on many subjects, including Mozart, Pater, and Renaissance painting; his *Early Renaissance* (1967) was awarded the Hawthornden Prize in 1968. Her marriage, she said later, "turned out to be a matter of serene happiness." It also became a public spectacle: at once a soapbox from which to vilify marriage as an immoral institution and a pulpit from which to preach conjugal harmony. According to her husband, it was her views on sex and marriage that brought her into disfavor. For instance, "I think it's highly unnatural to be married." "My husband is a wife." "I think that probably about ten per cent of the community have a talent for being married, and the rest shouldn't attempt it." "We don't make use of the social aspects of sex. We don't have enough three-sided relationships." "It is a pure myth that men are naturally polygamous and women are not." Hunter Davies reported their marriage for the *Sunday Times* with the bewilderment of Gulliver observing the Houyhnhnms. "They're too, too

reasonable to quarrel. They semantically differ. They thrive on a hot-bed of nonstop verbal intercourse. 'One is more brilliant at night,' said Michael Levey. 'Especially in bed. One is somehow more baroque.' "

The second novel, *The King of a Rainy Country* (1956), written before this relationship became public in this way, perhaps suffers from too much serenity. It is Brophy's most naturalistic book, an elegant picaresque tale about a Bohemian girl and her lover. Like one of its own characters it seems to shrink from the inside of things. But there are moments when the prose wriggles with sudden life, giving promise of hidden energy. The birth of Brophy's daughter Kate in 1957 seems to have released this energy. "The responsibility of becoming this person's mother obliged me to pause and define my own convictions, accounting to myself for how I could be both an artist and a rationalist, and both a Freudian and a Shavian evolutionist. The result was a colossal work of nonfiction, *Black Ship to Hell*." Published in 1962, this book—compared by Anthony Quinton in the *Daily Telegraph* to Norman O. Brown's *Life Against Death*—is an ambitious exploration of the dynamics of hate. Often maddeningly mechanical in its application of Freudian theory to life, it is still an intellectual tour de force. It was fiercely attacked by reviewers, but Peter Porter summed it up accurately in the *Listener*: "Miss Brophy has found a new way of being creative. She disguises her book as a critical work; it seems to me a loving fiction of opinion. Her respectable progenitors are the great entertainers and explainers Shaw and Auden. They fight for her soul with Colin Wilson."

Black Ship to Hell won Brophy the London Magazine Prize for Prose in 1962. It also seems to have stimulated her creatively. Between 1962 and 1964 her three most accomplished novels were published. *Flesh* (1962), dedicated to I[ris] M[urdoch], is a cunning fable about sexual awakening. The story is straightforward and concerns the meeting, the marriage, and the marital complications of two young north London Jews. Brophy describes it as "an almost distressingly cold-blooded little story which reads better in the French translation than in English, and which was the first of my novels to have a numerical as distinct from a highbrow success." A Sunday *Times* reviewer called it "not erotic but curious, exploratory, examining the feel of things, the shape of relationships. This detachedly clinical approach is perhaps characteristic of an age which has no moral knowledge, only scientific knowledge. And this, too, may explain why there has been a recent expansion of the comedy of manners." The book is clinical, but also poetic, with moments of animal tenderness such as the description of "deep, moist green" chestnut leaves which, "losing the pleated look of the flesh on a baby's hands, opened to their fullest like the palms of hundreds of adult, caressing hands." Again her father's writing comes to mind, in this case the celebration of hands in *Body and Soul*.

The Finishing Touch (1963), described by its author as a "lesbian fantasy," is a modestly evil comedy about a girls' finishing school on the French Riviera. It has been called "the most concentrated single example of Firbank's influence, really a posthumous monument to him." Again the events are simple. An English princess arrives at the school and innocently precipitates blackmail, scandal, and a startling denouement. The story is projected through the schoolmistress, a *fade*, highbrow Molly Bloom. The novel was highly praised. A reviewer in the *Times Literary Supplement* said "Firbank is almost too obviously both the inspiration and the victim of Miss Brophy's waspish and witty tale." A *Daily Herald* reviewer called it "an outrageously indelicate joke made in beautifully mannered prose."

It is her most decadent book—in *Don't Never Forget* she calls decadence "a rearguard revolutionary movement"—and, as the title suggests, an important contribution to the poetics of masturbation. Awareness of the relationship between literature and pornography led her to crusade publicly for the latter. In 1972 she published, in response to *The Longford Report on Pornography*, a pamphlet, *The Longford Threat to Freedom*, which attacked this "committee of theocrats, paranoiacs, simpletons and puritans" and proclaimed, "Masturbation is one of the few human activities that absolutely *cannot* do any harm to anyone."

The third and most celebrated of these novels is *The Snow Ball* (1964), a black comedy of manners. The plot is one of intrigue and seduction, the setting is a New Year's fancy dress ball, and the principal characters—dressed as Donna Anna and Don Giovanni—evoke Mozart and Tolstoy. Structurally, according to its author, the novel "attempts to transcribe in literature the erotic perspectives and the chilling effects of a baroque tomb." Such complexity may not be immediately apparent in the narrative, which leads through a series of festive encounters and witty conversations to a bedroom scene recommended by Olivia Manning as "a truer impress of The Act than the much-discussed passage in *The Group*." But something of Brophy's intention can be glimpsed from the way the main story—the

courtship and seduction of Donna Anna by Don Giovanni—is teasingly reflected and refracted by other events at the ball, from the rapid shifts of mood and setting, from the luxurious interiors and freezing exteriors, and from the somber conclusion.

Dust jacket for Brophy's "lesbian fantasy"

Both in style and subject matter *The Snow Ball* is a study in artifice. The characters, to quote the heroine, are—or aspire to be—"very beautiful, highly-coloured, fantastic reptiles." The best moments have a frigid brilliance. There was a lot of uneasy praise from the critics, and even those who disliked the book conceded its effectiveness. It was described by John Horder in the *Guardian* as Brophy's "breakthrough novel." Iris Murdoch praised it unreservedly in the *Sunday Times*, and it was dramatized on BBC television in April 1964.

The Snow Ball is dedicated to Charles Osborne, an Australian who emigrated to England in the 1950s and from 1958 to 1966 served as Assistant Editor of *London Magazine*. His favorable response to *Black Ship to Hell* led, in Brophy's words, "to my being invited to contribute to the *London Magazine* and by that route I entered journalism, becoming a critic and a propagandist of libertarianism (including liberty for animals) in the papers (most regularly the *Sunday Times* and the *New Statesman*)." She also began to broadcast on television and radio. (She was not quite a stranger to radio, for her father had broadcast regularly, and she had made her own first broadcast on 10 January 1943 in the series "Answering You," for which she received four guineas.) Her first adult broadcast, in July 1963, was entitled "The Novel as a Takeover Bid"; this and subsequent talks were later collected and published in *Don't Never Forget*. After her first television appearance on "Writer's World" in May 1964, she became a regular television guest throughout the 1960s and 1970s, appearing on "Not So Much a Programme More a Way of Life" in 1964 and 1965, "Late Night Line-Up" in 1965 and 1966, "Enquiry" and "Horizon" in 1965 and 1970, and "The Book Programme" in 1974 and 1976. She joined the Labor party and became one of the academy of writers who supported Harold Wilson in the 1964 election. She testified as one of the principal witnesses for the defense at the *Fanny Hill* trial in 1964. In the same year she subjected Kingsley Amis to what a *Daily Mail* reporter called "the most violent public attack on any author I have read since Dr. Leavis carved up C. P. Snow." She said it "deeply offended her to see authors who couldn't write to save their lives getting all the praise."

Her writing at this time became at best trenchantly witty, at worst harsh and arrogant. "The trouble with Miss Brophy," complained Peter Wilsher after a radio talk attacking Aldous Huxley in 1964, "is that her haymakers are so wholesale. The undoubted vigour of her invective begins to boomerang on her." Something of this defect mars her radio play *The Waste Disposal Unit*, broadcast in April 1964. The play, she says, "is written in American as a foreign language, the poetic expression of my lethal fascination with that alien tongue which is licking the brains out of my native civilisation." Peter Wilsher described it in the *Sunday Times* as "a good round-arm swipe at American language and the American way of life," but compared it unfavorably with the work of Edward Albee. "Let Miss Brophy in future reserve her Savonarola lashings for the British—they hate it." They hated it so much that when given the chance to retaliate they hounded her. When her first stage play, *The Burglar* (a Shavian farce about conflicting moralities), which had enjoyed a successful preliminary run in the provinces, came to the Vaudeville Theatre in 1967, the critics killed it. When it was published in 1968, Brophy prefaced it with a long *apologia pro vita sua*. Another reaction to the attempted literary assassination was to abandon language altogether. Her Prop-Art exhibition of 1969, prepared in collaboration with the novelist Maureen Duffy, consisted of polystyrene wigheads adorned with plastic carrots, toy drums, masks, etc.: an eloquent silence indicating "Words Fail Me."

Apart from broadcasts, plays, and the exhibition, Brophy's chief writing during the 1960s was criticism. In *Palace Without Chairs* (1978) there is a novelist who has abstained from writing novels, "developing a technique for dealing with his imagination when it preferred the nuclei of fictions: "a few he compressed into short stories, but most, even more clearly, he distorted into sometimes rather brilliant critical perceptions about other writers' work. 'All critical insight,' he began one of his critical essays, 'is autobiography by the critic.' " The critical books after *Black Ship to Hell* can be read as simultaneous attempts by the writer's rational self to expose the secrets of her imagination, and by her imagination to elude rational exposure.

The first of these critical works was *Mozart the Dramatist: A New View of Mozart, His Operas and His Age* (1964). Brophy says it was "detested by music critics but, happily for me, liked by composers." One of the reasons *Mozart the Dramatist* creates problems for the reader is that the title implies a study of Mozart's dramatic technique (along the lines of Joseph Kerman's *Opera as Drama*), whereas in fact the book is a penetrating study of the psychology of an artist in an age of rational enlightenment. Another reason is its abrupt manner. Although Brophy spotlights the difference between Mozart and Beethoven, her approach seems more akin to Beethoven than to Mozart: "Beethoven assaults our emotions head on, Mozart is the strategist who takes our breath away by the audacity of his plans. He is upon us and has captured the citadel before we had time to conceive that he might come by that route." That said, *Mozart the Dramatist* abounds in fertile suggestions. Like *Prancing Novelist*, it is radically perceptive about creative parricide ("Mozart was caught in the dilemma that he could please and satisfy Leopold only by surpassing him . . . he was casting about for an adoptive musical father whose music he could more genuinely admire and learn from than Leopold's"). It is also acute about the quality of the vocal line: "the melody itself is impermanent and unsolid, on the verge of

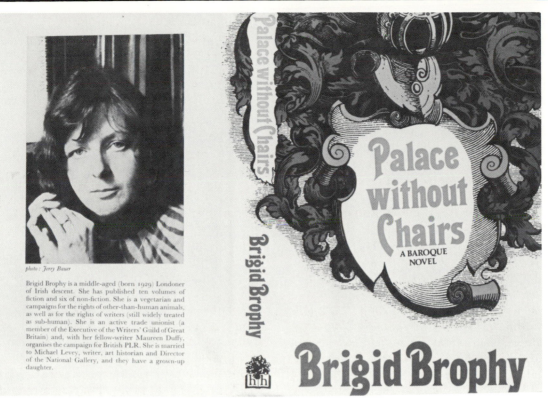

Dust jacket for Brophy's 1978 "psychological fable"

vanishing into the surrounding silence. The outline of the melody remains perceptible or deducible, but it is essentially *performer's* music."

In 1966 Brophy published a collection of selected journalism called *Don't Never Forget* (the title is taken from an inscription in English by Mozart: "Don't never forget your true and faithfull friend"). "People (even those who do not mean to be rude)," she wrote in the preface, "often ask me whether my journalism interferes with my serious writing. As a matter of fact, my journalism *is* serious writing." *Don't Never Forget* bears out this claim. It can stand comparison with W. H. Auden's *Forewords and Afterwords* (1973) in range and wit. Its subjects include the rights of animals, marriage, opera, detective stories, writers from John Cleland to Patricia Highsmith, and a radio talk on the Profumo affair (commissioned and withheld by the BBC), "The Nation in the Iron Mask." Ian Hamilton attacked the collection for its "mincing aggressiveness and grey slabs of polemical rightmindedness." There is some truth in what he says, but only if the book is read as the sum of its parts. The parts, like poetry in Walter Bagehot's definition, are memorable and emphatic, intense, and *soon over*. She says that wit "is always some form of analysis" and goes on to pro-

vide proof, sometimes epigrammatically, sometimes aphoristically. On Ivy Compton-Burnett: "It's like reading a Wilde comedy in algebra." Katharine Mansfield "had a cannibal imagination. Her *aperçus* are the world glimpsed by an assassin." On her mother: "Antecedents do not explain my mother. Her background is interesting less for what it made her into than for what she made of it."

Aggressiveness is more damagingly apparent in the work in which she collaborated with Michael Levey and Charles Osborne. *Fifty Works of English and American Literature We Could Do Without* (1967) is a debunking survey of fifty English and American classics which was received by reviewers in the spirit in which it was written. Bernard Levin gave it the toughest treatment, declaring that "the three authors have established themselves as incomparably the three biggest twits in Britain." The main trouble is that the authors are unable to make up their minds whether or not it is important *not* to be earnest about the classics. The result is a mongrel mixture of the facetious and the pharisaical. For all that, *Fifty Works* is a useful antidote to the hagiography that often passes for literary criticism.

In *Black and White: A Portrait of Aubrey Beardsley* (1968) Brophy turned her attention to the psychology of graphic art. *Black and White* is not quite a pioneering study (there was a Beardsley exhibition in London in 1966) and, like much of Brophy's criticism, it is more an attempt to explain the artist to herself and herself to the artist than an exploration of the wider implications of his success. William Empson hinted as much in his otherwise favorable review in the *Listener*: "This is what needs explaining: why did the quality of his line suddenly get under people's skins, a thing which hasn't happened since to any major artist?" But it again demonstrates her gift for condensed precision. And the real value of the book is suggested by the fact that W. H. Smith banned it from their display shelves—not because of the text but because of the pictures.

During the middle and late 1960s Brophy's engagement with public opinion and events was at its peak. In October 1965 the *Sunday Times* published her influential essay "The Rights of Animals." This case against vivisection led her into an increasingly active campaign for animal liberties. She spoke in Trafalgar Square in 1967 against factory farming, describing herself later, in an interview in the *Daily Mirror*, as "white with terror standing on that bloody plinth in the pouring rain." Her campaign continued throughout the 1970s and

still continues. She contributed a paper called "The Darwinist's Dilemma" (arguing that Darwinism encourages society to regard animals as failed humans) to the Animal Rights Symposium at Cambridge in August 1977, and she is closely associated with the British Union for the Abolition of Vivisection. In addition, she joined the Arts Council's literature panel in 1966, but resigned in 1967 in protest against the dismissal of one of the members (Barry Miles, co-owner of *International Times*, a fortnightly newspaper for hippies) for appearing to advocate in his paper the use of drugs by young people. And, again in 1966, she lectured with missionary zeal to the Fabian Society against religious education in state schools. The lecture was published as a Fabian Tract in 1967, arousing intense hostility and widespread discussion.

In the late 1960s Brophy's slight lyric grace was nearly destroyed by her tough unreasonableness. In *The Human Face* John Brophy wrote that Hugh Walpole and T. E. Lawrence "were both men in whose personalities there raged a secret civil war, and neither of them fully understand what the conflict was about." *In Transit* (1969) is Brigid Brophy's most self-exacerbated book. Fundamentally it expresses the plight of an imaginative writer who has tried too hard to rationalize her irrationality. "Our

Dust jacket for Brophy's 1969 book, described as an "anti-antinovel"

them, where he half-closed the door behind ~~them~~ him.

'Don't press the matter further for the time being', he said in a low voice, feeling that the conspiracy was betraying him into betraying his wife — and on the very point where, of all points in their life together, he most concurred with her and she commanded his most vivid allegiance.

'You understand, Papa —'

'Papa, you as a man —'

He put his finger to his lips. 'Let a little time ~~pass slowly~~ elapse', he said. 'It will pass ~~before~~ quickly, [?]'

Both boys nodded, conspirators with him, and walked soft-footed away.

He turned and went back into Madame Bolsanier's drawing room, feeling that he had betrayed not only her but his own most urgent wish — which was that time should draw itself out slowly, since this was the last possible day on which he could hear, as new information, ~~words~~ sentences and thoughts that had originated in the mind of Ferdy.

❧ 5

'Monsieur le marquis'.

A haughty turn, as though the mere naming had offered the insult of physical contact; an inclination, correct but the minimum, a mere nod in which,

Manuscript of a work in progress

programme," it proclaims at one point, is "Undo the Normative Conquest." Though subtitled "an heroicycle novel," *In Transit* is less a novel than a cross between a neurotic essay in criticism and a farcical nightmare. The setting is an airport, and the basic subject of the deracinated protagonist's speculations is loss of social and sexual identity. The surreal narrative, which throws together a variety of bizarre styles and characters, includes an antibaroque opera (*Alitalia*), an antithriller, and an Irish antihero, O'Dysseus. The book is best described as an anti-antinovel. Its hero/heroine remarks at one point, "I am hateful to myself through claustrophobia." *In Transit* followed hard on the heels of Gore Vidal's *Myra Breckinridge* (1968), to which it alludes. But unlike *Myra*, the protagonist of *In Transit* is nothing more than a voice, though one which manages to epitomize the flat spin of the late 1960s in its jokes, puns, syllogisms, and scissored wordplay.

Self-exasperation shows again in *Prancing Novelist: A Defence of Fiction in the Form of a Critical Biography in Praise of Ronald Firbank* (1973), which is as long and unruly as its title suggests. "Here is Brigid Brophy," wrote Philippa Pullar in the *Sunday Times*, "whose strength and beauty lies in her lyric brevity, writing a fat and heavy volume about someone whose own strength and beauty also lies in lyric brevity." P. N. Furbank in the *Listener* called it "a rum go, a vast ramping book at once so bad and so good one doesn't know whether to cheer or to weep." *Prancing Novelist* is as much about Firbank as D. H. Lawrence's *Study of Thomas Hardy* (published in *Phoenix* in 1936) is about Hardy. It is her most quixotic book: a work of creative dissatisfaction and anticriticism, raging in the dark about the most inexplicable artistic property, invention: "the magical faculty which conjures something into thereness where nothing existed before." It is quixotic, but also antiquixotic: in a brilliant chapter, "Cervantes and the Label on the Sauce Bottle," Brophy invokes Don Quixote and St. Teresa as opposites who meet in creative madness, the one from an excess of the literary, the other from an excess of the literal. Indeed, her evocation of the character of St. Teresa comes closest to explaining the quality of this sometimes unreadable and occasionally unforgettable book: "Saint Teresa's personality is in strange suspension. It did express itself in art, yet it was, in its capacity as artist's personality, frustrated, because it would not admit its self-expression to *be* art."

The Adventures of God in His Search for the Black Girl (1973) represents a recovery from solipsism: a series of fables—including a poignant reworking of

"The Crown Princess," called "The Singularly Ugly Princess"—and a philosophical novella. A. S. Byatt, reviewing it in the *Times*, objected to "a humour based on an apparently colossal optimism." But as Brophy wrote in her preface to *The Burglar*, "I would hardly have survived the assassination [of *Black Ship to Hell*] had I not transformed myself from masochist and coward into the tough stoic, obstinate egoist or rash Irish lunatic I have been ever since." And anyway, as Dylan Thomas said, "Comic writers can't expect society to be comic just for *them*."

Her most recent works of fiction are *Pussy Owl: Superbeast*—a charming tale of a boastful hybrid "noted for wisdom, intelligence, agility in flight, linguistic ability and for jumping on anyone who gives me cheek," broadcast on BBC television in March 1976 and published in the same year—and *Palace Without Chairs* (1978), a psychological fable set in a wintry mid-European Arcadia where everything has gone wrong. It is the most frigid and sterile of all her books. The prose has lost its spring, so that each sentence hits the same flat, dull note. There is, however, a new vigor in naming. Characters called Frumgeour and Skimplepex suggest that her fiction might take a new direction, away from Shavian enlightenment toward the rococo-gothic of Firbank and Peake.

Palace Without Chairs, dedicated to Michael Foot, is prefaced by a note to readers pointing out that British writers are not paid for the borrowing of their books from public libraries and asking readers to support Public Lending Right. Despite other activities—serving as vice-president of the National Anti-Vivisection Society from 1974, and as vice-chairman of the British Copyright Council from 1976—Brigid Brophy's chief public activity in the 1970s was the establishing, with Maureen Duffy, of Writers' Action Group, with the aim of negotiating a Public Lending Right. The idea was originated by John Brophy in 1951, who named it "the Brophy penny" (that then being the amount library users were to be asked to pay). Though the concept initially aroused intense controversy, nearly thirty years later, in 1979, Michael Foot steered the Public Lending Right Bill through Parliament.

"I would very much like to let go and sing out," said Brigid Brophy in a recent interview. Victims of what she obdurately insists on calling her reasonableness may believe she has let go quite sufficiently. And the quality and quantity of her work already make it one of the chronicles of the time. But although the battle between herself and society has tested virtually every combination of her complicated identity, two remain as yet untried. One is a dramatic encounter of a kind she adumbrates in a vivid image in *Don't Never Forget* while describing Sartre's analysis of Genet: "There he stands, the gangling and admirable professor, goggling through his global spectacles, making lunges with his butterfly net—and above him swoops, sombre and solid, dazzling in smoothed black-and-white marble, a vast, wing-spread, baroque angel of death." The other is implicit in John Bayley's comment on W. H. Auden: he "is most simply himself when his verse is at its most entrancingly mannered." Brigid Brophy has earned the right to be simply herself.

Play:

The Burglar, London, Vaudeville Theatre, 25 February 1967.

Radio Script:

The Waste-Disposal Unit, BBC, 1964.

Other:

Elizabeth Smart, *By Grand Central Station I Sat Down*

and Wept, introduction by Brophy (London: Pantheon, 1966);

"The Young Mozart," *Opera 66* (London: Alan Ross, 1966);

Jane Austen, *Pride and Prejudice*, introduction by Brophy (London: Pan Books, 1967);

The Waste-Disposal Unit in *Best Short Plays of the World Theatre 1958-1967* (New York: Crown, 1968);

M. Hill and M. Lloyd-Jones, *Sex Education: The Erroneous Zone*, foreword by Brophy (London: National Secular Society, 1970);

Libretti of *Die Zauberflöte* and *Die Entführung aus dem Serail*, translated by L. Salter with introduction by Brophy (London: Cassell, 1971);

"The Way of No Flesh," in *The Genius of Shaw*, edited by Michael Holroyd (London, Hodder & Stoughton, 1979);

"The Darwinist's Dilemma," in *Animal Rights: A Symposium*, edited by D. Paterson and R. D. Ryder (London: Centaur Press, 1979).

Periodical Publication:

"Lucretius: The Liveliest Latin," *Times* (London), 6 July 1968.

Christy Brown
(5 June 1932-7 September 1981)

Cathleen Donnelly
University of Delaware

BOOKS: *My Left Foot* (London: Secker & Warburg, 1954; New York: Simon & Schuster, 1955); republished as *The Story of Christy Brown* (New York: Pocket Books, 1971); republished as *The Childhood Story of Christy Brown* (London: Pan, 1972);

Down All the Days (London: Secker & Warburg, 1970; New York: Stein & Day, 1970);

Come Softly to My Wake (London: Secker & Warburg, 1971); republished as *The Poems of Christy Brown* (New York: Stein & Day, 1971);

Background Music: Poems by Christy Brown (London: Secker & Warburg, 1973; New York: Stein & Day, 1973);

A Shadow on Summer (London: Secker & Warburg, 1974; New York: Stein & Day, 1975);

Wild Grow the Lilies (London: Secker & Warburg,

1976; New York: Stein & Day, 1976);

Of Snails and Skylarks (London: Secker & Warburg, 1977; New York: Stein & Day, 1978).

Christy Brown is best known for his autobiographical novel *Down All the Days* (1970), a work which reflects the influence of Thomas Wolfe and, closer to Brown's milieu, James Joyce. It is a powerful book, and its drama is all the more compelling because of what Brown had to accomplish to write it. He was born, and remained all of his life, almost completely paralyzed by cerebral palsy.

Brown first received notice in 1954 with the publication of *My Left Foot*, a straightforward, concise account of his early life and his persistent struggle to function in spite of his handicap. In addition to *Down All the Days*, Brown wrote two other novels, *A Shadow on Summer* (1974) and *Wild Grow the Lilies* (1976), neither of which received the critical acclaim that accompanied *Down All the Days*. He also had three volumes of poetry published: *Come Softly to My Wake* (1971), *Background Music* (1973), and *Of Snails and Skylarks* (1977).

Brown was the tenth of twenty-two children born to a Dublin bricklayer and his wife. Thirteen of the Brown children survived into adulthood. Well into his adolescence, Brown could not speak intelligibly, and he could move only his left foot. His autobiography dramatically recounts his discovery, at age five, that he could control his foot sufficiently to write on his sister's chalk slate. His mother, who had never believed that her son was retarded despite repeated diagnoses by doctors, taught him to write the alphabet, to spell, and to read. As a teenager, Brown painted industriously, mostly with water colors, using his left foot, and read voraciously, chiefly nineteenth- and early twentieth-century novels. In the late 1940s, Robert Collis, an orthopedist and amateur playwright, heard about Brown's handicap and made the acquaintance of Brown and his parents. Through Collis's efforts, Brown was able to obtain therapy, which improved his muscle coordination and his speech. Collis urged Brown to put his thoughts on paper and actually oversaw the writing of *My Left Foot*. It was during the writing of his autobiography that Brown met David Ferrer, his first editor, who remained a close friend and literary advisor.

In 1972, Brown married Mary Carr of Killarney; the couple settled in Parbrook, Somerset, where Brown did most of his writing. He and his wife designed and constructed many devices to make their home more accessible and to improve Brown's mobility. He impressed most all who met him as a cheerful and gregarious man, though he never overcame the impediment which made his speech almost unintelligible to those who did not know him well. Brown died in September 1981 at the age of forty-nine.

After completing *My Left Foot*, Brown did not have anything published until 1970, when *Down All the Days* appeared. The work, which was published in fifteen countries, received wide critical attention, much of it favorable. The story is Brown's own, told from the perspective of a mute and crippled but remarkably sensitive boy whose brothers' and sisters' willingness to push him about in a homemade wagon allows him to observe, if not participate in, the street life which is often the only childhood Dubliners know. The book's characters are familiar in Irish fiction: a hard-working, hard-drinking, and

Christy Brown

often brutal father; an enduring mother who refuses to succumb to bitterness; an array of children alternately infuriated and heartbroken by their circumstances. The boy's brothers become soldiers; his older sister runs off to London to escape her father's capricious wrath. The boy remains a mute observer, coping with ridicule, which he is intelligent enough to understand, and with sexual longing and frustration, which he is sensitive enough to be confused by and even afraid of. Brown also supplies the requisite trappings: drunks, bawds, lusty young men, compliant young women, brawls, dreams, and wakes. Yet the book is not formulaic or trite. Brown's ability to convey the intensity of the emotions around and inside him and his fine ear for dialect distinguish this novel from others of its kind.

While recognizing Brown's potential, several reviewers quite rightly criticize his tendency to overwrite, his endless descriptions, and his occasional mawkishness. An impressionistic work, *Down All the Days* is essentially plotless, though many of the events are clearly recreations of the anecdotes included in *My Left Foot*. Brown later dismissed the early work as "the kind of book they expected a cripple to write—too sentimental and corny." The narrator of *My Left Foot* is essentially an adolescent—all hope and naivete, still somewhat astounded by the relative success of his painful struggle. In *Down All the Days*, an older, somewhat embittered Brown seems intent on exploring the pain involved in that struggle and in the more general struggle of lower-class Dublin life. Though there is no overt sentimentality in the novel, Brown does not wholly avoid the excesses that often result from introspection and over-analysis.

Over-analysis also characterizes Brown's second novel, *A Shadow on Summer*, published in 1974. Another autobiographical work, the novel centers on Riley McCombe, a handicapped young writer who has "arrived" on the English-American literary scene. McCombe, visiting America for the first time, becomes a kind of artist-in-residence at the Connecticut shore home of Don and Laurie Emerson. Don, a rather bland, nondescript fellow, is nothing if not a devoted husband; his wife is rather more high-minded, with a literary bent. Inevitably, she falls in love with Riley, who resists both his feeling for her and her attempts to influence his writing. At one of his obligatory cocktail parties (all inhabited by shrewd publishers, their glittering wives,

and successful but disillusioned playwrights), Riley meets Abbie Lang, a winsome, waifish photographer who loves Riley even though she doesn't understand his work. The novel deals with the several conflicts which ensue, including those between Riley and his work, Riley and his women, and Riley and the artificiality of the commercial literary world. The action moves from the affluent Connecticut shore to the counterculture of Greenwich Village. None of the characters is quite fully drawn and much of the novel is taken up with Riley's excruciating self-consciousness—about his sexual inadequacy, about the literary process, about his own response to the people and environment that surround him.

Critics were generally unimpressed with *A Shadow on Summer*, again faulting Brown for overwriting. It is a flaw which Brown himself recognized ("Why this endless love affair with *words*?" Laurie asks Riley in exasperation) but did not quite know how to correct. Brown's powers of description were immense, but the ability to construct characters of any dimension or to put an original cast on ordinary events is not evident in *A Shadow on Summer*.

Wild Grow the Lilies, Brown's third novel, is less verbose than the others, but no less full of cliches. Brown abandoned the autobiographical mode; but

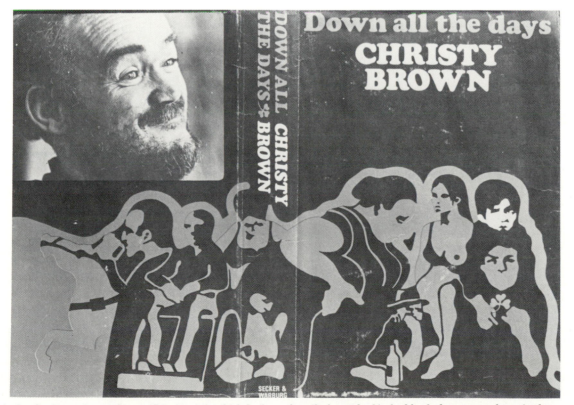

Dust jacket for Brown's autobiographical novel, which he later described as "the kind of book they expected a cripple to write"

this novel seems largely an exercise in wish-fulfillment nonetheless. Luke Sheridan, the main character, is a good-looking, charming, and gifted writer whose rakish lack of discipline prevents him from producing anything more important than sensational pieces for a local scandal sheet. Cavorting across the Irish countryside, Luke gets more than his share of alcohol and women (who fight for his favors), and the narrator contrives to get him into several scrapes with characters more vulgar and less entertaining than those encountered by Henry Fielding's Tom Jones. The alcoholic-sexual escapades become tedious after a while, and the entire novel rings a bit hollow. One critic dismissed the work as "full of utter falseness . . . interminable, contrived, and untrue."

Brown's poetry is pleasant, containing many a lilting phrase and reflecting his keen eye and flair for imagery. But, like his novels, his poems are undisciplined and unpolished. The three volumes published before his death are enjoyable rather than brilliant, interesting rather than provocative.

Brown did not reach maturity as a novelist or as a poet before his sudden death in 1981. He had less difficulty refining short, lyrical pieces of poetry than taming his own created expanses of landscape and emotion and character, but neither his poems nor his novels reflect a fully developed artistic vision or sense of craftsmanship. Because of his handicap, writing was for Brown a laborious process; editing, which is essential to the art, was no doubt equally difficult. A reviewer has characterized his prose as "static, given lengthily to pursuing and explicating the sensations of each slow moment, very much the product of living at the edge of immobility."

Just before his death, Brown submitted the manuscript for another novel, entitled "A Promising Career." There could be no more fitting title for a final manuscript. The words clearly characterize Brown's own career: he had much promise, but he never achieved the greatness of which he seemed capable.

George Mackay Brown
(17 October 1921-   )

Thomas J. Starr
University of Delaware

SELECTED BOOKS: *The Storm* (Orkney, Scotland: Orkney Press, 1954);

Loaves and Fishes (London: Hogarth Press, 1959);

The Year of the Whale (London: Hogarth Press, 1965);

A Calendar of Love and Other Stories (London: Hogarth Press, 1967; New York: Harcourt, Brace & World, 1968);

Twelve Poems (Belfast: Queen's University Festival Publications, 1968);

A Time to Keep (London: Hogarth Press, 1969; New York: Harcourt, Brace & World, 1970);

An Orkney Tapestry (London: Gollancz, 1969);

A Spell for Green Corn (London: Hogarth Press, 1970);

Lifeboat and Other Poems (Bow, Crediton, U.K.: Richard Gilbertson, 1971);

Poems New and Selected (London: Hogarth Press, 1971; New York: Harcourt Brace Jovanovich, 1973);

Fishermen with Ploughs (London: Hogarth Press, 1971);

Greenvoe (London: Hogarth Press, 1972; New York: Harcourt Brace Jovanovich, 1972);

Magnus (London: Hogarth Press, 1973);

Hawkfall and Other Stories (London: Hogarth Press, 1974);

The Two Fiddlers: Tales from Orkney (London: Chatto & Windus, 1974);

Letters from Hamnavoe (Edinburgh: Gordon Wright, 1975);

Edwin Muir: A Brief Memoir (West Linton, Scotland: Castlelaw Press, 1975);

The Sun's Net (London: Hogarth Press, 1976);

Winterfold (London: Chatto & Windus, 1976);

Pictures in the Cave (London: Chatto & Windus, 1977);

Selected Poems (London: Hogarth Press, 1977);

Witch and Other Stories (London: Longman, 1977).

George Mackay Brown is probably the greatest living Scottish writer. Since 1954 he has had published eleven volumes of poetry, which have met with both critical and popular success. At the age of forty-five Brown delved into the area of prose as well, and since the publication of his first volume of short stories, *A Calendar of Love* (1967), he has established himself, in the words of critic Alan Bold, as "one of the finest living prose stylists."

Brown was born on 17 October 1921 in Stromness, a small seaport town in the Orkney Islands of Scotland. The Orkneys, an archipelago just off the northernmost tip of Scotland, were formed during the Ice Age; their history dates back to the Stone Age. The town of Stromness, with only one serpentine street and fewer than 2,000 inhabitants, deserves some attention. Brown has seldom left the town since his school days, and he has lived in his house at 3 Mayburn Court since the death of his mother in 1967. He has written two tourist guides, a book of essays, and a number of journalistic pieces on the Orkneys and Stromness; the islands have been the center of his fictional universe, the town the "Hamnavoe" of his poetry and fiction. A majority of his works are set in Orkney, dealing largely with the history of these ancient islands and town as it bears on the present; they have thus, along with the works of Brown's mentor, Edwin Muir, immortalized the area for twentieth-century readers.

Brown's father, John, born in 1875, was a tailor by trade and later a postman. In 1910 he married nineteen-year-old Mhairi Sheena Mackay, an Irish-speaking woman who had come to work in a hotel in Stromness. They had six children: five boys, one of whom died in infancy, and a girl; George Mackay was the youngest. His father was fond of hymns and music hall ballads, but otherwise the family had no particular artistic or literary inclinations. One brother became a bartender, another a banker, and the third a schoolteacher; his sister became a teacher as well.

Brown first began to write at Stromness Academy, which he attended from 1926 to 1940. He became ill and, a year after leaving school, was admitted to the sanatorium at Kirkwall to be treated for tuberculosis. This confinement imposed upon Brown a long period of introspection, during which he wrote mainly poems, journalism, and, in 1948, the text for an illustrated tourist guide, *Let's See the Orkney Islands*.

Just when Brown was beginning to get restless in 1951, the Director of Further Education for Orkney, Alex Doloughan, invited him to attend Newbattle Abbey, an adult education college in

George Mackay Brown

Dulkeith, near Edinburgh. Here Brown was to form the most important relationship of his literary career. Edwin Muir, the famous writer and Brown's fellow Orkneyman, had become Warden of Newbattle Abbey in 1950, when the school had reopened after World War II. In 1940 Brown had read Muir's *The Story and the Fable*, a book which greatly influenced his approach to life, literature, and Orkney. In this book the everyday life of Orkney is turned into myth and legend; it was Muir's philosophy that behind everyday events— the "story"—lay an external extension of them—the "fable." This idea was to permeate Brown's work for the rest of his career.

In his year at Newbattle Abbey Brown met Muir and his wife, and the famous author took Brown under his wing. He admired Brown's poetry and, in 1952, recommended to the *New Statesman* what was to be Brown's first national publication: a poem called "The Exile." A year later Brown was back in Kirkwall Sanatorium after another attack of tuberculosis, and fifteen months later he was back out again and writing. In 1954 came his first book of poetry, *The Storm*, a volume of fourteen poems about Orkney. Published by the Orkney Press, it was introduced by Edwin Muir.

In 1956 Brown went back to Newbattle to prepare himself for entry into Edinburgh University the following fall; Muir had left Newbattle to accept a professorship at Harvard. In 1958 Muir—without Brown's knowledge—sent a collection of Brown's poems to the Hogarth Press; the result was *Loaves and Fishes* (1959), a great critical success. By this time—Brown was thirty-eight years old—his poems did not have the immaturity or the tentativeness of the first-published, but instead a clear, mature direction and style.

Brown graduated from Edinburgh University in 1960 with an M.A. degree in English literature. As after two of his three previous periods of schooling, he promptly suffered another attack of tuberculosis and was sent to Tor-Na-Dee Sanatorium in Aberdeen. When he recovered his health, he reentered Edinburgh, doing postgraduate work on Gerard Manley Hopkins from 1962 to 1964.

In 1961 Brown officially became a Roman Catholic. This was not a sudden conversion—he had been interested in Catholicism since his mid-teens. He was always fascinated by the majesty of Catholic ritual and the mystery of its images. Like D. H. Lawrence's, although to a lesser degree, Brown's faith is not all-accepting; he questions the work of the Reformation in particular. Yet there is little doubt that his religion has added a deeper

sympathy and richness to his fiction. Again, like Lawrence, Brown champions the instinctual nature of the working man; Lawrence's farmers and collierymen are Brown's crofters and fishermen. All coexist with the rhythm of the four seasons, the circle of life: seed, birth, harvest, and death. According to Alan Bold, both Lawrence and Brown look to the everyday miracles of life: in the miracle of the resurrection of Christ's body from the dead, Lawrence saw the revitalization in man of his physical, sexual nature; in the miracle of the loaves and fishes, Brown perceives "the way crofters and fishermen wrench a living from the obdurate soil and the vindictive sea."

After his postgraduate work at Edinburgh, Brown produced another volume of poems, *The Year of the Whale* (1965), and in 1966 he won the Arts Council Award for Poetry. In 1967, when he was forty-five, his first collection of short stories, *A Calendar of Love*, appeared.

In *A Calendar of Love* Brown has not merely decided to "dabble" in the short story; this collection has the mark of a mature writer with a considered direction. It includes all of the major characteristic features which distinguish Brown's later work. The stories deal with Orkney's past and present, ranging in time from 1150 A.D. to the 1960s. The story "Witch," for example, is set in the sixteenth century with Brown imitating the prose style of that era; the title story takes place in 1962; and "The Three Islands" presents a comparison of the two eras. Brown also gives signs of his preoccupation with numbers as a thematic and structural technique; "A Calendar of Love," for instance, is broken into months of the year as well as into stanzas and sections. There are three principal characters, a trinity—the two male protagonists revolving around the female. Numerical titles are also found in "The Three Islands" and "Five Green Waves."

In *A Calendar of Love* Brown introduces his use of counterpoint. In "The Three Islands," the present is counterpointed against the past; each island is given its own section (again, a trinity), with the pressure of the present being set against the permanence of the past. Brown links the three islands and links present and past as well through a voyage. Three fishermen pass by each of these ancient islands, preoccupied with their own thoughts and totally unaware of the rich history of these Ice Age formations.

In "A Calendar of Love," Brown develops his recurrent theme of the revitalizing nature of the seasons. Jean Scarth, whose father has just died, is promptly pursued by Peter, a religiously devout fisherman, and Thorfinn Vik, a crofter who drinks excessively. In March, Brown's season of "seed," Jean makes love to both men and is impregnated. In November the first pure, forgiving snowflakes fall—on Peter, now a religious fanatic; on Thorfinn, a violent alcoholic; and on Jean and her newborn baby, as if from heaven, welcoming the child as a creature capable of renewing Jean's world.

The final stylistic technique which Brown introduces in *A Calendar of Love* is akin to his use of counterpoint. His stories in this and in other collections are noticeable for their disparity of length and intensity; there are many five-page stories interspersed with the richer thirty-five-page tales. The briefer works are satisfied more to expand an anecdote than to weave the elaborate symbolism of his longer pieces.

In *A Time to Keep*, published in 1969, Brown parlays these same themes and techniques into a superb short-story collection, which won for him in 1969 the Scottish Arts Council Literature prize and, for the title story, the Katherine Mansfield Menton Short Story prize. In this collection—especially in the shorter stories—Brown reminds one much of Ernest Hemingway, although he claims no particular influence from the American author. The two writers merit comparison, however. Brown, like Hemingway, can be brief and simple. If Hemingway romanticizes the wilds of early twentieth-century Michigan, then Brown romanticizes the seaport bustle of Orkney; if Hemingway glorifies the stoic rituals of hunting and bullfighting, then Brown glorifies the Orkneyan rituals of farming and fishing. Rather than to "tell," Hemingway and Brown prefer to "show"; the strength of their prose lies in a sort of pointed simplicity. Perhaps without realizing it, Brown builds his short stories—indeed, his novels—upon Hemingway's "iceberg" theory: only one eighth of the total structure is visible to the eye; the remainder, a "sub-text," is an interpretation which lies beneath the story's surface.

"The Wireless Set" is one such story. In these four or five pages Brown shows not only his pointed simplicity but, again, a Lawrentian contempt for the contemporary faith in progress. Here the "wireless set," or radio, is the villain; it disrupts the entire community. In 1939 Howie Eunson brings to his home the first wireless set ever seen in his community. His family listens to the radio with enjoyment every evening—with enjoyment, that is, until it brings the horrors of the war into their home and foretells the death of Howie, who has gone to the war in the meantime. The Eunsons—indeed the entire town—thus see the radio as a harbinger of

evil; it is to blame because it coincides with the death of Howie, and his father smashes it to pieces. Like the locomotive engine in Lawrence's "Odour of Chrysanthemums," the wireless rudely intrudes upon the simple, primitive, nonmechanized world of the crofter. The pessimism of this story and of others of Brown's works stems, therefore, from a fear that this addiction to progress will deprive the people of Orkney of their rich heritage. His deep appreciation of the past has made Brown suspicious of the mechanized world of the present, with its potential to obliterate tradition: "There is a new religion, Progress, in which we all devoutly believe, and it is concerned only with material things in the present. . . . It is a useless utilitarian faith, without beauty or mystery. . . ."

Like *A Calendar of Love*, *A Time to Keep* uses counterpoint. Yet in the latter collection, when imagination is pitted against reality, reality emerges the victor; if a character possesses a romantic vitality, his dreams are shaped by the economic poverty that overwhelms him. This is why *A Time to Keep*, perhaps, is Brown's most unromantic book; but his vision again turns optimistic in his later writing.

All this time Brown continued to publish poetry, which mirrors in theme and in vision his now-renowned short stories. In 1968 came *Twelve Poems*; in 1971 *Lifeboat and Other Poems*, *Fishermen with Ploughs*, *Poems New and Selected*, and the Scottish Arts Council award for verse. In 1972 Brown was included in *Penguin Modern Poets 21*.

With *Greenvoe* (1972), Brown completed his full artistic circle from poem to short story to novel, reaching, at age fifty, the peak of his artistic powers. After having poetry and short stories published in London and New York, in his first novel Brown finds a fictional form commensurate with his expansive thematic concerns and his capacity for experimentation in form and structure. His stylistic features are the same as in his short stories and poetry, if more full-blown: the mingling of story and fable, the juxtaposition of present and past, the preoccupation with numbers as a structural and thematic device, the evocation of miracle, the use of myth and folklore, and the usual setting of Orkney.

Brown is more than able to sustain his thematic material and dramatic intensity over such an extended structure. *Greenvoe* is not a conventional novel in that most of the real action takes place in the last chapter, when the mythical village of Greenvoe is destroyed. In the remainder of the book Brown portrays the way of life of the inhabitants in this fishing village by describing the five typical days that precede its fall. The seemingly

Stromness

Old Houses Stromness

The Double Houses, Stromness

Sylvia Wishart drawings of Stromness, Brown's hometown. These illustrations were included in **An Orkney Tapestry.**

banal events of each working day—"Dear Tom, . . . Not a thing happens in this place . . ."—are actually leading to the gradual self-destruction of this eight-hundred-year-old town set on the imaginary island of Hellya. Its fall is presented on three distinct levels.

The first level includes a trinity of fishermen, Samuel Whaness, Bert Kerston, and "The Skarf." Whaness is an industrious, devout fisherman—forever praying for the coming of heaven—who is almost drowned at sea. Bert Kerston, a habitual drunk, is later beaten up by his son for neglecting his pregnant wife, Ellen. And The Skarf, an atheist and Marxist, has given up fishing to impose on anyone who will listen his history of the island. Brown compares the lives of the three fishermen with those of the lesser characters in the book. The ferryboat captain makes passes at the sexually frustrated schoolteacher and the stuck-up boarding-school granddaughter of the laird. Alice Voar, unmarried at age twenty-nine, has had seven illegitimate children by seven different fathers. Timmy Folster, a retarded beachcomber, drinks the methanol the shopkeeper gives him for his stove. The parish minister is an alcoholic, and his mother is haunted by imaginary inquisitors who are in reality her conscience.

Such is the questionable state of affairs in Greenvoe. But there is hope, Brown tells us, in the tradition of Hellya itself—in the rich heritage of this thinly disguised Orkney. Here is the second level of significance. For The Skarf is writing, in an old cash-book, the complete heritage of the island—in four pieces of historical narrative interspersed throughout the novel, The Skarf presents the story of Hellya.

The novel's third level of significance is introduced as The Skarf describes the Broch of Ingarth as the "seminal" point of the island. Near this broch, in the year in which the novel takes place, a timeless ritual is being observed at the Bu farm. The Ancient Mystery of the Horsemen is a secret society which holds its meetings in the stables of the Bu, three miles from Greenvoe. Mansie Anderson, the "Lord of the Harvest," is taking his son, Hector, through the initiation rites of this ancient society.

Brown presents this ritual in dramatic form, at the end of each chapter. There are six initiation rites, corresponding to the six chapters of the novel. Each takes place at the chapter's end, at dusk, so that the next chapter can begin with a new day and a hope of renewal. The six rites embody, symbolically, the crucifixion and the resurrection: Chapter one ends with the Station of the Plough; chapter two

with the Station of the Seed; chapter three with the Station of the Green Corn; chapter four with the Station of the Yellow Corn; and chapter five with the Station of the Dead. It is at this point that the sixth and final chapter begins, and instead of just another day, the town is faced with the catastrophe of "Operation Black Star."

Operation Black Star is a military technological project which requires the physical island of Hellya—but not, of course, its people. The village is to be obliterated and, with it, the past—again, as in "The Wireless Set," the mechanical present is imposed upon the primitive people of the island. The inhabitants are ruined, and eventually Operation Black Star is aborted, but only after it has already done its damage; the authorities seal off the island so that it cannot be contaminated by humanity.

The sixth and final rite of the Ancient Mystery of the Horsemen takes place ten years later, when Mansie Anderson returns with seven men to Greenvoe. By completing their initiation rite, they hope to invoke the spirit of resurrection on the island, to restore its agricultural life and thus bring back its people. The novel ends on a positive note, with its promise of renewal; the seven men stand in the new morning sun, seeking resurrection:

> The Lord of the Harvest raised his hands. "We have brought light and blessing to the kingdom of winter," he said, "however long it endures, that kingdom, a night or a season or a thousand ages. The word has been found. Now we will eat and drink together and be glad."
>
> The sun rose. The stones were warm. They broke the bread.

A year after *Greenvoe*, Brown's second novel, *Magnus* (1973), was published. It deals with the notion of redeeming society by the weaving of a "Seamless Garment"—a biblical reference to Christ's seamless robe at his crucifixion. Legend says that the garment may be rewoven by a saint and, not surprisingly, for his story Brown chooses the Orkney saint, Earl Magnus. Basically, the novel retells the story of Magnus's martyrdom. Earl Thornfinn, the mighty ruler of Orkney, has died and left his sons, Paul and Erland, as joint rulers of the state; it is inherited then by Paul's son, Hakon, and Erland's son, Magnus. They vie for sole control of the islands for seven years and finally agree to a peace conference on Easter Sunday in 1117. Magnus arrives with two ships, as agreed, but Hakon comes with eight. The public demands an im-

George Mackay Brown

GREENVOE
A Novel

One

Slowly the night shadow passed from the island and the Sound. In the village of Greenvoe lights burned in the windows of three fishermen's cottages above the pier

A small dark knotted man came out of one of the doors. He picked up a half-dozen lobster creels from the white wall and carried them across to the pier and down a few stone steps. A motor-boat called the _Ellen_ was tied up there. Bert Kerston stowed his creels on board. He untied the _Ellen_ and pushed off. He swung the starting handle. The _Ellen_ kicked and coughed into life. Her bow tore the quiet water apart.

From the second open door came a mild chant. Samuel Whaness the fisherman was reading Scripture with his wife Rachel. 'He maketh the deep to

The opening passages of Brown's first novel

mediate solution and, judging from Hakon's evident military superiority, thinks he would be the more suitable ruler; Magnus, realizing his disadvantage, asks to be imprisoned or banished rather than to die. But the public will accept nothing but death and, by his own preference, Magnus has Hakon's cook hammer an ax into his forehead.

Brown does, of course, work this story into his own artistic terms. In the very opening of the novel, for example, Mans, a peasant, is plowing his hill. His ox is lame, so Hild, his woman, must pull the plow; they make seven furrows on the hill. Directly across the bay, barely within the sight of Mans, a wedding is taking place—the marriage of Erland and Thora. As the peasants sow their seed into the furrowed earth Erland, on his wedding night, sows his human seed in his wife; thus the seed of Magnus is planted.

Brown also adds elements to the story of the Seamless Garment, for which Magnus is fated (by The Keeper of the Loom) to quest during the rest of his life. For Brown there are, in fact, not one but three Seamless Garments. The first is the coat of "hand-to-mouth" existence, the coat of social protection which embraces all levels of society. The second is the heraldic coat-of-state; it is worn by the Earl of Orkney at certain ceremonial occasions. The third Seamless Garment is the garment of sanctity, the white coat of innocence. If the first garment is practical and the second political, the third is religious—holy, in fact.

Before Magnus can gain control of this Seamless Garment, however, he must face five tests. First, he must use a psalter instead of an ax at the battle of Menai Straits. Second, when he feels lust he must cool himself with holy water. Third, he must remain a virgin, which means not consummating his marriage to Ingerth. Fourth, he must refuse an offer to become the sole Earl of Orkney by murdering Hakon. Fifth, he must decline the chance to become a monk, realizing that he cannot die a quiet death, that he must be martyred so that the world will know of his sacrifice.

This novel has no particular stylistic or thematic flaws, but it may have little appeal for non-Catholic readers. Magnus has no free will—his actions are predetermined by an angel, The Keeper of the Loom; he has no real choice in the matter of his death, so it is hard for the non-Catholic to see anything particularly saintly in it. Furthermore, the entire novel relies on the image of the Seamless Garment of sanctity, which may be unmoving for the unreligious or non-Catholic. As Alan Bold says, "An image illustrates a text but cannot entirely comprise it."

In 1974 Brown returned to the short story, and the result was *Hawkfall and Other Stories*. He used the word "hawkfall" in his "The Eye of the Hurricane" to suggest death and destruction—a pilgrimage to Jerusalem had been made to "delete from history the Viking hawkfall." It is not surprising, then, that only two of the eleven stories in this volume deviate from this theme of death and destruction.

The most characteristic story in the collection is "The Interrogator." The narrator, who is this interrogator, has come to Norday to investigate the death of a young girl. Six witnesses, all called up from the dead, are questioned about the mysterious death in 1862 of Vera Paulson; four of them bear false witness before Vera herself is summoned. She tells the true story of her death: she was rejected by her father because of her pregnancy out of wedlock; rejected by the father of the child, Theodore Melzie; spurned by the moralistic townspeople; and nearly raped by the ferryboat captain. Thus, unable to bear the scorn of the public, she drowned herself in the sea. This belated confession of her suicide will no doubt ease the agony of Theodore, who has since degenerated into poverty and drunkenness. Vera's death by water is, too a purification—a remission of her sin, a rite of passage into the eternal world.

Brown writes of death nine times in this volume and still makes his subject matter interesting. He treats death with neither fear nor overly pious stoicism—rather with a humanistic warmth that stems from his religious vision. For Brown does not see death as a terrible finality; he regards it as a provocative mystery, and a provocative mystery must be explored.

If *Hawkfall* is an Orkney Book of the Dead, *The Sun's Net* (1976) is a book of the living—a book of birth. Four of the ten stories concern acts of impregnation or birth; the remaining six are much more diverse than the stories of any of Brown's earlier, more unified collections. Three are interesting examples of the way Brown reworks stories from Orkney folklore. "The Book of Black Arts" is about a great black book with white Latin text. This book exacts a terrible price from those who use its powers; it is fated to be purchased and then sold for less than its cost until it comes to one who pays merely a farthing for it; he is fated to burn in Hell. First, a Hamnavoe landlord buys it for a shilling; he uses it to popularize his infamous tavern, but then he loses everything in a thunderbolt. He sells the book to Rob Skelding, a poor farmer who envies his neighbor's fertile soil. Skelding uses it to get one good year of crops while his neighbor's land suffers, but eventually his crops die, and he dies with them. The book is sold to others until Teenie Twill, a sexually frustrated nurse, buys it for a farthing. She bears a child, who dies, and she is ostracized by everyone in her parish until she finally gives the book to the minister, who burns it.

"Perilous Seas" and "The Pirate's Ghost" are both about the eighteenth-century pirate John Gow, whose ship anchored at a spot visible from Brown's Mayburn Court window. An Orkneyman and son of a respectable merchant, in "The Pirate's Ghost" the buccaneer Gow leads a mutiny aboard the *Caroline* en route to Genoa in 1724. Returning to Stromness, Gow appears to be the illustrious captain of his ship; he is a frequent guest at the house of the wealthy merchant James Gordon, who encourages Gow to make advances to his daughter, Thora. Gow is forced to flee when his crew arouses the suspicions of the local people, but not before he has made a love pact with Thora. When he is finally captured, tried, and hanged in London, his body is left hanging and tarred as an example to the public. His ghost, tormented by his unfulfilled love, returns to Stromness to haunt Thora. Finally, to release the ghost from her love, she must go to Execution Dock and shake hands with the tarred corpse.

Brown's stories are marvelous examples of his ability to turn Orkney folklore into living legend. In "The Three Islands" he uses his technique of counterpoint to show the constant pressure of the present upon the past; "The Wireless Set" shows Brown's disdain for contemporary faith in progress; and the stories in *Hawkfall* reveal his stoicism in the face of death. In *Magnus* Brown uses his Catholic philosophy to portray the Orkney saint who bears on so much of his fiction. But it is in *Greenvoe* that Brown most successfully weaves all of these elements into his own seamless garment. The plot compellingly describes life in twentieth-century Orkney, its fears and its struggles. Its characters are thoroughly and sympathetically explored by Brown. The form is experimental in its use of numbers as both a thematic and a structural device, and in putting all of the novel's main action in the final chapter, with the dramatic incidents of the Ancient Mystery of the Horsemen initiation ceremony interspersed throughout. *Greenvoe* is, then, the culmination of all of George Mackay Brown's fictional concerns. But its greatest strength is in its faultless prose style—Brown is, without question, a master craftsman, a prose stylist with a poetic vision. His novel ranks with *The Great Gatsby, Mrs. Dalloway*, and *The Spire* as among the great prose poems of this century.

Plays:
Witch, Edinburgh, 1969;
A Spell for Green Corn, Edinburgh, 1970.

Other:
Penguin Modern Poets 21, includes poetry by Brown (London: Penguin, 1972).

Reference:
Alan Bold, *George Mackay Brown* (Edinburgh: Oliver and Boyd, 1978).

Papers:
Collections of Brown's manuscripts are at Scottish Library, Edinburgh, and at Edinburgh University.

Anthony Burgess

(25 February 1917-   )

Geoffrey Aggeler
University of Utah

SELECTED BOOKS: *Time for a Tiger* (London: Heinemann, 1956);

The Enemy in the Blanket (London: Heinemann, 1958);

English Literature: A Survey for Students, as John Burgess Wilson (London: Longmans Green, 1958);

Beds in the East (London: Heinemann, 1959);

The Doctor Is Sick (London: Heinemann, 1960);

The Right to an Answer (London: Heinemann, 1960; New York: Norton, 1962);

One Hand Clapping, as Joseph Kell (London: Peter Davis, 1961); as Anthony Burgess (New York, Knopf, 1972);

Devil of a State (London: Heinemann, 1961; New York: Norton, 1962);

The Worm and the Ring (London: Heinemann, 1961);

A Clockwork Orange (London: Heinemann, 1962; New York: Norton, 1963);

The Wanting Seed (London: Heinemann, 1962; New York: Norton, 1963);

Inside Mr. Enderby, as Joseph Kell (London: Heinemann, 1963); enlarged as *Enderby*, as Anthony Burgess (New York: Norton, 1968);

Honey for the Bears (London: Heinemann, 1963; New York: Norton, 1964);

The Eve of St. Venus (London: Sedgewick & Jackson, 1964; New York: Norton, 1970);

Language Made Plain, as John Burgess Wilson (London: English Universities Press, 1964); as Anthony Burgess (New York: Crowell, 1965);

Malayan Trilogy, as John Burgess Wilson (London: Heinemann, 1964)—includes *Time for a Tiger*, *The Enemy in the Blanket*, and *Beds in the East*; as *The Long Day Wanes: A Malayan Trilogy*, as Anthony Burgess (New York: Norton, 1965);

Nothing Like the Sun: A Story of Shakespeare's Love Life (London: Heinemann, 1964; New York: Norton, 1964);

Here Comes Everybody: An Introduction to James Joyce for the Ordinary Reader (London: Faber & Faber, 1965); republished as *Re Joyce* (New York: Norton, 1965);

A Vision of Battlements (London: Sedgewick & Jackson, 1965; New York: Norton, 1966);

Tremor of Intent (London: Heinemann, 1966; New York: Norton, 1966);

The Novel Now: A Student's Guide to Contemporary Fiction (London: Faber & Faber, 1967; New York: Norton, 1967);

Enderby Outside (London: Heinemann, 1968);

Urgent Copy: Literary Studies (London: Cape, 1968; New York: Norton, 1969);

Shakespeare (London: Cape, 1970; New York: Knopf, 1970);

MF (London: Cape, 1971; New York: Knopf, 1971);

Joysprick: An Introduction to the Language of James Joyce (London: Deutsch, 1973; New York: Harcourt Brace Jovanovich, 1975);

159

Napoleon Symphony (New York: Knopf, 1974);

The Clockwork Testament; Or Enderby's End (London: Hart-Davis, MacGibbon, 1974; New York: Knopf, 1975);

Beard's Roman Women (New York: McGraw-Hill, 1976);

ABBA ABBA (Boston: Little, Brown, 1977);

Ernest Hemingway & His World (New York: Scribners, 1978);

1985 (Boston: Little, Brown, 1978);

Man of Nazareth (New York: McGraw-Hill, 1979);

Earthly Powers (New York: Simon & Schuster, 1980).

Widely regarded as one of the foremost contemporary fiction writers in English, Anthony Burgess began his long and prolific literary career while living in Malaya during the late 1950s. In 1949 he had written a fictional account of his wartime experiences in Gibraltar, but this did not appear until 1965 as *A Vision of Battlements*. He started writing fiction during his Malayan years "as a sort of gentlemanly hobby, because I knew there wasn't any money in it." At the time, he was an education officer with the British Colonial Service, and the fiction he was writing included realistic portrayals of actual events and personalities. Since it was regarded as indiscreet for one in his position to have such fiction published under his own name, he adopted the nom de plume "Anthony Burgess," which consists of his confirmation name and his mother's maiden name. His full name, which he seldom uses, is John Anthony Burgess Wilson.

Abundantly reflected in Burgess's fiction is his Roman Catholic background, which is part of an ancient regional and family heritage. He comes from an old Lancashire family whose Catholic heritage reaches back through centuries. Like other Catholic families, his forebears suffered severely for their faith during the penal days of the Reformation, and one of Burgess's ancestors, also named John Wilson, was martyred during the reign of Elizabeth I. Moreover, being Catholic, the family lost what land it possessed. Its later history parallels that of other steadfastly Roman Catholic Lancashire families. During the Civil War, it "hid its quota of undistinguished Royalist leaders in Lancashire cloughs, and supported the Pretenders after 1688." Burgess renounced Catholicism at about age sixteen, but the renunciation gave him little joy. Although intellectually he was convinced that he could be a freethinker, emotionally he was very much aware of hell and damnation, and to some extent he still is.

His most persistent youthful ambition was to become a composer, and when he entered the University of Manchester, he wanted to study music. However, lacking the science background required by the music department, he had to take English language and literature instead. His personal tutor, whom he admired, was Dr. L. C. Knights, author of *Drama and Society in the Age of Jonson*, coeditor of *Scrutiny*, and one of the leading exponents of New Criticism. Through Knights, Burgess met critic F. R. Leavis and came under his influence, as well as that of I. A. Richards. He was struck by their method, which enabled one to assess a novel critically by close analysis and explication of the text.

Burgess managed to get through the required courses at Manchester without much effort, but he tended to neglect subjects other than English. The energy he failed to spend on course work he poured into editing the university magazine, *The Serpent*, and into the dramatic society. Unlike many of his contemporaries, who were involved in some form of political activity, he had no interest in politics. The university's Socialist society had no more appeal for him than its Fascist society, and he maintained, as he has maintained since about age fourteen, a stance neither radical nor conservative nor anything but "just vaguely cynical." This point of view manifests itself in his fictional conflicts between "Pelagians" and "Augustinians."

While at Manchester, he met a Welsh girl, Llewela Isherwood Jones, a distant cousin of Christopher Isherwood. Four years younger than Burgess, she was an economics honors student at the university. They were married in 1942, and the marriage lasted until her death in 1968, after many years of severe illness.

In October 1940 after taking his degree Burgess joined the British army and was assigned to the Royal Army Medical Corps. He was then sent to join a small entertainment group as a pianist and arranger. The group, all of whose members except Burgess had been professional entertainers, gave concerts at camps and lonely batteries, relieving the boredom of soldiers who were sick of the "phoney war." Then in 1943, having been transferred to the Army Education Corps, he was sent to Gibraltar, where he remained until 1946. The story of Richard Ennis in *A Vision of Battlements* is "pretty close to my own story." Like Ennis, Burgess lectured to the troops and taught them useful skills, such as map reading and foreign languages. Unlike Ennis, however, he was involved with Army Intelligence in cipher work. It was a frustrating, dreary time for him. He composed a good deal of music, including a symphony and a concerto, but very little literature.

Burgess's first year on Gibraltar was made especially miserable by the news that his wife was hospitalized in London with severe injuries. She had been assaulted on the street by American GI's, deserters bent on robbery, who had beaten her and caused her to abort the child she was carrying. In time Burgess overcame the consuming rage he had felt initially against all American soldiers, but his horror of the action itself, senseless male violence against a defenseless woman, remained undiminished. Clearly, this horror was the inspiration for the most shocking scene in *A Clockwork Orange* (1962), the brutal assault on the writer and his wife, as well as the woman-beating incidents in *The Right to an Answer* (1960).

After his discharge from the army in 1946, Burgess's career oscillated between music and teaching. For a time, he was a pianist with a little-known jazz combo in London and did arrangements for Eddie Calvert, "the Man with the Golden Trumpet." Then he became a civilian instructor at an army college of education, a lecturer in an emergency training college for potential teachers, and finally a senior master in a grammar school in Banbury, Oxfordshire, where he remained for four years.

The situation of grammar school teachers was, as he says, "ghastly beyond belief in those days." Negotiations were going on for a new salary scale, but nothing came of them, and Burgess's salary was so wretched that he found it "increasingly impossible to live." His dismal situation was essentially the same as that of Christopher Howarth in *The Worm and the Ring* (1961). Discouraged and desperate, he kept applying for jobs to better himself. Then one night in a drunken stupor, he "quite unconsciously" scrawled out an application for a teaching post in Malaya. He was subsequently offered a post on the staff of a public school for Malays in Kuala Kangsar, Malaya, which he accepted with little hesitation.

Burgess found Malaya a fascinating, indeed fantastic, cultural and linguistic melange, and he was eager to record what he saw. As a musician, his first impulse was to orchestrate it, and he actually composed a symphony in which the different ethnic groups reveal themselves in snatches and strains. But the symphony was not well received, and he sought another medium. The resultant oeuvre, *The Malayan Trilogy* (1964), may be likened to a symphony or a giant canvas upon which Burgess has painted portraits representing most of the generic types he knew. He introduces Malays, Tamils, Sikhs, and Eurasians, as well as a collection of largely maladapted British colonials. The vocabu-

lary of the novel is enriched by the addition of numerous words and expressions in Malay, Urdu, Arabic, Tamil, and Chinese. A glossary is included in the back of the book, but, as he does in *A Clockwork Orange* (1962), Burgess weaves the strange vocabulary into the context so the meaning is readily apparent.

The trilogy—*Time for a Tiger* (1956), *The Enemy in the Blanket* (1958), and *Beds in the East* (1959)—is unified by Malaya and by the presence of Victor Crabbe, a young British schoolmaster who has come to the Far East in search of a new life. Like Richard Ennis of *A Vision of Battlements* and other Burgess protagonists, Crabbe is guilt-ridden (oppressed by the memory of a wife he accidentally drowned in an English river), and, like many of the protagonists, he feels the inexplicable pull of a darker civilization. Crabbe's presence links the trilogy, but because the focus of the book is much broader than any individual, he is primarily a witness. Attention is focused mainly on the people he meets and their experiences, which reveal the heart of Malaya itself.

The first novel of the trilogy, *Time for a Tiger* (originally published in 1956) concerns the hilarious trials and adventures of a gigantic colonial police lieutenant named Nabby Adams, whose raison d'etre is alcoholic drink, preferably "Tiger" beer. As his name suggests, by its closeness to Nabi Adam (Arabic for "the prophet Adam"), Nabby is a true son of Adam, for within the thematic framework of the novel, he represents the condition of man. He helps introduce Crabbe to the East and reconciles him to "going forward," despite his name. Nabby has already achieved what Crabbe longs for: acceptance by, indeed absorption into, the East.

As Burgess introduces Malaya through the experiences of these and other characters, he reveals some of the reasons why the British raj must pass. Crabbe and his wife and, to an extent, Nabby Adams gain the affection and respect of segments of the native population, but they do so at the expense of alienating the rest of the British community. Most of the British colonials are content to remain in lofty isolation from the native community. The native Malayans have little reason to love the British, but they do have reasons to be grateful to them. For one thing, the British provide protection against the Communist guerrillas who infest the jungle. Also, the British promote, albeit unwittingly, some degree of interracial harmony. The Chinese, Indians, and Malays despise each other, but the British presence gives them a unity of resentment. Unfortunately, the departure of the

British will immediately liberate the old racial antagonisms. Crabbe's school is a microcosm of Malaya and a vision of its dismal future, but Crabbe is a liberal optimist, a believer in human reasonableness and it will be a long time before he finally begins to lose hope that racial strife will yield to reason.

The problems of adjustment to a darker civilization are dealt with lightly in *Time for a Tiger*. Crabbe chooses to "let down the side" (fraternize with the natives) and Nabby Adams drowns himself in Tiger beer. In *The Enemy in the Blanket*, Burgess deals with more complex cases, shifting the scene to a different Malayan state and introducing a "very white man," an albinic lawyer named Rupert Hardman. At the time of Crabbe's arrival in the state to take a new teaching post, Hardman is about to become reluctantly absorbed into the Islamic culture. Hardman's experience shows how Islam might lose its enchantment for an Englishman, as it once did for Burgess himself, even if he has much to gain by embracing it. Under desperate financial pressure, Hardman decides to marry 'Che Normah, a fiery, voluptuous, and wealthy Malay widow, who has been attracted by his "very white" skin, indisputable proof of his racial identity and his status as a professional man. Unfortunately for Hardman, who derives no pride from being an albino, she is also a strong-willed and orthodox Muslim. His "very white" skin and his profession are about the only vestiges of his former self she will permit him to retain.

Although Burgess does not focus exclusively on colonials in this novel—he is as much or more concerned with presenting the native community—there are other colonials who take up considerable attention and who provide a great deal of hilarity. One is Talbot, a fat, moon-faced creature who exhibits the same devotion to food that Nabby Adams had to drink. As with Nabby, most of Talbot's sexual drives seem to have been either rechanneled or replaced by the demands of other viscera. He is perpetually gorging himself, but far more nauseating than his gluttony is his lyric poetry, in which he celebrates the pleasures of the table. His wife, Ann, clings desperately to her sanity chiefly by means of affairs with other men; inevitably she and Crabbe have an affair. Ann is a small, dark-haired girl, physically resembling Crabbe's dead wife. One of the means whereby Crabbe placates his former wife's "unquiet ghost" is making love to vague images of her, such as Ann Talbot. This practice drew him earlier into an affair with a Malay divorcee, and he hopes to find his dead wife reincarnated again and again as he becomes absorbed into Malaya.

In his new academic position as head of a college, Crabbe must supervise the teaching of Malays, Indians, Chinese, Tamils, and Eurasians. This is trying enough, but he must also contend with the vigorous hostility of some subordinates, including a not-very-bright Tamil senior master who had been bribed with the promise of the headship before Crabbe's appointment and who intrigues ceaselessly against him. The Tamil finds an unwitting ally in Hardman, who indiscreetly mentions Crabbe's undergraduate leftist activities at the English university they had both attended. This revelation leads to the resurrection of Crabbe's Marxist juvenilia in old issues of the student magazine and their circulation in typed copies among members of the staff and community. With the Communist guerrillas still at their bloody work in the jungles, such relics of youth could be troublesome for Crabbe. But the smears of his enemy are not the worst threat. Thanks to the thievery of his Chinese cook, Crabbe has actually been feeding the guerrillas. Oddly enough, these dangerously embarrassing associations are part of an incredible chain of accidents that eventually ingratiate him with the natives. His undergraduate utopianism proves attractive to some members of the faculty who are supposed to be scandalized, and a large group of Communist guerrillas surrender to Crabbe, considering him their benefactor. It is one of the few times in the trilogy that he is actually able to do something for Malaya. For the most part, he has no real control over events and, all his benevolent efforts notwithstanding, he can only watch the coming of independence with helpless concern, unable to make any meaningful contribution.

The good fortune that makes Crabbe temporarily a hero of the people allows him to continue in his liberal optimism. As the novel concludes, he is preparing to take a new assignment, an important administrative post in which he hopes to accomplish something before he is replaced by a Malayan. His wife leaves him with his memories, just as Talbot's wife leaves him with his food and poetry, and Hardman makes an unlucky escape from 'Che Normah—unlucky in that the plane Hardman pilots to freedom apparently crashes.

Beds in the East, the last novel of the trilogy, begins with a description of a Malay family arising on one of the last days of British rule; it concludes with a description of a lovely Tamil girl wiping away a tear for the dead Victor Crabbe as she is pulled onto a ballroom floor. Nearly all of the novel is concerned with native Malayans, members of

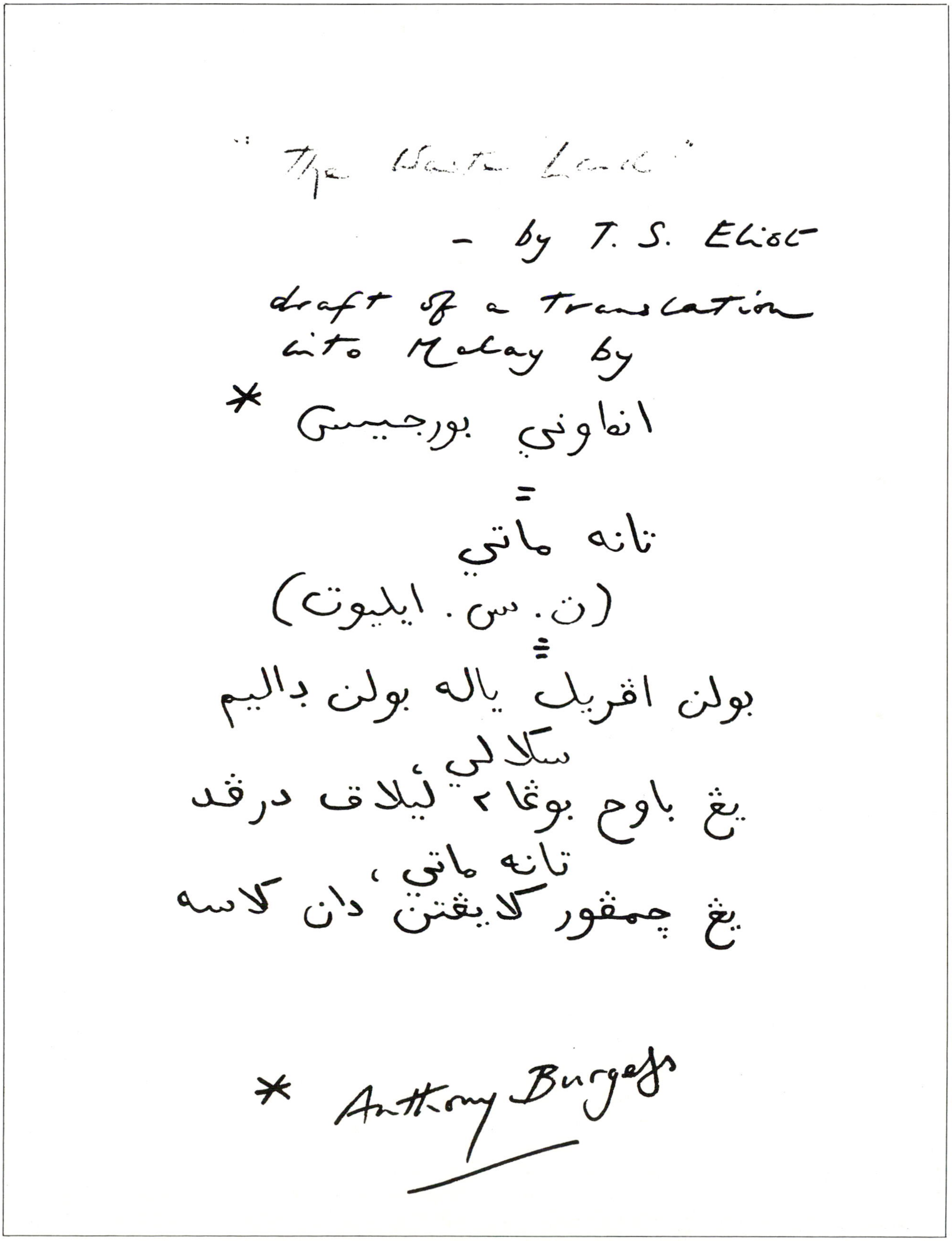

"The Waste Land"

— by T. S. Eliot

draft of a translation
into Malay by

* انطاوني بورجيسي

=

ثانه ماتي

(ن . س . ايليوت)

بولن اقربيل ياله بولن بداليم
سكلالي
يغ باوح بوڠا٢ ليلاق درقد
ثانه ماتي ،
يغ چمڤور كايڠتن دان كلاسه

* *Anthony Burgess*

Draft of Burgess's translation of The Waste Land *into Malay* groups Burgess has introduced briefly in the first two books. For them it is the "dawn of freedom," an illumination of the problems of freedom. As anticipated, the only change in interracial relationships is an intensifying of mutual hostilities.

Before his death, itself partly a result of interracial hostility, Crabbe engages in a number of benevolent activities that are little appreciated, including a daring attempt to promote interracial harmony by bringing together members of the principal ethnic groups at a cocktail party. The party is a hilarious disaster, but then a scheme potentially more effective for promoting racial amity presents itself in the form of an eighteen-year-old Chinese boy who is a bona fide musical genius. The boy is, Crabbe feels, capable of becoming Malaya's answer to Jean Sibelius and Manuel de Falla, someone capable of giving Malaya what Burgess had tried to give it, a musical monument. This benevolent scheme, like all of his others, is destined to fail, but thanks to his violent death, Crabbe is spared complete knowledge of the failure.

Throughout the trilogy Crabbe has yearned for the wife he had left dead at the bottom of an English river, and his yearning quest for her finally ends upcountry in an unbearable reunion of revelation that shatters all his illusions about his relationship with her. This is followed by a watery destruction he had shunned since her death. His disillusionment and death must inevitably arouse our pity and perhaps a degree of fear as well, since he is typical of the bulk of enlightened, well-meaning but ineffectual humanity. In presenting Crabbe's destruction, Burgess has clearly intended to evoke pitying laughter rather than tragic purgation; Crabbe and his dreams are devoured— perhaps by a crocodile or the river itself—while Malaya, in the form of a Tamil veterinarian, stands by in studied unconcern.

Although Burgess might have become a major novelist without going to Malaya and writing the trilogy, the importance of this experience in his development as a novelist was in many ways analogous to the importance of *Endymion* in Keats's development as a poet. His success in capturing so much of Malaya's cultural variety in an extended piece of fiction seems to have been a tremendous impetus for him toward writing other fiction dealing with other worlds he either knew or imagined. He also had the encouragement of perceptive critics.

Burgess enjoyed his teaching in Malaya in spite of a tendency to clash with administrative superiors. After a quarrel with one headmaster, he was assigned to Malaya's east coast as a senior lecturer in a teacher training college. Then in 1957 Malaya gained her independence and the future of British expatriates grew doubtful. Shortly thereafter the Malayan government generously provided each erstwhile colonial with a sum of money and then deported him. Burgess soon found another teaching post in Brunei, Borneo. Despite the favorable reception of his Malayan books, he viewed himself not primarily as a novelist, but as a professional teacher who simply wrote novels "as a kind of hobby."

In Borneo, as in Malaya, Burgess refused to join the British colonials in their isolation from the native community. His perfect command of Malay and genuine interest in the people enabled him to mix freely with them, and, at the expense of antagonizing his fellow colonial officers, he won their trust and respect. This relationship led to an invitation to lead the people's Freedom party, which he refused. Even so, rumors about his loyalty began to circulate within the British community, and he was stuck with the appellation "bolshy." The antagonism of his fellows and superiors was further augmented by an incident during a garden party in honor of Prince Philip, who was in Brunei on an official visit. As the prince wandered dutifully from group to group, he inquired casually about local conditions: "Everything all right?" All the dazzled colonials replied appropriately that indeed everything was as it should be—all, that is, except Burgess's fiery Welsh wife, who according to rumors, was supposed to be British socialist Aneurin Bevan's sister. She replied bluntly and insultingly that "things bloody well weren't all right," and that, moreover, the British were largely to blame. After this episode, Burgess's days in Brunei would probably have been few even without the physical breakdown that finally sent him back to England. Not long after the garden party, Burgess was giving his students a lecture on phonetics when he suddenly collapsed on the floor of the classroom. He now suspects that it was "a willed collapse out of sheer boredom and frustration." Whatever the cause, with incredible dispatch he was loaded aboard an airliner for England, where doctors at the National Hospital for Nervous Diseases diagnosed his ailment as a brain tumor. The neatness with which he was thereby eliminated as a source of official embarrassment in Borneo leads him to guess that his hasty removal had as much to do with his general intransigence and the garden-party incident as with his collapse on the classroom floor.

The political situation in Borneo was now

among the least of his worries. The existence of the brain tumor had been determined primarily on the basis of a spinal tap, which revealed an excess of protein in the spinal fluid. Other excruciating tests followed. Initially the doctors considered removing the tumor, and Burgess was apprehensive, lest "they hit my talent instead of my tumor," but they then decided that removal was impossible. Burgess was told he would probably be dead within the year, but that if he managed to live through the year, he could infer that the prognosis had been excessively pessimistic and that he would survive. His situation was extremely dismal in that he had no pension, was unable to get a job, and saw no way of providing for his prospective widow. Fortunately they had been able to bring a bit of money with them from the Far East. His wife, Llewela, having graduated in economics from the University of Manchester, was knowledgeable in money matters, and she shrewdly invested on the stock exchange the £1,000 they had taken out of Malaya. The stock exchange was a free organization in those days; one could buy and sell on margins, and, in a few years, she had doubled, then quadrupled, the original sum. The initial sum enabled them to live through the year, from 1959 into 1960, that Burgess had been told would be his last. Instead of moping about in self-pitying depression, he began writing novels, chiefly to secure posthumous royalties. Surprisingly, he felt more exhilarated than depressed, and his "last year on earth" was one the most productive he has ever known. The five novels he produced—*The Doctor Is Sick* (1960), *One Hand Clapping* (1961), *The Worm and the Ring* (1961), *The Wanting Seed* (1962), and *Inside Mr. Enderby* (1963)—include some of his best work, and they were not the only things he wrote. Thus he launched himself as a professional novelist under less than favorable and quite accidental circumstances. But, as he says, "most writers who actually do become novelists do so by accident. If a man deliberately sets out to become a novelist, he usually winds up as a critic, which is, I think, something less."

His productivity astonished the critics and, paradoxically, alarmed his publisher. The fecundity of writers such as Charles Dickens, Anthony Trollope, and Henry James had long been forgotten in England, where there was an unfortunate trend to believe that writers of quality followed the example of E. M. Forster and produced a canon of perhaps four or five books over a period of eighty to ninety years. Fecundity, Burgess found, was looked upon as a kind of literary disease. His publisher suggested that he conceal the malady by taking

another pseudonym, so that *Inside Mr. Enderby* (one of his comic masterpieces) and *One Hand Clapping* were published under the name Jospeh Kell. But the two books were not widely reviewed and sold poorly, mainly because no one had ever heard of Joseph Kell. (Since then both novels have been republished profitably under the name Anthony Burgess.) A comical result of the Kell business was that Burgess was asked to review one of his own novels. The editor who sent him the book did not know that he was Joseph Kell. Appreciating what he took to be the editor's sense of humor, Burgess wrote the review—and was never again allowed to write for that journal.

As the novels came out, his health improved steadily, and he began to take various nonfiction writing chores as well. For a time, he was both music critic for *Queen*—a British magazine read in the United States—and drama critic for the *Spectator*. One of the trials of this dual role was being dogged by spies assigned "to see whether I really saw an opera and a play on the same night." He also wrote a number of television scripts, including one on Shelley and Byron in Switzerland and another on Joyce. Other projects included a play written at the request of the Phoenix Theatre, London; another one for the BBC; and still another for Independent TV, as well as a new translation of Berlioz's *Enfance du Christ*. In addition, he was becoming more and more in demand as a book reviewer, and his average yearly output in reviews alone was estimated by one reporter at 150,000 words. But Burgess was and is primarily a writer of fiction, and most of his boundless energy during the early 1960s went into the writing of novels. He also wrote some short fiction and, although he finds the short story a constricting form, contributed a sizable number of stories to the *Hudson Review*, *Argosy*, *Rutgers Review*, and other periodicals. He also contributed verse to various periodicals, including the *Transatlantic Review*, *Arts and Letters*, and the *New York Times*; the latter commissioned him to write a poem on the landing of Apollo II.

He has never, however, remained rooted to his writer's chair. Always restless, he has traveled a great deal, and so far as his fiction is concerned, one of his most productive trips was a visit to Leningrad in 1961. His purpose in going "was to experience life in Leningrad without benefit of Intourist—i.e., as one of the crowd." Before the trip, he spent about six weeks reviving his Russian, acquired during the war; his use of the language enabled him to gain a great deal from the experience. One of his first discoveries in Russia was that it was possible to enter the country without a passport. One simply left the ship long after everyone else, after the immigration officials had gone off duty. If one were really willing to live dangerously, one could also reap a tidy profit selling smuggled Western goods. One could smuggle a man out of the country by securing a deluxe cabin with a bathroom in which he could be hidden. Burgess actually did some of these things himself or heard about others who had succeeded in doing them. On top of all this, he found that one could get to know the secret police on a friendly basis. Late one evening, these stock villains of Western spy thrillers were kind enough to take Burgess home, drunk, in one of their cars. This and other experiences finally led him to conclude that "the Russian soul is all right; it's the state that's wrong."

One of the fruits of this hair-raising "research" was *Honey for the Bears* (1963), a hilarious entertainment in which an unconsciously homosexual ("gomosexual") antiques dealer goes to Russia to sell smuggled dresses and in the process loses his wife to a lesbian. Another product was *A Clockwork Orange*, a seriously philosophical picaresque tale narrated by a demonic young hoodlum who could be either Russian or English or both. Burgess and his wife encountered some of his prototypes late one evening outside a Leningrad restaurant. As they were finishing their meal, they were startled to hear loud hammering at the door. Having been filled with the usual Western propaganda, they immediately had the terrifying thought that the hammerers were after them, the capitalist enemy. In fact, these hardfisted young toughs, called "stilyagi," were after different prey. When the Burgesses wanted to leave the restaurant, the stilyagi courteously stepped aside, allowed them to pass, and then resumed their hammering. Burgess was struck by the Nabokovian quality of the incident, the way in which their conduct reflected the "chess mind": "Even lawless violence must follow rules and ritual." He was also struck by their resemblance to the English teddy boys of the 1950s whom they were copying, and he went home with an even sturdier conviction that "Russians are human." (When he described this incident during a recent lecture, he accidentally said "Humans are Russian," but he would not correct the slip, considering it *ben trovato*.)

As time passed and his "terminal year" receded, he became less worried about his own health but more about his wife's. She had never fully recovered from the injuries she received in 1943, and the years in the Far East had been hard on her. She died in 1968 of portal cirrhosis, brought on partly by alcoholism but mainly by years of vitamin starva-

tion in Malaya and Borneo. Although there was little Burgess could really do to ease the pain of her last years, he was still burdened with a strong residue of guilt about her death, and this conflict may be reflected in one of his novels, *Beard's Roman Women* (1976).

Some months after his first wife's death, he married a lovely, dark-haired Italian contessa, Liliana Macellari, whom he had known for several years. She is a philologist and translator, whose works include Italian translations of Thomas Pynchon's *V* and Lawrence Durrell's *Alexandria Quartet*. Burgess finds the latter project "hard to forgive," not because of the quality of her translation, but because he considers the original hardly worth translating, especially into Italian, which he knows and reveres. (At present he and Liliana are looking forward to working together on a project of appalling complexity—translating *Finnegans Wake* into Italian.)

With their son Andrea, the Burgesses moved to Malta in 1969, where they lived, between lecture tours and a teaching stint in North Carolina, for

Burgess teaching at City College of New York, autumn 1972

nearly two years. They soon found that the island had little to recommend it besides its Mediterranean climate. The repressive rule exercised by a church-dominated government made life exceedingly dreary if not intolerable. Yet during his brief, unhappy residence on the island, Burgess managed to produce two books: a biography of Shakespeare and the novel *MF* (1971), which is set in the United States and a tyrannically ruled Caribbean island called "Castita." The striking resemblance this supposedly chaste little island bears to Malta would appear to be more than coincidental.

In 1971 Burgess and his wife purchased a flat in Rome (the flat that appears in *Beard's Roman Women*) and acquired a house in the nearby lakeside town of Bracciano (the house that appears in the conclusion of *MF*). Between tours and visits abroad, they lived alternately in the two residences until 1976. Although they found the atmosphere in Rome a good deal more civilized and bearable than that of Malta, after five years they felt compelled to move again. Italy, Burgess believed, was on the verge of civil war. There was a state of general chaos, prices were rising intolerably, and shortages were becoming more than irksome. In addition, there was the omnipresent danger of his son Andrea's being kidnapped, since Italians tend to believe that all foreigners, especially foreign writers, are rich and capable of paying high ransoms. To escape these nuisances and threats, Burgess moved his family to Monaco, where they presently reside.

Although Burgess has been a professional writer for many years, he still does a considerable amount of teaching. He has taught widely in the British Commonwealth and Europe as well as in the United States, and he is fairly impressed by the quality of American students "from a human point of view": "They're good and sincere, aspirant and very different from their parents. They do question everything. But it worries me that they lack basic equipment. They haven't read very widely. I don't mind their cutting themselves off from the 1930s or '40s, but I do object to their cutting themselves off from the Roman and Hebraic civilizations which made our own. It means that if one is giving a lecture on Shakespeare or Marlowe, one cannot take it for granted that they know who Niobe was, or Ulysses, or Ajax. And this is undoubtedly going to get worse in America; may indeed lead to the entire cutting off of America from the whole current of culture which gave it birth. A man like Benjamin Franklin, a great American, may become an unintelligible figure to modern Americans. This is very

frightening." He objects as well to the utilitarian view of literature held by many American students, their insistence that it is to be valued primarily in terms of the "messages" it conveys, and their concomitant tendency to regard a purely aesthetic aim as "irrelevant," "sinful," or "reactionary."

Though he enjoys university teaching, he does not see himself as an intellectual ("If I am one, I'm fighting against it all the time"). He does not want to become too much a part of the rarified, cerebral campus atmosphere in which the enwombed academic thrives. His attitudes stem largely from his view of the nature of literature and indeed reality itself. To some extent, he agrees with the Shakespeare/Burgess composite hero of *Nothing Like the Sun* (1964) that literature is "an epiphenomenon of the action of the flesh": "I don't think it's an intellectual thing. It's not made out of concepts; it's made out of percepts. People often think you're being trivial or superficial if you think it's important to describe a bottle of sauce or beer as neatly, as cleverly, as evocatively as you can. It's really more important to do that than to express an idea or concept. I believe the world of physical things is the only world that really exists, and the world of concepts is a world of trickery, for the most part. Concepts only come to life when they're expressed in things you can see, taste, feel, touch, and the like. One of the reasons I have a sneaking regard for the Catholic Church is that it turns everything into tangible percepts. There's no mystical communion with God as there is in Hinduism or Buddhism. Instead you get God in the form of a meal, which is right, which is good."

With regard to religion, Burgess still maintains a "renegade Catholic" stance that is oddly conservative in some respects. He despises liberal Catholicism, which seems to have become another religion in the process of gaining acceptance in the modern world. The ecumenical movement repels him, as do the liturgical changes and the use of the vernacular: ". . . when I say that I am a Catholic now, I mean solely that I have a Catholic background, that my emotions, my responses are Catholic, and that my intellectual convictions, such as they are, are very meager compared with the fundamental emotional convictions. Certainly, when I write, I tend to write from a Catholic point of view—either from the point of view of a believing Catholic, or a renegade Catholic, which is I think James Joyce's position. Reading *Ulysses*, you are aware of this conflict within a man who knows the Church thoroughly and yet has totally rejected it with a blasphemous kind of vigor."

To an extent, he subscribes to the Manichean heresy, although he agrees with the Church that it should be condemned as heresy. He shares the Manichean belief that there is a perpetual conflict between two forces that dominates the affairs of the universe, and whether the forces can be accurately labelled "good" and "evil" is by no means certain. They might as reasonably be designated by terms such as "right" and "left," or "x" and "y" or even "hot" and "cold." All that is certain is that the opposed forces exist, that they are in conflict, and that earthly turmoils, such as the present conflicts between East and West, are relatively trivial affairs which merely "figure" the great cosmic clash. Burgess believes that the man who is aware of this conflict yet deliberately and cynically refuses to involve himself in it is a contemptible self-server. He believes that the rivalry between America and Russia reveals "an unconscious recognition that this is the nature of life—the two opposed forces, as exemplified in these big political blocs, the West and the East and their opposed ideologies. In this respect, I call myself a Manichee. I believe, if you like, that God and the Devil are possibilities, but it is not foreseeable, it is not inevitable that God should win over the Devil."

The five novels Burgess produced during his "terminal year" develop themes which he was to develop again and again in the course of the next twenty years—the role and situation of the artist vis-a-vis an impinging world, love and decay in the West, the quest for a darker culture, and his view of history as a perpetual oscillation or "waltz" between "Pelagian" and "Augustinian" phases. (In the following discussion, these and other novels will be considered in roughly the order in which they were composed. However, where it is illuminating to consider together novels that are closely related thematically, the discussion will not adhere to this order.)

The Pelagian-Augustinian theme is the central focus of *The Wanting Seed*, Burgess's first Orwellian proleptic nightmare. The novel presents a horrifying, though richly comic, picture of life in a future world freed of the scourge of war but overpopulated beyond Malthus's most fearful imaginings. As the novel opens, it is apparent that a suffocatingly crowded England is applying what Malthus would call checks through "vice" and "improper arts." Homosexuality, castration, abortion, and infanticide are much encouraged by a desperate government. The leaders share Malthus's belief that the educated classes can be persuaded rationally while the proletariat cannot. Hence, while the state makes little attempt to sway the "proles," it seeks to influence the more "responsible" classes by education, propaganda, and social pressure. Everywhere posters blare "*It's Sapiens to be Homo.*" A "Homosex Institute" offers both day and evening classes. People are able to improve their social and economic positions only if they can maintain a reputation either of "blameless sexlessness" or non-fertile sexuality. The protagonist, Tristram Foxe, misses a deserved promotion because, as a superior tells him, "A kind of aura of fertility surrounds you, Brother Foxe." Among other things, Tristram has fathered a child, and, while each family is legally allowed one birth, "the best people just don't. Just don't."

But even if the "best people" can accept these inverted standards, the gods cannot. (The term "gods" is used advisedly since Burgess's Manicheism is clearly evidenced in the novel.) Blights and animal diseases reduce the food supply severely. Malthus's checks through "misery" come into play in the form of famine and bloodshed. Starvation causes a total abandonment of the restraints imposed by the perverted society. People are murdered and devoured by anthropophagic "dining clubs." Frequently these cannibal feasts are followed by heterosexual orgies "in the ruddy light of the fat-spitting fires."

In a fairly short time order is restored by a hastily created army, and it becomes apparent that the experience of cannibalism has suggested to government leaders new methods of population control. Implementation of these methods requires a re-creation of war as it had been fought long before, during the twentieth century. The objectives of the war and the character of the enemy are top secret matters, but an uninformed civilian population cheers on an equally uninformed soldiery, and only the government and civilian contractors know that the heroes are bound for a Valhalla where they will be processed for consumption. Although few people are aware of the real nature of this "warfare," there is a widely held assumption that canning makes cannibalism a relatively civilized affair. As one soldier tells Tristram Foxe, "It makes all the difference if you get it out of a tin."

The cyclical theory of history Burgess illustrates in this novel is one he had partially formulated in *A Vision of Battlements*. In that novel an American officer describes how the Pelagian denial of Original Sin had spawned "the two big modern heresies—material progress as a sacred goal; the State as God Almighty." The former has produced "Americanism" and the latter, "the Socialist process." In *The Wanting Seed* all government history is seen to be an oscillation between Pelagian and Augustinian "phases." When a government is functioning in its Pelagian phase, or "Pelphase," it is socialistic and committed to a Wellsian liberal belief in man and his ability to achieve perfection through his own efforts. Inevitably man fails to fulfill the liberal expectation, and the ensuing "disappointment" causes a chaotic "Interphase," during which terrorist police strive to maintain order by force and brutality. Finally, the government, appalled by its own excesses, lessens the brutality but continues to enforce its will on the citizenry on the assumption that man is an inherently sinful creature from whom no good may be expected. This pessimistic phase is appropriately named for the saint whose preoccupation with the problems of evil led him, like Burgess, into Manicheism. During "Gusphase" there is a capitalist economy but very little real freedom for the individual. What Burgess appears to be suggesting is that a Godless society which accepts Augustine's view of unregenerate human nature is apt to be a Fascist dictatorship.

In *Inside Mr. Enderby* and its sequel, *Enderby Outside* (1968), Burgess is primarily concerned with the condition of poetry and the poet in the latter half of the twentieth century. He intended *Inside Mr. Enderby* to be "a kind of trumpet blast on behalf of the besieged poet of today—the man who tries to be independent, tries to write his poetry not on the campus, but in the smallest room in the house," where he can have some privacy.

The protagonist of Enderby novels, F. X. Enderby, is a middle-aged poet who is able to practice his art only in the monastic seclusion of his own lavatory. There, poised on the water closet, his bathtub filled with notes and rough drafts, he produces lyric poetry that is published and read with admiration by a few individuals who are still interested in poetry. His lyric gift depends to some extent on the state of prolonged adolescence he is able to maintain in his isolation. In *Inside Mr. Enderby* he emerges long enough to accept a publisher's award, which he impulsively spurns in a sudden effusion of liberal indignation, and then he returns to his water closet study. The event has little impact on his art, but he is brought into contact with two people who are destined to exert a fatal influence on it. Vesta Bainbridge, an attractive young widow, tries to force him to mature sexually, while Rawcliffe, a ruined poet inordinately proud of the fame accruing from one short piece "in all the anthologies," jeeringly reminds him of the mortality of the lyric gift. Under these and other pressures, Enderby eventually loses his gift, and the recognition

of his loss causes him to attempt suicide. The attempt leads him into the benevolent hands of psychiatrists who seek to rehabilitate him by changing his identity. The fact that the psychiatrists are succeeding as *Inside Mr. Enderby* concludes would suggest that this is one of Burgess's more melancholy comedies. (Burgess's attitude toward psychiatrists who accept the premises of behaviorist psychology may be inferred from his picaresque masterpiece, *A Clockwork Orange*, in which the psychopathic teenage protagonist triumphs gloriously over will-sapping behaviorist reformers and regains an utterly depraved self that is somehow morally superior to the well-behaved "not-self" the reformers force upon him.)

In *Enderby Outside* the behaviorists are again vanquished as Enderby regains his lyric gift and returns to the practice of poetry. Abandonment of his art has been an essential part of his rehabilitation, and his publication of a poem drives one of his psychiatrists into a rage bordering on insanity. The insanity of psychiatrists is not, however, the principal focus of the novel. Burgess is primarily concerned with the practice of poetry and its significance in the mid-twentieth century, and, as in most of his novels, he provides more questions than answers.

The formidable question of what makes a poet is one that exercises Burgess in his splendid reconstruction of Shakespeare's love life, *Nothing Like the Sun*. In that novel, and in *A Vision of Battlements*, he seems to accept the Joycean verdict that, in Shakespeare's case at least, it was "overplus of Will." Shakespeare's achievement was largely the result of satyriasis. In the epilogue to *Nothing Like the Sun*, WS scornfully dismisses the spiritual pretensions of his most gifted contemporary, John Donne: "Let us have no nonsensical talk about merging and melting souls, though, binary suns, two spheres in a single orbit. There is the flesh and the flesh makes all. Literature is an epiphenomenon of the action of the flesh." Burgess, fully aware that this explanation explains little, carries the investigation much further in the Enderby books. The gift Enderby loses in *Inside Mr. Enderby* and regains in *Enderby Outside* is an ability to write technically competent verse in a variety of traditional forms. He favors the sonnet especially, but he also essays more ambitious forms such as the Horatian ode, and in *Inside Mr. Enderby* he is involved in a long allegorical piece concerning the role of original sin in Western culture. "Uninspired" would be the wrong word to apply to Enderby's verse, for it is inspired by something. But what? He can write competent love lyrics, but he fears all women, associating them with his loathsome stepmother. Much of his poetry concerns religion, but he has long since abandoned his own religion. His art and the matter of his art really have nothing to do with one another.

The question of whether or not Enderby and others like him have what it takes to write significant poetry is left in the air in *Inside Mr. Enderby*. However, it is answered unequivocally in *Enderby Outside* by a mysterious young girl, who seems to be either Enderby's Muse or her representative. She tells Enderby that he lacks courage and that "Poetry isn't a silly little hobby to be practised in the smallest room of the house." However, after this devastating indictment, she tries to rescue him for poetry, offering herself as a delectable golden avenue to the commitment he needs to make in order to achieve anything truly great. But Enderby, visualizing himself "puffing in his slack whiteness," is paralyzed with fear. The episode effectively defines his limitations: " 'Minor poet,' she said. 'We know now where we stand, don't we? Never mind. Be thankful for what you've got. Don't ask too much, that's all.' " Great poetry, then, cannot be expected from fearful little men who have "opted to live without love."

Burgess also focuses on other claimants to the title of "poet" that flourished in the 1960s. Yod Crewsy, whom Enderby is accused of assassinating, is a representative of the rock singers who received much critical acclaim at that time both as poets and as musicians. Burgess has always maintained a consistently contemptuous attitude toward their artistic pretensions which he has expressed in various novels besides *Enderby Outside*. In *Enderby Outside* he focuses special attention on their claim to significance as poets, which even such Establishment organs as *Time* and *Life* were taking seriously. Enderby, serving as a barman in a London hotel, is horrified to hear his own verse being clumsily read by Yod Crewsy (leader of the group "Crewsy-fixers"), who has just become a Fellow of the Royal Society of Literature. Enderby's ex-wife, who has married the Crewsy-fixers' manager, has provided the singer with some of Enderby's old manuscripts, and these have secured for Crewsy considerable recognition as a poet. A large group of admiring notables, including the Prime Minister, is assembled to celebrate the artistic triumphs of the Crewsy-fixers, and Crewsy gratifies them with a ghastly recital of Enderby's verse followed by a crude piece of noisy rock. The latter treat is interrupted by a shot, and Enderby suddenly finds himself framed for the shooting of Yod Crewsy.

Enderby manages to flee successfully from England to Tangier where he comes in contact with another type of singer, the poet spawned by the so-called psychedelic revolution. He wanders into a cafe in Tangier where a group of soi-disant literati, mostly expatriate Americans, are trying to induce creativity with drugs. One of them favors Enderby with a short piece of verse addressed to "mod and rocker" on behalf of "peyote chiefs," "Zen roshis" and other "psychedelic guides." Enderby is unimpressed, but he is led into searching questions concerning the status of his art in the 1960s. He wonders if perhaps these acid-inspired makers are not closer to the truth of art than he is: "Was it right that art should mirror chaos?" He wonders if Marshall McLuhan's widely accepted pronouncements on media and the universe have not made the whole business of putting words together in an ordered meaningful relationship a pointless exercise. "That Canadian pundit," however, does not trouble him greatly. The sort of relationships McLuhan perceives are "too elegant . . . too much like Mallarmé or somebody. Old-fashioned too, really. Surrealist."

Burgess's point of view on these questions is hard to perceive clearly. He seems to expect as little in the way of significant verse from the chaos-obsessed and acid-inspired as he expects from rock singers or fearful little men like Enderby. The hope for poetry, if there is any hope, seems to lie in a synthesis of the qualities and artistic points of view of these pretenders. Enderby himself possesses the most vital prerequisites, technical skill and saturation in the works of the masters; but he lacks courage and fears "the young and the experimental and the way-out" and the evil represented by "the black dog" in his dreams. In contrast, the rock-singers and the acid heads have youth and courage but lack skill and knowledge. As they are now, Burgess implies, little can be expected from any of these would-be poets. In the concluding chapter, a strange persona leading a tour of schoolchildren through Tangier sneers: "They are small artists, all. Here there is a *rue* Beethoven, also an *avenida* Leonardo da Vinci, a *plaza* de Sade. But no artist here will have a square or thoroughfare named for him. They are nothing."

Burgess once rated "the whole *Enderby* book in its American form, which is the form I always wanted," as his highest achievement so far in the novel: "It's the book in which I say most, mean most to myself about the situation of the artist." For precisely these reasons, the whole Enderby book might be rated beneath some of his others, such as *Nothing Like the Sun, Tremor of Intent* (1966) and *Napoleon Symphony* (1974). The first Enderby book is a little comic masterpiece, but the sequel is flawed by didacticism and a tendency to lecture through various mouthpieces on the "role of the artist." The same flaw is apparent in other novels, most notably *MF* and *Beard's Roman Women*.

Besides *Inside Mr. Enderby* and *The Wanting Seed*, Burgess produced two other first-rate novels during his "terminal year": *The Doctor Is Sick* (1960) and *The Worm and the Ring* (1961). The latter novel is a mock epic, or, more exactly, a mock opera, a burlesque of Wagner's *Der Ring des Nibelungen*. Wagner's allegorical tale of a struggle for power between Nibelung dwarfs, giants, and gods is translated into a struggle for the control of a grammar school in a little English borough. Wotan, ruler of the gods, becomes Mr. Woolton, headmaster of the school and an old-fashioned liberal humanist. Fafner, the giant who seizes all and turns himself into a dragon, is "Dr." Gardner (Gard-drag-dragon), a cynical academic Babbitt who has managed to ingratiate himself with members of the business community. With these back-slapping connections, the prestige of a doctorate (earned with a plagiarized dissertation), personal wealth, and a Machiavellian ruthlessness, he is bound to triumph. Woolton has no allies among the smug burghers of the town who despise not only his weakness and inefficiency as an administrator, but also all of the humanistic values he represents. They want Gardner and, as the novel reveals, they deserve him.

Gardner is wormlike in every respect (Anglo-Saxon *wyrm*=serpent, dragon), but he is destined to emerge triumphant, unscathed by the hero, the ruler of the gods, or anyone else—a bitter reflection which extends well beyond the arena of school politics. One of Woolton's few allies is the protagonist, Christopher Howarth. Howarth, an ineffectual Siegfried, is a thirty-nine-year-old assistant master who teaches German and leads an ungratifying existence. In addition to feeling the conflict between Woolton and Gardner (whose dissertation is actually one of Howarth's essays), Howarth is under a number of personal pressures. For one thing, his relationship with his wife is tense, partly because of their poverty, but mainly because of her submission to the rules of the Catholic Church.

The wretchedness of Howarth's poverty, the stupid tyranny of Catholic orthodoxy, and the philistinism of the English borough are all presented with angry force. But Burgess's anger does not cause him to present any of his criticisms simplistically. If the society is drifting toward philistinism and the rule of the worm, it is not entirely due to the strength or cunning of philistine "giants." The liberal humanism of Woolton, his unshakable faith in human goodness, gives him excuses to shirk responsibility. In the face of the insidious intrigues of Gardner, which contradict Woolton's whole liberal view of human nature, he retreats into his books and makes no real attempt to defend either himself or his humanistic intellectual values on the battlefield of public opinion. Burgess's treatment of Woolton's reptilean antagonist is similarly balanced. Gardner is repulsive, more like a worm or an insect ("a quick smart darting beetle") than a man, but unlike Woolton he is capable of ruling the Valhalla of education, and he is unhampered by any illusions about human nature. An epilogue provides a depressing glimpse of the school's future under his rule, but the feeble liberalism of Woolton has failed to provide any alternative that would satisfy the community's craving for stability.

This balanced critical treatment of the extreme of rule based on liberal idealism versus the extreme of cynical autocracy agrees with Burgess's other novels. As in his dystopian books, *The Wanting Seed* and *A Clockwork Orange*, Burgess exposes the inadequacies and dangers of both as governing philosophies. At the same time he suggests that Western society is becoming increasingly incapable of accepting a sane, realistic mixture of the two philosophies that would insure the preservation of individual human dignity. That he intends this power struggle in the grammar school to have broader political implications is indicated in the thoughtful response of one of the teachers to Gardner's announcement that under the new state plan designed to insure "the realization of a genuinely democratic education" all pupil segregation will be eliminated. In reply, the teacher remarks "how the pushing of a thing to its logical limit seems to turn into its opposite . . . real democracy is anarchy, and anarchy is Hobbes's state of nature, and then we have to have a large police force to keep chaos in check, all the apparatus of totalitarianism."

The other significant novel Burgess produced during his terminal year, *The Doctor Is Sick*, was based to some extent on his experiences in Borneo and as a patient at the National Hospital for Nervous Diseases. The protagonist, a thirty-eight-year-old philologist named Edwin Spindrift, collapses on the floor of a classroom in the Far East, is flown back to England, and is told that he must undergo brain surgery, whereupon he escapes into the night clad like a concentration-camp inmate in striped pajamas and undergoes a series of ordeals in London's seamier districts.

Before his escape, Spindrift has been blessed with the innocence and smug pedantry that can survive only in a hermetically sealed academic atmosphere. Holder of a doctorate in linguistics awarded by the University of Pasadena for a thesis "on the semantic implications of the consonant-group 'shm' in colloquial American speech," he insists upon being addressed as "Doctor Spindrift" and is prepared to present the ocular proof of a diploma he carries inside his coat pocket. For him the important reality, perhaps the only reality, is within a purely verbal realm. He tends to elevate words above the mere phenomena denoted by them, and his resultant inability to cope effectively with the world of tangible percepts is the basic source of the troubles he is destined to experience in the course of some informal, although rigorous, postdoctoral studies.

Once outside the "safe" confines of the hospital, Spindrift goes in search of his faithless wife, Sheila; his pursuit of her becomes, among other things, a search for love, or more precisely the meaning of love. This is one of the many respects in which it parallels the quest of Leopold Bloom in *Ulysses*. This novel, like a number of Burgess's others, structurally parallels Joyce's masterpiece and may be regarded as one of his own treatments of Joyce's major themes. For instance, Spindrift's descent from disembodied philology into the world of tangible reality in London is like the progress of Stephen Dedalus from a world of words, in which he is an acknowledged master, to the world of Leopold Bloom. In the third part of the *Telemachia* section of *Ulysses*, Stephen is walking along the seashore pondering the nature of reality and attempting to encompass the shifting, treacherous Protean world of material phenomena in language. To an extent, he succeeds, and through philology he manages to achieve a partial victory over Proteus; but it is only a partial victory. He needs Bloom, for Bloom represents the world of the flesh, which Stephen has not mastered, although he has mastered words and ideas. Burgess's protagonist parallels the transition from Stephen's world to Bloom's by passing from his sphere of disembodied words, in which he is an acknowledged "doctor," to the sphere of organic and economic reality in which only the knowledge of medical doctors or technicians or worldly-wise members of the London demimonde really matters.

In terms of experiences, Spindrift and Bloom have much in common. Both have adventures and encounter obstacles that parallel, and parody, those of Odysseus. Spindrift's visit to the office of his superiors in London, for instance, like Bloom's visit to the newspaper office, seems to correspond to the sojourn of Odysseus in the cave of the wind god Aeolus. Spindrift, like Odysseus, is given a gift of "wind," although he, unlike Odysseus, actually needs another gift. Both men, like Odysseus, are detained by monsters and nymphs. A masochistic monster who detains Spindrift shares with the Cyclops and the Laestrygonians an insatiable perverted appetite, and his business of dealing in stolen watches may also have analogues in the *Odyssey*. The Calypso in Spindrift's odyssey is a hardworking London prostitute who picks him up and finds him a totally unrewarding customer, except in a financial way. Like Bloom, he is questing toward a reunion with a Penelope who has been unfaithful to him, but unlike Bloom, he will not be able to revive her love.

The concluding section of *The Doctor Is Sick* is analogous to the *Book of the Dead*. Spindrift encounters an old schoolmate, Aristotle Thanatos, from whom he receives a great deal of sympathy and promises of assistance. With the entrance of this new "agency of the world," as he describes him, Burgess begins to introduce a new level of interpretation that may confuse a reader if he overlooks significant details and hints, perhaps the most important of which are conveyed by the name "Aristotle Thanatos." That "Thanatos" means death strengthens the suggestion that Spindrift's three days in the "underworld" have been just that. But Aristotle Thanatos clearly represents more than death: he is both literally and symbolically a Dionysian figure. Since his last meeting with Spindrift, he has become a prosperous vintner, and he is attending a convention to promote Greek wines in England. Like Osiris, the Egyptian counterpart of Dionysus, he leads Spindrift from the underworld into a heavenly realm where he is judged and permitted to make a "Negative Confession" that he is not as wretched as he appears to be.

In introducing the mysterious Mr. Thanatos, Burgess evokes mythic treatments of death and rebirth, and connected with these regeneration motifs is an "Aristotelian" one that should not be overlooked. Spindrift, in descending from disembodied philology to a world where words are attached to things, has had to make a plunge comparable to that of Plato's true philosopher returning from the sunlit world of concepts, or forms, to the cave of percepts. The difference is that Plato's philosopher will supposedly be granted an infallible grasp of how the world of perceptible things ought to be ordered. Spindrift's career in the immaterial world of verbal forms, on the other hand, has made him simply unable to cope with the world of matter. If he is to get anything out of the world of percepts, he must completely cast off his old Platonic self and assume a new Aristotelian one. He must be ready to come to terms with the changing matter in which forms are dynamic principles. This Aristotelian motif is related to the Joycean parallels mentioned above. Stephen Dedalus, too, looks to Aristotle, the great classifier, for assistance in taming the world of matter. The motif is also related to the *Book of the Dead* analogue in that Spindrift's Aristotelian grasp of reality will draw him toward a state of oneness with the ever-changing universal being, the world of things "ripe for the picking."

Compared to these other products of Burgess's "terminal year," *One Hand Clapping* is a slight book, and, largely because it appeared under the pseudonym Joseph Kell, it did not receive much critical attention. Like *The Right to an Answer*, it is a first-person commentary on life in England at the time. Janet Shirley, the narrator-protagonist, is a fairly clever but ill-educated young Englishwoman, a product of what Dr. Gardner in *The Worm and the Ring* called "the realization of a genuinely democratic education." She has been required to take courses in deportment and dress senses, ballroom dancing, "and what was called Homecraft," along with some courses in English and history ineptly taught by teachers who want to be "real cool" and "with" the times.

Janet is happily married to a good-looking, upright young man named Howard, who possesses an uncommonly efficient photographic brain which is capable of assimilating incredible amounts of factual data. He can also formulate probabilities on the basis of accumulated data. Thus he is able to succeed first in winning £1,000 on a television quiz show and then multiplying that amount over and over again in the potentially ruinous game of horse racing. Having become affluent, the Shirleys soon discover that money does not "make for happiness, really." And like other Burgess protagonists, Howard becomes disgusted with the modern age, and he decides to express his disgust by suicide. He also tries to force his wife to join him, but she resists and kills him in self-defense with a coal hammer. She then departs for the continent accompanied by Redvers Glass (a poet hired by Howard to celebrate their suicide in verse) and Howard's body in a pigskin trunk. She seems happy enough with her new love, free of guilt and regrets, but one gathers that the poet had better watch his step. As Glass thinks about the quality of life in modern England,

he begins to indulge in morbid musings, and Janet thinks about the coal hammer she still keeps handy.

One Hand Clapping is a weak novel, but it gives an authentic picture of England in the 1960s through a young Englishwoman's mind. A reader may be startled by the callousness and ruthlessness she exhibits near the end of the novel, but eliciting this response seems to be one of Burgess's purposes. As a product of her society, Janet is so lacking in stable, meaningful values that the transition from loving wife to calculating murderess is an easy one.

Certainly the best of Burgess's early 1960s novels which focus on the decadence of modern England is *The Right to an Answer*, an account of an expatriate's experiences while visiting from the Far East, based partly on Burgess's own experiences on a visit. The narrator-protagonist, Mr. J. W. Denham, is a plump, balding middle-aged businessman who takes what he can out of life in pleasure and novel experiences. After living in the Far East, he feels alienated, but he is troubled more by the spectacle of "irresponsibility" and "instability" in hideous, TV-haunted England." What he has seen of life in East and West has given him a Hobbesian view of human affairs. He values stability more than freedom and is convinced that "you definitely can't have both."

Although the scenes of action in *The Right to an Answer* range from England to Japan and back again—with stops in places such as Singapore, Colombo, and Aden—much of the action originates in a single drinking spot within the "rather large smug Midland city" where Denham goes to visit his retired father. This spot, the Black Swan, has a Shakespearean connection that is also its most important customer-drawing asset: the landlord himself, an extremely likable man named Ted Arden, whose connection with the family of Shakespeare's mother is proclaimed both by his name and his appearance; moreover, he has an irresistible charm that effectively transforms what is actually a dreary little pub into a place where one feels privileged to spend one's money.

Denham usually visits the Black Swan in company with his father after they have been partially lobotomized by an evening in front of the "telly." There they encounter other patrons, including some who have spent the evening in the same way and some who have spent it in more sordid fashion. The so-called suburban switch, considered by some Americans to be a peculiarly American institution, is shown to be a British sexual pastime as well. They also meet Ted Arden's three helpers named, incredibly, Cedric, Cecil, and Selwyn. The latter character suggests an Eliot-Pound reference. One is apt to think of Ezra Pound's autobiographical poem *Hugh Selwyn Mauberly*, especially if one happens to have seen the Wyndham Lewis sketch of the poet in which his spectacles are like Selwyn's "idiot's spectacles filled with light." *Hugh Selwyn Mauberly* is an indictment of modern materialism, as is another long poem Pound influenced, T. S. Eliot's *The Waste Land*, in which the blind seer Tiresias appears. The major themes of these poems—the sterility and philistinism of modern culture, the loss of values and meaning accompanying a lack of belief in anything—are certainly treated in *The Right to an Answer*, and the novel demonstrates that such indictments are more valid in the age of television than they were earlier.

The brief glimpses of dreary or sordid suburban life are a prelude to the entrance of Mr. Raj, a character who provides yet another view of England from the vantage point of Far Eastern experience. He has come to England to carry out research for a thesis on "Popular Conceptions of Racial Differentiation." He tries to bridge some gaps between East and West by attempting to have an affair with a woman who has been involved in the game of wife-swapping, and the results are tragic.

In many ways the story of Mr. Raj resembles the story of Othello. Like Othello, Mr. Raj is fond of self-dramatization. He has the same tendency to idealize in an unrealistic fashion a golden-haired woman he does not understand, and he is prone to fits of insane jealousy that have fatal effects. Like Othello, also, he is under the illusion that he is accepted fully by the fair-skinned society around him—only to find, during moments of stress, that those who seem to accept him are, like Brabantio, secretly repelled by his blackness. Although Mr. Raj is not created by Ted Arden, as Othello is by Shakespeare, the drama of his attempt to achieve "contact" with the West is presented largely in the theater of Ted's establishment, and it is appropriate that a man who is himself an authentic piece of Shakespeariana should provide much of the setting for an updated tragicomic version of *Othello*.

The range of subjects treated in *The Right to an Answer*—from culture clashes to love and moral responsibility—is considerable; yet the relevance of each subject to the others is clearly evident. Denham himself, whose commentaries serve to clarify the connections, is more than a mouthpiece. He is a well-developed and delightful character, despite his essential selfishness and stuffy conservatism that conflicts with his hedonistic impulses. What repels

him initially is Mr. Raj's radiant human warmth, a warmth that, by the end of the novel, he longs to acquire himself. But what most impresses about Denham, even more than his progress in humanity, is his wit. Even a dreary event such as a Sunday dinner at the house of his sister becomes hilarious, and his description of a voyage back to the Orient aboard a Dutch liner is a marvelous piece of comedy worthy of any anthology. *The Right to an Answer* is Burgess's funniest treatment of love and decay in the West, as well as his meatiest.

Devil of a State was a Book Society Choice when it first appeared in 1961, and like so many of Burgess's novels, it received mixed critical response. A *New Statesman* reviewer observed that its comic devices would have been more effective "if Mr. Burgess hadn't been Scooped long ago." He and others had noted that the book seems to echo Evelyn Waugh's early satires, *Scoop* and *Black Mischief*. Indeed, the African setting and the sardonic detachment with which Burgess presents the chaos of life in a newly emergent state are liable to give a reader of the Waugh satires a sense of *deja vu*. Burgess has acknowledged a general indebtedness to Waugh, as well as to Joyce, Sterne, and Nabokov; but the book is essentially Burgess's own vision of life in such a state, and he likely saw the same things in the Far East that Waugh saw in Africa. "Dunia," the imaginary caliphate in *Devil of a State*, is, Burgess has said, "a kind of fantasticated Zanzibar," but one senses that the real setting may be Borneo. One is tempted to toy with possible etymological connections between "Brunei" and "Dunia"; perhaps Burgess is dropping a hint that he has transferred a "brown" culture from the East Indies to Africa. Actually, *Dunia* is the Arabic word for "the world" in its Far Eastern form, but one might still view it as a Joycean etymology making Brunei and Dunia at least dream cognate.

Like Burgess's earlier novels dealing with states of transition in British colonial territories, *Devil of a State* presents a richly comic gallery of natives, Europeans, and various ethnic mixtures. Again, much attention is focused on the trials of a guilt-ridden Englishman haunted by the memory of his first wife, whom he believes is dead. But Lydgate, the fifty-year-old protagonist, has little in common with Victor Crabbe, besides guilt, bad luck, and a fondness for darker, warmer civilizations. He is an adventurer who has tried everything from importing in Nairobi to gold prospecting in Malaya. Unlike Crabbe, he has few altruistic impulses. Thoroughly selfish, he tends to use other people as means rather than ends and to dodge responsibilities. He had married his first wife, an older woman, for her money, only to find life with her impossible. Unable to endure her religious fanaticism, he had deserted her, and much of his wandering from place to place has been continual flight to avoid her. When he believes she is dead, he remarries, only to be divorced and remarried again.

For all his problems with women, Lydgate adjusts to Dunia more easily than most of the other Europeans in the novel. Among the more sympathetically drawn and pathetic characters is the Honorable Mr. Tomlin, United Nations adviser, a competent, conscientious veteran of the British colonial service. One can see in the presentation of British administrators generally in this novel a bit more sympathy than was shown in the *Malayan Trilogy*. Burgess, a former colonial officer, may have become fed up with the abuse heaped on the British by those who had gained from them as much as or more than they had lost.

Overall, however, this novel is more comic than bitter, and some of the funniest effects are provided by an Italian, Nando Tasca, and his son, Paolo, who have been brought to Dunia to complete the marblework on a new mosque. Their relationship is as utterly without either filial or paternal devotion as one could imagine. The son feels wronged by the father, the father by the son, and each looks forward to a day of retribution. The son falls under the influence of native revolutionaries who see in him a potentially moving symbol of the plight of the downtrodden native working classes under "the oppression of paternal white rule." They elevate him to glory, and one suspects that Burgess's depiction of them was heavily influenced by his own experiences with revolutionaries in Borneo, including the invitation to lead their Freedom Party. (Such conjectures about the relevance of his experiences in Borneo are based on the predominance of Asians in the novel and the fact that most of Burgess's fiction is based on his own experience.)

The novel's protagonist, Lydgate, like backward-looking Victor Crabbe in the *Malayan Trilogy*, progresses toward a terrible reckoning with his past, and his progress, like Crabbe's, is set against the chaotic progress of a former British colony toward independence. But while it is possible to become involved with Crabbe and the Malaya he loves, in *Devil of a State* Burgess does not permit involvement with Lydgate and Dunia. He compels instead sardonic detachment from the horribly comic spectacle of irresponsibility and its fruits both

on the individual and on the state level. The book is both farce and parable. Like the satire of Jonathan Swift, it points in many directions and sustains its irony throughout.

In 1962 what was to become Burgess's most widely read novel, *A Clockwork Orange*, was published. (Even before Stanley Kubrick filmed it, it was his most popular novel, a fact that does not greatly please Burgess, who values some of his other works more.) Like *The Wanting Seed*, *A Clockwork Orange* is a proleptic nightmare with antiutopian implications. Although it can be read as an answer to and a rejection of the main ideas of the psychologist B. F. Skinner, Burgess was less directly influenced by Skinner's ideas in particular than by accounts he had read of behaviorist methods of reforming criminals that were being used in American prisons with the avowed purpose of limiting the subjects' freedom of choice to what society called "goodness." This effort struck Burgess as "most sinful," and his novel is, among other things, an attempt to clarify the issues involved in the use of such methods.

The setting of *A Clockwork Orange* is a city somewhere in either Western Europe or North America where a civilization has evolved out of a fusion of the dominant cultures east and west of the Iron Curtain. This cultural merger seems partly the result of successful cooperative efforts in the conquest of space, efforts that have promoted a preoccupation with outer space and a concomitant indifference to exclusively terrestrial affairs, such as a maintenance of law and order in the cities. In light of recent events, a reader is apt to assume that Burgess was thinking of the United States when he envisioned this situation of the future. In fact, he was more influenced by what he had seen during his visit to Leningrad in 1961. At that time, Russia was leading in the space race, and the gangs of young thugs called stilyagi were becoming a serious nuisance in Russian cities. At the same time, London police were having their troubles with the teddy boys. Having seen both the stilyagi and the teddy boys in action, Burgess was moved by a renewed sense of the oneness of humanity, and the murderous teenaged hooligans who are the main characters in *A Clockwork Orange* are composite creations. Alex, the fifteen-year-old narrator-protagonist, could be either an Alexander or an Alexei. The names of his three comrades, Dim, Pete, and Georgie, are similarly ambiguous, suggesting both Russian and English given names.

A reader may miss these and other hints completely, but what he cannot overlook is the effect of

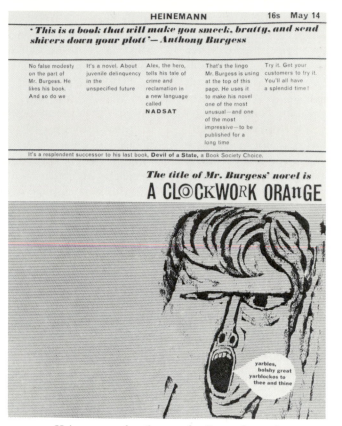

Heinemann advertisement for Burgess's novel

the cultural fusion on the teenage underworld patois in which the story is narrated. The language, Burgess's invention, is called *nadsat*, which is a transliteration of a Russian suffix equivalent to the English suffix "-teen," as in "fifteen." Most, but by no means all, of the words nadsat comprises are Russian, and Burgess has altered some of them in ways that one might reasonably expect them to be altered in the mouths of English-speaking teenagers. For instance, the word *horrorshow* is a favorite adjective of nadsat speakers meaning everything from "good" to "splendid." The word sounds like a clever invention by an observer of teenagers who is aware of their fondness for films such as *I Was a Teenage Werewolf* and *Frankenstein Meets the Wolfman*. Actually, it is an imagined development from *Kharashó*, a Russian adjective meaning "good" or "well."

Many of the non-Russian words in nadsat are derived from British slang. For example, a member of the city's finest, the ineffectual safeguards of law and order, is referred to as a "rozz," a word derived from the English slang term "rozzer," meaning "policeman." The American edition of the novel has a glossary, prepared without Burgess's consultation, which is not entirely accurate either in its translation of nadsat words or in the information it

gives concerning their origins. Actually, after a few pages of the novel, a reader of even moderate sensitivity should not need a glossary and will do well to refrain from consulting this one, whose translations, even when they are accurate, may substitute terms which lack the rich onomatopoeic suggestiveness of Burgess's language.

The novel is more than a linguistic tour de force. It is also one of the most devastating pieces of multipronged social satire in recent fiction, and, like *The Wanting Seed*, it passes the test of "relevance." The protagonist, Alex, is one of the most appallingly vicious creations in recent fiction. Although his name suggests his composite Russian-English identity, it is ambiguous in other ways as well. The fusion of the negative prefix *a* with the word *lex* suggests simultaneously an absence of law and a lack of words. The idea of lawlessness is readily apparent in Alex's behavior, but the idea of wordlessness is subtler and harder to grasp, for Alex seems to have a great many words at his command, whether he happens to be snarling at his "droogs" in nadsat or respectfully addressing his elders in Russianless English. He is articulate but "wordless" in that he apprehends life directly, without the mediation of words. Unlike the characters who seek to control him and the rest of the society, he makes no attempt to explain or justify his actions through abstract ideals or goals such as "liberty" or "stability." Nor does he attempt to define any role for himself within a large social process. Instead, he simply experiences life directly, sensuously, and, while he is free, joyously. Indeed, his guiltless joy in violence of every kind—from the destruction or theft of objects to practically every form of sexual and non-sexual assault—suggests, however incongruously, innocence to the reader. Alex also has a fine ear for European classical music, especially Beethoven and Mozart, and although such widely differing tastes within one savage youngster might (again) seem incongruous, they are in fact complementary. Knowing his own passions, Alex is highly amused by an article he reads in which some would-be reformer argues that Modern Youth might become more "civilized" if "A Lively Appreciation Of The Arts," especially music and poetry, were encouraged.

The first third of the novel is taken up with Alex's joyful satiation of all his appetites; and as rape and murder follow assault, robbery, and vandalism, the spectacle of pleasure in violence overwhelms. While it might be argued that psychopathic delight could not be experienced by a sane person, there is no implication in the novel that Alex is anything but sane—sane and free to choose what delights him. Since his choices are invariably destructive or harmful, it appears that society's right to deprive him of his freedom, if not his life, can hardly be disputed. What the novel does dispute is society's right to make Alex less than a human being by depriving him of the ability to choose a harmful course of action.

Partly as a result of his own vicious activities and partly as a result of struggles between Pelagian and Augustinian factions in government, Alex is destined to experience life as a well-conditioned "good citizen." (Although the labels "Pelagian" and "Augustinian" are not used, it is not difficult to recognize these factions by their policies.) The Pelagian-controlled government that is in power as the novel opens is responsible by its laxness for the enormous amount of crime that occurs. When Alex is finally caught, while attempting to escape from a burglary involving a fatal assault on an old woman, it is mainly because his gang has betrayed him and facilitated the capture. He is sentenced to fourteen years in prison, and while there he will feel the effects of a major change in government policy.

The failure of liberal methods of government generates the usual DISAPPOINTMENT and the concomitant yearning for Augustinian alternatives. Realizing that the terrorized electorate cares little about "the tradition of liberty" and is actually willing to "sell liberty for a quieter life," the government seeks to impose order by the most efficient means available. Unlike the Augustinian-controlled government in *The Wanting Seed*, this body does not resort to mass murder. Instead, it relies upon the genius of modern behavioral technology, specifically the branch of it that aims at the total control of human will. When Alex brings attention to himself by murdering a fellow inmate, he is selected as a "trailblazer" to be "transformed out of all recognition."

The purpose of Alex's transformation is to eliminate his capacity to choose socially deleterious courses of action. Psychological engineers force upon him what B. F. Skinner might call "the inclination to behave." Strapped in a chair, he is forced to watch films of incredible brutality, some of them contrived and others actual documentaries of Japanese and Nazi atrocities during World War II. In the past, violence has given him only the most pleasurable sensations; now, he is suddenly overcome by the most unbearable nausea and headaches. After suffering a number of these agonizing sessions, he finds that the nausea has been induced not by the films but by injections given beforehand. Thus his body is being taught to associate the sight or even the thought of violence with unpleasant sensations. His responses and, as it were, his moral progress are measured by electronic devices wired to his body. Quite by accident, his body is conditioned to associate not only violence but also his beloved classical music with nausea. The last movement of Beethoven's Fifth Symphony accompanies a documentary on the Nazis, and the connection of the two with bodily misery is firmly fixed.

Having gratified his rehabilitation engineers with proof that he is a "true Christian," Alex is free to enter society again—if not as a useful citizen, at least as a harmless one—as living proof that the government is doing something to remedy social ills and therefore merits reelection. He is not only harmless but helpless as well. Shortly after his release he is the victim of a ludicrous, vengeful beating by one of his most helpless former victims, an old man assisted by some of his ancient cronies. Unable to endure even the violent feeling needed to fight his way clear, he is "rescued" by three policemen. The fact that one of his rescuers is a former member of his own gang and another a former leader of a rival gang suggests that the society is experiencing a transitional "Interphase" as it progresses into its

Augustinian phase. These young thugs, like the "greyboys" in *The Wanting Seed*, have been recruited into the police force apparently on the theory that their criminal desires can be expressed usefully in the maintenance of order on the streets. Again, it is tempting to suppose that Burgess was influenced by conditions in some American cities where, as he has remarked, the police seem to represent little more than "a kind of *alternative* criminal body."

Having been beaten by his rescuers, Alex drags himself to a little cottage that was the scene of the most savage atrocity he and his droogs had carried out before his imprisonment. One of his victims, a writer named F. Alexander, still lives there. The writer's political and philosophical ideals incline toward Pelagian liberalism and he has remained, in spite of his experience as a victim of human depravity, committed to the belief that man is "a creature of growth and capable of sweetness." Because of this view, he remains unalterably opposed to the use of "debilitating and will-sapping techniques of conditioning" in criminal reform. To some extent, he is an autobiographical creation. Like Burgess, he has written a book entitled *A Clockwork Orange* with the purpose of illuminating the dangers of allowing such methods. The fact that he has had the sincerity of his beliefs about criminal reform tested by the personal experience of senseless criminal brutality is something else he shares with Burgess. Recall that during the war, while Burgess was stationed in Gibraltar, his pregnant wife was assaulted on a London street and suffered a miscarriage as a result. But here the resemblance ends. Although Burgess believes man is capable of sweetness and should not be turned into a piece of clockwork, he is no Pelagian, and his book, unlike F. Alexander's, is no lyrical effusion of revolutionary idealism.

Although F. Alexander and his associates seem motivated by the loftiest of liberal ideas, they are incapable of seeing Alex as anything but a propaganda device. To them Alex is not an unfortunate human being to be assisted, but "a martyr to the cause of Liberty" who can serve "the Future and our Cause." When F. Alexander begins to suspect that Alex is one of the attackers who invaded his home, he and his associates decide that Alex will be more effective as a dead "witness" against the government than as a living one. Utilizing the responses implanted in him by the government psychologists, they attempt to drive him to suicide, and they nearly succeed. Thus Burgess effectively underlines what Pelagian idealism shares with Augustinian cynicism. The Pelagian preoccupation with the tradition of liberty and the dignity of man, like the Augustinian preoccupation with stability, will make any sacrifice for "the Good of Man" worthwhile, including the destruction of Man himself.

The government receives ample amounts of embarrassing publicity concerning Alex's attempted suicide, but somehow survives. One day Alex awakens to find himself fully as vicious as before his treatment. More psychological engineers, using "deep hypnopaedia or some such slovo," have restored his moral nature, his "self," and his concomitant appetites for Beethoven and throat cutting. In this "depraved" condition, he cannot further embarrass the Augustinian government.

At this point, the American edition of *A Clockwork Orange* ends, and Stanley Kubrick, following the American edition, ends his film. In its earlier British editions, however, the novel has one additional chapter that makes a considerable difference in how one may interpret it. This chapter, like the chapters that begin the novel's three main parts, opens with the question, "What's it going to be then, eh?" The reader has been led to believe that, aside from imprisonment or hanging, the two conditions presented are the only possible alternatives for Alex. The omitted chapter, however, reveals yet another alternative; Alex is shown becoming weary of violence. Having met one of his old comrades who has married and settled down, he realizes that this is what he wants for himself. He wants to marry and have a son, whom he will try to teach to avoid his own mistakes, though he knows he will not succeed.

Burgess's American publisher insisted on omitting this chapter so that the book would end "on a tough and violent note," and Burgess agrees that the omission was in some ways an improvement. The missing chapter in effect suggests that individuals are capable of growing and learning through suffering and error. It suggests further that suffering, fallen human beings, not behavioral technology or the revolutionary schemes of idealists, bring "goodness" into the world.

Between 1962 and the end of 1980 Burgess produced fifteen novels. Some of these, such as *The Eve of St. Venus* (1964), *The Clockwork Testament*, *Beard's Roman Women*, and *ABBA ABBA* (1977), are rather slight books. The most significant are *Nothing Like the Sun: A Story of Shakespeare's Love-Life*, *Tremor of Intent*, *MF*, *Enderby Outside*, *Napoleon Symphony* and *Earthly Powers* (1980).

One of Burgess's most remarkable achievements in the novel is *Nothing Like the Sun*, a book which, unfortunately, did not receive its due from critics at the time of its appearance in the year of the Shakespeare quadricentennial. Its setting is a classroom somewhere in Malaya or Borneo; the narrator, as Burgess states in a prologue, is "Mr. Burgess" who has just been "given the sack" by his headmaster, and it is time to bid his students farewell. His farewell speech, a last lecture, will be primarily for the benefit of those "who complained that Shakespeare had nothing to give to the East." It is a long discourse, but he is well fortified with a potent Chinese rice spirit called *samsu*, a parting gift from his students. The *samsu* and his considerable knowledge of Shakespeare enable him to transport himself and his class back into sixteenth-century England. In a sense, however, he also brings Shakespeare forward into the twentieth century through identification with himself. As his lecture progresses, accompanied by much *samsu* swigging, the identification becomes stronger and stronger until finally, in the epilogue, we are able to hear the voice of a Shakespeare-Burgess composite hero.

The lecture begins with a vision of an adolescent Master Shakespeare at home in Stratford. As a youth, he dreams of a "goddess," a dark golden lady who is his muse, his ideal of beauty, and his forbidden fruit. He finds her literally embodied in various dark-complexioned country maidens, and occasionally she inspires verse. Next we see "WS the

married man," who has been trapped into marriage with a fair-complexioned lady, Anne Hathaway. Burgess's characterization of her reveals how she might have served as a model for Regan in *King Lear*, Lady Ann in *Richard III*, and Gertrude in *Hamlet*.

A position as a Latin tutor enables WS to escape for a time from Anne and the glove-making trade, and this experience gives birth to Shakespearean comedy in *The Comedy of Errors*, which is based on a Latin play, Plautus's *Menaechmi*. A careless bit of pederasty ends his teaching career, but the play enables WS to join a touring company of players with a completed script in hand. Soon he is with Philip Henslowe's company, and a number of events occur that are destined to influence his art. Perhaps the most momentous is his meeting with Harry Wriothesley, third earl of Southampton, who is to become "Mr. W.H." of the sonnets. Like the poet himself, Harry is sexually ambiguous, and when he seems to favor other effeminate young lords and a rival poet named Chapman, WS is wracked by jealousy.

As he rises to prominence as both playwright and poet, WS is drawn on by occasional glimpses of his goddess. No longer an unsophisticated country boy, he does not see her embodied in every dark-haired wench, but when he catches a glimpse of

Malcolm McDowell as Alex in the film version of Clockwork Orange

Fatimah, more commonly known as Lucy Negro, a brown-gold girl from the East Indies, the old yearning to know his goddess fully in the flesh overwhelms him again. His conquest of this dark lady is a long and arduous process, but he finally succeeds and finds himself in a state of desperate sexual bondage.

His deliverance from this enchantment is painful and disillusioning. His two "angels" (as he describes them in Sonnet 144) meet each other and, knowing the lady's courtly ambitions and Wriothesley's voluptuous nature, he must before long "guess one angel in another's hell." Eventually he is reconciled with Wriothesley, but then his refusal to join the young man in supporting the Essex revolt causes another break, which is permanent. Eventually, too, he is reconciled with the dark lady, whose relationship with Wriothesley has been terminated by a pregnancy for which WS is probably responsible. The golden son she bears is to be raised as a gentleman and sent to her homeland in the Far East, and the poet is exhilarated by the thought that "his blood would, after all, flow to the East." Unfortunately, she also bears within her "hell" the fatal spirochete, a gift of Mr. W.H., which will have a profound influence on the development of Shakespeare's art.

With the poet's discovery that he is syphilitic, Mr. Burgess is near the end of both his lecture and the *samsu*. In the "Epilogue," the voice of the poet merges completely with that of the writer-lecturer, and, although the latter is not himself syphilitic, he describes how the disease molded "his" art even as it ravaged his body. Burgess has observed that students of serious literature may owe as much to the spirochete as they do to the tubercle bacillus. Tuberculosis and syphilis would seem to be the most "creative" diseases, and it is significant that Keats, who had "an especially good hand," had both, Mr. Burgess says. The list of syphilitic poets is long, including such widely differing talents as Baudelaire and Edward Lear, and to this list Burgess would add the greatest name of all. His reasons are based chiefly upon close study of the poet's later works and the actual experience, while he was serving with the Royal Army Medical Corps, of seeing genius flower in individuals suffering the last stages of the disease.

This is not to suggest that Burgess simply used his imagination in lieu of doing his homework. His knowledge of the late Tudor period and its well-documented events is considerable, and by his deft use of allusion and descriptive detail, as well as his imitation of Elizabethan idiom, he gives us an ex-tremely convincing picture of the vigor, violence, filth, and color of Elizabethan town and country life.

In 1966 Burgess, having already experimented successfully with a wide variety of subgenres of the novel—mock epic, historical romance, picaresque, proleptic satire—turned his hand to a type that seems to be, by its very nature and purpose, fatally constricting to a writer with Burgess's philosophical and artistic concerns. *Tremor of Intent* is a spy thriller, and upon the well-worn framework of Ian Fleming's James Bond formula Burgess has fleshed out and molded a tale of intrigue that must fire the senses of even the most Bond-weary aficionado of the spy thriller. The typical Bond feats of appetite are duplicated and surpassed, sometimes to a ridiculous extent. The protagonist, Denis Hillier, has bedroom adventures that make Bond's conquests seem as crude and unfulfilling as an adolescent's evening affair with an issue of *Playboy*. His gastronomic awareness is such that Bond is by comparison an epicurean tyro. In addition, Hillier possesses a mind that is good for something besides devising booby traps and playing games with supervillains.

Hillier is one of Burgess's Augustinians, a believer in original sin and a pessimist about human nature, and the novel focuses on the course of his spiritual progress as he tries to carry out a final mission for Her Majesty's Secret Service. He must sneak into Russia in disguise and kidnap a British scientist who has defected to Russia. The scientist, Dr. Edwin Roper, is an old friend.

In the course of attempting the kidnap, he encounters an obese supervillain by the name of Theodorescu, who exemplifies the state of self-serving "neutrality" that Burgess regards as the most contemptible and evil moral attitude a human being can assume. He agrees with Dante that such human beings are unworthy of the dignity of damnation. His protagonist, Hillier, discovers that the world is full of such "neutrals," and his mission for his government, which is dominated by bureaucratic neutrals, becomes a search for a way to make a meaningful commitment of himself against evil in the modern world. He is assisted in his spiritual progress by two women, who represent stages in a Dantesque progress through Hell into Heaven. One of them, an Indian woman named Miss Devi, is herself a "hell," in the Elizabethan sense of a locus of sexual excitement. The other, a young girl named Clara, becomes for him a Beatrice figure. Eventually Hillier finds his way back into the Catholic church, which he had left as a youth because of its puritanical view of the flesh. Only the church can satisfy his craving for commitment in the great conflict between the forces of "God and Notgod" that dominates the universe. Like other Burgess protagonists, he has become a Manichee.

Burgess has accomplished something amazing in *Tremor of Intent*. He presents violence and a variety of sensual experience with an evocative linguistic verve that must dazzle even the most jaded sensibility. At the same time, he makes some provocative eschatological statements and conjectures. This in itself is amazing because the spy thriller by its very nature tends to avoid eschatology. In the hands of a less competent novelist, any involved religious or philosophical questions would be a fatally distracting burden; but *Tremor of Intent* is such a brilliantly integrated package that somehow we pass easily from an irresistible, corrupting, and vicarious involvement in gastronomy, fornication, and bloodshed to involved questions of ethics and eschatology and back again.

In a number of his novels, notably *The Wanting Seed, The Eve of St. Venus, The Worm and the Ring,* and the Enderby novels, Burgess builds deliberately upon mythic frames and, like his master Joyce, even reveals some mythopoeic tendencies. Many of Burgess's characters are ironically modified archetypes who undergo archetypical experiences or ironic parodies of such experience. However, none of these novels fits wholly within a mythic frame, presumably because Burgess found archetypes too confining for his purposes. In his novel *MF*, however, he found a framework large enough to accommodate his total artistic design. He fused incest myths—Algonquin Indian and Greek—and gave them new meaning as a devastating satiric indictment of contemporary Western cultural values that goes well beyond the criticisms levelled in the Enderby novels.

The novel's title, *MF*, derives in part from the initials of the narrator-protagonist, Miles Faber. It also stands for "male/female," a valid human classification that the book implicitly contrasts with various false taxonomies, and it has another reference to the all-encompassing theme of incest, especially when certain racial factors, bases of false taxonomies, are revealed in the conclusion. While the obscenity *motherfucker* has a wide range of usages in the North American black idiom, Burgess reveals that the range can be widened further to encompass all the maladies currently afflicting Western culture.

The novel consists mainly of Faber's recollections of youthful experiences. As a young man he

had been gifted with an Oedipean skill as a riddlesolver. This talent emphasizes his role as an archetypal MF, and it becomes more and more important as the mythic design of the novel unfolds. Like "that poor Greek kid" who had been crippled and left to die, he is propelled unwittingly but inexorably toward a solution to the riddle of his own origins and destiny. The gods have managed to place him under the influence of a professor who introduces him to the works of one Sib Legeru, a poet and painter who had lived, created, and died in almost total obscurity on the Caribbean island of "Castita." The samples he has seen of Legeru's work lead Faber to hope that the main corpus will reveal the "freedom" he passionately yearns to see expressed in art—"beyond structure and cohesion . . . words and colors totally free because totally meaningless." To be vouchsafed this vision, he must make a pilgrimage to the island and seek out a museum where Legeru's works have been decently interred.

In the course of relating the story of this pilgrimage and the events that take place on the island of Castita, Faber reveals the connections between riddling and incest. In developing this theme, Burgess was heavily influenced by Claude Lévi-Strauss's essay *The Scope of Anthropology* (1967), which discusses the parallels between American Indian myths involving incest and the story of Oedipus. Riddling and incest, Lévi-Strauss argues, have become associated in myth because they are both frustrations of natural expectation. Just as the answer to a riddle succeeds against all expectation in getting back to the question, so the parties in an incestuous union—mother and son, brother and sister, or whoever—are brought together despite any design that would keep them apart.

Burgess uses the Algonquin-Greek mythic framework to encompass much of Western culture and especially those branches that seemed to be flowering in North America during the late 1960s. Clearly Burgess's American experiences, perhaps as much as his reading of Lévi-Strauss, had a great deal to do with generating his vision of incest. According to Miles Faber's grandfather (who may or may not be expressing Burgess's own point of view), incest "in its widest sense" signifies "the breakdown of order, the collapse of communication, the irresponsible cultivation of chaos." This same character, who had a Tiresian vision of the world's corruption as a result of a long lifetime's immersion in it, observes that the totally free (because totally meaningless) "works of Sib Legeru exhibit the nastiest aspects of incest. . . . In them are combined an absence of meaning and a sniggering boyscout codishness. It is man's job to impose order on the universe, not to yearn for Chapter Zero of the Book of Genesis. . . . Art takes the raw material of the world about us and attempts to shape it into signification. Antiart takes that same material and seeks insignification." For a number of reasons, one may suspect that these are Burgess's sentiments. For one thing, they echo sentiments expressed by the semi-autobiographical Shakespeare (WS) in *Nothing Like the Sun*. In refusing to support Essex's revolt, WS explains that "the only self-evident duty is to that image of order we all carry in our brains," and this duty has a special meaning for the artist: "To emboss a stamp of order on time's flux is an impossibility I must try to make possible through my art, such as it is." Recall also the opposition between the honest, technically competent poetry of Mr. Enderby and the utterly chaotic, meaningless drivel of the chaos- and acid-inspired makers who scorn him.

The focus of *MF* is actually much broader than art. The whole pattern of Western culture, as Burgess sees it, is incestuous. Race consciousness in particular, which has in no way diminished in recent years, is symptomatic of an incestuous pull. In Burgess's view, "the time has come for the big miscegenation." He had ridiculed white racial consciousness in a number of his earlier novels, including the *Malayan Trilogy* and *A Vision of Battlements*. In *MF* he focuses on what he regards as the equally absurd and incestuous black preoccupation with race. Some months before he began writing *MF*, he observed "that it's about time the blacks got over this business of incest, of saying they're beautiful and they're black, they're going to conquer, they're going to prevail." In *MF*, he attempts to jolt his readers out of their race consciousness by allowing them to finish the entire novel before he reveals a racial factor that most writers would feel compelled to clarify on their first page. And one of the "alembicated morals" he offers the reader is "that my race, or your race must start thinking in terms of the human totality and cease weaving its own fancied achievements or miseries into a banner. Black is beauty, yes, BUT ONLY WITH ANNA SEWELL PRODUCTS."

Burgess has invited the recognition of the incestuous pattern on the racial plane as it mirrors the incestuous yearning in art or, rather, antiart. The two are related in that they both reveal a colossal willed ignorance and laziness on the part of Western man. Just as it is a good deal easier to shirk the burdens of true art in the name of "freedom," so it is easier to allow oneself to be defined and confined by a racial identity so that the search for truths that

concern "the human totality," truly a "man's job," can be put off. Both the "freedom" of the artist who incestuously allows his own masturbatory "codishness" to create for him and the "identity" of the black or white racial chauvinist are pernicious illusions that the artist, perhaps more than anyone else, is bound to expose.

Burgess's next important novel after *MF* was an attempt to fuse his two major interests, the novel and music. *Napoleon Symphony* presents the life of Napoleon Bonaparte, from his marriage to Josephine until his death, in the "shape" of Beethoven's *Eroica* Symphony. What this means is that he has deliberately matched the proportions of four "movements" within the novel to each of the four movements within the symphony. He began the project by playing the symphony on the phonograph and timing the movements. He then worked out a proportionate correspondence of pages to seconds of playing time. He worked with the score of the *Eroica* in front of him, making sections within his prose movements match sections within the *Eroica*; thus a passage of so many pages corresponds to a passage of so many bars. Beyond this, he sought to incorporate the actual dynamics of the symphony, the same moods and tempo. The project probably would not have astonished Beethoven, for, as Burgess observed while he was in the process of writing *Napoleon Symphony*: "Beethoven himself was a more literary composer than many people imagine. He was a great reader of Plutarch's *Lives*, which of course always deal with two parallel lives. And he seems to have done something like this in the *Eroica*, though we have no external evidence to prove it. It has seemed to many musicologists that the first two movements of the *Eroica* deal with a sort of Napoleonic man. We see him in action, then we hear his funeral oration, and after that we get away from the modern leader and back to the mythical. The scherzo and the finale of the *Eroica* both seem to deal with Prometheus. In the last movement Beethoven puts all his cards on the table because it is a series of variations on a theme taken from his own ballet music about Prometheus and his creatures." This left Burgess with the task of writing a set of variations on a Promethean theme. After his death on St. Helena, Burgess's Napoleon turns into a Promethean character in the last two "movements" of the novel, and there is a posthumous resurgence of the triumphant mood of the earlier movements, with Napoleon being crowned for having, despite all obstacles, at least partly fulfilled his dream of a united Europe.

Reading *Napoleon Symphony* is a pleasure despite the complexity of its form. Napoleon emerges as a human being in a way he has seldom been allowed to emerge from lengthy historical tomes or even other works of historical fiction. Like Coriolanus, he is simultaneously tragic and ridiculous, a grand comic creation demanding sympathy as well as laughter. He is seen from within engaged in spectacular rationalization and romantic self-delusion, and from without through the eyes of the lesser creatures who follow his fortunes—cynical political observers in Paris, wretched foot soldiers in Egypt and elsewhere, and his faithless empress. The disastrous effects of his Promethean efforts are in no way softened, but there is sympathy for the dreams inspiring the efforts.

Napoleon Symphony was followed by *The Clockwork Testament*, which outraged many New Yorkers, and two novellas, *Beard's Roman Women* and *ABBA ABBA*. The latter two works represent, Burgess says, "a sort of farewell-to-Rome phase." In

Beard's Roman Women, he draws upon his experiences as a scriptwriter and, as he does in *The Clockwork Testament*, puts cinematic art in its proper place, well below literature, in the hierarchy of artistic achievement. *ABBA ABBA* is primarily a collection of sonnets by the blasphemous dialect poet Giuseppe Giocchino Belli (1791-1863), which Burgess translated, maintaining the Petrarchan rhyme scheme, ABBA ABBA CDC CDC. The collection, seventy-two of Belli's nearly three thousand poems, is introduced by a brief novella about John Keats's death in Rome and his possible meeting there with Belli in 1820 or 1821. Another poetic exercise for Burgess, written at about the same time as *ABBA ABBA*, is a long original poem in free verse entitled *Moses*. As he explains, the poem was actually the "source" of the script for the television epic *Moses the Lawgiver*, starring Burt Lancaster, which in turn became a film for the movies: "I was trying to get a rhythm and a dialogue style, and verse-writing

Burgess composing music

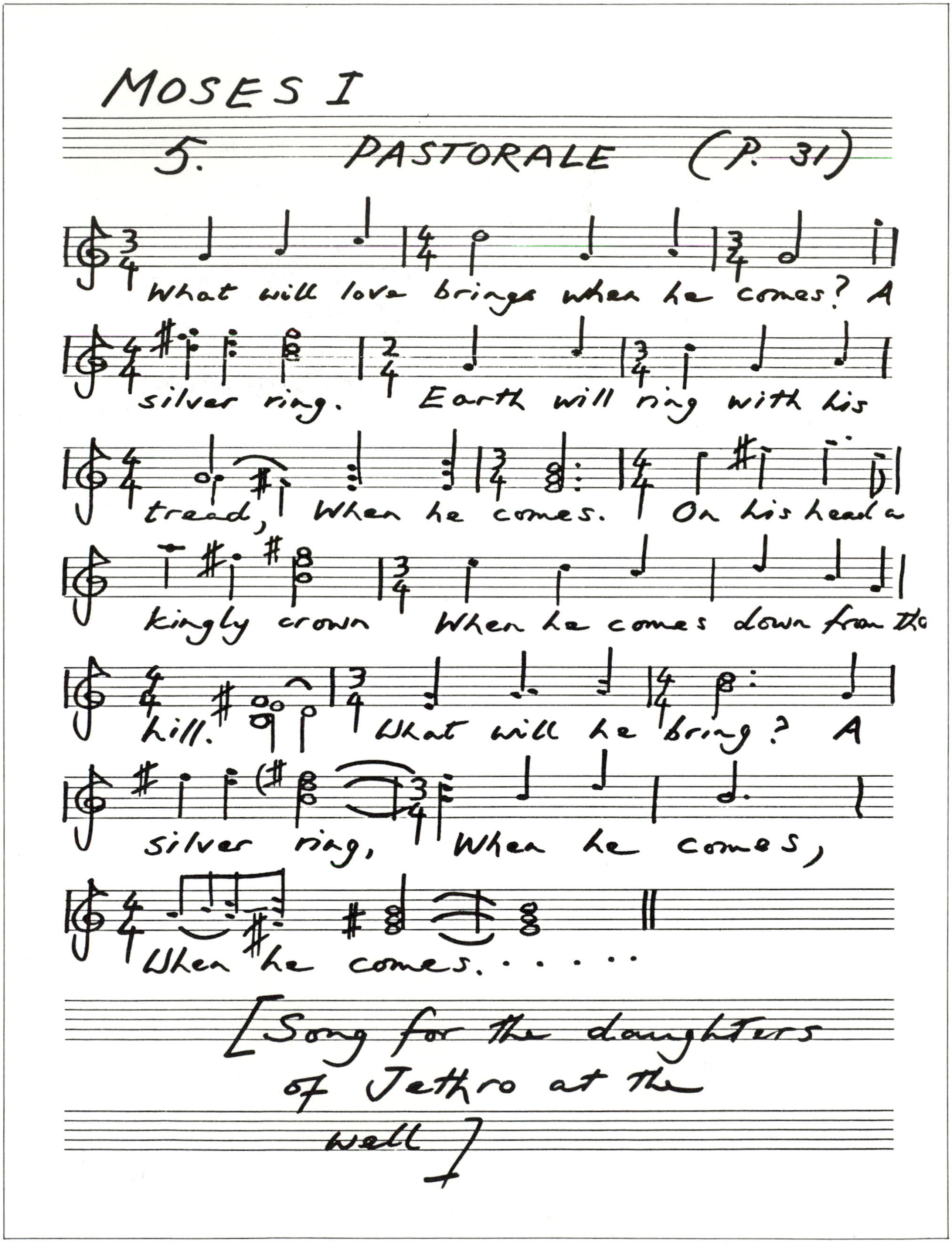

Burgess's musical adaptation of Moses

helped." The *Moses* epic was part of what Burgess calls his "TV tetralogy," which also includes specials on Shakespeare and Michelangelo and the widely acclaimed *Jesus of Nazareth*. As a result of the highly favorable reception of these productions, he was asked to write scripts for several others, including a six-hour television epic on "Vinegar Joe" Stillwell, who hated the British; a Persian film on Cyrus the Great; and a disaster epic for Zanuck and Brown of Universal, "ultimate, really, since it's about the end of the world."

Burgess remains, however, primarily a novelist, and in December 1980 he had published what many regard as his masterpiece, *Earthly Powers*. It is a long book, about the length of *Ulysses*, and it took Burgess nearly a decade to complete it. The novel's original title was "The Affairs of Men." Then it became "The Prince of the Powers of the Air" and finally *Earthly Powers*. The second title was taken from Thomas Hobbes's description of Satan and his kingdom in Part IV of *Leviathan*.

The protagonist, Don Carlo Campanatti, is modeled on the late Pope John XXIII, a pontiff whom Burgess neither revered nor admired. He has referred to him as a "Pelagian heretic" and an "emissary of the devil" who caused the Church enormous damage by raising unrealistic hopes that there would be radical doctrinal changes to accommodate the pressures of twentieth-century life. His character Don Carlo is a Faustian figure who made a bargain with the devil in return for the earthly powers of the papacy.

Perception of Don Carlo is dependent upon another protagonist, Kenneth M. Toomey, an eighty-one-year-old homosexual novelist-playwright modeled deliberately on W. Somerset Maugham. The ubiquitous references to Maugham and the obvious parallels between Toomey's career and Maugham's make the identification virtually explicit. Toomey has throughout his long life acted in accord with his nature and his occupation as a writer. Where they have brought him is clearly revealed in what he himself calls the novel's *"arresting opening"*: "It was the afternoon of my eighty-first birthday, and I was in bed with my catamite when Ali announced that the archbishop had come to see me." Especially suggestive in this first sentence is the word "catamite," evoking as it does an image of refined decadence and pagan luxury in a quasi-Olympian setting. Generally acknowledged "greatness" as a writer has eluded Toomey, but he has achieved a kind of Olympian eminence of fame and wealth and the freedom of fleshly indulgence that goes with wealth. The Ganymede (a Greek name

from which the Latin word *catamite* derives), however, is no downy-chinned little Greek boy, but a fat, sadistic drunkard named Geoffrey Enright, whom Toomey keeps and who may be modeled on one of Maugham's secretary-companions. Burgess demonstrates that the freedom of fleshly indulgence is also the bondage. Enright is only one in a line of lovers who have made Toomey pay for their favors with more than money. To escape the pain of loneliness he has had to repeatedly endure humiliation, spite, and treachery.

As with so many of Burgess's novels, the Pelagian versus Augustinian theme is central to *Earthly Powers*. He introduces it subtly in several places in the novel by means of a fragment from Catullus: "*Solitam . . . Minotauro . . . pro caris corpus.*" In other Burgess novels, notably *The Worm and the Ring* and *Inside Mr. Enderby*, the Minotaur is described as a Greek mythic analogue of Original Sin, and Theseus (who killed the monster) is analogous to the heretic Pelagius, who denied Original Sin and asserted that man was capable of achieving perfection without the aid of divine grace. Enderby is in the process of writing a long poem about Theseus and the Minotaur, the argument of which is "Without Original Sin there is no civilization."

Earthly Powers is mainly about the monsters that abide within the labyrinth of the human soul. That there are such monsters is something Toomey and Don Carlo both believe. For Toomey, one of Burgess's "Augustinians," the monsters are the forms of badness that are part of fallen human nature. His personal monster is his homosexual nature, which he has managed to overcome only once, through the experience of a nonphysical love for another man that in effect drove out all desire. The death of this man, which is the result of diabolical machinations, in effect deprives Toomey of a grace bearer, indeed the only source of grace in his life, leaving him prey to the monster of his own nature and the monstrous relationships his nature demands. For Don Carlo, on the other hand, the monsters within are all intruders who have come from the kingdom of darkness. Since man is God's creation, he is perfect. Evil is wholly from the devil, who taught man how to be evil and is still teaching him. God permits this because He will in no way abridge human freedom. Man is free to reverse the consequences of the fall: "the return to perfection is possible." These beliefs shape Carlo's theology and his career. Toomey emphasizes and re-emphasizes their importance in his thinking. Initially, they lead him into prominence in the field of exorcism, and Toomey sees him in action against devils in Malaya and the devils inhabiting Italian mobsters in Chicago. Wherever the devil is at work, it seems, he may expect to encounter Carlo.

While Carlo sees himself as Satan's enemy and a champion of mankind against the powers of darkness, it is suggested early in the novel that he is vulnerable to these same powers, and the reader must be attentive to these suggestions if he is to accept some of the later developments in the novel as plausible. The genuinely heretical nature of Carlo's beliefs in human perfectability is made clear in a treatise he writes which includes, among other things, a defense of Pelagius.

Burgess effectively juxtaposes Carlo's and Toomey's views and explanations of various evils in the twentieth century, and he suggests that both views are to some extent partially correct, but both are also significantly limited. Toomey would attribute such triumphs of evil as Nazism wholly to innate human depravity, while Carlo would credit them wholly to the devil. Burgess's depiction of events suggests, however, that there is an interaction, a cooperation between the demons that are a part of man's nature and the devil himself. Failure to recognize the existence of both may lead to dreadful consequences.

Earthly Powers has been generally praised by critics, and it was a Book of the Month Club choice. Enormous in scope, encompassing much of twentieth-century social, literary, and political history, it inevitably has some flaws; parts of the book are wearisome, and the language is occasionally pedantic. These flaws are, however, minor and unavoidable in a work so large and ambitious. Overall it is a magnificent performance.

Another recent novel, *1985* (1978) was less well-received by critics than *Earthly Powers*. Originally conceived as an introduction to George Orwell, it begins with a 106-page dialogue-discussion of *1984* which suggests, among other things, that Orwell's vision of England in 1984 was shaped essentially by his vision of England in 1948. The remaining 166 pages present Burgess's own proleptic vision, one that differs markedly from that of his *A Clockwork Orange* and *The Wanting Seed*, as well as that of *1984*. One of Burgess's more sympathetic critics has argued convincingly that this latter section of *1985*, Burgess's fiction, is intended as an ironic counterpoint to *1984*, one that presents a near future that is "harrowing but not horrific." The England of Burgess's *1985* has left behind any belief in moral absolutes, is populated almost entirely by small people who are moral neutrals. What

makes it such a bad place is the all-pervasive dullness that is the end result of social impulses carried too far, thus leveling intelligence, taste, and knowledge.

Although Burgess is a novelist, his nonfiction works also bear mention. The earliest of these is a useful overview of British literature entitled *English Literature: A Survey for Students* (1958). He has also written several works intended to introduce the "average reader" to the fiction of James Joyce. *ReJoyce* (1965) focuses on *Dubliners, Ulysses,* and *Finnegans Wake. A Shorter Finnegans Wake* (1965) is an abridgement with linking commentaries designed to guide the reader through the complete novel. *Joysprick* (1973) is an introduction to Joyce's language. *Shakespeare* (1970) is an entertaining biography, full of fanciful conjecture, and useful to the beginning student. *Language Made Plain* (1964) is an introduction to linguistics that persuasively encourages readers to become involved in the matter of language and in languages other than their own. *Urgent Copy* (1969), a collection of essays and reviews on various topics, mostly literary, contains an essay on Claude Lévi-Strauss that is of considerable interest to readers of Burgess's *MF. The Novel Now* (1967) is a survey of the contemporary novel in various languages. Burgess intends to update it to include "more Americans." *Ernest Hemingway and His World* (1978) is a critical biography. Burgess is a perceptive, sympathetic critic of the works of other writers, and students of his fiction will find that he frequently illuminates his own work in the process of discussing the works of others.

Translations:
Michel de Saint-Pierre, *The New Aristocrats* (London: Gollancz, 1962);

Jean Pelegri, *The Olive Trees of Justice* (London: Sidgwick & Jackson, 1962);

Jean Servin, *The Man Who Robbed Poor Boxes* (London: Gollancz, 1965);

Edmund Rostand, *Cyrano de Bergerac* (New York: Knopf, 1971);

Sophocles, *Oedipus the King* (Minneapolis: University of Minnesota Press, 1972).

Bibliographies:
Beverly R. David, "Anthony Burgess: A Checklist (1956-1971)," *Twentieth Century Literature*, 19 (July 1973): 181-188;

Carlton Holte, "Additions to 'Anthony Burgess: A Checklist (1956-1971),'" *Twentieth Century Literature*, 20 (January 1974): 44-52;

Paul Boytinck, *Anthony Burgess: An Enumerative Bibliography with Selected Annotations*, second edition, with foreword by Burgess (Norwood, Pa.: Norwood Editions, 1977);

Jeutonne Brewer, *Anthony Burgess: A Bibliography*, with foreword by Burgess (Metuchen, N.J. & London: Scarecrow Press, 1980).

References:

Geoffrey Aggeler, *Anthony Burgess: The Artist as Novelist* (University, Ala.: University of Alabama Press, 1979);

Samuel Coale, *Anthony Burgess* (New York: Ungar, 1982);

A.A. DeVitis, *Anthony Burgess* (New York: Twayne, 1972);

Carol M. Dix, *Anthony Burgess* (London: Longman, 1971);

Modern Fiction Studies, special Burgess issue, 27 (Autumn 1981);

Robert K. Morris, *The Consolations of Ambiguity: An Essay on the Novels of Anthony Burgess* (Columbia: University of Missouri Press, 1971).

Papers:

Most of Burgess's papers are collected at the Mills Memorial Library, McMaster University, Hamilton, Ontario.

Alan Burns

(29 December 1929-   )

David W. Madden

California State University, Sacramento

SELECTED BOOKS: *Buster*, in *New Writers One* (London: John Calder, 1961; New York: Red Dust Books, 1972);

Europe After the Rain (London: John Calder, 1965; New York: Day, 1970);

Celebrations (London: Calder & Boyars, 1967);

Babel (London: Calder & Boyars, 1969; New York: Day, 1970);

To Deprave and Corrupt (London: Davis Poynter, 1972);

Dreamerika! (London: Calder & Boyars, 1972);

The Angry Brigade (London: Allison & Busby, 1973);

Palach (London: Penguin, 1974);

The Day Daddy Died (London & New York: Allison & Busby, 1981);

The Imagination on Trial (London & New York: Allison & Busby, 1982).

It is no exaggeration to say that Alan Burns is currently one of the most original and innovative British novelists. He is a highly experimental writer whose works have been variously described as "surrealistic" and "infrarealistic," and who invites comparison with American novelists such as John Hawkes, Robert Coover, and Donald Barthelme. Relying on an aleatoric method, Burns strives to create accidental juxtapositions, and, as he has described it, "the kaleidoscopic, dialectical effect."

Burns was born in London into a middle-class family to Harold and Anne Marks Burns and educated at the Merchant Taylors' School. When he was thirteen his mother died, as did his older brother two years later; both deaths profoundly affected him both emotionally and artistically. Burns has described the impact of these separations by writing, "The consuming nature of this experience showed itself not only in the disconnected form but also in the content of my work." The most obvious treatment of these experiences is in *Buster* (1961); however, the theme of death pervades all his novels. From 1949 to 1951, Burns served in the Royal Army Education Corps, stationed at Salisbury Plain. After his discharge, he traveled through Europe; he married Carol Lynn in 1954. He was called to the Bar in 1956 and practiced as a London barrister until 1959, when he spent a year as a postgraduate researcher in politics at the London School of Economics. For the next three years, Burns was assistant legal manager for Beaverbrook Newspapers, "vetting [appraising] copy for libel and copyright."

While walking down Carey Street on his lunch hour one day, he saw, in the window of a jeweller's, a

photograph of a man and woman kissing, which reminded him of a photo of his mother and father on their honeymoon. Having previously felt stymied in his attempts to write, Burns describes the artistic significance of this moment: "I understood, in literary terms, the value of the image because I saw that I didn't have to grapple, as it were in essay form, with the endless complexities and significances of the love and other feelings that existed between my mother and father, and what they meant to me. I could let it all go by the board, let it take care of itself; I could, in the time-honoured phrase, show, not tell. . . . I could tell this story in a series of photographs, which is to say, a series of images, and let the stories emerge and the ideas emerge from that series of fragments, and that's how I found myself able to write that first book, *Buster*."

Although quite different from the novels which follow it, *Buster* suggests a number of the fictional concerns and techniques Burns employs in all his works. Central to his fictions is the technique of fragmentation, and although *Buster* is more conventional than any of his other novels, it too employs a limited form of fragmentation. Events in the work follow one another rapidly, and the temporal links between incidents are implied more often than they are stated. The effect is one of an associative rather than of a temporal pattern of organization.

The novel's protagonist, in fact, hints at the truncated method in Burns's later works when he attempts to write a story that concludes with the lines, "Uniqueness demanded disjointedness. Irrelevance was the key." The hero goes on to define some of the author's attitudes concerning the nature and function of language when he thinks, "Words don't describe, they point, and poets hit the source in history, the shadow behind each word. . . . Words are abstract isolate ancient huge, flipping and floating in coloured balloons in fanlight air." The quality of disjointedness and the idea of the "shadow behind each word" play increasingly larger roles in the compositional techniques of later novels.

Buster chronicles the growth from childhood to maturity of Dan Graveson, apple of his father's eye and failure in the eyes of others. At an early age the boy loses his mother when she is blown apart by a bomb before his eyes, and soon after that his older brother dies in military service. Graveson then deliberately flunks out of school, is dismissed from the army for Communist sloganeering, initiates and abruptly quits a peace committee, fails his law exams twice, and is eventually evicted bodily from his apartment. The novel ends with Graveson returning to his father's home where he greedily consumes the meal left on the pantry for his parent.

The domestic theme presented by this autobiographical novel predominates in many of Burn's others. Beginning and ending with the line, "They stood over him," *Buster* records the joys and suffocations that domestic life breeds. Continually feeling the pressure to succeed and please his trusting father, Graveson inevitably fails at every undertaking, and the novel's epigraph, which is a collection of dictionary definitions of the title, describes Graveson's fate—"to fall or be thrown."

Buster also introduces readers to another significant feature of Burn's fiction: his keen eye for detail, often rendered in arresting descriptive and figurative language. Frequently he will interrupt or clarify the ambiguity or disjointedness of a scene with a vivid metaphor or image, as in the following passage in which the narrator describes the condition of the dead mother's body: "The foot had a slight unnatural twist at the ankle. She could not have bent her foot like that if she had been alive. The difference was small, an angle of ten degrees. But alive she could not have done it without breaking the bone, gouging one bone into the other, wrenching the muscle enough to make her scream with pain or come as near screaming as an ill middle-aged woman can, not a young clean scream, but a choke, a sob, a cough, a constriction in the throat caused by too much trying to escape at one time."

With the publication and favorable critical reception of *Buster*, Burns ended his legal career, and on a monthly £50 subsidy from publisher John Calder, moved to Dorset where he spent the next four years writing. During this period his son, Daniel Paul, and daughter, Alshamsha, were born. In 1965 Calder published his second novel, *Europe After the Rain*. Taking the title from a painting by Max Ernst, Burns creates a horrifying vision of lives and of a landscape devastated by war. He was inspired not only by Ernst's painting, but also by a transcript of the Nuremberg trial and by a report on life in Poland after World War II. He set his novel in an indefinite future in which people and events lack logic and hope. Wandering throughout this waking nightmare, the unnamed narrator searches for an unnamed girl he may have loved at one time. Held prisoner by a rampaging commander, the girl eventually murders him, escapes, and then wastes away. To say this much is to imply a greater cohesiveness than the plot actually offers.

Developing his fragmented style, Burns presents the reader with a phantasmagoric assortment of horrors and brutalities as anonymous characters struggle against one another to survive an intolerable life. Sentences are terse and clipped, employing almost no subordination or transitional devices. Consequently, images and events take on an intensely isolated, disconnected relationship with each other, where linguistic austerity mirrors the austere conditions of the environment. Burns has explained that much of the novel's fragmentation results from the semihypnotic state in which it was composed. Glazing his eyes over as he typed, Burns wrote "from the unconscious" by emphasizing only the strongest and most clear words, usually nouns. It is a technique he has compared with that of many landscape painters.

In *Europe After the Rain* the domestic theme reappears, but here in a less evident way than in many of the other works. Although the narrator is the focus of the reader's attention, one knows less

about his family than about the nameless girl's. Like the children in Burns's other works, this girl has been separated from her father by the commander of an opposing political faction, and her eventual reunion with her parent leads not to a new life but to a physical decline. Family is finally an ineffective alternative to the violence and chaos of this world and may perhaps even contribute to the widespread devastation.

As in *Buster*, the images of death in this second novel are especially compelling, and they abound everywhere. Besides the sterile landscape, the reader witnesses the stabbing of a dog whose legs are dislocated, people who fight over corpses for their gold tooth fillings, a commander who is stoned and crucified, and a woman who tears a leg from a corpse and eats it. In each case, Burns renders the events with detailed precision, in a thoroughly prosaic tone. The disturbing qualities of a passage such as the following one stem not only from their graphic nature, but more importantly from the matter-of-fact manner in which the narrator relates such carnage: "Disturbed, she gave the cry, went up to the body and touched it, dragged it down as the others crowded round, clamoured for it, each one desperate for it. She wrenched off the leg, jabbed it, thick end first, into her mouth, tried hard to swallow it, could not get it down, the thicker part became less visible, there was nothing but the foot, she twisted off the protruding foot." The critical reaction to *Europe After the Rain* was mixed and thus initiated a pattern of response that would continue with the publication of many of Burn's other novels.

In 1967 Burns received an Arts Council Maintenance Grant and saw the publication of his third work. In a much more obvious way than *Europe After the Rain*, *Celebrations* explores the tensions and ambushes of family life, and similar to the pattern in *Buster*, this novel presents a family in which the woman is dead and one of the sons, Phillip, is killed when his brother crushes him under a machine. Overseeing these two is the father, Williams, who as factory boss dominates his sons as both parent and employer. After Phillip's death, father and remaining son, Michael, compete for the affections of Phillip's wife, Jacqueline, and for leadership of the company. Although she weds Michael, Jacqueline sleeps with and controls each man.

Once again, the narrative technique is a disjointed one, as events crowd ridiculously and inexplicably in upon each other. Punctuating the details of the familial rivalry are descriptions of the various rituals that form the "celebrations" of the work. Beginning with Phillip's inquest and funeral,

Burns catalogues Michael and Jacqueline's wedding, their advance in wealth and social stature, Williams's physical and professional decline, his death and funeral, Michael's unexpected death, and Jacqueline's remarriage. The novel grows from "a mosaic of fragments" as Burns uses these celebrations to create absurdly comic and surreal sequences, in, for instance, Williams's funeral march: "A procession of black castles slowly through the suburbs, patience of the dead face, his clothes taken from him, his feet buried in nettles, there was no significance. Black walnut, brick wall. Michael asked for a carton of coffee, it was water heated up. A brick wall advocated huge white letters hidden by coal. A seizure. Vegetable houses. A grubby bird, fancy-dress Spaniard, did not stay long. The living were talking." As in surrealist paintings, striking and outlandishly dissimilar images are juxtaposed, producing new, comic, and startling effects.

Like the novel which preceded it, *Celebrations* regularly eschews rational logic for the logic of the dream. Thus the reader moves between different levels of time and of consciousness, discovering a pattern of thought and emotion beneath the sequence of the narrative's events. One of the best examples of this condition is the description of Williams's death in a car accident, one which leaves the details ambiguous but the result certain: "In the street there were few people, he had not begun, it was unfair, life had gone badly, he had begun and ended." It is passages such as this which remind the reader of Burns's preoccupation with the theme of death and the spare, abrupt manner in which he renders its horrors, inevitability, and finality. The novel enjoyed a favorable reception, with reviews by B. S. Johnson and Robert Nye being particularly perceptive.

In 1969 Burns received a second Arts Council Maintenance Grant as well as a £ 2000 Writing Bursary from the Arts Council. During this period he and B. S. Johnson founded "Writers Reading," a collective to "establish a circuit, organize bookings and publicity, create a recognized 'norm' for fees, [and] be generally a co-operative centre for otherwise isolated and scattered fictioneers." They produced a booklet with photos and biographies of twelve writers, among them Ann Quin, Alan Sillitoe, Barry Cole, Carol Burns, Stephen Themerson, and Eva Figes, and organized a number of readings throughout London, Wales, and other areas of the United Kingdom. Although the organization began to fade by 1972, it was officially terminated with the deaths of Johnson and Quin in 1973.

Dust jacket for Burns's 1967 novel, which "explores the tensions and ambushes of family life"

In the same year that "Writers Reading" began, Calder published Burns's fourth novel, *Babel*. Inspired once more by a painting, in this case Brueghel's "Babel," Burns took his fragmented, snapshot method as far as possible. His most truly experimental, surreal, and difficult work, *Babel* is composed of a series of isolated paragraphs which occasionally center on an identifiable character and which frequently lead to incidents or personages in later paragraphs. More often than not the effect is nonsensical because "I used the cut-up method to join the subject of one sentence to the object from another with the verb hovering uncertainly between." Thus Burns rejects the methods of traditional storytelling, and his novel is best viewed as a series of voices competing with one another for the reader's attention. Using the biblical image of the tower of conflicting languages and purposeless action, *Babel* details the chaos, dislocations, and disjunctions of modern life.

Like the style in his earlier novels, Burns's prose is sparse, concise, and thoroughly compressed, while thematically the work expresses the writer's concern with the power of the state. Describing this feature, Burns writes: "*Babel* described not the obvious apparatus of dictatorship but the hints nudges nods assents implications agreements and conspiracies, the network of manipulations that envelops the citizens and makes them unaware accomplicies [*sic*] in the theft of their liberty. In *Babel* the crude despots of the earlier books, camp commander, factory manager, death, are re-constituted in the subtle dominance of the amorphous State." The critics, however, either glibly dismissed or bitingly denounced *Babel* as a failure.

During the summer of the following year, Burns gave a single lecture on censorship for the National County Libraries Summer School, and he was approached by producer Charles Marowitz to write a play. The result was *Palach*, which was performed at London's Open Space Theatre on 11 November 1970 and was published four years later. Presenting four separate stages, speakers blaring various voices, and actors interrupting and speaking over one another's lines, the play concerns the self-immolation of the Czech student, Jan Palach, who died in January 1969 protesting the Soviet invasion of his country. The various stages and conflicting voices remind one once again of Burns's commitment to random methods of storytelling, and the play's theme also reinforces the author's concern with the sacrifice of youth and the overwhelming power of the state.

In the following year, for ten summer weeks and with a stipend of £600, Burns became the first holder of the Henfield Fellowship at the University of East Anglia, Norwich, where he spent most of his time writing. Here, he gave a pair of lectures ("Writing by Accident," which explored various aleatoric writing methods, and "The Novel of the Future"), held weekly writer's workshops, and helped found and edit a magazine of student creative writing.

In 1972 Burns had two of his works published; the first, *To Deprave and Corrupt*, is a study of pornography and censorship, and the second, *Dreamerika!*, is his fifth novel. Since he had gone as far as he felt he could with the fragmented technique in *Babel*, Burns attempted to give the reader of *Dreamerika!* points of reference for his many images in the figures of the Kennedy clan. Using offset litho printing, the novel combines a fantastic vision of the family with cuttings from newspaper headlines which act as commentaries and counterpoints to the fiction's activities. As Burns describes it, "I played hell with the documented facts, made crazy distortions of the alleged truth, in order to get some humour out of it, and also to raise questions about the nature of documentary realism. Screwing up the story made some very undocumentary truths emerge."

Once again the themes of the power of the state and of the family, which is fueled by rivalry and torn apart by death, are immediately recognizable. In Burns's hands, the Kennedys become the embodiments of the American dream in all its most mercenary and exploitative fashions, with the reality of the dream suffusing all action and painting an emotional landscape of a culture gone awry.

Although roundly criticized as bitter and cruel, the work is an especially important one in the scope of Burns's career because it marks a turning point in his artistic development. While it uses the cut-up, collage effects of *Babel* and the surreal exaggerations of his earlier works, *Dreamerika!* also represents a recovery from the artistic dead end that *Babel* implied. By linking the fragmented method to a comprehensible narrative line, Burns was able to give this "surrealist fantasy," as he calls it, the cohesion that his earlier work lacked. The penultimate chapter, in which grandson Joe Kennedy dallies with communes and Marxism, foreshadows the lost revolutionaries who people Burns's next novel, *The Angry Brigade*.

In 1973 Burns was again awarded an Arts Council Bursary and held the C. Day Lewis Writing Fellowship at Woodberry Down School in London. In the same year, he and eleven other writers, among them Margaret Drabble, B. S. Johnson, Piers Paul Reid, Stephen Themerson, and John Brunner, published a "group novel" entitled *London Consequences*, a work commissioned and published by the Greater London Arts Association. Meeting one evening in Drabble's house in Hampstead, the group decided that each contributor would write a separate chapter, and the entire project was completed in ten weeks.

Also in 1973 another novel, *The Angry Brigade*, was published. Here Burns again experiments with documentary realism; his novel is ostensibly a collection of tape-recorded interviews of six London revolutionaries. Continuing with his method in *Dreamerika!*, he relies less on the subconscious for his material than on found pieces which he weaves into a fictional framework. While in the preface the author contends that he met and interviewed six people, Burns admits in a letter to David W. Madden that the work is entirely fictional. However, he did interview subjects, "mainly friends who agreed to talk with me about many matters unconnected with the book's content. I transcribed the tapes and then altered them to suit my purpose, the book's purpose. Thus I retained, I hope, the convincing rhythm of real speech and thus helped maintain the fiction of a journalistic *coup*—real interviews with real members of the Brigade. As an example, one of very many: I talked with and taped a friend who'd been on a series of visits to the dentist. She'd been scared and nervous about the visits. Also the dentist and his nurse had had the habit of talking to each other, rather intimately, 'over the patient's head.' The resulting discomfort-tending-toward-paranoia characterised the story my friend told. I transcribed the tape and then changed, particularly the nouns, to make the story fit one of my character's recollection of attending meetings of a faction of the Brigade at which she had felt rather intimidated, a bit scared, and had the sense that the others were discussing rather dangerous topics 'over her head.'. . ."

Divided into six chapters, which are then broken into the language and recollections of the four men and two women, *The Angry Brigade* presents the ignorant, misguided, and selfish attempts of a group of young, disaffected street kids and pseudo-intellectuals who vainly try to make a "political statement." Such statements result in the occupation and defacement of the Ministry of Housing, an action which brings about the five-year imprisonment of one member; the bombing of a railway embankment, which blinds a child, leads to the arrest of one of the women, and causes the escape of another member back to his native India; the bombing of the Post Office Tower, which kills a waitress; and an ambush on police, the casualties of which are uncertain.

Employing his now characteristic political theme, Burns shows the conflict between the powers of the state and the personal sacrifice made by some of the youths. However, the seriousness of many of the revolutionaries' actions is undercut by an acid irony that reveals their own internecine power struggles and forms of personal and sexual inequity. Ultimately, the novel reveals not only the state's deadly powers but also the ways in which victims and the exploited can easily turn into victimizers and exploiters.

Although it uses the collage technique once again, the book is scrupulously controlled and concise. Unlike the profusion of voices that confound

the audience of *Babel*, the differing voices in *The Angry Brigade* establish varying points of view for the same incident and thus question one's convenient assumptions about the nature of verifiable facts. This is not to say that the work does not contain ambiguous incidents; it does. However, Burns uses this ambiguity to reinforce the tension and paranoia that animate these lives. And like the children in his earlier novels, the youths in this fiction, dispossessed of their biological families and frightened by their own confusion and isolation, strive to create a pathetic substitute family in their commune. Casually dismissed by many critics, *The Angry Brigade* is actually one of Burns's strongest works.

Feeling artistically exhausted and financially strapped, Burns accepted a position in 1975 as Senior Tutor in Creative Writing at the Western Australian Institute of Technology in South Bentley, Australia. He spent his time there teaching fiction writing and also oversaw a student production of *Palach* that was performed at the National Australian Student Drama Festival in Sydney. In the same year, Hutchinson published *Beyond the Words*, an anthology, edited by Giles Gordon, of works by eleven contemporary British novelists. Burns's contributions consist of a particularly revealing essay about his fictional methods and concerns and a short story, "Wonderland."

Prepared to remain permanently in Australia, he nevertheless returned to London the next year to accept an Arts Council Fellowship. There, attached to the City Literary Institute, Burns enjoyed a good deal of free time for writing and the generosity of a £4000 stipend. In the following year he returned to teaching, accepting a tenure-track position at the University of Minnesota, where he is currently an associate professor in the English Department. In 1979 he and his second wife, Jean, had a child, Katherine Anne. While on leave in England, Burns worked on notes and materials he had been collecting for five years, which resulted in his seventh and most recent novel, *The Day Daddy Died*, published in the fall of 1981. Returning to the domestic theme, the novel presents a tough, working-class woman, Norah, who, despite repeated pregnancies and financial difficulties, perseveres. During the Depression her father loses his job and later dies, leaving a lonely, adolescent Norah to find a succession of lover-father surrogates. Despite her poverty she manages to raise five children, the eldest of whom commits suicide, but unlike Burns's other fictional families which ultimately tear one another apart, this family bands together and eventually buys the woman her first house.

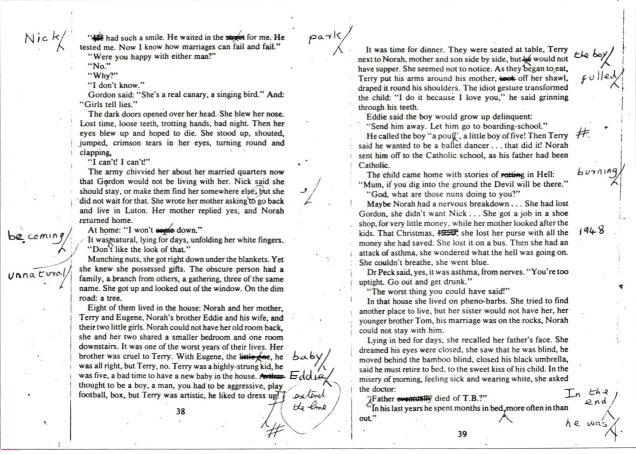

"He had such a smile. He waited in the street for me. He tested me. Now I know how marriages can fail and fail."

"Were you happy with either man?"

"No."

"Why?"

"I don't know."

Gordon said: "She's a real canary, a singing bird." And: "Girls tell lies."

The dark doors opened over her head. She blew her nose. Lost time, loose teeth, trotting hands, bad night. Then her eyes blew up and hoped to die. She stood up, shouted, jumped, crimson tears in her eyes, turning round and clapping,

"I can't! I can't!"

The army chivvied her about her married quarters now that Gordon would not be living with her. Nick said she should stay, or make them find her somewhere else, but she did not wait for that. She wrote her mother asking to go back and live in Luton. Her mother replied yes, and Norah returned home.

At home: "I won't come down."

It was natural, lying for days, unfolding her white fingers. "Don't like the look of that."

Munching nuts, she got right down under the blankets. Yet she knew she possessed gifts. The obscure person had a family, a branch from others, a gathering, three of the same name. She got up and looked out of the window. On the dim road: a tree.

Eight of them lived in the house: Norah and her mother, Terry and Eugene, Norah's brother Eddie and his wife, and their two little girls. Norah could not have her old room back, she and her two shared a smaller bedroom and one room downstairs. It was one of the worst years of their lives. Her brother was cruel to Terry. With Eugene, the little one, he was all right, but Terry, no. Terry was a highly-strung kid, he was five, a bad time to have a new baby in the house. Arthur thought to be a boy, a man, you had to be aggressive, play football, box, but Terry was artistic, he liked to dress up!

38

It was time for dinner. They were seated at table, Terry next to Norah, mother and son side by side, but he would not have supper. She seemed not to notice. As they began to eat, Terry put his arms around his mother, took off her shawl, draped it round his shoulders. The idiot gesture transformed the child: "I do it because I love you," he said grinning through his teeth.

Eddie said the boy would grow up delinquent:

"Send him away. Let him go to boarding-school."

He called the boy "a pouf", a little boy of five! Then Terry said he wanted to be a ballet dancer . . . that did it! Norah sent him off to the Catholic school, as his father had been Catholic.

The child came home with stories of rotting in Hell: "Mum, if you dig into the ground the Devil will be there."

"God, what are those nuns doing to you?"

Maybe Norah had a nervous breakdown . . . She had lost Gordon, she didn't want Nick . . . She got a job in a shoe shop, for very little money, while her mother looked after the kids. That Christmas, 1950, she lost her purse with all the money she had saved. She lost it on a bus. Then she had an attack of asthma, she wondered what the hell was going on. She couldn't breathe, she went blue.

Dr Peck said, yes, it was asthma, from nerves. "You're too uptight. Go out and get drunk."

"The worst thing you could have said!"

In that house she lived on pheno-barbs. She tried to find another place to live, but her sister would not have her, her younger brother Tom, his marriage was on the rocks, Norah could not stay with him.

Lying in bed for days, she recalled her father's face. She dreamed his eyes were closed, she saw that he was blind, he moved behind the bamboo blind, closed his black umbrella, said he must retire to bed, to the sweet kiss of his child. In the misery of morning, feeling sick and wearing white, she asked the doctor:

"Father eventually died of T.B.?"

"In his last years he spent months in bed, more often in than out."

39

Corrected page proofs for The Day Daddy Died

Interwoven with this narrative, which is delivered in a conversational, straightforward manner, is a second story of a girl who has a love affair with her father. This narrative strand is highly surrealistic, and the novel shifts back and forth between the two modes. Interspersed with both of these are also photo-collages by Ian Breakwell, which form a parallel narrative of memories and imaginings that float through the book. Despite the generally cool response, a review in the *Times Literary Supplement* was especially favorable and insightful.

Several months later Allison and Busby published another book, *The Imagination on Trial*. Co-authored with University of Minnesota colleague Charles Sugnet, this work is a study of twelve contemporary British and American novelists, including Burns, Alan Sillitoe, John Gardner, John Hawkes, J. G. Ballard, Michael Moorcock, Eva Figes, Grace Paley, Ishmael Reed, Wilson Harris, Tom Mallin, and B. S. Johnson. It offers a series of interviews which examine the ways each writer's ideas germinate and evolve into fictions.

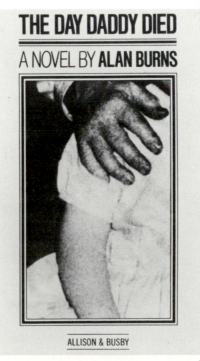

Dust jacket for Burns's most recent novel

While it is obviously difficult to predict where a writer like Burns is heading, the second strand in his most recent novel suggests that he will continue to employ the methods of surrealism to reveal, as René Magritte once said, "the magic of unforeseen affinities." At the same time, the evidence of *Dreamerika!*, *The Angry Brigade*, and the other strand from *The Day Daddy Died* indicates that Burns sees the need for some methods of traditional storytelling to balance the ambiguities and confusion of his surrealism. Continually concerned with the political and domestic pressures on individuals, Burns has his characters repeatedly struggle with and against their environments, and in each of his works it is his scenes of death that are usually the most compelling and fully realized. As Burns has said, ". . . if you are not willing to risk making a fool of yourself, you won't do anything worth doing." And while he does not make a fool of himself, Burns continues to experiment and to challenge himself and his audience with visions that call into question our most comfortable social and artistic assumptions.

Play:
Palach, London, Open Space Theatre, 11 November 1970.
Other:
Untitled chapter in *London Consequences*, edited by Margaret Drabble and B. S. Johnson (London: Greater London Arts Association, 1973);
"Essay" and "Wonderland" in *Beyond the Words*, edited by Giles Gordon (London: Hutchinson, 1975);
"Writing by Chance," *The Times Higher Education Supplement* (29 January 1982): 11-12.
Interviews:
John Hall, "Novels from the Unconscious," *Guardian* (30 April 1970): 9-10;
"The Disintegrating Novel," *Books and Bookmen*, 15 (15 September 1970): 6-7, 53;
Paddy Kitchen, "Surrealism and Sculpture in Words," *Times Educational Supplement* (18 September 1970): 21;
I. G. Leask, "The Value of the Image," *FallOut* (Spring/Summer 1980): 20-22.

A. S. Byatt

(24 August 1936-   )

Caryn McTighe Musil
La Salle College

BOOKS: *The Shadow of a Sun* (London: Chatto & Windus, 1964; New York: Harcourt, Brace & World, 1964);
Degrees of Freedom: The Novels of Iris Murdoch (London: Chatto & Windus, 1965; New York: Barnes & Noble, 1965);
The Game (London: Chatto & Windus, 1967; New York: Scribners, 1968);
Wordsworth and Coleridge in Their Time (London: Nelson, 1970);
Iris Murdoch, Writers and Their Work Series (London: Longman, 1976);
The Virgin in the Garden (London: Chatto & Windus, 1978; New York: Knopf, 1979).

Although thus far she has written only three novels, A. S. Byatt has nonetheless achieved a distinguished place as a person of letters in the last two decades. As novelist, critic, reviewer, editor, and lecturer, Byatt offers in her work an intellectual kaleidoscope of our contemporary world. Demonstrating awesome competence in an astounding variety of areas, she is at ease whether exploring the Renaissance, teaching a Wallace Stevens poem, editing Willa Cather, discussing van Gogh, writing for the *Times*, or broadcasting for the BBC radio. Her novels, like her life, are dominated by an absorbing, discriminating mind which finds intellectual passions as vibrant and consuming as emotional ones. With the publication in 1978 of her most recent novel, *The Virgin in the Garden* (the first in a projected tetralogy), Byatt has come fully into her own as a fiction writer and has guaranteed her place in literary histories of the future.

Antonia Susan Drabble was born in Sheffield, England, whose Yorkshire county landscape contains the wild beauty of the Brontë moors as well as the blackened scars of Lawrence's coal pits. Born of

A. S. Byatt

only finished off if you could write them down." From her early school days, Antonia continued to write in notebooks until she finally had her first novel published when she was twenty-eight. She shares her penchant for writing with other members of her family, for her barrister father, sister Margaret Drabble, and several aunts have all had novels published. Not surprisingly, one theme running through Byatt's novels is the struggle of the individual to discover and then live out her own identity, an identity etched out only with enormous effort and determination.

Always an exceptionally bright student, Antonia won major scholarships to both Somerville College, Oxford, and Newnham College, Cambridge. Choosing the latter, she had a distinguished career and received her B.A. in 1957 with first class honors. After a year of postgraduate work at Bryn Mawr College on an English-Speaking Union Fellowship, she returned to England to begin work on a doctorate in seventeenth-century literature under Helen Gardner at Oxford. Leaving Oxford in 1959 without completing her degree, she married (on 4 July of that same year) an economist, Ian Charles Rayner Byatt. The couple moved to Durham, where their first child, Antonia, was born in 1960, followed by their second child, Charles, in 1961. In addition to raising two children, Byatt also taught part-time and began work on her first novel, *The Shadow of a Sun*, which was published in 1964. It was followed a year later by *Degrees of Freedom*, a book of criticism on Iris Murdoch, a novelist with whom Byatt herself is often compared and who is an obvious influence on Byatt's fiction. What had been locked in notebooks, voluminous drafts, and Byatt's imagination was at last made public as she began in earnest her career as a writer.

An unwavering pattern for Byatt's creative process was set very early. Her novels have a long gestation period, gain substance through notebooks, and eventually are transformed through several painstakingly rewritten drafts. Her first novel, *The Shadow of a Sun*, for instance, was conceived as a hypothesis when she was seventeen, before she went to Cambridge. She continued to think about and work on the novel while at Cambridge and Bryn Mawr. It was not until she returned to Oxford to work on her doctorate that her true vocation crystallized. Byatt had been working on *The Shadow of a Sun* side by side with her thesis in the Bodleian library, thinking it quite possible to do both simultaneously. According to Byatt, Helen Gardner, under whom she was studying, said one day, "My dear girl, every English graduate thinks

parents who both studied at Cambridge despite working class origins, Byatt is the eldest child of four. Like several of her heroines, she was impatient with childhood. "I remember thinking when I grow up I will write that I couldn't stand it. I will not write that it was a happy time." Because she was asthmatic, she read a great deal, which only increased her discontent with childhood. "I hated being a child because I didn't like any of the things children did. If you've read *Anna Karenina* by the time you are twelve, after all, and Shakespeare, and there you are puttering around with Pooh bear."

Although she describes herself as an agnostic, her parents (Marie Bloor Drabble and John Frederick Drabble), who became Quakers only later in life, sent Antonia to a Quaker school in York for her education. While her memories of those days are not fond, she did begin writing there once she had devised a hideout in the boiler room where she could have privacy and scribble in her big black notebook by the light of the fire. In an interview with David Gerard in 1980, Byatt explained, "From being very little, reading and living were all to me she can write a novel. Ninety-nine per cent of them can't. Get on with your thesis." Helen Gardner then mentioned that she was reading Proust, but not in French. In a rage over Gardner's remarks, Byatt claims she "fled out of the room and went to Blackwells where I purchased Proust in French, read all of his work, and stopped writing my thesis. I needed to read Proust to learn how to write from him at that time, and Proust is all over *Shadow* in big chunks." Proust is still the novelist with whom Byatt feels the greatest affinity today.

Looking back at her first book, Byatt sees it as a very feminist novel. "I thought you'd be trapped by decisions of marriage unless you thought through your decisions very carefully." In the Bildungsroman tradition of James Joyce's *Portrait of the Artist as a Young Man* (1916) or Doris Lessing's *Martha Quest* (1952), *The Shadow of a Sun* traces the adolescence and young adulthood of Anna Severall, a sensitive, aspiring young writer riddled with self-doubt yet determined to carve out an identity and a future all her own. Paralyzed in her own growth in part because of her novelist father, Henry, a man of towering presence who "looked like a cross between God, Alfred Lord Tennyson, and Blake's Job," Anna has protected her precarious ego primarily by being passive and withdrawn. Her other defense is to run. The first view of Anna is of her on the run, escaping visitors and her parents' house. "Something would be destroyed if she did not get away and hide," Anna says. In a narrative reminiscence, Anna describes a previous abortive attempt to escape that had resulted in absolute failure and had only confirmed her sense of her own insignificance. She had left her boarding school one Sunday morning, taken a train to the nearest city, York (where the novel also ends), and fantasized about a life of beauty, reflection, and writing. Her early ebullience soon faded in the dreary, cramped hotel room. Her first "room of her own" was, in fact, desolate, colorless, depressing, and ugly. "She felt suddenly and finally trapped." When she pushed open a window to see the sky, "She was confronted by a blank wall and a dark window." Having returned home in defeat, Anna thought "that all her actions had no weight and no importance, that she was living in a vacuum and might as well do any one thing as any other."

It is in such a state of imaginative paralysis that Oliver Cannings discovers Anna at seventeen in part one of *The Shadow of a Sun*. A literary critic who has won his reputation by writing about Henry Severall's work, Oliver arrives for a long visit at the Severalls' home with his wife Margaret, a woman whose entire life is tragically defined by the presence of a man, at this point Oliver. The shifting dynamics between Henry/Anna and Oliver/Margaret determine the larger structure of the novel as the two women trade dependencies. Determined to invade Anna's defensive privacy, Oliver orders her to take charge of her own life but then promptly begins to make decisions for her. Though a skinny little beardless patriarch, Oliver is as potent and suffocating a figure for Anna as her father is. " 'But what must I do?' Anna asked, mesmerized by Oliver's fierce face, and the harsh little lecturing voice, into accepting his view for a moment absolutely." While Oliver does tutor Anna so she can eventually go to Cambridge, his motives are complex. Pitting himself against a powerful male, Oliver delights in usurping Henry's role, derives heady pleasure playing Pygmalion, and ultimately claims a warrior's spoil when he eventually takes Anna sexually. Throughout the novel Anna is torn between what she sees as her only two options, each represented by one of the two men: the first is her father's life as a visionary, a creator, one who transcends the mundane world to a place apart and beyond it; the second is Oliver's as a realist, a critic, a commonsense practical man who resigns himself to limitations and somehow has contempt for what he sees as Henry's imaginative indulgences. Anna finds herself helplessly trapped between the two men and the two world views, using each man and each view as armor against the potentially obliterating weight of the other.

A temporary resolution comes at last one night when everyone else is asleep. Feeling like "gas in a narrow jar" growing and yet "confined in a little space" which would soon explode, Anna is desperate to imitate her father's escape: "He had found the third way, neither in the enclosure, nor out into Oliver's myriad concerns, but an extension, a development, of what she thought she had already." Awaiting a gathering storm outside that parallels her internal one, Anna sits at the window and finally has her vision. Holding a glass while it catches the light, she now is confident: "I can do something with this that matters." By the time Oliver joins her to trap her again into recognizing limitations, she can say as the lightning flashes, "Sometimes . . . I think perhaps I have no limitations." Furious at her achieved independence, Oliver kisses her violently, but Anna says with detachment, "It isn't important" and muses, "Poor old Oliver." Part one ends with Anna poised, capable of generating her own visions like her father does, freed from Oliver's control, released at last from paralysis.

Part two opens, however, with Anna drunk at a party at Cambridge, once again immobilized by a world of men to which she surrenders without overt resistance. Anna finds she has not escaped her father by coming to Cambridge. As before, she retreats in self-doubt to passivity and abdicates her life to Peter Hughes-Winterton, a golden, classically heroic aristocrat. Oliver reappears, takes possession of Anna once again against an opposing male figure, and this time sleeps with her. Anna welcomes the affair with Oliver because it seems safe, postpones decisions about her future, and, she erroneously thinks, has no consequences. A frequent lesson for Byatt's heroines is that actions always *do* have consequences, though they may think at first they are acting in total freedom.

Thinking about leaving Cambridge and striking out on her own, Anna leaves Oliver one afternoon; while walking on a bridge she stares at a green bottle floating in the river and waits expectantly for a vision. "This will change me" and "be a clue to how to begin." But no illumination comes. "The possible glory was gone." Anna muses despondently, "I don't think I am going to know. . . . I can't make it. I shall never make it." And the moment of realization "would cast a shadow on things always now." Unlike Joyce's Stephen Dedalus who plunges into the river where he has his vision of his vocation as a priest of art, Anna is left desolate. The vision she does experience is biologically induced, for her nausea on the bridge is her first clue that she is pregnant. In speaking of Anna's behavior, Byatt says, "You do things you think are temporary and they turn out to be permanent because of woman's biology."

Anna's pregnancy alters all her plans, and she is left once again with a set of choices, a repetitive pattern in the novel. Peter offers to marry her and, in fact, whisks her off to his family estate. Anna really does not want either to have the baby or to marry Peter, so she bolts once more from a house and from a family. Her goal is the York train station and independence. In riding to the station, Anna decides not to have an abortion, a decision characteristic of her passive behavior. Her other escape route is thwarted as well when Oliver catches her at the station and she succumbs to what she sees as her fate. The novel ends with her resigning herself to being trapped, limited, and controlled. Anna says carelessly, "I was just going. . . . But it doesn't matter. I wouldn't have gone far I suspect."

In reflecting about the origins of her first novel, Byatt says it was inspired by two ideas. The first, a literary idea, was the notion that if the great

D. H. Lawrence critic F. R. Leavis (who taught at Cambridge while Byatt was a student) had met Lawrence, the two really would not have gotten along. Henry is Lawrence, Oliver is Leavis, and Anna, Byatt claims, is her own mind stuck between the two. Seeing herself as part of both men, Byatt understands the conflict as her "fear of the dictatorialness of the critic as opposed to the tentativeness, and ease, and solitariness of the writer." The conflict was a very personal one for Byatt, who reveals, "And that was another choice I had to make, of course. I knew I was a good critic but I didn't know if I could write at all. So that first novel was all choices."

The second inspiration for the novel, Byatt explains, was the particular challenge to ambitious women in the 1950s who were encouraged to go back into domestic roles. "I was afraid of not going on as a writer or not being a woman." Anna is like George Eliot's trapped heroines, Byatt says. "In a sense I put Anna in a house so I could be out of one." Anna's fear of loving someone and her pattern of always choosing a romantic attachment that is impossible to achieve grew out of Byatt's conviction then that "if you got wound up in love too badly, you were done for."

Although Anna does not escape either houses, domesticity, or her conviction of her own limitations, completing *The Shadow of a Sun* seems to have freed A. S. Byatt to define herself as *both* critic and novelist, as *both* mother and visionary. Alternating between Henry's world and Oliver's, Byatt wrote a critical study of Iris Murdoch between the publication of her first novel and the appearance of her second, *The Game* (1967). Byatt explains that she started *The Game* while at Bryn Mawr in 1957-1958 and completed a draft between beginning and ending the final version of *The Shadow of a Sun*. *The Game* was among other things to Byatt "a technical exercise in which I worked out how to do metaphors." Writing in a more polished, tightly controlled, and confident voice, Byatt demonstrates her success in this novel layered with imagery of snakes, Eden, and jungles—all interwoven in a dialectic tension between the medieval and modern world, spiritual and sensual expression, good and evil.

With epigraphs from both Charlotte Brontë and Samuel Taylor Coleridge, *The Game* is centrally preoccupied with the power of the imagination. Brontë in "Retrospection" recognizes the power of fantasy to grow larger than the real, while Coleridge sees the serpentine wisdom of the imagination become a world unto its own. For Julia and Cassandra

Corbett, the sisters in the novel, however, their shared fantasy life assumes ominous and ultimately fatal proportions. Fictions each has woven about the other obliterate the actual person herself. Although Byatt insists that the characters are largely inspired by other models, the germ of *The Game* is also Byatt's exploration of the fear of sisters. The publication of her manuscript, as well as the critical reception of it, was complicated by Margaret Drabble's 1963 book, *A Summer Bird-Cage*, a novel also about sisters which critics assumed was inspired by Margaret's relationship with her older sister, Antonia. When Byatt finally had *The Game* published in 1967, the comparisons between the two books as opposing versions of the Drabble sisters' relationship interfered with critics' focusing on *The Game* for its own remarkable merit. Today Byatt is understandably reluctant to discuss the book's autobiographical implications and prefers to avoid the painful intrusion into her personal life the novel has generated.

The primary drama of the novel is the battle between the two sisters, Cassandra and Julia, each of whom imprisons herself in an imaginary sibling fantasy. The elder sister, Cassandra—an Oxford don in medieval studies—is unmarried, withdrawn, hidden, constricted. Convinced that love deforms and kills and that the real world only consumes and destroys, Cassandra lives a defensive life of self-denial which keeps her impulse to risk herself in ritualized check. Like Anna in *The Shadow of a Sun*, Cassandra tries as a child to run away, but unlike Anna, Cassandra succeeds in walling herself off from worldly intercourse. Adorned with layers of chains, locks, and crosses, Cassandra retreats into her room, her journal, her imaginative and spiritual life. The younger sister, Julia, appears at first glance an exact opposite. Julia is flamboyant, sensual, successful in worldly terms as a novelist, television personality, wife, and mother. Much of Julia's life, however, is defined by her insecurity and need to have other people affirm her significance. Even more than through the various men in her life, Julia needs that affirmation from her sister. In fact, because of her determination to have Cassandra take her into account, she deliberately married Thor Eskelund, a man whom she had known for only two months. Julia hoped her marriage would shock her older sister into seeing her. The marriage did no such thing, and by the time the novel begins with the sisters in their thirties, they are as distrustful and alienated from each other as ever.

Only the serious illness and eventual death of their father forces the sisters back into each other's company. It is then that we learn of two incidents that have insured their hostile and defensive posture toward each other. As children, Julia and Cassandra shared a common imaginary world through inventing and playing The Game. With an oilskin and clay figures, the two girls created characters with castles, knights, queens, romance, and adventure. Through the mythology of their game, they could reach each other in symbolic ways. Their battles for control, however, were played out even in The Game, for Cassandra's stories gave Julia nightmares and Julia kept trying to invent happy endings to avoid Cassandra's grim conclusions. When Julia published an adolescent story that contained references to her imaginary world with her sister, Cassandra refused to play any more, and their imaginative partnership totally disappeared. The second incident to separate the sisters involved Simon Moffit, a young man to whom Cassandra became passionately attached just before she went off to Oxford. Having met at the post office while each was mailing a letter to Cassandra, Simon and Julia became friends; when Cassandra returned home on holiday, she felt like an outsider. Even as an adult, Cassandra refuses to forgive either Simon or Julia for what she defines as a betrayal.

When the novel opens, Simon, now a herpetologist doing scientific investigations in the Congo, is broadcasting a television series which both Julia and Cassandra watch with avid intensity. His reappearance both on television and in the flesh in London is the dramatic incident that triggers the final confrontation between the sisters. A temporary reconciliation after their father's death is shattered by the real experience of trying to trust each other. Julia's visit to Cassandra at Oxford makes Cassandra feel like an outsider again and confirms her view of Julia as menacing. Shattered by her one effort at reentering the human world of trust and involvement, Cassandra—desperate to confront and contain the tangled natural world—begins a fatal battle with the real world of objects by giving up Sir Thomas Malory and taking up painting. With only the paper as a thin bulwark between madness and sanity, Cassandra, dressed in her yellow sou'wester, paints obsessively at the botanical garden, a place echoing Simon's jungles, and, of course, the biblical Eden.

Encouraged in her triumph over Cassandra at Oxford, Julia decides to write a novel, *A Sense of Glory*, whose protagonist is a version of her sister. The novel concerns a woman whose imaginary life is invaded by the flesh and blood presence of the man she dreams about but would never dare reach out to claim. When he shows up in her life, "Does his real presence free her to live in the world without him or does the loss of her illusion kill her?" Despite misgivings about the effect of the novel on Cassandra, Julia has it published anyway, in part to free herself forever from her sister's domination. By making a fiction out of an imagined fear, Julia hopes to diminish Cassandra's presence, make her human, and in the process, lovable.

As in other Byatt novels where the consequences of one's actions are far different from anything imagined, Julia's novel does not free her from Cassandra. "The net was tight and constricting as ever, and she herself had fastened it more securely. We think, Julia thought, that we are releasing ourselves by plotting what traps us, by laying it all out to look at—but in fact all we do is show the trap up for real." Cassandra, having confronted in real life, through Simon's surprise visit to her at Oxford, the incident Julia's novel imagines, refuses to be trapped into fiction and controlled by Julia. Recognizing she is in fact not the "rag doll" in her sister's novel, she also acknowledges that such fantasies "were fed and watered by me, too much of my energy went into their growth for me to be able to clear them away, or make myself a space to inhabit." Cassandra decides, "I can choose, at least, to put out the light that throws it. I want no more reflections." In a logical metaphoric extension of her relation to the world, Cassandra kills herself by withdrawing to her room, locking her doors, stuffing cracks with clothes, taking sleeping pills, and turning on the gas.

When the real Cassandra dies, Julia is herself confronted with the very situation her novel claims happened only to the Cassandra figure. Julia's own imaginary construct of Cassandra is gone, and even the real person is gone, as indeed Simon Moffit is from Cassandra's life. Will Julia survive without her illusions? "All her life Cassandra had been the mirror where [Julia] studied the effects of her actions. It was Cassandra's reactions that proved her existence, now she had lost a space and a purpose." The novel ends with Simon's returning to the jungle, having offered no traditional romantic rescue for either Julia or Cassandra. Even Julia's husband finally leaves her to follow his obsession to be self-sacrificing on a global scale. Julia is left, then, with the challenge of finding her significance from her own measure of herself, not from without. "She would not depend on other people's thoughts of her." She is determined to be a new woman, a survivor, to live, but knows "it couldn't be done at one blow, or in one movement. . . . But the will to change was there. Julia knew it was there."

A piece of technical virtuosity, *The Game* is also a taut novel that explores with a courage and determined honesty greater than Lawrence's the deepest levels of antagonism that come with intimacy. Widely reviewed, especially in Great Britain, *The Game* established Byatt's reputation as an important contemporary novelist, though the book's readership was not extensive. Elaine Showalter in *A Literature of Their Own: British Women Novelists from Brontë to Lessing* (1977) says it is "a brilliant novel that should be much better known."

In her usual fashion, Byatt wove a book of criticism, this time *Wordsworth and Coleridge in Their Time* (1970) between *The Game* (1967) and her latest novel, *The Virgin in the Garden* (1978). The study of early Romantic poets continues to reflect the obvious fascination Byatt has for such visionaries which so inspired Henry Severall's character in *The Shadow of a Sun*. Typical of Byatt's own fiction, too, her critical work on the Romantic poets roots the poetry and poets to a cultural and historical context. Per-

Dust jacket for the first volume in a projected tetralogy: "I think I am naturally inclined like Proust to write novels that are endless."

sonality is subordinated to a broad and lively description of the social history that shaped individuals, even ones so awesome as Wordsworth and Coleridge. The eight-year interval between her book of criticism and her next novel is largely explained by a series of personal dramas in her life. After divorcing Ian Charles Byatt in 1969, she married Peter J. Duffy in the same year, moved again, and had two more children, Isabel in 1970 and Miranda in 1973. In addition to reviewing regularly for magazines and newspapers, writing academic articles, and doing several radio broadcasts, Byatt also accepted a full-time teaching appointment at University College, London, in 1972, a position she still holds. She was also stunned into silence when her eleven-year-old son, Charles, was killed by a car in 1972. Having written one third of *The Virgin in the Garden* by then, Byatt says she had to scrap the novel and start all over much later "because it along with everything else had died." In her rewritten version there is a character, Mrs. Thone, whose son has died suddenly from a fall off a park bench. Byatt explains, "I had to put a character in my novel now who understood what I was feeling."

The Virgin in the Garden is also a far more ambitious novel than any Byatt had thus far attempted, and it is part of an even grander scheme for a tetralogy that promises to span not only several decades in the characters' lives, but several in the author's as well. "I think I am naturally inclined like Proust to write novels that are endless," Byatt asserts. She has found in this book what seems congenial to her intellectual and imaginative life. Although Byatt used to keep two sets of notebooks, one for her intellectual thoughts and one for ideas about her current novel, she now weaves the two together. Holding a slim black volume, she says, "That's my intellectual life, but it is also the plot of my novel, and I just wind it all together. There are about twenty of these as I am writing my next novel, 'Still Life.' " In an interview with David Gerard, Byatt describes *The Virgin in the Garden* as "a novel of ideas . . . a novel that thinks as it goes along like a Proust novel." All of her novels have characters, especially heroines, who are intelligent and who think. Linking herself in a literary tradition to George Eliot, Byatt insists that Eliot realized that "the intellect had saved her." In the same interview Byatt also talks about how her academic life nourishes her imaginative life. "I work very much off verbal echoes and . . . I am one of those people to whom a good book is at least as powerful an experience as another person." Whenever she writes a novel, Byatt reads around her subject

widely and seriously, uses deliberate cross-references as she writes and rewrites her drafts, and works out of "a conscious need to keep the English language complex and flexible." The result in all her novels—but especially her third and latest one—is a density that can be problematic to some who complain of overloading and extravagance. To others, however, the result is spellbinding, intriguing, and—described more positively—brocaded, allegorical, and tapestried.

The Virgin in the Garden's origins go back to Byatt's thesis begun at Oxford in 1959 and took form as an idea for a novel in the early 1960s. She was intrigued by the technical problem of how to put an accident into fiction, an accident which transforms a person's life forever, is never anticipated, yet after it happens, defines one's life entirely by its occurrence. The accident in her tetralogy, she confides, has not yet occurred.

The novel's central symbol is Queen Elizabeth I, a monarch Byatt sees as surviving because she used her mind and thought things out, unlike her rival, Mary, Queen of Scots, who was "very female and got it wrong." Here again one sees Byatt's repetitive themes of love as a danger for women and intelligence as a way to achievement and selfhood. In *The Virgin in the Garden* the small Yorkshire town of Blesford is planning to celebrate the 1953 coronation of young Elizabeth II by performing a verse drama written by a talented, delicately attractive English professor, Alexander Wedderburn. Just as producing the drama unites the town and puts odd sorts in relation to one another, so does it shape her novel and stand as its controlling metaphor.

With a panoply of characters rivaling Dickens, the novel gains structure by weaving alternating accounts of the events of 1953 in the lives of the three Potter children: Stephanie Potter, twenty-one, bright, sensual, passive, and soft, who after a first at Cambridge returns to teach English at her alma mater, Blesford Girls' Grammar; Frederica Potter, seventeen, fiery, impulsive, desperately anxious to be through her childhood, who is chosen to play the young Queen Elizabeth in the drama; and finally Marcus Potter, the youngest child, sensitive, withdrawn, nearly autistic, and haunted by visions he cannot understand. The three children define their actions in part in defiance of their domineering, intrusive father, Bill Potter, who fumes, rants, and sputters through much of the novel just as his wife, Winifred, survives stoically in his blanketing shadow. Bill is a senior colleague of Alexander's at the Blesford Ride School. To her own surprise and to her militantly agnostic father's horror, Stephanie finds herself agreeing to marry the local curate, Daniel Orten. A huge man physically, Daniel is also humanitarian, loving, warm, and passionately involved in human beings' private tragedies. He claims Stephanie as his own and pursues her until she finally agrees to marry him. Their curious courtship, disappointing first intercourse, and early married life are some of the best-written passages in the novel. The final view of the couple, however, suggests that external circumstances will squeeze the laughter and light from their lives. Already living in contracted geographic space in their tiny flat, they find that their house, like their lives, is continually invaded by people who turn to them with voracious need. Even Daniel begins to be oppressed by the consequences of living out his love for people. By the novel's end he dreams both of murdering and being murdered: "And, most terrible of all, a blanket terror of smothering: his own bulk accidentally weltering on . . . the child, some unknown damp and heavy monstrosity pressing and choking away his own life." On her part, Stephanie silently accepts life's burdens; but the last portrait of her, immobilized on her couch by the weight of her brother's sagging head and her own pregnancy, making her look "like some unnatural and ungainly Pietà," is a chilling tableau.

Parallel to Daniel's determined pursuit of Stephanie is Frederica's of Alexander Wedderburn. Frederica's portrait is a marvelous account of the painful adolescence of a very bright yet very inexperienced girl who, while greedy for life, has an aesthetic and moral sensibility that prevents her from being an undiscriminating hedonist. When she wins the part of the young Elizabeth, Frederica also wins an entree to a world beyond the meager fare of her confining school and home. The bacchanalian banquet held at Matthew Crowe's Long Royston, the estate where the play is performed, satiates some of Frederica's appetites and quells other longings. When, however, the play is over, the stage dismantled, and Frederica is driving out of the gates of Long Royston, she reflects: "She had somehow imagined she would become a welcome visitor there. . . . She heard behind her the faint crash of breaking glass. Fled is that music. It really was like being shut out of Paradise." Like Milton's Eve and Henry James's Isabel Archer, Frederica has the world laid all before her as she looks elsewhere for her earthly paradise. She seems momentarily to find it in Alexander, who at last surrenders to her siege and agrees to a rendezvous. Panicked that Alexander will discover her virginity, she fails to show up for their assignation. While their romance

goes unconsummated, its very failure convinces Alexander that like Frederica he must also move out beyond the stifling gates of Blesford. In our last view of him he drives out of town to meet the worldly opportunities awaiting him because of the critical success of his verse drama on Elizabeth. Meanwhile, Frederica eases herself into womanhood with a man safer than Alexander; she learns how to have sex without violating her private self, a lesson that seems crucial for Byatt's young sexually active heroines: "She had learned something. . . . You could sleep all night, with a strange man . . . and be more self-contained than anywhere else. . . . It removed the awful either/or from the condition of women as she had seen it. Either love, passion, sex, and those things, or the life of the mind, ambition, solitude, and others." Frederica's desire to have both a sensual and an intellectual life echoes the same hunger Anna had in *The Shadow of a Sun*. Unlike Anna, Frederica learns how to claim both.

Frederica, who closes the novel in a conversation with Daniel, appears in the novel's prologue set in 1968. We know, then, from the novel's opening that Frederica is a survivor who continues to live a life of risks and adventures. She promises to be at the center of "Still Life," the second in the planned series and the book Byatt describes as her autobiographical volume. Byatt has revealed that Frederica will go to Provence to be an au pair girl; there she will again meet Alexander, who is staying in Matthew Crowe's European house while he writes a piece on van Gogh. Byatt spent the summer of 1980 traveling in Provence to revisit and take notes about the house and landscape where as a young woman she herself was an au pair girl.

Marcus Potter's drama in *The Virgin in the Garden* is the most difficult part of the novel to describe, though to many critics it is the most powerful. Largely nonverbal, Marcus retreats without much control into his private photic visions, visions that a teacher of his, Lucas Simmonds, discovers and tries to study and systematize. Lucas's involvement with Marcus is complex. A fanatic visionary himself, the seemingly drab, nondescript and pathetic Lucas assumes a sinister control over Marcus's life. His attempt to manipulate either Marcus or Marcus's visions ultimately fails, and the failure is assured when Lucas makes a homosexual overture to the frightened Marcus, who likes neither to touch nor be touched by anyone. Lucas's shame for what he sees as his sexual weakness drives him to attempted suicide, which in turn propels Marcus beyond his self-enclosed world to reach Lucas. In a moving scene in a mental hospital where Lucas has been

(118)   <u>Polite Essays</u> p. 60

Coleridge spoke of   "the miracle that might be wrought simply by one man's feeling a thing more clearly or more poignantly than anyone had ever felt it before." The last century showed us a fair example when Swinburne awoke to the fact that poetry was an art, not merely a vehicle for the propagation of doctrine. England & Germany are still showing the effects of his perception. I cannot belittle my belief that Mr. Hueffer's realization that poetry should be written at least as well as prose will have as wide a result. He himself will tell you that it is "all Christina Rossetti" and that "it was not Wordsworth" for Wordsworth was so busied about the ordinary word that he never found time for <u>le mot juste</u>.'

Further prologue: opposite flayed/dead lady
in BM.
     I once saw a woman flayed alive
      The image itself

It occurs to me today that the lecture and the aesthetic chapter can be written <u>in tandem</u>. Both being abt developments of techniques of impressionism.

STC   on symbol   —   Van Gogh's chair.
<u>Not</u>   the Symbolistes.

Noel Forster on Provence & Van Gogh. 'You could just drive up a removal van and drive great slices of it away.'

(119)

Van Gogh — yellow chair & mot juste &
'impressionism'.

   | Color adjectives — Pound on
   | A's verse containing colour adjectives about chair
   | Containing Van G's explanations of color adjectives
   | Containing symbolism of apparently for-themselves
objects.
   Containing Proust's expl. of symbol that <u>is</u> & says —
closeness, primitive.
   Cf Gauguin who came to be the green-and-red
'noir-rouge' villain. ~~But~~ Brothels and Bernard &
Alexander's own sexual innocence of Van G.
   Correspondence of this with Casesbakh — cut-out parts of
woman.
   Correspondence of le mot juste with Ford on Flanders fields.
It is <u>F</u> who says OK tackle it — who puts
Sara Tê Kali & madness into his Vext — he is afraid
of what he has found, of the changing gear.

   More like <u>Sweeney Agonistes</u> than like <u>Venus Observ'd</u>
Rhythm of letter to Bernard abt sun & madness.
   3 bits. Van G & postman & letters alone.
   Dialogue with sex in: Van G — Gauguin. Electricity.
Collapse. Dramatic scenes.
   Coda by Gauguin.
St.-Rémy and the foreshadowing — the avoidance of
the Christian
   (use also for God piece.)

Byatt in her office at the University of London, beside a travel poster depicting the setting of her novel in progress

taken after his breakdown, Marcus reaches out and holds Lucas's limp hand assuringly, although Marcus himself must clutch the side of the iron bedstead to control his revulsion. The effort to get beyond himself to others totally exhausts Marcus, and the novel ends with his taking refuge in Daniel's house and Stephanie's bosom.

Like D. H. Lawrence, Byatt ends her novel in the middle of a conversation, a conversation between Frederica and Daniel, the two aggressive and active characters, who are discussing what to do next. It is a conversation that leaves us eager for the book's sequel. Byatt has indeed written a Proustian novel whose fictional life interweaves with the continuing intellectual life of the author. Layered with references to Milton, Spenser, the flowery Elizabethan Age of intrigue and discovery, Byatt's novel roots her characters in a historical and literary continuum with the past. She uses the Elizabethan Age with its iconography, mythology, and ornate language as a literary metaphor for understanding her own age and expressing that age in fiction.

With the publication of *The Virgin in the Garden*, A. S. Byatt initiated the middle phase of her career as a novelist. Much denser and dependent on her readers' erudition, the novel achieves a style that suits Byatt. It blends her acquisitive, intellectual bent with her imaginative compulsion to tell stories. Though she expects the style of "Still Life" to change when the metaphor for the novel shifts from Queen Elizabeth and the Renaissance to Vincent van Gogh and the post-Impressionists, she recognizes a potential aesthetic problem. She plans to write plainly and clearly as her new novel demands, yet she is still determined to weave in the necessary layers of allusions and cross-references whose cumulative accretions give her novels and style their singularity.

Although her reading audience in Great Britain is small, Byatt has an enthusiastic following. Despite having been widely reviewed in the United States, she has not yet reached a wide American reading audience and deserves far more critical attention. When asked if she were not by her very intelligence and breadth going to reduce her possible reading audience, Byatt acknowledged the possibility but seemed resigned to being "a dinosaur . . . writing long and complicated novels."

She has already enlarged the boundaries of our contemporary literary tradition, and we are all the better off for her refusal to become extinct.

Other:
"The Lyric Structure of Tennyson's Maud," in *The Major Victorian Poets Reconsidered*, edited by Isobel Armstrong (London: Routledge & Kegan Paul, 1969), pp. 69-93;

"People in Paper Houses: Attitudes to 'Realism' and 'Experiment' in English Postwar Fiction," in *The Contemporary English Novel*, edited by Malcolm Bradbury and Edward Arnold (Stratford-upon-Avon Studies, 1979), pp. 19-41;

George Eliot, *The Mill on the Floss*, edited with introduction and notes by Byatt (New York: Penguin Books, 1979);

Grace Paley, *Enormous Changes at the Last Minute*, preface by Byatt (London: Virago Modern Classics, 1979);

Paley, *The Little Disturbances of Man*, preface by Byatt (London: Virago Modern Classics, 1980);

Willa Cather, *My Antonia*, preface by Byatt (London: Virago Modern Classics, 1980);

Cather, *A Lost Lady*, preface by Byatt (London: Virago Modern Classics, 1980).

Periodical Publications:
"The Obsession with Amorphous Mankind," *Encounter* (September 1966): 63-69;

"Real People and Images," *Encounter* (February 1967): 71-78;

"Wallace Stevens: Criticism, Repetition, and Creativity," *American Studies*, 12, no. 3 (1978): 369-375.

Angela Carter
(7 May 1940-   )

Lorna Sage
University of East Anglia

BOOKS: *Shadow Dance* (London: Heinemann, 1966); republished as *Honeybuzzard* (New York: Simon & Schuster, 1966);

The Magic Toyshop (London: Heinemann, 1967; New York: Simon & Schuster, 1968);

Several Perceptions (London: Heinemann, 1968; New York: Simon & Schuster, 1968);

Heroes and Villains (London: Heinemann, 1969; New York: Simon & Schuster, 1969);

Love (London: Hart-Davis, 1971);

The Infernal Desire Machines of Doctor Hoffman (London: Hart-Davis, 1972); republished as *The War of Dreams* (New York: Harcourt Brace Jovanovich, 1974);

Fireworks (London: Quartet, 1974; New York: Harper & Row, 1981);

The Passion of New Eve (London: Gollancz, 1977; New York: Harcourt Brace Jovanovich, 1977);

The Sadeian Woman (London: Virago, 1979; New York: Pantheon, 1979);

The Bloody Chamber (London: Gollancz, 1979; New York: Harper & Row, 1980).

Angela Carter's fiction poses precisely the question of what is central, what eccentric in contemporary British writing. "We live in Gothic times," she wrote in an afterword to her 1974 collection of tales, *Fireworks*; and all her work reflects that perception, in technique as well as in setting and subject. "Gothic" here is not used in the rather special American sense, but implies the European tradition that goes back to (at least) the eighteenth century (one of her recent books is a polemical rereading of the Marquis de Sade) and is a category that overlaps with other subgenres—romance, pornography, detective fiction, science fiction. To say "We live in Gothic times" is to suggest that the subgenres are now the appropriate and (paradoxically) central ones, since the times themselves are splintered and fraught with violent mythology. These assumptions—and the speculative, parodic style that stems from them—have made "placing" Angela Carter particularly difficult. Writers as diverse as Anthony Burgess and John Hawkes have expressed great admiration for her work; some reviewers, unimpressed, have greeted it with incom-

Angela Carter [signature]

prehension or vague revulsion. And for many readers "Gothic" is only acceptable when it stays boxed in its corner, or imparts a slight shading to a narrative, not when it demands direct and sustained attention. However, both her writing and its reception changed between the 1960s, when she won two major literary prizes, and the 1970s, when she became more notably, and more problematically, a literary outsider.

Angela Carter grew up in South London. In view of her later interest in conditions of rootlessness, it is perhaps worth noting that her family was new to the city (her journalist father, Hugh Stalker, came from Scotland; her mother, Olive Stalker, from a mining district in Yorkshire) and to the middle class. Following recent family tradition, she passed the "11-plus" qualifying examination, and attended a local (direct grant) grammar school, before beginning a brief apprentice career in journalism. In 1960 she married, and in 1962 she went back to school, to Bristol University, where she read English and specialized in medieval literature; however—perhaps because she was four years older than most undergraduates, perhaps because of her background—she seems to have practiced some-

thing of an autodidact's resistance to the English curriculum. Certainly much of the reading that informs her fiction is in French literature, as well as in psychology, anthropology, and social science. When she was graduated in 1965, she settled in Bristol, and it is there—or more precisely, in the provincial bohemia reborn in Bristol, as in other English cities, during the 1960s—that three of her earlier novels are set.

Shadow Dance (1966) is a Gothic detective novel, a murder story, and its main setting is a junk shop selling newly fashionable Victorian rubbish. A patina of meretricious charm spreads over the characters and their present world too—echoes of fairy tale (beauty and the beast) and of other fictions lend an eerily familiar and even decorative air to the violent, grubby, chaotic feelings and events. The plot involves an ambiguous threesome: impressionable Morris; his hippie partner in the antique business, attractive and vicious Honeybuzzard; and Honeybuzzard's discarded and now self-mutilated girl friend Ghislaine, come back for more. Much of the "action" consists of scavenging expeditions through derelict houses, where the decay of ordinary possessions into "antiques" forms a fitting metaphor for the decay of the characters' experience into theater. Anthony Burgess's prepublication comment noted the novel's impressive timeliness: "I've read this book with admiration, horror, and other relevant emotions, including gratitude that we seem to have here a very distinctive talent that's going to be a major one. Angela Carter has remarkable descriptive gifts, a powerful imagination and—what I admire and envy more than anything—a capacity for looking at the mess of contemporary experience without flinching." Angela Carter's intimacy with the cruel 1960s dandyism that took up, displayed, and discarded feelings like fashions was particularly disconcerting, combined as it was with a lucid aesthetic distance. She wrote of the secondhand trade in an idiom that was itself self-consciously secondhand, literary: the ending of *Shadow Dance*, when, in a deserted house, Morris discovers Ghislaine's body carefully covered with oilcloth, a bowl of disinfectant under the bed, is an ironic act of homage to Fëdor Dostoevski's *The Idiot* (1868). And while Morris is shocked by this piece of Honeybuzzard's handiwork into finally "betraying" him, the book's message, inevitably, is cooler and more ambivalent.

Her next novel, *The Magic Toyshop* (1967), again focused on the play culture, the trade in dreams, but this time with the stress on inner space. Fifteen-year-old Melanie and her younger brother and sister are suddenly, bleakly orphaned—in the manner of countless children's stories—and are whisked unceremoniously from their comfortable, middle-class home in the country to the dirty, sinister South London shop where unknown Uncle Philip makes his all-too-lifelike toys. The shop, with its vertical, decaying house beetling above, becomes their world, and their nice, clean, vague childishness is sharpened, bit by bit, into vivid and shocking definition. The plot, in short, is about growing up—a Freudian fairy tale about supplanting mother (Melanie knows she somehow caused her parents' death in a plane crash when she tried on her mother's wedding dress) and symbolically sleeping with father, played by gross, domineering Uncle Philip, who now stands between Melanie and her future.

The fantasy motifs lurking in the background in *Shadow Dance* come into their own in *The Magic Toyshop*. Uncle Philip's household, seen with stunned literalness through Melanie's eyes, is nonetheless a place of timeless enchantment, where like an ogre he holds in thrall his starveling Irish wife Margaret (struck dumb on her wedding day) and her two threadbare, wild brothers, Finn and Francie. They are his creatures, as surely as the toys he carves; and the point is spelled out when Melanie realizes that his true obsession is not the shop, but the very private puppet theater in the basement. To escape, she must fight her way out of Uncle Philip's world of artifice (which involves playing Leda in his climactic "production" of Leda and the Swan—with a Jove-sized swan) and join forces with his desperate, red Irish captives, who have their own archaic rituals (including a frontal assault on the incest taboo) to set against his deathly games. The ending has something of a fairy tale's happy-ever-after promise; it serves, however, to emphasize the novel's entirely contemporary knowingness—the fact that its symbols are known as symbols, and that the main struggle is with unreality. *The Magic Toyshop* won the John Llewelyn Rhys Memorial Prize for 1967.

Her third novel, *Several Perceptions* (1968) won the Somerset Maugham Award and established her, seemingly, as one of the distinctive voices of the times. Set in Bristol, among a pageantlike array of "fringe" figures who subsist on 1960s tolerance for impromptu, narcissistic performance, it has much the same period flavor as *Shadow Dance*. Joseph, the hero, attempts suicide in the first chapter, after the manner of Samuel Beckett's *Murphy*—exploding the gas—and thereafter is forced, against what is left of his will, to rejoin the "real"

world which is, of course, quite the reverse. The novel is constructed rather like a strip cartoon, or a "flicker-book," in which the motion of the pages turning sets the separate frames in illusory motion: a geriatric music-hall artiste playing an imaginary fiddle; a richly aging call girl; a bisexual self-appointed master of the revels who collects misfits in his house, while his mother lies in bed in a coma listening to show songs of the 1930s; an analyst who says (to Joseph) things like, "You're wedged in the gap between art and life." The climax, at a Christmas party, stages a series of ironic miracles, so that the fiddler suddenly plays a real violin, the call girl's wartime boyfriend comes back, and so on. Joseph decides not to be mad any more. As the title's rather throwaway tone suggests, *Several Perceptions* occupied its author's now distinctive imaginative territory ("wedged in the gap between art and life") with almost casual expertise.

She had, it seemed, found herself a niche. From 1966 on, she reviewed occasionally for *New Society* and the *Guardian*, using her insight into the iconography of clothes, gestures and idioms; and the first three novels, while they mocked the culture of marketable myths, also reflected it. *Heroes and Villains* in 1969 broke out of this pattern. Its speculative allegory (set in future Dark Ages) pushes the implications of imaginative dandyism to newly radical conclusions—and in a form (Gothic-science fiction) with disreputable connections. There is continuity with the earlier books, both thematically and technically (the opening, for instance, parodies the opening of Jane Austen's 1816 novel, *Emma*), but the writing is unmistakably more aggressive and more schematic. Her Dark Ages world is divided between Professors, who wryly mull over history's disasters in their high towers, and Barbarians, vagrant, predatory scavengers who threaten the outposts of rationalism. The heroine, Marianne, a Professor-child who sees her brother brutally murdered in a Barbarian raid in the first scene, wanders traumatized and fascinated into the forest; the book's action concerns her violent initiation into Barbaric life and her chillingly efficient acquisition of the strategies necessary for survival outside the pale of reason.

Barbarian existence, with its bizarre costumes (beads, fur, bits of mirror glass), its superstitions and its collage of half-forgotten, half-invented rituals, allows fantasies of aggression and possession to blossom into action. Marianne becomes the ravished "bride" of a beautiful, savage youth called Jewel; Jewel himself, bleakly narcissistic, becomes for her (and for the reader) an object of desire, "a phallic and diabolic version of female beauties of former periods." Possibly the new order will be a matriarchy. Just as important as the reversal of sex roles, however, is the fact that in *Heroes and Villains*, fantasy—*systematic* fantasy—has taken over. Discussing this transition in a 1977 interview in the *New Review*, Angela Carter remarked that in her first three novels she had not been consciously at odds with the realist tradition: "I thought I was a social realist." With *Heroes and Villains*, however, she became a deliberate analyst and interrogator of mythologies: ". . . I have done it consciously, because I do think we're at the end of a line, and to a certain extent I'm making a conscious critique of the culture I was born to. In a period like this of transition and conflicting ideologies, when there isn't a prevalent ideology, really all artists can do is to go round mopping up." In a sense, turning to speculative fiction was an act of self-recognition rather than a major change of direction. *The Magic Toyshop* had been wittily constructed after a Freudian blueprint. The difference, though, is real enough: Freud as invoked in the earlier novel did represent a "prevalent ideology"; from *Heroes and Villains* on, her choice of myths and mentors would be more arbitrary and more conditional. The *New Statesman* reviewer, not untypically, regretted her addiction to the "Gothick" (letting spelling imply his distaste for the whole genre) and found the objects of her parody "obscure."

A glance at her publishing history makes the same point in a different way. *Heroes and Villains* was to be the last of her novels published by Heinemann in England and Simon and Schuster in the United States. Since then, she has become something of a nomad, with several publishers in both countries and no single, secure arrangement. The break with Heinemann signaled the end of the brief period in which—at least in her case—"central" and "eccentric" tastes overlapped. She became, in part deliberately, in part inevitably, a figure of the counterculture: the paperback version of *Heroes and Villains* was one of the first titles published under the new (and consciously "experimental") Picador imprint. (Interestingly, it is again, in 1981, one of the first novels in the revived King Penguin paperback list. It seems to be a book that symbolizes breaks and beginnings.) Carter's personal life was changing at this time too. She separated from her husband (their divorce was to become final in 1972), and she traveled. She visited Japan in 1969, and in 1970 she went to live there for two years, as if to confirm her displacement and add to her collection of "conflicting ideologies." Before leaving Great Britain,

however, she completed *Love* (1971), an immaculately ironic salute to the passing of the 1960s. Although in some ways reminiscent of *Shadow Dance* (it is again set in hippie Bristol and has a sexual triangle at its center), *Love* is altogether blacker, more erotic, and more lucidly nasty. Buzz, Lee, and Annabel live—and in Annabel's case die—in an atmosphere polluted with images. A moment that catches the novel's tone fairly exactly is one in which Lee, challenged by Annabel, has his heart tattooed on his chest—in green, the most painful pigment. Annabel is a devotee of passive suffering. Her paintings are full of trees with breasts and carnivorous flowers; gradually she substitutes dreaming for painting; and eventually she dies (horrifically) in the full conviction that doing so is a way of entirely controlling the world.

Love offers a distinctive moral—that dream images are vampiric and will possess you unless you actively possess them. Its style, too, elegant near-pastiche, is characteristic of Angela Carter's writing from the beginning and survives the shift to systematic, speculative forms, in which the pastiche only becomes more explicit. In the 1977 *New Review* interview she describes one particularly effective piece of scene setting in *Love* ("In the street where the brothers lived with their aunt, during their childhood, it always seemed to be Sunday afternoon") as "my tribute to Balzac," and suggests that there is little that is "native" in her language: "the minute I read Racine, I knew that it moved me much more savagely than Shakespeare. . . . Anybody who's had a stiff injection of Rimbaud at eighteen isn't going to be able to cope terribly well with Philip Larkin, I'm afraid. . . . It made the circumstances of my everyday life profoundly unsatisfactory. Later the surrealists had the same effect"; and again, "I'm quite distressed I'm too old, I'll never be able to write in French. It's the structure of the sentences—French has got a much more subtle grammar than English . . . you can do so much more with the subjunctive and the passive and what have you."

Her various displacements converged, in 1972, in *The Infernal Desire Machines of Doctor Hoffman*, written while she was in Japan. Her experience there does not figure directly in the novel; however, it is possible to infer from one or two of the short stories collected in *Fireworks* two years later what she made, fictionally speaking, of Japan. It became the land of appearances and of illusionist dimensions, where people take shockingly for granted that there is no distinction between existence and essence. A passage from "A Souvenir of

Angela Carter, 1974

Japan," one of the short stories, illustrates the mingled pleasure and dread of the discovery:

> Speaking of mirrors, the Japanese have a great respect for them and, in old-fashioned inns, one often finds them hooded with fabric covers when not in use. He said: 'Mirrors make a room uncosy.' I am sure there is more to it than that although they love to be cosy. One must love cosiness if one is to live so close together. But, as if in celebration of the thing they feared, they seemed to have made the entire city into a cold hall of mirrors which continually proliferated whole galleries of constantly changing appearances, all marvelous but none tangible. If they did not lock up the real looking-glasses it would be hard to tell what was real and what was not. Even the buildings one had taken for substantial had a trick of disappearing overnight. One morning, we woke to find the house next door reduced to nothing but a heap of sticks and a pile of newspapers neatly tied with string, left out for the garbage collector.

This passage reveals, as her writing rarely does, something of the processes by which social observation is made over into exotic fictive hypothesis. In *The Infernal Desire Machines of Doctor Hoffman*, the Doctor has found out how to set the unconscious free, and he begins to infiltrate reality with guerilla images that slide out of mirrors to mingle with the citizenry.

The Infernal Desire Machines of Doctor Hoffman, retitled *The War of Dreams* in the United States, is about a protracted encounter between the reality principle and the pleasure principle—an intricate and graphic exploration of the repertoire of fantasy. The narrator, Desiderio, looks back on the time when he, almost single-handedly, saved reality: for the common good perhaps, but also because in the end he could not contemplate the lineaments of gratified desire, and so for him the impossible remained impossible. His quest for the Doctor leads him through a fearful wonderland of cultures and institutions, each described with ironic anthropological and sociological accuracy: a community of River Indians, for example, who adopt him into the innermost recesses of their lives and their rituals in exchange for his miraculous ability to read and write: it is only with the greatest reluctance that he realizes, on the eve of his marriage and final absorption, that of course they mean to eat him at his own wedding feast, in order to imbibe his unnatural skill. Other encounters include a Sadeian marquis who takes Desiderio to a surreal brothel where android prostitutes enact the transformation of flesh into vegetable, animal, machine; and a community of eminently rational centaurs, close cousins of Swift's Houyhnhnms, who worship a Great Stallion and punish their human halves with pain and repression. Throughout his travels he meets and re-meets one lover in many disguises—Albertina, the Doctor's shape-shifting daughter, whom he finally destroys, only to want her forever. The novel ends with, in its hero's phrase, "insatiable regret" that we sustain the possible by outlawing the impossible. It is an extraordinarily self-conscious and sophisticated piece of myth breaking—along the lines suggested by *Heroes and Villains*, but picaresque in structure and tighter and more informed in its depiction of alternative societies. Carter described it as "an inventory of imaginary cities," and—despite the plot to "save" reality—it marked her more decisively than any of her work up to that point as an aggressive anti-realist.

In 1972 she came back to England. She stayed in London for a year and then returned to the West Country, this time to Bath. By now, however, she

*my ~~heart~~ heart well nigh stopped with
apprehension when I ~~allowed myself~~ to*
                                                                    9.

exceedingly ~~f afrix~~ afraid, ~~for every visitor, even the most~~

~~fleeting, soon heard some whisperings of the man they called~~

~~"La Bestia."~~ ~~xk~~ ~~whose passion for cards alone drove him out~~

~~of the absolute seclusion in which he lived, to whom, it seems,~~

~~I must now play the whore for the sake of my father's raddled~~

~~reputation.~~ *now, it seems, I must play the whore for the
sake of my ~~father's raddled~~ reputation, ~~a~~ to a ~~man~~ who,
in all his ~~posses~~ seems ~~to have no other name~~ bit Beast*

*My fat
Mrs B. old
nurse, now dead,
~~who~~ ~~she had~~
~~forsky~~
told me
a boot*

~~My~~ English ~~nurse~~ ~~once~~ ~~told~~ me about a tiger-man she saw, in

London, when she was a little girl, (to scare me into good   *my charge*

behaviour ~~x~~ for ~~x~~ I ~~was~~ a wild wee thing ~~and she could~~ not ~~tame~~   *who could   he tamed*

me into submission with the bribe of a spoonful of jam or a   *cherry*

ribbon or a frown.) If you don't stop ~~plag~~ plaguing the nursemaids,   *pestering   sliding*

down the bannisters, singing on a Sunday,   ~~my beauty,~~ the tiger-man will come and take you away to his ~~cave~~   *den*

in the mountains, *my beauty.* They'd brought him from Sumatra, in the Indies,

she said; ~~and~~ his hinder parts were all hairy and only from the

head downwards did he resemble a man. And yet La Bestia goes   *cannot*

always masked; ~~so~~ it ~~cannot~~ be his face that resembles mine.   *with my can no   own*

But the ~~gitx~~ tiger-man, in spite of his hairiness, could take a

glass of ale in his hand like a good Christian and drink it down.
Nana   sink his pint,
Had ~~she~~ not seen him ~~do so~~, at the sign of "The George," by the   *high*

steps of Upper Moor-Fields, ~~When~~ she was just ~~as old as me,~~ ~~a lisped~~

Then she would sigh, for ~~London, across the North Sea of seperation~~   *toddled too,*

~~and~~ the lapse of years ~~and~~ ~~circumstance.~~ But, if this young lady   *no higher than
her charge, a
lisped a toddled, too*
                                                                    her boiled cabbage
was not a good little girl and ate up her crusts and ~~boiled~~

~~beetroot~~ ~~beetroot,~~ the ~~Tif~~ Tiger-man would put on his travelling   *left   wool,*

coat of thick, black ~~wool,~~ just like your daddy's, and ~~take~~ ~~jump astride~~
                                        his tall, black horse that was made
~~ship at Tilbury~~ ~~across the~~ ~~War~~ ~~waves until~~ ~~he stepped ashore at~~
                    of the wind a ride through the night as fast as
~~the harbour of Riga and hire a~~ ~~kax~~ ~~horse to ride through the night~~   *the wind*

~~as fast as the Erl-king on his galloper~~ of wind and... come

straight to the nursery and –
Yes, my beauty, Gobble you up!

was no longer settled in the way she had perhaps seemed five years before; and she was no longer winning literary prizes. The nine tales in *Fireworks* (1974) mapped out something of her range of fictional interests and styles: the Japanese pieces already mentioned are studies in disorientation and enchantment. "Elegy for a Freelance" is an unusual and not entirely successful foray into barely-future urban terrorism; "Reflections" steps through the looking glass, where a palindromic Anna rapes/is raped by the tweedy hero; two lush tropical jungle tales reenact—with crucial differences—the myth of the fall ("Penetrating to the Heart of the Forest") and the story of Robinson Crusoe ("Master"); most memorably, she revisits Transylvania in "The Executioner's Beautiful Daughter," which mischievously and meticulously constructs a sullen, mountain community fixated on incest, and in "The Loves of Lady Purple," which is about a vampire puppet that comes to life. "The Loves of Lady Purple" engages openly in the perverse delights of self-parody ("warlocks continually practised rites of immemorial beastliness in the forests"); it also elegantly displays her fascination with the problem of imagining freedom: when Lady Purple has murdered the puppet-master and run in an instant through the newfound scales of emotion, she makes her way unerringly—for all the world as if she were still on strings—to the town brothel.

The afterword appended to *Fireworks* sketches out a quizzical attitude toward reality and realism: "The tale does not log everyday experience, as the short story does; it interprets everyday experience through a system of imagery derived from subterranean areas behind everyday experience. . . ." Angela Carter was beginning to make a new space for herself on the British literary scene. At this time, too, she became a regular rather than an occasional contributor to *New Society* and the *Guardian*; and in 1976 London became, as it remains, her base, though she spent two years (1976-1978) as Arts Council Fellow in Creative Writing at the University of Sheffield. A rueful comment, again from the *New Review* interview in 1977, suggests something of the difficulty she faced in explaining herself in a context in which "subterranean areas" are often relegated to subgenres of fiction: "One's washing around with all these things going on in one's head, and there are all these people unmoved by the notion. The savage sideshow."

Nonetheless, her next novel, *The Passion of New Eve* (1977), made few concessions to "everyday experience." It was conceived as part of a projected speculative trilogy (along with *The Infernal Desire Machines of Doctor Hoffman*); however, the third volume has not yet appeared, and in any case, the connections are generic and thematic rather than narrative, so that the book is perfectly capable of standing on its own. Indeed, it offers one of the most radical visions of the dissolution of the merely possible in contemporary fiction, and—to compound the offense—does so with both wit and conviction. While the genre of speculative fiction and its symbols may be disreputable, we are invited (or instructed) in the opening pages of the novel to take them entirely seriously: "Our external symbols must always express the life within us with absolute precision: how could they do otherwise, since that life has generated them? Therefore we must not blame our poor symbols if they take forms that seem trivial to us, or absurd. . . ." In this case, the main symbols in question are Hollywood movie goddesses, from the 1930s on, layered over with two generations' projected yearnings, and personified in *The Passion of New Eve* in a composite idol, Tristessa St. Ange, a silver wraith who lives forever in two dimensions.

The plot concerns bringing the dead travesty of a woman to life, in more senses than one. Evelyn, the English hero, a cool customer and one of Tristessa's fans, rejects his black love, Leilah, in New York, and in full flight from his guilt (and her bloody abortion) sets out across the continent. Again, the form is primitive and picaresque, though this time Evelyn's encounters reveal a scandalously clear pattern: a technological matriarchy in the desert where, under the scalpel, he becomes a centerfold Eve; a stay at the Manson-style ranch of a demented guru called Zero (who teaches him/her all she needs to know about oppression); and the final meeting with Tristessa in her morgue of a glass house in the middle of nowhere. Tristessa turns out to have been a transvestite all along. Eve makes love to what is left of him and ends by embarking from the West Coast, pregnant, into an unknown future. It is characteristic of Angela Carter to have operated on the sex roles in this Frankensteinish fashion, and it is equally characteristic that the writing retains a mocking charm. Tristessa's absurd hobby, for instance—"sculpting" glass teardrops by plopping barrowloads of molten glass into her swimming pool from the diving board—is at once satirically accurate (in the fan magazines, all stars had a hobby) and mythically suggestive, the contemporary symbol of all the crystal tears shed by suffering Gothic heroines from the eighteenth century on.

Some reviewers were, again, deeply uneasy: "any poor male reader," wrote Jill Neville protectively in the London *Sunday Times*, "would feel like a cat having its face rubbed in its own excrement." The violence with which the book's characters are made and unmade takes a great deal of sexual history for granted. Indeed, the concerns on display here clearly relate to those of *The Sadeian Woman* (1979), Carter's only nonfiction book, a polemical exploration of the uses of pornography, which itself boldly exploits Sade: "In the looking-glass of Sade's misanthropy, women may see themselves as they have been and it is an uncomfortable sight. He offers an extraordinary variety of male fantasies about women and, because of the equivocal nature of his own sexual response, a number of startling insights. . . ." Her choice of Sade as an (unwitting) collaborator has an edge of vengeful humor about it; it also reflects her conviction that the most subterranean, unrespectable mythologies constitute a key to imaginative life—that "deviance" is never just that. *The Sadeian Woman* spells out the politics of Carter's present position as a fiction writer: "Flesh comes to us out of history; so does the repression and taboo that governs our experience of flesh. The nature of actual modes of sexual intercourse is determined by historical changes in less intimate relations, just as the actual nature of men and women is capable of infinite modulations as social structures change. . . ." It would be misleading, however, to suggest that the politics are separable from, or prior to, the image making and image breaking of the fiction. Nevertheless, it seems likely, from the noisy and often enthusiastic reception of *The Sadeian Woman*, that its forceful and cruelly explicit reading of the codes of pornography may help to provide a context in which the strategies of her fiction can be better understood.

The Bloody Chamber, also published in 1979, is a collection of adult fairy tales which reveals, after all, the continuity of her career as a writer. The main theme is the collusion between artificial and animal nature, and "Beauty and the Beast" is the story running through the stories. The characters range from dreamy puppets to nameless, pulsing bundles of claws and hair. There are many patterns of relationship to be made out of the book's motifs, since the process of transforming one tale into another is in part what it is "about," but the major figures are two, the *homme* and the *femme fatale*. Bluebeard presides over the first half of the collection, Sleeping Beauty over the second, and both are pried loose from their timeless roles and persuaded to live them out again—and again—differently.

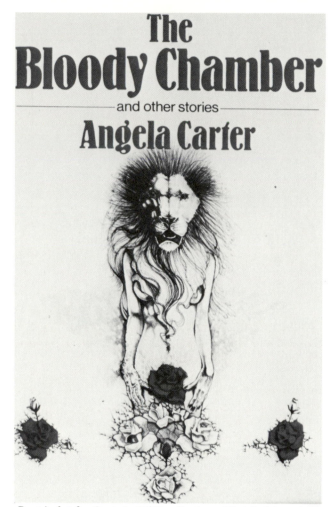

Dust jacket for Carter's 1979 collection of "adult fairy tales"

The Bloody Chamber won the Cheltenham Festival Literary Prize; however, it would be true to say that Angela Carter is still difficult to "place." And this is perhaps appropriate, since her preoccupations as a writer—deepened and defined over the years—remain radically at odds with the puritanism and the conventional realism that characterize much British fiction.

Translation:
The Fairy Tales of Charles Perrault (London: Gollancz, 1979).

Reference:
Lorna Sage, "The Savage Sideshow, A Profile of Angela Carter," *New Review*, 39/40 (June/July 1977): 51-57.

Juanita Casey

(10 October 1925-   )

Fleda Brown Jackson
University of Arkansas

BOOKS: *Hath the Rain a Father?* (London: Phoenix House, 1966);

Horse by the River (Dublin: Dolmen Press, 1968);

The Horse of Selene (London: Dolmen Press, 1971; New York: Grossman, 1972);

The Circus (London: Dolmen Press, 1974; Nantucket, Mass.: Longship Press, 1978);

Juanita Casey: A Sampling (Newark, Del.: Proscenium Press, 1981).

Juanita Casey is a highly individualistic Irish yarn spinner. Her short works reflect a blend of comedy, irony, and tragedy peculiarly intense and poetic. Her stories are mythic definitions of the collective Irish spirit as well as highly metaphorical and personal dramas. Most often they are tales of animals, particularly horses, which serve not only as well-known snorting and grunting creatures but also as emissaries of a "secret ageless darkness," metaphors of an eternity that is "all horse." (Her original fictional horse, Blondie, "had begun ten thousand years before and was still here, and would

go on being Horse for ever.") Frequently, her animals serve as catalysts to a clear vision of the human situations she describes.

Casey's life has been lived among the animals. Born 10 October 1925, in England, she is the daughter of gypsies. Her mother, Annie Maloney, was an Irish Traveler, a tinker, and her father, Jobey Smith, was an English Romany. Their marriage resulted in her father's banishment from his tribe, and so the independent couple traveled together alone until the birth of Juanita, during which Annie Maloney died. (She was at this time about sixteen or seventeen). When his daughter was a year old, Jobey Smith pulled into the fields of Walter Barlow, an animal buyer for the Mills-Fossett Circuses, left Juanita with a goat (for milk), and disappeared. Having been banished from his people, he likely went off on his own.

Casey was not adopted by members of either her mother's or father's tribes, so she remained with her surrogate "uncle," using through childhood the surname Barlow. Her life was split between the

Juanita Casey

213

circus atmosphere of the farm and private boarding schools. She attended four—which she claims were probably the making of her, since she had no other conventional schooling—but she hated school. At Rooksbury Park, in Hampshire, she says, she learned nothing but fear, and the swimming pool was full of frogs. At another school in Dorset, she found some diversion in dinosaur footprints that covered the countryside. At Elmer's Court, still another boarding school, she taught boxing in the shrubbery. Haile Selassie, the Ethiopian monarch, lectured there during her relatively brief stay. While there, she caught and broke a wild Forest pony, then ran down the school chaplain in the kitchen gardens and fell off the horse into a bed of nettles. Casey was expelled later that year for going without permission to a fair, where she bumped into the games mistress. During these school years, she sometimes stayed with her uncle's wealthy brother, Gerald. Her unhappy visits there possibly influenced her later haunting stories "Pipistrelle" and "The Well," which are studies of a child's isolation and fear while wandering in the courtyard of a nearly deserted, elegant house.

Casey left school at age thirteen, worked as a "lad" with racehorses for a year, and then worked for a variety of farmers. When she was sixteen, she was hunting for a young horse for a farmer when she met John Fisher, who became her first husband. She found him lying half under his horse in a ditch and pulled him out. He proposed marriage there and then, and Casey accepted. Her adopted parents bribed her to stay home with an offer of a horse she had been hunting, but John offered her three, so he won. They were finally officially married in 1945. Fisher, over twenty years her senior, owned a huge Elizabethan farm in Dorset, which Casey claims was host to a Negro ghost, a butler from the slave-trading days of the 1700s. According to her, the sounds of the ghost's complaining about the cold and of an old bucket being brought up from a grassed-over well pervaded the house. Fisher sold the farm, and he and Juanita lived on the *Star of Bethlehem*, a Cornish gaff-rigged cutter; a Loch Fyre *Zulu*, another fishing sailboat from Scotland; and the *Provident*, a Brixham trawler. Then they separated and Fisher sailed in a schooner for the West Indies. (He died in 1980 after thirty years in the West Indies, leaving nothing but a book of poetry behind.) William, born in 1947, is the only child of this marriage.

Casey's second husband, Sven Berlin, whom she married in 1953, was a Swedish poet, sculptor, and artist. The one child from this marriage, a son,

Jasper, was born in 1953. In addition to helping her husband pour bronze for his castings, she had stud Appaloosas and trained liberty groups for circuses. Among the horses at stud was Queen Elizabeth's Russian stallion "Zaman." Because of an article Casey wrote for *Horse and Hound* magazine, the queen asked her for information about the breeds of two Russian horses presented to her by Khrushchev and Bulganin in 1956. Casey's knowledgeable response prompted a gracious thank-you letter from the queen.

Casey has lived in tents, caravans, and cottages in the New Forest in Cornwall, Kerry, Drogheda, county Clave, Dublin (in the orchard of the house where J. M. Synge lived), Coole Park (for a night when no one was looking), and under Ben Bulben. Besides working with horses, she has also trained zebras, considered the most dangerous of all wild animals. She met and fell in love with Fergus Casey, who became her third husband, when he worked as a groom, helping her to train her last zebra. They were married after her divorce from Berlin; Sheba, the one child of Casey's third marriage, was born in 1963. The couple traveled around Ireland with the infant, a pram, a Siamese cat, and an Irish wolfhound. They also ran a newspaper for six weeks before it collapsed. Fergus Casey later vanished in an alcoholic disaster-trip to Galway and was washed up on the beach there.

Casey's reading has included Thomas Hardy and the work of a not-well-known Dorset man, Theodore Powys, whose brother, novelist John Cowper Powys, was a good friend of Hardy's. She feels a kinship with Hardy's county of Dorset, his nihilism, his pessimism, and his sense of being God-haunted. She considers that Theodore Powys's "very, very odd, quirky little stories rubbed a moth dust off onto me." She does not, however, consider herself well-read, and she feels that her work has been little affected by her reading.

Casey wrote as a child, but her work was not published until she reached mid-life. Earlier minor works include a radio play, *Stallion Eternity*, which was produced by BBC in 1956, and "Fields of Praise," an article on horses for *Riding*, a specialty magazine. In 1960, she contributed a section, "Gypsies of the New Forest," to a work titled *The New Forest*, a composite book by authors of that region.

Her first significant publication came in 1966 when her volume of short stories, *Hath the Rain a Father?*, was published by Phoenix House of London. The stories were written in a stable in Cornwall where Fergus was a gardener, and Casey finished the drawings for the book during the family's tour of Ireland. She illustrated the twelve stories with her own line drawings of animals, mostly horses, which resemble Etruscan cave representations except for their haunting suggestions of sensibility—their eyes, mouths, and the stretched, aspiring quality of their bodies.

Casey's stories typically have a strong sense of the teller. She successfully uses word order or selected idiomatic phrases to give the impression of Irish dialect without actually resorting to imitation of native pronunciation. Although the narrator is seldom a character, he is a participant in the meaning of the narrative, the mythological structure defined by the story. Her tales revolve around animals—both real and mythical. In the title story, Casey delineates in the young girl's relationship with her horse what "horse" is to mean throughout her fiction—a real animal which becomes a symbol of the unknowable or of the instinctual, to be revered. The girl's horse, Blondie, takes shape in the dawn like an eternal thing, becomes most realistic at midday, then finally melts into dusk until the night itself is like the horse, and "the crescent of the horse's white face" is like a new moon. All the animals of her stories are similarly ambiguous: the line between reality and the supernatural is as blurred as dusk.

The twelve stories in this volume are fables and myths, simply told. Often, they are darkly deterministic: "The Sacrifice," a story of a he-goat that gores and kills a girl-child dressed in ritual white during a village celebration, suggests "something that must be fulfilled down in the dark caves of man's brain." The goat is neither good nor evil, but is simply the cold agent of necessity.

The stories evidence several varying "distances" of narrator. One type is the Irishman storyteller who has actually witnessed the events and muses on their implications, or who simply tells the story as an interesting event and leaves its resonances to the listener. The narrator's viewpoint in this case influences the story's meaning. These stories often have an air of unreality, but are not purely magic, for the quality of legend inspired by the native folkteller allows for exaggeration or distortion. "We, the old men" tell the story of "The Return of Sagittarius," acting as a chorus. The orphaned and silent young Jenny Malone, who lives a hermit's life after the death of her only relation, has always been secretive; but after a cataclysmic night with a great black horse, she keeps "the light of the moon in her eye" and becomes known as "Crazy Jenny." After Jenny's death, yellow-haired Sara is drawn away by the same black horse. There is a

The Pony from Ladakh, *drawing by Casey*

stampede. Near her trampled body lies the "terrible body" of what clearly must be half-man, half-horse Sagittarius, his gentle face still longing for companionship. Now, only the old men remember, and what they know dies with them.

Sometimes the narrator is an epic storyteller whose rhythmic catalogues, frequent parallel sentences and phrases, and heavy reliance on coordination create an incantatory tone. "The Sea Beast and the 'Queen of Heaven,' " a simple, overly coincidental tale of the life of Barra the porpoise, who in old age follows the hulk of a long-remembered ship to destruction among the rocks, draws its energy from the pure enthusiasm of the telling. In its simplicity, it could be understood by a child.

This same teller, even further removed from participation in the events, becomes the dispassionate reporter of unmistakably magic events. These stories tend toward fable, are generally strongly moralistic, and are least successful. Typical is "The Hounds." Henry O. (for Oisin) Riordan, a ruthless archaeologist who cares nothing for myth, is pursued by the red-eared hounds of hell after his death, thus fulfilling the prophecy of his name. Another story, "The Silver Bullet," tells the tale of Farmer Stevens, who shoots a hare with a silver bullet, knowing full well that the hare is magically the hermit, Genty Lovelace, whose land he wants. As a result of his cruelty, his farm (Overlong) deteriorates, Farmer Stevens accidentally shoots himself, and hundreds of hares dance around his dying body.

Most distanced, yet strongly emotional, are the nonhuman narrative voices of the seals in "The Mermaid." The most highly poetic of the tales, the story seems to roll out of the metered voice of the sea: "He slept small sleeps in the sun or by the fire, and his mind wrinkled and moved like the mind of the sea." The sentimental tale of black-haired Lucia (who befriends Shoonah the seal and is shot by Black Isaac, her senile father, when he mistakes the two for a mermaid) is typical of Casey's treatments of the tension between human love and need and cold, irreversible destiny.

A small volume of Casey's verse, *Horse by the River*, was published in 1968 by the Dolmen Press of Ireland, which typically prints foremost lyrical Irish writers. Inscribed to Fergus and including two more horse drawings, the volume consists of seventeen poems, frequently more casual than her prose—often simple metaphorical equations: "Wisdom is an old horse / Down by the river / Who stretches his neck among the leaves / And bites an acorn." Although Casey's comic vision is evident in her prose,

it is dominant in her poetry. In emphatic, frequently two-stress lines, she designs sometimes bitter, sometimes ironic dramatic situations which successfully avoid the sentimentality occasionally evident in her earlier stories. Her themes are the animal (especially the horse) as the portal to wisdom and poetic truth; the animal as an instrument to reveal and heighten human sentience; death; and human idiocy.

While living in a tent on Achill Island during the very wet summer of 1964, Casey began a new novel—at a gallop, she says. It was finished in six weeks, with no corrections. She and Fergus then went down to Puck Fair in August and rented a cottage in the New Forest, where Fergus, always supportive of her work, typed out the manuscript. The novel, *The Horse of Selene*, was published in 1971, also by Dolmen Press. It combines a dense poetic prose, what one critic has called her "enormous talent to perceive and evoke," with her comic-ironic vision.

The main character, Miceal, a young Aranchilla islander, is a product of the land: "of darkness and thought, from rocks and waters of endurance, of the quick light." His life is structured by the conscience of Father Muldoon and the rule of the church. He meets six young people of various nationalities who have come for a holiday to the western island. Miceal is fascinated by these irrepressible, intellectual vagabonds whose lives are so much less fettered than his. Among them is Selene (named for the moon goddess, who is also a horse driver). From among the many wild horses roaming the island, the dark-haired girl becomes fascinated by a streaked grey stallion: "The spots and splashes all over him mingled and reformed with his movements, as though someone was painting him into life's startling design, writing him into the eye." Characterized by her companion, the poet Ran, as being a horse herself when she is not thinking about horses, Selene is determined to ride the extraordinary stallion.

Miceal is smitten by Selene and finds that he desires her. However, when he meets her among the sheep at Coolnay he discovers that, although she is willing and even eager to make love with him, he simply cannot. He is afraid of his lust for pleasure and freedom. Meeting her later after a dance, he does finally make love with her, but afterward feels overwhelming remorse and turns away. She says she will stay with him and marry him if he wishes, since she wants such a man of the earth. At his rejection of this offer, she upbraids him, assuring him that he will die in his fear and love of God, in his cave, his little death he calls life. He assures her that she will have neither him nor the speckled horse. Selene turns to breaking and riding the stallion, a feat she accomplishes with the same concentration and desire she had turned upon Miceal. When Selene and her companions leave the island, Miceal's thoughts settle again. The men of the island gather for a roundup of the wild horses, which have become a menace. When Miceal goes after the stallion and slips the halter over him, the horse throws him against a rock, smashing his skull.

The Horse of Selene is essentially about Ireland under domination by the church. Selene is temptation, chaos in an ordered yet ruthless place, a threat to Miceal, a chunk of Irish earth. She is entirely outside his comprehension, yet she claims they are alike in their love of animals and in the free and easy way they fit into their environment, like animals. Still, she rides the horse that kills him. Selene can roll over the surface of life with little damage to herself, but Miceal is like a barnacle clinging to a wave-washed rock. He must remain attached or die.

Although the plot is tragic, Casey's view of the Irish people is full of ironic wit and occasionally even broad humor. She catalogues whimsical vignettes of the islanders as they go about their everyday tasks: John Mulloy reaches under his chicken for an egg, but gets a handful of something else; Mrs. Letitia Baggot, a butcher, dreams of slicing her husband and hanging up his remains, "a sort of fleshly mobile" on the shop ceiling; John Joseph Fenny answers questions half an hour after they are asked, which leads to peculiar conversations; his brother Re-Peter Fenny repeats himself constantly.

Ran, the dissident Irish poet, is Casey's mouthpiece to gather up and clarify the story's disparate visions of the Irish people and their relationship to the church. Because "Our queens are dead, our goddesses turned into pimply saints, and we have turned our Great Mother of all earth into an impossible virgin," he says, "we drink. O brother, do we drink . . . and we suffer dismal and uproarious and old-fashioned disasters . . . and we tear each other to bits with our arms round each other's shoulders."

Casey embeds the central action of the story in an expansion both backward into her characters' histories and forward into their futures. Thus, the reader is not allowed to imagine the island experience as anything but an interlude in a wider drama. There is no punctuation to set off direct quotations in the novel. The effect of this steadily forward-moving prose is to make less sharp the distinction between thought and utterance, becoming at times stream-of-consciousness. The novel was received favorably by reviewers. Most praised Casey's poetic prose but occasionally complained that its density often obscures the profundities she is trying to suggest.

In 1973 Casey's play, *30 Gnu Pence*, was read in the Peacock Theatre, Dublin, with some of the Abbey players. The inspiration for the play came while Casey was drinking coffee at Bewley's in Dublin. A man came in one day—not drunk, she says, but completely mad. He sat in the corner babbling for hours, words pouring out, talking only to himself while everyone else ignored him. Casey rushed home and wrote a drama the theme of which is the concurrent powerfulness and powerlessness of words.

The main character of the postmodernist play is A Chara ("Dear Sir" in Irish). In a garage arranged as a cafe, he wanders among tables of unresponsive diners who all sit under open umbrellas. He pours forth an endless stream of words which often include brilliant satire and colorful images, but which amount to little sense. He is confronted by several groups of people who wander in: the Religious, the Legal, the Circus, the Public, the Hippies. Each group speaks a bastardized, satirized jargon appropriate to itself, but which has no real coherence. In succession, the groups adopt A Chara for use in espousing their causes. The Public puts him up for election; the Religious people make a savior of him, hang him on a hatrack, and gag him. The Judge condemns him in more of the same omnipresent satirical jargon. But his execution is accomplished by a "nice" elderly, shabby-genteel couple, Normal and Dear, who run their umbrellas playfully through his suspended body while spouting disconnected platitudes. The hippies praise the whole situation as "cool." All exit, and a gypsy enters, collects usable items (showing no concern for A Chara on the hatrack), while the jukebox plays "Same Old Story." Words—"all the understanding, solflanding, upstanding, never bending never ending words"—will go on forever, Normal asserts. Those people wedded to their umbrellas are protected and unaffected by the meaningless cliches.

In 1973, Casey was asked to take on the training of horses, zebras, camels, and llamas at Roberts Brothers circus. She spent the winter of 1973 with them and part of 1974, but when her most recent novel, *The Circus*, was published, she left Kerry.

The Circus, like *The Horse of Selene*, was written quickly—in about eight weeks. As Casey explains in a 1972 interview in the *Journal of Irish Literature*, its subject is a child: "It starts off with one [a child]

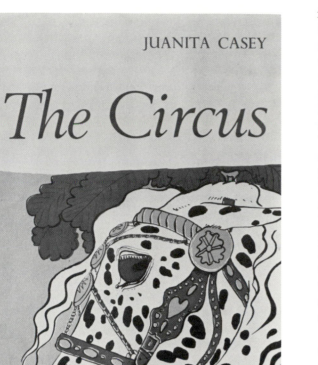

Dust jacket for Casey's second novel, based on her experience as animal trainer for the Roberts Brothers circus

about four. You know when you were young—before words really sort of crystalized and formed. . . . It's a step forward from earlier work, the stories, as different as the later James Joyce is from the early Joyce. It's just about a kid who wants to go to the circus and never gets there. When she does . . . it's completely spoiled, utterly spoiled. Words are beginning to harden into their real meanings. When you're a kid, it's *you* do this, and the *you* and the *I* gradually come together, and you can look forward. You can never look forward when you're a child. I suppose she gets to the age of about seven, when she can see birthdays coming at last, like telephoning down the years."

In lyrical stream-of-consciousness, Casey explores the same strongly autobiographical territory of previous stories: a gypsy orphan who is more sensitive than her adopted parents, she longs to regain touch with the world of her heritage. She

finds in horses an image of her father's power; and in the woods, the earth, the moss, she finds a nurturing mother. But the mind of Deffy, the child who wants to go to the circus, is more fully exposed than that of any of Casey's previous characters. Casey presents Deffy's brilliantly imaginative world broken only by short proverbial messages and occasional italicized patches of adult conversation. These interrupting windows correct Deffy's fantastic vision, just as her thoughts provide sharp, intuitive truth to an often hypocritical adult world. To Deffy, her adopted mother's love is leaning and smothering; her father's is cold and drawn inward. Her parents fear her gypsy blood. They want her to be normal and civilized. They worry when she hangs around the stable-keeper and when she evidences great fascination for vagabonds, gypsies, and circuses. She is a silent child. Her teacher says she has no imagination, and her parents wonder if she is subnormal.

Meanwhile, rioting in her head is a metaphorical wonderland. She learns words, numbers, and music: "2 has a lovely arched neck for a prince's golden bridle, and 6 has left another bit wriggling under the spade. . . . 3 looks back and is sorry. 4 is a clergyman. . . . DOG is completely final, even upside down. Verily wags its curly tail. . . . The devil says Disaster like a trayful of black teacups."

As she struggles to contain her "me that God put in," Deffy feels sharply the sensations of a world outside. She watches a mouse her father has almost killed struggle back to life. She sees the aftermath of a bloody accident and overhears a policeman say, "Poor devil," and she is sorry that one of the Devil's lives has been snuffed out. Casey presents the dramatic irony of the child's focus always with a gentle comic touch.

Deffy's succession of birthdays, her wait for the circus, her parents' refusals to take her, the missed circuses, and finally the circus event parallel her internal changes. Her thoughts are first subjective and merge with the external world so that perceptions and events just "happen like flowers." As she grows, her sense of self begins to form, and with her severing of the primal connections comes a new awareness of external reality and of the passage of time.

The climactic event is her first real sexual encounter. She wanders into the garden, full of the joy of anticipation of her first circus. There she finds Dino, an elephant trainer from the circus, whom she imagines is a satyr. He joins in her game, promises to show her his goat's hooves, and seduces her.

Afterward, reality comes into focus, and she knows that he is not a satyr, that men and satyrs are "all different, all the same." For her the circus is now "full of just circus . . . with people showing through like a spoilt cathedral." Deffy's new self-containment which places her midway between the past and a future of possibilities almost compensates for this bleak destruction of her imaginative world, but not quite.

Reviewers of her latest novel have called Casey's style "Joycean." The general critical reception has been favorable, but some have considered the book perhaps too esoteric and oblique to gain the favorable acceptance *The Horse of Selene* received. As it has evolved, Casey's work has become less sentimental and didactic, more abstract and poetic, and she tends to examine character more deeply in her later works than in her earlier stories. After the death of Fergus, she wrote little for a while, spending much of her time hunting fossils and gardening. But she is now at work again in Okehampton, Devon, on a third novel which she calls "Azerbaijan!"

Play:
30 Gnu Pence, staged reading, Dublin, Peacock Theatre, 1973.

Radio Script:
Stallion Eternity, BBC, 1956.

Other:
"Gypsies of the New Forest," in *The New Forest* (Essex, Conn.: Gallery Press, 1960; revised edition, London: Phoenix House, 1966);
Journal of Irish Literature, special Juanita Casey issue, includes contributions by Casey, 1 (September 1972);
Paddy No More, includes contributions by Casey (Dublin: Wolfhound Press, 1978);
"A Grab-Bag of Juanita Casey," *Journal of Irish Literature*, 10 (May 1981), pp. 5-36.

Interview:
Gordon Henderson, "An Interview with Juanita Casey," *Journal of Irish Literature*, 1 (September 1972): 41-54.

David Caute
(16 December 1936-   )

Gerald Steel
King's College, London

SELECTED BOOKS: *At Fever Pitch* (London: Deutsch, 1959; New York: Pantheon, 1959);
Comrade Jacob (London: Deutsch, 1961; New York: Pantheon, 1962);
Communism and the French Intellectuals, 1914-1960 (London: Deutsch, 1964; New York: Macmillan, 1964);
The Left in Europe Since 1789 (London: Weidenfeld & Nicolson, 1966; New York: McGraw-Hill, 1966);
The Decline of the West (London: Deutsch, 1966; New York: Macmillan, 1966);
Fanon (London: Fontana, 1970; New York: Viking, 1970);
The Demonstration (London: Deutsch, 1970);
The Occupation (London: Deutsch, 1971; New York: McGraw-Hill, 1972);
The Illusion (London: Deutsch, 1971; New York: Harper & Row, 1972);
The Fellow-Travellers (London: Weidenfeld & Nicolson, 1973; New York: Macmillan, 1973);
Collisions: Essays and Reviews (London: Quartet Books, 1974);
Cuba, Yes? (London: Secker & Warburg, 1974; New York: McGraw-Hill, 1974);
The Great Fear (London: Secker & Warburg, 1978; New York: Simon & Schuster, 1978).

David Caute has a reputation as both a novelist and a historian. He has written plays, including works for radio and television, as well as essays and journalistic pieces. A writer who combines sophisticated and wide-ranging experiments in the techniques of the modern novel with a strong commitment to left-wing political issues, and who brings a wide knowledge of European (particularly French) intellectual traditions into English fiction, he is one of the most intellectually stimulating novelists of recent decades in England—a "public" rather than a "private" writer.

John David Caute was born in 1936 in Alexandria, where his father, an army dentist, was stationed at the time. He was the only child of British parents who were themselves of mixed descent. His father came from French and Irish Catholic families. Because the elder Caute was repeatedly transferred by the army to different parts of the world (leaving his family in England) and then died when David was aged eleven, father and son did not see much of one another. However, the army and the mentality of some types of army officers were to become important subjects in Caute's novels, and his firsthand experiences of military life during his period of national service became an important source of material. Caute's mother was of Austrian Jewish descent, the daughter of a rabbi and composer named Asher Perlzweig. She graduated in physiology and later taught nutrition. Caute has subsequently referred to himself as "half-Jewish." He was educated at reputable British public schools—at Edinburgh Academy in Scotland and then Wellington College in Berkshire, England. He describes his schooling as "academic and middle-class." Caute's eighteen months in the army were spent in the African Gold Coast colony which became the independent state of Ghana in 1957, the year after his departure. On his return to England Caute studied modern history on scholarship at Wadham College, Oxford. He was elected a Fellow of All Souls College in 1959, and then went to Harvard University as a Henry Fellow for 1960-1961. He returned to All Souls and remained there until 1965. In 1961 he had married Catherine Shuckburgh. They had two sons before separating some years later.

In this early period of university life, Caute emerged first as a novelist and second as a historian; the two modes are clearly related. While an undergraduate student he wrote his first novel, *At Fever Pitch*, which was published in 1959. Indebted to Caute's experience of British army life on the Gold Coast, it tells the story of Michael Glyn's struggles to achieve sexual maturity and virility after a period of homosexual activity, in a context of loathed colonial army life—morally dissolute, snobbish and racially prejudiced—as well as the wider context of African political struggles and intrigue. Central to the action are Glyn's relationships with his African servant,

David Caute

Sulley, and his bullying superior officer, Brigadier Ridley-Smith. Equally important are the conflicts within the triumvirate that is steering the colony to independence, the demagogue-leader Bandaya, his English-educated minister Bruce, and the boorish soldier Atuhope. In the climax of the book, British and African themes combine in an ironic twist of the story, in which Glyn's achievement of virility is followed by his shooting of twenty-five Africans during a riot. In this novel, Caute made his first exploration of the sexual psychology of militarism, and showed the contradictions in African nationalism between residual European traditions and native or tribal ones. Caute tells the story through a variety of styles and experiments: conventional third-person narrative, montage, imitations of African poetry, Joycean stream of consciousness. *At Fever Pitch* was favorably reviewed and won the London Authors Club Award and the John Llewelyn Rhys Memorial Prize (both in 1960). V. S. Naipaul wrote in the *New Statesman* that "Mr Caute has applied a genuinely creative imagination to his African experience." However, he found the novel "unbalanced. . . . The emphasis on sex is disproportionate and unnecessary. The British characters are well observed but the African politicians are unconvincing."

Comrade Jacob, Caute's second novel, was published in 1961. It is dedicated to the historian Christopher Hill, who had been one of Caute's tutors at Oxford, and the subject of the story derives from his work. Hill is renowned for his studies of seventeenth-century England, in particular his interpretations of the Civil War, which he had termed "the English Revolution," and his studies of radical sects of the period (such as the Diggers and the Levellers). *Comrade Jacob* tells the story of the Diggers' leader and apologist Gerrard Winstanley as he attempts to sustain a rural collective settlement on St. George's Hill in Surrey. The Diggers' only aim is to live apart and be economically self-sufficient, but their belief in a fundamental right to hold land in common (as opposed to individual ownership) is seen as a threat by local vested interests, which persecute the settlement and eventually destroy it. Ironically, this hostility comes from parties which had fought on the same side as the Diggers in the Civil War: Platt, the Puritan minister whose true religion is property, and Gladman, an army captain and ruthless careerist. Gladman represents a historically emergent type of classless opportunist, and his sadism is allied to his atheism. In the middle of the conflict is General Fairfax, a tolerant aristocrat who is impressed by Winstanley's powers of argument. Finally Platt outmaneuvers Fairfax and has the settlement destroyed. But Caute's central creation is Winstanley. He makes him a genuinely revolutionary hero, but a flawed one, compromised first by the economic pressures that force him into a liaison with Platt's wife in order to secure money for the Diggers, and second by his egotistic need for the power of leadership. Winstanley develops away from theological convictions toward a political commitment based on humanism: ". . . we were the pioneers of a great movement, a great ideal, which will one day come to fruit, not when God wills it, but when man wills it."

He again uses a variety of styles and shifting points of view, but the overall impression is of a compressed and very readable work. Much of it is dramatized conversations on religion and politics between Winstanley and his opponents; these scenes are terse and ironic. Again critical response was favorable. In the character of Winstanley, wrote the *Times Literary Supplement* reviewer, "Mr. Caute achieves a masterpiece of sympathetic personification." Anachronisms in the language were noted; but the book was called "a remarkable and moving evocation of a stirring and significant experiment in English history." V. S. Naipaul was also enthusiastic.

He praised Caute for producing a convincing historical novel while avoiding too much distracting historical detail: "By seeming not to explain the age, he makes it live." Adverse criticism came from the *Spectator*, whose reviewer, Bernard Bergonzi, commented that Caute viewed events through "Marxist spectacles" and concluded that "Mr. Caute seems more concerned with debate than drama, and *Comrade Jacob* is a *roman a these* rather than a true novel of ideas." However, the book had some success (Caute has commented with amusement that it proved popular with "squatters") and was later made into an attractive film, *Winstanley*, directed by Kevin Brownlow (1975).

Even at this stage of his career, Caute revealed a willingness to attempt different kinds of writing, and a commitment to writing history as strong as his ambitions in the novel. In 1960 he wrote his first play, *Songs for an Autumn Rifle*, which was given a "fringe" production at the Edinburgh Festival the next year. The play focuses on the dilemmas posed for British Communists by the Russian invasion of Hungary in 1956. In retrospect, Caute has described the play as "shaped in the spirit of banal realism." However, the political, philosophical, and ethical problems for the European left of commitment to the Soviet Union were to form an important theme in much of his subsequent historical writing. His first work in this mode was *Communism and the French Intellectuals, 1914-1960* (1964), a study of many of the figures who supported the French Communist party during that time. It was this book which first revealed his deep and informed interest in French intellectual traditions. The work was greatly admired and established Caute's reputation as a historian. He followed it with a shorter study, *The Left in Europe Since 1789* (1966), which was received more ambivalently. However, by the mid-1960s he had become known as both novelist and historian.

In 1966 *The Decline of the West* was published. Caute's largest and most ambitious novel to date, it drew on many of the concerns of his previous writings, bringing them all together in one extended fiction. The story is one of civil war and counter-revolution in a newly independent African state, formerly a French colony, based to some exent on the Congo. The large array of characters includes James Caffrey; his father-in-law, Soames Tufton, a mining executive and diplomat with strong philosophical tendencies; the Paris-educated African liberationist, Amah Odouma; Laval, a reactionary and sadistic French army officer; and Jason Powell, a wealthy young Negro student from Harvard. Much of the story is told in retrospect. The African political struggles of the novel's present are set by Caute against narratives of the characters' past history, so that he presents the politics of Africa as dependent on an interplay of traditions from the West. Caute frequently develops the themes and methods of *At Fever Pitch*. Again he explores the relationships between sexual and political behavior; particularly he posits links between sadomasochism and military violence (Laval), and between sexuality and racial consciousness (Amah and his mistress, Dominique). Another theme of equal importance is the rise of European philosophies that justify colonial oppression and violence (German philosopher Oswald Spengler, from whose work the title derives, and French philosopher Georges Sorel) and the challenge these present to humanism or belief in man's capacity for goodness and justice. In intellectual range, Caute went far beyond his previous novels. He seemed to draw simultaneously on his recent research in French intellectual history, his year at Harvard in 1960-1961, and his early experiences as a soldier in Africa. Parts of the novel are indebted to his childhood experiences in England and at Edinburgh Academy.

For all its scope and interest, however, the book had a mixed reception, and reviewers tended to speak strongly either for or against it. Martin Seymour-Smith in the *Spectator* found the story impressive. Several reviews noted that Caute had combined aspects of the Congo struggles with others from the Algerian war of independence. Christopher Ricks strongly attacked the book in the *New Statesman*. Noting first that some of Caute's material was taken from *Communism and the French Intellectuals*, he described the work as a "novelette" and went on to accuse Caute of plagiarism by showing that his extensive descriptions of the torture of Amah and his sister were based on a work entitled *Gangrene* (1959). This was an English translation of *La Gangrene*, a collection of statements published in Paris in 1959 by Jerome Lindon and suppressed by the French government. The authors, Algerians living in Paris, alleged in the book that they had been arrested by the French police and violently tortured; they described the brutalities in detail. Ricks was correct in his source (although Caute did not acknowledge it in his book), but he did not consider the part that these scenes play in Caute's fiction, and his dismissive literary verdict has not received universal assent. The torturer Laval's revealed sadomasochism is contrasted with the humanism of various kinds advocated by other characters in the novel, and the tortures be-

come test cases for these philosophies. Documentation strengthens their value here, rather than weakening it. Late in the novel James Caffrey realizes that "the true humanist and the true Christian alike must be first and last a humanitarian."

During the early 1960s Caute participated in some important political activities at Oxford, being one of the leading organizers of the Oxford "teach-in" on the Vietnam war (1965), and supporting a campaign for reform within All Souls College. Resigning his fellowship when the college failed to admit graduate students, he published a witty, biting denunciation of the collegians' entrenched conservatism in *Encounter*. He returned to the United States as visiting professor at New York University and Columbia University (1966-1967), and afterward returned to England to take up the post of reader in social and political theory at Brunel University, Uxbridge, near London (1967-1970). In 1970 he gave up university teaching to devote himself wholly to writing. In recent years he had also become increasingly interested in new developments in French literary criticism, particularly in works arguing for "committed" writing and in those critics attempting to elaborate a Marxist theory of literature. He published highly praised articles on the philosopher Jean-Paul Sartre, whom he greatly admires, and on the critic Lucien Goldmann. In 1967 he edited a selection of *Essential Writings of Karl Marx*, and in 1970 his monograph on the political writer from Martinique, Frantz Fanon, was published.

The experiences of university politics in Oxford, his return to the United States, and the widespread political activity among university students during the 1960s all provided Caute with material for his next substantial work of literature, *The Confrontation: A Trilogy*, consisting of a novel, *The Occupation* (1971); an essay, *The Illusion* (1971); and a play, *The Demonstration* (1970). Caute has said that the three works should be considered together. All of them concern the partly autobiographical character Stephen Bright, a university teacher. Bright is the supposed author of *The Illusion*, an interesting and wide-ranging essay on literature, criticism and politics. Both this essay and the play *The Demonstration* show the influence of the anti-illusionary ideas of the German dramatist Bertolt Brecht. In the play Bright (now middle-aged) is confronted by militant students of the "New Left" who challenge his hitherto progressive ideas on drama. The novel, *The Occupation*, shows a younger Bright in New York again confronted by militant students, but it is not clear to what extent these clashes are products of his own imagination. Bright, who is rejected by his student-mistress and estranged from his English wife, embarks on a series of comic sexual and social adventures, real or imaginary. The novel continually experiments in form and repeatedly breaks the fictional illusion of the narrative. Brecht's theories are clearly relevant, but Caute himself acknowledges the influence of Philip Roth's *Portnoy's Complaint* (1969). The result for Caute is a new, largely successful departure into humor. With regard to themes, he has turned inward somewhat, writing about a literary and academic career that parallels his own. He carries his experiments with different styles further than before. The trilogy was well reviewed. The dramatist Dennis Potter praised it (in the *Times*) while challenging Caute's argument, put forth in *The Illusion*, that "the lie of illusionism" is easier in the theater than in the novel. Robert Nye in the *Guardian* was also enthusiastic. Motivated perhaps by a scene in *The Demonstration* satirizing the novelist Norman Mailer, Nye offered this scale of comparison: "If Mailer equals zero and Sartre six then David

Caute is about three and a half. . . . Three and a half is serious and intense and useful. . . . This mongrel trilogy—a novel, a long essay, a play—stands testament to an energy and an intensity rather rarer than they should be in contemporary writing in English." The philosopher Anthony Quinton (*Sunday Telegraph*) was full of praise for the three works but denied that *The Occupation* was politically serious: "The novel is an intensely passionate and subjective work. . . . The ideological content of this work, or—which is much the same—of Stephen Bright, is zero. At most, his off-stage commitment to the politics of the young is a weapon in his anxious struggle with the fear of becoming middle-aged."

In 1970 Caute was legally divorced from his first wife. He married Martha Bates in 1973; they have two daughters. Caute remained an independent writer until the late 1970s, when for two years he held the post of literary editor of the *New Statesman*. In the period following publication of his trilogy, he continued to pursue a career as a dramatist, experimenting in different media. *Fallout* (1973) was written for radio. His next play for the theater, *The Fourth World* (1973), was performed at the Royal Court Theatre in London. It is a comedy about an English novelist in the United States, reminiscent of Bright in *The Occupation*. Caute's continuing interest in Brecht led to a play for television, *Brecht and Company* (1976). Always a versatile and energetic writer, he meanwhile continued his career as a historian and also produced literary and political journalism. Nineteen seventy-three saw the publication of *The Fellow-Travellers*, a highly regarded study of Western intellectuals' support for Stalinism. The following year two works by Caute appeared— *Collisions*, a collection of essays and reviews, and *Cuba, Yes?*, a travel book. A further period of historical research resulted in *The Great Fear: The Anti-Communist Purges Under Truman and Eisenhower* (1978). This book was praised for its exhaustive research and massive documentation. Caute's performance as a novelist slackened as he devoted himself to this historical work. Since 1973 his published fiction has consisted only of two popular thrillers published under a pseudonym. He has said that he is working on another serious novel. He also plans a further collection of his critical essays and reviews, and at present he is writing a book about the newly independent state of Zimbabwe (formerly the British colony of Rhodesia). As literary editor of the *New Statesman* in 1979-1980, Caute enlivened its columns by publishing outside contributors' articles on recent developments in Marxist philosophy in Britain and by writing a series of articles on Jean-

Dust jacket for the third volume of Caute's autobiographical trilogy, The Confrontation, *consisting of a novel, an essay, and a play*

Paul Sartre, his favorite author.

David Caute has been criticized for faults of style, for bringing his left-wing commitment into his novels; most important, it has been alleged repeatedly that he writes about subjects that lie outside his own experience. It is true that his writing contains flaws and is occasionally repetitive. His committed approach to the novel is in the tradition of Sartre; Caute declares his interest in socialism and in Marxist philosophy, but he is also a widely read and eclectic writer who refuses to hold allegiance to any single school of thought. Finally, while some of the subjects of his first three novels are derived from his reading and research, he treats his material in ways that reveal a genuine, often powerful, historical imagination. In his later work he has become more willing to explore "private" themes. In 1976 he commented: "Perhaps the tension between man's private and public existences is the central 'problematic' of my thinking and writing. Nowadays I'm more preoccupied by questions of literary form than I used to be. Another thing: it scarcely used to occur to me that I owed my readers an occasional smile or even laugh, but I'm learning now to open the cage on humor a bit."

Other:

Essential Writings of Karl Marx, edited by Caute (London: MacGibbon & Kee, 1967; New York: Macmillan, 1968).

Gerda Charles
(14 August 1914-   )

Priscilla Martin
University of East Anglia

BOOKS: *The True Voice* (London: Eyre & Spottiswoode, 1959);

The Crossing Point (London: Eyre & Spottiswoode, 1960; New York: Knopf, 1961);

A Slanting Light (London: Eyre & Spottiswoode, 1963; New York: Knopf, 1963);

A Logical Girl (London: Eyre & Spottiswoode, 1966; New York: Knopf, 1967);

The Destiny Waltz (London: Eyre & Spottiswoode, 1971; New York: Scribners, 1972).

Gerda Charles has written five novels and some short stories. Although her fiction has won several literary prizes, it has been somewhat neglected, in view of her subject matter. While in the early 1960s she attracted a good deal of interest as one of a number of Anglo-Jewish writers, her characteristic areas of concern should be familiar to a much larger readership. She says that her ambition is to show "what it's like to be ordinary." In particular, her central characters are possessed by the suffering of being ordinary and undergo quotidian crucifixions unnoticed. As the hero of *The Destiny Waltz* (1971) puts it: "Everybody understands tragedy; nobody understands pain. . . . Nobody even wants to go outside the accepted categories of pain . . . if I could be granted one gift

Gerda Charles

from the Gods, it would be just that; the ability to extend the boundaries of pain; to force attention on the small murderous humiliations, the tiny killing leaks of blood that no one sees, no one sees. Or seeing, discounts." Her characters are ravaged by desolate Sunday afternoons, silent telephones, banal relatives, social exclusions, the empty promise of urban summers. In fiction, this territory is her own; in life, most of us have inhabited it. Reading Gerda Charles produces a groan of recognition.

She was born Edna Lipson in Liverpool in 1914. She sometimes refers to herself as "provincial," and a horror of the provinces and the suburbs runs through her novels. (Four of them are set in London: the narrator of *A Slanting Light*, 1963, has specifically escaped to the capital from her despised girlhood and marriage in Liverpool.) Edna's father died when she was a year old, leaving her mother in poverty. Mother and daughter formed a lonely unit, living together until Mrs. Lipson's death in 1981. They led a marginal existence: they moved often; Mrs. Lipson did unskilled work and took in lodgers; their life was hard and—worse— humiliating. Gerda Charles with bitterness speaks of her youth and of her mother's family, who had abandoned them: "We were two women alone, no father, no husband, no brother," an invitation, in her view, to predators. She formed a personal philosophy: the world is divided into the vulnerable and the powerful. Her fiction comprises a report, as indignant as it is compassionate, on the human jungle in which the weak—those deprived by virtue of sex, class, appearance, talent or its absence, personality, environment, or address—are savaged by the strong. And this indifferent success-loving cosmos encloses vicious microcosms, whose oppressed are doubly injured, scorned by the contemptible, enslaved by petty despots. "It's better," says Charles, "to be trampled on by a tyrant than a worm. It's more dignified."

Young Edna's formal eduction was sporadic and ended at the legal minimum age of fifteen, by which time she had attended nine different schools; she did not take the School Certificate, the school exit examination. After she left school, she and her mother moved to London. Apart from five days work in a chilly bookshop, Edna never had a job other than helping her mother run a boarding-house. She later discovered that evening classes offered intellectual and social sustenance. In 1957 she wrote an assignment for a Morley College class called "Forgotten Books," an account of some of her favorite childhood novels which most people had never heard of. Her tutor was impressed and the

essay was published in the Morley College magazine. Then it was reprinted in *Books*, the house magazine of the National Book League. Fan mail arrived from other readers who remembered the forgotten books; some sent copies of novels she had not seen since childhood. The novelist Paul Scott, then a literary agent, wrote to inquire if she had work in progress. She showed him an amorphous passage of prose fiction that, with Scott's encouragement, became her first novel, *The True Voice* (1959).

The meeting with Scott was a turning point. She wrote five novels in about a decade. "It was like a tap being turned on," she recalls. But she still felt vulnerable; until *The True Voice* received favorable reviews, only her mother, Paul Scott, and the publisher knew that Edna Lipson had written a novel. She used the pen name Gerda Charles in case the book should be a failure. The choice—"Gerda" a composite of "Edna" and her mother's name, "Gertrude"; "Charles" a family name—argues a sense of kinship and connection at odds with biographical facts. Her fear of public humiliation seems to have centered on the idea of scorn from the family and was not disarmed by the moderate success of *The True Voice*. Charles did not find authorship and professional recognition the key to personal fulfillment and family approval. She says that her mother, for all her pleasure in the achievement, would have preferred her to marry and produce grandchildren. And she endorses the priorities behind the disappointment: "Life matters more than art."

The True Voice is a polemical title, making a claim crucial to Charles's novels, that she is prepared to tell truths generally ignored in fiction. The narrator, Lindy, is the archetype of the characters Gerda Charles likes—a "brain-worshipper," shy but self-righteous, intelligent but inarticulate, with limited experience and perfect judgment, sensitive, socially desperate—expressing their hunger in its purest form: "I knew no one whom I was proud to know." Her quest is to escape the confines of Staveley Park, for Charles a potent symbol of spiritual blight. Staveley Park, though crude and tedious, displays in microcosm the savagery of all human societies: "I have often found [Staveley Park] to serve me in the way a native tribe serves a sociologist by revealing on the surface what more sophisticated communities cover but do not kill." Lindy makes several timid ventures into a better class of world: a sad and solitary vacation in a village reputed to be popular with artists; an ego-bruising affair with a dislikable minor poet who lectures to her evening class; some work for a political organization which enables her to bask nervously in the presence of a glamorous public figure; she even stands outside the flat of a woman novelist and gazes up at the windows (a motif repeated in various guises in future novels).

Her yearning to better her personal circumstances is matched by her inability to take advantage of any occasion for doing so. She is inarticulate, her true voice buried beneath the platitudes of Staveley Park: "Unused to speaking with my inner voice, I kept forgetting that I must not speak with the false, unthinking voice which it had become second nature to me to use. I forgot that everything I had used speech to conceal I must now use words to reveal." She usually manages to muff any promising moment and (another recurring theme in the novels) has to look on while less deserving opportunists reap the social rewards.

The story of the search for personal improvement has a long tradition in the English novel, but here Charles insists on revising the traditional goals, money and marriage. Her subject is the poor in spirit. Lindy contests any dismissal of her social deprivation as relatively trivial: "What was economic help compared with the relief of such poverty as I *and others* endured?" For her the real injustices of life are immutable accidents of nature, which cannot be ameliorated by political systems. She also values friendship over love, denying that sex brings major emotional aid. Lindy desires her teacher Andrew not because he is a handsome man, but because he has published poems and been to Spain. She wants to go to parties, rather than to bed, with her next idol. With the failure of these bids at vicarious glamour, Lindy is left to find her true voice for herself. The novel closes on a lyrical and tender scene in Kensington Park Gardens, with Lindy's perceptions, a chance meeting with an acquaintance who wants to know her better, with an invitation in her own right. *The True Voice* was favorably received by the reviewers and was the Book Society choice of the month.

Charles describes *The Crossing Point* (1960), begun the day she finished *The True Voice*, as her "Jewish novel." Brian Glanville and Frederick Raphael produced books at about the same time, and the three were grouped together by the critics as a new school of Anglo-Jewish writers, a connection Charles regards as artificial. She sees only contrast between Glanville and Raphael's sophisticated backgrounds, their world of glittering prizes, and her own. The label did, however, attract Jewish

attention to her work, and in 1967, shortly before the Six-Day War, she and her mother visited Israel at the invitation of the Israeli government. Despite her religious commitment, Charles is critical of Jewish society and wishes to desentimentalize its image. In the introduction to *Modern Jewish Stories* (1963) she suggests that modern Jewish writers indulge in a nostalgic vision of their ancestors comparable to the romanticized concept of "Merrie England": "The lives they portrayed in the little *shtetls* [towns] . . . are now looked back on as dreams of pastoral simplicity and warmth—though stranded, unlike other peasant societies, always with an adoration of learning." Charles finds this mythical love of learning and culture absent from most contemporary Jewish society. In the United States, she argues, "The raw blatant life of the immigrant masses was so horrifying—and worse, constricting—to live that the Jewish artist's first thought on lifting his head was to escape from it." In England she finds in Jewish lower-middle-class life a philistinism equal to any Gentile version of Staveley Park. But her view of the positive aspects of Jewish experience is profound: "There is, in the greatest Jewish short stories, a kind of wise, patient, accepting forgiveness for all our faults. And with it goes equally an unashamed emphasis on the necessity of goodness." Her second novel paints a particularly bitter human experience and suggests, without sentimentality, that it can be reinterpreted in the light of the spirit. The work also introduces an idea central to the later novels: the Jew as symbol of all the oppressed.

The Crossing Point is set in the Jewish community of Manor Green, a London suburb, "a deadening and self-deceiving society" described with vividness and humor. The major characters are Rabbi Leo Norberg and some of his congregation, in particular the Gabriel sisters, Sara and Essie, trapped at home with their appalling and bigoted father. This "Jewish novel" is also in several ways a nineteenth-century novel. In her first, third, and fourth novels Charles employs first-person narrative and female centers of consciousness. *The Crossing Point* has a broader canvas and focuses on Leo as well as the sisters. It is narrated from the orthodox but critical perspective of the author, who permits herself considerable homiletic address, and in her closing words tentatively entrusts to the "Spirit of God" even the dreadful Mr. Gabriel. Lindy's mild and solitary epiphany at the end of *The True Voice*, her locating of the potential for growth and happiness within herself, is as much a modern theme as money or marriage is a conventional Victorian finale. Lindy unknowingly stands in a direct line of descent from Joyce's Stephen Dedalus and Lawrence's Paul Morel.

Marriage is central to *The Crossing Point*: it would be the solution to the rabbi's loneliness and "shame of being alone"; it would be escape for Sara and Essie. Charles's heroines notably lack the modern ladders of university education and professional careers. The Gabriel girls are described as living in an "eccentric nineteenth century corner" and are explicitly compared with the Brontës. Their entire community is as preoccupied with marriage as Jane Austen's, even to the point of hiring "agents" and discussing dowries. Essie flees into an ominously unsuitable marriage with a Gentile: "there was nothing else to do—except grow old." Sara, left alone with her father, accepts her imprisonment. She loves Leo: he is moved by her goodness but desperately proposes to a personable girl whom he does not love. He rejects Sara because "her gift is for the soul"; in convincing anguish he opts for the worldly and presentable rather than a pacific wife and a shaming father-in-law. Ultimately, he reflects, the reasons for war or for marriage are those of status: the worst pain of loneliness or poverty is the humiliation, the visible lack of success.

Sara is radiant, yet tainted, with failure. She is the moral center of the book, but Leo's flight from her patience is understandable. The very unattractiveness of passive suffering deepens the suffering, and perhaps with it the virtue. Sara describes the old as "the Jews of life"; their suffering centrally consists in inaction. Leo sees as specific to Jewish spirituality a quiet acceptance over the centuries of suffering in obscurity. Sara's domestic martyrdom, that of the self-sacrificing unmarried daughter familiar from Victorian fiction, is placed in larger and ancient contexts of oppression and endurance. The novel was well received and several reviewers commented on the combination of generosity and impartiality in her picture of Anglo-Jewish life. John Coleman wrote in the *Spectator* of "the human warmth and complexity of the society Miss Charles creates," but added "she also has a sharp eye for Jewish failings and some pages will be fuel for the wrong people." Similarly, the *Times Literary Supplement* reviewer judged her "a courageous chronicler, rigidly honest in her examination of Jewish character and paradox . . . she allows no prejudice or sentiment to intrude on her hard-hitting yet compassionate commentary."

This theme recurs in *A Slanting Light*, which won the James Tait Black Memorial Prize in 1963.

The novel consists of letters written from Ruth in London to the husband she has left behind in her native Liverpool, her departure having been triggered by a glimpse of the contents of a neighbor's shopping bag, a vision of intolerable gracelessness. Ruth describes herself as "a new kind of woman . . . a type of intellectual Englishwoman who has hitherto never been found outside the upper classes . . . a new kind of provincial-urban, intellectual Bovary from the sooty-brick, mean streets and the sweet shop on the corner." She becomes housekeeper to the Jewish-American dramatist Bernard Zold, who is living in London with his feather-brained wife, disturbed child, and querulous mother during the production of his latest play.

Despite his talent and success, Bernard is as isolated as Ruth: he lacks personal charm, he suffers from and for his family's difficulties, he cannot make friends in London. Ruth perceives him as an expatriate in both countries. Sympathetic to each other, they have frank and competitive conversations. Ruth pits the stifling English provinces against the tedium of "Hicksville." Bernard insists that the "slanting light" of his writer's imagination, which she envies, is separate from the rest of his life and brings it no comfort. The obliquity of the writer's imagination is reflected in the indirection of the novel's epistolary form, as well as in failures of connections between people: Ruth participates in the life of the family by eavesdropping through the kitchen hatch; the climax is an act of masturbation; the anticlimax is Bernard's exclusion from his first night party.

Bernard's description of his work can be applied to *A Slanting Light*: "My country is the region of everyday hurt, the things everyone seems agreed are trivial and even ridiculous." Ruth comes to recognize the importance and seriousness of Bernard's unspectacular patience, his unfashionable nineteenth-century virtues, and to see him as the archetypal Jew "obliged not by choice but rather by a mystical necessity to exemplify the suffering, the humane, the pacific, the compassionate strands in the composite human nature of society. That these are mistaken for cowardice, lack of will, failure of energy . . . the misunderstanding is an intrinsic part of the very role itself." Conversely, she perceives in the sadism of malicious cocktail chatter "every reasonless lynching mob in the world. . . . I saw and understood for the first time the concentration camps." Finally these forces are polarized as in a morality play: faced with the goods of this world which she finds most seductive—sophisticated and

successful people—Ruth feels the "pull of goodness" and resists.

The critical response was enthusiastic, with
many comments on the author's seriousness and
commitment to unfashionable virtues. Richard
Brickner described it in the *New York Times* as "a
memorably deep and disturbing revelation of our
time's greatest anguish: the struggle of 'goodness' to
keep its head above water." R. V. Cassill reviewed
the novel in *Bookweek* with unsurpassed generosity
but with a significant caveat: "The author's verdict
on some of her characters is unproved . . . But
within the area of her sound achievement she ticks
off marvel after marvel. If a lot of the edges are
ragged this is partly due to the abundance of a
first-rate writer with a lot to say . . . If only somewhere in the book there were an intelligence detached enough to measure Bernard's responsibility
with something more than passion, I think we
would have had a masterpiece."

Rose Morgan, the "logical girl" of the next
novel, published in 1966, also connects the perse-
cution of the Jews and the rise of Hitler with the
springs of human evil which she sees in her home, in
her daintily tyrannical sister-in-law, her blindly ap-
peasing father, and, finally, in her jealous propen-
sities for vengefulness. *A Logical Girl*, set in 1943 in
the seaside town of Peach Bay, where Rose and her
family run a boardinghouse, brilliantly describes
the "invasion" of American servicemen. Charles
says that, like Rose, she was fascinated by the
America of the movies, "filling our empty, grasping
imaginations starved for fable with fantasies of a
heaven across an ocean." That she did not visit the
United States until 1972 for the publication there of
The Destiny Waltz is surprising: her ear for transatlantic speech patterns is acute, her evocation of both
the American dream and Zold's Hicksville vivid.

Peach Bay falls collectively in love with its
Americans. For Rose, placed like other Charles
heroines, on the margin of the action, the GI's embody all she has craved: they are exotic, varied,
articulate, chivalric. Charles admires contemporary
American fiction more than British because of its
greater candor, its confrontation of the painful
"and—what's worse—the embarrassing." Rose values in particular the seriousness with which the
Americans discuss and give attention to psychological problems. She sees in some of the Americans
(almost for the first time in her life), real quality.

The power of the illogical is revealed when the
most distinguished of them, Tim Rousseau, a
guarantee of "the world's goodness and human
wisdom," becomes engaged to the drabbest of the

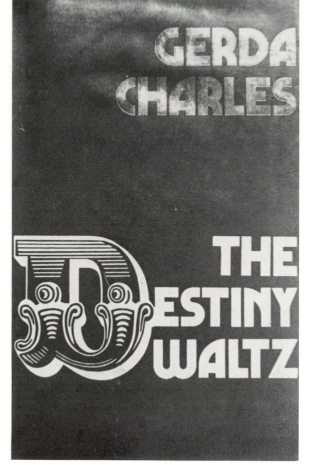

*Dust jacket for Charles's most recent novel, winner of the 1971
Whitbread Fiction Award*

Peach Bay girls. In her personal and epistemologi-
cal distress Rose is uncharacteristically bad-
tempered with her peripheral boyfriend. Her testi-
ness excites him into proposing to her, more evidence of cosmic perversity: "He did not like me
suffering, tolerant, controlled, he liked me angry
and self-willed. And I realised again the appalling
dichotomy between what we are told about how to
be with others and what in fact *works*." But Rose
refuses to deform herself to fit the shape of her
world, to marry beneath her ideals merely because a
single person looks untidy in the social order.

The reviewers were less wholehearted in their
praise of *A Logical Girl* than of its predecessors.
Doubts were raised about Charles's assessment of
her central characters. In the *Nation* she was described as "an extremely gifted writer, a writer of
unfashionable moral seriousness and exceptional
narrative power." The review continues: "One can
take her female protagonist seriously or regard her
as an object for subtle satire. Miss Charles has not
quite brought her themes and characters under the

control of her hard unsentimental intelligence." Some critics expressed unqualified hostility. For example, Louise Armstrong in the *New York Times Book Review* dismissed Rose as "one of the most tiresome women fiction has produced for some time," yet apparently admitted her verisimilitude: "the most tenacious adolescence I have ever seen outside of real life."

The Destiny Waltz, which won the Whitbread Fiction Award in 1971, recounts the making of a television documentary about Paul Salomon, a fictitious poet who lived in obscurity and died young. Georges, the director, enlists the aid of Michele, the author of a book on Paul's poetry, and Jimmy, who had been a friend of Paul's since their childhood in the Jewish East End of London. As the three work together for some weeks, Michele and Jimmy are both strongly attracted to the exquisite and sympathetic Georges. Jimmy, now sixty-three, retired and lonely, was a famous dance-band leader in the 1920s and 1930s. His retirement has been "banishment to the world of the ordinary," but the apparent friendship of Georges and the television crew temporarily restores him to a buzzing world of talent and limelight. However, as the documentary nears completion Georges becomes impatient and elusive. His charm has been meretricious; no longer useful, Michele and Jimmy are being dropped. They realize, however, that they love each other. Jimmy reflects that destiny has given him another chance, and the novel ends warmly.

No comfort can be salvaged from Paul's destiny. The platitudes of self-help—"You get out of life what you put into it"—are dismissed as "smug and dangerous rubbish." One gets out of life the hand which destiny has dealt: the cards may or may not include the courage, talent, or charm to better one's lot. Jimmy seems to be playing an eternal game of "yes, but . . ." as he defends the author's determinism against the increasingly barbed consolations of Georges. More laborious, perhaps more pessimistic than Charles's other works, *The Destiny Waltz* seems through Jimmy to state the other novels' premises pugnaciously and to combat the obvious criticisms of their indulgence in snobbishness, envy, and self-pity. Envy and self-pity, Jimmy argues, are doomed losers' intelligent and justified responses to the inequities of life. Snobbishness results from an objective appraisal of the facts and a preference for quality.

However, some readers may, like Georges, finally refuse to sympathize. This novel certainly vexed some of the reviewers, who reported that its opinionated tone was destructive of its great poten-

tial. The *New Statesman* complained of "a disproportionate amount of sermonizing." The *Times Literary Supplement* reviewer conceded that "it is rare to find a novelist tackling moral problems as explicitly and as seriously as Gerda Charles does," but found the tone "too humorless for comfort." J. W. Charles in *Library Journal* wrote that the novel "is busting with moral seriousness but the didactic tone that occasionally threatened her fine novel *A Slanting Light* has now taken over completely . . . characters by the novel's end have become earnest humorless puppets tidily for or against her issues. The most exasperating aspect is that she *has* written an important novel in spite of her excesses and misjudgments."

The novels are clearly fueled by personal unhappiness: this charges them, not only with their undoubted power and authenticity, but also with an insistent buttonholing quality which can repel. The author is (except, perhaps, in *The Crossing Point*) positioned uncomfortably close to her central characters; she is soft on her aggrieved heroines with their hypersensitivity to every slight and their damning judgments of others. Ruth dismisses the cultured inhabitants of St. John's Wood: "Their lives are not *living*." Rose, so frantic for company, is amazed, almost incredulous, when her father sulks at not being included in a party. Charles is surely right to locate all human capacity for good or ill in minute particulars. (Yet is it merely morally obtuse to object to Rose's identifying herself with the Jews and her sister-in-law with Hitler? Or to fail to be outraged when Sara is offered "an undistinguished biscuit from the meagre assortment"?) At times Charles's vision may impress us less with its sensitivity than with its lack of perspective.

Charles feels born into the wrong century as well as into the wrong class. She demands of her readers the same seriousness and compassion as a nineteenth-century novelist. She has much in common with Charlotte Brontë: awkward heroines, a concern with loneliness, restriction, and frustration, the moral passion, the romantic fervor, the stress on the particular emotional and social problems of women. Charles does not, however, share Brontë's feminism. Skeptical that human nature can be changed, she is contemptuous of the women's movement. Yet, although Charles scorns much in the twentieth century, her central characters express modern hedonism as much as they condemn it. Despite her admiration for Victorian fortitude and humility, her heroines sometimes expect an emotional welfare state, unearned benefits of personal fulfillment. As Sara says about being unmusical: "I feel that I'm missing something, that I'm being cheated out of my rights." Her slightly ironic tone is unusual among Charles's protagonists, yet essentially they are right; life does not distribute evenly. People are usually justified in minding who they are born and what they are born into.

During the 1970s Charles cared for her mother, whose declining health required full-time

attendance until her death in 1981. The next novel, about the Six-Day War, remains unfinished, and Charles feels diffident about the prospect of further novels.

Other:

Modern Jewish Stories, edited by Charles (London: Faber & Faber, 1963).

Barry Cole
(13 November 1936-   )

Theresa M. Peter
University of Delaware

SELECTED BOOKS: *Blood Ties* (London: Turret Books, 1967);
Ulysses in the Town of Coloured Glass (London: Turret Books, 1968);
A Run Across the Island (London: Methuen, 1968);
Moonsearch (London: Methuen, 1968);
Joseph Winter's Patronage (London: Methuen, 1969);
The Visitors (London: Methuen, 1970);
The Search for Rita (London: Methuen, 1970);
The Giver (London: Methuen, 1971);
Vanessa in the City (London: Trigram Press, 1971);
Pathetic Fallacies (London: Eyre Methuen, 1973).

Although he considers himself more a poet than a novelist, Barry Cole writes exceptionally precise and enjoyable prose. His novels involve colorful but very realistic people in familiar situations and surroundings, usually centered in London. Cole catches the essence of British life in the late 1960s and early 1970s in a style that is witty and fresh.

A Londoner all his life, Barry Cole was born in Woking, Surrey, on 13 November 1936, the eldest of five children of Jennifer Ryder and Leslie Herbert Cole. His father, the son of a self-made antique dealer, was rather a jack-of-all-trades; his mother was the daughter of a Durham coal miner. The family was quite poor while Barry was growing up, and he left Balham Secondary School at age fifteen in order to supplement the family income. Brief summaries of Cole's life often emphasize the early termination of his formal schooling, sometimes even stating that he failed his exams. However, he was always a voracious reader and educated himself by reading whatever he got his hands on. Books,

periodicals, and the public libraries were Barry Cole's university, and the success of such an education is evident in his outstanding command of the English language. He continues to read five weeklies, ten to twenty poems, and as many as five books each week, in addition to three daily newspapers.

At fifteen, Cole became a clerk for a firm of solicitors in London. He served in the Royal Air Force from 1955 to 1957 and afterward found a variety of jobs. In June of 1958 he married Rita Linihan. In that year, also, he was hired by Reuters news agency as a clerk. By this time he was reading the *Listener* regularly and becoming interested in writing journalism. He eventually worked his way into the field while with Reuters. In 1964 he was hired by the Central Office of Information in London as a reporter with the title of Assistant Information Officer.

After publication of his first novels and books of poetry, Cole was granted a Northern Arts Fellowship in Literature at the Universities of Durham and Newcastle-upon-Tyne and taught post-war British literature—novels and especially poetry—from 1970 to 1972. As he puts it, he entered the university from the top, gaining the perspectives of both an insider and an outsider to academia. He associated with academics, yet he did not have their formal education. The same was usually true in his journalism jobs. Between 1972 and 1974, Cole worked as a free-lance writer. He returned to the Central Office of Information in 1974 and is still employed there as a senior editor. His government work, he says, is completely separate from his creative work.

It was at age thirty-two that Barry Cole actually

became a published novelist. He had written some verse before that, and a number of his poems had been published in magazines, periodicals, and anthologies. A small independent publisher, Turret Books, published his first collection of poetry, *Blood Ties*, in 1967 and *Ulysses in the Town of Coloured Glass*, a single twelve-part poem, in 1968. Both were limited publications and are unobtainable now. Later in 1968, Methuen published a major collection of Cole's poetry entitled *Moonsearch*, which won him a Poetry Book Society Recommendation in 1969. In 1968 Methuen also published *A Run Across the Island*, Cole's first novel.

The novel is written as the memoirs of Robert Haydon, a young man who has been living alone on a desolate island for two years. Although within rowing distance of the British mainland, the island, known as M 38, contains little more than an abandoned oil derrick and Robert's sparsely furnished hut. Alternating between reminiscences of his life on the mainland and accounts of his eccentric activities on the island, the novel reveals not only the increasing social pressures that have driven Robert

to seek refuge on the island, but also much about his own peculiar character. His childhood memories revolve around his three stepmothers, Polly I, Polly II, Polly III, to whom he attributes many of his later thoughts and impressions. His father, he says, was a small but forceful man, whose wrath Robert feared as a boy, but often risked through his own preposterous behavior. Robert tells how, on the eve of his nineteenth birthday, he finally succumbed to the urge to pillage his father's desk, an incident that accidentally caused the older man's death from a stroke.

Robert has reacted to the deaths of relatives and friends in the novel with unusual detachment, a coolness and almost lazy indifference that typify his general behavior. He has never actually fallen in love, although he has been strongly attracted to several women and has always sought physical enjoyment and security. He has had affairs with Hedda, the present wife of his close friend, Carl Gilbert, and with Carl's first wife, Susan Willis, with whom he lived and who supported him while he remained willfully unemployed. A short stint as a fine arts dealer once put him deeply in debt. After suddenly marrying Susan and moving with her to Edinburgh, he realized that he could no longer stand the life that others were leading for him, so he has fled to the island. Summarizing his relationships with other people, Hedda at one point told Robert that he was selfish and emotionally immature, "a cardboard cut-out, a comic strip, a nothing, a parasite." Hedda's words have continued to haunt him, and he draws some conclusions about himself. He wanted, he says, "not only to know I was free from other people, but to be able to *see* that I was free from them. . . . I wanted to break society into static fragments." Most of Robert's narrative, however, is not so analytical. He reveals no malice and no self-pity in his character—just deadpan wit and a nonchalance that allows for keen, objective descriptions. These two qualities are, of course, attributable to the author, and they are the hallmarks of all Barry Cole's fiction.

Cole's second novel, *Joseph Winter's Patronage* (1969), was called by John Lucas in *Contemporary Novelists* (1976) "the most touching and warmly sympathetic novel that Barry Cole has so far written." Like *A Run Across the Island*, it deals with alienation and the tenuousness of human relationships. Joseph Winter is a very old man, but he is also very spirited and unwilling to relinquish his authority. Before coming to the Manor (the small, exclusive old people's home in which he lives), he was a successful entrepreneur and a business bully. The most orthodox and least mysterious of his enterprises was a pub, The Checquered Lamb, which his son Jago and daughter-in-law Carrie have inherited. Jago is sexually impotent and socially inept. He is unable to keep the business solvent and depends on Joseph occasionally for funds to keep things going. While disgusted by Jago's weakness and ineptitude, Joseph finds Carrie attractive and makes advances to her whenever he can, especially when he knows Jago has instructed her to beg money from him.

The narration is third person, but the focus variously shifts from Joseph to Jago, Carrie, and the other elderly occupants of the Manor. Many passages derive from the old men's memories, not as conventional flashbacks so much as subtle lapses into the past. For Joseph they are thoughts of his younger days of fast living, hard work, and sexual prowess. Bill, a somewhat feebler old man, sits reading dictionaries and reminisces through word association. Bentham constantly reads novels, and when he reminisces, he describes images and events in the precise, eloquent language of romantic literature. Here, Barry Cole captures the feeling, the mentality, of old age, especially as revealed in strong emotional attachments, such as Joseph Winter's to the stone wall that surrounds the Manor. The book ends on a note of indignation at the patronizing attitude of society toward the elderly, and critics have praised the novel for isolating "what is, after all, *the* problem of old age."

The Search for Rita (1970), Barry Cole's third novel and his favorite one so far, is his liveliest, wittiest, and cleverest. It deftly captures the spirit of London in the 1960s and while amusing, it also reveals sinister undertones. The plot is vague and subordinate to the characters, who are highly developed and vividly described. Among them are Sigmund Ames, a reclusive old foreigner who enjoys sending parcels (e.g., a sweater made of lint) to people chosen at random; Gwendolene Leyday, a typical Victorian young woman transposed into the twentieth century (Cole was reading George Eliot's *Daniel Deronda* at this time, and she is deliberately modeled after Gwendolene Harleth, Eliot's heroine); Jonathan, Gwendolene's rich husband, from whom she is separated; and Jean Caspar, an only child whose naivete and desire for excitement lead her to become the victim of various sexual perversions, beginning with a rape which she completely fails to comprehend.

Throughout the novel, these characters' lives become increasingly intertwined, but the central figure who emerges is the mysterious narrator. He treats the others objectively, includes passages about his own life, and makes sudden appearances in their lives. It is never certain whether he is an eccentric and lazy private eye, an unemployed man half-heartedly searching for his own vanished lover (the elusive Rita), or an amiable author who is attempting to please his characters. He is in some ways all three. He is hired to search for several characters and investigate others, but his unorthodox methods yield few results. He spends most of his time observing—staring out of his window or watching passersby in cafes and underground stations, waiting for Rita to happen along while making no active attempt to find her. He chats with Jean now and then, he seduces Gwendolene, and for no discernible reason he is the recipient of grotesque gifts from Sigmund. With such an ambiguous story line, the novel has a necessarily dubious ending. It leaves the reader with a melange of impressions, simultaneous amusement, bewilderment, delight, and apprehension. "A lavish piece of writer's self-indulgence," Roger Baker of the London *Times* wrote, "but extremely witty, sinister, and immaculately composed."

In *The Search for Rita*, Cole's stylistic techniques are evident: his emphasis on language and skillful

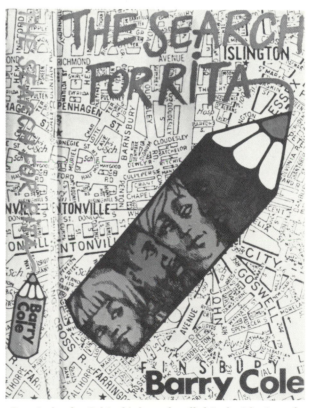

Dust jacket for Cole's third novel, called "a lavish piece of writer's self-indulgence"

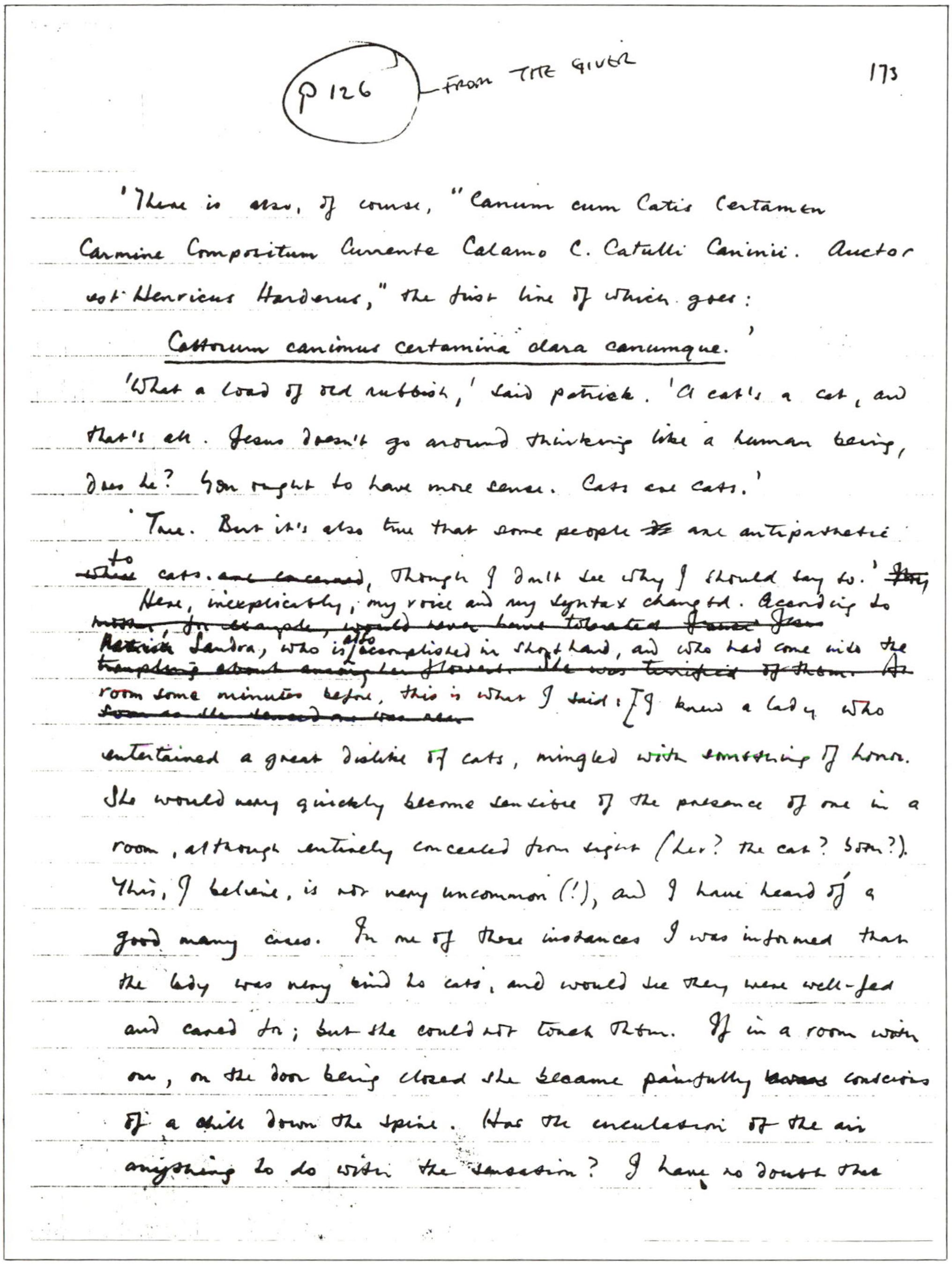

p 126 — FROM THE GIVER 173

'There is also, of course, "Canum cum Catis Certamen
Carmine Compositum Currente Calamo C. Catulli Caninii. Auctor
est Henricus Hardenus," the first line of which goes:
Cattorum canimus certamina clara canumque.'
'What a load of old rubbish,' said patrick. 'A cat's a cat, and
that's all. Jesus doesn't go around thinking like a human being,
does he? You ought to have more sense. Cats are cats.'
'True. But it's also true that some people are antipathetic
to cats, though I don't see why I should say so.'
Here, inexplicably, my voice and my syntax changed. According to
Sandra, who is also accomplished in shorthand, and who had come into the
room some minutes before, this is what I said: [I knew a lady who
entertained a great dislike of cats, mingled with something of horror.
She would very quickly become sensible of the presence of one in a
room, although entirely concealed from sight (her? the cat? both?).
This, I believe, is not very uncommon (!), and I have heard of a
good many cases. In one of those instances I was informed that
the lady was very kind to cats, and would see they were well-fed
and cared for; but she could not touch them. If in a room with
one, on the door being closed she became painfully conscious
of a chill down the spine. Has the circulation of the air
anything to do with the sensation? I have no doubt that

Manuscript for The Giver

selection of words, his use of cinematic flashbacks and scene transitions, and the obvious lack of chapters. Chapters are unnecessary in Barry Cole's novels; in fact, he regards them as artificial devices in fiction generally. His text is divided into sections, which occur more or less naturally and can consist of anywhere from two sentences to several pages. The fluctuation of scenes and perspectives keeps his novels from becoming stagnant. A distinctive trait of Cole's fiction is that it is always brisk though never frenetic.

Cole's cleverness overruns his fourth novel, *The Giver*, published in 1971. He admits that in writing it he was playing with words to an extreme, almost showing off. Many of the passages are turned around, transmuted, reexecuted. The speaker is Stephen Blackpool—the name, that of a Dickens character, being the first of numerous literary allusions in the novel—and he is very conscious of his role as writer. ". . . After all," he says at one point, "my own subjects are those which occur to a man almost wholly occupied with writing." The narration gives the impression of being candid and impromptu, and yet considered and manipulated at the same time. Sometimes the narrator is quoted, sometimes not, but other characters respond to him either way. Stephen lives in a large, almost empty house which he has inherited from his mother. Sandra, a former tenant, comes back to live there during her pregnancy, and responsibility for her well-being automatically falls upon Stephen. His only other companion is Patrick, a vagrant who establishes squatter's rights in the cottage behind the house and adopts a cat he calls Jesus. Stephen speaks of his other ex-tenants from time to time—Dr. Bhatax, Mr. Levin, Sandra's supposed boyfriend John, and Rachel, Stephen's onetime lover—but he makes few real social contacts. When he ventures into the outside world, it is as a burglar and then as an almost absurd rebel in state-occupied territory. But Stephen has neither malice nor political savvy; his escapades seem worthless.

The Giver explores moral principles and the nature of human relationships, but quite obscurely. There is no plot as such; the novel is more a prolonged exercise in syntax and phraseology. The critics' response was not positive. "One fights the steely wit of this experiment," a *London Times* reviewer remarked, calling *The Giver* a "twisted crossword whose answers do not fit, but whose clues demand a response." However, the same creative imagination, precise description, subtle absurdities, irony, and wit that characterize Barry Cole's other fiction are all present, though *The Giver* ultimately remains enigmatic.

Prose writing has never hindered Barry Cole's production as a poet. Since 1970, he has had five volumes of verse published. His most recent collection, underway for some time, is scheduled for publication as "New Poems."

In addition to his four published novels, Barry Cole has written four others that have not been published: "Into the Hub-Tub" in 1968, "A Gathering of Bones" in 1969, "Cat and Glove" in 1971, and "Doctor Fielder's Common Sense." Methuen contracted to publish the latter in 1972, but because of financing problems, that contract has not been fulfilled. Publishers have had to cut back, and unfortunately Cole's novels have been among those shelved. Never a "popular" novelist, despite critical praise, he presently has no novels in print but is currently at work on a new one entitled "The Cutbush Capers." Simple, comic, and typically anecdotal, it involves a graduate student who sets out to become a criminal but fails through his lack of common sense. One passage describes the character's attempts to disguise his getaway car, but what he uses is poster paint. It rains during his holdup and the result is disastrous.

"Anyone can write a novel," Barry Cole says. He would rather write a fourteen-line poem than an entire novel, because he feels writing verse is more of a challenge and more satisfying in the end. "Poetry is a craft," he believes, ". . . the art of prose writing is more innate." His abilities to write both poetry and prose improve with age and experience, he says. Yet his poetry collections continue to be better received by the critics than his novels.

While Cole does not write "poetic" prose, some comparisons can be drawn between his poetry and his fiction: verbal meticulousness, simplicity of subject, familiar details, and fresh imagery. Descriptions such as "a toffee coloured sun" and "bottletop eyes" flavor his poems and novels. Cole is never concerned with philosophies in his writing; his themes are subtly developed. Although his work lacks the social significance usually prerequisite for literary immortality, this is deliberate. Cole's novels provide insight into human nature and relationships—love, friendships, rejection, isolation—but draw no lofty conclusions. Words are everything to him; he calls himself a "frustrated lexicographer" and challenges anyone to find a solecism in his work.

Cole's other trait that is manifest in his writing is his knowledge of literature. Direct and indirect allusions are abundant in both his novels and his poetry. His favorite author is George Eliot, he is fond of Dickens, and in general, he prefers nineteenth-century picaresque novels.

Barry Cole has reviewed novels for various periodicals: the *New Statesman*, the *Spectator*, the *London Times Educational Supplement*, and many others. He still does impromptu book reviews from time to time. His personal test for the merit of literature, whether fiction or verse, is whether he wishes he had written it (although he admits with a smile that this is probably egotistical). Regarding twentieth-century fiction, Cole asserts that there is

actually no such entity. Whatever is written in a given period is inevitably influenced by all literature that has come before it. Thus, fiction writing is a synthesis, something Cole is aware of in his own writing.

Barry Cole presently lives near the Angel, Islington, in London with his wife, Rita, and their three daughters, Celia, Becky, and Jessica. He enjoys his work, his family life, and holidays in Italy. He continues to write at the energetic pace that has marked his first fifteen years as a creative writer, a habit that augurs well for more fiction and poetry of interest to his readers.

Isabel Colegate
(10 September 1931-   )

Sarah Turvey
Roehampton Institute of Higher Education, London

BOOKS: *The Blackmailer* (London: Blond, 1958);
A Man of Power (London: Blond, 1960);
The Great Occasion (London: Blond, 1962);
Statues in a Garden (London: Bodley Head, 1964;
    New York: Knopf, 1966);
Orlando King (London: Bodley Head, 1968; New
    York: Knopf, 1969);
Orlando at the Brazen Threshold (London: Bodley
    Head, 1971);
Agatha (London: Bodley Head, 1973);
News from the City of the Sun (London: Hamilton,
    1979);
The Shooting Party (London: Hamilton, 1980).

Isabel Colegate's novels chart the fortunes of the moneyed classes in twentieth-century England, from the weekend shooting parties of the Edwardian aristocracy to the anachronistic antics of the upper classes in the 1950s. In doing so, the novels are also about history and the efforts of representative individuals to recognize it, to direct it, or to accommodate themselves to it. Her books are equally about myth, and the shifting relationship between history and myth governs their development and constitutes her importance as a contemporary novelist.

Colegate grew up in Lincolnshire, the youngest child of Sir Arthur Colegate and Lady

Colegate Worsley. After being taught at home by governesses she went to boarding school, but because, as she has remarked, she "never quite got the hang of being taught," she left at sixteen. At nineteen she went to work as an assistant for literary agent Anthony Blond. In 1953 Colegate married Michael Briggs. They have three children: Emily, Joshua, and Barnaby.

Colegate continued working for Blond after her marriage, and when Blond turned publisher, Colegate's novel *The Blackmailer* (1958), was one of his earliest undertakings. The book focuses on the development of a bizarre relationship between a would-be blackmailer, Baldwin Rees, and his victim, Judith Lane. The absent center of the novel is Judith's husband, Anthony Lane, a war hero of mythic proportions, Rees's commanding officer in Korea, and the object of Rees's rancorous envy. The myth, however, is false: Lane was a coward and perhaps also a traitor, and Rees uses this knowledge to blackmail Judith. Appalled at Rees's threat to sell the story to a Sunday newspaper, Judith pays and continues to pay while each becomes increasingly fascinated by the other. The curious grotesqueness of the relationship is epitomized by their weekend trip to visit Anthony's wealthy and snobbish family. Though ignorant of Rees's role as blackmailer, the family members snub him for his vulgarity. Thereafter the relationship disintegrates and moral proprieties reassert themselves. Rees stops extorting money from Judith, and she returns to her job at the family publishing house.

The novel's fascination is with power, represented by both the myth of Anthony Lane and the reality of Baldwin Rees. There is a compelling quality in its depiction. At the same time the book is very much a first novel. Colegate's characteristic style is full of syntactic deferrals which in her later novels are not only elegantly disciplined but also major constituents of meaning. The deferrals in sentence structure mimic the books' awareness of the deferred meanings of history, which is given coherence only retrospectively. In *The Blackmailer* this style has not yet been brought under control, and it has a clumsy and stumbling quality. A contemporary reviewer referred to the "whimsical" feel of the novel, and it certainly is peopled with a strange generic mix of characters—there are echoes of both Nancy Mitford and the detective thriller. The strangeness of the novel is partly accounted for by what Colegate remembers as her determination *not* to write an autobiographical book. The most bizarre character was apparently modeled on a midget who used to walk his dogs in the area of Chelsea where

she was living at the time. The resemblance did not go unnoticed by one reviewer who was also familiar with the area and telephoned her to express his delighted shock of recognition. That phone call, she says, did as much as anything else to encourage her in her writing, though she was still uneasy in the realms of the symbolic. There is a resultant defensiveness in statements like: "That night [Judith] dreamt, dispensing with the subtleties of symbolism, that they were in bed together." Perhaps the most interesting aspect of the novel is the portrait of Anthony Lane's family, representatives of a class in retreat before forces it cannot understand. Mrs. Lane insists to Judith: "The world's changed. People have no sense of values, no decency, they're all out for what they can get. Our sort of people get pushed aside by all the lies and ingratitude. The Welfare State—it's just a means of sheltering these liars and slanderers and upstarts. I brought Anthony up in the old-fashioned way, to be what his father was before him." Part of the effort of the later novels is to understand what "the old-fashioned way" meant and the nature of the forces before which it retreated.

The title of Colegate's second novel, *A Man of Power* (1960), clearly declares one of its major themes. The man in question is Lewis Ogden, a nouveau riche but immensely successful businessman who has tired of his submissive wife and ex-secretary, Jean, and has turned his attentions instead toward the aging but aristocratic and still fascinating Lady Essex Cooper. Ogden divorces Jean who subsequently suffers a mental collapse and eventually kills herself. Though Essex is unattracted by the man himself, she nonetheless allows the relationship to develop to the point of impending marriage while she and her circle of parasitic admirers devote themselves to spending Ogden's money. Eventually she and her lodger-cum-lover, Alexander, are discovered by Ogden in Ogden's own home, and a team of hired detectives quietly ushers the couple and their hangers-on out of his house and out of his life.

The real interest of the novel is provided by its narrator, Essex's daughter Vanessa, who is fascinated by both her mother and Lewis Ogden. At one point in the book, reference is made to Henry James's *The Awkward Age* (1899), and there are evident thematic and stylistic parallels. Both novels deal with the education of upper-class young girls, and, like Nanda, Vanessa finds herself relegated—through both her knowledge and her desires—to a position of spectatorship, as she tries to comprehend the personalities and relationships around her. Part of the continuing struggle of Colegate's novels is the search for an adequate narrative position, somewhere between participation and detachment. Her novels are about a class with which she is intimately familiar, but from which she is constantly trying to distance herself. The use of Vanessa as narrator offers a kind of double detachment: Vanessa is isolated from the antics of the other characters, but she is also distanced from the author and the reader through her evident and extremely naive fascination with them. Finally she is partially rescued from this fascination through her acquaintance with the enigmatic Tom Jones. Like all of Colegate's characters with leftist political sympathies, Jones is a distanced figure, but he offers Vanessa a way out of her stifling class existence: "Tom Jones was at least something of a mystery, something to be found out about, and there was a hope—surely there was a hope—that through him I might find a life less futile than was offered by Mme Sobiska's Bureau, or my mother's antique shop, or Betty Carr's charity committees. I didn't know but it was worth trying."

The Great Occasion (1962) is Colegate's most autobiographical novel and—perhaps relatedly—the most narratively assured of her earlier works. Its setting in the early 1950s is lovingly created through telling details which are close to those recounted in an article she wrote much later about growing up in Lincolnshire as the youngest of four daughters. The novel, similarly set in Lincolnshire and describing a family of girls, traces their various attempts to create futures for themselves in a changing society which no longer provides women with the constricting security of a preordained position. Patriarchy is losing ground: there is no son to inherit and continue the family dynasty, and the father, Gabriel Dodson, is ineffectual, most definitely *not* a man of power. The eldest daughter, Penelope, does attempt to fit herself into an older mold. She marries a rising politician and devotes herself to the furtherance of his career. Her husband, Ham, is the epitome of upper-class conventionality and obtuseness, but even in his family the lines are not holding. He is the younger brother, but while he struggles to fulfill his traditional role, Lord Trent, the son and heir, has turned the ancient family seat into an indoor zoo where he lives in homosexual seclusion with his lover and ex-bearkeeper, Fergus.

Colegate has said that of all her novels, *The Great Occasion* is "about least" in terms of plot or theme. She regarded it rather as "an exercise in technique, an attempt to keep five major characters

on the go for the length of an entire novel." In many ways the five Dodson daughters provide prototypes for many of Colegate's later women. While Penelope is to some extent a woman of power, her sister Susan gives herself entirely to the safe-keeping of her husband, Bill. She denies herself completely and as a result suffers the same mental collapse which is experienced by Jean in *A Man of Power*, and later Judith in *Orlando King* (1968). Angel is one of the group whom Colgate has described as her "man-made" women. At the beginning of the novel, the narrator says that Angel should have been at the "awkward age," a reference which suggests comparison with Little Aggie in James's novel. Like Aggie, and like a number of Colegate's other women, Angel is beautiful, but she is constructed as a sexual object by the male characters whom she encounters in the novel. Unlike the others, however, Angel does achieve redemption through motherhood, though the tone in which her salvation is described leaves room for less happy conjectures about her future. Charlotte attempts to free herself through her art and through her marriage to the talented but unpedigreed artist Smith Pennington. In marrying Pennington, however, she denies her work in favor of his, a denial far more depressing than her eventual death of cancer.

Selina is the youngest daughter, and she is the most enigmatic character in the book, arguably because of the autobiographical elements in her creation. Selina spends her childhood in the henhouse, writing a novel which mimics the style of whatever she happens to be reading. (Colegate says that her first novel, written when she was eleven, "turned out to be exactly the same as the latest Arthur Ransome.") At the end of *The Great Occasion* she too is claimed by a man, but there is a strong feeling that she will resist the claim and attempt to create her own life.

In discussing her career, Colegate has remarked that two of her novels were especially important to her in terms of her development. One of these is *Statues in a Garden* (1964). Her first three novels, she says, she wrote "quite easily. I was trying to write books like other books, because I like books." All three were well received, but she was disappointed that *The Great Occasion* sold no more copies than *The Blackmailer*. In response, and feeling that she had little to lose, she decided to write a novel which "would not try to please" but which would enable her to experiment with new techniques and a new historical setting.

Statues in a Garden, which takes place in the summer of 1914 and is centered upon the Westons, a leisured, aristocratic family whose collapse occurs in the shadow of World War I, is nonetheless intensely personal. Sir Aylmer is a liberal politician and a member of Prime Minister Asquith's cabinet; Lady Cynthia is his beautiful and gracious wife. In addition to their own charming children, there is Philip, Aylmer's orphaned nephew and adopted son. Philip is an intelligent, disruptive force. He recognizes that: "There is a whole new force coming up, based on everything that's been suppressed til now." The complexity of this new order and of Philip as its representative are beyond the understanding of the family. To them Philip is "alright really. Just a bit complicated." All right, that is, until he breaks the rules and sleeps with Cynthia, his adopted mother. The act flouts not only the ideal of graciousness which the society upholds, but the "incestuousness" of the act also threatens the foundations of the family structures on which the society is actually based. When Aylmer learns of the affair he kills himself; Philip abandons Cynthia, and she disintegrates into a pathetic sexual adventuress. The outbreak of the war comes at the end of the novel, claiming among its casualties the family's son and heir, Edmund.

Statues in a Garden is the most experimental novel of the corpus. It is also Colegate's most tentative book, both in terms of narrative technique and in its effort to engage with a nexus of history, myth, and fiction concepts which are to be taken up again and again in her later work. The identity of the narrator is withheld until the end of the novel and even then it is less than certain: "And I, I suppose, was Alice, but it was a long time ago." Alice is the governess and more spectator than participant in the events she recounts. The use of such an ambiguous figure seems to indicate the conflicting urges which characterize the book: first person narration is a device which tries to satisfy the simultaneous effort toward involvement and withdrawal. Above all, it is a means of refusing omniscience and authority about a historical period of which the author had no personal experience. Near the beginning of the novel the narrator states: "We are not trying to recapture an age as it was or to write history: we are trying to remember the background for a fable. A private background for a private fable." There is a strange tension between this claim and the choice of a particularly portentous moment in history for the setting of the novel, recreated with a specificity and precision that indicate extensive historical research. At the same time, however, the years which preceded World War I have been the subject of considerable historical mythmaking about the "golden twilight" of a class, shattered by the single, cataclysmic event of war. The myth possesses elements of truth and exercises a powerful appeal, but it is not adequate historical explanation. *Statues in a Garden* is caught in these contradictions, and Colegate seems uncertain how to negotiate fiction between history and myth. As a result it fluctuates between an effort toward historical detail and a denial of history: "London 1914. People said there was too much money about, the old standards were going (Rand magnates, American heiresses). Bitterness in politics, talk of civil war in Ireland, of a general strike in the autumn; suffragettes. . . . It was during the summer of 1914 that all this happened; but it might have happened at any time; at least I suppose it might. I suppose in fact that these same events take place all the time in one shape or another, or might take place, and it is only the human inclination for myth which requires them to have happened once and for all at some specific moment in time. . . ." For all these reasons, *Statues in a Garden* is a troubled and fascinating novel, and a watershed in Colegate's development. Critical response was generally favorable, but it reflected the novel's own ambivalence toward history. The *Times Literary Supplement* reviewer, for example, asserted that "No responsible literary advisor could have recommended such a theme" to Colegate, but then went on to praise the book for its evocation of the period without any of the "staginess that undoes so many period novels."

The trilogy published between 1968 and 1973 is the most ambitious fictional project Colegate has undertaken. The three novels trace the fortunes of Orlando King, and subsequently his daughter Agatha, in the years between 1930 and 1956. The personal drama is played out against a background of punctuating historical events: the rise of Hitler and Moseley; the Munich accord; World War II; and finally the Suez Canal crisis and the Hungarian uprising. However, the trilogy is also clearly structured around a reenactment of the Oedipus myth, producing close parallels of event and character. The novels attempt to work through some of the questions which are raised by *Statues in a Garden*.

The first part, *Orlando King*, focuses on the years between 1930 and the Blitz in 1940. Orlando is raised by a reclusive Cambridge professor on a remote island off the coast of Brittany. Appropriately he comes to London at twenty-one, the age of initiation. Through a letter of introduction he is employed by Leonard who, unknown to either of them, is his father. In the course of the 1930s Orlando's career takes a meteoric rise. By the outbreak of war he has achieved both extreme wealth and a position as a Cabinet minister. After unwittingly precipitating Leonard's death, Orlando marries his stepmother, Judith. In her marriages to both Leonard and Orlando, Judith's role is that of beautiful and alluring woman; however, she is older than Orlando, and as she becomes increasingly unable to sustain the role, she tries to kill herself and eventually dies in a state of complete mental collapse. After Orlando discovers his father's identity and is then partially blinded during the bombing of London, he abandons his career and goes into voluntary exile in Tuscany.

Both the time scale and the pace of the story contract in the second novel, *Orlando at the Brazen Threshold* (1971). Set in 1951, it spans only the last few months of Orlando's life. The setting moves between Tuscany and London, and the book concentrates upon the reunion and developing relationship of Orlando and his seventeen-year-old daughter, Agatha. Until now Agatha has been raised by Judith's brother, Conrad, formerly a powerful politician, but by the 1950s a disaffected aristocrat.

The final novel, *Agatha* (1973), is set in 1956 and concerns her relationship with her husband, Henry, and with her stepbrother, Paul, the child of Leonard and Judith. Paul is a friend of Guy Burgess and a convicted traitor for whose escape from prison Agatha pays, both financially and with a prison sentence at the end of the novel. The final scene is a confrontation between Agatha and her father-in-law, Conrad, over the morality of her actions. Her defense is a paraphrase of E. M. Forster's famous remarks about the choice between treachery toward a brother or toward a country. Her speech to Conrad is an impassioned insistence upon the subversive power of love and personal politics.

One of the problems faced by any historical novel is the negotiation of a position between the seemingly contradictory claims of the individual and of the historical forces beyond the grasp of the individual. In the trilogy this problem is compounded by the narrative reluctance to arrogate authority either about historical processes or about the contributions made by individuals to those processes. The result is a characteristic tentativeness: "What do you think Orlando would have thought coming to London for the first time in 1930? It was December. Nearly 1931. That's a year we've heard of. Would he have seen the dole queues, hunger marchers?" Arguably the presence of the Oedipus parallel lessens the pressure of historical specificity, but finally the meshing of history and myth pro-

duces an uneasy alliance which declares its uncertainty through the ambivalence of the narrative tone: "We know the story of course, so nothing need be withheld. . . . We choose a situation in the drama to expose a theme: passing curiosity must look elsewhere, we are here profoundly to contemplate eternal truths. With ritual, like the Greeks. With dream like Freud. Let us pray." What constitutes the interest of the trilogy is its awareness of these contradictions, an awareness voiced most explicitly by Graham Harper, a friend of Orlando's, but also a committed Socialist who fights and dies in the civil war in Spain. Even as the novel is busy rescuing Harper from historical obscurity and granting him a kind of fictional reality, Harper recognizes that: "I can go and do all that I have ever wanted to do which is to achieve anonymity. I can march behind another man, shooting when he shoots. . . . I can lose myself in action. But the action will not be mine it will be history's, that's why I can count on anonymity." It is also this awareness which invests all three novels with considerable power.

Critical reaction to the trilogy was mixed, but in general the reviews of the last part, *Agatha*, were favorable. By the time it was published, however, both *Orlando King* and *Orlando at the Brazen Threshold* were out of print. Colegate admits that she was depressed by this situation; in consequence she turned her energies to reviewing and an attempt to break into the television play market. Increasingly she realized that writing novels was actually what she wanted and needed to do. Thus, she wrote *News from the City of the Sun* (1979), the second of those novels which she has described as being particularly important to her. She recalls that while writing it she felt strongly that "if nobody's listening, I'm not going to shout." The result is a novel which seems to represent a new phase in her development.

The book takes its title from a biblical reference to a nonearthly paradise. The quotation on the title page continues: "For we have no continuing city; but we seek one to come." The novel traces the history and eventual collapse of a self-sufficient community established sometime before 1930 by three brothers, each with different and ultimately conflicting aims. The site of the community is an old and crumbling abbey, formerly occupied by a nonorthodox religious group. Fisher believes in nonviolent anarchism and the perfectibility of man, while Arnold advocates a variety of cooperative socialism. The third brother, Hamilton, is a recluse obsessed by the effort to restore the shattered stained glass windows of the abbey, which even in their original state were "Weakly executed pieces of

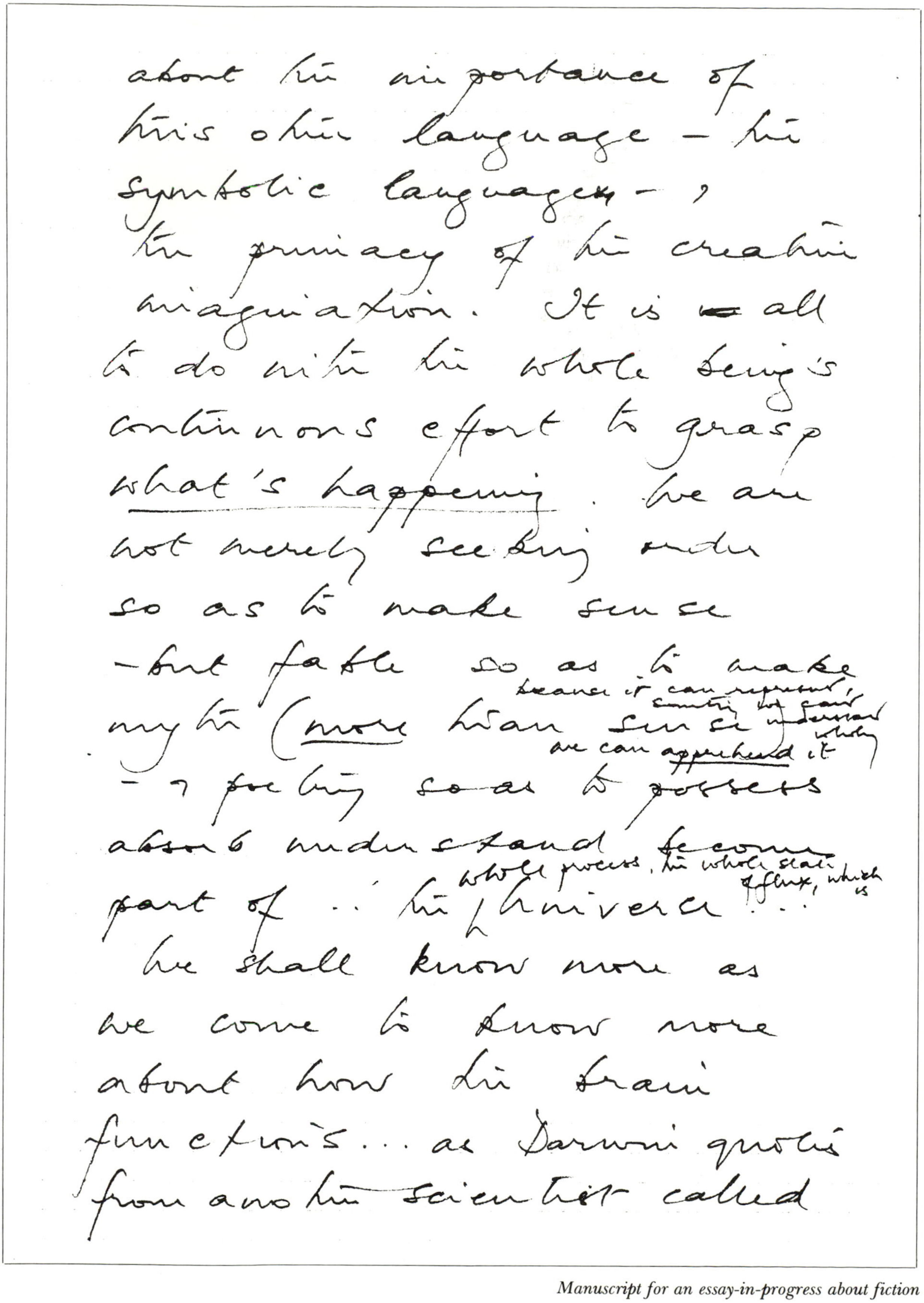

about the importance of
this other language – the
symbolic languages – ?
the primacy of the creative
imagination. It is all
to do with the whole being's
continuous effort to grasp
what's happening. We are
not merely seeking order
so as to make sense
– but fable so as to make
myth (more than sense because it can represent, something we can't understand wholly
we can apprehend it)
– & feeling so as to possess
absorb understand become
part of .. the whole process, the whole state of flux, which is the universe ..
We shall know more as
we come to know more
about how the brain
functions ... as Darwin quotes
from another scientist called

Manuscript for an essay-in-progress about fiction

Richler ... 'The dream is an involuntary kind of poetry." – "Fiction is a voluntary kind of dream".

30 mins: So we come round to some sort of answer to our question – why write – equally why read (because the reader of course re-creates what the writer writes –)

, the answer is more or less , oversimplifying grossly – because we have to have ~~we need~~ this continuous process of setting out ~~in another language~~ our deepest preoccupations in another language – the language of dream, of image, symbol, fable, parable, myth .....

Think of some of your

sentimentality, memories to the appalling taste of Fr. Augustine, the fraudulent monk who lived in the Abbey around the turn of the century." The novel spans the years between 1931 and the early 1970s. The social and political changes which occur during this time are registered by the nature of the people who arrrive at the community: from the unemployed miners in the Depression years to the hippies of the 1960s and the female revolutionaries of the early 1970s. All of these changes are observed by Dorothy Grant, who grows up near the abbey and becomes its long-standing and sympathetic witness.

What differentiates the novel from Colegate's previous work is its tone. In place of the sometimes painful involvement and uncertainty of the earlier books, the narrator of *News from the City of the Sun* is ironically detached both from the characters and from the history which weaves itself about them. The reward for detachment is confidence and assurance; no questions are asked about the status of the recreated past, and as a result it flows effortlessly. In this respect the narrative position parallels that of Dorothy. Like Vanessa Cowper in *A Man of Power*, Dorothy is a spectator of most of the events of the novel, but through this nonparticipation she preserves her freedom and is enabled to make choices about her own life at the end of the novel. Critical response to *News from the City of the Sun* focused most favorably on the novel's stylistic achievement. Reference was made to Colegate's Flaubertian "detachment" and to "the precise economy of style." In some of the reviews, however, this praise was qualified by claims that the characters in the novel seemed to exist too little in their own right and too much as illustrations of particular historical events or movements, "like figures in a historical pageant."

Colegate's most recent novel, *The Shooting Party* (1980), is also her most widely acclaimed. It was awarded the W. H. Smith Literary Award in 1981, the first novel to win it in nine years. Like *Statues in a Garden*, it is set in the months immediately prior to World War I, about which time she has remarked: "I'm fascinated by that period. The calm, unruffled surface of post-Edwardian England and everything boiling away like anything underneath."

In the wake of Vera Brittain's *Testament of Youth* (1933), the autobiographical account of an unmarried woman's experience during World War I, and the highly successful television serial *Upstairs, Downstairs*, Colegate's publisher suggested that she write a saga of the western front. Her reply to this

Dust jacket for Colegate's most recent book, the first novel in nine years to win the W. H. Smith Literary Award

suggestion is typical of her wry humor: "Not unlike God, I'm not prepared to do that to my characters. But on the other hand I've got this little idea I've had in my mind for ages and he said, to my delight, Yes, do that."

The Shooting Party is set in the Oxfordshire estate of Sir Randolph Nettleby—"Baronet. A country gentleman"—where a variety of guests assemble for a weekend shoot during the pheasant season. The action of the novel occurs both on the grounds of the estate and at the ritualized meals which interrupt the bouts of hunting. The narrative shifts between the upper-class host and guests and the people who organize their pleasure: the servants of the house and the gamekeeper and the beaters (those who rouse the game) on the estate. Most of the book is dominated by the private preoccupations of its characters: their rivalries, their love intrigues, and their concern for the seamless progress of the weekend. At the end of the novel these preoccupations are disrupted by the accidental but careless shooting of one of the beaters, an event which produces a variety of telling responses from the assembled cast.

The achievement of the novel lies partly in the skill and economy with which the characters are created and reveal themselves through dialogue. As in many of Colegate's novels, the opening is enigmatic but revealing: "You could see it as a drama all played out in a room lit by gas lamps . . . and then a fierce electric light thrown back from a room beyond, the next room, into which no-one has yet ventured, and this fierce retrospective light through the doorway makes the lamplit room seem shadowy . . . and the people, well discernibly people, but people from a long time ago, our parents and grandparents made to seem like beings from a much remoter past. . . ." For all the ease and assurance of this introduction, there is also a strong element of protective preempting in it. The past has become fictional drama and the narrative arms itself against accusations of nostalgic misrepresentation. What is more interesting is the extent to which the *characters* are aware of themselves as performers, though whether as fictional creations diverting an audience or as representatives of a class whose existence was a public act remains uncertain. In either case, the novel offers a spectacle from which both narrator and reader are completely distanced. The characters may struggle to escape, but they are forced to resign themselves to the myths which have been created around their class and their historical period. As one of the guests tells Sir Randolph, "You are part of the myth, you see. That's why you

say you don't believe in it, because you're inside it. It doesn't look the same to you, how could it?"

The narrator's collusion in the myth is demonstrated through the tendency toward caricature, evident in all the characters, but significantly acute in the portrait of Cornelius Cardew. Cardew is a Fabian who strides through the novel and the grounds of Nettleby Park, daring to challenge the mythic, unchangeable quality of the society depicted. Lest the reader attempt to escape from myth through identification with Cardew, he is made not just an ineffectual figure, but a ridiculous one through whom the narrator issues a solemn warning: "the cure could not come from a nonparticipant, from someone who was not part of the game, for how could a mere spectator expect to be listened to when he wanted to tell the players not just that they were using the wrong rules but that they were playing the wrong game?" What makes the book fascinating is the self-conscious quality of the narrative's collusion, a self-consciousness epitomized in the casual reference at the end of the novel: "By the time the next season came round a bigger shooting party had begun, in Flanders."

In addition to her novel writing, Colegate has reviewed for various literary journals, and she contributes regularly to the *Times Literary Supplement*. One of her major concerns, however, is with what she describes as "the common reader," whom she feels is not particularly well-served by such journals. In her opinion, reviewers generally are "catering more and more for academics and librarians" and do little to foster the idea of the reader-writer community in which she strongly believes. She has also been outspoken on the necessity for publishers and booksellers to make more good books available outside of London and other major cities. Undoubtedly the narrow distribution of her own books has contributed to her comparatively small readership, despite a considerable reputation in critical circles. The 1982 Penguin publication of *The Shooting Party*, however, may help to extend her reading public. She is presently at work on a tenth novel, which she has described as being "much more concerned with contemporary life." Whether this focus will result in the further consolidation of the narrative assurance which has characterized her last two novels or whether it will result in greater experimentation are open questions.

Periodical Publication:
"The Youngest of the Young," *New Review*, 4 (Spring 1978): 19-23.

Lionel Davidson

(31 March 1922-   )

Rosemarie Mroz
University of Delaware

SELECTED BOOKS: *The Night of Wenceslas* (London: Gollancz, 1960; New York: Harper, 1961);

The Rose of Tibet (London: Gollancz, 1962; New York: Harper & Row, 1962);

Soldier and Me, as David Line (New York: Harper & Row, 1965); republished as *Run for Your Life* (London: Cape, 1966);

A Long Way to Shiloh (London: Gollancz, 1966); republished as *The Menorah Men* (New York: Harper & Row, 1966);

Making Good Again (London: Cape, 1968; New York: Harper & Row, 1968);

Smith's Gazelle (London: Cape, 1971; New York: Knopf, 1971);

Mike and Me, as David Line (London: Cape, 1974);

The Sun Chemist (London: Cape, 1976; New York: Knopf, 1976);

The Chelsea Murders (London: Cape, 1978); republished as *Murder Games* (New York: Coward, McCann & Geoghegan, 1978);

Under Plum Lake (London: Cape, 1980).

Lionel Davidson is a writer of adventure stories and thrillers which have attained both commercial and critical success. While the former is not unusual for books of this type, what sets Davidson apart from other writers of action-packed "quick reads" is that his novels offer the reader more than they usually get from the genre.

Davidson is not a prolific writer, but he is a versatile one. His books are both original and entertaining; he expertly combines dialogue and descriptive prose to produce convincing, lively fiction with memorable characters and settings. His books contain interesting twists of plot, fast action, suspense, and enough historical and scientific information to add credibility. Davidson also manages to include subtle humor in his novels. Each work takes him in a slightly new direction.

Once Davidson has an idea for a novel, he spends much time researching, obtaining a command of his subject matter, before beginning to write. While formulating his plot, he looks for loopholes in the facts or forks in the road, and he considers the outcome of events if things had taken a different turn. Much of what Davidson learns during his investigations and uses in his novels, which adds dimensions of believability to the action, he often forgets afterwards.

His first novel, *The Night of Wenceslas* (1960), was awarded the Silver Quill by the Authors' Club as the most promising first novel of its year. It also received the Golden Dagger Award from the Crime Writers' Association as the best crime novel of 1960. (Davidson also received the Golden Dagger in 1967 and again in 1979; he is the only author who has won this award three times.) *A Long Way to Shiloh* (1966) was a Book Society Choice in Britain and Book-of-the-Month Club Choice in the United States. *Smith's Gazelle* (1971) proved to be another award winner, receiving the President's Prize for Literature in Israel.

Lionel Davidson was born on 31 March 1922 in a poor section of Hull in Yorkshire, England. His father, a Pole, died when Davidson was two years old, and when he was six his Russian-born mother moved with her nine children to London. He left school at age fourteen, being unable to afford any further education. He obtained a job as an office boy for a shipping firm, and then later for the *Spectator*; at fifteen, his first story was published in this paper. The story resulted in a job with a Fleet Street agency, where he both wrote and edited. He left this job to join the Navy and served in submarines in the Pacific during World War II. In 1949 Davidson married Fay Jacobs. After the war he returned to the agency post for a year and then went to Europe as a free-lance journalist.

During this time in Europe Davidson got the idea for his first novel. It was written almost as a lark, and he thought it was a failure since he heard no news of the book's progress (what delayed its publication was actually only a strike). When the book was finally published in January 1960, it became, much to Davidson's surprise, both a bestseller and an award winner. Comparisons were drawn to the works of John Buchan, Graham Greene, Kingsley Amis, and Eric Ambler.

The Night of Wenceslas opens in London where the cocky Nicholas Whistler soon finds himself tricked by a pseudo-lawyer, Stephen Cunliffe, into believing that his Canadian uncle has died and left him money. Cunliffe gives Whistler money (which he promptly spends) and then informs Whistler that it was all a hoax; a favor is owed. Nicholas next finds himself on the way to Prague where he is to visit some glassworks and obtain what he believes to be a formula for unbreakable table glass. Cunliffe has made all the necessary arrangements and Nicholas is given a carefully planned itinerary. Everything runs smoothly except that the formula Nicholas returns with is incomplete. He must return to Prague. This time complications arise and Nicholas discovers that he is smuggling formulas of greater importance than any for special glass. The state security police go after him and there is an exciting and comical chase scene in the middle of a People's Festival as Nicholas runs to the British Embassy, where he is interrogated and eventually released.

Although the use of a will in the initial trickery and the mix-up of maps during the smuggling are perhaps trite, Davidson provides enough twists to keep the reader, along with Nicholas, guessing

about the intentions and involvement of others in both London and Prague. The novel does not dwell on descriptions, but the setting is nonetheless easily visualized, as are the characters. Nicholas sees in Prague the familiar sights of his youth in the new setting after the Communist takeover. Davidson visited Prague in 1947 and again in 1955; therefore, he has had the before-and-after experience that the reader witnesses through Nicholas's eyes.

During the time that Davidson believed his first novel to be a failure, he began a second thriller, primarily for commercial reasons. He had 30,000 to 40,000 words already written when *The Night of Wenceslas* was finally published. He completed his second book, *The Rose of Tibet*, not especially caring for it; but in 1962 when it was published, it became another bestseller. It is a first-class adventure story that takes place (as the title suggests) in the Orient. The novel is written as a frame tale, with sections devoted to the author's descriptions of his source and the writing process. Although the frame is fictional, it helps make the action seem closer to actual fact. The different levels of reality that the technique provides make the novel all the more entertaining.

The story revolves around Charles Houston's search for his half-brother, a member of a film crew,

THE ROSE OF TIBET

"Is Lionel Davidson today's Rider Haggard? His novel has all the excitement of 'She' and 'King Solomon's Mines'"
—*Daphne du Maurier*

LIONEL DAVIDSON

Dust jacket for Davidson's best-selling thriller set in the Orient

245

305

was only because of the illusion of height. The thing to do was to put this illusion out of mind. I was simply having this slow sort of walk along a ledge a few feet off the ground, and the only difficulty was ~~this kind of wall that might topple you off~~ the proximity of the wall. It wasn't a real difficulty ~~if you weren't careful. Not that it would, of course~~; plenty of room, if somewhat smooth now and less secure underfoot. Perhaps it would be best, all things considered, if I turned in to the wall and went sideways. No difficulty at all, then; how could there be?

I turned in to the wall and went sideways, arms outstretched on the rock. There was no difficulty except the mental one of accepting that I was just a few feet off the ground. The sudden effort required from the right leg ~~now~~ indicated quite clearly now that I was climbing, and climbing very steeply. I shuffled sideways for a few minutes ~~or two~~ more, and stopped for a breather, and incautiously looked down between ~~through~~ my legs, and saw the gorge about two miles below and nearly fell off.

I leaned sickeningly in, head on the rock, and felt it lurching and wheeling as I fought the screaming horrors of vertigo. ~~I'd had a sharp mental vision of myself stuck there~~ I was stuck on the sheer rock face like a fly on the wall. ~~I'd been sick once x~~ My knees were trembling, delicate fly's knees, and they'd give in a moment and I'd drop, drop, drop.

They were giving. I could feel them giving. There was nothing to hold on to, nothing to lean in ~~on~~ to. The rock ~~seemed to be~~ itself was leaning out, and I was leaning out with it, stuck there ~~only~~ for seconds only ~~by~~ by tactile adhesion, by the ~~sweaty~~ pads on my fingers, by the film of sweat ...

The rock swung, and I fought it, and leaned in again and I could lean in with it, shaking all over, wet with sweat, ~~and~~ suddenly very cold. I could hear my teeth rattling, and above it the calm hiss of the wind.

Revised typescript for A Long Way to Shiloh

who is missing in Tibet. Houston enters the country illegally and winds up in the village of Yamdring where his brother is being held in the monastery. He finds himself subject to Tibetan prophecies and superstitions; he is at first feared as a reincarnation of an evil Chinese, Hu Tzung, and later exalted as a trulku (Hu Tzung's alter ego). He also falls in love with the abbess, Mei-Hua. A Chinese invasion compels Houston to flee along with the abbess (and her emeralds), a few villagers, and the other Europeans. They soon find themselves confronted with not only foreign forces but also those of nature: extremes of geography, fierce winter weather, and a grumpy bear. Most of the party is lost. Houston finally makes it back to England missing an arm, the abbess, and his brother—but a very wealthy man.

Davidson visited Israel and thought that it would provide a good setting for a novel; *A Long Way to Shiloh*, another thriller-adventure novel, takes place there. Dr. Casper Laing, an English archaeologist, has been asked to help in the search for an old and valuable menorah. Going on scanty information from an ancient scroll, Laing and his helpers try to find the menorah before the Arabs do; tension mounts as the mystery is cleverly unravelled. J. T. Winterich in the *Saturday Review* said that the essential historical, social, political, and religious backgrounds are summarized without detracting from the story, and he referred to the novel as more than a "fictionized documentary."

A Long Way to Shiloh (republished in the United States as *The Menorah Men*) was number one on the best-seller list for most of the summer of 1966, a fact demonstrating public acclaim for Davidson's third novel. Davidson was pleased. His ability to blend fact and fiction smoothly, as well as his ability to capture the spirit of people and place, makes the book more than simply a commercial success.

The novel that followed, *Making Good Again* (1968), takes the reader to an altogether new setting, as Davidson attempts to capture the spirit of postwar Germany. The book deals with the current feelings in Germany towards Jews, the Holocaust, and Nazism, and, as the title implies, the possibility of making good again. The theme is revealed through a complicated plot as three lawyers, James Raison (an Englishman), Yonah Grunwald (a sickly, modern Shylock and concentration camp survivor, coming now from Israel), and Heinz Haffner (an impotent German) attempt to sort out a compensation case involving the fortune of Helmut Bamberger, a wealthy Jewish banker who vanished during the war. The Swiss bank that holds the for-

tune insists on proof that Bamberger is in fact dead before it will release any of the funds. As the lawyers wrestle with the dilemma, Davidson reveals some of the different attitudes found in the modern world: lingering anti-Semitism and fascism, guilt, the desire to provide restitution and the efforts towards that end, as well as the ignorance and confused feelings of the post-war generation. A moving scene, Grunwald's visit to the site of a concentration camp, accentuates the more somber side of the novel. *Making Good Again*, however, is not without the usual women and humor: Raison's affair with Haffner's daughter, Elke; the antics of her fascist aunt, Magda; and the opening scenes in the London underground provide comedy.

Making Good Again marks Davidson's first attempt to write a novel of a more serious nature. Less entertaining and not quite as successful as his first three novels, owing in part to its theme and somewhat cumbersome plot—as many reviewers noted—the novel's message still comes across and it succeeds in provoking thought on a touchy topic.

After writing this novel, Davidson moved in 1968 with his wife, Fay, and their two sons to Israel, where they lived for the next ten years. Davidson sometimes found it strange to be writing in English in a foreign country, but Israel proved to be what he calls a creative place, and his next two novels were written and set there.

The first one shows Davidson taking still another direction. *Smith's Gazelle*, an allegorical fable, is about a deformed Bedouin shepherd, Hamud, who, after avenging his wife's murder, seeks shelter in a ravine near the Golan cliffs. There he discovers a rare (and pregnant) gazelle. A superstitious man, he believes himself chosen to oversee the propagation of this delicate species. He works in the ravine, transforming it into a self-contained unit for the gazelles and himself, separate from the problems of the Israeli and Syrian civilizations that surround it. Two young boys, an Arab (Musallem) and an extraordinary, mischievous, and bright Jew (Jonathan), accidentally meet, reconcile their differences, and enter the crazy shepherd's world. The onset of the Six-day War disrupts their normal routine, the presence of the gazelles is discovered, and an attempt is made to move them from the ravine. The story ends with the escape and destruction (by land mines) of almost the whole herd, with the exception of one male and one female that disappear over the horizon. Steven Kroll in *Book World* suggested that the gazelles are a symbol of the Israelis' survival as a people.

The book is written in a simple, clear style.

One of its greatest merits is the appreciation it gives the reader for the variety of life-styles and peoples who claim the Holy Land as their homeland. In spite of the violence and turmoil that surround its events, the book, with its zany characters and storyline, is delightful, particularly in its treatment of the world of natural beauty.

The second of Davidson's novels written while he was residing in Israel, *The Sun Chemist* (1976), is a thriller which he researched at the Weizmann Institute. It is based on the work of Dr. Chaim Weizmann, scientist, founder of the state of Israel, and its former president. When Davidson stumbled across a second-hand copy of Weizmann's autobiography in Tel Aviv, he opened it to a section on oil research and decided to build a story around it (at that time oil and energy were much in the news). The result was a story close to fact. Since it was based on real events, Davidson decided to use names of real people in this fictional work.

Igor Druyanov relates the story of his editing of the late Chaim Weizmann's papers for the years 1931 to 1935. As information is pieced together, it becomes almost a detective story, and the reader is kept in suspense until the puzzle begins to take shape, revealing bits of data from Weizmann's work on a cheap energy source from the fermentation of sweet potatoes. The information Igor collects proves to be extremely valuable, and he finds himself becoming fearful, not without cause. The story's denouement is a night chase in the ruins of an old fortress. Igor's pursuer turns out to be a scientist, Ham Wyke, a candidate for the Nobel prize, whose chances will be ruined by the information Igor is uncovering. As with his other works, critical reception was mostly positive.

Davidson's next novel, *The Chelsea Murders* (1978), was inspired by the many wall plaques of famous former Chelsea residents that he observed on a trip back to England. He wanted to write a murder story that somehow tied in with these historic markers. Initially he had some difficulties with the plot, but ultimately he had fun writing this book that mocks the murder mystery genre of which it is part. A few pages into the book the reader witnesses the first of several frightening and gruesome murders. Suspicion is cast primarily on three young men involved in making a bizarre film. The police and a reporter, Mary Mooney, independently seek the killer. Clues come to the police as fragments of poetry by notables whose initials correspond to those of the victims. The reader is kept in the dark until the killer is apprehended; the pace slows as the murderer's story and motives are explained. At the novel's end there is an unsolved and apparently unrelated murder, an extra little twist that Davidson includes to poke fun at detective stories and murder mysteries.

Besides his earlier work as a journalist and later work as a novelist, Davidson has been involved with adapting screenplays and writing filmscripts. He has also written children's stories (under the pseudonym David Line). His second, *Mike and Me*, was not published in the United States because it dealt with British institutions unfamiliar to an American audience. Most recently, Davidson has had published another children's story, *Under Plum Lake* (1980), which appeared under his real name. He considers it his best book. It was difficult to write, he says, because it is told by a child as he ventures into the fantasy world of Egon and because it contains many philosophical thoughts. He rewrote it nearly a dozen times over a period of two years. Although published to appeal to adults as well as children (in the vein of Tolkien), it is, Davidson says, simply (but not simple-mindedly) a high-level children's story without hidden meanings. It is characteristically imaginative, different, and pleasing to read.

Davidson, currently living in England, hopes to write more about Israel, a series of thematically linked short stories, and another adventure story. His versatility, originality, and narrative skills, and (as he claims, not unjustifiably) his "knack for action" will undoubtedly result in the success of whatever he chooses to tackle next.

Margaret Thomson Davis

(24 May 1926-   )

Patrick Lyons
University of Glasgow

BOOKS: *The Breadmakers* (London: Allison &
Busby, 1972);
A Baby Might Be Crying (London: Allison & Busby,
1973);
A Sort of Peace (London: Allison & Busby, 1973);
The Prisoner (London: Allison & Busby, 1974);
The Prince and the Tobacco Lords (London: Allison &
Busby, 1976);
Roots of Bondage (London: Allison & Busby, 1977);
Scorpion in the Fire (London: Allison & Busby, 1977);
The Dark Side of Pleasure (London: Allison & Busby,
1981);
The Making of a Novelist (London & New York: Alli-
son & Busby, 1981).

Margaret Thomson Davis's novels have centered on Glasgow, Scotland's largest city, a city that
has tempted few novelists. That antiurban strain
which can narrow the English novel may exert no
comparable force on Scotland, but other Scottish
writers have not found their own cities as persistently rewarding as she has. The case against Glasgow has been put most vehemently, as if the city can
prove especially uncooperative when there is imaginative work to be done: the Glasgow painter and
playwright Alasdair Grey, in his novel *Lanark*
(1981), renamed his city "Unthank"; the poet Hugh
MacDiarmuid raged, frequently and furiously, at
what he saw as the city's "drivelling imbecilities," its

contentment with the image of itself in the dull mirror of sociologists' commentaries, its positive glee in the reductive simplicities of "Auld Lang Syne" and pawky music-hall sentimentality, at what might be summarized as resistance to any imaginative transformation. Aware of the challenge in this assessment, Davis appears to relish a head-on encounter: "right from the start," her autobiographical *The Making of a Novelist* (1981) says, "I felt a need to portray the character of Glasgow." Invoking as the novelist's motto James's insistence on "the power to guess the unseen from the seen," she goes on to recount how composing from the details of place and circumstance, prejudices and furniture precisely recorded, could eventually provide "the thrill of having made a whole new world." She summarizes her version of truth in Alfred Hitchcock's phrase "like real life with the dull bits cut out." The Glasgow of her novels is, as Glasgow has been in her life, a character as much as a setting, and often a particularly troublesome character, ever ready to retell a story in its way, so that independence is impossible without either challenge or some judicious accommodation.

Glasgow has been home for Margaret Thomson Davis—apart from a period of evacuation during the war—since she was three. Samuel Thomson, her father, had been a railway employee in Bathgate (in the Eastern Lowlands of Scotland) where she was born; in Glasgow he worked as a clerk and had an evening job in a local library. Stimulus to be a storyteller came from the tales with which he amused his children in the evenings, but ample discouragement from any ambition to set stories on paper was part of the ethos of working-class Glasgow. "Writers were a different breed from us. . . . They lived in a different world . . . far removed from the tenement flat in Glasgow in which we lived. For anyone in such an environment to have writing pretensions was treated with the utmost suspicion. More than that, it aroused in friends, neighbours and relations, acute embarrassment, shame, discomfort, and downright hostility."

She was to learn later how other natives of her city had shared the "obsession for committing words to paper" and had been discouraged at the start by the world they inhabited: one, she recalls, became disheartened on finding that "no one he knows regards writing as work." Her first attempt to move in a world where books were not improper showed more canniness; sidestepping the Puritan preference for work over fiction, at the age of fourteen she secured a job in a bookshop; her mother persuaded her not to take up writing as it

would not be "respectable." And years afterward, when she was in her late thirties and had been married once, her first announcement that her work had been accepted by a publisher "was met by total and utter silence. Eventually my mother, or someone, remarked on the weather. . . . I felt terribly ashamed."

The Making of a Novelist transforms as it records this background, hindsight and some maxims from other writers turning what might otherwise be recalled with bitterness into positive encouragement. "Respectability" can be said to have developed a storyteller's skill: deprived of a present one poverty-stricken Christmas when her mother had spent what there was to spend on a present for her brother, it was still necessary to save face and family decency; so, young Margaret told other children that her present had been a chocolate handbag, which contained a chocolate purse full of chocolate money. (This was a clever story; no proof could have been demanded because, as any wise child knows, in a poor world chocolate must be devoured immediately.) A novelist is not poorer for firsthand lessons in "the difference between what people say—the image they project of themselves—and what they *do* and *are*." Even deep-seated and lasting pain—"the feeling that my mother hated and rejected me"—can have its benefit, once Tolstoy's proclamation that "real art depends first on feeling" is recalled: "so my mother brought to intense life my instincts and my emotions." The emphasis is on invention, and there is distinct unwillingness to be seduced to masochism, or to a reductive reading of how a novelist works with suffering. Davis cites an anonymous friend who lists instances where women in her novels have felt rejected: in *The Breadmakers* trilogy (1972-1973), for instance, Catriona is hated by her mother and marries a widower still in love with the memory of his first wife; Madge is married to a Don Juan; and Julie's mother-in-law hates and rejects her; Celia, the eponymous *Prisoner* (1974), is married to a man in love with Owen, his business partner; Regina, in the novels of Davis's eighteenth-century trilogy, is abandoned by her husband and rejected by her mother; and Augusta, her nineteenth-century heroine, is thrown out from home by her mother and then is unwanted by her husband. Their stories turn out differently, or, as Davis comments wryly, "There's more, however."

Her view is that "without conflict there's no story," and that the novelist must know desire and obstruction, the ways to "trap the characters in the conflict." This could all be learned in her parents' household—"a continuous battle-ground." Davis's father was a committed atheist, her mother given to Christian pieties. Her father cherished a splendid hide chair, a private space where he could think and read; her mother knew how to impede these attempts "to hang on to a bit of himself," most effectively by littering his chair with linen for the wash. When the writer's younger brother died in early manhood, her mother clung to his widow while blaming her husband for a death he could in no way have prevented. "They fought tooth and nail until the day he died." Then her mother, in public still a cheerful woman who played the piano at parties (she was a trained musician who had squandered her talent), became an anxiety-ridden widow, dependent on her daughter, terrified to be alone, but ready to joke with strangers even when death was imminent. Recording this as the novelist's gain results in a narrative sorry for everyone except its author, a perspective that reappears in her novels, and might account for their breadth and their compassion.

Although she had begun writing stories when she was sixteen, Davis kept this activity to herself until, when in her late thirties, she joined the Glasgow Writers' Club. She entered a story in a BBC competition, it was broadcast, and an agent became interested in her work. Further stories were translated and broadcast overseas, in Scandinavia, Switzerland, and Australia, for example. She set out to understand what she calls "the market-place of publishing" by studying magazines, avidly reading "agony columns" to discover what might interest different readerships. At the same time, she worked at a variety of jobs, prompted by curiosity about how differently people lived. Her stories became a technical apprenticeship, sometimes a matter of understanding different editors. ("You had to learn to do it *their* way.")

It was a training that would, later, buy her some freedom: she learned how to write popular romance, and still occasionally writes romantic fiction under a pseudonym for easy money. Her summary of what the short story requires of a writer suggests she was beginning to feel limited by that medium: "either the situation in which the characters are placed undergoes a change, or the characters adapt to fit the situation. If no change occurs, then it is a sketch, not a story . . . the short-story illuminates rather than develops. (A novel develops)."

Margaret Thomson divorced her first husband, George Baillie, whom she had married in 1951. In 1958 she married Graham Davis, her pres-

ent husband. As well as rearing Kenneth Baillie, her son from her first marriage, she reared her stepson by her second marriage, cared for her widowed mother, and ran the Davis household. For most of the 1960s, while both the children were young, her free time for writing was limited, and she continued to concentrate on short stories.

Her decision to embark on a novel came at a conference at the Writers' Centre, Swanwick (where she is now a regular lecturer). It sounds like a simple decision: "If I can get short work into print, I can get long work into print." Her account of what happened next is one of hard work. Determined to write about Glasgow, about working-class poverty and the laughter hardship breeds, she decided to set the novel in a fictional part of Glasgow, Farmbank, which is similar to the districts of Govan and Balornock. A bakehouse suggested itself as a place where people meet and gave her a title: *The Breadmakers* (1972). She remembered hearing of a fair in Govan in 1936 and took that year as her starting point, making her heroine, Catriona, sixteen years old (older than Davis had been at that time). She talked to bakers and then talked to people who worked for bakers. She was delighted to find that they saw bakers differently from the often smug way bakers liked to see themselves. This assessment gave her the start for old Duncan MacNair, the bullying master baker. She began to keep notebooks, one for each character as she went on inventing, each a full biography itself, with ample supporting detail the novel was never to incorporate. With her conviction that there must be conflict, and a sense that "one must push characters to their limits," she continued to invent on the basis of contrast: Catriona begins the novel dreaming that marriage will make her safe and secure; Melvin, the man she is to marry, is her opposite, an aggressive and conceited bully whose cruelty feeds on her insecurity. In contrast to Melvin, Davis invented Jimmy, a sensitive confectioner's apprentice who dreams of becoming a concert pianist. Davis based his character, to an extent, on her brother, who had taught himself piano; another character, Rab, was in part based on her father. Her sense that she was becoming bound to models prompted further invention, and in contrast to Sammy, a pacifist, she developed Alec, a soldier.

The novel was a study of women in wartime. Because *The Breadmakers* told only part of the story, Davis decided to expand her work into a trilogy, continuing with *A Baby Might Be Crying* and *A Sort of Peace* (both published in 1973). More notebooks were filled to span the city: "By the time I came to

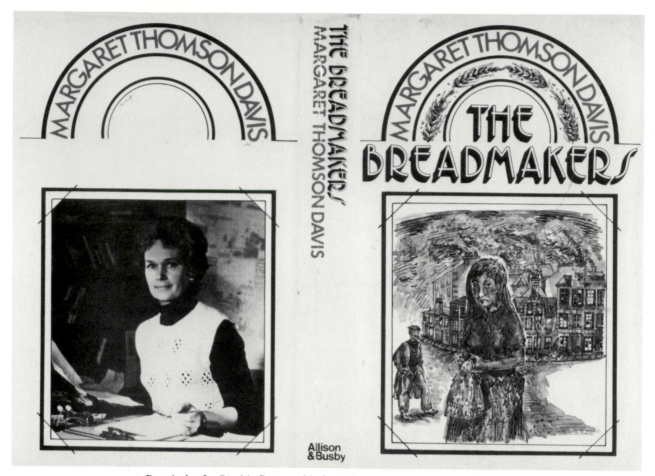

Dust jacket for Davis's first novel in her trilogy about women in wartime

the third book . . . I hadn't yet characterised the East side and the West side. . . ." To her heroines Catriona and Madge (one tormented by her husband, the other neglected), she added Julie, a girl from the Gorbals, who will marry Alec and find herself ostracized by his West End mother. A fourth woman, Sarah, developed in the course of writing the novels, independently of the notebooks; she is driven to murder and becomes the center of a fraught trial scene. All these narrative strands are interwoven and carried through with remarkable skill, from crisis to crisis, with considerable intensity and often with broad (and sometimes earthy) humor. Minor flaws are occasioned by the need to provide each separate volume with a stopping place; but an overall assurance is particularly evident in the deft management of the crowd scenes—the 1938 Empire Exhibition, Victory Night in George Square, for instance—which catch the sense of individuals suddenly become anonymous, finding themselves part of a city rather than a village.

Before the entire trilogy appeared, a curious coincidence led Davis to change her residence. While researching the locality where Julie's mother-in-law was to live, she had fallen into conversation with a woman who lived in Glasgow's West End. When her mother's health required that she move to a home in that locality, Davis heard from her friend in the West End of a flat for sale nearby. It so corresponded to the one she had invented for her novel that she moved there (from Bearsden, an outlying suburb). That these circumstances prompted her to write a novel set in Bearsden is not altogether surprising: her choice of wartime Glasgow for her first novel corresponded with the period in her lifetime when she had been absent from a place she knew well. Her autobiography describes people in Bearsden as "so well-fed, so well-dressed, so sure of themselves in their comfortable routines . . . [cushioned] from any disturbing ripples," and *The Prisoner* studies life in such a cage. Appropriately, it is a short, concentrated piece, almost a novella, without the scope her trilogy had enjoyed.

Davis has since described Celia, the central

figure in *The Prisoner*, as "a very frustrated woman who thinks about nothing but sex all the time." With some wit, but little humor, the novel begins with Celia sitting on a park bench, speculating angrily that a man nearby might be trying to pick her up, and then—when this proves incorrect—continuing to sit mesmerized while another man touches her leg, before eventually walking away to enjoy self-righteous disgust at the way men behave. Endlessly attentive to her hair and clothes, Celia is unaware that her husband, who was a young officer when they married, has for years been sexually involved with a man he met while a prisoner of war, now his business partner. Several subplots fail to bring any resolution; Celia finally discovers Peter (her husband) in bed with his partner, Owen, and sets fire to their home, from which she flees in confusion. Some measure of the novel's daring is that a considerable number of its first reviewers could not bring themselves to mention the homosexual love that underlies it. In no sense radical—in one scene, Celia feels humiliated as Owen constantly addresses her as "girlie," although she can give herself no clear reason why this should be taunting, or why it should embarrass her husband—the homosexual love is nonetheless presented with some sympathy; it is love as tormented and fevered as Celia becomes through her dedication to "keeping up appearances."

In its concentration on a narrower world than that explored in her first trilogy, *The Prisoner* considerably sharpens Davis's acute attention to the details that make up social surfaces, details that betoken obsession and that can indicate where a crack will appear. As Celia notices flowers arranged in her hall, she guesses (correctly) that Owen has come to visit, and can grasp his unease from the elaborateness of the flowers, hinting that there has been some offense whose nature she cannot begin to understand. To develop its study of ignorance that possesses some awareness, some peripheral vision, point of view is also managed with more artfulness. The compassionate and generous sweep of *The Breadmakers* allowed some latitude, and one after another its various characters occupy the center of consciousness in a sympathetic manner. With *The Prisoner*, Celia's viewpoint dominates, and her claustrophobia is emphasized as she shifts into reminiscences, at first in nostalgic indulgence, then less voluntarily, as her unease is confirmed by a past that is only comfortable in short and well-edited selections. A few chapters are told through other characters, but each brief excursus ends in return to Celia, more and more deeply absorbed in her in-

vented world, her genteel prison.

One particularly telling shift begins as she fantasizes the gallantry of a local politician from a rougher part of the city—McGurk, whose son and Celia's schoolgirl daughter want to marry because the girl is pregnant—imagining his sexual yearning for her as he discusses the plight of their children over lunch, and then provides her with a seat in the public gallery of the local council chamber. As the council debate continues, he becomes aware of, and horrified at, Celia's callow lust, and he returns home to his sluttish wife, relieved to escape from the hothouse Celia was beginning to fashion around him. Only later does she realize he is not attracted to her in the way she had been imagining, and her horror grows as she registers what the reader already knows. There is no room in *The Prisoner* for pain to heal; Julie, in *A Sort of Peace*, established friendship with her mother-in-law once her child was born; Celia can only insist her daughter have an abortion, and it is left to the McGurks to offer an alternative to the children. While humor was bounteous in the trilogy, the little humor allowed in *The Prisoner* has a sour edge: Mrs. McGurk's coarse tongue; her unwillingness to wash laundry, which drives her more fastidious husband to buy nylon shirts he can rinse out each night in secret. The ending, too, is more uncompromising and cheerless, despite some rhetoric on Celia's part: she knows no other world that can accommodate her, and she has shown no skill at building accommodation for herself yet she has set fire to her prison-house.

The technical gains benefited Davis's next project, which explored some of the areas *The Prisoner* had touched. Again taking the format of a trilogy, with the increase in scope she knew it could offer, she turned to examine Glasgow in another guise, as an eighteenth-century city, a world she could only know at some distance.

The Prince and the Tobacco Lords (1976) begins with a state of siege in the background. The prince is the Stuart pretender to the English throne; the tobacco lords are the merchants who trade from and govern Glasgow, and who favor Hanoverian rule for Scotland and England, because it fosters their trade and their profits. The novel opens in 1745 with a Highland army mustered by the prince threatening to sack Glasgow unless the merchants pay for uniforms for the entire army. The army is billeted in the city, and the novel examines the reaction to invasion. The previous novel was concerned with the threatening impact of a devious invasion of domestic comfort, but with invasion relegated to a background space, there is greater scope for comedy: in one hilarious scene, for instance, mourners on their way to a funeral become so drunk they forget the body. An unusual aspect of eighteenth-century Glasgow, which may have its origins in Scotland's strong historic links with continental Europe rather than with England, was that its tenement dwellings were inhabited by a mix of social classes: a single building might have gentry on one floor, their servants on another, the poor in a basement, and a beggar sleeping under the common staircase. This arrangement allows Davis to draw together a group of characters in the way the bakehouse gave her common ground for the characters in *The Breadmakers*; in *The Prisoner*, class barriers were implicit, in the self-defenses of Bearsden; the housing arrangements of the earlier century allow class differences to be presented more vividly, through contrasts among a group living in close proximity. What the political and social background provides is immediate potential for conflict.

The central concerns of this trilogy are love and treachery, intertwined but open to exploration and not, as in *The Prisoner*, frozen. There is much tenderness in the treatment of affection between brother and sister. Regina and Gavin are the children of a Highland woman, reduced to living in a Glasgow hovel. Brought to an extreme state by poverty and humiliation, the girl is rejected by her mother, whereupon her brother, Gavin, takes up employment in the service of a wealthy merchant, Adam Ramsey, to care for his sister. Although Ramsey is loyal to the English cause, his daughter, Annabella, is swept up in the sheer excitement the invading troops bring to the city, and she follows a French officer (with whom she gets drunk) to Inverness. Regina is responsible for the death of Annabella's lover and, terrified of Annabella's vengeance, flees to America disguised as a boy. In Virginia, she marries a plantation owner, but continues to fear that her happiness will be shattered, somehow, by Annabella. As in Davis's earlier studies of insecurity, Regina's has a real basis: Annabella has married a staid minister of the church, and already is on her way to Virginia, where she will catch up with Regina. Where *The Prisoner* had ended in flight, the final volumes of this trilogy explore whether old jealousies and old treacheries can be escaped. Quin, a Glasgow beggar, becomes a traveling companion and part-time narrator. (Like Sarah in the earlier trilogy, he is a character who developed independently of Davis's preliminary re-

search and planning notebooks; unlike Sarah, he is a survivor, which may indicate the author's growing confidence in the sheer capacity to write.) Although this use of multiple narrators marks a shift away from the claustrophobic single point of view approach, flight is only a partial resolution: even the ship to America bears the past in its name, *The Glasgow Lass*, and the stories begun in the city's conflicts are played out to the end.

Persistent in Davis's work, the sense of a community that imposes a destiny on the individuals who belong to it most afflicts her women. The opening of one chapter of *The Breadmakers* illustrates this perception:

> The Band of Jesus was having a special meeting in the front room. The proper meeting hall was in town in Dundas Street, a forbidding Victorian building of sooty black stone above the entrance of which a neon sign made a startling contrast, with bright busy letters telling the people of Glasgow that Christ died for their sins.
>
> Special meetings of the Matrons, however, were held in the front room. The opening hymn wailed loud and long, some voices strong, others continually stumbling. . . .
>
> Catriona felt as if there were a big placard hanging round her neck, shouting to the world in foot-high letters, IT IS ALL MY FAULT!

Catriona's independence is at stake, and it is about to be crushed unless there can be some defiance of the way the community reads events, some other way to tell the story. And this passage also shows, in brief, that the community imposes because it too is evading conflict within: not only do the Matrons differ in ability to sing, they hive off separately, suggesting division that cannot wholly be recognized, joining voices where other unity and coherence is missing, while distress remains private. In her picture of a city that is an attenuated community, built around internal barriers that are known but not always admitted to exist, Davis taps a source of conflict richer and less easy to resolve than simplistic accounts of lonely souls pitted against united opposition.

Her most recent work has continued to hunt out new contexts in which to explore this world. *The Dark Side of Pleasure* (1981), which reaches back into her father's experience with the railways, is set in the early nineteenth century, when railways were being extended across Scotland. Although shifting location more frequently, if less dramatically, than her eighteenth-century sequence, the narrative centers on Glasgow, where its heroine has to remap the limits of her life, while the railway lines are being mapped onto Scotland. Its main innovation is a more intense presentation of violence between men: a contest between two pugilists, before Queensbury rules had been devised, develops in brutality to gratify gloating spectators; a scene in a public house has spectators again gloating at suffering as animals fight for survival in a rat pit. The horror built up in these scenes may reflect Davis's Quaker pacifism. Awaiting publication, "A Very Civilised Man" returns to contemporary material; although the city in which it is set remains anonymous, the title suggests that concern with the demands made by public canons of decency, which can prove ambiguous in their effects, remains a central theme.

In *The Making of a Novelist*, Davis describes other projects awaiting publication. One is a novel based on diaries kept by her father prior to 1913, exploring a Scotland which has touched her directly, although she did not inhabit it. Another is a contemporary work centered on a lodging house with tenants as diverse as those of her eighteenth-century tenement. To prepare for this novel, she has been moving among immigrant communities, and has been befriended by several Pakistani families: the absence of racial prejudice in Glasgow (other than at football games against English teams) makes immigrants ideal outsiders (like Quin the beggar), observing the conflicts of the world to which they find themselves adapting. Davis has been particularly fascinated by the older women, who had been "hidden in the burkah [a heavy tentlike garment with just a tiny grating-type window for the eyes to peer out] all their lives before coming here." From a life where "nobody could see you, no need to smile" the protective covering was "ripped off in a strange land." Her phrasing here suggests how violence, and violation, may lurk where there are no tell-tale marks, and can shift the angle of vision on what might otherwise be a familiar world.

In less than ten years as a novelist, Davis has won considerable popular success. A 1980 survey by the Library Association of England found that her novels were, in one week, borrowed more frequently from public lending-libraries than those of any other author. Her success outside Scotland continues to surprise her: *The Breadmakers* trilogy sold successfully in paperback in the United States as well as in Britain; and in 1980 it was republished in hardback, presumably so that libraries might replace worn-out copies. It has become a reviewers' cliche to compare her with Catherine Cookson, although Davis's sales are far from the millions of copies that bring royalties to the Teesside writer. Though both are sometimes counted as "regional" writers, Cookson's interest in specific regionalism is confined to details of idiom, where Davis has been concerned to explore her specific city from new and even daunting perspectives. They share a toughness, a readership that will accept passion shown in adversity, not in the glamorous realms of romance. In tackling a social web that has cowed other writers, Davis is well on the road to building a world all her own.

Margaret Drabble
(5 June 1939-   )

Barbara C. Millard
La Salle College

BOOKS: *A Summer Bird-Cage* (London: Weidenfeld & Nicolson, 1963; New York: Morrow, 1964);

The Garrick Year (London: Weidenfeld & Nicolson, 1964; New York: Morrow, 1965);

The Millstone (London: Weidenfeld & Nicolson, 1965; New York: Morrow, 1966); republished as *Thank You All Very Much* (New York: New American Library, 1969);

Wordsworth (London: Evans Bros., 1966; New York: Arco Literary Critiques, 1969);

Jerusalem the Golden (London: Weidenfeld & Nicolson, 1967; New York: Morrow, 1967);

The Waterfall (London: Weidenfeld & Nicolson, 1969; New York: Knopf, 1969);

The Needle's Eye (London: Weidenfeld & Nicolson, 1972; New York: Knopf, 1972);

Virginia Woolf: A Personal Debt (London: Aloe Editions, 1973);

Arnold Bennett: A Biography (London: Weidenfeld & Nicolson, 1974; New York: Knopf, 1974);

The Realms of Gold (London: Weidenfeld & Nicolson, 1975; New York: Knopf, 1975);

The Ice Age (London: Weidenfeld & Nicolson, 1977; New York: Knopf, 1977);

For Queen and Country: Britain in the Victorian Age (London: Deutsch, 1978; New York: Seabury Press, 1979);

A Writer's Britain: Landscape in Literature, text by Drabble and photographs by Jorge Lewinsky (London: Thames and Hudson, 1979; New York: Knopf, 1979);

The Middle Ground (London: Weidenfeld & Nicolson, 1980; New York: Knopf, 1980).

Margaret Drabble's rise as one of the most important and well-known British novelists writing today has been steady and sure. She has received serious attention in Great Britain since the appearance of her first novel, and since the publication of *The Needle's Eye* (1972) she has established an impressive reputation in America as well. Behind her is a solid body of work including several volumes of criticism and biography, television and film scripts, and numerous pieces of short fiction and journalism, in addition to the nine novels which have

brought her both popularity and critical acclaim. She is a traditionalist in form and a pioneer in subject. From her first novel, written immediately after graduation from Cambridge, Drabble has recorded the conflicting sensibilities of the "new," educated woman seeking her place in the modern world. Her heroines are self-aware, articulate, intelligent, career-concerned; they are also wives and mothers caring for and redeemed by their children, while desirous of emotional, moral, and economic autonomy.

Drabble's fiction has grown in scope, richness, and sophistication, as have her female protagonists. Her angle of vision has shifted from the psychological interiors of single female characters to omniscient panoramas of men and women struggling with the ambiguities of life in contemporary Britain. As Elaine Showalter has observed, Drabble's early concern with self-analysis and female realism has combined with twentieth-century sociological and political issues. While her literary credo deliberately reflects her admiration for the "Great Tradition" of the British novel, her particular contribution to the novel emerges from her experience of the human situation and her reflection on it. "I try to confront the problems that confront me . . . but I now find myself increasingly interested by and able to tackle more general subjects," she has said recently. "I think literature is one of the ways of mapping out territories and problems. I'm trying to find out where we are going." Consequently, Drabble has explored the individual's search for identity; the particular self-awareness of womanhood; the individual's relationship with his own and his country's past; the interaction of fate, chance, and character; and the guilt and anxieties of the liberal conscience. In her role as chronicler of contemporary Britain, Drabble aims in her fiction for the amplitude, centrality, and autonomy of the major novelist.

The second of four children, Margaret Drabble was born in Sheffield, Yorkshire, on 5 June 1939 to Kathleen Bloor and John Frederick Drabble. Her family and she have since moved south, but Drabble's strong ties to the region of her birth are reflected in her recent work. Her family tradition claims kinship with Arnold Bennett, and Drabble identifies with him in her roots: "We had the same kind of Methodist upbringing . . . a rather repressive, dull family background like that of my grandparents." Her parents, however, broke from family roots by attending the university and separating themselves from strong religious practice. Although her immediate family changed houses often, Drabble always regarded her grandparents' cottage as home. Growing up in an intellectual, middle-class, liberal household, she absorbed a small amount of puritan guilt and a large amount of the work ethic which she believes is "good for the soul." Her family is both industrious and illustrious. Her father, also an author, was a barrister and then a circuit judge until he retired in 1973; her only brother is also a barrister. Before and after childrearing, her mother taught English; her younger sister is an art historian, and her older sister, Antonia, is a novelist of considerable reputation who writes under the name A. S. Byatt.

Despite the context of a large family, Drabble describes her childhood as lonely. Often ill, she saw herself as a "Maggie Tulliver": "I had a bad chest and was always rather feeble—hated games. I certainly did not feel I was part of the main stream." She spent her time alone writing, reading, and "just being secretive." Her early love of literature became an affair of constant duration. She read books about Boadicea and the Lady of Shalot, and, like Rose Vassiliou in *The Needle's Eye*, was profoundly affected at an early age by John Bunyan's *Pilgrim's Progress*. Like the Brontë family, the Drabble children composed magazines, stories, and plays together.

Drabble was educated at an old Quaker boarding school, the Mount School, where she made many friends and became more socially oriented. Like her father and her older sister, she went on to Cambridge with a major scholarship. She read English literature at Newnham College, and "enjoyed it so much," she says, "that I really think it

Margaret Drabble

took me a long time to get over it." While at the university, she stopped writing stories in her head and started acting, with some success, because "it was so much more sociable." When she did write anything at Cambridge, she kept it to herself because she found the critical atmosphere "forbidding and difficult." Drabble still challenges a critical standard so high that it discourages the young writer who cannot know at eighteen whether he will be "a minor writer or a major writer."

In 1960 Drabble took a B.A. degree with first-class honors, and she might have stayed on as a lecturer if she had not wanted to be an actress. She married Clive Swift the week after she left Cambridge and went with him to work with the Royal Shakespeare Company, understudying Vanessa Redgrave and doing occasional walk-ons. Drabble describes her life at this point as without an objective, consisting of "jumping over obstacles: marriage, having babies." Bored with such small roles as a fairy in *A Midsummer Night's Dream* and expecting her first baby, she began writing her first novel, *A Summer Bird-Cage* (1963), to fill the time and disprove the theory that "one kind of creativity displaces another." Other causes contributed to the start of her career as a novelist. She was encouraged in her choice of genre by her perception that writing novels was an open-ended profession in which English women had a strong tradition. She was also encouraged by recent British and American fiction to write something "human and contemporary." Finally, Simone de Beauvoir's *The Second Sex* presented her with material personally important to her. "It was material that nobody had used and I could use," she told Peter Firchow in 1972, "and nobody had ever used as far as I could see as I would use it." Drabble still sees this as an exciting time for women to be writing, since the writer—like her characters—has to find her own path among the profusion of choices.

Drabble began *A Summer Bird-Cage* in Stratford-upon-Avon during the first year of her marriage. She describes with characteristic candor the process of learning to write by doing: "I just wrote, day after day, like a very long letter, with no conscious sense of form or plot at all." A better novel than such a description would indicate, *A Summer Bird-Cage* reflects the experiences of Drabble and her contemporaries upon leaving the university, unemployed and without focus. The title comes from John Webster's observation: " 'Tis just like a summer bird cage in a garden, the birds that are without despair to get in, and the birds that are

within despair and are in consumption for fear they shall never get out." As the bird outside in her black and drab-green clothes, Sarah Bennett is fresh from a first at Oxford and a summer interlude as a tutor in Paris. With her "shiny, useless new degree," she returns to England for the wedding of her beautiful older sister, Louise. The first-person narration is primarily a record of Sarah's attempt to find the direction of her life. She drifts into a BBC job "filing things" and ponders the mystery of her sister's motive for her marriage to the snobbish, obsessive writer, Stephen Halifax.

The real thematic center of the novel, however, is the relationship between the two sisters, which involves competition, jealousy, self-definition, the failure of love, and Sarah's fear of subsiding into nothingness. Sarah looks to the soaring, white and lavender Louise to teach her success, but she must find her own way out of the social dislocation and lack of commitment she feels. Contemptuous of her sister's marriage for money and convenience, Sarah rejects the other roles modeled by foil characters, including the high-powered Simone who lives a "wholly willed, a wholly undetermined life," but who is finally sexless. Sarah wants the best of worlds: "I should like to bear leaves and flowers and fruit, I should like the whole world . . . oh, I should indeed." She begins her quest by liberating herself from her study-bound conceptions of human nature in the appropriate arena of London. Ultimately, Louise's revelation of her extramarital affair and Sarah's confrontation with her sister result in a new intimacy between them and a firmer sense of self for Sarah.

Drabble's style is witty and urbane, her narrative salted with the literary allusions and bons mots of the graduate narrator. More indicative of Drabble's later technique is her use of literary and folk myths of female relationship to provide an archetypal structure for the novel. Despite the book's thematic strength and vigorous imagery, Drabble's apprenticeship is evident in the self-consciousness of the narrator's voice. The introduction of characters and events is sometimes plodding, the minor characters are caricatured, and Drabble's authorial tongue-in-cheek style sometimes intrudes in what she calls a "female love-love story." Although the book was not a commercial success, Drabble found the critical response enthusiastic and encouraging. Reviewers immediately appreciated the novel's panache, its ability to capture the tone of contemporary life, the author's good humor, and her acknowledgment of her limits in the narrative form.

Drabble wrote her second novel in her dressing room at Stratford. Expecting her second child and discouraged with her acting career, she wrote *The Garrick Year* (1964) rapidly, expressing her situation and surmounting it simultaneously: "I know that partly I was writing these books in order to assert myself against the environment which I felt was hostile and unbelievably boring." Actually Drabble was understudying the role of Imogen in *Cymbeline* and playing a walk-on in *The Taming of the Shrew*. The central episode in the novel mirrors her concern about children drowning literally and women drowning figuratively in the Avon.

Emma Evans, the narrator—a former model ("all bones, no blood") and a young mother with a predilection for physical facts—is rescued from an extramarital affair by her daughter's nearly drowning. Frustrated and resentful, Emma had sacrificed a job as a BBC announcer to follow her egotistical and unfaithful actor-husband to a provincial theater festival. In retrospect, Emma sees the year as a turning point in her problematic marriage and in her search for self-purpose. Asking if there is life after motherhood, the novel portrays Emma's coy hide-and-seek affair with the "glossy" director Wyndham Ferrar, her idyllic return visit to an aunt's cottage, a timely car accident, and the drowning scene with its mutual rescue. The long-delayed consummation of her intrigue is a disturbingly sterile experience which does little to reinforce her sense of identity. Recuperating from her collisions with the automobile and with Ferrar, Emma recognizes both her strength and her mistake in "trying to relapse into self-pity" or romantic self-centered indulgence. In fighting against domestic chaos, she has almost capitulated to her "dangerous nature." Having survived, she vows to protect others (especially her children) from herself. Saving her daughter, Flora, convinces her that the domestic imperative is her lifeline, at least for the present, even if she cannot "patrol the bank" for the rest of her life. If the children root her in the earth of her unsatisfactory marriage, they also keep her from sinking in the river of despond. This solution is not only temporary, but also far from ideal: "Time and maternity can so force and violate a personality that it can hardly remember what it was." Emma insists on confronting the truth unflinchingly, if quietly, and Drabble's concluding emblematic image clarifies how destructive Emma's choice of motherhood over sexuality and self-definition can be. During a day in the countryside with her family, Emma sees a snake clutching at the belly of a sheep,

but maintains wryly that "one just has to keep on and to pretend for the sake of the children not to notice. Otherwise one might just as well stay at home."

Although criticized for thin plot and some superficial characterization, the novel drew praise for its delicacy of nuance and the psychological portrait of its protagonist. The pertinence of Emma's conflict was especially recognized by feminist critics. Virginia K. Beards commented: "As a portrait of the frigid-seductive woman with a muddled concept of both male and female sexual rights, the novel is wise and complete." Both *A Summer Bird-Cage* and *The Garrick Year* are primarily character studies in which the protagonists resolve their uncertainty about the future to some extent, but fall short of real autonomy. Since *The Garrick Year* Drabble's novels have become more dense psychologically and more involved with exploring the implications of the characters' socioeconomic pasts. Drabble attributes some of this growth in scope to her experience with motherhood: "Having children gives you access to an enormous common store of otherness about other people."

During her third pregnancy, Drabble wrote her third book, *The Millstone* (1965). At this point, having produced three of each in five years, she saw clearly that children and books could be managed together, but that an acting career could not fit in. She was also involved in some radio and television work (which included the 1964 television play *Laura*). Abandoning acting and working at night after her children were asleep, Drabble completed *The Millstone*. A moral fable, the book takes its title from Matthew's Gospel (18:6) and suggests that the child born out of wedlock to the heroine, Rosamund Stacey, is both a millstone and a salvation. Drabble later wrote a film script based on the novel, which bears the title *Thank You All Very Much*, a line from the film. Consequently, a later edition (1969) of the book is so titled. Since its emergence in a casebook edition (1970), *The Millstone* has been one of Drabble's most popular books.

Rosamund Stacey, like her predecessors, is young, attractive, intelligent, and possesses a "strange mixture of confidence and cowardice." The offspring of socialist, middle-class parents, she is a virgin at twenty-five who lives in her parents' comfortable flat while writing a doctoral thesis on the Elizabethan poets. Considering her limited sexual activity "misguided" in this age and deploring a figurative scarlet letter on her bosom that stands for Abstinence, Rosamund succumbs to a BBC announcer whose reticence and detachment resemble her own. This one "pointless" encounter leaves Rosamund pregnant. When her attempts to abort fail, she decides to have the baby without informing George, the father, or her parents. Her experiences with gestation and the National Health Service teach Rosamund what many hours at the British Museum did not: "the human limit" of her female body, her common bond with the poor women at the clinic, and her susceptibility to forces "not totally explicable." Similarly, her baby, named for the feminist Octavia Hill, teaches her what the sonneteers could not—the trauma and necessary selfishness of love.

Rosamund's education in the quality of life does not hinder her academic project, but it does necessitate a compromise of her independence and privacy. When she takes in a roommate for financial help, she becomes the subject of her lodger's novel; and it is no meaningless accident that Octavia chews up this manuscript. The literary allusions which spring to Rosamund's lips throughout the first-person narration may give meaning to the facts of life as she discovers them, but Octavia is a paradox that all her erudition will not resolve. The baby exposes her and saves her at the same time. When Rosamund finally encounters George at the end of the novel, Drabble thwarts any expectation of a conventional ending. George's indifference on viewing the baby he unknowingly fathered convinces Rosamund that she has grown beyond his numbness. He is the image of what she would have been, but for the grace of motherhood. George remains a shadowy character throughout the novel because Rosamund sees him only with the "half-knowledge" of adult affection rather than with the certainty of parental love which imparts luminescence to Octavia. Since childbirth does not ultimately interfere with the completion of Rosamund's thesis or her later academic career, she finds in Elizabethan poetry the analogue by which to assess the condition of the modern woman. This Rosamund's "complaint" is, therefore, an ironic reversal of the heroine's in Samuel Daniel's poem (1592). Though his Rosamund is punished with death for her sexual transgression, Drabble's heroine finds that the accident of her sexual act and her fate to bear children liberate her from a sterile solipsism and an emotional paralysis. However, while her maternal love may be pure, her cold and unethical treatment of George indicates that her "salvation" is not complete.

Critics have noted the moral ambiguities of this novel, its psychological subtlety and its more sophisticated narrative skill. The subject and theme of *The Millstone* drew much attention, especially feminist, and led to Drabble's identification as "the novelist of maternity." If some reviewers dismissed these issues as insignificant, they admired her wit and were impressed by the Jamesian nuance of her style. Commenting that Drabble's "deliberate unpretentiousness" led her to concentrate on the ordinary and "hide her lights in rough homespun," Peter Firchow characterized her writing as unmistakably distinctive. *The Millstone* continues to be a commercial success, but after its publication, Drabble was still unsure that she could be financially independent as a writer. She characterizes her life at this time as bourgeois and domestic and her writing as both limited and enriched by her familial obligations. Shortly after *The Millstone*, she produced her first critical book (1966), a monograph on Wordsworth, whose heightened sense of the ordinary life and the beneficence of children echoes in the themes of *The Millstone* and her later novels.

In December 1966 Drabble received the John Llewelyn Rhys Memorial Award, a travel grant which enabled her to take her children to Paris for six months, where she finished *Jerusalem the Golden*. Published in 1967, this novel unites a more elaborate structure with more intense personal feeling in the narrative. Unlike her detached predecessors, Clara Maugham is intense, insecure, greedy, upwardly mobile—and a young woman already heavily burdened with her past. Drabble describes Clara's tension as a cross between her own mother's reactions to her family history and Drabble's, yet she personally finds Clara to be the toughest, most unsympathetic of her characters. A third-person narration explains immediately that Clara's personal unease began with her name and continued with her family and intelligence. Clara's love-starved childhood with a vicious, puritanical mother has left her desperate to escape from her stifling house and narrow midland town and find a glittering life. Carefully selected boyfriends and a class trip to Paris provide her with moments of glamour until she breaks away by means of a scholarship to the university.

Clara's personality is inhibited from expressing itself in any outward way. Like Rosamund, she is amazed at the fortuitous aspect of her meeting Clelia Denham. Through Clelia, whom Clara finds a more fascinating alter ego than the reader does, Clara gains admission to the decadent, middle-class opulence of the Denham household. If Clara's family is hopeless and its members mutually repelling, the brilliant Denhams are full of promise, mutually attractive, and dependent. They embody Clara's fantasy of an alternative social and economic realm, the Jerusalem of the title: "a terrestrial paradise, where beautiful people in beautiful houses spoke of beautiful things." Clara's inevitable affair with the romantic but married Gabriel Denham has spontaneity and passion, but is clearly motivated by his elegance, good looks, and money. Moreover, the affair introduces Clara to the chic circles of London and Paris where she discovers the perimeters of her personal strength and independence.

Returning alone to Northam after a rift with Gabriel, Clara weathers the recrimination of a deathbed scene with her mother and accepts the impossibility of reconciliation. Browsing through her mother's girlhood journal, Clara belatedly discovers the truth of her mother's aspirations, the degree of hopelessness in her adult life, and her own "true descent" from her mother. Clara, however, is able to separate herself from her mother's death, and, confident of her survival and success, she is all the more determined to realign herself in a starry conjunction with Clelia and Gabriel.

Once again Drabble conveys moral ambiguity through metaphor. Clara's fable of the two weeds suggests that superficially she may resemble the glorious flowering plant, but that as a result of her tough tactics for survival she may finally emerge as the low, brown one. Despite determination, Clara is as isolated as her family—and Drabble's other heroines—in a world of her own hypersensitive perceptions. Although her sense of profound despair at the pull of hereditary fate strikes familiar and sympathetic chords, her personality frequently alienates. Her notion of love is inextricably woven with her admiration of class and money; her sexuality is inevitably exploitive. One is ambivalent as to whether her new pattern of life is too costly, too cold. Just how well Clara succeeds in escaping her grim history is also uncertain.

Although noting the "mandarin" coolness of Drabble's style, British reviewers saw *Jerusalem the Golden* as living up to the promise of her earlier works. The particularity of her subject generally met with greater enthusiasm in Great Britain than in America. A reviewer for the *New York Times* quibbled with both characterization and plot but appreciated the novel's "promising depths." Noting that Drabble asserts rather than depicts, another critic found her heroines, especially Clara, annoyingly self-satisfied. Despite the harsher judgments, Drabble's work was beginning to command wider and more serious attention in the United States.

With the publication of *Jerusalem the Golden*

Drabble began to realize her goal of a financially independent career. While her husband continued to tour in the theater, she settled with her three children into her present home in Hampstead, a handsome red-brick house which backs onto the "Keats" house. In 1968 she received the James Tait Black Memorial Book Prize. Confident that her writing career was established and that her books "were bound to get printed," Drabble began the regimen she still follows and moved her writing to daylight hours. With her children in school, she was able to take an office in Bloomsbury where she could escape interruptions. She writes in the mornings, rarely for more than three hours at a stretch. She composes easily, she says: "If a book is going reasonably well, I write terribly fast. And I don't rewrite very much either. . . . I think that this is because I've always been short of time. I've always been saving up the time to work so that by the time I actually get to the typewriter . . . it's all there waiting."

A devoted mother, Drabble has so closely harmonized her professional life and her domestic life that she has steadily been able to increase her professional commitments. If necessary, she manages "by cutting out a lot of things that other people find necessary, like social life." As a result, the time between 1968 and 1969 was productive for Drabble and brought her often into the public eye. She began lecturing to adults in evening classes at London College. The film *Isadora* (for which Drabble wrote the dialogue) was released, as was the film version of *The Millstone* (as *A Touch of Love* in England), and her play *Bird of Paradise* opened in London. Thus, she became a radio and television personality, and her fifth novel, *The Waterfall* (1969), was published to a waiting audience.

As an outgrowth of Drabble's writing about Wordsworth and his vision of a "flood" of love, *The Waterfall* depicts a woman paradoxically saved and destroyed by her discovery of sexual love. The paradox is related to those in earlier novels in which the agents are children. In *The Waterfall* Jane's baby is only tangential to her mother's rebirth. The novel's title ostensibly refers both to the watery vision of the Goredale Scar and to a card trick whereby cascading cards are a metaphor for orgasm in coitus. Drabble uses the sublime waterfall in the scar to represent the reality of true romantic passion between Jane Grey and her lover (and cousin's husband), James Otford: "It is impressive not through size, as I had perhaps expected, but through form: a lovely organic balance of shapes and curves, a wildness contained within a bodily limit."

As the novel opens, Jane Grey is suspended in frigidity, immobile. Her husband gone, her second child due, she has relinquished control of her life in an effort to absolve herself of responsibility: "If I were drowning, I couldn't reach out a hand to save myself, so unwilling am I to set myself up against fate." Embracing fate more passionately than prior Drabble women, Jane stops all effort to maintain her home or herself; she informs neither her husband of the child's birth nor her parents of her husband's desertion. Deliverance from her "dry integrity" comes with the delivery of her baby and her seduction of James during her convalescence in a warm, womblike bedroom.

The duality of female existence structures the novel. Deliberately commenting on the continuity of female doom and moral conflict as registered in the tradition of the novel, Drabble's heroine exclaims: "These fictional heroines, how they haunt me. Maggie Tulliver had a cousin called Lucy, as I have, and like me she fell in love with her cousin's man. She drifted off down the river with him, abandoning herself to the water. . . . In this age what is to be done? We drown in the first chapter." Drabble's layered fiction presents a hierarchy of female creative form. It begins with the gestation and delivery of her child Bianca Gray, moves from Jane's poetry to the double-point-of-view narration of her affair, and culminates in the all-encompassing control of Drabble's irony. The reader must participate in this fiction by integrating Jane's "schizophrenic" point of view: her objective, controlled third-person description of her life and her first-person impassioned account of her feelings about her experience. While the third-person narrative is a contemporary story, the first-person voice is at once a more honest expression and a neurotic parody of Victorian sensibility. "Lies, lies, it's all lies. A pack of lies," the narrator says of the third-person narrative, "I've even told lies of fact, which I had meant not to do. . . . Reader, I loved him: as Charlotte Brontë said."

When Drabble's Victorian-named heroines find themselves in uncharted waters, they often fall back on literary precedent. Jane especially reflects this thesis that art can teach us about life when she argues with Jane Austen's solutions: "Emma got what she deserved in marrying Mr. Knightley. What can it have been like, in bed with Mr. Knightly? Sorrow awaited that woman." Denying that the book is experimental, Drabble accounts for her split-point-of-view technique as indigenous to her material, the dualism of Jane's experience: "I wrote the first chunk in the third person and found it impossible to continue with, because it did not seem to me to tell anything like the whole story. . . . I thought the only way to do it was to make Jane say it." Drabble's controlling device for this narrative structure is the network of images and symbols mostly derived, like the water imagery, from Romantic poetry and Victorian novels. If Drabble's structure presents the dualism of reality and fiction, of character and author, Jane's divided vision presents the novel's theme: death in love, virtue in guilt, and pleasure in pain. After a car accident alerts Lucy to her husband's affair, Jane must decide on an ending for the story: James's death, his impotence, or her relinquishment. Preferring to "suffer," Jane opts finally for a continuation of the affair which began with Bianca's birth and culminates in the price a modern woman must pay, the threat of thrombosis from the pill or neurosis: "one can take one's pick."

The Waterfall has become Drabble's most controversial book. She wryly calls it "a wicked book" which brought serious attack from those "who say that you should not put into people's heads the idea that one can be saved from fairly pathological conditions by loving a man." Critical response to *The Waterfall* tended generally to divide along lines of sexual politics. Several male critics expressed concern that Drabble was becoming "more of a woman novelist" with an obsessive quality to her style, "particularly when characters are going through the motions of love." Noting as well the domestic character of her journalism, Bernard Bergonzi saw both *Jerusalem the Golden* and *The Waterfall* as close to "women's magazine fiction." However, other (notably female) critics came to view *The Waterfall* as an intriguing sequel to the spectrum of liberationist issues in Drabble's first four novels. More recently, Ellen Cronan Rose has asserted that *The Waterfall* is the most female of Drabble's novels because it is the most nearly androgynous. In it, Rose says, Drabble has discovered female nature to be divided between male and female form "which amalgamates feminine fluidity and masculine shapeliness."

The critical debate as to the feminism or femininity of her work has prompted Drabble to declare the autonomy of her art. Denying that her books are "about feminism," she specifies that her concerns are privilege, justice, salvation, equality, and egalitarianism. Justice for women is for her not a subject, but a tenet so basic that it "is part of a whole." From the beginning, Drabble has written independently of outside, even editorial, influence. Although she writes many articles and reviews for income, she has not been concerned about the commercial success of her novels, her most serious work. After the publication of *The Waterfall*, however, she began to respond to the pressure of analytic criticism. Charges that her heroines were of a similar, autobiographical pattern have made her "cagey" in responding to queries about her life, although she acknowledges that she uses incidents from her experience and that the truth of her characters' emotional response derives from her identification with them to a certain extent. She avoids reading reviews while she is writing, but, an astute critic herself, she has found constructive criticism helpful.

The Needle's Eye, a pivotal novel in Drabble's career, seems to have been encouraged by comments like those of William Trevor, who in the *New Statesman* urged her to expand her range. She also credits Doris Lessing with having influenced her development of technique. Politically, philosophically, and technically more complex than her previous fiction, *The Needle's Eye* seems to reflect Drabble's increased involvement with public activities such as her literary tours for the British Arts Coun-

cil and her research on Arnold Bennett. Preferring the social sympathy of Bennett to the elitism of Jane Austen or Henry James, Drabble set about blending the humanity of the former with the sensibility of the latter in her novel of contemporary British manners.

When the *Guardian* asked her to write an article on child custody cases for the women's page, Drabble conducted extensive research on the subject. Instead of the article, she wrote *The Needle's Eye*. According to Drabble, her favorite novel not only introduces her first fully developed male character as narrator, but it also tests for her a certain lifestyle in Rose Vassiliou's eccentric and passionate rejection of wealth and middle-class status. Whether she plays "lady of the manor" in the shabby neighborhood she forces herself to embrace or experiences true religious and philosophical integrity is an interpretive question not easily resolved. One admiring but skeptical perspective on Rose's self-imposed martyrdom is provided by the attorney, Simon Camish. Drabble skillfully balances the two points of view within a complex temporal structure. Rose's chosen life "in the depths" suggests Wordsworth's philosophy of plain living and high thinking, but also reverberates with the neurosis and guilt of John Bunyan.

A lonely, self-effacing child, Rose Virtue Bryanston was warned of her spiritual danger by Bunyan's Pilgrim and her nurse, Noreen, who was given to intoning such biblical texts as that of the camel and the eye of a needle. Rose's adult life is propelled by the Pilgrim's own question: "What must I do to be saved?" Meditating on the hopelessness of his marriage and disinterested personality, Simon meets Rose at a trendy dinner party and drives her home. Fascinated by her vitality and unpretentiousness, he becomes involved in her legal and personal affairs. As he immerses himself in the sensational newspaper accounts of Rose's past—including her defiant marriage to a poor Greek, her legal battles with her parents, and her nasty divorce case—Simon must confront his own motives for marrying a wealthy but superficial woman. His working-class history makes him sympathetic to Rose's scruples about money, and, like her, he operates from a sense of duty and decency. He gradually takes refuge in the warmth and authenticity of her home and advises her on her husband Christopher's custody suit for the children.

Their platonic, domestic love and Christopher's desperation bring the action to its climax in a series of scenes reminiscent of a Noel Coward comedy: a police-and-lawyers race, a rendezvous in

Dust jacket for Drabble's favorite among her novels, which established her as a major writer

the garden of the Bryanston's country house, a confrontation in the drawing room, and a picnic for all parties on the beach. Unable to deny Christopher his children and unable to give up the grace they impart, Rose can only yield to the dilemma. Her self-sacrifice in readmitting Christopher and giving up Simon is an act of puritan desperation, a "leap off the ladder even blindfold into eternity, sink or swim, come heaven come hell." As part of the frustration of all Rose's choices, even her run-down neighborhood becomes fashionable and redeveloped. Thwarted in the design of her life (her husband keeps making money; Rose must inherit more), she strives to remain the ordinary person she believes nature intended her to be. She continues to defy the fatal accident of wealth, but clearly, at the end of the novel, her "living death" with Christopher cannot last. The "dry light of arid charity" and duty to her former husband is as questionable a virtue as her haphazard donation of her fortune to a revolutionary African regime.

Although *The Needle's Eye* has been seen as a defeatist novel because of Rose's impasse, its main thematic thrust is Simon's agonizing Shakespearean question: why should man have such exquisite perception of justice, equality, and the eternal, when he is possessed of "just enough lumination . . . to suffer for failure and too little spirit to live in the light, too little strength to reach the light." Drabble, however, insists that she intended the novel to be optimistic in its portrayal of people struggling to live as best they can in a difficult situation. For its moral intensity *The Needle's Eye* was almost universally praised as a mature and impressive expression of Drabble's talent. Joyce Carol Oates commented that Drabble, like Rose Vassiliou, had made "an extraordinary leap forward" in this intelligent and densely-textured novel: "Drabble is not a writer who reflects the helplessness of the stereotyped 'sick society,' but one who has taken upon herself the task . . . of attempting the active, vital, energetic, mysterious recreation of a set of values by which human beings can live." In the general praise, some commentary took exception to the ratio of interior monologue to plot and questioned the plausibility and coincidence of events. The consensus, however, was that *The Needle's Eye* established Drabble as a major writer. The novel was especially appreciated in the United States and drew the attention of academics to Drabble's work. Articles on her books proliferated in scholarly journals, and the American Academy of Arts and Letters awarded her the E. M. Forster Award in 1973. Subsequently all of her novels have been in print in both Great Britain and the United

States, and most have been translated into several languages.

Also published in 1972 was *London Consequences*, the collaboration of several young writers, which Drabble edited with her sister, A. S. Byatt.

Margaret Drabble, early 1970s

Although the early works of the sisters portray sibling rivalries, both writers have discouraged the comparative articles (and their hints of competitive friction between the women) which have appeared in London tabloids. Despite her reticence on the subject, Margaret's relationship with Antonia appears to be personally important if professionally complex.

Separated from her husband and eventually divorced in 1975, Drabble did not produce another novel for three years after *The Needle's Eye*. Writing nonfiction steadily during this interval, she had her literary biography of Arnold Bennett published in 1974. Drabble intended, in doing this project, to stimulate a reappraisal of Bennett's work, but a by-product of her research was a reexamination of her own provincial origins and a deeper commitment to social realism in her fiction. She looked more intently to the public domain for material for her novels. Newspapers still provide her with stories she can connect to the personal tragedies of people she knows. To assure accuracy, she researches extensively and conducts interviews with those involved in the sphere of her interest.

Inspired by stories "about old ladies dying alone in cottages," especially one starved woman who had eaten the family Bible, Drabble began *The Realms of Gold* (1975), a novel which employs archeology as a controlling metaphor for fragmentation of contemporary families. In addition to reading and interviewing archeologists, she took part in an archeological expedition to gather background for the novel. *The Realms of Gold*, which contends with *The Needle's Eye* as Drabble's best novel, is actually a work about the survival of human community. Her return to Yorkshire while working on the Bennett biography suggested her story of a family plagued through three generations with "hereditary depressions." Speaking with an interviewer before she finished the novel, Drabble commented: "It would fit in very nicely with my interest in predestination and fate and whether you can escape your destiny—whether it's right to escape it by taking drugs or just being happy in other ways; whether it will get you in the end anyway." Certainly many of the novel's physical details derive from the landscapes of her childhood—the cottages, the ditch, even the newts.

All of the primary characters in *The Realms of Gold*, except Frances Wingate's lover, are related by blood, and all are afflicted in some way with the Ollerenshaw family's "Midlands sickness." The various ways in which the characters cope with this depressive tendency make up most of the story. Frances Wingate, the novel's chief protagonist, is far removed from Drabble's earlier, agoraphobic women. Feminist issues are not a problem for Frances, a golden girl who has emerged unscathed from a dissolved marriage. Despite occasional bouts with the family malaise, Frances successfully pursues her career as an archeologist, rears four children, and wins the devotion of her lover. Her mobility, freedom, financial independence, and professional security are offset dramatically by the foil characterization of her cousin Janet, the more familiar Drabble housewife, incarcerated in a "tiled hygienic box" with a nasty husband and a teething baby. Nevertheless, while freed from the more personal female problems, Frances must face the stress of the Ollerenshaw neurosis and that of the larger human community: boredom, a sense of the futility of endeavor, isolation, and, occasionally, an overwhelming sense of spiritual desolation. Her suicidal nephew fuels her more despairing vision by asking

her to convince him that life has meaning: "How can you possibly imagine," he taunts, "that the things you do are worth doing?"

An expert in reconstructing the era of the ancient Phoenicians, Frances struggles to discover her past and come to terms with her family's Darwinian climb up the beanstalk of economic and educational opportunity. Her perspectives are tempered by those of her historian lover, Karel, and her geologist cousin, David. She understands such scientific endeavors as theirs and hers to be "a fruitless attempt to prove the possibility of the future through the past. . . . We seek golden worlds from which we are banished, they recede infinitely for there never was a golden world, there was never anything but toil and subsistence, cruelty and dullness." Only when her reclusive great-aunt dies grotesquely from starvation does Frances begin to find some answers. Huddled in her aunt's overgrown and womblike cottage, Frances comprehends the simple dignity and integrity in the elemental human struggle for survival. Her moment of grace is alternately replenished and diminished by the return of her lover and the deaths of her nephew and his baby. Unlike his Aunt Frances, Stephen is convinced by the old lady's death of the indignity of life and chooses the "pure triumph" of suicide. For lack of any other "revelation," Frances eventually accepts death and love as the only inexplicable absolutes. Oriented by her relationships of the heart and "wedded" to culture, process, and human effort, she accepts Stephen's death as a sacrificial act intended to save all of the Ollerenshaws from their sad inheritance. The novel concludes with tears for the dead and joy for the survivors, including marriages, middle-age adjustments, and renewed family ties.

Perhaps in response to criticism about her other heroines' fates, Drabble invites the reader to "invent a more suitable ending if you can." She further knits her several points of view together by means of a network of symbols, images (especially archeological), and parallel or juxtaposed scenes like Janet's and Frances's separate visits to their great-aunt's May Cottage. She balances the images of a golden existence, which sustain Frances, Karel, and David, with the apocalyptic visions of the abyss into which Stephen, Frances's sister Alice, and great-aunt Con leap. The novel is textured with descriptions of natural phenomena—muddy ditches, glaring sun, desert sands—and threaded with the labyrinths of human intellection. Both the interior and exterior landscapes have their "black holes" and precious lodes.

Although *The Realms of Gold* was praised for such detail, some critics questioned its efficacy. A *Spectator* review quipped that Drabble "sometimes dabbles in the still water of tedium" and indulges in a "misplaced seriousness" in some sections of this lengthy novel. The high level of coincidence and fairy-tale resolutions have been challenged as well. Yet the extension of Drabble's imaginative sympathy in this novel "exposed the narrowness of ours," according to critic Patricia Sharpe, who finds the improbabilities appropriate to the "drama of discovery" reflective of the John Keats sonnet from which the title comes. And Roger Sale, who had previously charged Drabble with a willingness "to settle for superb parts and inferior wholes," declared that the title was the true name for the quality of this fiction. For him, the joy at the end "overwhelms disbelief."

Drabble's narrative technique in this novel successfully presents a triptych of discovery through the three cousins' points of view. Compared to her previous novels, *The Realms of Gold* contains a looser plot, a more complex temporal structure, and daring shifts in narrative style. Drabble deliberately uses a humorously self-conscious authorial voice whose omniscience, she slyly admits, "has its limits." While examining the multiplicity of the characters' responses to the same issues, this voice often archly baits the reader about his response: "And that is enough for the moment of Janet Bird. More than enough, you might reasonably think, for her life is slow, even slower than its description, and her dinner party seemed to go on too long to her, as it did to you." Such tone indicates Drabble's self-assurance in this novel which reviews some of her earliest themes—fate, luck, sexual relations, identity—on its way to presenting new, more profound concerns. The ambiguity expressed in the resolutions of her other novels finds a definitive shape in this one as a truth unearthed by Frances both in the desert and in her heart: there is no finished truth, no definitive past, no inevitable future. The hope and terror of such a perception has provided the focus of her next two novels.

However much the subject of critical debate, Drabble's themes and her stylistics have inspired a rash of "pseudo-Drabblerians," according to the Society of Authors. Drabble continued to write for such periodicals as *Spectator, Guardian, Punch, Ms.* and *Saturday Review*. In 1976, the University of Sheffield presented her with the honorary degree Doctor of Letters. As her involvements with committees of cultural and social organizations increased, so did her interest in the public characters

and private quality of British life. In her next novel, *The Ice Age* (1977), Drabble continued to reduce plot and emphasize the characters' contemplation of their past and present situations, but she alternated soliloquies with detailed vignettes of the contemporary British scene. She has said that the impetus for *The Ice Age* was Oliver Marriott's book *The Property Boom* (1967), which detailed the fortunes people made by speculating in real estate and property development in the 1950s and 1960s. A visit to redeveloped Sheffield, while researching the Bennett biography, convinced Drabble that the issue was a complex and intriguing one. The title of the novel refers both to the disastrous economic freeze of the 1970s and to the spiritual wastes of modern life. Consequently, *The Ice Age* has a fair measure of the naturalistic pessimism glimpsed in *The Realms of Gold*.

The novel's central metaphor suggests that the individual character's malaise is part of a larger crisis created by the drastic, enormous changes in the nature and quality of life in the last hundred years. Particularly, the moral and financial decline of several characters seems to parallel that of Britain, a "shabby, mangy old lion now." Like the northern wastes and dumping sites they have created, Drabble's land speculators are now bankrupt, "living in the ruins of their own grandiose excesses." Designed as a more universal portrait of modern times, the novel includes almost every imaginable social theme: ecology; television; the failure of the upper class and the liberal arts; dissolution of traditional forms; the dissipation, self-centeredness, and aggression of youth; the sexual promiscuity of everyone; the plight of the elderly; prison conditions; the Americanization of the world; inflation; oil and energy conservation; Arabian acquisition in Britain; terrorism; and the IRA. Behind the topical issues lurks the central problem of a paralyzed, disillusioned middle class and its loss of ethos: "a huge icy fist, with large cold fingers, was squeezing and chilling the people of Britain, that great and puissant nation, slowing down their blood, locking them into immobility, fixing them in a solid stasis, like fish in a frozen river."

"Fed up with women—slightly," Drabble chose a male character as the primary focus of her omniscient narrative. A middle-class, thirty-eight-year-old Oxford graduate, Anthony Keating abandons a comfortable but static career in television production to go out of his depth in a partnership with two shrewd and manipulative land developers. While riding the crest of the development boom Anthony "was a modern man, an operator, at one

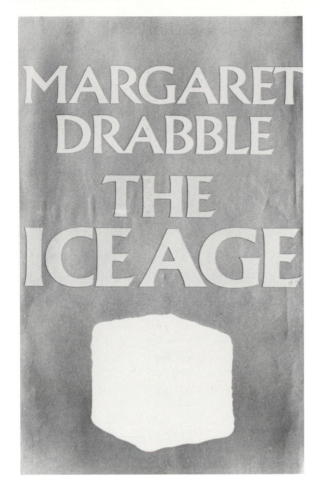

Dust jacket for Drabble's 1977 novel, about the economic and spiritual freeze of the 1970s

with the spirit of the age." As the novel opens, however, Anthony is retired in his heavily mortgaged country home, recuperating from a heart attack and awaiting financial ruin and prosecution for his part in a recent development scheme. Since Anthony must eschew the ordinary panaceas of his culture—food, alcohol, and sex—he is defenseless against the ennui that has stalked him as it has Drabble's other protagonists, a "profound, disabling, terrifying boredom." Amicably divorced, Anthony has had a long-running if limping affair with a woman who has abandoned her acting career to care for a child afflicted with cerebral palsy. Obsessive in her devotion to Molly, Alison Murray incurs the resentment of her other daughter, sullen teen-aged Jane. The novel shifts narrative focus from Anthony's meditations in his garden to draw parallels with Alison's fruitless vigil in a Communist bloc country where Jane awaits trial for dangerous driving. The Alison-Anthony separation is placed in counterpoint with that of Len Wincobank, an

entrepreneur in prison for fraud, and his mistress, Maureen Kirby. As Drabble had observed about Jane's dinner party in *The Realms of Gold*, art mirrors life. Alison's futile wait in Wallacia, Anthony's boredom at Rook House, Len's tedium in prison, and Maureen's frustration without him are all projected by the absence of plot in part one, which surveys one day in the lives of the characters and their several pasts through lengthy flashback and exposition.

Thereafter the novel has little action. The energetic and ruthless characters like Len Wincobank and Giles Peters continue to scheme and deplete themselves. The survivors like Maureen Kirby and her new lover, architect Derek Ashby, move steadily upward, cutting competently through the ice to self-satisfaction and a brave new world of their own making. The victims—Molly, Max (murdered by a terrorist bomb), and Maureen's displaced aunt—are silent. The lost and seeking, Anthony and Alison, learn to accept failure in childrearing and real estate and find only their own mortality. Alison returns alone to England, only to learn that her loss is total, that she is no longer indispensable to Molly. Having found her identity in both her beauty and her devotion to Molly for one half of her life, she faces the mid-life crisis of Drabble's other recent heroines and sees no basis for the second half. Worse, the surrealistic images of London offer no rescue to her failed imagination. Reunited with Anthony at Rook House, Alison watches him dwindle to triviality and wonders "what next, what next, what next?" Convinced that "ill-thoughts" and poor choices bring our fate, Alison believes she bears the terrible weight of a retribution which reflects the chaos of the economic-social sphere. Her generation had its certainties when young, but they have since "fragmented and dissolved into uncertainty." After such knowledge as theirs, Drabble asks, what action?

Her answer to this thematic question has elicited conflicting responses. Anthony survives his financial crisis only to fall victim to his own quixotic impulse. As a result of the sermons he found in his stony garden, he rushes off to rescue Jane and incidentally to spy for Whitehall. He reaffirms the old beliefs with grim determination and succeeds in rescuing Jane despite his contempt for her callousness. After an unconvincing arrest episode, Anthony becomes a contemplative in prison, gets "high on suffering," and is spiritually reborn. Unlike *The Realms of Gold*, *The Ice Age* presents no alternative to the dreadful revelation experienced by its female protagonist. There is no fairy-tale ending for Alison: "Her life is beyond imagining. It will not be imagined. Britain will recover, but not Alison Murray."

The Ice Age begins with patriotic exhortations by Milton and Wordsworth, and the rest of the novel is spotted with allusions to Shakespeare's island jewel and Milton's puissant giant. The promise is that England will recover even if she has replaced the cathedral spire with the gasometer as her inspiration. The sun which thaws the ice age is literally a golden one, and the discovery of oil in the North Sea may produce "a senile Britain, casting out its ghosts. Or a go-ahead Britain, with old rig men toasting their mistress in champagne in the pubs of Aberdeen." Drabble's ambivalence toward such renewal is conveyed by style as well as by image. Double negatives like "without implausibility" or "not unattractive" set the tone, as does an ironic authorial voice. Expanding a tactic initiated in *The Needle's Eye* and developed in *The Realms of Gold*, Drabble speaks to the reader about her art: "It ought now to be necessary to imagine a future for Anthony Keating. There is no need to worry about the other characters, for the present." The characters alternate between choice and an existence determined as often by that authorial voice as by accident of plot.

Valerie Grosvenor Myer's assertion that Drabble's early novels contain a dominant judgmental vein has been disputed by other critics. However, puritan fatalism becomes a dominant tone in *The Ice Age*, not only in Alison's determined view, but also in the authorial voice: "Evelyn Ashby, who has not been allowed to appear, will not remarry; she will grow eccentric and solitary, and refuse to see her own children." Such comments prompted James Gindin, who admired much in the novel, to observe that Drabble's shift in perspective has placed many of her characters in double jeopardy, up against the rock of fate and the "hard edge" of the author's disapproval. Since the author creates a "determined immobility" for the characters, he argues, she punishes Alison unfairly and makes the possibility of a "recovery" for anyone other than Anthony a matter of fantasy. While acknowledging Drabble's superior talent, Granville Barker also found her characters in this novel singularly unattractive and "masochistic." Moreover, he considers her style too journalistic and insists that, by concentrating on exploiters rather than their victims, she "sacrifices the essential dramatic and moral validity of her subject." Nevertheless, her more aggressive style has won the applause of critics like Maureen Howard, who finds event and character convincing because they are given "full thematic and emotional support." As is the case with such large and ambitious novels, *The Ice Age* received few unmixed reviews, but won general notice as an important work. More than any of Drabble's other novels to date, *The Ice Age* takes the shape of a nineteenth-century novel and draws from its traditions: elaborate structure, expansive focus, coincidence, a definitive social context, interlocking lives, and meaningful resolution. In her authoritative stance, Drabble admits to technique and the self-consciousness of her art in a way that imparts vigor to the form. With its panoramic view of British society and its multiplicity of character and theme, *The Ice Age* is her most ambitious novel so far, but in the particularity of its issues, it may also become her most dated.

Drabble had intended her next book to be "a public health drama" about the immunization program of the national health care system, but she "threw it away" in preference for *A Writer's Britain* (1979), a book on literary landscapes. In her novels, London settings have a specific presence and are portrayed with exquisite attention to detail: inhuman traffic circles, fortress-like office buildings, a vacant lot with chickens roosting in a chair, a littered tube station. Her attention to countryside herb and flower rivals that of Thomas Hardy. Descriptions of the microscopic life in a ditch, of wild and formal gardens, have the power of incantation. Understandably, Drabble was "over-excited" about this book, and her contribution (along with the many handsome photographs by Jorge Lewinski) illustrates her conviction that physical setting is a large part of the determined aspect of a character's personality and life.

Commenting on her movement from private to public concerns in her novels, Drabble has said that, having come to terms with her own interior life, she no longer felt the need to write about it. Instead, she is "very interested in the way society works." Yet her latest novel, *The Middle Ground* (1980), returns to issues germane to her present circumstances and combines them with several of the larger social problems depicted in *The Ice Age*: the alarming fluctuations of youth, the economy, social injustice, and foreign immigration. Drabble also returns to the female narrator. Like Frances Wingate, Kate Armstrong is a vigorous, sexy, slightly bohemian, divorced woman; like Alison Murray, she stands at the edge of her childrens' independence and feels the loss of definition; like Anthony Keating, she is bored with her career as a journalist writing about women's matters.

In a recent interview Drabble has said that Kate "could be an analogy for the novelist who is fed up with the feminist critics." Her character has reached the stage where she is "fed up with the narrow little ditch that she's got herself stuck in," and worst of all, she is "bored with herself." At the crossroads of her life, Kate wonders where to go next. Toward the novel's end, she goes back to her hometown to trace the subsequent lives of her childhood friends. Ostensibly she is working on a television documentary on women (again), but in actuality she is looking for herself. The daughter of a sewer worker, Kate is self-educated and self-made. She is limited not as a woman but, like most people, as a person with few talents. In the process of her evolution she has traded sexual guilt for feminist guilt, feminist guilt for ennui.

Drabble's comment about the book, that "nothing really happens in it at all," accurately describes the novel's Woolfian temper. People drift in and out of Kate's house: miscellaneous friends of her teenaged children, punks, and musicians "crash" there; an old sot and former mentor gets sick on the floor; an Iraqi student seeks refuge from political trouble; and a close friend and fellow journalist, Hugo Mainwairing, finds the impetus there to resume his career as a foreign correspondent. The narrative consists mostly of the characters' retrospection. Things that have happened in the past are reviewed in detail: Kate's marriage to a bohemian artist "done in" by her capability; her abortion; the hate mail sent to her anonymously by her brother; her affair with her best friend's insensitive and egotistical husband; the friend's problems with her adolescent children and her cases as a social worker. Even the attack on the friend, Evelyn Stennett, by the husband of one of her clients is revealed after the fact.

Characters from Drabble's other novels reappear. Gabriel Denham has survived *Jerusalem the Golden* as a television producer and a potentially romantic lead in *The Middle Ground*, and Kate has invited *The Millstone*'s Rosamund Stacey to her party. Drabble may be building a saga, but she is surely suggesting the closed circuit of London chic. There are snappy set pieces, including Kate's contemplation of underwear advertisements on billboards and the phenomenon of planned, "edenic" suburban communities. Portentous occurrences of animal and bird deaths continue an ominous motif begun in *The Ice Age*. The book concludes with a "Mrs. Dalloway-type party" and with what Drabble calls a note of "guarded optimism." Before the party, Kate enjoys her first automobile ride with her nineteen-year-old son as driver. This ride, her son's adult demeanor, a bouquet of flow-

ers, and the prospect of intrigue at the party suddenly combine to buoy Kate with hope. Her life, after all, has the potential of a soap opera: "Will Stuart be civil to Ted; will Ted make a pass at Rosamund Stacey? . . . Anything is possible, it is all undecided. Everything or nothing. . . . Something will happen." A child calls her downstairs to reality; the doorbell rings, signaling possibility; the telephone rings, reestablishing contact with the outside world; and Kate "rises" to embrace life.

Once again Drabble asserts the miracle of children and the real spiritual benefit to rearing them. Kate's children have their abominable stages but return, like Mark, the eldest, capable and caring. The necessity of caring within reason has been a steady chord in Drabble's composition, played in counterpoint to the paradoxical theme of the inevitable failure of male-female love relationships. The paradoxical mode characterizes Kate's mid-life experience. Whereas earlier novels embody opposing perspectives in a pair of female characters,

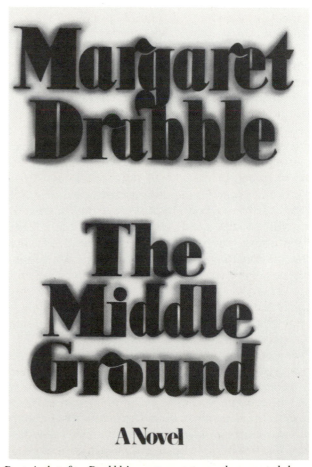

Dust jacket for Drabble's most recent novel, narrated by a character who "could be an analogy for the novelist who is fed up with the feminist critics"

such as Louise and Sarah in *A Summer Bird-Cage, The Middle Ground* presents a divided self in Kate, the image of middle age. She is set in her convictions about the quality of life (she knows what she wants, as distinct from earlier heroines who knew only what they did not want), but she is full of questions and doubts about its meaning now. The division is, in one way, a conflict of past and present: "Those two selves, that prattling chattering journalist in Kentish town, with her smart views and expensive boots and trendy house . . . and the child in its skimpy cotton dress, lonely, cast out, cut off—what had they in common?" She is "settled-in," tired, jaded, but also unsettled. Things in the outer world seem to be in total flux; in the inner world all is moribund. Only Kate's resilient personality glues her together at the end. Fittingly, she rises to a social occasion, accepting the challenge of facing "everything or nothing."

Drabble's theme has its logic in the development of her work, but it inspires a style that suffers from imitative fallacy. *The Middle Ground* often exhibits, to use one reviewer's phrase, "narrative paralysis." In describing Kate's situation, Drabble characterizes the novel. Her plot, like Kate's middle years, "stretches back too densely. . . . No wonder a pattern is slow to emerge from such trivia, from such serious but hidden connections. Everything has too much history." Similarly, Kate goes to a play by and with famous people, only to be bored stiff because "Nothing happened at all. The characters talked and talked." For every opinion Drabble's cast members express, they offer a counteropinion; for every question they pose, they continue with a catalogue of qualifying or opposing questions: "Oh dear, oh dear, thought Kate, . . . the trouble is, anything *could* mean anything. Or its opposite." Presenting paragraph after paragraph of such speculation, the novel is an epic quandary and thwarts every expectation of revelation.

The novel has its admirers, who consider Drabble at the top of her form in expressing Kate's "articulate doubt." A *New Statesman* review totally disagrees, observing that "assertion is about all we ever get." Drabble's authorial voice still addresses the reader, but the tone has changed and it has dropped its ironic stance towards the characters' self-indulgences. Perhaps Hugo Mainwairing's comment about his own writing explains Drabble's intention in this novel: "Now that . . . is really bad writing despite the fact that I mean every word of it. . . . The more I try to tell the truth, the worse I write. But surely, at my age, I ought to have the courage to write badly? What do I fear to lose?"

Margaret Drabble, 1982

Drabble refers to her book as a "document" and reminds us that if we see Hugo as "a depressing spectacle," that is our choice. Drabble anticipated that *The Middle Ground* might be regarded "as a true feminist tract" or as "a complete failure," and said she did not care: "The truth is more important than ideology." For all its fault, *The Middle Ground* is an honest book. One hopes with a *Spectator* reviewer that, the "crisis of confidence" passed, Kate's reasserted hope may be the author's as well.

In any event, with the publication of her ninth novel, Drabble is no longer at a crossroads in her reputation. Her corpus is strong enough to assure her a primary place among contemporary writers. Beset by the claims of popularity and critical regard, Drabble has learned to become even more chary of her time, more careful in her commitments, more protective of her privacy. Generally appearing unruffled, she is much sought after for interviews, appearances, and reviews. She made her first trip to the United States in the summer of 1974, financing her journey with funds received from a grant from the American Academy of Arts and Letters. Currently she is editing the *Oxford Companion to English Literature*. In the fall of 1980, at a Buckingham Palace ceremony, the Queen Mother dubbed

Margaret Drabble a Commander of the British Empire. Possessing immense creative energy, Drabble does not regard herself as remarkable, but—in keeping with her themes—"ordinary," fated, and lucky. By her own admission, her novels reflect her progress from graduate and actress, through housewife and mother, to novelist and critic. Like her characters who escape self-absorption by establishing links with their communities, Drabble has increased her public involvement, sitting on committees because she believes she should. She maintains, however, that what she does for pleasure, money, or society will always be secondary to her commitment to writing serious novels. When not writing or serving, she is reading: "I find out about living and about the values of living—and a lot of my beliefs in life and my feelings about people and what to do—from reading novels." *The Middle Ground* indicates that, having safely traversed the crossroads, Drabble will continue to address sensitive social issues against an authentic contemporary background, but without abandoning the private purpose, the conscious autobiographical element. Bent on developing her craft, but eschewing modern experimentation, she still studies the classics of Western literature to learn what can be done with the medium of the novel. "I'd rather be at the end of a dying tradition which I admire," she said in 1967, "than at the beginning of a tradition which I deplore."

Drabble began testing the parameters of human life through a feminist consciousness. Her discoveries led to the creation of male and female characters who perceive yet wryly question their circumspection in their domestic and social spheres. Believing that striving, not happiness, is important to human fulfillment, Drabble sets her characters to moral choice in today's society. Like Hardy, about whom she has written, she locates her fatalism in both the human condition and the nature of society. In her novels, she perpetually seeks to define the relationship between accident and plan. Her attention to detail and nuance has led to her identification as a novelist of manners, and therefore to comparisons with Jane Austen and Henry James. Noting her focus on female discovery and aestheticism, critics have also aligned her with George Eliot, Virginia Woolf, and Doris Lessing. Drabble's art bears comparison as well with those classic and contemporary novelists she admires: Angus Wilson, Iris Murdoch, the Brontës, Arnold Bennett, and Saul Bellow. But finally, Drabble's voice is her own. She is a lucid, intelligent writer whose wry humor, incisive wit, technical skill, and sensitivity to the minutiae of events have become the hallmarks of her style. A novelist on whom nothing is lost, Drabble is articulate about what she is attempting in her novels, yet she refuses to define any single meaning. As she avoids strong closure in the novels, so she rejects solutions. The ambivalence with which her characters meet their fates, the dualism of their perceptions, and the ambiguity of the narrative tone all reflect Drabble's variousness and her vision of the novel: "There is no answer to a novel. A novel is like a person's life. It's full of complexities and therefore any explanation is unsatisfactory. It's the constant flux, the going to and fro between various emotions that makes fiction interesting to me." Drabble's work has steadily achieved maturity; many critics and readers expect that in its maturity it will achieve greatness. One might say of her novels what she has said of Arnold Bennett's, that they deal with material never encountered in fiction but only in life.

Plays:
Bird of Paradise, London, 1969.

Screenplays:
Laura, Granada Television, 1964;
Thank You All Very Much, Columbia Pictures, 1969; as *A Touch of Love*, Palomar Pictures, London, 18 August 1969.

Other:
"The Reunion," in *Winter's Tales 14*, edited by Kevin Crossley-Holland (London: Macmillan, 1968);
"The Gifts of War," in *Winter's Tales 16*, edited by A. D. Maclean (London: Macmillan, 1970);
London Consequences, edited by Drabble and A. S. Byatt (London: Greater Arts Association, 1972);
Jane Austen, *Lady Susan, The Watsons, Sanditon*, edited with introduction by Drabble (London: Penguin, 1975);
New Stories #1, edited by Drabble and Charles Osborne (London: Arts Council of Great Britain, 1976);
"Hardy and the Natural World," in *The Genius of Thomas Hardy*, edited by Drabble (London: Weidenfeld & Nicolson, 1976; New York: Knopf, 1976): pp. 162-169.

Periodical Publications:
FICTION:
"Hassan's Tower," *Nova* (June 1966): 100ff.;
"Voyage to Cytherea," *Mademoiselle*, 66 (December 1967): 98-99, 148-150;

"Faithful Lovers," *Saturday Evening Post*, 241 (April 1968): 62-65;

"A Pyrrhic Victory," *Nova* (July 1968): 80ff.;

"Crossing the Alps," *Mademoiselle*, 72 (February 1971): 154-155;

"Success Story," *Ms.*, 3 (December 1974): 52-55;

"Homework," *Ontario Review*, 7 (1977-1978): 7-13.

NONFICTION:

"Margaret Drabble Talking about Discipline," *Guardian* (10 January 1966): 6;

"The Fearful Flame of Arnold Bennett," *Observer* (11 May 1967): 12-14;

"The Sexual Revolution," *Guardian* (11 October 1967): 8;

"Women," *Listener*, 79 (4 April 1968): 425-426;

"Stepping into Debt," *Guardian* (12 August 1968): 7;

"Denying the Natural," *Listener*, 80 (5 December 1968): 750-751;

"Wordsworth: So Honourably Born," *London Times* (14 December 1968): 17;

"Money as a Subject for the Novelist," *Times Literary Supplement* (24 July 1969): 792-793;

"A Shocking Report," *Author*, 80 (Winter 1969): 169-171;

"A Myth to Stump the Experts," *New Statesman* (26 March 1971): 435;

"Perfect Ending," *Listener*, 85 (1 April 1971): 420-421;

"Doris Lessing: Cassandra in a World Under Seige," *Ramparts*, 10 (February 1972): 50-54;

"How Not To Be Afraid of Virginia Woolf," *Ms.*, 1 (November 1972): p. 68ff.;

"A Woman Writer," *Books*, 11 (Spring 1973): 4-6;

"Lawrence's Aphrodite: The Life of Frieda van Richthofen," *Encounter*, 41 (August 1973): 77-79;

"The Writer as Recluse: The Theme of Solitude in the Works of the Brontës," *Brontë Society Transactions*, 16 (1974): 259-269;

"T.V.," *Ms.*, 4 (February 1976), 32;

"Travels of a Housewife," *Spectator* (21 February 1976): 20;

"Jane Fonda: Her Own Woman at Last," *Ms.*, 6 (October 1977): 51-53;

"Elders and Betters?," *Observer* (9 October 1977): 13;

"A Woman's Life," *New Statesman* (3 November 1978): 585-586;

"Rape and Reason," *Observer* (10 December 1978): 9;

"No Idle Rentier: Angus Wilson and the Nourished Literary Imagination," *Studies in the Literary Imagination*, 13 (Spring 1980): 119-129.

Interviews:

Bolivar Le Franc, "An Interest in Guilt: Margaret Drabble," *Books and Bookmen*, 14 (September 1969): 20-21;

Terry Coleman, "A Biographer Waylaid by Novels," *Guardian*, 106 (15 April 1972): 23;

Nancy S. Hardin, "An Interview with Margaret Drabble," *Contemporary Literature*, 14 (Summer 1973): 273-295;

Joseph McCulloch, "Dialogue with Margaret Drabble," in his *Under Bow Bells: Dialogues with Joseph McCulloch* (London: Sheldon Press, 1974): pp. 125-132;

Nancy Poland, "Margaret Drabble: 'There Must Be a Lot of People Like Me,'" *Midwest Quarterly*, 16 (April 1975): 255-267;

Peter Firchow, ed., *The Writer's Place: Interviews on the Literary Situation in Contemporary Britain* (Minneapolis: University of Minneapolis Press, 1975): pp. 102-121;

Barbara Milton, "Art of Fiction LXX," *Paris Review* 74 (Fall 1978): 40-65;

Iris Rozencwajg, "Interview with Margaret Drabble," *Women's Studies*, 6 (1979): 335-347;

Dee Preussner, "Talking with Margaret Drabble," *Modern Fiction Studies*, 25 (1980): 563-577;

Diana Cooper-Clark, "Margaret Drabble: Cautious Feminist," *Atlantic Monthly*, 246 (November 1980): 69-75.

References:

Virginia K. Beards, "Margaret Drabble: Novels of a Cautious Feminist," *Critique*, 15 (1973): 35-46;

Colin Butler, "Margaret Drabble: *The Millstone* and Wordsworth," *English Studies*, 59 (August 1978): 353-360;

Cynthia Davis, "Unfolding Form: Narrative Approach and Theme in *The Realms of Gold*," *Modern Language Quarterly*, 40 (1979): 390-402;

Lee Edwards, "*Jerusalem the Golden*: A Fable for Our Times," *Women's Studies*, 6 (1979): 321-335;

E. Fox-Genovese, "Ambiguities of Female Identity: A Reading of the Novels of Margaret Drabble," *Partisan Review*, 46 (1979): 234-248;

Peter E. Firchow, "Rosamund's Complaint: Margaret Drabble's *The Millstone*," in *Old Lines, New Forces: Essays on the Contemporary British Novel, 1960-70*, edited by Robert K. Morris (Rutherford, N.J.: Fairleigh Dickinson Press, 1976): pp. 93-108;

Nancy S. Hardin, "Drabble's *The Millstone*: A Fable for Our Times," *Critique*, 15 (1973): 22-34;

Mary M. Lay, "Temporal Ordering in the Fiction of

Margaret Drabble," *Critique*, 21 (1979): 73-84;

Marion V. Libby, "Fate and Feminism in the Novels of Margaret Drabble," *Contemporary Literature*, 16 (Spring 1975): 175-192;

Joan Manheimer, "Margaret Drabble and the Journey to the Self," *Studies in the Literary Imagination*, 11 (1978): 127-143;

Valerie Grosvenor Myer, *Margaret Drabble: Puritanism and Permissiveness* (London: Vision Press, 1974; New York: Barnes & Noble, 1974);

Ellen C. Rose, "Surviving the Future," *Critique*, 15 (1973): 5-21;

Rose, "Feminine Endings—and Beginnings: Margaret Drabble's *The Waterfall*," *Contemporary Literature*, 21 (February 1980): 81-99;

Rose, *The Novels of Margaret Drabble: Equivocal Figures* (London: Macmillan, 1980);

Roger H. Sale, "Williams, Weesner, and Drabble," in his *On Not Being Good Enough: Writings of a Working Critic* (London: Oxford University Press, 1979): pp. 42-53;

Patricia Sharpe, "On First Looking into 'The Realms of Gold,'" *Michigan Quarterly Review* (Spring 1977): 225-231;

Susan Spitzer, "Fantasy and Femaleness in Margaret Drabble's *The Millstone*," *Novel*, 11 (Spring 1978): 227-245.

Maureen Duffy

(21 October 1933-   )

Gerard Werson

BOOKS: *That's How It Was* (London: New Authors Ltd., 1962);

The Single Eye (London: Hutchinson, 1964);

The Microcosm (London: Hutchinson, 1966; New York: Simon & Schuster, 1966);

The Paradox Players (London: Hutchinson, 1967; New York: Simon & Schuster, 1967);

Lyrics for the Dog Hour (London: Hutchinson, 1968);

Wounds (London: Cape, 1969; New York: Knopf, 1969);

Love Child (London: Weidenfeld & Nicolson, 1971; New York: Knopf, 1971);

The Venus Touch (London: Weidenfeld & Nicolson, 1971);

The Erotic World of Faery (London: Hodder & Stoughton, 1972; New York: Avon, 1980);

I Want To Go To Moscow (London: Hodder & Stoughton, 1973); republished as *All Heaven In A Rage* (New York: Knopf, 1973);

Capital (London: Cape, 1975; New York: Braziller, 1976);

The Passionate Shepherdess: Aphra Behn 1640-89 (London: Cape, 1977; New York: Avon, 1979);

Housespy (London: Hamilton, 1978);

Inherit the Earth: A Meditation on Family History (London: Hamilton, 1979);

Gor Saga (London: Eyre Methuen, 1981).

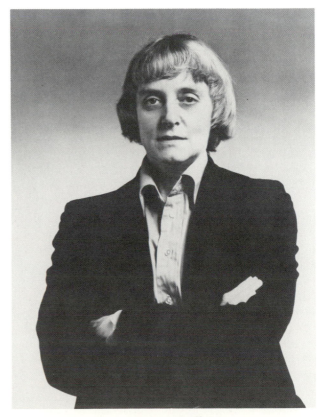

Maureen Duffy

Maureen Duffy's writing, in the many genres she has attempted, reflects both her involvement in contemporary society and her uneasy place in the English social system, as a Socialist, a lesbian, and an artist aware of her illegitimate and working-class origins. Her work, with its ambitious range, its versatility, and its vitality of language, is impressive. Her best novels are characterized by their brilliancy of style, their elegance of structural form, and their ability to suggest questions that haunt the mind. Several of her novels have received both critical and popular acclaim in Great Britain and the United States, but her fiction has not yet secured a large and widespread readership.

Duffy was born in Worthing, Sussex, to Grace Wright and Cahia P. Duffy, into an environment proletarian and impoverished. Her autobiographical first novel, *That's How It Was* (1962), describes the combination of maternal affection and material deprivation she experienced. The exceptional child from such a background, Duffy has sardonically observed, is "ever so bright and clever and lovely. . . . There's only one thing, I think, that works after that sort of attention, and that is a perfect emotional and sexual relationship. That is the only way in which what you lost can be put right. That's what I meant to convey in the last sentence of *That's How It Was*. That's how it was, and where the hell do I go from here? This is the basis of one's romanticism, of course. And even of one's classicism in the sense of the need for discipline. . . . It is cleverness that prevented you being stuck there, and destroyed by it, but once you are out, what you escaped from is what feeds you."

At age six she was evacuated with her mother to Trowbridge in Wiltshire, where she later began to write poetry. When she was fourteen she returned to her family home in Stratford, London, where she attended grammar school. She taught for two years at the City Literary Institute, Drury Lane, London, before she went to King's College, London, to read English, and after graduation in 1956 she taught for five years in various state schools. In 1972 she founded with colleagues a pressure group that swiftly achieved the parliamentary support necessary to pass the Public Lending Right rewarding authors from a central public fund whenever their work is borrowed from public libraries. Duffy is also closely involved with antivivisection pressure groups, and her interest in animal welfare crucially informs two of her novels, *I Want To Go To Moscow* (1973) and *Gor Saga* (1981). Until she wrote her first novel, she regarded herself as primarily a poet and a dramatist, and she has continued to work in the theater and to publish poetry. In 1961 she won the City of London Festival Playwright's Prize with *The Lay-Off* and in 1969 her play *Rites* had its premiere at the National Theatre. She has lived virtually all her adult life in London, the city she celebrates in *Capital* (1975).

Duffy's versatility, perhaps, has not succeeded in attracting readers who prefer the mixture of poetry, prose, and drama. Her poetry, her stage work, and her fiction all reflect, however, her desire to capture the truth of the moment in its emotional significance. In order to convey these truths Duffy confronts courageously the problem of achieving her own style, and this impression of struggle, of her attempt to achieve poetic precision, distinguishes her contributions to many different genres, and gives her best work a peculiar quality of felt life.

The dominant themes of Duffy's fiction can be traced to autobiographical sources: a preoccupation with education and "social engineering"; the status of outsider she bestows upon her major characters; her emphasis that love is in both personal and social terms a vital creative and redeeming force; her need to describe truthfully the varieties of sexual experience; and, of central importance, her commitment to the vernacular shaped by her artistry. Underlying these themes is a deep-rooted recognition (rendered in a bright, sensitive yet sinewy prose) that for all its grossness and frequent disregard for human and animal life, this world is the only world we possess: our attitude toward it ought, therefore, to be constructive.

Kit, the jealous Cupid who narrates *Love Child* (1971), contemplates the death and destruction she/he has caused, in a cadence which concludes the novel "She will have no more lovers except me. . . . I am my mother's lover now. But I didn't know, I didn't know." A poignant counterpoint between idealism and experience is thus described in language far removed from the language Duffy has condemned as the "terrible television, mid-Atlantic, jargon-ridden, technologised muck that people are learning to speak now." The force of idiomatic vernacular is seldom absent from Duffy's work, and when replaced in *Love Child* by a mandarin style appropriate to the world described in that novel, the effect is perhaps rather startling to some of her readers. This reliance upon the vernacular, the storehouse of communal wit, assists a prose style which is for the most part terse yet imagistic. "[N]o amount of repetition," remarks Mike, the narrator-photographer of *The Single Eye* (1964), "will give a scene more meaning. Better one clear picture than an endless repeating because in the end . . . we retain one, one that has all the essentials, and that is the essential." Duffy's fiction is rooted in realism, yet, as she acknowledges, realism is for her a form of metaphor. The major influences upon her style she notes as Joyce Carey, James Joyce, and Virginia Woolf and, among the Americans, F. Scott Fitzgerald, Upton Sinclair, and Theodore Dreiser. The resulting blend is unlike the conventional, often rather tepid English novel written by such contemporaries as Susan Hill and Margaret Drabble, and Duffy feels "more of an affinity with continental writers."

The autobiographical *That's How It Was* begins with the birth of its heroine, Paddy, but this is no satisfactory bourgeois event: "Lucky for me I was born at all really, I mean she could have decided not to bother. Like she told me, she was tempted, head in the gas oven, in front of a bus, oh a thousand ways." Paddy's mother, a "small fierce flame," provides the warmth necessary to sustain a child in the poor, cold 1930s; her father, "the loveliest dancer and the most terrible liar," disappears two months after her birth. Suffering with pleurisy, "that fantastic running battle she kept up for twenty years," the mother sustains the daughter through the war years, their wanderings in search of a home, her marriage into a large and rowdy family, and the constant struggle to provide Paddy with the education with which she can climb out of poverty. The novel focuses on the relationships between Paddy and her mother, her stepbrothers, her school friends and the schoolteacher on whom she has a "crush." It concludes with the death of her mother and the girl's adult awareness that she has lost what has inspired her. *That's How It Was* in one of the few authentic accounts in British fiction of a working-class childhood and is one of the most successful. Shaped with the tact and the discipline of an accomplished novelist, its style is remarkably assured. The dramatic immediacy characteristic of this writer's work is conveyed through an exact, precise notation: "By the time truth has been strained through someone else it's not the same colour anyway, that's why I'm putting all this down now. It's like trying to catch a flea on a sheet. You pin it down under your forefinger and just as you shift ever such a bit, its away and the chase is on again." The narrator adds: "When you finally catch it and crack it between your thumbnails, there's a little pop and a nasty mess and that's that."

The novel's events of emotional significance unfold against their historical backgrounds: the hunger marchers are seen as "grey shuffling men putting one foot before the other with the abstracted concentration of inanition." The narrator's controlled anger registers its point through deft characterization: "[Aunt Liddy] knew all her tables up to fourteen times, the Kings and Queens of England, the stories of the Maid of Norway, the princes in the Tower, how King Charles hid in the oak tree, and all about the Great Fire and the famous battles of the last century: the Factory Acts somehow got left out." Duffy's laconically accurate style expels sentimentality, and the narrator does not act as a commentator, thus removing any suggestion of patronage and contributing to the immediacy of the work. The honesty and generosity of spirit of mother and child are reflected in the quality of the prose, which suggests Ernest Hemingway's definition of courage as grace under pressure, and also several of Stevie Smith's idiosyncratic and arresting poems. The novelist has had to organize a great deal of material, and the controlled style of her narrative imposes an order upon the chaos of grief and loss. After their street has suffered bomb damage and her mother has disappeared, the lonely Paddy maintains a vigil in the front-room window: "in the afternoon of the fourth day, I saw her—a tiny figure far off but I knew it . . . she came on doggedly towards me as I gazed out of that front-room window, down the road, in those daft boots, and she was alive."

Two years elapsed after the enthusiastic critical reception of *That's How It Was* before Duffy's second novel, *A Single Eye*, appeared. The narrator, the photographer Mike, is the first of the prominent male characters in Duffy's fiction. The author reverses customary expectations, in a schema that is too neat, by making Mike's Italian wife, Toni, a dark cloud of apathy and negation, and the Northerner Mike the gregarious partner desiring good companionship. Three relationships dominate the narrative: that between Mike and Toni; the affair between Mike and his sister-in-law; and the homosexual attraction expressed toward Mike by his colleague, Colin. An adulterous affair conducted by another of Mike's colleagues develops the novel's theme of the variety of emotional and sexual response, which stands in ironic contrast to the novel's title. *A Single Eye* is, in form and style, Duffy's most conventional work, although its atmosphere reflects the early days in England of the "Permissive Society." The construction of narrative and dialogue is skillful, yet (inevitably in a work including an element of allegory) characterization is often registered through externals: the novel is patently manufactured. It asserts, as does most of Duffy's work, the vital relevance of art and love to the human condition. The art eagerly adopted by Mike's working-class adolescent students is photography, twin of the cinema and the most democratic art form invented. Toni is a failed artist, and her incomplete work mirrors her failure of spirit; Mike's success with his camera accompanies his desire and regard for his sister-in-law. Locked into their unhappy marriage ("a strange condition of isolation where we mocked at the rest of the world"), Mike is physically ill and comments "If I loved [Toni] and gave her security, she would get better. You can't believe the whole world is terrible if you love someone, it makes an exception, a chink to let the light through until everything is flooded with it."

A Single Eye makes explicit the author's attitude toward homosexuality. Her discovery of her sexuality, she has remarked, was "unifying. . . . To understand takes away a lot of the residual pain and worry. It never seemed to me in the least unnatural or immoral or even, once I'd made the intellectual discovery, particularly unusual." Yet the contemporary climate of opinion obliges her to defend her position and that of many of her characters, and she sketches three main strategies: "we love many people of all ages and sexes," Mike observes. "Mother love, supposedly the most beautiful in the world, can take on some pretty hideous faces"; previous ages have felt differently, Colin observes, listing a few of the many great names who preferred the company of their own sex; and Mike's friend Kate, invoking Christian charity, remarks, "I've got too many sins of the flesh of my own to come down heavily on other people's." Underlying these defensive arguments is the author's detestation (expressed by Colin to Toni) of the "steadily advancing theory of psychological conformity, the well-adjusted personality, mature, happy, accepting the standards of its own society." He adds: "You can find thousands in any ant-heap or beehive," and twice in *A Single Eye* the response of the heterosexual toward the homosexual is a test of his liberalism and his integrity.

The Microcosm is, to date, Duffy's only novel to deal almost exclusively with the topic of female homosexuality, and it earned enthusiastic reviews when it appeared in 1966. Unlike the majority of male writers (themselves almost invariably gay) who present the subject of homosexuality within a framework of incessant moralizing (Marcel Proust, Jean Genet) and employ frequent images of violence, despair, and instability (John Rechy, William Burroughs, Hubert Selby), Duffy gives the reader a book which is credible and illuminating and avoids the sentimentality that infests E. M. Forster's

Maureen Duffy

Maurice. Duffy's homosexual characters are not always drinking the brandy of the damned. The novel draws upon the author's experience as a schoolteacher, and also on her fascination with, as she describes it, "the whole queer club metier, and . . . the Dantesque atmosphere of the 'underground.'. . ." The book was originally conceived as a nonfiction study, and the author incorporated "lots of characters I had interviewed, and others I knew personally . . . so that I could get as full a range as possible in the Dantesque sense. . . ." The novel mixes several modes of narrative, including a stream-of-consciousness monologue and a brilliant pastiche of Daniel Defoe's wordy and loving descriptions of Moll Flanders. (It anticipates the method of *Capital*, a novel that attempts to give the reader a panoramic view through many shifts of perspective.)

The Microcosm opens in a nightclub, the House of Shades, and the opening pages are mosaics of almost Firbankian dialogue, both inviting and disorientating the reader. His confusion is analogous to that experienced by the homosexual victims of majority prejudice, and the novel throughout mirrors this confusion in its lack of lucidity. Duffy's

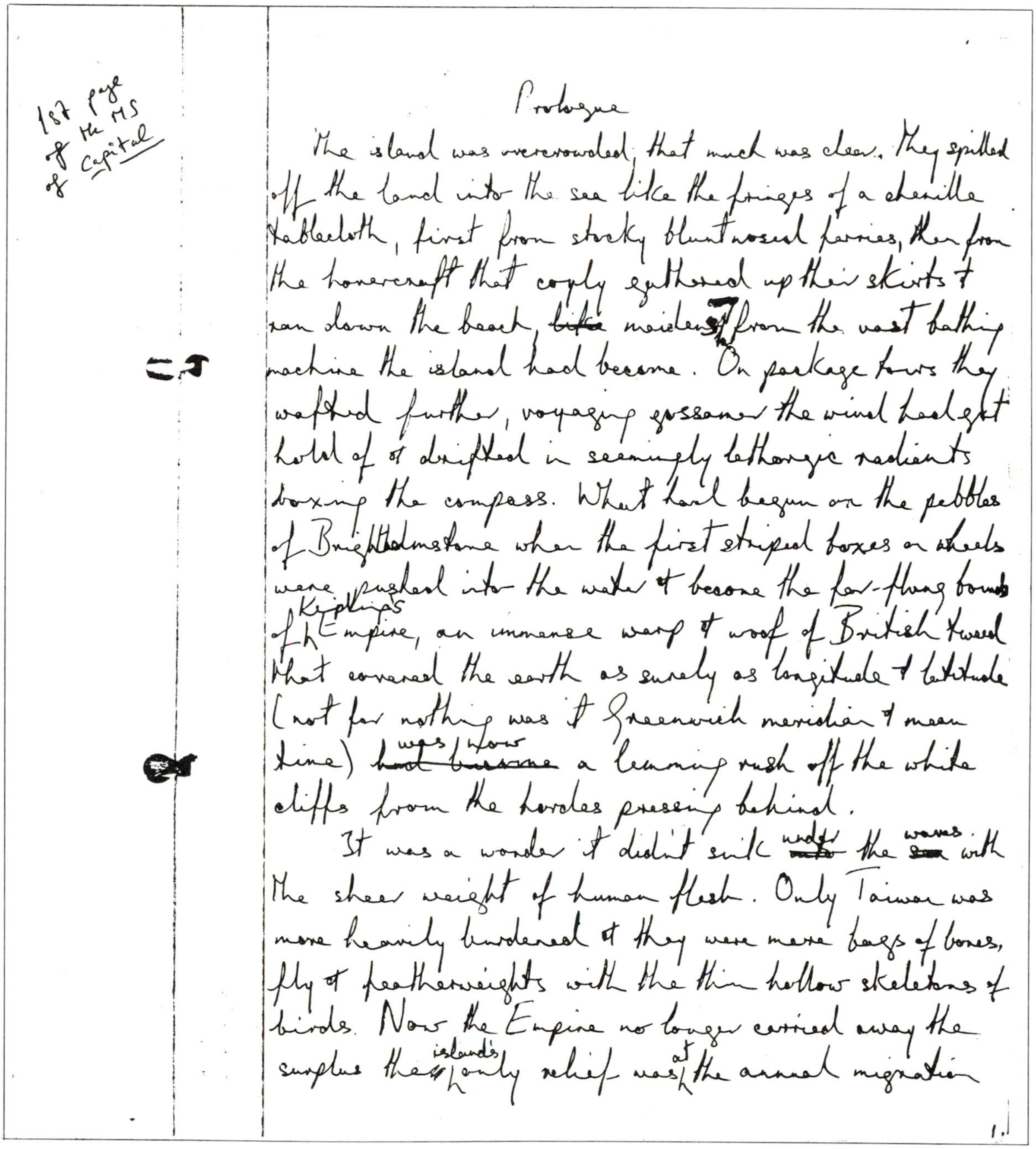

1st page
of the MS
of Capital

Prologue

The island was overcrowded; that much was clear. They spilled off the land into the sea like the fringes of a chenille tablecloth, first from stocky blunt-nosed ferries, then from the hovercraft that coyly gathered up their skirts & ran down the beach, like maidens, from the vast bathing machine the island had become. On package tours they wafted further, voyaging gossamer the wind held light hold of & drifted in seemingly lethargic radients boxing the compass. What had begun on the pebbles of Brighthelmstone when the first striped boxes on wheels were pushed into the water & became the far-flung bounds of *Kipling's* Empire, an immense warp & woof of British tweed that covered the earth as surely as longitude & latitude (not for nothing was it Greenwich meridian & mean time) *was / how* had become a lemming rush off the white cliffs from the hordes pressing behind.

It was a wonder it didn't sink *into* the *sea* with the sheer weight of human flesh. Only Taiwan was more heavily burdened & they were mere bags of bones, fly & featherweights with the thin hollow skeletons of birds. Now the Empire no longer carried away the surplus their *island's* only relief was the annual migration

Capital, *first page of manuscript*

work is seen to its best advantage when her prose luxuriates in a strict but elegant economy of style, but *The Microcosm* gives the impression of an undigested mass of notes and jottings, almost as if a conventional novel—focusing on the three major characters Steve, Cathy, and Matt—has been clumsily mixed with more experimental ingredients. The reader is impressed with the author's penetrating eye: the descriptions of the schoolmistress, Steve, in her class and her staff room; the bus conductress, Cathy; and the women working in a factory assembly line are captured with Duffy's quick, accurate sketches. She demonstrates the truth of the dictum from Louis MacNeice's poem "Snow and Roses" (the epigraph to *The Microcosm*): "World is crazier and more of it than we think, / Incorrigibly plural." The attempt to describe a range of varying social classes and occupations in this world in miniature is not free of a sense of artificiality and strain. There is also a polemical coarseness about the conclusion of the novel that is perhaps inseparable from the era in which it was published.

The publication in 1967 of *The Paradox Players* confirmed the impression of Duffy's versatility of theme and style. It draws upon the novelist's experience in its description of a colony of exiles from society living in houseboats moored on a small Thames island near Hampton Court. The central character, Sym, is an unsuccessful writer, and the novel begins with his attempts to clear his writer's block. After an unhappy affair with his neighbor Sassie, he discovers that he is able to write, but that his manuscript is no substitute for the loss of the beloved. In the opening pages of *The Paradox Players* lurks a suspicion of Muriel Spark's self-conscious game-playing with fiction, but Duffy is too much a realist to detain us there for long, and she quickly takes up Sym's struggle for survival and his attempt to create a new identity in this colony of dropouts. Sym and his neighbors wish to reject society, yet their unavoidable emotional and financial links with each other provide an element of understated comedy. The anarchist Walden, who spends much time contemplating the pleasures of the body but who has not made love to his wife for more than a year, returns to the city in order to provide for his wife and children; Sassie knowingly rejects the possibilities of love. Although it skillfully displays characterization and lively incidental detail, the novel lacks dramatic momentum, and the issues of choice and responsibility confronting the exiles are not addressed with sufficient force and complexity. If Henry James's question, "What is the ado here?" were posed, it would be difficult to produce an answer of substance, and the novel has the hallmarks of experience that has not undergone alchemy into art.

In *Wounds* (1969), however, Duffy displays the mastery of style and organization evident in her first novel. *Wounds* is in part a gloss on the lines from John Donne's "The Good-Morrow": "For love, all love of other sights controules, / And makes one little roome, an everywhere." The novel depicts a contrast between an unnamed man and woman exploring their physical desire for each other, and the world surrounding them. The novel's title is all-inclusive: Duffy's major and minor characters experience almost everything except freedom from pain. Characters are introduced periodically into the episodic structure and are gradually woven together, while the image of the lovers is used throughout as a leitmotiv. Duffy's shortest novel to date and one of her most harmonious combinations of style, narrative design, and characterization, its greater integration of style and content also marks a development in her career: with the publication of *Wounds* and its successors, Duffy secured and consolidated her position as one of the major novelists of postwar Britain.

In a novel preoccupied with language, a black immigrant nurse who dislikes English hypocrisy, fastens upon "their words that were sharp and cold, untextured, adding no richness of layered color but defined, precisioned, tooled so that the language they spoke didn't give themselves, wasn't offered out of them in generosity, the sounds tumbling, breaking into colored bubbles, the punctuation cries of love or pain, but etched them into age, class, sex and left you to make your bid because you had to and then they would slide away." The lovers are capable of a rich, textured language, yet outside their bedroom the wounds of class division and racial and sexual prejudice persist. The contrasts between black and white; rich and poor; educated and uneducated; heterosexual and homosexual; and kindness and malice surround the lovers, yet the combination of fortitude and irony peculiar to Duffy's major works knits it together stylistically.

Similar virtues inform *Love Child*, which received on publication in 1971 a critical reception marked by indifference and hostility. The novel is narrated by a child (whose sex is not specified) who begins in magical fashion: "It was I who christened my mother's lover." Kit is identified with Cupid, and his/her mother, is Venus, to the child, the name she bears throughout the book. Kit is also an artist, and the plot he/she fashions gives the mythology of art. Yet the brilliant child is only able to grasp truths through a cold ratiocination and is, in the grip of his/her jealousy, incessantly elaborating upon his/her mother's infidelity, and remains ignorant of the heart's reasons. Kit's adoration of Venus is based on self, and in order for him/her to transcend this egotism (if this is indeed signaled in the ambiguous conclusion) Kit triggers the death of his/her mother's lover. Self-knowledge is gained at the price of pain caused to the beloved.

Love Child is set in Italy where the child with the skill of a spy watches a love affair develop between Venus and Ajax, the father's secretary. A work that has much to say about its creation and about the nature of art, the book wears its Freudian allusions with ease, and it is written with a brilliancy marred only by its stilted discussions of aesthetics. The book is unusual among her works in that matters of social and political importance are raised by implication. "One of the points I wanted to demonstrate," Duffy observes, "by making the family so rich was that political questions did not apply to them . . . throughout *Love Child* I try to show that when you've solved the political problems, the emotional ones will still exist. It is also one of the reasons for returning to childhood again, because you are not then conscious of the political and social, yet it is impinging upon you." Narrated by Kit in a cool and elegant style, the voices that break through his/her obsession are foreign: American dropouts and his/her Italian accomplice, and at a finishing school in Switzerland, Jude: "Where her hands moved flames licked up so that I was powerless to pull away as she undid the zipper. 'You're a virgin,' she said. 'You'll go like a bomb.' I braced my leg muscles to keep me from falling and as the pain and pleasure bit through me I heard her say, 'It isn't love, Kit, it isn't love.' My mouth filled with ash." Several key images in the novel, perhaps most notably the scene in which Kit spies on Venus and Ajax through a periscope, are effective in their ability to support great concentrations of meaning.

I Want To Go To Moscow, published in 1973, takes us into a world of terrorism conducted by middle-class and aristocratic men and women who are determined to prevent cruelty to animals by any means necessary. Their organization, AHIAR (All Heaven In A Rage), contrives the escape from prison of the beautifully named Jarvis Chuff in return for his criminal expertise. The novel is presented through the eyes of Chuff (though not narrated by him) and therefore narrated in the speech of ordinary working people. This rich idiom guides our response upon the discovery that the princess is none other than the music hall artiste, Lottie Shoe;

the padre is a con man who has done time in prison. Also admirable is the courage of AHIAR in its futile attempt to achieve by force what can only be accomplished through persuasion and legislation. Jarvis is assisted by the glamorous Philomela in a partnership that owes something to the thriller genre, which is affectionately and thoughtfully parodied in *I Want To Go To Moscow*.

Several of the gang's exploits (a raid on a mink farm, the destruction of an abattoir) are imagined with an almost hypnotic combination of swift action and surreal detail, but what knits together the disparate elements of the novel and holds attention is the "hero" Chuff. He is an intelligent man, who can quote a little William Blake, yet who rejected the welfare state education seized by his classmate Edwards: "It seemed a straight choice: either you went their way, the way of Crawler Edwards, or you were bolshie and went your own way, the way you'd been brought up in. Neither, it seemed to Chuff, would give him the onion-domed dream city, jewelled and loud with bells." The novel explores with skill the play between legality and illegality, that which is morally wrong, yet not legally prohibited. It is a tribute to her skill that Duffy is able to combine credible characterization and style with a novel of ideas with little sense of strain.

Capital presents a central character, an autodidact, around whom revolves a novel of ideas, and an element of farcical comedy that is a welcome addition to Duffy's style. An ambitious novel, *Capital* attempts to celebrate London as James Joyce celebrated Dublin in *Ulysses* (1922). The narrative gives three points of view: through London's past, evoked through a variety of characters (introduced are Arthur and Merlin, Dick Whittington, Sir Thomas Wyatt, King Elisabeth [sic], Oscar Wilde in Reading Gaol); through London's present, evoked through the letters of a university lecturer to his beloved; and through the adventures of the central character, Meepers. The lecturer asserts that the eighteenth century, a period he teaches, was harsh, but, unlike our own, it remained in touch with reality: for him the city has meaning only when it houses the woman he loves. Meepers loves neither man nor woman but London, and his present is its past and future as he attempts to prove that the great city lived through the so-called Dark Ages, that its salvation lies in its historical continuity.

Meepers informally attends the university lectures at Queen's College where he works as a porter. He sleeps at night in a succession of little sheds in public parks. In a fascinating and strangely plausible passage he "ran his mind through Lon-

I London

1st page of
the MS of
Housespy

'And the lady is a lush,' Sir John Harpieson said & let go
the firing pin on the miniature dun camouflaged field gun,
Great War vintage, sited on the blotter in front of him, so that
it whammed a matchstick salvo across the room with deliberate
eccentricity.

They loved it of course, Scully thought, his minions giggling
nervously behind the filing cabinets. Old Harpie they called
him or 'CRB', standing for Clean Round the Bend, though it
was, 'Yes, Sir John,' to his face & rarely, 'No, Sir John,' when
that was what he expected. Something about _quin_ & the subjunctive
for questions expecting the answer 'no' flitted involuntarily, & no
doubt erroneously, through Scully's upper mind like a sunbeam
through water to rest teasingly on the bottom of his consciousness where it would lie, a meaningless bright focus of half
attention, until he could blot it out.

'American wives also expect to earn their keep by taking
a quite needless interest in their husbands' jobs. This one is
the same, expecting to be invited, included, even, I imagine,
in the safety of the marital home or bed, consulted, told. There ought
to be a directive that all men in responsible positions should
marry well trained British, preferably of course & English, wives
who know nothing & expect to know nothing. But there isn't.
They go on conferences & pick them up like clap. The League
of American Nations organises manhunts for distinguished
foreigners with their divorced daughters as bait & everyone

Housespy, *first page of manuscript*

don's monuments," his rucksack on his back, thinking of places to stay: "He was too old for the liftless heights of Nelson's Column or the Monument." Meepers's homeless and disorientated state indicates the poverty and the decay of our great cities. (Fewer people live in London today than in 1901, although the national population levels are virtually the same). With its vivid skill and ambition, *Capital* is only a partial success, and there is a discord between characterization and structural form that results in a lack of unity.

Housespy (1978) and *Gor Saga*, Duffy's most recent novels, are perhaps her best-plotted fictions and are impressive demonstrations of her power as a stylist, as a novelist of ideas, and as a creator of real people. The note of farcical comedy present in her two previous novels is allied here with a bleak statement of our cupidity and cruelty. Her fiction takes on a richer, darker coloring, and its structure becomes more intricate and complex. Duffy is never simply a pessimist, and there is little sense in her work of the novelist's personal frustration masquerading as analysis of the ills of society, yet in her recent work there is a distance from the statement in *The Single Eye*: "It was all clear to me. The suffering was unimportant. It was part of the pattern, part of growth, but it was never final, the last word. The last word is always positive."

Housespy, published in 1978, is an espionage thriller (in a sense Duffy's best works are all thrillers) and is a superb example of the genre. It has all the elements of the bestseller—sex, politics, treachery in high places, murder—and its inability to date to secure wide sales is puzzling. What gives the novel its distinction is its patterning, its design: it is, stylistically, a tour de force. Scully, the housespy, is a senior policeman assigned to protect the Socialist Minister for Economic Planning. The minister's rich American wife, Danny, causes Scully unease with her excessive drinking, and her flight from home raises the possibility of blackmail and takes Scully abroad in pursuit.

The novel is a wilderness of mirrors, and the reader is constantly surprised by the detonation of appearances, of surface reality. Scully, a liberal and intelligent man, is a stranger in his own department. Harpic, a high-ranking civil servant, is not faithful in his vow of allegiance to Her Majesty's government, yet the toy weapons with which he plays indicate his real nature. Scully's daughter leads a separate life, and her boyfriend is revealed as a police informer instructed to watch Scully. The minister, Oldfield, is by background and education an establishment man, yet his accent does not reflect his origins. Danny does not behave as a Cabinet minister's wife ought; Oldfield is attempting to bypass Parliament with his radical legislation; his secretary, who does not behave in bed as Scully expects her to, is also an informer. The pretty girl Scully dances with in a nightclub is in fact a boy; Scully is a little in love with Danny, who cannot return his response; her friend, the lesbian Martha, is raped and murdered by a man who remarks, "I didn't know whether she was dying or coming." The dialogues of the major characters are brief, often garbled, and secretly recorded. Scully (a mirror-image of Jarvis Chuff) and Oldfield are untypical of their social classes and professions, and all are exiled by sexual proclivity, beliefs, temperament, or nationality.

Gor Saga, published in 1981, is a fable (with certain resemblances in style and content to those by George Orwell and Aldous Huxley) and is one of the few works of its kind not to suffer by comparison. It is recognizably set in the near future and is rooted in the present political climate of England. The novel combines two of the author's most pressing concerns: the nature of socio-political organization, and (an intrinsic part of that organization) human response to the knowledge that man is part animal in nature and desire. Gor is not human, remarks his creator, the scientist Forrester, who is also Gor's father, he is "just humanoid: the test-tube product of a gorilla ovum and human sperm." Like his author-creator, Gor is illegitimate and is brought up in a working-class environment. Forrester creates Gor, in a parody of the artistic impulse, to demonstrate to his colleagues that his scientific miracle can be achieved. Of lowly origins, Forrester is one of the few to rise through the rigid caste system, and he sends Gor to a military college to perfect his creation and to give the boy, of simian appearance, the manners of a gentleman. Gor, having escaped the conformist forces that created him, resorts to the nomadic poverty suffered by those who refuse to accept subsistence in the shanty towns.

The key image in this novel, imprisonment versus creativity, is repeated several times. The ability to cage human regard for self and others is reflected in the English caste system, and Forrester's loveless marriage and the elitist snobbery of the ancient English universities share characteristics of a cold universal selfishness and obsession with wealth. It is a sorrowful and angry vision (resembling at times Charles Dickens's view in *Little Dorrit*, 1855-1857, of life and society as a vast cage): Emily, a major character in *Gor Saga*, "suddenly saw the world as bound together in layers of suffering, an imprisoning mesh from which here a face looked out or there a hand grasped at the air outside and was drawn back."

The dominant mood of the novel is not resignation. The physical prowess of Gor and his skill as a painter of murals compel his classmates' admiration, and he is befriended; the constant of maternal affection is present (though shown toward the baby and adolescent Gor by foster mothers); freedom of choice allows Forrester's wife to leave him, and also bonds together the oppressed who are determined to resist their betters. As in Duffy's first novel, individual acts of kindness shine out in a dark world. The celebrated fictions in this genre (those by Yevgeni Zamyatin, George Orwell, Aldous Huxley, David Karp, and several writers of science fiction) had, it seemed, looted the precious seam of its gold, but Duffy presents a version of the future that is distinctive in its structure and its ideology. In a didactic work of this kind, it is difficult for the author not to insist, and some elements (the rich speech of Emily's mother; the flowers and dancing in the streets of the urban guerrillas) are pointed up too explicitly; but the novel's disciplined and economic control of its subject matter is admirable.

Duffy's new fiction will undoubtedly evidence the versatility of theme and subject she has displayed in the past, and an artistic control similar to that demonstrated in her recent works. This versatility has made it difficult for publishers and readers accustomed to novelists repeating the mixture as before to ensure for Duffy a wide publication and readership. The republication in hardback and paperback of her major novels—*That's How It Was*, *Wounds*, *Love Child*, *Housespy*, and the wide sale of *Gor Saga*—ought to be a matter of urgent concern to those who care for serious fiction. This writer is one of the few major novelists of postwar Britain who is both in touch with the contemporary England familiar to ordinary people, and who is able to convey that reality through fiction written with grace, intelligence, and passion.

Other:
Rites in *New Short Plays* (London: Methuen, 1969);
A Nightingale Sang In Berkely Square in *Factions*, edited by Giles Gordon and Alex Hamilton (London: Michael Joseph, 1974).

Reference:
Jane Rule, *Lesbian Images* (London: Peter Davies, 1976).

Papers:
The largest collection of Duffy's papers is at King's College University of London.

Janice Elliott
(14 October 1931-   )

Virginia Briggs
University of Delaware

BOOKS: *Cave with Echoes* (London: Secker & Warburg, 1962);
The Somnambulists (London: Secker & Warburg, 1964);
The Godmother (London: Secker & Warburg, 1966; New York: Holt, Rinehart & Winston, 1967);
The Buttercup Chain (London: Secker & Warburg, 1967);
The Singing Head (London: Secker & Warburg, 1968);
Angels Falling (London: Secker & Warburg, 1969; New York: Knopf, 1969);
The Kindling (London: Secker & Warburg, 1970; New York: Knopf, 1970);

The Birthday Unicorn (London: Gollancz, 1970);
A State of Peace (London: Hodder & Stoughton, 1971; New York: Knopf, 1971);
Private Life (London: Hodder & Stoughton, 1972);
Alexander in the Land of Mog (Leicester: Brockhampton Press, 1973);
Heaven on Earth (London: Hodder & Stoughton, 1975);
A Loving Eye (London: Hodder & Stoughton, 1977);
The Honey Tree (London: Hodder & Stoughton, 1978);
Summer People (London: Hodder & Stoughton, 1980);
Secret Places (London: Hodder & Stoughton, 1981);

Janice Elliott

The Country of Her Dreams (London: Hodder & Stoughton, 1982).

Both British and American reviewers have praised novelist Janice Elliott's control of events, use of dialogue, descriptive prose, and imagery as being "outstanding in her generation." In addition, she has been called "one of the best novelists writing in England at the moment (and no sexual qualification is needed)." Having served as a book reviewer for nearly eighteen years, she has apparently learned what pleases and what does not, and she has used this knowledge to her advantage in her fiction. In 1982, with fifteen novels and two children's books to her credit, she still reviews fiction for the *Sunday Telegraph* every three weeks.

Janice Elliott was born in Derbyshire in 1931 to Douglas John and Dorothy Wilson Elliott. Her father was an advertising executive. She has written and read nonstop from the age of five, although

nothing of her early work survives. Her recent novel, *Secret Places* (1981), draws heavily on her school days, but she is careful to point out that the book is not autobiographical—she is neither Laura nor Patti, the book's two heroines. Educated at St. Anne's College, Oxford, where she read English and was active in dramatics (she played Queen Eleanor in the Oxford University Dramatic Society's production of *King John* and wrote four verse plays as well), she took an honors degree in English in 1953. She began her professional writing career as a journalist, working first as a subeditor for *House and Garden* magazine. Then during the 1950s and early 1960s she worked for various periods as a staff journalist for *House Beautiful*, as beauty editor for *Harper's Bazaar*, and as a full-time journalist for the London *Sunday Times*'s women's page. She began her first novel, *Cave with Echoes* (1962), in 1959 while still working for the *Sunday Times* on its newly formed *Colour Magazine*. Also in 1959 she married Robert Cooper, public relations manager for Esso. In 1962 the Coopers moved from London to Partridge Green, Sussex, into a sixteenth-century Tudor cottage that they fell in love with. They now live in Fowey, Cornwall.

In Sussex, relatively isolated from London, Elliott began devoting more time to writing novels, having left her enjoyable but demanding job with the *Times*. She worked as a free-lance journalist and reviewer first for the *Sunday Times*, then for the *Times*, and in 1968-1969 for the *New Statesman*. In 1969 she became a columnist for *Twentieth Century Magazine*, a position she held until 1972. She also began reviewing for the London *Sunday Telegraph* during this period. Although at age thirty she began to have novels published, it was not until she gave birth to a son and had her third novel published that she felt she was "wholly committed" to writing fiction. With regret, she abandoned journalism almost altogether in 1972, retaining only her position as book reviewer for the *Sunday Telegraph* (again as assurance of a steady income).

Written in her spare time, Elliott's first novel, *Cave with Echoes*, is narrated by a man on the edge of madness who looks back on his life and his struggle to be accepted. Jonah defends himself against the pain of rejection, first from his mother, who thoughtlessly uses him to keep her husband. He is sent to public school, where he unsuccessfully tries to win friends, and then to Oxford, where he briefly steadies his unstable personality with the help of his roommate's affections. Through his roommate, Sparrow, he meets Agnes, with whom he falls in love and marries, and for a time he becomes integrated into London society. His happiness is short-lived, however. Shunned another time by the one he loves, he is left on the verge of a total breakdown. The depth of characterization in this book is typical of Elliott's style, and her effort was acclaimed by the *Times Literary Supplement* reviewer as an "unusual first novel, colourful and fascinating."

Elliott's second novel, *The Somnambulists* (1964), resembles her first not only because it deals with upper-middle-class morals and the theme of love and rejection, but also because she develops her characters naturally and realistically. In this novel she first introduces the theme of war and its effects on British society, one of her favorite and most successful fiction topics. The story centers on twins Jessica and Andrew Purdy, who, along with their younger brother, David, were orphaned at an early age. Jessica becomes increasingly attached to and possessive of Andrew as they grow up under the supervision of the "Moon Faces," their guardians at the estate their parents have bequeathed to them. When Andrew leaves for Oxford, Jessica tries to strike out on her own; becoming involved with a Nazi organization, she meets and falls in love with "Piggy" Price. When he is killed in a riot at a political demonstration, Jessica withdraws into herself and struggles to regain security through Andrew's love. When Andrew decides not to marry Alice Molteno, a frivolous upper-middle-class girl he has known from childhood, Jessica recovers the control over him that she desperately needs.

While still holding her journalism position, Elliott produced her third novel, *The Godmother*, in 1966. Its leading character, Helen Porter, an old, eccentric, upper-middle-class woman, has been compared to the type of character found in the novels of E. M. Forster or Virginia Woolf. The story begins with the christening of Helen's nephew, James, and develops around the influence she exerts not only upon him and his mistress, Anne, but upon everyone else with whom she comes in contact. She feels she has discovered the secret of life—to be thoroughly oneself—and lives to pass it on to her many "children." The novel has been described as "thoroughly convincing within the limitations of a strictly private outlook."

The Buttercup Chain (1967) followed this success and proved to be the only one of Elliott's novels that has not been well received. Critics argued that the work created "an artificial emotion and rarified humbug" brought out both in the dialogue (the characters never speak except in the language of young children) and in the incidents affecting the speakers. Frances and Margaret, Fred and Manny,

the principal characters, are placed in a situation so idyllic that it becomes forced and unnatural. Taking a holiday from their studies, they travel together from Oslo to Venice to a Greek island, and in the process learn who they really are: to their relief they discover that they are "very ordinary people." Elliott wrote the novel in three months, mainly for fun. Although it failed with the critics, it was filmed by Columbia Pictures. Directed by Robert Ellis Miller, the film premiered in May 1970 to adequate reviews, despite the phoniness of the story.

Elliott redeemed herself with the critics a year later with *The Singing Head* (1968). Using imagery from Greek mythology, she produced her first novel that works well on two different levels. On the surface, the plot concerns a campus scandal into which Marcus Wilson, a teacher of English at Crowfield College, Sussex, finds himself drawn. He is falsely accused of homosexuality in order to divert attention from the numerous other disreputable undertakings of various staff members. Marcus is a man haunted by his past. His wife's suicide drives him into a state of passiveness which allows others to manipulate him, for he does not have the energy to turn away those who maliciously and wrongly implicate him. Somehow, though, Marcus always manages to wind up on top of the situation. Eventually, his accusers implicate their own falsehood, and Marcus regains a position of honor at the college. On another level, each character can be identified with a Greek deity: Athene, Apollo, Dionysus. Marcus resembles Orpheus, the oracle and poet who continued singing though his head was cut from his body and thrown into a river. Similarly, Marcus refuses to give in though his enemies apparently have defeated him.

The next year Elliott produced *Angels Falling* (1969), a novel she claims to have enjoyed writing so much that she could for the first time sketch out the chapters ahead. It won praise for its vivid and wide-ranging characterizations, an element which, from this point, became the driving force of Elliott's novels. Here she develops a realistic story about a family, using the form of myth: the father and mother are the king and queen, and their children are their subjects. At the beginning, Lily Garland, the mother and "queen," is on her deathbed, her family gathered around her. The sixty years of her life are recalled as characters come and go at her bedside. Among the extensively developed characters is her husband, Andrew, who fought courageously in the trenches during World War I until driven temporarily insane by the death of his best friend, whereupon he rebelled and became a

2

'And then,' she wrote, ' Deborah knocked three times, the door
swung open, and she entered the country of her dreams.'

2 line #
after full out line # throughout

─ 'Tomorrow we could have a picnic,' said Mary Lamb , reaching for a
fig and not displeased with any of this: her firm, round, brown arm,
the gold kxasakxkagix bangle against it, the   scrubbed, happily
loaded table beneath the trellised vine and her friends around it.
And her husband, Nicholas - she was certainly pleased with Nicholas.

 ' Yes, Mrs Ramsay.' Nicholas looked over his spectacles.

 ' ─Ramsay?'

Nicholas waved his paperback. ' Woolf.'

2

 ' Oh, her. ' Mary opened her mouth to ask Nancy Prewitt what she
thought of Woolf, then closed it because Nancy would tell her. Instead,
Mary split open the ripe fig . Its seeds spilled and the juice ran
down her arm . She licked and sucked. It's over-ripe, she thought, like
me - ah, well. ' Figs are like flesh,' she said.

 ' Cannibal.' Nicholas smiled and ░░░░░░░░░░░░░░░░░░░░░░
░░░░░░░░░░░░░░░░░░░ leaned towards her. She offered him the
open vulva of the fig - a private joke none of the others caught, married
complicity. Oh, she did love him.
         Come
 ' Painting tomorrow?'
H e shook his head.' ░░░ *Opening ceremonies. All that.'*

Joe Porterhouse, down the table, caught this. He leaned his big bulk
across Nancy Prewitt and waved his fork. ' You should get in on this,
Maria. You and your *books* ░░░░ .'

Mary smiled, ░░░░░ almost ░░░ yawned. Poor Nancy looked squashed,
sallow, frowned at her peach.
 ' The *Abri des Arts?* ░░░░░ Oh no, I don't think so. ░░░░░░░░ *Not children's stories.*
░░░░░░░░░░░░░░░░░░░░░░░░░░░░░░░░░░░░░░
░░░░

32

Setting copy for The Country of Her Dreams

pacifist poet. The scene in which he remembers picking up his friend's severed head and wandering across the battlefield with it recalls the Orpheus myth used in the preceding novel. Melvyn, the son accused of homosexuality who becomes a degrading, loudmouthed, yet popular alcoholic, proves to be the incarnation of Lucifer, the fallen angel after whom the novel is titled.

Fearing that her novels were becoming "elegant but meaningless" by dealing almost exclusively with the affluent classes, Elliott set her next work, *The Kindling* (1970), in the Midlands of her childhood. Noted for the "strange and convoluted relationships her characters have with one another," it deals with the dilemmas of a small industrial town in the mid-1950s, as seen through the eyes of Jack Wolstenholme. At age twenty, he finds himself working in a factory, longing to be a writer yet knowing he is trapped by his narrow working-class outlook. Four other characters are developed at length: Herbert Wolf, a teacher in the town whose encouragement makes Jack's generation restless and dissatisfied with their situation; Laura, Wolf's daughter, who comes home from Oxford and provides a necessary contrast between middle- and working-class virtues; Ted, who is satisfied to stay where he is; and Rose, who would do anything to escape her environment. Thus Elliott manages to incorporate a wider range of morality, attitudes, and opinions than was hitherto present in her work.

Over the next five years she composed her most substantial work of fiction: a series of three novels, *A State of Peace* (1971), *Private Life* (1972), and *Heaven on Earth* (1975), tracing the life of Olive Armetage. The first in the sequence, *A State of Peace*, was called Elliott's "most powerful and far-reaching novel to date," one that "captures brilliantly the mood of the times." The story develops around its many characters' responses to the bitter aftermath of victory following World War II. Olive, on whom the action is centered, breaks away from her upper-middle-class roots in Kensington to help the destitute and war-torn people of South London. Here she is drawn to her first husband, whose saintliness becomes appalling and drives her to her lover, Bob Wilson.

In *Private Life* Wilson becomes Olive's second husband (after an uncontested divorce from her first), and together Bob and Olive learn that life in London in the 1950s is not as simple as they thought it would be. One of the complications is that Bob's son, Alan, who is doing his National Serivce, and Willi, a refugee lodger in the flat above theirs, bring back the haunting memories of the war. Olive's quickly aging mother clings to her Kensington gentility and becomes a great source of guilt for Olive, who realizes how idyllic her vision of freedom has been. This novel was nominated for the *Yorkshire Post*'s Book of the Year Award.

The last novel in the trilogy, *Heaven on Earth* (a New Fiction Society choice), begins in the winter of 1968 when Olive witnesses a near-fatal accident involving one of the minor characters introduced in *A State of Peace*. The incident throws her back into the past, forcing her to question the path her life has taken. For the past twenty years she has contented herself with her family; raising her children has been her main concern. Now that they are all gone, she realizes that her marriage is falling apart. Her attempt to strike out against her personal crisis through a love affair ends in a violent and dangerous manner and in the near death of her husband.

A Loving Eye (1977) treats again a theme which appeared in the trilogy as well as in some of Elliott's earlier novels. The principal character, David Middleton, is a boy searching and longing for love. The novel is set in the Midlands in the 1930s, where David first seeks attention from his widowed mother, Carrie. But she disgraces him when her hypocritical religiousness ironically leads her into a

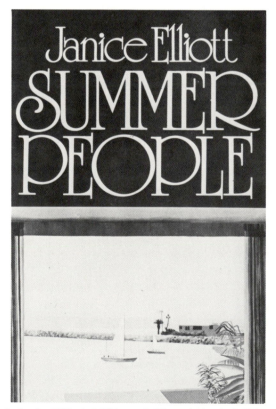

Dust jacket for Elliott's 1980 novel. The painting is California Seascape *by David Hockney.*

Dust jacket for Elliott's 1978 novel

scandalous relationship with the local minister. David struggles for his grandparents' love at their farm in Hopedale, but they are old and eventually die. Billy, his childhood companion, offers him affection, but when David goes off to public school he is no longer satisfied with Billy's attentions and strives for the love of Ned Banks. Ned betrays him with Mary Machin, soon to be his wife, and only after Ned's death does David learn of the weakness that forced Ned to deceive him. Even at the end, however, David remains a romantic, idealistically and trustingly searching for love.

A Loving Eye was followed by *The Honey Tree* (1978) and *Summer People* (1980), two novels of social criticism. Philippa Toomey of the *Times* praised Elliott for her "crisp, satirical touch" in *The Honey Tree*, which was a New Fiction Society choice. William Boyd, reviewing *Summer People* for *TLS*, was less complimentary about Elliott's talents, acknowledging her "deft touch" but finding her characters silly. Boyd faults the novel, set in the early 1990s, for failing to create the "apocalyptic doom-laden atmosphere" for which it strives.

Secret Places combines Elliott's themes of growing up in an upper-middle-class family, life in a British public school, and the effects of war. It is set in a girls' school in the 1940s where young women are shut away from the horrors of World War II, although not from the problems of growing up nor from an awareness of sexuality and its need for expression. One day, however, a refugee child joins the ranks of the schoolmates, bringing with her the reality of the horrors of war—and the concept of life as battle. Much of the novel is drawn from Elliott's experiences during her school days, but, as she has not drawn on them "emotionally," she claims it is not truly autobiographical. The "secret places" of the title include air-raid shelters, prisoner-of-war camps, the empty classrooms at night, and the secret recesses in every heart.

Besides her adult fiction, Elliott has had published two children's books which have been criticized for their highly political content. Both *The Birthday Unicorn* (1970) and *Alexander in the Land of Mog* (1973) deal with the many adventures of Alexander Columbus Banyana, a red-haired boy who lives with his family on top of the Ritz Palace Hotel in London. He is modeled after Elliott's red-haired son, Alexander Cooper, who was six in 1970, when the first book was published. Among the characters in *The Birthday Unicorn* are many who can easily be identified by those familiar with British politics. They include, for example, George Brown, Sir Alec Douglas-Home, and Jim Callaghan. Prime Ministers Harold Wilson and Edward Heath are absent because, as the text makes clear, they were turned into toads by the Unicorn when they refused to stop fighting in a House of Commons debate over how many currants to put into a bun. Thus the book works on two levels, but the fun is not spoiled for those unfamiliar with British politics. *Alexander in the Land of Mog*, less politically oriented, deals mainly with Alexander's extraordinary adventures with his friends, the Unicorn and the Dodo, and with the way he saves the day heroically when the Unicorn and the Lion try to measure their magic.

A prolific and able novelist—recently Bernard Levin twice referred to her as a "true artist"—Elliott is constantly at work on a book, and another novel, *The Country of Her Dreams*, has just been published.

"I try to start a new novel probably even the day I finish the old one," she has said. Her novels demonstrate her capacity to handle a broad range of characters and her skill in developing their relationships naturally and convincingly.

Interviews:
Pooter, *Times* (London), 30 August 1969, p. vi;
Malcolm Winton, "An Obsession like Writing," *Times* (London), 8 June 1970, p. 11;
Philippa Toomey, "Manuscripts, Angels, and a Process of Discovery Down in Sussex," *Times* (London), 7 March 1975, p. 8;
Anthea Hall, "Recipe for Writer's Block," *Sunday Telegraph*, 8 March 1981.

J. G. Farrell
(23 January 1935-12 August 1979)

T. Winnifrith
University of Warwick

BOOKS: *A Man from Elsewhere* (London: Hutchinson, 1963);
The Lung (London: Hutchinson, 1965);
A Girl in the Head (London: Cape, 1967);
Troubles (London: Cape, 1970);
The Siege of Krishnapur (London: Weidenfeld & Nicolson, 1973; New York: Harcourt Brace Jovanovich, 1974);
The Singapore Grip (London: Weidenfeld & Nicolson, 1978; New York: Knopf, 1979);
The Hill Station; and An Indian Diary, edited by John Spurling (London: Weidenfeld & Nicolson, 1981).

James Gordon Farrell's brief career as a novelist was marked by major literary prizes and the praise of contemporary critics, but was cut short by his untimely death. After some slight early works, he found his metier in three major novels which explored in a variety of ways the collapse of the way of life which had built the British Empire. His originality as a historical novelist was balanced by the objectivity and compassion with which he approached his task and by the careful research he conducted into the background of each book. He was helped, however, by his attachment to the old-fashioned world whose decline he sympathetically but faithfully recorded.

Farrell's parents were Anglo-Irish, and, though born in Liverpool, he spent much of his childhood in Ireland. He went to school at Rossall in Lancashire, a conventional English public school which, even after World War II, aimed with its emphasis on loyalty and duty to produce a race of empire builders, although the sun was already setting on the British Empire. (In 1956, the year Farrell went to Oxford, the disastrous Suez expedition marked the last attempt of Britain to assert itself as a world power.) Before going to Oxford, Farrell had worked at a school in Ireland and as a laborer in Canada. His academic career at Oxford was undistinguished; he left in 1960 with a modest third-class degree in French and Spanish. For the next ten years he did some teaching in France, but ceased teaching when, on the strength of his first two novels (*A Man from Elsewhere*, 1963, and *The Lung*, 1965), he was awarded a Harkness Fellowship to New York in 1966.

Farrell's first three novels are incoherent accounts of a central character alienated from the world in which he finds himself, with a beautiful but unapproachable girl hovering mysteriously in the background. His fourth novel, *Troubles* (1970), is named after the troubles that beset Ireland after World War I. This novel won Farrell the Geoffrey Faber Memorial Prize and enabled him to travel in India to do research for his next book, *The Siege of Krishnapur*, which was awarded the Booker Prize for 1973. *The Siege of Krishnapur* is a largely fictitious account of events in the Indian Mutiny, but Farrell made extensive use of letters, diaries, and other factual evidence of the Victorian period to substantiate his narrative. His sixth and last complete novel, *The Singapore Grip* (1978), is even more solidly based on fact. He worked for a long time in the Far East to prepare for it, and the novel is among other things an accurate picture of the collapse of British authority in the Malayan Peninsula, culminating in the capture of Singapore by the Japanese in 1942. Characters from life, like Field Marshall Wavell and General Percival, appear in the novel, to which is appended an extensive historical bibliography. Farrell did not confine his research to Malaya; he also spent weeks in Saigon shortly before its capitulation to the North Vietnamese. The ambitious scope of

J. G. Farrell, 1973

this novel makes Farrell's death on a fishing expedition in Ireland all the more tragic.

Farrell's first novel, *A Man from Elsewhere*, was published after he had spent two years in France. It is set in France and shows many signs of French influence; for example, a character called Luc, a film director, is difficult to fit into the thematic pattern of the novel, but is a reminder of the French cinema and of the famous director Jean Luc Godard. The main story hinges on the efforts of a journalist, Sayer, to unmask a famous former Communist, Regan, before he dies, showing him up for something shady he did in the war. The story in Regan's village is that he sacrificed a hero of the Resistance, Audin, to the German occupying forces because his wife had had an affair with Audin. This is the story spread by Audin's father, but Sayer, as he gets to know Regan and his mysterious daughter, Gretchen, begins to realize that the truth is different. He learns that Regan's wife had been unfaithful with the German commander, Heinrich, and that Gretchen is their daughter. Everybody, including the reader, is left vaguely dissatisfied at the end of this novel, which does, however, with its subtle interplay between public events and private sorrows, foreshadow Farrell's later successes. The London *Times* reviewer commended Farrell for handling his complex story with rare assurance.

The Lung focuses on the predicament of Martin Sands, married to Sally, but in love with his stepdaughter, Marigold. He is gravely ill and is confined to an iron lung in a hospital. He recovers and appears to win Marigold (who is a nurse at the hospital), but the novel ends with enigmatic gloom; "Perhaps I married my ex-stepdaughter and we had ten children and lived happily ever after. It was just terrible." The novel has much enigmatic gloom, and the plight of the other patients—with neither Marigold nor eventual recovery to sustain them—is gloomy indeed. It is difficult to see exactly what point *The Lung* is making; clearly the iron lung is equated to the artificial life of modern man, but it is not clear how Martin's imprisonment in the lung, or his escape from it, reflects this artificiality. The book received little critical attention.

In 1966 Farrell was awarded a Harkness Fellowship to New York, and in 1967 *A Girl in the Head* was published. The title is more appropriate in a way to the earlier novels where females— mysterious Gretchen and Marigold—are central. The most prominent female in this work, Inez, does not have a major part to play. The central role is usurped by Boris, a continental refugee who has arrived at the seaside resort of Maidenhair and has been embraced by the Dongeon family (whose daughter Flower he marries), but whose life is made unhappy by reveries about the past and prospects of future dalliance with Inez. The novel is curiously timeless and placeless. Maidenhair, in spite of its comic English name, has a continental air about it, and the Dongeons, although they speak no French, have a French name and a French disposition. Inez is Swedish in spite of her Spanish name; another key character is called Allesandro; and it is not surprising that Count Boris Slattery—in spite of his reminiscences about Atocha and Jena and Copenhagen and Nice—meets a man who greets him as Mick Slattery from Limerick. Some of Boris's reminiscences have a pre-1914 ring; some of his activities date to the 1960s. The *Times* reviewer saw faults in this novel but praised its sharpness of observation and even compared Farrell to Nabokov.

It is worth noting that after these limbolike false starts, Farrell's three major novels are firmly committed to a definite time and place. *Troubles* is set in County Wexford, Ireland, in 1919, the time of the complicated and difficult uprising of the Irish which eventually led to the partition of the island between Northern Ireland and an independent Eire. By coincidence, 1970 was the beginning of the troubles in Northern Ireland which have dominated the history of the province for the last dozen years, and this fact may have given the novel topical interest, although the Irish world evoked in *Troubles* seems oddly remote from Ulster in the 1970s.

Major Brendan Archer, after serving in World War I, comes to the Majestic Hotel, Kilnolough, the home of Angela Spencer, to whom he has become engaged. Angela displays little interest in the Major—or indeed in anything, except her faded triumphs as a beauty in Edwardian drawing rooms. Early in the novel she becomes ill and unexpectedly dies; the Major then falls in love with the more dynamic Sarah Devlin. Angela's father, Edward Spencer, fanatically loyal to the British, is unable to prevent the crumbling of his hotel or the collapse of British authority, and the novel ends with the Major recovering after an Irish attack which has destroyed the hotel.

The Majestic—huge but ramshackle, with innumerable rooms, luxuriant vegetation, and a host of cats—dominates the novel. Once magnificent, it now houses a few elderly guests who cannot pay their bills. As a symbol of the British Empire whose collapse Farrell is recording, it is effective (although, curiously, the British Empire reached its greatest extent at the time of the Irish troubles). At

times there is a nightmarish quality about the Majestic, surpassing its symbolic value, and clearly Farrell is operating at many different levels, or, as critic Bernard Bergonzi says, with many different codes. The pallid Angela and the rambunctiously eccentric Edward Spencer are representations of a dying breed of Empire builders; they are also comically Irish. Their way of life is deplored by the weakly liberal Brendan Archer, but so in a sense is the passing of their way of life. Farrell takes pains not to confine his novel to Ireland by interspersing contemporary accounts of troubles in other parts of the world—a practice which at times gives the novel a chaotic air.

Bergonzi has compared Farrell's novels to E. M. Forster's *Passage to India* (1924), a masterpiece of realism and symbolism. In *The Siege of Krishnapur* Farrell, whose style resembles Forster's, went to India for the story. It involves an incident in the Indian Mutiny in which Krishnapur, a minor garrison town, resists attack and siege and—after a heroic defense—is eventually relieved. The gap between Forster's twentieth-century and Farrell's nineteenth-century India is revealed in this bald summary of the plot; and though Forster is writing in the 1920s and Farrell in the 1970s, the latter is simultaneously more sympathetic to British imperialism's virtues and more incisive in showing its faults. Farrell declared that "the reason why I preferred to use the past is that, as a rule, people have already made up their minds what they think about the present. About the past they are more susceptible to clarity of vision."

The hero of *The Siege of Krishnapur* is the Collector, Mr. Hopkins, whose vision and energy enable him to organize the defense of the town. He is a man imbued with confidence in progress, inspired by the Great Exhibition of 1851, although at the end of the novel (in 1880) he is less confident. Victorian scientific and intellectual thought is carefully represented in the character of Mr. Hopkins, as it is in minor heroes like George Fleury, the Pre-Raphaelite aesthete, and his friend Harry Dunstaple, the cheerful, dutiful British soldier. At the end of the novel George marries Harry's sister, and Harry marries Lucy Hughes, a girl whose doubtful reputation is canceled by her noble conduct during the siege. Victorian womanhood is well represented by these two characters, and the scene in which Lucy, attacked by a cloud of large beetles, is stripped naked by the innocent George Fleury is at once comic, tragic, and elegiac.

At one level *The Siege of Krishnapur* is a simple

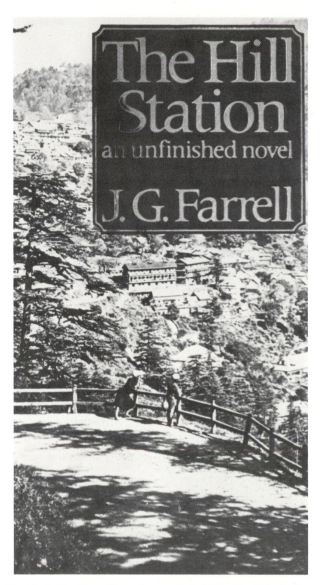

Dust jacket for Farrell's posthumously published book, including his 1971 Indian diary and a fragment of the novel in progress at his death

show the vulnerability of Victorian beliefs.

Farrell's last completed novel, *The Singapore Grip*, is less charitable than *Troubles* or *The Siege of Krishnapur*. One of the most sympathetic characters in it is Major Brendan Archer of *Troubles* (now in late middle age), who drifts through the novel in a purposeless fashion; but at least he is unselfish and practical in helping to organize the defense of the city and in trying to arrange an escape. Walter Blackett, a businessman blind to the Japanese peril, thinks only of the material prosperity of his rubber firm, and is as eccentric as Edward Spencer, but not so endearing. Blackett and his selfish elder daughter, Joan, escape from Singapore, while Matthew Webb, (Blackett's partner's son), the Major, and the mysterious Eurasian Vera do not. The novel ends in uncertainty, with speculation on the possible husband in 1976 of Blackett's younger daughter, Kate.

The Singapore Grip is more than a historical account of the fall of Singapore: it is a universal statement about the behavior of people trying to carry on normal lives when everything is crumbling around them. It is probably not accidental that a Frenchman, Dupigny, and an American, Ehrendorf, play a role in the story, reminding us of later similar collapses in Indo-China and Vietnam. Both behave sensibly and selflessly in contrast to the Blacketts, whose lives seem to revolve around trapping the unfortunate Matthew into marriage with the unpleasant Joan. In addition, the novel has many comic and tragic accidents and coincidences; it is touching—and a little sinister—to find the Japanese singing the Major's old school song which they have learned after a chance visit by the Major to Manchuria years before. Farrell's tight military narrative, faltering only in the problematic conclusion, is a vehicle for showing the role of chance in the affairs of men. The best laid plans go astray in war, in matchmaking, and in love, and the feckless Major, a confirmed bachelor, perhaps has the best answer.

Farrell's posthumous novel, *The Hill Station* (1981), dealing with the high noon of the British Empire, is little more than a fragment, but as his Indian diary shows, it is a work combining the same scrupulous accuracy and imaginative vision as his other historical novels.

adventure story with the heroic British winning in the end, and the Indians—who appear ridiculous, if not actually sinister—suffering an ignominious defeat. A tribute to Farrell's skill and fairness as a narrator is that a novel with such an old-fashioned attitude could win acclaim in 1973. The doubts of the Collector and the aestheticism of Fleury, as well as the failure of such minor characters as the clergyman in Krishnapur, unable to reconcile himself to the many deaths in the town, or the doctor, unable to recognize or treat the outbreak of cholera,

Reference:

Bernard Bergonzi, "Fictions of History" in *The Contemporary English Novel* (London: Edward Arnold, 1979), pp. 43-65.

Elaine Feinstein

(24 October 1930-   )

Peter Conradi
Kingston Polytechnic

SELECTED BOOKS: *In a Green Eye* (London: Goliard Press, 1966);

The Circle (London: New Authors, 1970);

The Magic Apple Tree (London: Hutchinson, 1971);

Matters of Chance (London: Covent Garden Press, 1972);

The Amberstone Exit (London: Hutchinson, 1972);

At the Edge (Rushden, Northamptonshire: Sceptre Press, 1972);

The Celebrants and Other Poems (London: Hutchinson, 1973);

The Glass Alembic (London: Hutchinson, 1973); republished as *The Crystal Garden* (New York: Dutton, 1974);

Children of the Rose (London: Hutchinson, 1975);

The Ecstacy of Dr Miriam Garner (London: Hutchinson, 1976);

Some Unease and Angels: Selected Poems (London: Hutchinson, 1977; University Center, Michigan: Green River Press, 1977);

The Shadow Master (London: Hutchinson, 1978; New York: Simon & Schuster, 1979);

The Silent Areas: Short Stories (London: Hutchinson, 1980).

Elaine Feinstein has excelled as both a poet and a novelist and is also a television playwright and a translator. Expertise in more than one genre is as

292

rare in England as it is in America; and suspicion of such generalism is frequently indicated by praise of Feinstein as a "poetic novelist," which, as an early reviewer pointed out, is a canting accolade often dumped on novelists who also write poems. Nevertheless, she did first discover herself as a poet, and her first novel was conceived, she acknowledges, as a prose poem. Her impressive progress as a novelist can be seen, she has indicated, as an emancipation of prose from a provincial sense of its limits, but one simultaneously conducted to protect it from the effects of excessive deracination and ellipsis. She is not easily grouped or categorized and is an original; but she could be said to have sought a novel form which might feel "no longer local either."

Feinstein was born in Bootle, Lancashire, to Isidore and Fay Compton Cooklin and brought up in Leicester in the English Midlands. Her grandparents had lived in Odessa in the Ukraine and came to England, like many Ashkenazi Jews from the Russian Pale, after the pogroms at the end of the last century. Her father's family settled in Liverpool and became small businessmen. Her father was a cabinetmaker who ran his own factory until money troubles forced him to sell and start again. Her mother's family, also from Odessa, was different. They were successful business people (her maternal grandmother came of Sephardic stock) who disinherited her mother when she married "beneath" her. Her paternal grandfather was a learned rabbi manque, and the family kept up some Jewish traditions, including kashrut.

Feinstein always knew she was Jewish. At school she gradually discovered that the rest of the world was not. After the war she came, like so many, to an understanding of the degree to which being Jewish could mean to suffer and live in danger. For her it was newspaper descriptions which irrecoverably changed her view of the world: The death marches; the fathers who gagged their children to prevent them from crying out (to cry out meant to be shot); the families who were walked to their deaths in any case. . . .

Though her background was typical of that generation of English men and women who profited early from the 1944 Butler Education Act, which set up a university grant system and made it possible for children from less well-off homes to enjoy higher education, Feinstein was a special case. This act spelled release for many from a constricting, provincial, lower-middle class, shopkeeper background (through newly accessible university education) into a world of larger and sometimes

guilt-producing opportunities. But Feinstein felt few of the anxieties and resentments about social location out of which some of her Gentile contemporaries wrote (for example, Philip Larkin's *Jill*; Kingsley Amis's *Lucky Jim*). Studying English literature at Newnham College, Cambridge (1949-1955) where she received her B.A. and M.A. degrees, made for her a fairly guiltless and uncomplicated escape.

She published her first book, a volume of verse, comparatively late, in 1966. The intervening years had been occupied with taking part 1 bar finals in law in London; working briefly for Cambridge University Press; teaching variously at a secondary school, a technical school, then a teacher's training college. From 1956, when she married Dr. Arnold Feinstein, a biochemist, she spent much of her time bringing up their three children.

For a time she supervised students at Cambridge and this brought her into contact with Donald Davie. When Davie moved to Essex University, he suggested Feinstein apply for a lectureship. Her application was successful, and while lecturing there (1967-1969) she was introduced to Russian literature. She later translated, and was importantly influenced by Marina Tsvetayeva. She also met Ed Dorn and a number of poets attached to Essex and attracted to American poetry. Feinstein became involved with a group which included Tom Pickard and Lee Harwood, who for a while in the late 1960s published poems weekly in the mimeographed "English Intelligencer." Sharing a common poetic, they were in reaction against the classical form that they felt the Group and Movement poets differently emulated; they were interested in opening out their verse to incorporate the spoken voice. Other dicta she would now find more questionable, including the notion that to correct one's poetry is immoral (this is connected with the urge toward spontaneity) and that there is a relationship between the poet's physiology and his work. The group hoped to become a coterie after the fashion of the Black Mountain poets in America, but disbanded after 1969. Their importance for Feinstein seems to have been, first of all, in the assistance they gave her (and one another) in finding a poetic voice; second, in the nature of her disagreements with them. They wished to de-Europeanize themselves, to make a cult of and to explore the history of their particular Englishness. This helped her define herself against any such cult, as a person who had never definitely "settled" in England and whose roots, if she had them and was not nomadic, were certainly not to be discovered in a nationalist version of "Little Englandism." In a sense, her novels thereafter can be read as an increasingly various quest for those roots in European history and culture.

The early chapters of *The Circle* (1970) were published in "English Intelligencer." This book incorporated some of the devices of her poetry: the use of two-em spacing, the use of pauses, and the fragmentation of syntax in order to evoke the rhythms by which the world is experienced, felt, and thought. This novel and her second, *The Amberstone Exit* (1972), both came out of domestic and personal experience whose woes and wonders they to some degree make lyrical. (Robert Creeley and William Carlos Williams were important poetic influences at this stage.) Like all her novels, *The Circle* uses language with a fine and effective thrift, pleasurably distilling the essence of her imaginative intention to good effect. The economy in this case is put at the service of depicting the "terrible continuous burden of relationship" suffered by Lena and her friends. Set in a South coast town not unlike Brighton, where Feinstein had once lived, the novel chronicles the variously successful quests of its characters, and especially its women characters, for that magic "which every human being must have if his life is not utterly dead with dependence." Lena is finally to find such magic, the end seems to promise, in "Her separate life. Her lonely life, the music of words to be played with, the books; yes, those long enemies of his [her husband's], the books; they would be her refuge; her private world. As his was this of the laboratory." A teasingly schematic book, in some ways the descriptions of Lena's children and their world are, arguably, among the best things in it, as many critics commented in praising this first novel.

Many of Feinstein's novels make good use of a time split. *The Amberstone Exit* begins with Emily rootless in London and about to give birth; it then moves back to her adolescence. The flashback charts her escape from Amberstone, a Midlands town reminiscent of Leicester, from her own family—her father is good but unsuccessful; and from the glamorous Tyrenes, wealthy German emigres, with all four of whom Emily has been entangled: the manic-depressive daughter, the powerful mother, the austere and frightening father with whom she has fallen in love, and their adopted child Frederick, the stripling whom she finally marries. "I want you all to go away, so that I can feel better," says the heroine to implicitly all the Tyrenes at one point. When Frederick and Emily finally come together the narrative voice comments in the

book's closing words: "Neither of them had the faintest idea what they were in for."

The Glass Alembic (1973; *The Crystal Garden* in America) came out of a sabbatical year in Switzerland where Feinstein's husband was employed in a well-equipped pharmaceutical laboratory. Basel, in which the novel is set, was the city of Paracelsus, one of the first to use drugs for cure of illness; and the novel charts the end of the drug culture of the 1960s in contrast to the somewhat hidebound Baseler Swiss culture, which is based not so much on marijuana as on valium, and against which the action takes place. Matthew, a research chemist working in Basel, is joined by his wife, Brigid, and their teenage son and daughter, whose fare from England has been paid by a mischievous, sexually ambiguous colleague who likes stirring things up. The colleague's boyfriend goes off with the daughter; other couplings ensue and most are inconclusive. The capacity of the human agents for change is reflected by that of the cells being studied in the laboratory: it is at least partly random, and finite.

About 1973 both Feinstein's parents died, and she naturally turned to investigating her past in a different spirit. It was about this time that she began to enquire into Jewish history more systematically and enlarge her reading. A wish to make her characters more securely substantial also entered into this investigation; the result was not merely more substantial characterization, but also more satisfying mythmaking. The three novels which followed all make profitable use of Jewish history. At this time also the Feinsteins took a trip to Poland where Dr. Arnold Feinstein's family had originated and where a cousin still lived. The cousin had survived the war hidden by a large number of different Polish families.

In *Children of the Rose* (1975) Feinstein's interest in the past is shared by her protagonists Lalka and Alex Mendez. Polish Jews who escaped the Holocaust and made a fortune, they are separated in middle age. Lalka stays in Cheyne Walk, Chelsea, while Alex furnishes a chateau in Provence. Alex sleeps with Lee, whose family once owned the chateau, and who thus knows what the gestapo did to refugees there. He now fills the house with disaffected and parasitical young people. Lalka goes back to Krakow and reacts violently to her confrontation with the past, suffering a collapse. She is brought back to the chateau and ends in the serene grip of a mental state close to imbecility. She may still be better off than the tormented Alex. "They say peace is good for you " is

- 2 -

Looking around she could have thought herself in a prison. The walls

were brick, and the green paint was peeling off them. Even the windows were

high as though to cut off the world deliberately. The room contained about

twenty beds, some open to her, and others curtained. From the curtained

booth on her left she could hear a low moan which rose and fell regularly.

Meanwhile from the far end of the ward a woman under blankets and holding a

black rubber mouthpiece over her face was wheeled by at great speed, just

as two domestics with tea wheeled in their own trolley.

—You should get up and walk around, you know, said the Irish nurse. That

brings it on.

—Thank you, said Emily. She was glad of the tea.

Across the ward, a fat woman attached by one wrist to an iron stand

shouted something companionable, so Emily got out of bed and went over to

sit next to her. Rosie, her name was.

—What? She said, surprised at Emily's ignorance: This is a sugar drip, love.

But when Emily asked her whether she thought anyone could hold a baby back

just by wishing it, she laughed until she farted under the sheets. Emily

~~stood here~~ sat holding the stand steady until she recovered.

About eleven a doctor came round and warned Emily not to walk about at

all in case the cord got twisted round the baby's neck. ~~which was a bit~~ She told him,

~~frightening to hear~~ she'd just forced herself to walk up and down the ward

twice. And he nodded a moment more over her belly, listening.

All the same she found she could eat lunch. Sitting up. Cautiously, on

her bed. She was just finishing off the dried apricots/ when there was a

great hooting from the bed opposite. The jolly fat woman had begun to thrash

35

Elaine Feinstein, 1978

the last sentence of the novel, which is exquisitely written and quietly done, as certain critics recognized.

Like Anna in Feinstein's story "The Grateful Dead" (in her collection *The Silent Areas* published in 1980), Lalka is in some sense reclaimed by a horrible past. In many of Feinstein's novels someone falls dangerously ill, sick beyond the reach even of modern pharmacy, and it is often the past which can be said figuratively to have sickened them, and which has returned to get them. In the early 1970s Feinstein was particularly influenced by novelist friends such as Angela Carter, J. G. Ballard, and Emma Tennant in the direction of programmatic antirealism. This group of writers reacted self-consciously against what they saw as a mendacious, desiccated, and limiting set of conventions in fiction. Like others, they felt that if realism were based on the consoling fantasy of a stable world, then fantasy would have to be the new realism. Only exploration of the grotesque, of science fiction, black farce, or gothic could adequately reflect the

ways in which both language and the world language creates were felt to have become destabilized. Feinstein's next two novels made a very personal use of the new gothic. In each, gothic provides a code or convention by which past time can bring its exotic revenges to the present. If these purposes were not always immediately understood by reviewers this says more about the timidity and conservatism of British reviewing than about the value of the new writing.

The Ecstacy of Dr Miriam Garner (1976) can be read as a brilliant and witty spoof of science fiction, but it clearly contains a serious novel, too. Its un- or anticonventional discourse enables a more serious quest for a sense of the past. Dr. Miriam Garner, a Jewish Arabist, returns home from abroad to find her father, also an Arabist, living in bizarre squalor in Cambridge with an eccentric housekeeper; her former lover, who is a sinister sadist, is in attendance. Apparently triggered by what she sees when she enters the wrong bedroom, Miriam is transported back in "a state of continuous orgasm," to medieval Toledo, where Jews, Christians, and Moslems lived amicably together. A number of possible explanations are proffered concerning the real nature and cause of Miriam's state, and they undercut one another: the myth of a guiltless, prelapsarian state of Jewishness, before Christianity had massively and symbolically handed on the stigmata to Jews—that is, had made Jews into symbolic scapegoats, like Christ—underlies it all. The novel is marvelously bodied forth—a witty, uneasy, and satisfying tale.

In *The Shadow Master* (1978) a Jewish Messiah, possibly a descendant of the seventeenth-century Sabbatai Zevi, emerges in contemporary Istanbul, where his putative ancestor earlier tried to bring about the millenium. "Does God enjoy puppet shows?" asks one character, who is asked in return, "Why not? Are we not all his puppets?" "Then the whole world is a black farce," replies the first speaker with distaste, suggesting a thematic framework for the novel. The exotic cast includes an expatriate astrologer, tourists, revolutionaries, businessmen, cosmopolitan spies, and chiliasts, and the setting moves deftly between the Bosporus, Prague, Amsterdam, and London. Feinstein likes this novel less than its predecessor and feels that it is only at the end that she ceases holding the numinous at bay and lets the reverential back into the book. Reviewers tended to feel the same division of purpose, between celebrating and secularizing the pieties exemplified by a religious millenarianism. Feinstein admires Isaac Bashevis Singer's *Satan in*

Goray not just for its specificity of setting but for the metaphysical struggle he allows to occur within it. She attempts a similar accomplishment in her novel, but despite the book's energy, wit, and intelligence, she feels she did not succeed.

Her impatience with *The Shadow Master*, for all its virtues, indicates the kind of novelist Feinstein would like to be and the kind of novel she feels she has so far actually achieved. In a symposium on the state of British fiction, she simultaneously commended the attempt of antirealist writers to recapture lost territory for the human imagination but, acutely, also charged writers of fantasy and grotesque fairy tales with not always avoiding the dangers of whimsy and, more important, of encouraging a "steely rejection of humanism, a fashionable resistance to compassion, which I believe is as much a luxury of our English innocence as the euphoria of the affluent flower generation."

Feinstein feels she has moved away from commitment to the gothic, which she used to largely humanist ends. Her commitment to developing a profounder psychological realism, neither tricksy nor "experimental," is, however, as strong as ever. She wants to write novels which *move* her readers, as the great novels of the past have done, and to involve them in the fate of her characters so that they will care about what happens to them. Her scorn of those who indulge facile and posturing rejections of humanism, and her impatience with writers who fashionably attitudinize, are both timely.

In *The Silent Areas* Feinstein produced a brilliant set of short stories which aptly point up her dilemma and heighten the reader's curiosity about where this gifted and inventive writer will move next. The success of her stories points to exactly those virtues which Feinstein clearly suspects. She pares down her language because she is also a poet and has a poet's eye and ear. She develops a bright and beautiful linguistic patina under which the realm of the implicit (that silent area within all of us) can gather its fearful and prophetic power. She succeeds because the short story is a form which, while much given to vivisection of heartlessness, can at once glory in its cold and impersonally elegant shining surfaces. In the more contingent and discursive novella, which she has so far made her particular vehicle, but out of which she shows clear signs of wishing to expand, reticence and neatness can operate differently and more treacherously. She is a writer who has made fragmentation and deracination her special topics; she has developed a language of formidable efficiency for evoking each, and for searching for authentication in the teeth of each. If her earliest books defamiliarized the ordinary world and the domestic self, her later books appropriately domesticated the exotic. She now wants to become a more accessible writer who would attract a wider readership. It is something her fine and invigorating talent deserves.

Television Scripts:
Breath, 1975;
Lunch, 1981.

Other:
Selected Poems of John Clare, edited by Feinstein (London: University Tutorial Press, 1971);
The Selected Poems of Marina Tsvetayeva, translated by Feinstein (London: Oxford University Press, 1971);
Three Russian Poets: Margarita Aliger, Yunna Moritz, Bella Akhmadulina, translated by Feinstein (Manchester: Carcanet Press, 1978);
New Stories 4, edited by Feinstein and Fay Weldon (London: Hutchinson, 1979).

Reference:
Valentine Cunningham, "Women Who Look Like Witches," *Listener*, 21 June 1973, p. 837.

Eva Figes
(15 April 1932-)

Peter Conradi
Kingston Polytechnic

SELECTED BOOKS: *Equinox* (London: Secker & Warburg, 1966);
Winter Journey (London: Faber & Faber, 1967; New York: Hill & Wang, 1968);
Konek Landing (London: Faber & Faber, 1969);
Patriarchal Attitudes (London: Faber & Faber, 1970; New York: Stein & Paul, 1970);
B (London: Faber & Faber, 1972);
Days (London: Faber & Faber, 1974);
Tragedy and Social Evolution (London: Calder & Boyars, 1976);
Nelly's Version (London: Secker & Warburg, 1977);
Little Eden: A Child at War (London: Faber & Faber, 1978);
Waking (London: Hamilton, 1981; New York: Pantheon, 1982).

Eva Figes is both a novelist of distinction and a writer of one of the classic texts of the women's movement, *Patriarchal Attitudes* (1970). In each capacity she can be seen to have defined herself against and to have questioned the traditional politics and pieties of the culture in which she lives. The 1960s and 1970s were decades in which many gifted younger writers turned against the realistic conventions of the immediate postwar British novel. For them, these conventions seemed cozily irrelevant. Figes's history has provided her with a unique viewpoint from which to focus and criticize that irrelevance, and from which to fund an alternative and innovative view of the novel's function.

Eva Figes was born Eva Unger in Berlin—a year before Hitler's rise to power—to Emil Eduard and Irma Cohen Unger, well-to-do German Jews. The elder of two children, she had a typically comfortable, culturally assimilated, upper-middle-class Berlin childhood, without religious education as a Jew. Her father, a textile-industry representative, was arrested on the notorious *Kristallnacht* of November 1938 and taken to Dachau prison camp where he fell ill. Since the gestapo was corrupt as well as brutal, the family was able to acquire the longed-for visa for England. Despite having missed the boat to Bangkok (a last, desperate escape route) due to her father's illness, they packed in March

1939 and, a few weeks before Figes's seventh birthday, made a lucky, late escape to England. The political realities of the Third Reich and of her father's imprisonment had been kept from Eva and her brother, to whom understanding came slowly and in fragments. England was hard to adapt to. In the North London Primary School where she was first sent, she was stigmatized not, ironically, as a Jew, but as a German. She was foreign and made to feel it. But she was intelligent, learned English fast, and discovered that the English language and literature comprised a world in which her sensitivity and imagination could find expression and release.

In her autobiographical *Little Eden* (1978) Figes describes how, like many children during the war, she was evacuated from London in 1940-1941. Hers was a strange idyll in Cirencester where she

Eva Figes

found intellectual if not physical nourishment. The bizarre carnival of English country life during these years continued unabated, and was haunted by few spectres any grislier than those provided by the English class system with its inherited arrogances and superstitions.

One afternoon just before the war ended in 1945, Figes's mother gave her ninepence and sent her off to the local cinema. "Go and see for yourself," she said. The small adolescent child sat in the dark and watched a newsreel of Belsen concentration camp. "Mounds of corpses, dazed survivors with huge haunted eyes staring out of skulls which had become too heavy for the frail emaciated bodies, mute evidence for the prosecution posing for the camera. At last I knew what it meant to be a Jew." At this time her family knew only that her maternal grandparents had been "deported." After the war Figes's mother discovered that her father had died in the Warsaw ghetto where he and his wife had been taken. A letter was received from him just before the ghetto was finally destroyed. His wife, on the other hand, was separated from him and presumably died in a camp.

While *Little Eden* elegizes her period in Cirencester, an article written for the *Observer* in 1978 suggests a different view of England and of Figes's sense of herself in relation to it: "England does not share the European experience. German troops never marched down Whitehall; men were not rounded up and shot or sent to labour camps; there were no gas chambers on the outskirts of Surbiton or Tunbridge Wells; no partisans, no collaborators and no bitter aftermath of retribution. This enabled a lot of English people to see life after 1945 as a continuation of life before the war."

Here the political innocence of England, which made it so attractive to a refugee family during the Holocaust, ironically kept it from reflecting the deepest cultural realities of the twentieth century. The continuities in England are aesthetic as well as political, Figes implies, and there is a conservative, parish-pump quality to English life and English letters which would be unimaginable on the continent. Her *Observer* piece ends with Figes declaring her sense of her own continuing statelessness: "But I am a European wrestling with a different reality. A piece of shrapnel lodges in my flesh, and when it moves, I write."

During her adolescence and early twenties Figes began to have a recurring dream in which she relived her family's departure from Berlin: "a grey day, the airport, and my grandparents standing, a forlorn little group, outside the airport building to wave goodbye as we sat in the plane waiting for take-off," she wrote in *Little Eden*. After describing the dream to a psychoanalyst in 1955, she found herself crying uncontrollably for those she had lost. The dream never returned. The *Observer* article states: "All Jewish survivors of the Holocaust have to cope with a sense of guilt, however irrational that sounds."

Her family had been the kind in which educational opportunities went first of all to the son. But she had excelled at school (Kingsbury Grammar) and won a state scholarship to Queen Mary College, London, where she was involved in drama, edited a magazine, and regretted not going to Cambridge since she preferred the tutorial system; she received a B.A. with honors in 1953. She also found herself at odds with academic criticism. Fifteen years with various publishing houses followed (1952-1967) during which she married and had two children. It was the breakup of her marriage to John George Figes, a graduate in history and a personnel manager, which led directly to the writing of her first published novel, *Equinox* (1966). It remains her most autobiographical work, chronicling a year of crisis in its heroine's life. The hope of escape into new relationships, with a child and later with another man, proves futile. She is finally left by herself, without convictions or allegiances, unable to act or use her talent or to see any point in living.

Franz Kafka, another Central European Jew, the great prescient poet-novelist of alienation, paranoia, angst, and the conspiratorial view of reality, had been the acknowledged major influence on Figes's early writing. ("He blew the top of my head off.") As a student she had written poetry and had been keenly interested in drama. Kafka seemed to demonstrate to her that the novel could, within its compass as an extended prose narrative, develop some of the potentialities of drama and poetry. Samuel Beckett was another influence, another poet of nightmare, of solipsism and depersonalization. Both helped Figes jettison the English realist tradition with its cautious social *rapportage*, its felt obligations to document public reality, and its occasional and consequent default on the exploration of the further reaches of inner consciousness. The difficulty that both her admirers and her detractors have found in her work is the consequence of her fastidious attempts to discover a new poetic language for the notation of private thought and feeling in fiction.

Winter Journey, one of her most satisfying novels, was published in London in 1967. W. L. Webb, literary editor of the *Guardian*, in awarding this novel the *Guardian* Fiction Prize for that year, commended the author for bringing alive the old protagonist (Janus) who, near to death, "struggles through the ceaseless traffic of another day in the London streets. But the living of that is neither quick nor simple; and it's the living, the whole texture alive in all its dimensions that Mrs. Figes enacts so intently, and sometimes so inwardly that we feel the stammer of that old heart, hear the grinding of the pack ice in his brain, and come to know, as if we had inherited it, the pain of his experience and the pulse of the will which keeps him going." Webb's account of this novel also illuminates the ways in which Figes's writings mock any attempt to summarize them. Without a continuous narrative, plot, or the character development which we think of as Victorian, the novel can become almost nebulous. Figes's novels share in part some of the resistance to critical penetration of Virginia Woolf's fiction half a century earlier.

In 1967 Figes gave up publishing as a career for writing full time. Her next book, *Konek Landing* (1969), was an attempt to come to fictional terms with her understanding of the Holocaust and with what her relatives had undergone in Europe. It is an imaginative, elusive, serious, and experimental fiction set in a nameless country where there are mainly victims and executioners. It takes its luckless protagonist, Stephan Konek, a stateless orphan, through a complex set of monologues and nightmare encounters. It was less well-received than either *Winter Journey* or her next book, *Patriarchal Attitudes*, the publication of which changed her life.

When *Patriarchal Attitudes* made the headlines, Figes became a name that editors were prepared to court. She was thus enabled to earn a reasonable living as a free-lance writer and journalist. The book is a levelheaded, politically undoctrinaire account of the ideology underlying male-female relations; it lacks the flaunting and provocative "personality" of Germaine Greer's *The Female Eunuch*. A friend remarked to Figes that if Greer's was the text most often read by men at this time then Figes's was that most read by women: the men who read it had often been pushed into doing so by their womenfolk. It was its very coolness and sobriety which, if anything, shocked readers. The following year she published an account of her legal battles with her husband over maintenance (alimony and child support) in an essay entitled "The White Road to Blackmail" in the collection *Woman on Woman* (1971). While it provoked further legal trouble, it is a passionate and powerfully argued personal testimony which ex-

tends the logic of *Patriarchal Attitudes* by its private witness.

Critical response to her next novel, *B* (1972), was again mixed, some reviewers finding it bleakly schematic, others excitingly innovative. It is an ambitious, intricate work which explores the nature of creativity itself, including its own. A self-conscious and self-reflexive novel in the vein of what has come to be called meta-fictionality, it concerns Paul Beard, a novelist who is writing about his relationship with another writer, B, whom he once knew or, possibly, invented. B is unsuccessful as a writer until Beard brings him into his own life and installs him in his cottage, where B writes a brilliant novel and then disappears. Simultaneously Beard loses control over his own life. "Reality" and "fiction" exchange places, and their concourse throws a violent, equivocal, and lurid light on the nature of each.

In the fall term of 1973 Figes took up a two term Cecil Day Lewis writer's fellowship at University College, London. As a student she had found herself disaffected with strictly academic criticism, and this period at University College did not arouse any new enthusiasm for it. During this time *Days* (1974) was published. In *Days* she continues to reject traditional English fiction and moves on once more to novelistic experimentation. A nameless wretch of a heroine lies ill in a hospital room meditating on her defeat and her suffering. There are signs of a portentous allegorizing at work whereby the cycle of male-dominated female lives and their deprivations are conflated (grandmother, mother, daughter). "I hate men," one of the women in the hospital thinks. "It was like a thought coming out of one's own head," another concurs.

In 1977 Figes took up a two year appointment as writer-in-residence at Brunel Unverisity where she lectured, started a magazine, saw students individually, and arranged for other writers to come and read. *Nelly's Version* (1977) grew from the donnee of a heroine suffering from amnesia. Nelly Dean catches sight of her own aging face in a hotel bedroom mirror and concludes that she must have been given the wrong room. It can be read as a thriller about the nature of identity itself, but a thriller whose outcome is characteristically equivocal.

After seven novels Figes remains a considerable enigma, and the self-questioning that lies behind her most recent novel *Waking* (1981) makes it clear that she is in more senses than one an unpredictable talent. In *Waking* she tries to move back to the intense poetic lyricism of her earlier work and chronicles seven waking moments, each separated by a number of years in the mind of her heroine (or heroines—Figes is deliberately ambiguous here). One of the paradoxes that Figes could be said to represent as a writer was identified by the reviewer of *Days* who wrote that those women whose lives and distresses were most accurately reflected in the book were precisely those least likely to read it and directly profit from it.

In her theoretical pronouncements Figes has written as though aesthetic and social experiment were directly linked. No such simple connection, however, exists. The old realist writers "trade in reassurances," which is dangerous, she says. "The price of survival is eternal vigilance," Figes grandly wrote in an introduction to her contribution in the collection *Beyond the Words: Eleven Writers in Search of a New Fiction* (1975). "Nobody really believes in [the old reassurances] any more," she continued. If no one believes them, then in what does their danger consist? "Having begun with an interest in the fragmentary nature of remembered experience I have found myself increasingly involved in making new connections, creating new networks which, if different in method from the traditional novel of the nineteenth century, nevertheless do create a narrative of a kind and do impose a sort of order on chaos. I am using a different grid, which I first have to construct by a painful process of trial and error."

In an epoch when many writers in England have been betrayed into caution and genteel restraint, her risk-taking may itself be something to admire. She has also avoided the opposite safety of obsessive formal preoccupation. In a 1978 *New Review* symposium on the state of British fiction she wrote a plaintive and combative piece which suggested that the continuing popularity of Jane Austen in England was due to Austen's capacity to "gently mock at a system of values which [the English] would really hate to see destroyed." The notion that Austen might be a more savage ironist than the nonacademic section of her audience often recognizes does not seem to have occurred to Figes. Such courageous innocence about literary history takes on a different light when the innocence concerns writers, like Virginia Woolf, whose formal curiosities seem to prefigure Figes's own. Figes has acknowledged the similarities of Woolf's work to her own, and for that reason she avoided rereading her until writing *Waking*, when she reread *The Waves*.

To dislike campus criticism is one thing, to write as if all literary history were a fictive conspir-

Dust jacket for Figes's seventh novel, which describes seven mornings in a woman's life

acy is another; and Figes seems sometimes to be painfully relearning lessons which are implicit in the brilliant innovations of Virginia Woolf more than fifty years earlier. Figes shares a commonly held view that television and film have taken over the old obligations of realism and that the novel must therefore primarily explore the neglected world of the self. Without the same external threats, Woolf felt precisely the same primary responsibility and established her genius at the risk of being found fey, portentous, whimsical, humorless, or simply incomprehensible as a result. Figes has taken similar risks and occasionally paid comparable prices. Her novels sometimes involuntarily demonstrate that the emancipation of the novel from some of its traditional debts can create, not a liberated zone, but a claustrophobia more tyrannically legislated than ever before. It may be for this reason that, while there have been reviewers who have consistently championed her, and while she clearly has a loyal if small readership, her critical reception since the well-received *Winter Journey* has been on the whole progressively less enthusiastic.

Figes's aesthetic courage and inventiveness, if not always her instinct for generating pleasurable new modes of coherence, are unmistakable. If she has so far attempted the kinds of novel which genius might enliven, but talent can only mock, then this may be preferable to that alternative, more traditional kind of postwar British writing, which genius would not have time to mock, and which talent, like a monkey gland, can only occasionally succeed in rejuvenating.

Other:
"The White Road to Blackmail" in *Woman on Woman*, edited by Margaret Laing (London: Sidgwick & Jackson, 1971);
"On Stage," in *Beyond the Words: Eleven Writers in Search of a New Fiction* edited by Giles Gordon (London: Hutchinson, 1975), pp. 113-127.

Translations:
Martin Walser, *The Gadarene Club* (London: Longmans, Green, 1960); republished as *Marriage in Phillipsburg* (Norfolk, Conn.: New Directions, 1961);
Renate Rasp, *A Family Failure* (New York: Orion, 1970; London: Calder & Boyars, 1970).

Periodical Publications:
"The Long Passage to Little England," *Observer*, 11 June 1978;
"The State of Fiction, a Symposium," *New Review* (Summer 1978): 14.

Penelope Fitzgerald
(17 December 1916-   )

Catherine Wells Cole

BOOKS: *Edward Burne-Jones: A Biography* (London: Michael Joseph, 1975);
The Knox Brothers (London: Macmillan, 1977; New York: Coward, McCann & Geoghegan, 1977);
The Golden Child (London: Duckworth, 1977; New York: Scribners, 1978);
The Bookshop (London: Duckworth, 1978);
Offshore (London: Collins, 1979);
Human Voices (London: Collins, 1980);
At Freddie's (London: Collins, 1982).

From virtually the outset of her career as a novelist, Penelope Fitzgerald's work has attracted serious critical attention. Her second novel, *The Bookshop* (1978), was shortlisted for the Booker Prize, which is Britain's most valuable literary award, worth £10,000 to the winner. She won the Booker Prize in 1980 with her third novel, *Offshore* (1979). Her writing couples a traditionally moral humanist approach with a supple, spare style; her novels are short, but not slight.

Fitzgerald sees herself as an encouragement to late starters—she was sixty-one when her first novel, *The Golden Child* (1977), was published. Born in Lincoln, England, in 1916, to Edmund Valpy and Christina Hicks Knox, she grew up in a literary environment—her father was the editor of *Punch* magazine, and her uncle, Ronald Knox, was a translator of the Bible and a writer of detective stories. She has written a biography of all four Knox brothers (1977), and feels that the quality she shares with them is that they are all, in her words "understatement people." She read English at Somerville College, Oxford, where she received a degree with first-class honors in 1939, and married Desmond Fitzgerald in 1941. Although she has worked in journalism, in the BBC, and in teaching, and still teaches part-time at a London tutorial college, she feels her most important work was rearing her three children. Work, however, which most people spend most of their time doing, is an area she thinks many novelists neglect: she has drawn on her own experience to present in each of her novels a small, specialist world which she opens for the reader's inspection.

In common with thousands of people in London in the winter of 1971-1972, Fitzgerald waited in line for hours to see the Tutankhamen Exhibition at the British Museum. Her mystery novel, *The Golden Child*, originated in her feelings of anger at the sheer length of the wait, and of anticlimax at the brief glimpse of the dimly lit treasures at the end of it. She felt that to discover, after all that, that the treasures were fakes could lead to murder! The *Golden Child* of the title is the centerpiece of an exhibition of the legendary treasures of the Garamantes on loan to a stately British museum. While the patient crowds wait daily outside, Fitzgerald opens, entertainingly, the ceaseless back-biting bureaucratic activity inside the museum, "a great hive, with the Golden Treasure at its heart." The organization begins to crack when the golden artifacts are discovered to be fake, and this discovery is followed by the murder of Sir William Simpkin, the "ancient ruffian" who discovered the treasure in 1913. Although the novel is densely and skillfully plotted, this is done with Fitzgerald's characteristic economy. Her publishers asked her to reduce her original 75,000-word draft to 50,000 words; subsequently she has written what she calls "microchip novels." Much of the reader's pleasure derives from the intricacy of the book's mechanics, and more from Fitzgerald's funny glimpses of archaeological bureaucrats, package tourists, and schoolchildren writing essays on the Garamantes: "They had gold; other people had salt, contrary to what we see in England today." To describe *The Golden Child* as a "comedy thriller," however, would be a disservice, implying that it is essentially trivial, a pastiche. While open to possibilities for comedy, it also shows that a genre usually treated in a facetious or cliched way can acquire resonance and depth. The murdered Sir William is a case in point: he is in many ways the heart of the museum; he alone of its senior staff cares about the people standing endlessly in the cold. He dies, caught between huge movable steel shelving units in the staff library, and the comically predictable cliche does not take away his dignity: "Sir William, who in his day had scoured the deserts and perilous ruins of the world, had ended as a body in the library."

The murder and the exposure of the treasures have the greatest impact on Waring Smith, a junior exhibition officer. He is pleasant, unassuming, and permanently worried about the mortgage repayments on his "very small terraced house in Clapham South." A recurring theme is his series of frustrated attempts at a reconciliation with his wife, Haggie; he teeters on the threshold of domestic happiness, but it is never realized in the novel. His efforts parallel those of the modern "pilgrims" to see the treasure, or those of the vast lines in Moscow (where Smith attempts to authenticate the treasure) waiting to see "the embalmed head and hands, and the ghastly

PENELOPE FITZGERALD

evening dress suit, of Lenin. . . ." Smith's encounters with the power structures behind the exhibition—the museum, the police, the foreign office, multinational corporations—though all lightly handled, add to his growing understanding of the "shoddy undertakings [controlling] every area of his life." He comes to a new perception of how the world is run: it is run by fakes.

Sir William's murderer is revealed to be the museum's urbane director, proving that a man who made a "lengthy TV series 'What is Culture?,' in which he had appeared in close-up against all the better-known works of art in Western Europe," can still be a villain. The novel questions value, power, and authority and explores the secrecy of their operation. Len Coker, the left-wing museum technician, believes that keys will be obsolete in future society. "Everything will be open to the people." The museum is a perfect model for a system at its most dangerous when at its most secretive. This element in the novel, distinct from its wit, has led to its being read, particularly in Eastern Europe, as a political parable. But as Fitzgerald says, it is hard for any novel which sets an individual against a "system" not to be read in this way.

Opposition is certainly to be found in *The Bookshop* (1978), which is a quieter examination of the operations of power. Less intricately plotted than *The Golden Child*, it is equally moral in its use of the techniques of comedy (characterization, observation, dialogue) for more serious purposes. In it Fitzgerald uses knowledge she gained working in a Suffolk bookshop in the late 1950s. This bookshop is still thriving, but the one opened in the novel by Florence Green, a middle-aged widow, fails.

The Bookshop is set in 1959, in the isolated Suffolk town of Hardborough. Its isolation is used not only as an excuse for description of flat marshland and clear East Anglian skies—though Fitzgerald creates a sharply poetic sense of these—but as an image to represent a town that is economically, politically, and socially almost stagnant. The River Laze is no longer navigable except by rowboat; getting to the nearest bridge involves a long detour by road; the railway closed in 1920. Parallel to Florence's efforts to convert the near-derelict Old House in the town center into a bookshop is the commercial failure of Mr. Deben, the fishmonger. The novel's brief references to him indicate marginally, but importantly, the decline of a whole industry and the economic realities of life in England before the booming 1960s. Not only these conditions are against Florence; she is also opposed by Violet Gamart, who sees herself as the leader of Hardborough society, and who wants to turn the Old House into "some sort of centre—I mean an arts centre. . . ." In fact, her opposition to Florence is not so specifically motivated—her name is an allusion to a character in Balzac's *Le Curé de Tours* whose motivation appears to be simply a refusal to be thwarted in anything. Fitzgerald is acute to the small but crucial class distinctions which make it possible for Violet Gamart to patronize and ultimately defeat Florence Green.

Courage rather than a crusading zeal for bringing culture to Hardborough makes Florence persist. Nonetheless, she has increasing difficulty in believing that "human beings are not divided into exterminators and exterminatees, with the former, at any given moment, predominating." Certainly the few friends and allies she makes belong to the latter category. Ten-year-old Christine Gipping, who comes to help in the bookshop after school, is presented with a total absence of sentimentality; her

two front teeth are broken because, in the previous winter when the washing on the line froze hard, "she was caught a blow in the face with an icy vest." Yet her failure in the eleven-plus exam, which means she must abandon hopes of going to the grammar school, suggests clearly the diminished prospects ahead of her and the injustice of a divisive educational system.

At the other end of the social scale, Florence makes an ally in Mr. Brundish, old and solitary, who belongs to an ancient Suffolk family and whom Violet Gamart invites in vain to her parties. Florence asks his advice as to whether she should resist the "threadlike pressures" of Hardborough (which always seem traceable to Violet Gamart) and sell Vladimir Nabokov's erotic best-seller *Lolita* in her shop. On this issue, in many ways a turning point in the novel, Florence's attitude is pragmatic and modest. She decides to stock the book for what are essentially moral, rather than crusading or aesthetic, reasons: "if *Lolita* is a good book, I want to sell it in my shop." It is a brave decision. In the face of economic decline, books, although a luxury, offer a means of opening up: when the van laden with *Lolita*'s arrives, the bystanders cheer; "Something new was coming to Hardborough." Ironically, the success of the book draws the big bureaucratic guns against Florence. In a rapid succession of legal moves, she is ousted from the Old House and from the town. Even the intervention of Mr. Brundish, who brings himself to visit Mrs. Gamart on Florence's behalf, cannot prevail: he collapses and dies going home, exterminated by the appalling Violet and the values she represents.

The Bookshop is concerned with self-preservation, courage, and defeat. Its surface is richly and intelligently comic, but at the end we share Florence's sorrow for the town that did not want a bookshop. Fitzgerald sees loss and failure as positive states, nobler (her own word) than any alternative she presents in her novels. *The Bookshop* was well received critically, and was shortlisted for the Booker Prize. As with her later novels, there was some debate on whether it was properly a novel or a novella. The critical consensus was that it achieves a totality greater than a superficial reading might suggest. Writing in the *Times Literary Supplement*, Valentine Cunningham found it "jagged and lucid as bits of broken bottle," and said "[it] is on any reckoning a marvellously piercing fiction. . . . fiercely, rousingly moral."

Her next novel, *Offshore*, creates what Frank Kermode has called its "illusion of total specification" from Fitzgerald's experience of living with her husband and three children on a Thames houseboat called *Grace* (this is also the name of one of the boats in the novel). The Fitzgeralds' boat sank; the community of boat dwellers on Battersea Reach in *Offshore* is, collectively, also unfortunate; and the novel charts the drift of their lives in a way that is comic as well as dreadfully sad.

The characters in the novel are different from each other: Willis, the elderly marine artist; Maurice, the male prostitute; Nenna, the vague mother of two young daughters; Richard, the London investment counselor who cannot bring himself to leave the river for dry land. Yet they are far from being a gallery of sharply observed eccentrics. Richard's wife, Laura, who hates the river life, is neatly judged by her use of snap summations: "there were very amusing people living on the Thames." The lives these people lead are as shakily moored, patched, and insecure as the creaking, vulnerable boats they live on. They are bound together by concern, affection, and friendship; when Willis's boat *Dreadnought* sinks, he is taken in by Woodie and cared for by everybody—Nenna patches and airs his underwear. The nature of the setting, the irregularity of where they live, makes this community something rare in English fiction—convincingly classless.

The ambivalences and uncertainties of their lives are reflected at all levels of *Offshore*'s carefully constructed narrative. The Thames is tidal at Battersea Reach; the characters spend half their lives on land, half on water. Every flood tide is a threat: "And each one of them felt the patches, strains and gaps in their craft as if they were weak places in their own bodies." The ebb and flow is ceaseless, but the analogy with the river is never obvious or obtrusive. The novel is too precise about the techniques of living on a small boat to get carried away with its implications, as when Martha, Nenna's daughter, is preparing supper: "Martha set confidently to work in *Grace*'s galley, which consisted of two gas rings in the bows connected to a Calor cylinder, and a brass sink. Water came to the sink from a container on the deck, which was refilled by a man from the boatyard once every twenty-four hours. A good deal of improvisation was necessary and Martha had put three tin plates to heat up over the hissing saucepan of beans." Yet this precisely evoked world is perfectly matched with the apparent inconclusiveness, the hesitancies and reticences, the ebb and flow of the book's construction. The narrative goes far beyond documentary observation, as can be seen in the presentation of the river. At times it is the Thames of Whistler: "The mist had cleared, and to

the north-east the Lots Road Power Station discharged from its four majestic chimneys long plumes of white pearly smoke which slowly drooped and turned to dun." At the same moment, it can be the sinister river of Dickens's *Our Mutual Friend*: "If the old Thames trades had still persisted, if boatmen had still made a living from taking the coins from the pockets of the drowned, then this was the hour for them to watch." Such aesthetic apprehensions later come under the dispassionate scrutiny of Tilda, Nenna's younger daughter, whom Willis takes to see the Whistlers and Turners at the Tate Gallery: "To Tilda, however, the fine pictures were only extensions of her life on board. It struck her as odd, for example, that Turner, if he spent so much time on Chelsea Reach, shouldn't have known that a seagull always alights on the highest point."

The narrative forces no value judgment between the imaginative and the practical view; similarly its characters both suffer and gain from their tideline existence. Their attempts to regularize their lives not only fail, but fail also to be depressing. Nenna has hesitated for months to get in touch with her husband Edward, who rejects what he sees as her irregular life on a houseboat. Finally she goes to his bed-sitting-room in Stoke Newington, but the attempted reconciliation is a failure. She returns to the Reach at dawn, to find Richard waiting to take her out in his dinghy; Fitzgerald avoids the romantic: "we can go up under Wandsworth Bridge as far as the Fina Oil Depot. . . ." But because of Richard's total practical competence, Nenna falls in love: "Small boats develop emotions to a fine pitch, and she felt that she would go with him to the end of the world, if his outboard was always going to start like that."

However, there are no happy endings: Nenna leaves for Canada, Richard for the country, and dry land has never been held out as a solution. The other resolution, the open sea, has no guarantees either. Tilda makes the escape in her imagination, seeing herself as ship's boy: "Men and women came out on the dock to watch as the great brown sails went up, with only a six-year old boy at the winch, and the *Grace*, bound for Ushant, smelt the open sea."

Tilda and Martha are important in establishing a perspective on the makeshift lives of the adults that is both knowing and innocent. Tilda knows what the capable Richard does not, that Maurice's boat is used as a repository for stolen goods. Being a child, she is a survivor in the novel, although the community as a whole does not survive. This closing sense of loss is controlled by the ambiguities of

Offshore's ending. The question of ending, in a novel constructed around and centrally concerned with a ceaseless ebb and flow, calls for exceptional resource in its author. What happens is that Edward, arriving too late to find Nenna, meets Maurice, who has "sat down with the whisky in the dark" at the thought of the emptying Reach, and the absence of friends. When they are both too drunk to notice, the storm outside looses *Maurice* from its moorings: "It was in this way that *Maurice*, with the two of them clinging on for dear life, put out on the tide." Like the novel, the ending is both hopeful and despairing, open and suggestive.

The critical response to *Offshore* was almost unanimously favorable. Lord Briggs, chairman of the Booker judging panel, found it "wholly original in matter and manner. A supremely honest novel, written with a sense of perception in no way derived from other writers or other sources." Victoria Glendinning, writing in the *Times Literary Supplement*, said: "[Fitzgerald] writes fluent poetic prose; yet the novel leaves an impression of sharpness and shortness. Only in writing about the river does she let the words flow . . . [she] has evolved a way of writing about people that compresses and therefore intensifies expression."

Human Voices (1980) is similarly technically as-

sured, managing briefly and unostentatiously to say a great deal. As with Fitzgerald's earlier work, an only half-inclusive plot synopsis would be longer than the novel. On the level of documentary, it concerns the workings of the British Broadcasting Corporation from May to September 1940. Fitzgerald worked at the BBC at this time, in the junior capacity of Recorded Programmes Assistant (RPA), and the novel is a funny and ironic account of the workings of this vast institution, "a cross between a civil service, a powerful moral force, and an amateur theatrical company."

The content of broadcasts is determined by historical events. France has just fallen, and England waits daily for invasion, while London suffers heavy bombing. Fitzgerald is rigorously selective, and totally convincing, in her use of period detail, such as the way household rubbish was sorted "into pigfood, henfood, tinfoil, (out of which, it seemed, battleships could be partly made). . . ." Tempting though it must have been, she is not engaged in an exercise of total recall; yet the novel's specific use of time and place is not merely a question of background. Although the novel's portrayal of the BBC is frequently funny, Fitzgerald has respect for its refusal, throughout the war, to peddle propaganda: "Without prompting, the B.B.C. had decided that

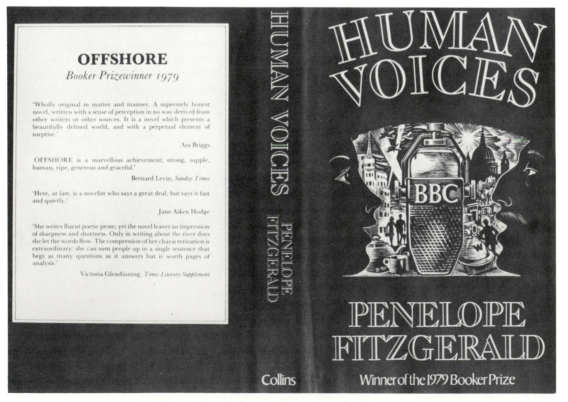

Dust jacket for Fitzgerald's novel about the BBC during the first years of World War II

asked for a long stay. Certainly the room was welcoming, with the 2 sagging red-cushioned wickerwork chairs. Perhaps her collection of post cards & tickets & theatre photographs was beginning to pile up a little, giving the place almost the air of a dressing-room. ~~she~~

She stood shaking the biscuit tin to see if there were any left, & wondering about him. But Carroll was much deeper sunk in himself than she had realised, almost out of her soundings.

'If I'd been able to choose my sin, Hannah' he said, 'I wouldn't have chosen jealousy.'

She watched the kettle, anxious that it ~~she~~ shouldn't start whistling when he was speaking seriously.

'Well, I don't know if our seven deadly sins are the same as yours, but I don't think jealousy was one of them.'

'They call it envy, but it's all the same.'

'And you wouldn't have chosen it.'

'No.'

'Which one, then?'

'I think, sloth. I have an elder brother who still lives at home with my mother and stays in bed every day till noon.'

'What does he do ~~with himself?~~ for a living?'

'Just that, but he enjoys it. He lies there wrapped in his blankets, dinner is brought up to him with the newspaper, and as I say he evidently enjoys himself. The jealous are wretched. The slothful are happy. And I'm not sure that my brother is

Manuscript for At Freddie's

truth was more important than consolation, and, in the long run, would be more effective." It is a decision she has made about her writing, for in *Human Voices* concern for truth becomes the matter as well as the manner of her fiction.

One of the novel's central relationships is between Sam Brooks, RPD (Recorded Programmes Director: Fitzgerald is sharp on the BBC's fondness for initials), and Jeff Haggard, DPP (Director of Programme Planning). Sam is monstrously selfish, obsessed by the need to make perfect recordings, and he thinks the progress of the war is less important than the microphone windshield he is developing. When his egotism upsets the establishment, Jeff always bales him out. Sam has no difficulty in communicating his problems; Jeff has never been heard to talk about his. This absence of articulation is significant in a novel which is thoroughly concerned with communication, and which works largely through dialogue, recorded voices. Visual description is minimal; this is the age of radio. The novel is concerned with what people say, and with how they say it; it is also concerned with silence and reticence, such as Jeff's.

The BBC has resolved to broadcast only the truth, but this must always be contingent—absolute truth is beyond its scope. Human relationships can also hope to achieve truth and this idea is developed through Annie Asra, Sam's new RPA from Birmingham, who speaks with the "scrupulously fair intonation" of the English Midlands. She also speaks the truth. Annie is sixteen, and an orphan—her father, a piano tuner, has recently died. A long, detailed passage describes how Annie, as a child, would watch her father at work, oiling pedals, loosening felts, tightening strings, until he could strike a "perfect chord." The minutiae of the job are not there simply for the sake of recording a craftsman at work (the BBC spends a lot of time doing this, in the novel); they also show that a "perfect chord" takes much hard work. As a final test, Mr. Asra would play a "torrent of chromatic scales," to the delight of the householders, who sentimentalize him as a concert performer manque, "letting himself go at last. . . ." But these flourishes were not the truth about Mr. Asra.

Annie brings the same dogged pursuit of an absolute to her work for Sam. He is completely insensitive to the fact that she soon begins to love

him, but against the odds her truth-telling (about his appalling selfishness) brings them together. Yet to isolate the "story" of Annie and Sam (or to discuss *Offshore* largely in terms of Richard and Nenna) is to oversimplify narratives which are denser, more allusive, and more seamless than a summary can make them sound. *Human Voices* is, deliberately, scrappy and full of hesitation, and these are means by which it demonstrates the failure of speech as well as the inability to speak. When Sam, by choosing Annie, involuntarily breaks the link that held him to Jeff, Jeff can only be laconic. Fittingly, they are talking on the telephone:

> "You're my oldest friend!" Sam roared.
> "No, I'm not."
> "I want to talk to you!"
> "You can't!"
> Nevertheless he hesitated.

Jeff goes out of Broadcasting House and is killed by a parachute bomb. *Human Voices* ends with the silence of death.

The "compressed intensity" to which many critics and reviewers responded in *Offshore* provides a critical focus for *Human Voices* also. In the *Times Literary Supplement*, A. S. Byatt praised its "absence, reticence [and] under-emphasis," finding these "essentially part of its theme and method." John Braine, in the *Sunday Telegraph*, also responded to the novel's deceptive simplicity, writing of its "elemental power beneath a smooth skin."

Although her output to date is small and her novels are short, Penelope Fitzgerald is an important novelist. The significant critical response which her work has evoked derives from an acknowledgment of her ability to compress and intensify some of the traditional concerns of the novel: personal relationships, social institutions, the interactions between the two. On a superficial reading Fitzgerald's novels may appear slight, but their real strength lies in what they omit, in what has been pared away. Their skill and grace is not simply displayed technical achievement, but derives instead from Fitzgerald's absolute concern, often conveyed through humor and comedy, for the moral values of the tradition she follows so precisely. *At Freddie's*, her most recent novel, was published in March 1982.

John Fowles

(31 March 1926-   )

Ellen Pifer
University of Delaware

BOOKS: *The Collector* (Boston: Little, Brown, 1963; London: Cape, 1963);

The Aristos: A Self-Portrait in Ideas (Boston: Little, Brown, 1964; London: Cape, 1965; revised edition, London: Cape, 1968; Boston: Little, Brown, 1970);

The Magus (Boston: Little, Brown, 1965; London: Cape, 1966; revised edition, Boston: Little, Brown, 1977; London: Cape, 1977);

The French Lieutenant's Woman (Boston: Little, Brown, 1969; London: Cape, 1969);

Poems (New York: Ecco Press, 1973; Toronto: Macmillan, 1973);

The Ebony Tower (Boston: Little, Brown, 1974; London: Cape, 1974);

Shipwreck, text by Fowles and photographs by the Gibsons of Scilly (London: Cape, 1974; Boston: Little, Brown, 1975);

Daniel Martin (Boston: Little, Brown, 1977; London: Cape, 1977);

Islands, text by Fowles and photographs by Fay Godwin (Boston: Little, Brown, 1978; London: Cape, 1978);

The Tree, text by Fowles and photographs by Frank Horvat (Boston: Little, Brown, 1979; London: Aurum Press, 1979);

The Enigma of Stonehenge, text by Fowles and photographs by Barry Brukoff (New York: Summit Books, 1980; London: Cape, 1980).

A novelist who writes for a living, says author John Fowles, is an altogether different creature from one whose art *is* his life. The latter, a "dynamic artist," seeks "to form new images and new methods of describing his world," while his less adventurous cousin, the "static artist," uses the traditional techniques of his craft to ensure the current "market value" of his work. As a novelist Fowles has managed to succeed in both categories. He has earned international prominence not only as an innovator seeking new methods of describing contemporary reality, but also as the author of five volumes of fiction that have ranked high on bestseller lists in the United States and abroad. In 1972,

Fowles's first three novels had sold more than four million copies in paperback reprints alone. Three of the novels—*The Collector* (1963), *The Magus* (1965), and, most recently, *The French Lieutenant's Woman* (1969)—have been made into motion pictures. Fowles's success in the marketplace derives from his great skill as a storyteller. His fiction is rich in narrative suspense, romantic conflict, and erotic drama. Remarkably, he manages to sustain such effects at the same time that, as an experimental writer testing conventional assumptions about reality, he examines and parodies the traditional devices of storytelling. Less known to the reading public are his published works of poetry and philosophy. Along with his numerous essays, articles, reviews, and translations, they reflect their

309

author's wide range of intellectual interests. Erudite in several fields of art and science, Fowles has written on subjects as diverse as medieval French literature, natural history, and biological evolution. He is one of the few writers today who command the attention of both a mass audience and the literary scholar and critic.

Born 31 March 1926 in a small suburb of London, Fowles describes his hometown as "dominated by conformism—the pursuit of respectability." A fierce individualist, he attributes his dislike of groups, of "mankind *en masse*," to the oppressive social pressures of his childhood. Fowles learned, however, to cope with these pressures by developing, in his words, "a facility with masks." This ability "to pretend to be what I am not" helped him to win popularity as a student leader at Bedford School, a suburban London preparatory school he attended between the ages of fourteen and eighteen. Fowles attributes his facility with masks to being English, to the way Englishmen "very rarely say what they actually think. That could derive from Puritanism— hiding emotions and wearing a public mask. I suffer from it like everyone of my type and background. I've played the game all my life." Many of the protagonists in Fowles's fiction share their author's facility with masks, and their success at masking their real feelings often proves a hindrance to their internal development.

During the years that Fowles was at Bedford School, excelling in scholarship and sports, World War II was at its height. At one point his family was forced to evacuate their home in order to escape German air raids, and Fowles left Bedford for a term to join them in Devonshire. Here, in the unspoiled southwestern countryside of England, he first encountered the "mystery and beauty" of nature—whose powerful attraction is evident in his fiction, philosophy, and lifelong avocation as an amateur naturalist. After preparatory school, Fowles served two years compulsory military service as a lieutenant in the Royal Marines, attending the University of Edinburgh for six months as part of this training. The war ended just at the time his military training did, so he never saw combat duty. Instead, he entered New College, Oxford, to read French and German languages and literatures. His study of French, especially, has had a lasting influence on his intellectual and literary development.

When Fowles was at Oxford, the French existentialist writers, Albert Camus and Jean-Paul Sartre, were being widely read and discussed. Fowles and his friends eagerly took up their ideas and imitated their philosophical stance, although he now points out that there was more fashion than substance to his understanding of existentialism at that time. All the same, much of Fowles's fiction reflects the existentialist's preoccupation with individual freedom and choice. The postwar existentialists were not the only French writers to have an abiding effect on Fowles's literary imagination. Of his other reading at Oxford, he says: "I was to discover later that one field of Old French literature refused to subside into the oblivion I wished on the whole period once I had taken Finals. This field— 'forest' would be more appropriate—was that of the Celtic romance." Fowles believes that the origin of modern fiction, of "the novel and all its children," can be traced to Celtic lore and its influence on medieval French tales of chivalry and courtly love. Many years after his graduation from Oxford, he paid tribute to his Celtic and French precursors. In a collection of his own stories, called *The Ebony Tower* (1974), he included a translation of Marie de France's twelfth-century French romance, *Eliduc*. In reading *Eliduc*, he says, the contemporary writer "is watching his own birth."

After graduation from Oxford, Fowles left England for Europe, teaching English first at the University of Poitiers in France and then at Anargyrios College, a boarding school for boys on the Greek island of Spetsai. On this island he rediscovered the enchantments of nature in a dazzling Mediterranean guise. The purity of the Greek landscape—the starkness of sea, sky, and stone— inspired his first sustained attempts at writing. Fowles did not think seriously about becoming a writer until he was in his early twenties. Then a "burning need to translate a French poem by [Pierre de] Ronsard" overcame his repression about writing. Fowles attributes this repression to "that stark, puritanical view of all art that haunts England, [the sense] that there is something shameful about expressing yourself." Although Fowles had done some writing while teaching school in France, his efforts intensified considerably in Greece. The two years he spent there, in 1951-1952, proved a formative influence on both his artistic and his personal life.

On the island of Spetsai Fowles met Elizabeth Whitton, the woman he married three years later in England, after her divorce from her first husband. It was on Spetsai, too, that he wrote a number of poems that later made up one section of his published volume of poetry. The Greek landscape had a direct influence on Fowles's first attempts to write fiction as well. In *The Magus*, a novel he began writing shortly after leaving Greece in 1952, the fictive island of Phraxos is directly modeled after Spetsai. Years later, Fowles described the powerful hold that the island landscape of Greece had on his literary imagination: "Its [Spetsai's] pine forest silences were uncanny, unlike those I have experienced anywhere else; like an eternal blank page waiting for a note or a word. They gave the curious sense of timelessness and of incipient myth. . . . I am hard put to convey the importance of this experience for me as a writer. It imbued and marked me far more profoundly than any of my more social and physical memories of the place. I already knew I was a permanent exile from many aspects of English society, but a novelist has to enter deeper exiles still."

This image of the writer as exile—one who lives in isolation and periodically voyages to regions unknown—persists both in Fowles's fiction and in his personal life. Since 1966, he has lived in the small coastal town of Lyme Regis, in Dorset county, on the southwestern tip of England. Hours away from the nearest city, Fowles frankly regards living in Lyme Regis "as a kind of exile." He says: "I have very little social contact with anybody; they mainly hold right-wing political views that have nothing to do with my own. The old idea of exile for an English writer was to go to the Mediterranean. To do what Durrell has done, or Lawrence did. For me, the best place to be in exile, in a strange kind of way, is in a town like this, in England. That's because novelists have to live in some sort of exile. I also believe that—more than other kinds of writers—they have to keep in touch with their native culture . . . linguistically, psychologically and in many other ways. If it sounds paradoxical, it feels paradoxical. I've opted out of the one country I mustn't leave. I live in England but partly in the way one might live abroad." With this paradoxical form of self-imposed exile, Fowles has apparently freed himself from the social and psychological restrictions of British middle-class life, which he has always hated, while at the same time remaining in close contact with the English landscape and language he has always loved.

At the end of 1952, Fowles left Greece and returned to England, where he taught for the next decade at various schools in and around London. He was also working on the first draft of *The Magus*, while experiencing an acute sense of loss at having left Greece. "It was agony," he says. "I thought I'd never get over having left." Yet in retrospect Fowles is glad of having left, believing it necessary to his development as a writer. "I had not then realized that loss is essential for the novelist, immensely fertile for his books, however painful to his private

being." Although he has settled permanently in England, having never returned to Spetsai, he continues to feel spiritually rooted in three countries rather than one: France, England, and Greece. His personal ties to the landscape of Greece and to the literature of France—as well as to the language, landscape, and literature of England—may help to explain Fowles's sense of living "in exile" within Britain, socially and politically. Both the themes and the settings of his fiction reflect his abiding sense of being "much more European than British."

On 2 April 1954, Fowles married Elizabeth Whitton and became stepfather to his wife's three-year-old daughter, Anna, by her previous marriage. For the next ten years the family lived in Hampstead, London. Here Fowles's teaching career continued to offer him exposure to a variety of social environments. He spent a year teaching English at an adult education institution, Ashridge College. At Ashridge, Fowles says, he "took strongly to the trade union and socialist side; and I haven't seen reason to change my mind since." With the success of *The Collector*, his first published novel, he retired from the teaching profession, having last served as the head of the English Department at St. Godric's College in Hampstead. Several years later he and his wife moved to Lyme Regis, in Dorset. They settled, at first, in an isolated old farmhouse on Ware Commons, a mile to the west of the town. Eventually finding the solitude too unbroken, the Fowleses moved into Lyme Regis in 1968. The pleasant old house they now occupy overlooks a garden enclosed by trees, sheltered from the sight of any other house in the environs. Fowles spends most of his time writing and rambling through his two-acre garden and along the Dorset coast, where he pursues his studies as a naturalist. He is also honorary curator of the little museum in Lyme Regis and has spent a lot of time, in recent years, researching the town's history. He says that his study of local history has lately begun to supplant that of natural history; but Fowles regards the two activities as "faces of the one coin."

Even as a boy Fowles was fascinated by nature. In Devonshire, where his parents sought to escape the German air raids during World War II, he developed a love not only for natural beauty but for natural history. During the summer holidays from Bedford School he shot, fished, and collected butterflies. But an increasing intimacy with nature led him to reject predatory sport for efforts, instead, to save nature preserves and threatened species. Some years ago Fowles told an interviewer, "I loathe guns and people who collect living things. This is the only thing that really makes me angry nowadays, I'm afraid—the abuse of nature." Among other things *The Collector* is the social and psychological analysis of a character who collects not merely "living things" but other human beings.

The Collector was not Fowles's first effort at writing fiction. By 1963, when this novel appeared in print, he had been writing for more than ten years and had produced seven or eight other manuscripts—most particularly *The Magus*, which was not published until 1965. *The Collector* was the first book Fowles sent to the publishers, because in his view it was the first manuscript he had completed satisfactorily. The others were "too large," and he found he lacked the technical mastery to bring them off. Set in London and its environs, *The Collector* is based on a central dramatic incident: the kidnapping of a young woman by a total stranger. Frederick Clegg, a nondescript clerk who works in a government office, kidnaps a twenty-year-old art student, Miranda Grey, as she is walking home from a movie. Although Miranda's family live across the street from the town hall annex where Clegg works, their world is remote from his. Miranda enjoys all the privileges of an upper-middle-class background and education. She is talented, beautiful, and surrounded by friends and admirers. Clegg is the son of lower-class parents whose marriage ended in disaster even before Clegg was orphaned at the age of two. Clegg is an introvert who suffers an acute sense of social and sexual inferiority. He spends most of his leisure time collecting butterflies, and he is attracted to Miranda as an amateur lepidopterist is drawn to a rare and beautiful specimen. Secretly he begins to follow her activities, suffering pangs of resentment as he observes her casually going out with other young men. He also indulges in romantic daydreams, picturing a cozy life with Miranda in a "beautiful modern home." His fantasies remain only that until, one day, he wins a huge sum of money—the equivalent in the early 1960s of $200,000—at the football pools, which he has routinely played for years.

Finding himself suddenly graced with "time and money," Clegg begins making plans to realize what before had been only a daydream. As he meticulously devises a plan by which to ensnare Miranda, he is not even sure that he will carry it out. Even after he buys an old cottage in the country, with a set of rooms hidden in the cellar, he does not fully admit his plan to himself. But the line between fantasy and reality is gradually crossed. Clegg furnishes the cellar room, stocks it with books and clothes he thinks Miranda will like, and finally brings her, chloroformed and gagged, to live in captivity.

The first half of the novel consists of Clegg's account of his relationship with Miranda. It is soon apparent that what he calls his "love" for the girl is really his desire to own her, to possess her not sexually but as one would acquire a beautiful object or butterfly. *The Collector* introduces a theme to which Fowles returns in his later works: how the obsession with "having" has overtaken modern industrial society. Clegg's actions dramatize the confusion inherent in contemporary values—society's failure to distinguish the urge for control from the liberating power of love. Clegg's confusion intensifies when, after he captures Miranda, the real and proximate human being proves very different from the remote and unchanging image he has worshipped at a distance. Miranda's verbal assaults, abrupt shifts of mood, and probing wit unsettle and bewilder her captor. At times driven to retreat altogether from her volatile presence, Clegg consoles himself with photographs he has secretly taken of the drugged and sleeping girl. As he says, "I used to look at them sometimes. I could take my time with them. They didn't talk back at me."

Following Clegg's narration, the second half of the novel launches a subsequent account of the same events, this time from Miranda's perspective. In her diary Miranda secretly records her responses to what has happened, along with an account of the thoughts and memories that occupy her in her cell. Now the reader gains a vivid sense of the stifling tedium and oppression of her daily life in captivity—the misery of confinement that ends only with her death. From Miranda's viewpoint Clegg's attempts to make his prisoner "comfortable" appear even more absurd. Gifts of perfume and chocolate can hardly compensate for her loss of freedom—for fresh air, sunlight, the sheer delight of unhampered being. Yet to this experience of freedom, precious and inalienable, Clegg remains persistently blind. As Miranda begins to observe and analyze her captor, she recognizes that he is the true prisoner. Trapped in an airless and dead existence, Clegg is mortally afraid of feeling, of human contact, of what is alive in himself and in others. Miranda records the discovered paradox in her diary: "He's the one in prison; in his own hateful narrow present world."

As Miranda vainly struggles to win her freedom, she begins to perceive Clegg's power over her as embodying "the hateful tyranny of weak people." Those who are themselves imprisoned by fear, ignorance, and resentment will naturally seek to repress and confine others, just as those who have a deadened perception of reality will tend to regard other people as objects. In his subsequent novels, Fowles's protagonists confront situations in some way analogous to Miranda's. Though not literally prisoners, as she is, they nevertheless struggle to assert their freedom and independence against the tyranny of the weak, ordinary, conventional—and most especially, against what, in their own psyches, is enslaved by fear or convention.

Hoping to convince Clegg to release her, Miranda strives to make him understand that she is a living human being, not a specimen he can keep in his private collection. Although totally in his power—Clegg prepares her food, buys her what she needs, determines whether she may be allowed a five-minute walk in the night air—Miranda nevertheless asserts her natural as well as her social superiority in their relationship. She calls him her Caliban (though he tells her his name is Ferdinand), because she regards him as more brute than human. Similar allusions to *The Tempest* recur throughout the novel, but the atmosphere of grim realism starkly contrasts with Shakespeare's famous romance. Miranda needles Clegg with questions he cannot answer, scorns his lack of taste in art and books, and even tries to educate him morally and intellectually. To her, Clegg represents the vulgar and unenlightened world of mass taste and education. He is one of "the Many," while she is struggling to develop the civilized and liberated values of "the Few."

The social dimensions of this conflict between Miranda and Clegg, the Few and the Many, were immediately recognized by critics and reviewers of the novel, some of whom charged Fowles with elitism and even cryptofascism. Responding to what he considered a misunderstanding, Fowles attempted to explain his intent. "My purpose in *The Collector*," he wrote in 1968, "was to attempt to analyse, through a parable, some of the results" of the historical confrontation "between the Few and the Many, between 'Them' and 'Us.' " He continues: "Clegg, the kidnapper, commited the evil; but I tried to show that his evil was largely, perhaps wholly, the result of a bad education, a mean environment, being orphaned; all factors over which he had no control. In short, I tried to establish the virtual innocence of the Many. Miranda, the girl he imprisoned, had very little more control than Clegg over what she was: she had well-to-do parents, good educational opportunity, inherited aptitude and intelligence. That does not mean she was perfect. Far from it—she was arrogant in her ideas, a prig, a

liberal-humanist snob, like so many university students. Yet if she had not died she might have become . . . the kind of being humanity so desperately needs." Fowles believes that society—the inequities of environment and social class—is largely responsible for the evils men commit against the system. In his next published book, *The Aristos* (1964), he states that "one cause of all crime is maleducation."

The author's expressed belief in the essential innocence of a man like Clegg may come as a surprise to readers of *The Collector*. It is questionable whether the novel really achieves this intended effect. The reader is naturally horrified as Clegg passively observes Miranda's slow death from pneumonia, which she contracts from the damp and unhealthy air of the cell. Clegg cannot bring himself to take her to a doctor, preferring to watch her die rather than to grant her freedom. At the end of the novel, soon after he buries Miranda's body under a tree, Clegg begins to follow the movements of a young woman in a nearby village who strikingly resembles Miranda. The future is grimly predictable. Considering Fowles's comments about the Few and the Many, are we to assume that Clegg would have been a good and productive citizen if he had been given a few of the benefits and privileges enjoyed by Miranda? The intended social parable may be lost on many readers, because the immediate effects of Clegg's actions tend to overwhelm any thoughtful consideration of their alleged social cause. The symptomatic expression of Clegg's fixation seems a more fit subject for clinical diagnosis than for social analysis. One tends to regard him as a psychotic, a pathetic madman, not as a product of social and historical forces. The Many are obviously victims of tremendous inequities in the social system; but while these conditions create unjustifiable human suffering and waste, they can hardly be said—by themselves—to produce madmen. Fowles may have intended that the reader perceive Clegg's deadened sensibility as an extreme product of the deceptively ordinary conditions of existence—rather as Beckett and Pinter ask us to see. Miranda observes that Clegg is "so ordinary that he's extraordinary." She recognizes that he is "a victim of a miserable . . . suburban world and a miserable social class"; and she identifies Clegg with "the blindness, deadness," "apathy," and "sheer jealous malice of the great bulk of England." When Miranda violently smashes the china ducks sitting on Clegg's mantelpiece, the reader knows she is expressing her hatred for the stifling banality of conventional taste and wisdom. Yet perhaps because this novel is rendered with such realistic detail, because the ordinary world is evoked in all its familiarity, Clegg appears too abnormal, too mentally disturbed, to function as a convincing emblem of the "dead-weight" of ordinary English life.

The Collector surprised Fowles with its commercial success. Even before the book was published, he had earned several thousand pounds from the sale of paperback, translation, and film rights. The novel was eventually translated into twelve languages; and a commercially successful motion picture—directed by William Wyler and starring Terence Stamp and Samantha Eggar— was released by Columbia Pictures in 1965. For someone who, until the age of thirty-five, could not at times afford a pack of cigarettes, such financial success must have proved a heady experience. Since then, Fowles has sold many more books and paperback, translation, and film rights. Yet what he says he enjoys most about being so well off is not the power to buy, but the freedom to live independently and do with his time what he chooses. Money appears, in fact, to have freed Fowles from *wanting* things: "I'm rich in a minor financial way," he says, "rich enough never to buy new clothes, never to want to go abroad, rich enough not to like spending money any more. I'm also rich in having many interests. I always have a backlog of books to read, there's the garden, nature, walking. . . ."

Taking advantage of the freedom success brings, Fowles made his next publication a book that was certain *not* to be a bestseller. A year after *The Collector* appeared, Fowles produced, in 1964, a work of informal philosophy, presented as a series of notes resembling Blaise Pascal's *Pensées* or Friedrich Nietzsche's more aphoristic writings. As the subtitle to the original edition indicates, *The Aristos: A Self-Portrait in Ideas* is the personal expression of the author's views on a wide range of subjects. "The notion I had," Fowles explains, "was that if you put down all the ideas you hold, it would amount to a kind of painter's frank self-portrait." He admits that *The Aristos* was in part a reaction to the commercial success of *The Collector*: "I didn't want to get docketed as a good story teller or as a thriller writer. *The Collector* . . . was widely reviewed in England as a thriller, it didn't even make the serious novel columns. Which is why I'm certainly tender towards the American critical scene. They at least realized it was simply borrowing something from the thriller form, but that, of course, the deeper intentions were quite different."

Four years after its initial publication, Fowles described the opposition *The Aristos* met even before it appeared in print: "I was told that it would do my

'image' no good; and I am sure that my belief that a favourable 'image' is conceivably not of any great human—or literary—significance would have counted for very little if I had not had a best-selling novel behind me. I used that 'success' to issue this 'failure.' " Fowles's disdain for the writer's so-called image suggests the irony of his situation, that of a "dynamic artist" seeking to work within the limits of a system dominated by the values of the marketplace. By making use of his commercial success to bring forth his "failure," he demonstrates his commitment to the moral and philosophical convictions set forth in *The Aristos*.

Presenting Fowles's views on such diverse subjects as human nature, evolution, art, society, religion, and politics, *The Aristos* provides a fruitful introduction to the major themes of his fiction. His main concern in this book is, as he says, "to preserve the freedom of the individual against all those pressures-to-conform that threaten our century." Like the existentialist philosophers to whom he pays tribute in *The Aristos*, Fowles is urgently concerned with the question of human freedom and the value of independent existence and action. The Greek word *aristos* means, as he explains, "best or most excellent of its kind," and "the Aristos" is Fowles's description of the individual most ideally suited to will and enact excellence under the conditions of existence as he perceives them. He takes the word and concept of the Aristos from Heraclitus, a pre-Socratic Greek philosopher whose thought has come down to us in the form of a few surviving fragments. To Heraclitus Fowles also owes his perception of the two opposing forces or principles at work in the universe: "the Law, or organizing principle, and the Chaos, or disintegrating one." The opposition of these two forces is what constitutes "the War" of existence, the tension between polar forces in which all forms of matter, including human beings, exist. Conflict and hazard, the operation of blind chance, are the inescapable grounds of existence.

Like Sartre, Camus, and other existentialist precursors, Fowles seeks a philosophical basis for human choice, value, and action in a universe that is not, so far as can be known, guided by a supernatural agent or power. Fowles's existential man inhabits a precarious universe that is constantly evolving but has no ultimate purpose. "All that is has survived where it might not have survived," says Fowles. Not only are the welfare and survival of human beings contingencies, but the very world we inhabit—this globe, those planets, our sun—is an accident, a contingent world that happened to "sur-

(94)

She reclined a little further back, and raised her knees; then extended one ~~███~~ leg in the air, turning and inspecting the slim ankle for a moment, before bringing it back to its partner.

"Actually ... oh well, there was something. *,I suppose I'd better tell you* Again, by pure chance, *was walking on my own and happened to* one day before he was given the boot, I passed near his beech-tree. It was terribly hot that day, too. I was rather surpised to notice he wasn't there, though all his smelly old sheep were. Then I remembered, Heaven knows why, that there was a spring nearby. *It* ~~███~~ came out of a cave and made a little pool ~~███████████~~. Anyway, I had nothing better to do, all this was in that absolutely marvellous time before the alphabet *and writing* was invented — my God, if we'd only realized ~~███~~ *We should be so* lucky ~~████████████████~~ *She ███ ███.* So I went to the pool. He was having a bathe. Naturally I didn't want to disturb his privacy, so I stepped behind some bushes." She glanced at the man on the chair. "Is this boring you ?"

He *shakes* ~~███~~ his head.

"You're quite sure ?"

He nodded.

"I was only fourteen."

He nodded again. She turned on her side, towards him, and curled up her legs a little. Her right hand smoothed the sheet.

"He came out of the ~~███~~ and sat on a rock beside it to dry. And then — he was only a simple country boy, of course. Actually, to cut a long story short, he began *... well,* playing with a rather different sort of pipe. He obviously thought he was alone. I was frankly

Actually it has our pool, it has supposed to be a kind of combined bath and bidet for my sisters and myself, but never mind .

Throws him a dark look.

the Pierian Fountain — that was Aunt Polly's prissy name for this pool —

vive where it might not have." Such a world—and its survival—has purpose only to us, because human beings have the conscious desire to see it survive, along with our race. Fowles wrests the responsibility for survival out of the hands of a putative god and places the burden squarely on the shoulders of human beings. Dispensing with myths of a golden age, whether the lost Garden of Eden or future utopias, man must confront and embrace the hazardous (in both senses of the term) conditions of existence, for they constitute his freedom. This freedom, like everything else, is relative because all people are limited—as Miranda is in *The Collector*—by circumstances and forces over which they have little or no control. Yet by asserting our freedom to will, choose, and act within such limits, we can constrain the blind power of chance in our lives or, conversely, seize the opportunities cast up to us by chance. By struggling to establish some measure of justice and equality in society, moreover, human beings may inhibit the harsher effects of social and biological inequities.

The Aristos is, in Fowles's view, the ideal man to contend with the hazardous conditions of existence, because he does not blind himself to the existential situation into which he was born. He "accepts the necessity of his suffering, his isolation, and his absolute death. But he does not accept that the War cannot be controlled and limited" for the benefit of himself and others. True to his recognition of the contingencies of existence, Fowles points out that the Aristos is an ideal model, not a real person. He is a goal, a potential toward which anyone may strive and which in some cases he may realize. "The Aristos is never always."

In 1968, Fowles had a revised edition of *The Aristos* published, stating in his preface that he hoped to clarify both the style and the organization of his ideas. In so doing, he cut much of the original material, restructured and occasionally retitled whole sections, and introduced new material that provides helpful transitions and more ample context for the development of particular ideas. Despite these noteworthy improvements, *The Aristos* is still not a wholly convincing work. Fowles admits that his manner of presentation is "dogmatic" rather than persuasive. He aims not to plead a case but, by "baldly" stating what he thinks, to provoke the reader into articulating his own ideas. Yet "bald" statements seem insufficient when the reader is faced with metaphysical questions concerning the origins of the universe and the nature of human consciousness. The loosely linked notes and paragraphs which *The Aristos* comprises frequently seem

an inadequate mode of discourse for such complex subjects. Moreover, the dogmatic nature of some of Fowles's assertions tends to contradict his avowed belief in the essential mystery of being. The "why" of existence and of the universe, he says, will never be solved by science or art. But his attitude toward "old religions and philosophies" is often condescending. He speaks of them as "refuges, kind to man in a world that his ignorance of science and technology made unkind." Fowles's assumption that the great religions and philosophies of former ages were merely a refuge from mystery—not a means of engaging it—seems an oversimplification, a manifestation of the "scientized" thinking he argues against later in the book. In the words of critic Walter Allen, *The Aristos* "falls short of what it promises . . . but at least it can be taken as an indication of [Fowles's] ambition." And ambition, Allen adds, "is probably the first thing that strikes one about Fowles's second novel, *The Magus*."

In 1964, the year *The Aristos* was published, Fowles resumed work on *The Magus*, which he had begun writing twelve years before. Over a span of a quarter century, he worked and reworked this book, so that it became inextricably bound up with his life. Having begun the novel shortly after leaving Greece in 1952, Fowles completed the first draft in London in 1953; then he dropped the project for new ones. Yet for the next ten years he returned to the novel from time to time, revising and rewriting various versions. In 1964, he collated and rewrote all previous drafts and, in 1965, the novel was published. As soon as the first edition appeared in print, Fowles knew he was dissatisfied, later remarking that the novel remained the "notebook of an exploration, often erring and misconceived." In interviews over the next several years, he candidly stated that he did not regard the work a success. Finally, in 1977, twenty-five years after it was begun, *The Magus* reappeared in a thorough revision, with stylistic or structural changes occurring on nearly every page of the new edition.

The novel's protagonist, Englishman Nicholas Urfe, is, like Miranda Grey in *The Collector*, a bright, well-educated person in his twenties. Having graduated, like Fowles himself, from Oxford University, Nicholas—for lack of a better idea of what to do with himself—accepts a job teaching English at a private boarding school for boys on a Greek island. As Fowles says in his introduction to the revised edition of the novel, he modeled the fictive island of Phraxos after Spetsai. But the school on Spetsai, Anargyrios College, where Fowles taught during 1951-1952, is apparently not the model for the Lord

Byron School, where Fowles sends his character Nicholas to teach. Although quickly bored with his job at this school, Nicholas remains enchanted with the gleaming Mediterranean landscape. The azure sea and sky give him the sense of inhabiting a pristine universe, an Eden untouched by human suffering or fear. Walking along the edge of a deserted beach, Nicholas feels like "the very first man that had ever stood on it, that had ever had eyes, that had ever existed, the very first man." But Nicholas is soon stripped of this illusion—the first in a series of illusions from which he will be separated. He meets Maurice Conchis, the wealthy owner of a villa overlooking this Eden. What Conchis says to him about Greece proves a more accurate description of the world Nicholas has entered: "Greece," Conchis says, "is like a mirror. It makes you suffer. Then you learn."

A cultivated European of Greek and English extraction, Conchis is a man of many and exceptional talents. Both scientist and artist, he has mastered disciplines as various as medicine, music, psychology, and the dramatic arts. What strikes Nicholas upon first meeting him is Conchis's extraordinary vitality: "He had a bizarre family resemblance to Picasso: saurian as well as simian; decades of living in the sun, the quintessential Mediterranean man, who had discarded everything that lay between him and his vitality." Among the things Conchis has discarded are those conventional patterns of thought and behavior that mark an individual as belonging to a particular nation or class. Conchis, like Picasso—or Prospero, to whom Nicholas later compares him—presides over a world of his own making, a world summoned into being by his creative energies and dominated by his will.

Like Prospero in Shakespeare's *The Tempest*, Conchis is a master of illusion. The "Magus," or magician, of the novel's title, he dominates an island which, like Prospero's, is a stage for dramatic spectacles and masques that bring revelation to their audience. Conchis's audience does not merely observe but participates in the dramatic action, which takes the form of a psychodrama. Nicholas soon becomes involved as actor-audience to the drama, and his spontaneous reactions contribute to the way it develops. What occurs between Nicholas and the Magus is, in Fowles's words, a kind of "godgame"; Conchis "exhibits a series of masks representing human notions of God, from the supernatural to the jargon-ridden scientific." By staging "a series of human illusions about something that does not exist in fact, absolute knowledge and absolute power,"

Conchis provokes Nicholas into confronting the essential mystery and hazard of existence. Conchis's motives for devoting his personal fortune and energies to such an elaborate enterprise are never fully explained in the novel. It is suggested, however, that the "godgame" is the result of a lifetime's study of human nature and the pursuit of a valid philosophy. Reflecting Fowles's existential vision in *The Aristos*, Conchis's philosophy is not a formal theory that can be systematically presented. The participant in the godgame discovers, through a series of concrete actions rather than a system of abstract logic, his capacity for free choice and action.

As Fowles suggests through numerous allusions to *The Tempest*, Homer's *Odyssey*, and medieval romance, the quest on which Nicholas embarks has romantic and mythic parallels. The island of Phraxos resembles that unknown other world to which the hero of ancient myth journeys in search of adventure and, ultimately, his true self. Fowles's final purposes are, however, those of the novelist, not the romancer. Nicholas is in no way an idealized hero, and the larger context for his adventure is the specific social-historical conditions of modern industrial society. Nicholas belongs to Fowles's own generation, coming of age immediately after World War II. According to Fowles, these college-educated young men grew up privileged, bored, and burdened with a sense of personal defeat and social exhaustion. Accepting few traditional beliefs or inherited values, Nicholas, like so many of his peers, feels incapable of sustaining a commitment to any person or ideal that might shape the course of his life.

In one sense, Nicholas is both Miranda Grey and Frederick Clegg. He shares with Miranda an interest in art and literature; and, like her, he desires to rise above the unexamined life of "the Many," to define himself apart from the stultifying conventions of respectable middle-class life. Yet Nicholas remains detached from life, an outsider looking in. Not mentally ill, as Clegg is, or afraid of human contact (he has already had numerous sexual affairs), he is reluctant, all the same, to give full range to his feelings. In *The Collector*, Miranda deplores Clegg's inhuman detachment from feeling. The "only thing that really matters," she writes, "is feeling and living what you believe—so long as it's something more than belief in your own comfort." Unlike Miranda, Nicholas has neither found what he believes in nor actively begun to seek it. As though subconsciously recognizing that feeling is the catalyst to both belief and action, Nicholas treats his emotional relationships with studied, even determined casualness. His impulse is not to "collect" women, but to use and dispose of them before he should have to commit himself to a lasting relationship. In some ways the result is the same, however; for Nicholas, like Clegg, purposely detaches himself from the object of his affections. In London, before leaving for his teaching post in Greece, Nicholas meets, and briefly lives with, a young Australian, Alison Kelly, whose affection for him is warm and spontaneous. But while he is sexually and emotionally drawn to Alison, he refuses fully to admit, or allow to flourish, his feelings for her. To others and at times to himself, he pretends that Alison is a mere convenience. When an old friend from his Oxford days runs into them, privately commenting to Nicholas that Alison is attractive, Nicholas feigns cool indifference. She is, he condescendingly remarks, "cheaper than central heating."

Behind Nicholas's cold and cruel remark lies a host of implications that Fowles directly addresses in *The Aristos*. There he describes the values of contemporary industrial society as based almost exclusively on the marketplace. Members of a marketplace or "agora" society tend "to turn all experiences and relationships into objects; objects that can be assessed on the same scale of values as washing machines and central heating, that is, by the comparative cheapness of the utility and pleasurability to be derived from them." Fowles criticizes the industrial societies for their tendency to reify experience, nature, and human beings, treating them as objects, or products, of consumption. Just as the relationship between Miranda and Clegg reflects the tensions existing within contemporary British society, so does Nicholas's dishonesty toward Alison reflect a profound social malaise. Nicholas is a representative not only of his particular class, generation, and nation, but also of the distorted values of the marketplace society now dominating Western culture.

Yet while he exhibits the confused values of his society, Nicholas is more than a product of social forces. Confused as to his real identity, he seeks to change this condition. The promise of discovering a new mode of existence draws him deeply into Conchis's drama. He experiences "an awareness of a new kind of potentiality," sensing that the "mess" of his life—"the selfishness and false turnings"—could "become a source of construction rather than a source of chaos." To Nicholas, the entry into Conchis's labyrinth feels "like a step forward—and upward." Even this initial sense of progress, of getting somewhere, will later prove to be one more in the

"series of illusions" that Conchis will shatter. As he seeks the answers to riddles posed by the dramatic scenarios orchestrated by Conchis and enacted by his company of actors, Nicholas discovers behind each question not an answer but another question, or a series of questions; and, mirrorlike, they all seem to double back on the seeker. Nicholas will not be granted, by the "god" of this game, any ultimate answers to his questions.

The twists and turns of the godgame, the false leads and dead ends into which Nicholas is led, are a dramatization of the essential mystery of existence. Existential uncertainty is, for Fowles, the ground of being; in that uncertainty man affirms not the answers to his questions but his freedom to seek them. As Conchis erects one version of reality after another like a series of stage sets, each collapsing as successive fictions dissolve before new versions of reality, Nicholas persists in seeking explanations for the drama itself. He wants to know whether each dramatic action has a basis in fact. He wants to find "the reality behind all the mystery." Gradually, however, he begins to recognize that the source, or truth, of the fictions is not the point. What is important is the culmination of the dramatic action—the way his own response becomes critical to the outcome. Not until the godgame on Phraxos draws to a climax does Nicholas suddenly perceive the point to which "all Conchis' maneuverings. . . , all the charades, the psychical, the theatrical, the sexual, the psychological," have brought him: to this moment of "absolute freedom of choice." Much earlier in the novel, Conchis has told Nicholas that "there comes a time in each life, like a point of fulcrum," which is a moment thrown up by pure chance, or hazard. The moment is pivotal to one's life because the choices one makes at this time affect "what you are and always will be." The truth of the godgame lies in the fiction itself, in bringing the participant to a "point of fulcrum" and self-revelation.

The labyrinthine complexity of *The Magus*—the mazes of the godgame, the multiple identities of its dramatis personae, the ambiguous nature of each version of "reality" devised by Conchis—disturbed many critics and reviewers when the novel first appeared. Yet the complexity of its form, so unlike the tightly compressed action of *The Collector*, is complemented by a greater complexity of characterization. In the earlier novel, the conflict between psychological polarities—between the Few and the Many, freedom and repression, love and possession, individuality and conformity—was played out, rather too neatly and with somewhat melodramatic effect, between Miranda on the one side and Clegg on the other. In *The Magus*, that conflict does not take place between polarized characters but *within* Nicholas himself. Thus, despite the latter novel's somewhat cluttered form and frequently mystifying effects, *The Magus* is a more convincing dramatization of Fowles's vision of human existence. For if, as Fowles believes, existence is conflict, then surely the primary battleground for this ongoing struggle between opposing forces is not merely external reality but the human heart and mind.

In part three of *The Magus*, Nicholas leaves Phraxos and returns to England. As one critic, Barry Olshen, has noted, Nicholas's journey from England to Greece and back is patterned after "the traditional quest story, involving a voyage to a distant land, the achievement of a mission or the acquisition of special knowledge, and the return home." Having acquired a degree of self-knowledge, Nicholas returns to London to confront Alison and resolve their relationship. But Nicholas is not the only one who has been changed by his journey; Alison, too, is not the same. Nicholas learns that she has secretly taken part in the godgame, and in London he discovers that the game is not over. Although the presiding figure of Maurice Conchis disappears, he is replaced by an equally extraordinary being, Lily de Seitas. Mrs. de Seitas, an old friend of Conchis and a veteran of the godgame, turns out to be the mother of two young women, Rose and Lily, who played major roles in the game on Phraxos. It is the younger daughter, Lily, with whom Nicholas has recently believed himself to be in love—only to have that illusion rudely shattered as well. In London, Mrs. de Seitas is the one who knows where Alison Kelly is and what terms Nicholas may have to fulfill in order to see her. Once again ordinary reality is temporarily suspended, and the actors in this new phase of the drama take on luminous significance as timeless figures of myth. In one of Nicholas's meetings with Mrs. de Seitas, she sits before him in a "corn-gold chair," appearing "like Demeter, Ceres, a goddess on her throne; not simply a clever woman of nearly fifty in 1953." The personal magnetism and power that make Conchis loom like Prospero on his island also emanate from Lily de Seitas. As Nicholas discovers, she and the other actors have all been through the harrowing spiritual journey on which he himself is embarked. This experience, as a seeker in the godgame, is what has given each of them such impressive vitality and courage. Like Conchis, Mrs. de Seitas seems to have "discarded everything that

lay between [her] and [her] vitality." She and Conchis are those rare individuals (and Nicholas may one day join them) who embrace their freedom, reject the values of the marketplace, and recognize the Aristos—the ideal individual—as their true model.

At the end of the novel Nicholas and Alison finally encounter each other, but their relationship remains unresolved. They are, as Nicholas realizes, at a "point of fulcrum," an experience of potential freedom that is the goal of the godgame. Here Fowles chooses to leave them, saying only that what happens to Nicholas and Alison after this "is another mystery." The apparent finality of endings is also an illusion. Like Conchis, the Magus, Fowles believes that mankind "needs the existence of mysteries. Not their solution." For mystery "pours energy into whoever seeks the answer to it." As a novelist Fowles seeks to provide his readers with that energy, too, bringing them to their "point of fulcrum." At the end the reader recognizes, if he has not already, that Fowles's novel is a godgame; the game's "two elements," "the one didactic, the other aesthetic," form a paradigm of the novel's own.

For the sake of the game, Conchis tells Nicholas, one must "pretend to believe." As a participant in the game between reader and author, the reader likewise obliges, pretending to believe in the staged illusions of the novelist until, in the last pages of the book, the author breaks the spell of his magicmaking and announces that we, like his "anti-hero," are also "at a crossroads, in a dilemma." "We too are waiting in our solitary rooms where the telephone never rings, waiting for this girl, this truth . . . this reality." The novel, like the godgame, is a metaphor for existence. What Fowles "teaches" in *The Magus* is not a particular set of truths, or solutions, but the unique responsibility of each individual to seek his own. In the foreword to the revised edition of the novel, Fowles emphasizes his reader's "freedom of choice," saying: "If *The Magus* has any 'real significance,' it is no more than that of the Rorschach test in psychology. Its meaning is whatever reaction it provokes in the reader, and so far as I am concerned there is no given 'right' reaction."

Though not as great a commercial or critical success as *The Collector*, *The Magus* won, in Ian Watt's phrase, "a special following among the under twenty-fives." Its popularity with the young may be explained by its being, in Fowles's own words, "a novel of adolescence written by a retarded adolescent." Though he finds this quality to be his novel's weakness, Fowles defends the novelist's right to "re-gress" in this manner. "The rest of the world can censor or bury their private past. We [artists] can-not, and so have to remain partly green till the day we die . . . callow-green in the hope of becoming fertile-green."

Although Fowles was dissatisfied with *The Magus* almost as soon as it was published, the novel aroused sufficient public attention to warrant a film version. Fowles wrote the screenplay, and he also spent some weeks on location, on the island of Majorca. Although he wrote the script, Fowles says he had little authority over the final product. It had to be altered to suit the director, and then "the producers wanted changes, the Zanucks had their ideas." To this "nonsense" was added "the wrong director" and bad casting. The resulting film, in Fowles's words, was "a disaster." Directed by Guy Green, it starred Anthony Quinn as Conchis and Michael Caine as Nicholas Urfe, with Candice Ber-gen and Anna Karina heading the female cast. While he regards the film made from his first novel, *The Collector*, as "just passable," he ranks *The Magus* and *Justine* (the movie made from Lawrence Dur-rell's novel) as "the two worst films of the Sixties." Ironically, Fowles speaks the first line of this motion picture "disaster." Because the director persuaded him, on the spur of the moment, "to do a Hitch-cock-style walk-on," as critic Robert Huffaker puts it, the novelist appears in the first scene of the film. He plays a Greek sailor who "casts a line ashore, turns to actor Michael Caine, and announces, 'Phraxos.'" Even this spontaneous attempt at a pri-vate joke contributed another mistake to the ill-fated film. As Fowles explains, "only Greek priests wear beards," so the appearance of Fowles as a bearded Greek sailor "set an inauthentic note from the beginning."

Despite, or perhaps because of, the failures associated with the first version of *The Magus*, Fowles decided, over a decade later, to revise this "endlessly tortured and recast cripple" one more time. In 1977, he had the new version published, explaining his intentions in the foreword. In re-writing the novel one final time, Fowles did not attempt to answer "the many justified criticisms of excess, over-complexity, artificiality and the rest that the book received from the more sternly adult reviewers on its first appearance." *The Magus* would have to remain a novel of adolescence, one that was, "in every way except that of mere publishing date," a "first novel." In what way, one might ask, did Fowles attempt to improve his young man's book, if not in conception? The answer apparently lies in the

mature writer's sense of responsibility to his craft and medium. Fowles wanted to rescue this novel from a clumsiness of style and structure he re-garded as criminal. Explaining why he rewrote *The Magus*, he says: "I do not believe that the intention matters more than the craft, idea more than lan-guage; and I do believe that almost all major human evils in our world come from betrayal of the word at a very humble level. In short, I have always felt with *The Magus* like an insufficiently arrested mur-derer." The novelist thus "paid" for his literary "crime" by rewriting phrases and paragraphs on almost every page of the novel and by recasting whole sequences of action and dialogue. He also corrected "a past failure of nerve" by strengthening the "erotic element" in two pivotal scenes. The ef-fect is a noteworthy improvement not only in the novel's formal qualities but in thematic clarity as well. Many of the novel's themes, rather obscurely buried in the original text, are more lucidly ren-dered in the subsequent revision. The analogy be-tween the strategies of the godgame and those of

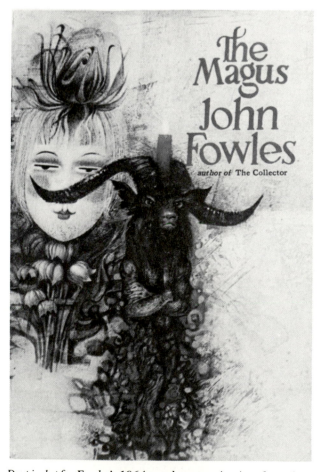

Dust jacket for Fowles's 1964 novel, an examination of a modern Prospero's "godgame"

the novelist is, for example, more fruitfully developed in the revised edition.

Nicholas's emotional and moral blindness also receives more emphatic treatment in the new version, as Fowles supplies him more opportunities to act like a cad. Nicholas more openly disavows his relationship with Alison, for instance, clearly betraying past affection as well as present loyalties. Brought to a harsher confrontation with the worst in himself, Nicholas more clearly perceives his own selfishness. Like Pip in *Great Expectations*—the Dickens novel Fowles most admires and the one that, by his own admission, influenced the writing of *The Magus*—Nicholas sternly judges his past behavior. But the rigor of his self-condemnation is also shown, as in Pip's case, to be a sign of moral growth. The new ending which Fowles wrote for the revised edition hints at a greater likelihood for reunion between Nicholas and Alison; yet the final scene is more open-ended. Nicholas demands that Alison choose, and choose now, whether they are to remain together. He then waits for her answer; and in this "frozen present tense" the author leaves his characters, and the reader, "suspended."

This withholding of any fixed solution, or resolution, to the story has troubled many of Fowles's readers, prompting some of them to write him angry letters demanding that he tell the reader what does in fact happen to his characters. Yet Fowles's purpose in sustaining ambiguity is not to shirk his responsibilities as a novelist, but to redefine them. In his next novel, *The French Lieutenant's Woman*, published in 1969, he overtly tells the reader that he does not exercise absolute authority over his characters. For him the novelist's traditional role as "omniscient god" is outmoded and untenable. Victorian novelists adopted this stance because they sought to model themselves after God himself, the all-knowing creator of the universe. But Fowles, a twentieth-century existentialist, rejects the notion of a universal creator; and in *The French Lieutenant's Woman* he announces his abdication from the throne of literary omniscience. He drives home the point by writing a convincing version of a "Victorian" novel—one that captures with detailed fidelity the manners and milieu of the time—but a Victorian novel that conspicuously lacks the assuring presence of an omniscient author. Thus, eighty pages into the novel, the narrator declares that his character, Sarah Woodruff, remains a mystery even to him. He confesses that his apparent omniscience is only a guise, an aspect of the literary game: "This story I am telling is all imagination," he says. "If I have pretended until now to know my characters'

minds and innermost thoughts, it is because I am writing in . . . a convention universally accepted at the time of my story: that the novelist stands next to God. He may not know all, yet he tries to pretend that he does." A remarkable evocation of the historical and social matrix of the Victorian age, *The French Lieutenant's Woman* is also a parody of the conventions, and underlying assumptions, that operate within the Victorian novel.

While Fowles's narrator draws attention to the contrasts in habits and ideas that exist between Victorian times and our own, he also reminds us that the Victorians' apparently stable and unchanging world was, in 1867, about to vanish forever. In this year Karl Marx published the first volume of *Das Kapital*; Charles Darwin's *Origin of Species* had already appeared in 1859. These eminent Victorians, steadily and without any violent action, helped to shatter the age in which they lived—its faith, morality, confidence. The shocks to the system that lie ahead—though unsuspected by Fowles's characters, who are naturally caught up in the present—are well known to Fowles's readers. This contemporary perspective imbues the historical elements of the novel with poignant irony. An example appears in the narrator's description of Ernestina Freeman, the pretty and pampered young lady engaged to the novelist's protagonist, Charles Smithson. Ernestina's doting parents, we are told, worry unnecessarily about their precious daughter's supposedly frail health. To these Victorian parents a genteel young lady is by definition fragile and must be treated like a porcelain doll. The narrator (sounding suspiciously omniscient) then provides the reader with some salient information to counter the assumptions of Ernestina's fond parents: "Had they but been able to see into the future! For Ernestina was to outlive all her generation. She was born in 1846. And she died on the day that Hitler invaded Poland." That Ernestina will live into an age when healthy young ladies are not treated like invalids is only the mildest indication of the forces of change about to unleash themselves on her world. For now, in the year 1867, Ernestina is a complacent, unsuspecting member of her class and generation. Her habits of thought and action are a straightforward reflection of the predominant attitudes of her day.

Fowles's parodic exposure of Victorian conventions serves as a springboard for testing not only literary devices but also cultural values and assumptions—those of the Victorian age and the present as well. The critical examination of one historical period against the background of another

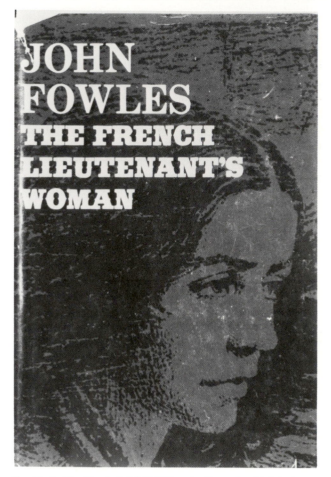

Dust jacket for Fowles's 1969 "Victorian" novel, which imitates the conventions and assumptions of that form

transforms this apparently historical novel into a truly experimental one. In a memorandum Fowles wrote to himself while working on *The French Lieutenant's Woman*, he says: "Remember the etymology of the word [novel]. A novel is something new. It must have relevance to the writer's now—so don't ever pretend you live in 1867; or make sure the reader knows it's a pretence." Both the experimental nature of this novel and its display of erudition—crammed as it is with scholarly information on Victorian mores, politics, art, medicine, science—could hardly have prepared one for the extraordinary popular success that greeted its publication.

For many months a bestseller in the United States, the novel also received enthusiastic reviews from distinguished critics such as Ian Watt, who said in the *New York Times Book Review* that Fowles's "immensely interesting, attractive and human" third novel is "both richly English and convincingly existential." Though less enthusiastically received

in Britain, as has steadily been the case for Fowles's work, *The French Lieutenant's Woman* was more warmly received there than his previous novels. In 1969, the International Association of Poets, Playwrights, Editors, Essayists, and Novelists gave Fowles its Silver Pen Award for *The French Lieutenant's Woman*, which also won the W. H. Smith and Son Literary Award in 1970. In September 1981, a filmed version of the novel was released, receiving wide public attention. The film's screenplay was written by the distinguished British playwright Harold Pinter, and its cast featured Meryl Streep as Sarah and Jeremy Irons as Charles.

Fowles himself was surprised by the critical and commercial success of this novel, whose conception had imposed itself on him while he was halfway through another. One predawn autumn morning in 1966, a vision of a woman standing on a deserted quay (one much resembling Lyme Regis harbor, which can be seen from Fowles's garden) came to him while he was still half-asleep. The woman was dressed in black and stood, with her back turned, gazing at the distant horizon. Readers of the novel will immediately recognize the figure as Sarah Woodruff, the "French lieutenant's woman." Chapter one of the novel ends with a description of Sarah, in black, standing "motionless, staring, staring out to sea, . . . like a living memorial to the drowned, a figure from myth. . . ." According to Fowles, these "mythopoeic 'stills' " often float into his mind. He ignores them at first, waiting to see if they are of the persistent variety that open "the door into a new world"—the new world, that is, of a new novel. Fowles ignored the image, but it duly persisted, the woman always appearing with her back turned. That turned back, Fowles began to perceive, signaled a rejection of the age she lived in, and Fowles already knew that the figure was Victorian. Ultimately the figure in black recurred with such power that it made Fowles's previously planned work seem a bothersome intrusion on a deeper and more compelling task. He had fallen in love with the French lieutenant's woman, and he set to work on the first draft of the book.

Unlike Ernestina Freeman in every way, Sarah Woodruff is, in both senses, the other woman in this novel. Mystifying everyone, including the author, Sarah rejects the values of her age, refusing to live by its conventions. She is an outsider, a nineteenth-century character with a distinctly twentieth-century cast of mind. The daughter of a tenant farmer, she has been sent to boarding school and thus educated beyond her station. Sarah also possesses a strong will, independent mind, and passionate heart—qualities that were hardly viewed as desirable in a young Victorian lady. By nature, temperament, and social circumstance, Sarah breaks the mold of respectable Victorian womanhood.

Between these two women, and the opposing values they represent, Charles Smithson, an intelligent though aimless Victorian gentleman in his early thirties, is driven to choose. Already engaged to Ernestina Freeman when he first encounters Sarah, Charles is at once fascinated and a little frightened by Sarah's striking presence. Rumors that she has been seduced and abandoned by a French lieutenant are adrift in the quiet little town of Lyme Regis, on the Dorset coast of England, where the novel is set (and where Fowles resides). On this lonely coast Charles first sees Sarah, in chapter one, staring tragically out to sea. Her isolation from respectable society and her "untamed" nature seem to require that Charles encounter Sarah in the wilds of nature rather than in a well-furnished drawing room. Their relationship thus develops outside the constraining walls, symbolic as well as literal, of Victorian society.

As this relationship (and the novel's plot) progresses, the "mystery" of Sarah's nature is not solved but augmented. She eventually tells Charles a different version of the tale concerning the French lieutenant, but she verifies the rumors of her seduction and abandonment. Not until much later, after a great internal struggle on Charles's part to resist her mysterious power over him, does he discover that Sarah's version of the story is also a fiction. She was not seduced by the French lieutenant at all. It is Charles, in fact, who deflowers her, never suspecting that she is still a virgin. Far from being seduced, however, Sarah orchestrates the events that lead to her brief tryst with Charles. And he, now in love with Sarah, finds it impossible to go through with his engagement to Ernestina.

Like Conchis, the Magus, Sarah Woodruff lives outside the bounds of social and moral conventions. And while she is drawn to Charles—and even, apparently, loves him—she desires not to make him happy, but to be free. This fierce desire for personal freedom is something that attracts Charles, though he does not understand it. He begins to discover the meaning of personal freedom through this relationship with Sarah. She is the mystery that gives him energy to seek answers; she is the catalyst for the discovery of his potential freedom. This slow and painful process takes place over a period of twenty months, beginning shortly after Sarah vanishes, upsetting all of Charles's romantic

expectations. Utterly alone and hopelessly confused, Charles is determined to find Sarah, vowing that "if he searched for the rest of his life, he would find her." On a train speeding toward London, Charles, having chosen an empty compartment, is abruptly joined by a bearded stranger, who sits down and eventually begins to stare at him with "cannibalistic" intensity. Here the author of this deceptively Victorian novel is making a brief theatrical appearance, in the nineteenth-century guise of a magisterial graybeard in a frock coat. Although his "prophet-bearded" persona gazes at Charles like an "omnipotent god," Fowles's narrator denies authorial omniscience. "What Charles wants," he admits, "is clear," but what Sarah, his more inscrutable character, wants "is not so clear; and I am not at all sure where she is at the moment." Appearances—even those of an author in his own novel—can be deceiving.

This playful introduction and ultimate debunking of the author's Victorian persona is a device by which Fowles reminds his readers, once again, that they are not engaged in a Victorian novel. The fact is, the present world of the author and the reader is at a century's remove from the Victorian era; and the enforced awareness of such temporal distance only augments the contemporary reader's sense of disjunction between the world—of any era—and its fictional representation. The contemporary writer cannot adopt the confident posture of omniscience so favored by his Victorian predecessors, because belief in omniscience, like God, is now dead. Fowles's narrator dramatizes his abdication, or fall, from omniscience by saying that his characters must be granted their freedom. Refusing "to fix the fight" and determine their fate, the author will present, instead, two alternative endings to the story. Now his bearded persona, whose aura of imposing authority has already begun to fade (he later reappears as a dandified impresario), flips a coin to decide which of the two endings shall be given the position of "last" chapter. The narrator regrets that in the novel's sequential narrative two versions of the ending cannot be presented simultaneously. He laments that the second ending inevitably "will seem, so strong is the tyranny of the last chapter, the final, the 'real' version." And this is exactly what happens in *The French Lieutenant's Woman*, though whether the novelist actually regards it as unfortunate is another question.

The author's expressed determination to grant freedom to his characters is an argument the reader may sympathize with but can hardly accept in a literal sense. Nor did Fowles intend that his provocative statements be taken literally. He has described, in an interview, what he feels to be the freedom of his characters. It is the "bizarre experience" of having his inventions, at some point in the process of writing, suddenly "start up on their own." Then, Fowles says, he has the strange feeling that these characters "know the line they ought to be saying" and that he must grope "around in the dark to find it." "Of course in reality," he adds, "the writer has the final say. And on the final draft you have to let the characters know it. Very often by then you know them so well that you are like a really skilled puppetmaster. You can make them do anything, almost. You have to guard against that. You have to say to yourself, this is just an assemblage of words and I can take my scissors and cut it where I want. In other words, you're cutting words, not some real person's skin and flesh." The novelist, as Fowles sees him, navigates a sometimes treacherous course between the insistent reality of his "new world" and the formal strictures of artistic creation. In *The French Lieutenant's Woman* he repeatedly draws attention to the paradox of literary creation, of having his characters take life in the imagination even while they are confined to the pages of a written text. This self-consciousness about the processes of art is a hallmark of much twentieth-century fiction. As a writer Fowles is as conscious of the limits on the life of a character as he is of the limits of his own omniscience. The freedom of an author's characters is metaphorical rather than literal, as is the reality embodied in his fiction.

The choices Fowles leaves to both his characters and the reader, in the form of open or alternative endings, reflect his existential preoccupation with human freedom. "How you achieve freedom," he told an interviewer, "obsesses me. All my books are about that. The question is, is there really free will? Can we choose freely? Can we act freely? Can we choose? How do we do it?" One of the ways we do it, Fowles appears to suggest, is through the process of literary creation. For the writer, "the novel is an astounding freedom to choose." With every word, every page, one makes a multitude of choices. Literary composition is thus bound up with the most essential principles of human life; and the novel, for Fowles, is a metaphor for the potential freedoms of that life. The novel will last, he says, "as long as artists want to be free to choose. I think that will be a very long time. As long as man."

By affirming his characters' freedom, Fowles also reminds his readers of their own. The reader, like the writer, is faced with choices; obviously, however, the choices he or she makes are inextrica-

bly bound up with the author's, which have already been made. Art, like life, has its deterministic principle; true freedom, Fowles affirms, "can never be absolute." Any choice the reader makes will be influenced or guided by the artistic choices the author makes—as, for example, when he provides two endings to the same novel. In *The French Lieutenant's Woman*, it is clear, the second ending proves more convincing because the artistry is more complete. This is the "tyranny" not only of the "last chapter," but of art itself. The author's persona may have flipped a coin in the railway compartment, but the real author, stationed in the wings, is arranging the sequence of endings just as he wants them. True, the novel's first ending is more emotionally satisfying, because the lovers are reunited after Sarah has "tested" Charles, but the reader, no matter how sentimentally inclined, cannot ignore the greater impact of the second ending, even though Sarah here rejects Charles. In the second ending, Charles does not discover that Sarah has given birth to his child. The scene does not end with Sarah's head modestly inclined on Charles's breast, in the manner of so many literary reconciliations of that era. It is as though Fowles were giving us a taste of old-fashioned assurances in the first ending in order to brace us for the harsh and lonely realities of the second. Only here, bereft of Sarah, past hope and expectations, does Charles discover "an atom of faith in himself, a true uniqueness, on which to build." The second ending, and the final chapter, of Fowles's novel closes with a line from Matthew Arnold's poem, "To Marguerite," which the narrator avows is "perhaps the noblest short poem of the whole Victorian era." Although the poem is Victorian, the image it offers of solitary human existence is an eloquent expression of Fowles's twentieth-century vision: men and women struggle alone, isolated one from the other like islands in the great "unplumb'd, salt, estranging sea." This vision, rather than the blessings of good fortune, Charles Smithson embraces in the second and final ending to the novel.

From the self-conscious artifice of *The French Lieutenant's Woman*, Fowles turned with admitted relief to his next project, a collection of poetry he had begun writing in 1951. This volume, simply entitled *Poems*, was published in 1973; it contains poems dating from 1951 through 1972. The personal immediacy of these poems, written in a compressed, even terse style, presents a striking contrast to the richly inventive language and structure of his major novels. Fowles says he regards poetry as a more honest reflection of the self, because the poet speaks directly from his thoughts and feelings. By contrast, the novel is "first cousin to a lie. This uneasy consciousness of lying," he adds, "is why in the great majority of novels the novelist apes reality so assiduously; it is why giving the game away—making the lie, the fictitiousness of the process, explicit in the text—has become such a feature of the contemporary novel. Committed to invention, . . . the novelist wants either to sound 'true' or to come clean." This impulse "to come clean" obviously manifests itself in *The French Lieutenant's Woman*, as Fowles's narrative persona self-consciously focuses attention on literary artifice and declares that "all is fiction." The novelist's clever and playful persona is a far cry from the quiet self whose voice we hear in *Poems*. In "Suburban Childhood," he describes a familiar world where "downstairs / the wireless droned immortally / important Sunday hymns." In the poem "In Chalkwell Park" the poet takes a walk with his aging father, quietly hoping that death will not take him soon. Despite the difference in tone and voice, many of the poems echo themes more amply treated in Fowles's novels. The poem "Crusoe," for example, treats the theme of the quest that underlies much of Fowles's fiction. Defoe's Robinson Crusoe is a symbol of the lonely voyager. People are "Crusoes, all of us. Stranded / On solitary grains of land." The image recalls the line from Arnold's "To Marguerite," with which *The French Lieutenant's Woman* concludes. Cast into the "unplumb'd, salt, estranging sea" of life, each man is an island.

The Ebony Tower, a collection of stories published in 1974, represents a further departure for Fowles from the extended form of the novel, a far more impressive departure than his poetry. It also reflects his continuing fascination with the literature and landscape of France, a fascination that began during his college years. Although Fowles does little traveling these days, when he does leave England he usually visits the French countryside, which provides the setting for several of these stories. Moreover, Fowles includes among the original stories in this collection his translation of a twelfth-century French romance, *Eliduc*, by Marie de France. The love of French literature that Fowles developed during his Oxford years is evident in the numerous translations and adaptations he has written since. In 1974, his adapted translation of Charles Perrault's seventeenth-century fairy tale, *Cinderella*, appeared. In 1977, he translated two classics of the French theater, Molière's *Don Juan* and Alfred de Musset's *Lorenzaccio*, for London's National Theatre. His translation of Claire de Dur-

fort's early nineteenth-century novella, *Ourika*, about a young Senegalese girl brought to France as a child and raised among Europeans, was published in 1977. In his foreword to this translation, Fowles admits that "the African figure of Ourika herself," a social outcast, must have subliminally inspired his depiction of Sarah Woodruff in *The French Lieutenant's Woman*. "The case history of an outsider," *Ourika* "touches on one of the deepest chords in all art, the despair of ever attaining freedom in a determined and determining environment."

In "A Personal Note" appended to one of the stories in *The Ebony Tower*, Fowles explains that the working title of this collection was "Variations," "by which I meant to suggest variations both on certain themes in previous books of mine and in methods of narrative presentation." Each of the stories is also a kind of variation on a mood, setting, or theme found in Marie de France's *Eliduc*. By including his prose translation of this romance among the original stories collected in this volume, Fowles encourages his readers to look for thematic correspondences and common motifs. He thus continues to provoke the reader's interest in the literary process as well as in the product. Fowles asks that his readers be as attentive to the way characters and events are portrayed as they are to the events themselves. Each of these stories is in some way about art, visual or literary; and at the same time it self-consciously reflects, or exposes, the process of its aesthetic creation. The author plants various self-conscious devices, announcing that "all is fiction," throughout. In the title story, also the longest—just under one hundred pages—one of the characters is reading a book entitled *The Magus*. David Williams, the protagonist of "The Ebony Tower," has never heard of the book, however, and assumes it is about astrology and "all that nonsense." The irony, shared by the author and reader alone, is that David Williams is about to undergo the kind of personal ordeal, or test, that Nicholas Urfe in *The Magus* faces at each stage of the godgame.

An abstract painter who also writes and lectures on contemporary art, David Williams travels to France to interview a famous British expatriate, the seventy-year-old painter Henry Breasley. Breasley, who lives with two young female companions in a secluded old manor house in Brittany, possesses the vitality that reminds one of Maurice Conchis, the Magus, or of Picasso. Through his encounter with Breasley—and with one of the young women living at the manor, a promising young painter—David finds the orderly "solutions" of his life suddenly thrown into question. Feeling a

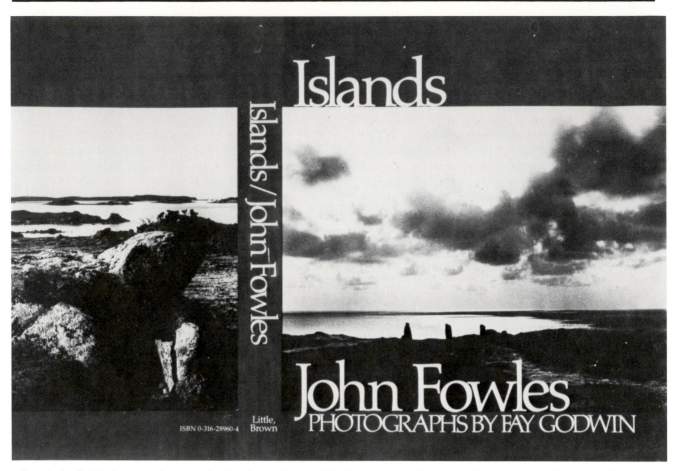

Dust jacket for Fowles's consideration of real and metaphorical islands, accompanied by Fay Godwin's photographs of the Scilly Islands

vital attraction to the young woman, David takes a fresh look at his comfortable, arid marriage. At Breasley's provocation, he begins to question the enterprise of abstract painting as well. (Fowles, whose stepdaughter, Anna, and her husband are both art teachers, says that their problems as art students helped him to understand the general problems of modern art as well as literature. He has, therefore, tacitly dedicated this story to them.) Breasley tells David that abstract painting exists in an "ebony tower," his designation for the obfuscating tendencies of contemporary art. A modern variant of traditional "ivory tower" idealism, the ebony tower signifies the contemporary artist's retreat from reality. Obscurity and cool detachment mask his fear of self-exposure and his failure to engage with life's vital mysteries. David gradually recognizes that he is such an artist, camouflaging the "hollow reality" of his paintings "under craftsmanship and good taste." He is a concrete example of the "static artist" described by Fowles in *The Aristos*.

The story culminates in a "point of fulcrum" for David Williams, but, failing to act at the critical moment, he loses the "chance of a new existence." Rejecting this chance, failing to seize it, David sadly realizes that he has arrested his further development as an artist. "Crippled by common sense," he has failed to embrace mystery, exploit hazard, and discover a way to self-renewal. The possibilities confronting Nicholas Urfe and Charles Smithson at the end of their ordeals appear closed to David. The conclusion of "The Ebony Tower" is final, not open-ended. As he goes to meet his wife at the airport, David awakens from the "dream" of a freer, more vital mode of existence. He has "a numbed sense of something beginning to slip inexorably away. A shadow of a face, hair streaked with gold, a closing door." With an inward, "drowning cry," David awakens to "jackbooted day" and "surrenders to what is left: to abstraction."

Like "The Ebony Tower," Fowles's next story, "Poor Koko," ends with an extended epiphany, or revelation, on the part of the main character. Like

David Williams, the protagonist of "Poor Koko" makes a discovery whose meaning extends beyond his personal life. David realizes that abstract painting is one symptom of the malaise in contemporary culture—a retreat from human concerns and reality into the "ebony tower." Similarly, the highly literate narrator of "Poor Koko" recognizes in what happens not only his own failure but the failure of his generation and the breakdown of society. He makes this discovery when he travels to a country cottage in North Dorset, which has been lent to him by friends so that he may finish, without interruption, his critical biography of Thomas Love Peacock (a nineteenth-century novelist admired by Fowles). Just after the narrator arrives at the cottage, a thief breaks in, thinking the cottage empty. The young robber ties up the narrator, but does not harm him. In fact, as the thief goes about his business, selecting things of value, he engages the narrator in a long conversation, even offering to make him a cup of coffee before he leaves. Before he goes, the young man suddenly, and without warning, destroys all the books, documents, notes, and drafts the narrator has accumulated—over a period of four years—for his book on Peacock.

This violent attack on his manuscript rather than on his person presents the narrator with an enigma he is still trying to solve nearly a year after the event. He keeps asking himself what could possibly have been the thief's motive. He arrives, finally, at a "tentative conclusion" that he relates to the reader. Being a man of letters, he focuses his attention on the verbal evidence. He recalls what the young man said to him and, what is more, what he might have been trying to say to him in the crude jargon adopted by contemporary, alienated youth. "Man, your trouble is you don't listen hard enough," the thief had told him. In that rebuff the narrator now recognizes "a tacit cry for help." He admits to himself that he was "guilty of a deafness." His manuscript thrown into the fire, he now perceives that "what was really burned was my generation's 'refusal' to hand down a kind of magic," the power of language. He blames himself, as a member of that generation, for such a catastrophic breakdown of social and cultural values. The younger generation, he perceives, has been deprived of the most vital source of personal energy and power a culture can bestow. They have been left to "doubt profoundly their ability to say" what they think and believe. The strongest evidence for the narrator's argument resides in the narrative medium of the story itself. The narrator's measured, precise delineation of feeling and perception, and the com-

passionate insight at which he ultimately arrives, could not be shared, or realized, had not the author's language worked its special magic here.

While the narrator of "Poor Koko" solves, at least to his own satisfaction, the enigma of what has happened to him, the mystery of the next story—aptly titled "The Enigma"—is not solved, but abandoned. In the process of investigating the sudden and inexplicable disappearance of John Marcus Fielding, a prominent London Member of Parliament, a young police sergeant named Jennings discovers for himself, and the reader, what Fowles had previously suggested in *The Magus*: the quest for answers to a mystery, rather than the answers themselves, pours energy into the seeker. While Michael Jennings searches for clues to a possible "sexual-romantic solution" to the M.P.'s disappearance, he unwittingly embarks on an amorous adventure of his own. *Cherchez la femme*, advises another M.P. whom Jennings questions about Fielding's disappearance; but the woman Jennings finally discovers is not the abstract one he thought he was looking for. His investigation leads, instead, to a remarkable young woman, Isobel Dodgson, who is the former girl friend of the vanished man's son. Jennings is immediately taken with her; and the mystery of love proves the abiding enigma of this story.

Not only is Isobel Dodgson exceptionally pretty and quick-witted; she also possesses the electric vitality and independence that characterize a self-motivated individual in Fowles's world. A fledgling writer, Isobel is aware of the parallels between the "game" of detection in which Jennings is engaged and the conventions of the detective story genre. "Let's pretend," she suggests to him, that "everything to do with the Fieldings, even you and me. . . , is in a novel. A detective story. . . . Somewhere there's someone writing us, we're not real. He or she decides who we are, what we do, all about us." Playfully taking up the writer's part in this predictable genre of fiction, Isobel teasingly suggests to Jennings a potential lead in the case—that is, her possible complicity in Fielding's disappearance. As the reader already realizes, however, Fowles's story transcends the narrow conventions of the detective story. Jennings rejects Isobel's playful solution as an obviously false lead, remarking that "it's not how I read her character." That Jennings has begun to "read" Isobel's character suggestively implicates the act of literary interpretation in the processes of life. In both life and literature readers seek meaning and a satisfactory mode of representing discoveries to themselves as well as to others.

The lack of a central lead or a neat key to

Fielding's disappearance prompts Isobel to observe: "If our story disobeys the unreal literary rules, that might mean that it's actually truer to life." For at the heart of life, as Fowles suggests throughout his fiction, lurks insoluble mystery. The uncertainty of real existence distinguishes actual human beings from conventional literary characters. The latter, because their fates are thoroughly "written" by a creator intensely interested in them, lack the freedom of real individuals inhabiting an apparently indifferent universe. It is also possible, in Fowles's view, to allow oneself to be "written" by a social system, or a fixed code of conventions, in real life. By unthinkingly conforming to a system of rules governing both thought and action, human beings can forfeit their freedom and unknowingly transform themselves into social puppets. In "The Ebony Tower," David realizes that, having allowed himself to be so written, he is an "artificial man" rather than a free one. By implicitly equating authorial control—being written—with social determinism, Fowles again raises the important question: how does an author who explicitly provokes his reader's awareness of the literary artifice hope to grant to his literary puppets a measure of personal freedom? One way is to insist that those of his characters who reflect human freedom—Maurice Conchis, Lily de Seitas, Sarah Woodruff, Henry Breasley, and perhaps the vanished man Fielding—retain an aura of mystery about them. They are, by virtue of their unpredictable humanity, not wholly solvable or determinable, either by the reader or by the author. The real mystery, or enigma, at the heart of Fowles's fiction provokes the reader to seek his own answers and thus partake of the energy that mystery generates. In the words of Conchis, the Magus, mystery "pours energy into whoever seeks the answer to it."

Abandoning the search for the solution to an abstract problem, Jennings recognizes the priority of the enticing mystery before him: "The act [Fielding's disappearance] was done; taking it to bits, discovering how it had been done in detail, was not the point. The point was a living face with brown eyes, half challenging and half teasing; not committing a crime against that." Part of Isobel's attraction for Jennings is her inscrutable air of independence. Her effect on him in some ways resembles Sarah's on Charles Smithson: "Something about [Isobel] possessed something that he lacked: a potential that lay like unsown ground, waiting for just this unlikely corn-goddess; a direction he could follow. . . . An honesty." The power Jennings perceives in

Isobel is associated with the source of growth, fertility, or fruition in nature. A "corn-goddess" whose vital power promises to nurture new life in him, Isobel recalls Lily de Seitas, who appears before Nicholas, the seeker in *The Magus*, "like Demeter, Ceres, a goddess" on her "corn-gold" throne.

The final story of the collection, entitled "The Cloud," is the most evanescent structurally and thematically. The opening paragraph, with its concrete evocation of a summer's day in rural France, proves nothing short of deceptive. In a matter of hours the azure sky of this "noble day, young summer soaring, vivid with promise," will be transformed by the precipitous appearance of a mysterious cloud, "feral and ominous"—the "unmistakable bearer of heavy storm." The style of the opening paragraph is deceptive as well. Its realistic tone and point of view will abruptly give way to a series of shifting narrative perspectives. To begin with, the reader is given a glimpse of the central characters at close range. On a terrace two young women lie outstretched on beach chairs in the sun; three other people, a woman and two men, are ranged about an outdoor table, while three children play below on the lawn. No sooner is this picture sketched than the point of view shifts to a position "across the river," from which the narrator gazes with a painter's detachment at the distant composition of these "eight personages" in a "leafy" and "liquid" landscape. The harmony of this composition suggests to the narrator a Gustave Courbet painting; the tranquility, however, is more apparent than real. "So many things clashed, or were not what one might have expected," he says, slyly adding, "If one had been there, of course." As soon as the narrator reminds the reader that he is indeed not "there," in the scene, he mysteriously finds himself—without any helpful transition—back in the midst of these "eight personages." The authorial sleight-of-hand reminds Fowles's readers that they are in a fictive universe, where imagining is the only form of being anywhere.

No matter from which perspective the characters are viewed—and in this story the perspective keeps changing—the sense of their interrelationships and ulterior motives is fleeting and elusive. The indistinct contours of the cloud, after which the story is named, come to suggest the impalpable human emotions lying beneath the visible surface of reality. A vaporous floating island adrift in the azure sky, the cloud also connotes the essential isolation of each of the characters, even as they embark on a group picnic by the river. Most isolated of all is the story's major character, a bitter young woman named Catherine, first glimpsed sunbathing on a beach chair. She is the recently widowed sister of Annabel Rogers, who lives with her husband, Paul, and their two children in a charming old mill by a river in central France. Visiting them are Paul's friend Peter; Peter's girl friend, Sally; and his son by a former marriage. Still mourning the loss of her husband, and consumed with bitterness over his suicide, Catherine resents the presence of the other guests; she feels both superior and hostile to their casual talk. Since the suicide of her husband, she has lost all sense of continuity in her life. For her everything has become "little islands, without communication, without farther islands to which this that one was on was a stepping-stone, a point with point, a necessary stage. Little islands set in their own limitless sea. . . . And the fear was both of being left behind and of going on." The terror and isolation Catherine feels, but cannot express to anyone, are revealed in the fairy tale about a lost princess that she tells to her little niece. The princess, having gone on a picnic with her royal family, falls asleep in the forest: "And when she woke up it was dark. All she could see were the stars. She called and called. But no one answered. She was very frightened."

At the end of "The Cloud," Catherine, like the lost princess, has been left alone by the other picnickers, who assume she has already started home. By this time, having noticed the ominous cloud that has suddenly appeared in the sky, they are eager to get back before it starts "thunder-and-lightning all night." As the picnickers, without Catherine, start walking back, the narrative viewpoint once again shifts "across the river." The reader watches the characters disappear from the scene, leaving the meadow empty. The landscape is silent, the composition of figures now removed from the setting. All that is left is "the river, the meadow, the cliff and cloud." No one, not even the reader, can see where Catherine is lying. The ambiguous final sentence of the story echoes a line from the fairy tale Catherine told to her niece: "The princess calls, but there is no one, now, to hear her." Catherine, it seems, is lost forever; perhaps she will commit suicide, a possibility that has haunted her throughout the day. Perhaps she is doomed not to death, but to that prison of despair from which she cannot call out—or, like the princess, calls out when it is already too late. The events of this story lead to no visible climax. Only the charged atmosphere of unspoken fear, hate, desire conveys the menace lurking in the otherwise bucolic landscape. The symbolic em-

bodiment of these elusive psychic realities is the cloud. A sign of the bad weather to come, the cloud also serves as a harbinger of impending human disaster.

As he announces the sudden appearance of the ominous cloud on the horizon, the narrator remarks: "And the still peaceful and windless afternoon sunshine . . . seems suddenly eerie, false, sardonic, the claws of a brilliantly disguised trap." In this story, the false "trap" of appearances has been staged by the author, but with obvious reference to the deceptions of both nature and art—most particularly, the deceptive surface "realism" of landscape painting. In "The Cloud" Fowles evokes the wilderness of the solitary human heart lurking beneath the innocent landscape, a wilderness, insubstantial but real, that every true writer seeks to embody in the concrete physical environment. In "The Cloud," imagery, style, and structure create a vivid impression of this protean reality without fixing it in final form.

In a *New York Times Book Review* of *The Ebony Tower*, Theodore Solotaroff qualified his warm praise of these stories by comparing them to Fowles's previous novels: "None of the four long stories . . . has the originality of those two novels [*The Magus* and *The French Lieutenant's Woman*] or even the tour de force quality of Fowles's *The Collector* . . . and they do tend to have a kind of relaxed, mopping-up feeling about them." Solotaroff's critical reservations may say less about the intrinsic value of *The Ebony Tower* than they do about the disadvantage any writer faces when he breaks with his past practices and tries out a new form or style. Although Fowles returned in his next work, *Daniel Martin* (1977), to the novel form, he was still committed to breaking new literary ground. His description of the novel as "a long journey of a book" is apt, for its writing occupied him for a number of years. (During those years he also conceived and wrote *The Ebony Tower* and completed his revision of *The Magus*—both of which were published before *Daniel Martin*.) Like much of Fowles's other fiction, this novel is patterned on the quest motif, the main character's search for an authentic self. *Daniel Martin* also reflects the author's journey toward greater authenticity as a writer. By his own admission, this novel is Fowles's most personal work. Aware of the obvious parallels between himself and his character, Fowles says: "I was brought up in a Devon village, the one in the book. Quite a lot of my ideas are spoken by [Daniel Martin]. I gave him two or three of my interests." The "authenticity" as well as the psychological intensity of this novel originate not in its autobiographical elements, however, but in Fowles's immediate and searching presentation of the main character's inner life.

A few years after the publication of *The French Lieutenant's Woman*, Fowles told an interviewer that he now wanted "to write more realistically. *The Collector* was a kind of fable, *The Magus* was a kind of fable, and *The French Lieutenant's Woman* was really an exercise in technique." He added, "of course style is *an* essential preoccupation for any artist. But not to my mind *the* essential thing. I don't like artists who are high on craft and low on humanity. That's one reason I'm getting tired of fables." Interestingly, he was preparing the final version of *The Magus*, attempting to atone for his literary "crimes" against language and craft in that "adolescent" book, at the same time that, in *Daniel Martin*, he was trying to move away from too much preoccupation with style and craft. Aware that his special gift as a writer was "for narrative"—a gift for telling stories that made people listen—Fowles had begun to wonder whether he had abused this gift by writing novels full of "literary gymnastics." While his earlier "betrayal of the word" had compelled him to rewrite *The Magus* one more time, his quest for a more authentic style in *Daniel Martin* apparently grew out of an awareness—now that he had mastered the techniques of literary invention—that craft alone is not enough. In an interview in 1977, shortly after *Daniel Martin* was published, Fowles referred to the novel as his "penance." The word suggests that for him this "journey of a book" was a kind of pilgrimage, an act of literary contrition for the artistic "sin" of having exploited, or hidden behind, his talent for narrative invention. *Daniel Martin* is not simply nor unartfully constructed; its design is extremely complex. But, unlike Fowles's previous novels, this one does not proceed with rapid forward momentum, catching the reader up in its ingenious twists and turns. Critics have, in fact, faulted the novel for its long paragraphs of unwieldly introspection and lack of dramatic tension. Fowles's intention, however, is clear. There is nothing superficially compelling about the action or plot of this long, ruminative novel.

The protagonist of *Daniel Martin* is an English playwright turned screenwriter. The idea for a novel about a screenwriter apparently took shape during Fowles's visit to Hollywood in 1969. He had gone there to discuss plans for filming a motion picture of *The French Lieutenant's Woman*. (Many abortive attempts to convert the novel to the screen were made prior to the version released in 1981.)

With a half hour to kill before his appointment with the head of production at Warner Brothers, Fowles wandered around the studio lot. Since nothing was being filmed, all the sets were empty. He had an intense impression of vacuity, and that sense of emptiness about the moviemaking industry inspired him to begin *Daniel Martin*.

A man in his late forties, Daniel Martin has arrived at a "point of fulcrum" in his personal and professional life. Although materially successful, with an established career in films, he is overcome by a sense of defeat and moral failure. It is, he says, "as if I was totally in exile from what I ought to have been." In an attempt to recover that neglected and abandoned self, Dan begins to contemplate, with considerable trepidation, the possibility of writing a novel about his life. The novel which Fowles's reader holds in his hand appears, at first, to be the one Dan ultimately succeeds in writing. By the end of the novel, however, Dan has not yet begun to work on it. Instead, in the last paragraph of Fowles's novel, Dan suddenly thinks of an apt concluding sentence for his projected work. Then, in the last sentence of *Daniel Martin*, the real author steps in to comment on his character's discovery of a last sentence: "In the knowledge that Dan's novel can never be read, [that it] lies eternally in the future, his ill-concealed ghost has made that impossible last [sentence of Dan's] his own impossible first." Daniel Martin's "ill-concealed ghost" is Fowles himself, who refers the reader to the "impossible first" sentence of his novel. This isolated fragment—"Whole sight; or all the rest is desolation"—makes little sense to the reader when he first encounters it. The full meaning only emerges after he has read Fowles's closing paragraph and returns to the opening of *Daniel Martin* to read the sentence a second time. Fowles's "journey of a book" thus describes a circle, tracing the archetypal pattern of the quest itself. In *The Magus*, Fowles describes this circular pattern, quoting from the last poem in T. S. Eliot's *Four Quartets*, "Little Gidding": "And the end of all our exploring / Will be to arrive where we started / And know the place for the first time."

At the end of *Daniel Martin*, the protagonist finds himself—like Fowles's other "seekers," Nicholas Urfe and Charles Smithson—poised on the brink of a possible new life, the "chance of a new existence." In contrast to Fowles's other novels, *Daniel Martin* concludes with a definitive happy ending—in the form of the main characters' reconciliation. In another sense Fowles still refuses to offer fixed solutions for his characters or readers. By self-consciously introducing himself, Dan's "ill-concealed ghost," into the novel's concluding sentence, Fowles reminds us that his character's projected novel is not the one, *Daniel Martin*, just read. Daniel Martin's book must lie "eternally in the future." Dan's past has been joyfully redeemed, but the future still holds its mysteries.

Most important, however, is the vision of wholeness achieved by Dan at the end of the novel. The discovery of "whole sight" is a culmination of his journey toward self-integration. To be whole Dan must recover that lost, or potential, self from which he has felt "exiled." The stages of this journey toward recovery and integration are embodied in both the events and the narrative structure of the novel. *Daniel Martin* astutely traces a mind's digressive movement back and forth over the critical events of a lifetime. These events loom like islands in the sea of Dan's consciousness, and he journeys back to them in memory while time carries him forward into the future.

In *Islands* (a long essay featuring a series of photographs of the Scilly Islands, published in 1978), Fowles remarks that the structures of his novels all seem to recall the voyage of consciousness to different islands in time and memory: "I have always thought of my own novels as islands, or as islanded. I remember being forcibly struck . . . by the structural and emotional correspondences between visiting . . . different islands and any fictional text: the alternation of duller passages, . . . the separate island quality of other key events and confrontations—an insight, the notion of islands in the sea of story." Although all of Fowles's novels loom as a series of islands in their author's mind, none has a structure more closely resembling this description than *Daniel Martin*. This "journey of a book" does not trace the linear movement one associates with a train or car, but the apparently wayward, drifting motion of a sailboat—tacking its way through a populous archipelago and halting at various points of interest. "Forward Backward" is the title of an early chapter in *Daniel Martin*, describing Dan's return to Oxford, England, where an old friend of his is dying of cancer. The friend, Anthony Mallory, is someone from whom Dan has been estranged for many years; in his last hours Anthony wishes to redress old wounds and make amends. The journey to Oxford from London, a literal progression forward in time, is for Dan a journey backward into the past. Here he must confront not only Anthony and his wife, Jane—with whom Dan was in love years ago, when they were students at Oxford, and whom he knows he should have married—but also buried regrets, fears, and

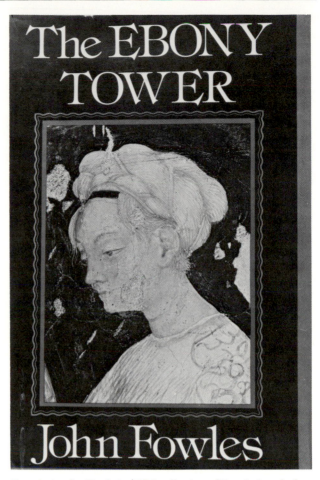

Dust jacket for Fowles's 1974 collection of "variations both on certain themes in previous books . . . and in methods of narrative presentation"

guilt. Up until this moment he has been living in flight from his past, fearing to face up to himself or to atone for past betrayals. Giving up writing plays for a career in films has also offered escape: "Film excludes all but now; permits no glances away to past and future; is therefore the safest dream. That was why I had given so much of my time and ingenuity to it."

The telephone call that brings Dan to Oxford from Hollywood, where he has been working on a script, is the catalyst for his delayed confrontation with the past and his lost self. When he hears, over the transatlantic telephone wires, the voices of Anthony's wife, Jane Mallory, and her sister, Nell (Dan's ex-wife), he already knows that the sea, and the voyage, have claimed him: "The decision is on him, almost before he knows it is there, and he feels—the image is from seeing, not experience—like a surfer, suddenly caught on the crest, and hurled forward." The surfer, riding the crest of the wave *back* to shore, is literally engaged in the "forward backward" movement that symbolizes Dan's inner voyage toward recovery of the past and "what he ought to have been."

The forward-backward movement of the novel's narrative also reflects the special Englishness of Dan's, and his race's, elusive nature. These special qualities comprise, according to Fowles, the basic subject of *Daniel Martin*. As Fowles has Dan realize in the novel, the reserve of the English is a manifestation of their "peculiarly structured imagination, so dependent on undisclosed memories, undisclosed real feelings." The real life of the English, Dan observes, takes place beneath the surface of the visible and present: "We are above all the race that live in flashback, in the past and the future; and by a long blindness I had got myself into the one artistic profession [filmmaking] where the essence of Englishness, this psychological and emotional equivalent of the flashback (or flash-forward, flash-aside) lay completely across the natural grain of the medium—which was a constant flowing through nowness, was chained to the present image." The Englishman's characteristic withdrawal into the privacy of the inner self is also expressed in Dan's love of the "sacred combe"—the hidden valley or forest retreat that provides sanctuary from the strictures of the everyday world. To this green world, a mythical Sherwood Forest, the English psyche retreats to encounter and be nourished by the essential mysteries of life. In *The Tree* (1979), an essay Fowles wrote to accompany a series of evocative photographs of trees, he describes the green refuge of forest and wood as "the best analogue of prose fiction." He adds, "Some such process of retreat from the normal world—however much the theme and surface is to be of the normal world—is inherent in any act of artistic creation, let alone that specific kind of writing that deals in imaginary situations and characters. And a part of that retreat must always be into . . . a complexity beyond daily reality, never fully comprehensible or explicable, always more potential than realized."

Dan's decision to write a novel is thus an expression of his "longing for a medium that would tally better with this real structure of my racial being and mind . . . something dense, interweaving, treating time as horizontal, like a skyline; not cramped, linear and progressive." Such a medium is embodied in the novel *Daniel Martin*. "Dense" and "interweaving" like a forest interior, the novel not only intertwines events from different time periods but also alternates between different narrative points of view. The narrative shifts from third to first person, from "he" to "I" and back as Dan intermittently engages in the "attempt to see oneself as others see one—to escape the first person, to become one's own third." His desire to escape the first person also manifests his fear of subjectivity, of "emotion and unreason." He knows that "the objectivity of the camera corresponded to some deep psychological need in him." This need for distance is akin to the emotional detachment Nicholas Urfe assiduously cultivates in *The Magus*. In some ways *Daniel Martin* represents a middle-aged version of Urfe, burdened by a sense of personal defeat and failure made heavier by his greater years and experience. The emotional rebirth, or recovery, of self which both characters undergo is, therefore, associated with their renewed apprehension of mystery—the fertile source, the green world, of "emotion and unreason."

The novel's frequent shifts in narrative point of view also serve to remind the reader of that authorial presence, Dan's "ill-concealed ghost," standing in the wings, waiting to declare himself at the end of the novel. As soon as Dan decides that "anything would be better than to present" his hypothetical novel "in the first person," the chapter breaks—and the next paragraph begins with the sentence, "I was also very tired that morning." It is not Dan but his author Fowles who is in ultimate control. This particular shift to first person occurs, moreover, just after Dan recalls the name Simon Wolfe, the name he is thinking of using for the main character in his projected novel. Later this "mythical Simon Wolfe" reappears in his thoughts as "S. Wolfe"; as several critics have noted, S. Wolfe is an anagram for Fowles. Fowles's self-conscious references to the act of reading and writing again draw attention to the analogies that exist between life and art. Consciousness makes all human beings readers and writers of reality—writing so that they may be read and interpreted by others. In *Daniel Martin*, this literary and existential process is reflected at all levels of the text. Behind the characters and events of the novel is glimpsed the shadowy presence of the author, John Fowles (S. Wolfe)—whose self, vision, and imagination have written the world of *Daniel Martin* into being.

In one sense, the novelist's characters are all versions, or representations, of his inmost self. They are the masks he invents for the purpose of defining what that self is, knows, experiences. In *Daniel Martin*, then, the author's role is recapitulated by Fowles's central character. As the narrating persona of the novel, Daniel Martin is engaged in the act of "writing himself." But writing himself in the present implies reviewing and interpreting his past. As he sets about doing this, Dan realizes that he has always been writing, producing, and acting versions of himself. He sees the Oxford student Dan Martin as a tour de force creation—with the author playing the role and serving as the audience, too. "I was writing myself, making myself the chief character in a play, so that I was not only the written personage, the character and its actor, but also the person who sits in the back of the stalls admiring what he has written." The description evokes both the world of the theater and the myth of Narcissus, who gazed with solipsistic admiration at his reflection in the pool. It also describes Dan's deep psychological need for what he calls "the objectivity of the camera." By detaching his public self, the one who performs and acts in the world, from his innate sense of being, Daniel Martin has sought to live at safe remove from the wellsprings of his deepest emotions. Of course, all versions of the self are to some degree masks constructed to act in the world, or to protect the individual from its harsh pressures. But some masks are more valuable, or more harmful, than others. Some, like Dan's glib persona at Oxford, may inhibit personal or artistic development by masking a human being's deepest impulses even from himself. Dan thus distinguishes between the "mask of excuse, a sacrificial pawn," behind which the wearer takes refuge from himself, and the mask that serves as "an emblem of some deep truth, or true presentiment."

The drama and destiny of the self is not the only issue confronted in *Daniel Martin*, however. Fowles appears more concerned than ever before with the relationship of the individual to his society, and with the necessary balance between personal freedom and social restraint—what he calls the "printed text of life." Recalling a "gratuitous sexual act" committed years earlier as a student at Oxford, Dan makes the following observation: "Our surrender to existentialism and each other was also, of course, fraught with evil. It defiled the printed text of life; broke codes with a vengeance; and it gave Dan a fatal taste for adultery, for seducing." The "printed text of life" is a communal code, created and validated by individuals united in a common concern, the health and welfare of their society. Coming of age during the years immediately following World War II, most of Dan's generation rebelled against the text and "broke codes with a vengeance." By doing so, they helped to usher in the "age of self." "All that my generation and the one it sired have ever cared a damn about," Dan observes,

"is personal destiny; all the other destinies have become blinds."

Like Gustave Flaubert's *A Sentimental Education* (1869), which Fowles has acknowledged as an influence on his novel, *Daniel Martin* is both the record of a character's personal history and the cultural history of a generation and its failures. Dan's recognition of the narcissism infecting him and his generation appears to convey his author's concern for the ultimate well-being of an entire culture. Significantly, in *Daniel Martin* the sexual-romantic relationships of the protagonist are, unlike those in Fowles's previous novels, linked to family relationships—relationships that bind the individual to society and the generations to each other. When Dan returns to England from America, he breaks off an affair with a younger woman and begins to pick up the pieces of his aborted, mangled friendship with Jane. In the tortuous process of their eventual reconciliation, and the gradual awakening of an affinity that lay in ruin for decades, Dan must examine and rebuild other relationships, too: the one with his daughter, Caro; with Jane's children; even with his ex-wife, Nell.

This "journey of a book" involves, then, not only Daniel Martin's quest for an integrated self, but also his gradual reintegration with others. The bonds existing between Dan's isolated self and others, in both his family and society at large, must be recovered in the quest for wholeness. Dan's renewed sense of loyalty and attachment suggests, within the context of this novel, the necessary commitment required of each individual if a sane and healthy social order is to be achieved. Fowles appears to say that a compromise between the needs of the self and the requirements of society is necessary. Dan comes to recognize, therefore, that compromise is not a denial of personal freedom but its realization in the actual world: "The only true and real field in which one could test personal freedom was present possibility. Of course we could all lead better, nobler . . . lives; but not by positing them only in some future perfect state. One could so clearly only move and act from today, *this* present and flawed world."

Daniel Martin's journey is a quest to discover "what had gone wrong, not only with Daniel Martin, but his generation, age, century; the unique selfishness of it, the futility, the ubiquitous addiction to wrong ends." What Dan accomplishes by reentering his past and attempting to put right what had gone wrong has a larger significance, suggesting the possibilities for moral and social regeneration. Anthony Mallory, Dan's dying friend, articulates the connection between personal and social history that Fowles develops throughout the novel. "I do have the strangest kind of optimism about the human condition," Anthony says. "I can't explain it. It's . . . just that we shall come through. In spite of all our faults. If only we learn that it must begin in ourselves. In the true history of our own lives." Dan's decision to write a novel about his true history appears to confirm Anthony's view that human progress begins "in ourselves."

When Dan, in Hollywood, receives the unexpected call summoning him to Anthony's bedside, he senses that a "door in the wall" of his existence has suddenly opened, "as in a fiction." He recognizes that this phone call breaks all laws of probability and plausibility, laws that he, as a writer, "might have flinched at breaking if he had been inventing the situation." Yet in this chance "unsettling of fixed statistical probability," Dan ultimately perceives "a release from mire, a liberation, a yes from the heart of reality to the supposed artifice of art." This "yes from the heart of reality" is tinged by irony, of course, since the phone call occurs not in reality but within the artifice of Fowles's novel. As a metaphor for existence, however, this artifice contains its own reality, conveys its own truth. By introducing this chance opportunity, this suddenly opened door into Daniel Martin's existence, Fowles knows he is breaking more than the code "of fixed statistical probability." He is self-consciously breaking with that overriding sense of doom and defeat that permeates so much contemporary fiction.

Apocalypse and absurdity seem indelibly written into the texts of life currently produced by the most noted writers of this age. It is, as Dan observes, "like some new version of the Midas touch, with despair taking the place of gold. This despair might sometimes spring from a genuine metaphysical pessimism, or guilt, or empathy with the less fortunate. But far more often it came from a kind of statistical sensitivity. . . , since in a period of intense and universal increase in self-awareness, few could be happy with their lot." Perhaps the "cultural fashion" of despair, Fowles suggests, is really a symptom of the "age of self," resulting from the extraordinary attention now focused on personal happiness, comfort, and reward. Rejecting the excesses of this age, then, Daniel Martin—and behind him his author, Fowles—refuses to create his novel in "deference to a received idea of the age: that only a tragic, absurdist, black-comic view . . . of human destiny could be counted as truly representative and serious." The thread of optimism that runs through Fowles's most recent novel, affirming

the possibilities for moral and social regeneration, suggests that Fowles wants to introduce more than formal innovations into contemporary fiction. In *Daniel Martin*, he attempts to free the novel not only from traditional conventions for depicting reality but also from a popular, doom-laden vision of reality itself. The "yes from the heart" of Fowles's novel may well embody the affirmation life can yield when established ways of seeing, as well as writing, give way and the resources of the individual are contemplated anew.

Readers of *Daniel Martin*, as Robert Huffaker points out, "have responded to the book generally less enthusiastically than they greeted his more flamboyant works." The more subdued character of this novel is a direct result of Fowles's decision to guard his integrity as an artist rather than to exploit his talents as a storyteller. Although *Daniel Martin* did not repeat the outstanding popular success of *The French Lieutenant's Woman*, several distinguished critics have regarded it as Fowles's most artistically ambitious work to date. Since the publication of *Daniel Martin* in 1977, no new fiction by Fowles has appeared. Instead, three consecutive works of nonfiction have been published. In each of these books, Fowles presents extensive, often wide-ranging commentary to accompany a series of photographic studies on a particular subject. Both *Islands* and *The Tree* (discussed previously) attest to the truth of Fowles's assertion that he "came to writing through nature." In the third and most recent study, *The Enigma of Stonehenge*, published in 1980, Fowles turns his attention from natural to man-made wonders. The site of one of the most intriguing artifacts of Stone Age civilization, Stonehenge is the "technological masterpiece" of Neolithic man. Standing on the Salisbury Plain in Wiltshire, England, are large circular formations consisting of huge upright stone slabs and lintels. The function of these massive stones, weighing as much as forty-five tons apiece, has long been the subject of scholarly speculation, and Fowles adds his own voice to the discussion of this ancient enigma. He provides both a detailed account of the archaeological evidence dating the phases of Stonehenge's construction and a survey of the various religious and scientific accounts that have arisen, from medieval times to our own, to explain the original function of this stone ruin.

In the book's final pages, however, Fowles characteristically shifts the focus of his discussion from what is known about Stonehenge to what is still unknown: "There are not yet enough facts about it to bury it in certainty, in a scientific, final solution to all its questions. Its great *present* virtue is precisely that something so concrete, . . . so individualized, should still evoke so much imprecision of feeling and thought." In an "increasingly 'known,' structured, ordained, predictable world," the enigma of Stonehenge—like the mysteries embodied in nature or great works of art—offers the human imagination "a freedom, a last refuge of the self." Here, as in his earliest fiction, Fowles identifies the quest for self and freedom with the presence of mystery and the energy it pours into the seeker. His own quest, it is clear, has centered on the imaginative adventures—and the very real risks—of writing fiction.

As a literary explorer, Fowles has investigated a wide range of styles, techniques, and approaches to writing; the history of this exploration is recorded and embodied in the rich variety of his published work. He has affirmed the resources of language and at the same time delineated the strictures inherent in representing reality within literature and art. By acknowledging these limitations, yet continuing to struggle against them, Fowles has indeed proved himself a dynamic rather than a static artist. Generations of readers will doubtless continue to be enlightened as well as entertained by his fiction.

Screenplay:
The Magus, Twentieth Century-Fox, 1968.

Other:
"Notes on an Unfinished Novel," in *Afterwords: Novelists on Their Novels*, edited by Thomas McCormack (New York: Harper & Row, 1969), pp. 160-175;

Sabine Baring-Gould, *Mehalah: A Story of the Salt Marshes*, introduction, glossary, and appendix by Fowles (London: Chatto & Windus, 1969);

Henri Alain-Fournier, *The Wanderer*, afterword by Fowles (New York: New American Library, 1971);

Sir Arthur Conan Doyle, *The Hound of the Baskervilles*, foreword and afterword by Fowles (London: John Murray & Jonathan Cape, 1974);

Charles Perrault, *Cinderella*, translated by Fowles (London: Cape, 1974; Boston: Little, Brown, 1976);

Piers Brendon, *Hawker of Morwenstow: Portrait of a Victorian Eccentric*, foreword by Fowles (London: Cape, 1975);

Claire de Durfort, *Ourika*, translated, with introduction and epilogue, by Fowles (Austin,

Tex.: W. Thomas Taylor, 1977);

"Hardy and the Hag," in *Thomas Hardy After Fifty Years*, edited by Lance St. John Butler (London: Macmillan, 1977), pp. 28-42;

"The Man and the Island," in *Steep Holm—A Case History in the Study of Evolution* (London: Kenneth Allsop Memorial Trust, 1978), pp. 14-22;

Marie de France, *The Lais of Marie de France*, foreword by Fowles (New York: Dutton, 1978);

Harold Pinter, *The French Lieutenant's Woman: A Screenplay*, foreword by Fowles (Boston: Little, Brown, 1981).

Periodical Publications:
"I Write Therefore I Am," *Evergreen Review*, 8 (August-September 1964): 16-17, 89-90;

"On Being English but Not British," *Texas Quarterly*, 7 (Autumn 1964): 154-162;

"My Recollections of Kafka," *Mosaic*, 3 (Summer 1970): 31-41;

"Is the Novel Dead?," *Books*, 1 (Autumn 1970): 2-5;

"Weeds, Bugs, Americans," *Sports Illustrated*, 33 (21 December 1970): 84ff.;

"*The Magus* Revisited," *Times* (London), 28 May 1977, p. 7; republished as "Why I Rewrote *The Magus*," *Saturday Review*, 5 (18 February 1978): 25-30;

"Seeing Nature Whole," *Harper's*, 259 (November 1979): 49-68;

"Book to Movie: *The French Lieutenant's Woman*," *Vogue* (November 1981): 266, 269, 271.

Interviews:
Roy Newquist, "John Fowles," *Counterpoint* (New York: Simon & Schuster, 1964), pp. 217-225;

Richard Boston, "John Fowles, Alone But Not Lonely," *New York Times Book Review*, 9 November 1969, pp. 2, 52, 53;

Daniel Halpern, "A Sort of Exile in Lyme Regis," *London Magazine*, 10 (March 1971): 34-46;

James Campbell, "An Interview with John Fowles," *Contemporary Literature*, 17, no. 4 (Autumn 1976): 455-469;

Mel Gussow, "Talk With John Fowles," *New York Times Book Review*, 13 November 1977, pp. 3, 84, 85.

References:
Robert Alter, "*Daniel Martin* and the Mimetic Task," *Genre* (Spring 1981): 65-78;

Ronald Binns, "John Fowles: Radical Romancer," *Critical Quarterly*, 15 (Winter 1973): 317-334;

Malcolm Bradbury, "John Fowles's *The Magus*," in

Sense and Sensibility in Twentieth-Century Writing, edited by Brom Weber (Carbondale: Southern Illinois University Press, 1970), pp. 26-38; republished as "The Novelist as Impresario: John Fowles and His Magus," in *Possibilities: Essays on the State of the Novel* (Oxford: Oxford University Press, 1973), pp. 256-271;

Patrick Brantlinger, Ian Adams, and Sheldon Rothblatt, "*The French Lieutenant's Woman*: A Discussion," *Victorian Studies*, 15 (March 1972): 339-356;

Dwight Eddins, "John Fowles: Existence as Authorship," *Contemporary Literature*, 17 (Spring 1976): 204-222;

Constance B. Hiett, "*Eliduc* Revisited: John Fowles and Marie de France," *English Studies in Canada*, 3 (Fall 1977): 351-358;

Robert Huffaker, *John Fowles* (Boston: G. K. Hall, 1980);

Barry N. Olshen, *John Fowles* (New York: Frederick Ungar, 1978);

Olshen and Toni Olshen, *John Fowles: A Reference Guide* (Boston: G. K. Hall, 1980);

William J. Palmer, *The Fiction of John Fowles* (Columbia: University of Missouri Press, 1974);

Elizabeth D. Rankin, "Cryptic Coloration in *The French Lieutenant's Woman*," *The Journal of Narrative Technique*, 3 (September 1973): 193-207;

Roberta Rubinstein, "Myth, Mystery, and Irony: John Fowles's *The Magus*," *Contemporary Literature*, 16 (Summer 1975): 328-339;

Robert Scholes, "The Orgastic Fiction of John Fowles," *Hollins Critic*, 6 (December 1969): 1-12;

Theodore Solotaroff, "John Fowles' Linear Art," review of *The Ebony Tower*, *New York Times Book Review*, 10 November 1974, pp. 2-3, 20;

Richard Stolley, "The French Lieutenant's Woman's Man: Novelist John Fowles," *Life*, 68 (29 May 1970): 55-58, 60;

David H. Walker, "Subversion of Narrative in the Work of André Gide and John Fowles," in *Comparative Criticism: A Yearbook*, volume 2, edited by E. S. Shaffer (Cambridge: Cambridge University Press, 1980), pp. 187-212;

Ian Watt, "A Traditional Victorian Novel? Yes, and Yet...," review of *The French Lieutenant's Woman*, *New York Times Book Review*, 9 November 1969, pp. 1, 74, 75;

Peter Wolfe, *John Fowles, Magus and Moralist* (Lewisburg, Pa.: Bucknell University Press, 1976).

Michael Frayn

(8 September 1933-   )

Malcolm Page
Simon Fraser University

BOOKS: *The Day of the Dog* (London: Collins, 1962; Garden City: Doubleday, 1963);

The Book of Fub (London: Collins, 1963); republished as *Never Put Off to Gomorrah* (New York: Pantheon, 1964);

On the Outskirts (London: Collins, 1964);

The Tin Men (London: Collins, 1965; Boston: Little, Brown, 1965);

The Russian Interpreter (London: Collins, 1966; New York: Viking, 1966);

At Bay in Gear Street (London: Fontana, 1967);

Towards the End of the Morning (London: Collins, 1967); republished as *Against Entropy* (New York: Viking, 1967);

A Very Private Life (London: Collins, 1968; New York: Viking, 1968);

The Two of Us (London: Fontana, 1970);

Sweet Dreams (London: Collins, 1973; New York: Viking, 1974);

Constructions (London: Wildwood House, 1974);

Alphabetical Order and Donkeys' Years (London and New York: French, 1976; London: Eyre Methuen, 1977);

Clouds (London: Eyre Methuen, 1977; London and New York: French, 1977);

Make and Break (London: Eyre Methuen, 1980).

Michael Frayn had five novels published between 1965 and 1973. The second and third of these, *The Russian Interpreter* (1966) and *Towards the End of the Morning* (1967), are conventional, the former a cold war suspense novel and the latter a

Michael Frayn

middle-class Londoners. Both are light, but also witty, stylish, and intelligent. The other three books are more original. While *The Tin Men* (1965) is tentative comic satire on the age of automation, *A Very Private Life* (1968) and *Sweet Dreams* (1973) are accomplished elaborate satiric fantasies. Perhaps because Frayn has mastered his unusual form of the fable in these two books, he has been unable to go any further as a novelist. His work since 1973 has been in the theater, and his future seems likely to be as a playwright.

Frayn was born in Mill Hill in north London; his mother was the former Violet Alice Lawson, and his father, Thomas Allen Frayn, was a salesman for an asbestos company. When the child was eighteen months old the family moved to Ewell, on the southwest fringe of London. Frayn says: "Everyone puts down the suburbs but they're very pleasant places to live. It's quite amazing how little they've changed in 40 years. They should be taken more seriously." He attended what he describes as "a dreadful private day school at Sutton, where the

headmaster used to cane about 20 boys every morning after prayers." He went on to Kingston Grammar School, which he found "merely rather dull and shabby, an imposing brick facade disguising an awful lot of corrugated iron."

He left with a State Scholarship to Emmanuel College, Cambridge, but first had to do his two years of national service, from 1952 to 1954. Starting out in the Royal Artillery, he was recruited to learn Russian—fourteen hours a day for eighteen months, billeted in villages near Cambridge. Instructors reminded him: "At any time, any time, you may be parachuted behind the Russian lines. You do understand that?" In his first year at Cambridge he read Russian and French, but found that though "he got on well with the language, when it came to the literature he couldn't see for the life of him what to write down." For his remaining two years, he changed to moral sciences (the department name has since been changed to the more usual philosophy). He wrote prolifically at Cambridge, producing columns in both *Varsity* and *Granta* and a strip cartoon each week for *Varsity* as well; he also wrote most of the 1957 Footlights show, the revue staged annually in May Week. He comments that in those years "the art-forms most passionately aspired to were musical comedy, revue, jazz, singing to a guitar, posters—anything that was predominantly entertaining and stylish. Our brand of humour was what was then called by its admirers 'off-beat,' which meant whimsical; carefully artless sub-Thurber cartoons, fantasies based, in what was hoped to pass for the style of Paul Jennings, upon archaic railway regulations and the like."

After leaving Cambridge he joined the Manchester Guardian as a reporter; although he was based in Manchester, in 1959 he spent a month in Moscow covering Prime Minister Harold Macmillan's visit to that city. The same year he moved to London with the task of writing a column, "Miscellany," three times a week. "As Frayn saw it, his job with Miscellany was to write cool, witty interviews with significant film directors passing through, but there were never enough film directors so he started making up humorous paragraphs to fill," explains Terry Coleman. He invented for the column the Don't Know Party and such characters as the trendy Bishop of Screwe; Rollo Swavely, a public relations consultant; and the ambitious suburban couple, Horace and Doris Morris. In 1962 his move from the *Guardian* to the London *Observer*, where his only duty was a weekly column, gave him more time for his own writing. The tone of the column, which he continued until 1968, slowly changed to a more serious examination of the contemporary urban liberal. Four collections of his columns were published in book form: *The Day of the Dog* (1962), *The Book of Fub* (1963), *On the Outskirts* (1964), and *At Bay in Gear Street* (1967). In 1960 he married Gillian Palmer; with their three daughters, Jenny, Susanna, and Rebecca, they eventually settled in Blackheath, in southeast London.

The whimsical tone of his first novel, *The Tin Men*, is almost that of a sustained *Guardian* column. The book is set in the William Morris Institute of Automation Research; its plot revolves around the financing and opening of a new wing. The collection of odd characters includes the sports fanatic who tries to be responsible for security, the would-be novelist who cannot get further than writing the blurb and reviews for his nonexistent book, and the researcher who reads everything backwards "setting himself and solving outrageous problems of comprehension in every paragraph." Most of the fun involves computers: the automating of football because the director believes "the main object of organised sports and games is to produce a profusion of statistics"; the programmed newspaper, which prints the core of familiar stories such as "I Test New Car" and "Child Told Dress Unsuitable by Teacher"; and Delphic I, the Ethical Decision Machine, which expresses the depth and intensity of its moral processes in units called pauls, calvins, and moses. The story ends: "Epoch IV is a computer that writes books and *The Tin Men* is its first novel." Amid the clever jokes, there is a kernel of anxiety about the dangerous potential of computers and the limitations of the men responsible for them.

Most critics, like Francis Hope of the *New Statesman*, found the book good fun: "Frayn's gifts include a Wodehousian felicity: the whole Institute rings with 'the bongling and goingling of steel scaffolding poles being thrown down from a great height.'" Similarly, Peter Buckman in the *Nation* noted, "It's farce from start to finish, without even a straight character against whom the weirdies can be compared." Julian Gloag in *Saturday Review* was more scornful: "You'll smile all right at *The Tin Men*, but it'll be the smile you give to a good joke you've heard before." He also complained about the characterization ("*The Tin Men* is repetitive. The two-dimensional characters do not change"), while the *Times Literary Supplement* faulted the framework: "The story is flimsy and ordinary. . . . Frayn's mind, his sense of the ridiculous and his actual writing are all too good to be trivialized in this way." William Trevor in the *Listener* inevitably judged the book

"like a particularly good Frayn piece blown up to size, with extra bits added and a plot thrown in." He cited Frayn, however, as "the only hatchet man of contemporary letters to combine a consistent attack with something that looks like a purpose."

Frayn's second novel, *The Russian Interpreter*, is about an English research student in Moscow. He serves as interpreter for a mysterious businessman who seeks ordinary Russians for exchange trips, and they become involved with a Russian girl. Though the streets and weather are carefully described, the action soon moves swiftly. Books are stolen and sought, someone is tricking someone else, espionage or smuggling is occurring, and the reader continues, waiting for the explanations. Even when the two Englishmen are imprisoned, the tone remains cheerful, and the book predictably ends with their release and flight home to England. The novel won Frayn a Somerset Maugham Award for 1966 (the prize money being spent on travel in the United States) and the Hawthornden Prize in 1967.

Critics treated the book gingerly, uncertain whether it deserved to be taken seriously. R. G. G. Price in *Punch* placed it as "just another novel making mild fun of cold war melodrama," and P. M. of the *Christian Science Monitor* saw only "an atmosphere of self-righteous dullness." Bill Byrom of the *Spectator* was amused: "There are eleven good belly-laughs, and the rest is trim and shipshape and elegant." The *New Yorker* reviewer, on the other hand, thought the humor harmed the novel: because it "is a comedy, nobody comes to grief—or even looks as if he might—which rather eliminates the possibility of suspense." The *Times Literary Supplement* was earnest about it: *The Russian Interpreter* was "a rather mournful story about the shabby half-world of deceit that surrounds dealing, on even the most personal level, between East and West."

The American title of the third novel, *Against Entropy*, points to opposing inertia and conformity; the British one, *Towards the End of the Morning*, to the growing sense of life's being circumscribed that comes in the mid-thirties (the hero "had spent his youth as one might spend an inheritance, and he had no idea of what he had bought with it"). Frayn's thirty-seven-year-old protagonist is a features editor, gathering crosswords and the columns for "Meditations" and "The Country Day by Day." Endlessly worried about repairs to his Victorian house with West Indian neighbors in London, S. W. 23, he dreams of escape and believes that appearing in a television panel could make this possible. The plot is a vehicle for the comedy of a newspaper office, and the story ends farcically as the man desperately tries to get a plane back from the Middle East in time for his television show. Some passages suggest that Frayn perhaps intends more, a fuller study of his hero's marriage and serious focus on the future of newspapers, but these are not pursued. He says of the sources of the book: "About two per cent is based on my time on the *Guardian*, two on the *Observer* and 96 on my imagination."

Some critics concentrated on the account of life in a newspaper office. Philip Howard wrote in the *Times* that the novel "catches the quirks and eccentricities of newspapers better than any previous book. . . . In parts it is uncannily like home life in our dear old Printing House Square. . . . Nobody has ever recorded so truthfully and so funnily the facts about the nutters who besiege the front door of a newspaper with messages from God, expenses, . . . galley proofs, and freebies." The *Times Literary Supplement* reviewer, however, recognized that more important was "the more serious and delicate theme of the journalists' home lives. . . . Frayn shows the private relationships within the public relations." Howard also identified that Frayn was "wistfully comic and perspective about the hang-ups of middle-class, middle-aged man, not sure about where he is going, or why, or if he will like it when he gets there." Stephen Wall in the *Observer* admired the characterizations of the women, "the clueless Tessa, Bob's girl, and Dyson's wife—are treated with much gentleness. The Dyson marriage, in fact, comes through with remarkable solidity." The theme for the *Times Literary Supplement* reviewer, finally, "is time, is change, is quite simply the business of people, institutions and society growing older."

A Very Private Life is written in future tense, beginning "Once upon a time there will be a little girl called Uncumber." In this world, "inside people" remain all their lives in windowless houses, making contact by "holovision" and receiving supplies by tube and tap. During their long lives they use drugs (such as Pax, Hilarin, and Orgasmin) for every experience. In chapters of two and three pages, Frayn explains how life has grown more private, first through physical privacy, then through the development of drugs to cope with anger and uncertainty. The opening pages set the scene slowly; then Uncumber, dissatisfied with her life, seeks out a man on the other side of the world, 515-214-442-305-217, whom she has met through a wrong number on holovision. Found, he turns out to be an "outside person," speaking a language unknown to her, living in a decaying palace by the sea

and going out daily to work. Eventually leaving him, she is lost in a jungle and spends a night with some bandits before being found by the Kind People and then rehabilitated as an "inside person."

The story is compelling, part fairy tale, as the opening implies, part fantasy, part morality tale. Certain details echo *Brave New World* (babies are decanted) and the distant future of *The Time Machine*, with weak Top People dependent on slaves. The *Times Literary Supplement* reviewer pointed out the relevance of Frayn's topics: "drugs, both medical and hallucinogenic, longevity, the treatment of personality, penology ('We don't think in terms of *guilt* and *innocence*. We just ask: are you happy, or are you unhappy?'), mass communications, dropping-out, the reduction of so many aspects of life to numbers or to strips of magnetic tape." Frayn's concern with where mankind is going, however, is focused on technology's making possible a new kind of isolation which excludes uncomfortable realities. The book is nevertheless a story: the moralizing remains discreet.

Though Uncumber has the name of a legendary saint, Frayn explained to Terry Coleman that much of the inspiration for the novel came from his observations in the United States: "The elite of the novel wear only dark glasses. To remove them is to be naked and indecent. This is the ritual covering and uncovering of American women, who wear dark glasses so that their eyes and their feelings shall not be seen. The insulated houses of the novel owe something to those of middle-class America, and in particular to those farmhouses in deepest Connecticut, abandoned when the farmers went west, surrounded by forest, and now being bought by city people to be alone in."

Critics were impressed with both theme and form in this fable. Stephen Wall interpreted in the *Observer*: "Frayn has realised that what technology looks like making possible is a new kind of isolation. When all needs can be satisfied by impersonal agencies, a man can become an island quite happily." Wall, however, was bothered by the style: "Its literary quality is uneven. The prose is sharpest when it's critical—when it has a bantering relationship with current cliches of thought and word; it is less impressive as an instrument of narrative." Frederick P. W. McDowell in *Contemporary Literature* identified different faults: "A thinness of line and elaboration perhaps obtrudes. Progression in the tale is always linear, and the complexities of Uncumber's problems are not all adequately delineated. Moreover, the characters lack the complexity which the inhabitants of his less allegorical satires reveal." Malcolm Bradbury in the *Guardian*, however, had high praise: "The book's ultimate virtue is the rigorous, brilliant intelligence with which Frayn holds its stuff within a totally consistent universe." The *Times Literary Supplement* reviewer called it a "book which nobody else could have written, and it ought to be put into the classic modern repertoire alongside *Animal Farm*."

Sweet Dreams, published in 1973, is dazzlingly clever. A typical middle-class, thirtyish, leftish, liberal Londoner is killed and finds himself in a heaven where he can fly, speak any language, change his age, and retrieve long-lost possessions. He is assigned to invent the Matterhorn, returns to England and writes an official report on its condition, drops out to enjoy the simple country life, and bounces back as right-hand man to God—who is rich, brilliant, and upper-class and says, "To get anything done at all one has to move in tremendously mysterious ways." Slowly we realize that the hero's heavenly evolution is markedly similar to his earthly one. Frayn tells with wit and flourish his shrewd and deceptively charming fable.

Julian Symons in the *Sunday Times* admitted to confusion: "It is difficult, though, to know just how to take Mr. Frayn, who offers without discernible irony a travel brochure Heaven.... Frayn's intentions are probably more serious than his manner, which is almost too light in its butterfly flitting from subject to subject." Janice Elliott in the *Sunday Telegraph* concluded that "in the last resort there are two elements missing: rage and love.... Within the limits of his humanity, man—even your decent liberal—is infinitely more various and flexible than Mr. Frayn would have us believe." The *Times Literary Supplement* reviewer was cautiously balanced: "Frayn is as deft as ever at characterizing a group of people whose most notable trait may well be their ability to be articulate in support of their latest volte-face. If the novel does finally seem a little indulgent to them and a little to disintegrate into more or less comic episodes, and if one does occasionally wish for more acid and even for more discussion, these are witty dreams and not uninstructive." In the *Guardian* P. J. Kavanagh stressed the humor: "All this is extremely gloomy and very funny. Packed with jokes, parodies and asides, most of them on slow fuses so you catch them a beat late: the quote from the Michelin Guide to Heaven is a masterpiece.... Frayn has the gift of making you laugh *at* someone, then he stands back mildly to watch whether you notice the joke is also on you." Margaret Drabble in the *New York Times Book Review* had only praise: "It is lucid, intelligent, delightful, stylish, extremely funny." Christopher Hudson of

Dust jacket for Frayn's fifth novel, a satiric fantasy about a modern-day, middle-class heaven

New Society also had no hesitations: the novel was "a small masterpiece, beautifully written, funny, perceptive."

Since 1973 Frayn has written only plays. He explains why he finds playwriting easier: "One of the pleasures of writing plays is that you never speak in your own voice. You speak through the voices of your characters. But novels have to be written in your voice alone."

His first play was in fact for television in 1968, *Jamie on a Flying Visit*. This comedy showed an old Oxford boyfriend coming to visit a married couple, then hurting his leg and being forced to stay; chaos ensues. *The Two of Us*, published two years later, consists of four short plays, each for a man and a woman, intended for performance by the same two actors throughout. The most amusing one deals with a couple returning to their Venetian honeymoon hotel with a new baby; the most ingenious one has five people, three being engaged in trying to keep an estranged husband and wife apart, and involves endless tricks of players exiting on one side and immediately reentering as someone else on the other. *The Sandboy* the next year was less successful: a television study of a day in the life of a clever and prosperous architect, interrupted by the muddled couple from next door. Frayn explains that the play is about coping with happiness: "Many people are happier than they admit. And not to admit you are happy is a terrible thing. Because if you feel or pretend that you're suffering more than you are, you decry the burden of those who really do suffer."

In fall 1975 BBC television broadcast a series of six plays by Frayn, *Making Faces*, written for Eleanor Bron. She played Zoya, involved with men at different stages in her life—as a student, teaching at a language school, as mistress of a Member of Parliament. Frayn described the series as "high-class sit-com. The BBC couldn't decide whether it was light entertainment or drama."

Alphabetical Order in 1975 returns to the newspaper world of *Towards the End of the Morning*. The play is set in the clippings library of a provincial daily, in which a new librarian orders what has previously been cheerful confusion. Frayn has argued that he has a philosophical point here: "You have to structure your life, otherwise it's impossible. But when the structure takes over you have to think again. Structures and institutions are never as solid as they seem. They may look safe, but meanwhile the mice are eating away at the wainscoting."

The very funny *Donkeys' Years* (1976) is set in "one of the smaller quadrangles, in one of the lesser colleges, at one of the older universities." Seven graduates return for a reunion after twenty years, establishing a pecking order similar to that of their college days: the woman who was once their number one fantasy lay and is now the Master's wife also farcically appears. *Clouds* (1977) seems the most seriously intended play: three journalists (two Britons, male and female, and an American) are taken around Cuba by a government official and a black driver. *Liberty Hall*, which only played a short run at Greenwich Theatre and did not transfer to the West End, is a curiosity, set in a 1937 Britain which has experienced a Communist Revolution twenty years earlier. Three "people's writers," Enid Blyton, Godfrey Winn, and Warwick Deeping, are seen installed in the palace at Balmoral. *Make and Break* (1980) ran for nearly a year in London in 1980-1981: this portrays a workaholic British businessman selling doors at a trade fair in Frankfurt. Frayn also translated two Russian classics for the National Theatre, Chekhov's *The Cherry Orchard* and Tolstoy's *The Fruits of Enlightenment*.

Frayn's search in his work is always for a comic framework which will allow him to make serious social and philosophical observations. He has twice succeeded in devising the right form, in the fables *A Very Private Life* and *Sweet Dreams*. In the other three novels, structure presents him with problems, and it now seems that he finds the form of drama more congenial. (One should note, too, that drama has been more profitable.) Frayn has such gifts for humor that his reputation is for comedy; however, he may be disappointed that the more solemn implications have yet to be perceived. His future may be in less comic theater, as he continues to focus mainly on people of his age, class, and education.

Plays:

The Two of Us, London, Garrick Theatre, 30 July 1970;

The Sandboy, London, Greenwich Theatre, 17 September 1971;

Alphabetical Order, London, Hampstead Theatre Club, 11 March 1975;

Donkeys' Years, London, Globe Theatre, 15 July 1976;

Clouds, London, Hampstead Theatre Club, 16 August 1976;

Liberty Hall, London, Greenwich Theatre, 24 January 1980;

Make and Break, Hammersmith, Lyric Theatre, 18 March 1980;

Noises Off, Hammersmith, Lyric Theatre, 11 February 1982.

Television Scripts:

Jamie on a Flying Visit, *Wednesday Play*, BBC-1, January 1968;

Making Faces, 6 parts, BBC-2, 25 September-30 October 1975.

Interviews:

John Grigg, "More Than a Satirist," *Observer*, 11 June 1967;

Terry Coleman, "Towards the End of Frayn's Morning," *Guardian*, 1 October 1968, p. 6;

Hugh Hebert, "Letters Play," *Guardian*, 11 March 1975, p. 12;

Ian Jack, "Frayn, Philosopher of the Suburbs," *Sunday Times*, 13 April 1975, p. 43;

Russell Davies, "Michael Frayn, Witty and Wise," *Observer*, 18 July 1976, p. 8;

Ray Connolly, "Playwrights on Parade," *Sunday Times*, 27 January 1980, p. 32;

Craig Raine, "The *Quarto* Interview," *Quarto*, 4 (March 1980): 3-6;

"Pendennis," "Tom Frayn's Son," *Observer*, 27 April 1980, p. 44.

Jane Gardam
(11 July 1928-)

Patricia Craig

BOOKS: *A Few Fair Days* (London: Hamish Hamilton, 1971; New York: Macmillan, 1972);
A Long Way from Verona (London: Hamish Hamilton, 1971; New York: Macmillan, 1971);
The Summer After the Funeral (London: Hamish Hamilton, 1973; New York: Macmillan, 1973);
Black Faces, White Faces (London: Hamish Hamilton, 1975); republished as *The Pineapple Bay Hotel* (New York: Morrow, 1976);
Bilgewater (London: Hamish Hamilton, 1976; New York: Greenwillow, 1977);
God on the Rocks (London: Hamish Hamilton, 1978; New York: Morrow, 1979);
The Sidmouth Letters (London: Hamish Hamilton, 1980; New York: Morrow, 1980);
Bridget and William (London: Julia MacRae Blackbirds, 1981);
The Hollow Land (London: Julia MacRae, 1981);
Horse (London: Julia MacRae Blackbirds, 1982).

Jane Gardam's earliest stories are children's stories, but only in the way that some of Katherine Mansfield's are: they recreate directly the sensations and impressions of childhood. Her first three books appeared on Hamish Hamilton's children's list; then came a collection of related short stories for adults, *Black Faces, White Faces* (1975), which was exceptionally well received: "Jane Gardam has taken the form of the short story as close to art as it is ever likely to reach," Peter Ackroyd wrote in the *Spectator*. There was praise, too, from Auberon Waugh who hailed Gardam as a "writer of talent and originality," but who treated the collection as a first work, as other critics did; in fact it won the David Higham Prize for Fiction, which is awarded for a first *novel*. (A later collection, *The Sidmouth Letters*, published in 1980, has also been described as a novel.) What is important is not the classification but the degree of acuity brought to bear on a theme; however, it seems unfortunate that those adults who take no interest in children's literature will miss, for example, *Bilgewater* (1976) and *The Summer After the Funeral* (1973), whose appeal should not be restricted by any factor of age in the reader.

Of the three Jane Gardam books unquestionably for adults, two are collections of stories and one, *God on the Rocks* (which appeared on the Booker short list in 1978), is a novel. She has also written two books unmistakably for the very young, *Bridget and William* (1981) and *Horse* (1982)—both published in the Julia MacRae "Blackbird" series—and a second group of related stories, set in Cumbria, *The Hollow Land* (also published—in 1981—by Julia MacRae, a children's imprint; but Isaac Bashevis Singer appears in their list, too). All of Gardam's work is marked by certain admirable characteristics: economy of style, exuberance and humor, a special relish for the startling and the unexpected.

Jane Gardam was born in Coatham, Yorkshire, on 11 July 1928, the eldest child of William and Kathleen Pearson. Her father was a housemaster at a boy's school (a position he kept for forty-two years, until his retirement). Her brother was born six years later. Although to an extent transformed in the course of writing, certain elements of Gardam's early life seem to have made a fairly consistent pattern in her books: the girl with a much younger brother; the schoolmaster or clergyman father; the Yorkshire or Cumbria locations. Each book, however, has a distinctive feeling, a mood and atmosphere all its own. Gardam repeats her motifs but not her effects.

She left Yorkshire in 1946, with a scholarship to read English at Bedford College (part of London University) under Kathleen Tillotson. London gave her a taste for wandering the streets (it was just after the war, when the appearance of the city had been dramatically changed) and for theatergoing—she went almost daily. After graduating, she stayed on at Bedford College to do research; then she worked for two years as a traveling librarian with the Red Cross hospital libraries—an experience which left her with a great deal of insight into the behavior of the elderly and the deranged. After a stint of working as an editorial assistant on *Weldons Ladies Journal*, she became assistant literary editor of *Time and Tide*, a position she held until the birth of her first child in 1956 (she had married David Gardam, an attorney, in 1952). The job taught her, she says, everything she needed to know about subediting: spelling, typing, cutting. (At one point she was reading 500 stories a week.) She left when her son Timothy was born, blithely declaring that she would be back at her desk in three weeks; in fact, it was some years before she was able to undertake work of any kind. Childrearing took all her time.

Her first book, *A Few Fair Days*, written in 1969-1970 and published in 1971, deals with memorable episodes in the life of Lucy, who "lived not so many years ago in a small cold town by the sea in the farthest part of the north of Yorkshire." Already the author's feeling for place and atmosphere is apparent. Lucy's age, which ranges from five to eleven, determines style as much as content. Gardam's method in this book is at the opposite extreme from Joyce Cary's, whose novels of childhood continually allow the adult narrator to interpret and comment on the child's behavior. Nothing outside Lucy's experience at these ages is included in Gardam's narrative. (*A Few Fair Days* and its successor, *A Long Way from Verona*, 1971, now seem to have a place in that small group of stylish works which helped to change children's fiction from an ill-considered genre to a highly regarded one; but

neither of these interesting books was actually written with juvenile readers in mind.)

In addition to its literal meaning, the title of Gardam's first book refers to a type of sponge cake popular in the district where Lucy is growing up. Lucy's escapades, from going off unescorted to wander on the beach, to getting her friends up at four in the morning to watch the sunrise, are recounted with fastidiousness and charm. One incident demonstrates the author's faculty for compression. Lucy is forced to spend an hour each week in the company of an awkward, boorish young man who ignores her.

> On the fifth Friday Lucy spoke. She said, all of a sudden in a queer deep voice that gave her a shock, "YOU HAVE GOT AWFUL EARS."
>
> The man immediately fell out of the car in a heap and spent the rest of the long, long hour pacing about, proudly examining first the sky and then his shoes and clenching his teeth on his pipe. "Nice young fellow," her father said the next day at tea-time. "Pity he can't drive us again. He's taken on extra cricket practice. Says he can't stand cricket either. Hard-working chap."

This passage tells us everything we need to know, and its brevity makes the incident seem funnier and more pointed than a longer account would have. Gardam is among the least prolix of authors; her economical use of words indicates a sound understanding of their value.

Words—highly colored, mysterious, and evocative—fascinate Lucy, who goes around chanting, "The magus Zoroaster, my dead child / Met his own image walking in the garden." Jessica Vye, in *A Long Way from Verona*, also falls under the spell of language. She gives her imagination free rein in a school essay, rejecting the usual formula for this type of work. "May I ask, Jessica, why you felt you had to write forty-seven pages?" her schoolmistress exclaims. Jessica's temper gets the better of her, and she is sent to sit in the shoe-bags, where her sobbing attracts the attention of Miss Philemon, the senior English mistress, dotty, intellectual, and kind. A tentative, delicate alliance is established between the two.

A Long Way from Verona is jauntier in tone than the earlier book, but it is also bleaker; it switches to first-person narration, and it is set in wartime, which adds a collective stress to the common, personal stresses of adolescence. A fair amount of horror and misery is accommodated in the text, unobtrusively. Life is suddenly full of grim possibilities, which are also exciting. Jessica's first experience of bombing occurs when she is in the company of a would-be social reformer who has taken her on an excursion to the Teesside slums. The aim of this person is to enlighten Jessica about social deprivation: both he and she are members of a professional class. Handsome, inappropriately named Christian Fanshawe-Smithe looks like the poet Rupert Brooke and calls himself a Communist. He compares Dunedin Street to hell, assuring Jessica that it ought to be destroyed. Immediately, it is. A bomb falls; two children are killed; and Jessica regains consciousness to find herself confronting a huge woman sitting in an armchair. "She had no legs and she was roaring with laughter." The tragic is effectively charged with outlandishness to diffuse its impact.

Jessica's personality is unformed, except in one aspect: her determination to be a writer. Her behavior, true to her age, is sometimes wayward or devious; she is by turns exhilarated, despondent, gregarious, and withdrawn. The novel is about growing up, which involves disillusionment and adjustment. Jessica's faith in a benign ordering of the world and the possibility of good fortune is shattered by the death of Miss Philemon, who is killed when a crashing English airplane unloads a bomb on her flat. It is some time before the girl can even acknowledge the event; and her reticence under the circumstances is entirely plausible and appropriate. Gardam always ensures that the emphasis falls in the right place.

What is instantly striking about the book, though, is its beguiling humor ("brilliantly witty and agonizingly true-to-life," the *Times Literary Supplement* reviewer described it). In an early scene, for example, Jessica and her friends are addressed by a peculiar lady, Mrs. Hopkins, who claims acquaintance with the great ("Churchill to all the world but he's Winston to me") and then goes on to compare the schoolgirls to four Juliets, quoting the line, "Younger than she were married mothers made," from Shakespeare's play to which the title alludes (though Gardam's heroines are more likely to descend from a balcony in confusion of spirit than to use one as a romantic prop). The girls find this hilarious; they are at the giggling stage. The lady is one of those will-o'-the-wispish eccentrics who make a vivid contrast to the dry, droll, and forthright in Gardam's fiction. (Examples of the latter type are Winnie the waitress in *The Summer After the Funeral*

and Paula Rigg, the young schoolmatron in *Bilgewater*.)

Jessica at one point finds herself encumbered with a large painting in an ornate frame and an orange (a wartime luxury). Her acquisition of these trophies, and her plans for them, have bizarre links with other elements of the story; the narrative pattern has a crazy-paving quality about it. The pattern recurs in *The Summer After the Funeral*, where the heroine, Athene Price, is burdened with a couple of unlikely objects: a crucifix and a rope ladder. "That's right," says phlegmatic Winnie, who can tell that trouble is in the offing, "likely you'll need the two."

Beautiful sixteen-year-old Athene, after the death of her father, an ancient rector, is sent to stay with various relatives and friends in the north of England—dim Aunt Posie, distressful Miss Bowles, and absent Auntie Boo (the arrangements go wrong, as might be expected). Athene's natural habits of discipline and resourcefulness are overtaken by confusion, insecurity, and guilt (there were times when she wished her father had been a younger man), and the result is a mood of hilarious desperation. But *The Summer After the Funeral* is also the most romantic in feeling of all Gardam's novels, true to the spirit of *Wuthering Heights* which it evokes continuously. The anarchic events which Athene sets in motion (fleeing from one inhospitable lodging after another, shedding first her luggage and then—perhaps—her virginity) have an oblique poetic quality, communicated by means of elision, suggestion, and ironic comparison. (The *Times* critic praised Gardam's "startlingly sure grasp of the passions and the eccentric course they are inclined to take.") As in Elizabeth Bowen's *A World of Love* (1955), the true romantic encounter is about to take place when the novel ends. And like Evelyn Waugh, Gardam makes splendid play with the humor of fortuitous conjunction.

Athene Price is plagued by repellent women who pop up inopportunely. (Gardam is thrifty in the matter of characters as well; the fullest use is made of each figure that appears.) Mrs. Messenger and loud-voiced Primrose Clark are garrulous, impertinent females who disconcert bereaved Athene with their tactless quizzing: "Is your mother over it yet? Not a penny I suppose." Primrose Clark catches Athene at Haworth with the young married schoolmaster, Henry Bell, destroying a moment of enchantment and causing the young man to take flight.

This aspect of the book is carried over to Gardam's next children's novel, *Bilgewater*, in which the eponymous heroine has trouble with a frightful, corpulent old body called Mrs. Deering who keeps appearing at inconvenient moments. Bilgewater—a corruption of "Bill's daughter"—is the frog princess who becomes desirable. "My mother died when I was born which makes me sound princess-like and rather quaint," her idiosyncratic narrative begins. She goes on to enumerate her defects—glasses, orange hair, squat figure, daftness, unsociability—but the rueful, chatty tone of the usual first-person teenage recital is replaced by something altogether stranger, more astringent, and wittier. Gardam makes high comedy of the fidgets and fancies of adolescence, with her heroine constantly on the brink of some contretemps or social disaster; but the narrative is charged as well with a kind of muted fairy-tale glamour. The effect is striking.

If *The Summer After the Funeral* is the most open about its romantic intention, *Bilgewater* is the most formal, intricate, and frivolous of Gardam's books. It is a comedy of false trials and misalliances. Bilgewater's troubles at the local comprehensive (where her intellectual ability is recognized rather

late); her infatuation with handsome Jack Rose (the darling of the sixth form), which ends chaotically; the willful emotional clumsiness which turns Tom Terrapin against her at a crucial moment—these make for narrative deviousness and richness. Grace Gathering, the headmaster's gaudy daughter, takes Bilgewater in hand, changing her clothes and hairstyle in a way that meets with the comprehensive fifth form's approval. But ordinariness fits Bilgewater like a choke. A more appropriate transformation occurs in Terrapin's tower, when the girl puts on some antique clothes once worn by Terrapin's grandmother. There is a dreamlike quality about parts of the book (though its sharpness of focus never fails), and it is with the crazy logic of dreams that bland Rose and wild Terrapin are replaced by studious Boakes, the third in the trio of boys who come close to Bilgewater.

Black Faces, White Faces was the book that got Gardam onto Hamish Hamilton's adult list. She wrote it after visiting Jamaica with her husband on business, and the tropical island is the setting for these tales of sexual frolicking, upheaval, and high jinks—all of them showing the effects of a more

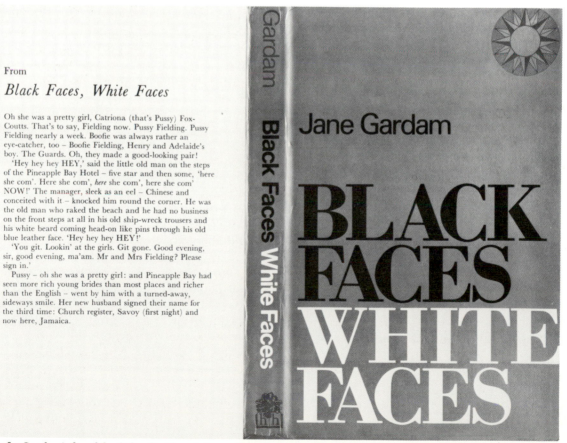

From

Black Faces, White Faces

Oh she was a pretty girl, Catriona (that's Pussy) Fox-Coutts. That's to say, Fielding now. Pussy Fielding. Pussy Fielding nearly a week. Boofie was always rather an eye-catcher, too – Boofie Fielding, Henry and Adelaide's boy. The Guards. Oh, they made a good-looking pair!

'Hey hey hey HEY,' said the little old man on the steps of the Pineapple Bay Hotel – five star and then some, 'here she com'. Here she com', *here* she com', here she com' NOW!' The manager, sleek as an eel – Chinese and conceited with it – knocked him round the corner. He was the old man who raked the beach and he had no business on the front steps at all in his old ship-wreck trousers and his white beard coming head-on like pins through his old blue leather face. 'Hey hey hey HEY!'

'You git. Lookin' at the girls. Git gone. Good evening, sir, good evening, ma'am. Mr and Mrs Fielding? Please sign in.'

Pussy – oh she was a pretty girl: and Pineapple Bay had seen more rich young brides than most places and richer than the English – went by him with a turned-away, sideways smile. Her new husband signed their name for the third time: Church register, Savoy (first night) and now here, Jamaica.

Dust jacket for Gardam's fourth book, her first for adults, a collection of related short stories that won the David Higham Prize for Fiction

colorful environment on reserved English tourists. Everyone is affected in one way or another by the Jamaican flair for merrymaking. Some of the visitors rediscover a faculty for enjoyment; one little family is taken in tow by an extroverted guide, Jolly Jackson, who embarrasses the parents and delights the child. In "The House Above Newcastle," pretty Pussy Fielding, who has been warding off her bridegroom's sexual advances with a teddy bear, finds that she is an adult after all. In one of the funniest stories, "The First Declension," a sedate wife, who chose to stay at home in London, becomes alarmed when her husband writes to tell her that he found Cuba considerably larger than he had imagined ("like essays or letters we did at school on Sunday afternoons," she reports to a friend). And a couple of priceless old schoolteachers, Miss Gongers and Miss Dee-Dee, familiar to more than one generation of pupils at Harrogate Hall in England, have an eventful time among gunmen, urchins, and vultures in the Blue Mountains. Ghosts flourish in the overheated air as well as orchids. But the book is by no means all effervescence and sunshine ("with sudden cold horror she saw her husband think, 'My God—she's silly.' "). Its sparkle is tempered with asperity.

One of Gardam's greatest strengths as a writer

Jane Gardam

is the ability to confine her observations to the most telling; every detail is there for a purpose. She is also an excellent mimic, assuming without fuss (as she demonstrates in her second collections of stories, *The Sidmouth Letters*) the exact tones of the grand, the effete, the well-intentioned, the anxious, the obsessed, even—in "The Great, Grand Soap-Water Kick"—the unwashed and inarticulate. Two of these stories, "The Tribute" and "The Sidmouth Letters," have been made into plays for television. Even "Hetty Sleeping" and "Transit Passengers," the closest her writing comes to magazine fiction, are enlivened by some acerbic touches.

Jane Austen looms in the title story which imagines the survival of a couple of her love letters written in 1801. An American academic, an intolerable professor who specializes in finding moral flaws in the great, is trying to track them down, but he is foiled by the heroine of the story. A young scholar and novelist herself, she finds that there is only one way in which her moral conflict can be resolved: "I burned both envelopes and both letters with my cigarette lighter." The theme is arresting, and it is handled with audacity and skill.

Gardam's novel *God on the Rocks* is more subdued in manner. The usual preoccupations—childhood, derangement, and the havoc caused by failures of sensitivity—are here; but bleakly, almost painfully. It could be described as an antidote to the guilelessness and freshness of *A Few Fair Days*. The time and setting are the same: a northern seaside town in 1936. But the house on Turner Street, which is the home of eight-year-old Margaret Marsh, is contaminated by religious fanaticism. Margaret's father, a bank manager, reserves his enthusiasm for lay preaching on behalf of an exacting sect. Her mother, when the novel opens, seems relentlessly self-effacing and conscientious, ministering to her baby son and taking pains to ensure that fractious Margaret does not feel neglected.

In *A Few Fair Days* Lucy had the grounds of an empty house to romp on; Margaret, too, finds a perfect playground in the gardens surrounding an institute for the insane. Here old Mrs. Frayling, the previous owner of the house, who donated it to charity to spite her Socialist children, is now a patient—suffering from a form of paralysis, not mad like the other inmates. She lies out-of-doors in a pramlike contraption reviewing her past life. She put a stop to the incipient romance between her weak son Charles and Margaret's mother Elinor ("Ellie the dustman's daughter"). Now Charles and his sister Binkie are back in the neighborhood.

'It's Lydia' said Margaret & fell
silent

'Yer not that different,' Lydia said
will ya — er — have a roll? asked
Birkie

No thanks. Yer toller that's all.
''You're not that different either' said
Margaret. [From far below the soldiers
were busy at getting at the water. Their
shouts came up unevenly, their little
black bodies were like Insects running,
in strings & groups. The water only
steady in being as helpful for the
shifting drifts of sand. There usual
was the sound of the birds on the wind
about the heads, tippy & lilting
their eyes brilliant & black seeing
it as urgent for them to covered
it as well as urgent for men.
'What'll ye do all the long Lydia?,
'I lived on at Birkp. I is, mountains'
'Did you seem sorry?'
Never. I'm at the daft' She leant
~~the sea~~ her by the head and laughed
& until the sea filled 'but they
barmy?' she asked Birkie

These are the ingredients of the plot, with rosy, voluptuous Lydia, the Marshes' housemaid, thrown in to raise the action to a high level of disorder. Lydia is attracted by the prospect of salvation at the hands of Margaret's bible-thumping father, who seems at first (with rare unworldliness) to have only her spiritual welfare at heart. But eventually Lydia discovers otherwise as the bank manager's pent-up sexuality makes him incautious. His assault on the housemaid is carried out in full view of first his daughter and then his wife. Disaster ensues.

Like Henry James's Maisie, in *What Maisie Knew* (1897), intelligent Margaret (who is pert at times) observes without fully understanding the sexual complications and guilts discomposing the adults around her. The emphasis, firmly on Margaret and her view to begin with, later shifts to one avid grown-up after another. Gardam avoids moral comment, however; her concern is with quirks of temperament, compulsions, self-deceits, and passions both insufficient and excessive, but not the moral implications of any of these. The novelist's function is to observe and record with sharpness and energy. As in all her work, illuminating eccentricities are subjected to scrutiny: " 'He thinks I've gone wonky,' she thought. 'Thinks I'm a bit funny.' " She is interested in the discrepancy between the face one presents to the world and one's actual feelings, and in the comedy which results from loss of face. Her approach is always subtle and oblique.

With *The Hollow Land* Gardam reverts to the "linked stories" framework of *Black Faces, White Faces*, though the location for this book is the Cumbrian moors, and it moves in time from the present up to the year 1999, when a total eclipse of the sun is expected (the background to the long concluding story, "Tomorrow's Arrangements"). The book opens with a scene of desolation, reminiscent of the Scottish Highlands after the Clearances or of the poorer parts of Ireland at any time: "All down this dale where I live there's dozens of little houses with grass growing between the stones and for years there's been none of them wanted. They're too old or too far out or that bit too high for farmers now. There was miners once—it's what's called the hollow land—but they're here no more. So the little houses is all forsook." The speaker is Bell Teesdale, a native of the place, who, at eight, strikes up a lifelong friendship with young Harry from London (whose family rents one of the deserted farmhouses, Light Trees). But the melancholy note, though effective, is not definitive. This is a story of domestic, country life felicity; summer sultriness and winter frost; the interesting peculiarities of neighbors; boys' escapades in the open air; the granite fastness of the uplands. It is utterly lucid in feeling, and its charm lies not in the decorative flourishes and freaks of circumstance found in *Bilgewater*, for example, or the high spirits of the earlier stories, but in a more orderly, even-toned arrangement of incidents. It sets out a world in which continuity is understood as a kind of grace. And it reminds us that the fanciful and highly colored in Gardam's work are always disciplined by a northern toughness and plainness of expression. In the ten years since her first books were published, Jane Gardam has shown herself to be a novelist of rare inventiveness and power, and her work has been justly acclaimed.

Penelope Gilliatt
(25 March 1932-   )

Thomas O. Calhoun
University of Delaware

BOOKS: *One by One* (London: Secker & Warburg, 1965; New York: Atheneum, 1965);
A State of Change (London: Secker & Warburg, 1967; New York: Random House, 1968);
What's It Like Out? (London: Secker & Warburg, 1968); republished as *Come Back If It Doesn't Get Better* (New York: Random House, 1969);
Sunday Bloody Sunday (New York: Viking, 1972);
Nobody's Business (London: Secker & Warburg, 1972; New York: Viking, 1972);
Unholy Fools (New York: Viking, 1973);
Jean Renoir: Essays, Conversations, Reviews (New York: McGraw-Hill, 1975);
Jacques Tati (London: Woburn Press, 1976);
Splendid Lives (London: Secker & Warburg, 1977; New York: Coward, McCann & Geoghegan, 1978);
The Cutting Edge (London: Secker & Warburg, 1978; New York: Coward, McCann & Geoghegan, 1979);
Three-Quarter Face: Reports & Reflections (New York: Coward, McCann & Geoghegan, 1980);
Quotations from Other Lives (London: Secker & Warburg, 1981; New York: Coward, McCann & Geoghegan, 1981).

Penelope Gilliatt, who retains the surname of her first husband, is a writer of short stories; novels; television and film scripts; and film, book, and theater criticism. She has been awarded a fiction prize by the American Academy of Arts and Letters, and is a fellow of the Royal Society of Literature, London. She was born the redheaded daughter of barrister Cyril and Mary Douglass Conner in London on 25 March 1932. She grew up in and around Northumberland but lived in London during the war years; later, she attended Queens College, London, and spent a year (1948) as a student at Bennington College, Vermont. Her first marriage (1954), to professor Roger William Gilliatt, ended in divorce, as did her second (1963), to playwright John Osborn, the father of her daughter, Nolan Kate.

Gilliatt is best known for the screenplay *Sunday Bloody Sunday* (1972), which won prizes from the

National Society of Film Critics, the New York Film Critics, and the British Film Writers' Guild and received an Oscar nomination for best original script. The film, produced by Joseph Janni for United Artists and directed by John Schlesinger, profiles three characters—two men and a woman—against the multileveled social backdrop of contemporary London. Inner conflicts of the main characters are crucial to the plot, and the action (episodes in a ten-day sequence) has mainly to do with the departure of one character from the lives of the other two. In its character selection, setting, and plot, *Sunday Bloody Sunday* is typical of Miss Gilliatt's novels and many of her short stories.

A character trio is central to her first novel,

Penelope Gilliatt at twenty-eight

349

One by One (1965). The book chronicles the disintegrating marriage of Polly and Joe Talbot, Polly's pregnancy, and the birth of her first daughter. The setting is contemporary London during a fictional epidemic. A third-person narrator establishes the novel as a mordant social satire, yet narrative point of view is limited, by and large, to perceptions of the characters she creates, and dialogue is the most important medium of exchange. The dialogue is idiomatic; we hear the concerned voices of the educated, professional middle class, the hounding of journalists, the euphemisms of bureaucrats, and the clipped, idiosyncratic voices of Britain's abiding upper class.

The narrator sets an external conflict: a mysterious plague threatens all in London. The characters reveal inner conflicts which threaten their psychic lives and their capacity to sustain social or marital relationships. Joe, a veterinarian who wishes he were a "real" doctor, is contaminated not by the plague but by a deep sexual confusion and by his inability to withstand the oppression of his mother's upper-class expectations for and perpetual dissatisfaction with him. Polly's life is threatened by the hysteria of the society in general, by her husband's withdrawal and breakdown, by the problems of pregnancy, and mainly by her lack of experience in managing an independent life. She is subject to loneliness, depression, and fainting spells, and after her husband commits suicide she is unable to leave their house for six months.

As in satires, the central characters in *One by One* appear both specific and representative. The man, in postwar England, suffers from the burden of traditional and family expectations, from failed ambition, from a sense of incompetence and of the inconsequence of life. He is unable to explain himself, to himself or others, withdraws to an ever more sterile seclusion, and develops a self-loathing that becomes more acute in the company of a woman who loves him. In his isolation, he involves himself in ideas of death: cultural, professional, personal. He seeks excuses and an easy way to die. The woman also suffers from the burden of the past, especially as her social and professional roles are confined by tradition and male domination. She is ill-equipped, historically and emotionally, to survive and nourish new life in the wasteland of contemporary London. If she is to live, the past cannot much count. Thus the awesome future remains at bay, and the present tense becomes her medium. There she must learn to manage. Her limitations and resolve become a kind of moral for the professional middle class who must work hard with only

marginal hope for a better life and with considerable regret for the past that is lost. Polly, with the aid of a friendly doctor, determines to face and solve the practical problems of doing things by herself, for herself and her child.

The plot of *One by One* engages a prominent third character, Coker, who has remained Joe Talbot's best friend since boyhood. A central mystery of Joe's past involves some form of homosexual relationship with Coker, and their present friendship shades into a dependency. Coker dies, a victim of the epidemic, just prior to Joe's suicide.

The trio, one a shared lover of the other two, reappears in *A State of Change* (1967), Miss Gilliatt's second novel, published two years after the first. Here, Kakia Grabowska (a woman who reflects her author's interest in the Soviet Union and her fluency in Russian) flees from Warsaw to Moscow and then arrives in London, in hopes of pursuing a career as a cartoonist. Kakia meets Don Clancy, a British media celebrity, and Harry Clapton, a doctor. The two men, here old Oxford friends, and the woman, a visual satirist and "observer of history," reconstitute the dramatic trio of Gilliatt's first novel.

The three engage in contests of affection and loyalty, while each encounters a personal crisis. Kakia must resolve her relationship with Andrzej, her authoritarian, Marxist ex-husband, now married to a professor of church history from New England. The crises of Don and Harry are sketched as a reversal. At first, Don rides high on the social crest as public celebrity and trendsetter, but Harry is stricken from the Medical Register and jailed for performing an abortion on an unmarried girl without a psychiatrist's sanction. Then, upon his release from prison, Harry settles down to a rural life with Kakia and begins to feel the forces of life, conviction, integrity, and hope returning. But Don, whose relationships with women are all for show, sees in Harry's new happiness his own hollowness and artifice. He is essentially spent, canceled out, for he cannot imitate the male-female bond achieved by his friends. He is capable of only an introverted, empty parody.

A State of Change is centered in London and its environs, but the novelist extends her concern for place by reflecting, through Kakia, on the terrifying memories of World War II and on the Communist-bloc/pan-European tensions of the 1950s and 1960s. The external events that matter are locked in memory or anticipation: heritage and childhood; custom and class; aging and death. The outer or public world, fragmented and artificial, drives characters in on themselves. Like a memento

Dust jacket for Gilliatt's first novel

mori, it encourages self-absorption, inner probing, the result of which for Kakia and Harry is a determined and darkly comic commitment to living in amenable juxtaposition with the past. Coming to terms with one's heritage and family allows at least a handhold on the future.

The manner of coming to terms, like the manner of interpersonal relations which change the lives of both parties, is improvised—an invention forged from old material. Gilliatt's characters, for example, play spontaneous word games. One cites a term, and the other responds with a definition or saying. The originator elaborates upon the response, and both are lifted from involuted states of languor and despondency. Kakia asks Harry:

> "What's a mimmybrace?"
> "Ah, that's a very interesting word," he said heavily.
> "You're stalling."
> "No, I'm not. It's a small loop made of tapestry and leather."
> "You're stuck on things about tapestry. This isn't going to be any good."
> "Oh yes it is. As I say, it's a small loop of tapestry and leather used in the 18th century to hold back a woman's skirt on side saddle."
> "That's not at all bad. But I'll tell you what it really is. . . . You know the little boys of nine or ten who were pressed into the Navy to be midshipmen in whatever century it was? When they were sent into the crow's nest to keep a lookout they were often so tired that they fell asleep on the watch so the second officer used to put a mimmybrace, which was a long narrow board studded with nails, inside their jacket to keep them awake."

The game, ridiculous on the surface, forms two kinds of bond. The characters are joined in present conversation, and the past, echoed in the definitions of some constraining device, is obliquely invoked and probed. It does not matter what a "mimmybrace" is, but who Kakia and Harry are does matter. Through this kind of dialogue, something like a verbal Rorschach test, they awaken to one another.

Critical responses to Gilliatt's novels nearly always stress the author's concentration upon verbal styles by which people reveal themselves. Critical receptiveness often depends upon the reader's response to cultural values or tastes implicit in the dialogue. Anthony Burgess, for example, admires innovative repartee and appreciates the verbal cultivation of Gilliatt's fiction. Others, including a reviewer for the *New Leader*, have accused the writer of "fatuous elitism"—a charge directed largely at the British class and culture which she typically represents in her subjects. Gilliatt's ear for good talk gets her into trouble, too, with critics for whom plot is the key element of a good book. But such social or structural biases aside, it is sometimes not hard to regard the author's point of view as that of one of her characters.

In *A State of Change*, Kakia's is the prominent perspective. She appears at times to be the author's spokesperson, and like Gilliatt "her humor [is] grim, but it [is] not about grievance. It [is] a style of frosty stoicism, absorbed with death not as a romantic theme but as the cliff face on which it had to find purchase." Like Gilliatt as well, Kakia's professional expertise lies in sketching characters. This skill is particularly apparent in the shorter fiction. *What's It Like Out?* (1968), a collection of short stories all but one of which appeared first in the *New Yorker* magazine, is in essence an ensemble of character sketches or fictional profiles. The characters are solitary people, often eccentric; many are aging or elderly. They engage in various forms of practicing dying.

A poet wanders daily on the Northumbrian moors (site of Gilliatt's childhood), "humming Anglican hymns, whose verbal schemes he admired for their metrical embodiment of depression." Albert, a jobless alchoholic whose wife lives with his best friend, fears that any move or change will be for the worse. So for him, "even the most dismal and unstable circumstances can be something to be clung to." Harriet, the title character of "The Redhead," quarrels with her father over her sudden decision to become a Roman Catholic and leaves home. "For two nights she slept on the Thames Embankment. It was really the misleading start to her whole punishingly misled life, because it gave her an idea of herself that she was absolutely unequipped to realize. She started to think that she had a vocation for heroic decisions, but it was really nothing more sustaining than a rabid kind of recklessness that erupted suddenly and then left her feeling bleak and inept." Briskly, succinctly, Harriet's character is sketched. She believes in one form of life and lives

an inadequate parody of it. Professor Henry Tenterden, a less volatile melancholic, says: "I can't put it right. My real life is the one I don't lead." "Of course," replies his wife. Gilliatt's people confront their solitude, often in the inverted reflection of a foil character, and in recognition of their personal version of death-in-life they improvise modes of sustaining themselves.

The title story, "What's It Like Out?," and one other, "The Tactics of Hunger," are about the lives of the aged. In the former, Franklin and Milly Wilberforce, aged eighty-nine and eighty-six, Oxford conservative and middle-class liberal, shroud their vital intimacy with a manner of indifference, a shield against physical infirmity and the fear of dying. The characters are approached and observed by an uncomprehending young interviewer. In "The Tactics of Hunger" a younger daughter's perspective is juxtaposed against the eccentric defenses of her elderly parents. Old Lord Grubb does not talk much, but he leaves notes all around the house, suggesting to his wife that she ought to eat properly. She refuses to answer the notes, though she knows about them, for she (too) is dying and cannot admit it to him. Nor will she be "bullied." "He'll die first and he knows it," says Lady Grubb. "Then I'll be on my own. I have to practice being on my own." Denials, of food or of communication, are rehearsals for dying.

Death and its forms in life—denials, detachment, loneliness, abandonment, alienation—are the unifying reality underlying class, economic, and ethnic stratifications of the English society Penelope Gilliatt sees. One's proximity to real death, the index of one's participation in dying, determines the characterizations and social strata of the film script *Sunday Bloody Sunday*. Gilliatt portrays her characters on three levels. The parents of central characters Daniel (a homosexual Jewish doctor) and Alex (a divorced professional woman) are fixed in traditional ways. Daniel's family is permanently entrenched in London's Jewish "ghetto." Alex's parents are as inflexibly residing in the upper-class world of property and investment banking. Daniel and Alex are at stages of middle life. They are attempting to live on their terms, to adapt to the freedoms of contemporary urban culture (he through sexual preference and casual observation of religion; she by divorce and by quitting her job as a business efficiency expert), but both are becoming more immobile and solitary. Bob Elkin, age twenty-five, the lover shared by Daniel and Alex, is a young pop artist who acknowledges no conventions (though his art is more parodic than iconoclastic), affiliates with no culture nor nationality, and is so self-centered that his motives are as ambiguous as his sexuality. He does what he wants to, when he wants to, but he is nearly dimensionless in his freedom. Personal or sexual relationships mean more to his partners than to him.

To both Daniel and Alex, Elkin is a satisfying lover as well as a representation of life lived on one's own terms. Not surprisingly, Elkin is bound for America, the land stereotypically free from tradition (though thereby capable of only a commercial, pseudoculture). Elkin's departure from the lives of

and collected under the title *Nobody's Business* (1972), include the surreal comedy "Property." This one-act play was later performed at the American Place Theatre in New York.

The play presents three characters, two aging men and the woman they share as their "property," who are able to move only a little since they are attached by wires to the electrocardiograph machines fixed to their beds. In the otherwise bare, Beckett-like space which is defined by technological constraints that prevent much action or any physical contact, the Gilliatt trio tell their stories. In this play,

Peter Finch, Murray Head, and Glenda Jackson in a scene from Sunday Bloody Sunday, *for which Gilliatt wrote the screenplay*

Daniel and Alex is the film's memento mori. On a Sunday, a day set aside for nothing, when British lives lose the shape and rhythm provided by scheduled work, Daniel and Alex meet, briefly and by chance. In the encounter there is a self-recognition for both—an awareness of age, of loss, and of the tenuous durability of their lives.

Sunday Bloody Sunday is a brilliant portrayal of the character trio Gilliatt had been molding in prior novels and stories. Glenda Jackson (Alex), Murray Head (Elkin), and especially the late Peter Finch (Daniel Hirsh) realize the gesture and intonation, the diffidence, defense, and insularity so crucial to Gilliatt's dialogue, and the character sketches come fully to life in these expert performances. Other of Gilliatt's film, television, and radio scripts (two of which, written for BBC, are adaptations of short stories: "Flight Fund" and "Fred and Arthur") have not been published, but her second volume of short stories, nine works first published in the *New Yorker*

as in *Sunday Bloody Sunday* and in much of the fiction, time is contracted into brief episodes which are abruptly entered, performed in dialogue, and then interrupted or discontinued. Just as the characters arrive at no clear understanding of what awaits them, there is no clear sense of ending or denouement. What happens is that one character becomes a foil for the other two. Two pair off against one; the alignment shifts, then shifts again.

Nobody's Business is distinguished by other stories based on conflicts between uprooted, displaced people and machines or systems which ironically have been devised to aid communications. "Frank," the Family Robot Adapted to the Needs of Kinship, is an absurd mechanical substitute for missing relatives. In "An Antique Love Story," little Izolska pays her touch-tone tuition and idly, pathetically, attends a computerized school by telephone. Sara Flitch runs a chain of toy stores where plastic nursery objects "properly researched by

Dust jacket for Gilliatt's second short-story collection, nine works first published in the New Yorker

child psychiatrists to be fit for middle-class children" are sold. Yet her own grandchild prefers to make models of erotic Indian figurines (and she is punished for doing so). Systematic, Freudian analysis is the enemy in "As We Have Learnt from Freud, There Are No Jokes." Newsjournal astrology provides the grounds for irrational choice and action in "The Position of the Planets." The title story, an excellent character study of an elderly British judge and his Russian-born wife, reveals a life-giving intimacy shared by the main characters. The love perseveres in spite of past indiscretions, and it is revealed in spite of efforts of two young interviewers who ask the wrong questions and perceive what they preconceive. The interviewers are engaged in a study of the "mechanics" of humor; they think of their subject "as though it were a problem in engineering." In the author's view, these technical experts are the least capable of understanding others, or themselves.

The world of analytical systems, of electronics and computer technology, displaces or conceals authentic human feeling in any developed nation. Gilliatt's characters, however, are often twice-removed from their heritage and themselves since many have been forced by circumstance or urged by economic opportunity to relocate in a foreign country. To counter these dislocations and other effects of "what life does" to people, "*stare decisis*," announces Emily Prendergast, wife of the judge in "Nobody's Business." "Stand by decided matters." This is as close as Gilliatt comes to engaging detailed behavior and speech with an explanatory principle. Just as she distrusts technology and analysis as measures of character, her stories here veer away from the traditional theme-bearing plot, moving toward tangentially embodied speech, which, if it signifies something other than what actually is said, points within to a remote core of feeling and motive. We overhear, mostly, verbal movement on the surface of inner worlds that are assumed but (like the past, like memory) are neither directly nor fully accessible. The third-person narrator is often limited to the functions of microphone and camera: listening, observing, and chronicling.

During the five years between publication of *Nobody's Business* and her third collection of stories, *Splendid Lives* (1977), Gilliatt published profiles (short biographical sketches with film histories) of French movie directors Jean Renoir and Jacques Tati (in 1975 and 1976), as well as a collection of critical reviews and articles, mainly on films, titled *Unholy Fools* (1973). A longtime film and drama critic for the London *Observer* (1961-1967) and cofilm critic (with Pauline Kael) at the *New Yorker* (1968-1979), Gilliatt has enjoyed a journalistic career that has run nearly parallel to her life as a fiction writer. The two pursuits are complementary. A third-person dramatic point of view, adapted from traditional theater and cinema, dominates the fiction; the episodic plot, linked by expository flashbacks and jump cuts, bears resemblance to cinematic script form and editing techniques. Reciprocally, Gilliatt's most perceptive comment as a film critic often has to do with literary aspects of the visual medium. But an interest in comedy is the most substantial bridge between the two forms of writing.

Highlighting *Unholy Fools*, along with feature reviews of Polish and Czech "new wave" directors, is a series on classic and contemporary film comedy. Buster Keaton, Harry Langdon, Charles Chaplin, Harold Lloyd, and Mack Sennett are studied; so are

Samuel Beckett, Eugene Ionesco, Jacques Tati, Richard Lester, Robert Downey, Monty Python, Woody Allen, and others. Incongruities, regarded as the common denominator of comic performances, appear throughout Gilliatt's fiction in paired components of a single character, in the pairing of characters, and in the juxtaposition of character and setting or occupation. Consider Felix of "The Last to Go" (*Nobody's Business*): "an affectionate, forgetful, hypomanic man passionately expert in animal physiology and the history of Communism." Consider Andrzej, the authoritarian Marxist, and his church historian wife. Emily, of "Nobody's Business," is a Russian-born Englishwoman who writes low comedy for radio shows and is married to a scholarly British judge. The title story of *Splendid Lives* features a retired bishop whose passion is a racehorse that will not eat unless its passion, a female pigeon, is present in the stable. Verbal incongruities serve the purposes of humor as well. "The poor Pope was praying for peace at the United Nations and was reported in translation as saying that he hoped the nations of the world would let their arms fall from their hands," laughs the bishop.

The nine stories collected in *Splendid Lives*, six of which appeared first in the *New Yorker*, sustain a comic vision in the face of an international political background that grows ever more grim. An America where parents abandon children in order to pursue careers and avoid taxes; a London where doctors strike and postmen burn mail; a welfare democracy that shuns the elderly and keeps the poor alive to face old age; a third world where developers exploit, natives riot, and dissidents are tortured and killed: these are contexts for displaced characters whose lives may be raised, if only a little, above the tawdry or the terrifying and made splendid through eccentric resistance to the forces that would pull them down. A seventy-four-year-old English widow living in Detroit and the young grandson abandoned to her care fly thirty-seven consecutive round trips between New York and Rome, soaring ridiculous and grand above their ruined families on the earth below. A child, neglected by parents whose interests are in raising and sheltering money, is sent to live on a tax-sheltered island where his father banks. There the boy burns £ 10,000 of his father's hoarded money, his own unwanted inheritance, while racial animosities on the island break into overt and pointless violence. The boy and the black islanders may appear to be fools, but only to one who shares the dehumanizing

values both are resisting. In the sadly comic story "Phone-In," an eighty-one-year-old man and his eighty-two-year-old wife set up a radio show. He pretends to be young and shrewd; she pretends to be the influential Mr. Big Director. Together, sustaining a foolish illusion, they accept calls and offer consolation and advice to lonely, aging people living in immobilized mobile homes. Two stories are about aging, working-class women who live in South London and maintain a marginal existence for themselves, their jobless, idle husbands, and children who think they are crazy to work so stoically and hard, for endless hours, for next to nothing.

Gilliatt's most recent novel, *The Cutting Edge* (1979), is a tacit reflection upon previous characters and situations. Like *A State of Change*, it has an international setting—this time ranging from England eastward to Paris, Italy, and Turkey. Like both previous novels, *Sunday Bloody Sunday*, and many of the short stories, it features three characters: two men and a woman. As if to suggest their prototypes, or to suggest that they themselves are in a sense abstractions, the men (brothers) are usually referred to not by their names, Peregrine and Benedick, but as Brother A and Brother B. Lurking in the background is another mirror pair, illegitimate twin boys spawned late by A and B's father, a retired professor. Brother B loves and marries Joanna, who loves Brother A, who loves Brother B. Brother B envies, emulates, and is always "mending the ramshackle life" of Brother A. Benedick and Joanna divorce; the novelist focuses on the narrowing relationship between the two brothers; A and B alter their appearances to resemble one another exactly; A and Joanna meet in Paris; B arrives in Paris, and the triangle is reformed as a quasi-pairing: the woman and two men who have become, virtually, one. The novel, having achieved the mathematical magic of $3 = 2$, ends. But this new symmetry bears only an obscure relationship to the psychology, expectations, and futures of the characters involved. It is a tenuous balance. What the three will do next is anybody's guess. Their stories are less concluded than adjourned.

According to Goedel's theorem, a mathematical proposition overheard by Brother A one night in a Paris cafe, "there exist meaningful statements in mathematics which are neither provable nor disprovable, now or ever. Logical systems in Goedel's sense are by nature incomplete." The narrator at this point intervenes and provides a summary vision of her characters and the novelistic geometry that encompasses them. "The subject they were dicussing was ambiguity . . . talking in the way that France has uniquely perfected, making abstractions a matter for conversation . . . the sound of souls buzzing in a glass prison of a world which they cannot escape but still try to understand, fluttering without clear hope but with many a keen pang, many a rank problem of the imagination, and much fine music." The music referred to here is meant literally, as literally as the motif from "Così fan tutte" that runs ironically through *Sunday Bloody Sunday*, but the music Gilliatt recreates is that of occasional, topical, refined speech. We overhear some fine talk from characters existing in the midst of lives governed by an obscure but relentless geometry. We witness in these characters' uncertain movements the unfinished parody of their lives'

clusiveness.

In 1980 Gilliatt produced *Three-Quarter Face: Reports and Reflections*, a second volume of film criticism collected from articles previously published in the *New Yorker* and augmented by reflections on an interview with Vladimir Nabokov first published in *Vogue*. She continues to reside in London and New York, and her stories continue to appear in the *New Yorker*. She has recently completed profiles on John Huston, Woody Allen, and Katharine Hepburn, and she has completed a three-act play called "But When All's Said and Done." Her fourth collection of short stories, *Quotations from Other Lives*, was published in 1981. She has also finished work on a libretto, "Beach of Aurora," commissioned by the English National Opera.

Jacky Gillott
(24 September 1939-19 September 1980)

June Sturrock
Simon Fraser University

SELECTED BOOKS: *Salvage* (London: Gollancz, 1968; Garden City: Doubleday, 1969);
War Baby (London: Gollancz, 1971);
A True Romance (London: Hodder & Stoughton, 1975);
Crying Out Loud (London: Hodder & Stoughton, 1976);
Providence Place–Animals in a Landscape (London: Hodder & Stoughton, 1978);
The Head Case (London: Hodder & Stoughton, 1979);
Intimate Relations (London: Hodder & Stoughton, 1980).

Jacky Gillott's early death seems a great waste. Her five novels show considerable and unusual talents: a strong sense of the possibilities of structure, an outlandish humor, a capacity to deal with public events with the assurance with which she dealt with private life, and above all a willingness to commit herself strongly to her own moral and political principles. At the time of her suicide at age forty, her achievements had by no means matched her apparent abilities.

Jacky Gillott was born in Bromley, England, in 1939. In 1960, she took her B.A. at University Col-

lege, London, where she studied English, and went on to work as a reporter on the Sheffield *Telegraph*, following a well established English theatrical and journalistic tradition of gaining experience in the provinces. In 1963 she began to establish her long career as a radio journalist, working for the BBC's *Radio Newsreel*. Later she became the first woman reporter for Independent Television News, but she retained her interest in radio: she worked for a long time on *Kaleidoscope*, the BBC radio arts program, and until the end of her life she was an occasional radio columnist for the *Listener*.

The producer of *Radio Newsreel* in 1963 was John Percival, whom Gillott married four months after meeting him. They later had two sons, Matthew Edward (1964) and Daniel John (1965). Gillott has written of her gratitude for her husband's loving encouragement and support, especially in connection with her writing. A year after their marriage she began writing one novel after another: "Three I wrote without stopping," she said, "while the washing went unironed, and brown wallpaper . . . peeled in sad streamers down the walls." She describes these early writings as "rubbish."

All the same, her first published novel, *Salvage* (1968), is one of her most successful books and

Jacky Gillott, 1976

shows even then the ability to handle a complex structure which is consummated in the legerdemain of her last (and best) novel, *The Head Case* (1979). *Salvage* has a double time scheme, beginning ominously with the protagonist contemplating suicide and following her day of escape (not quite an escapade) with a man from whom she hitches a ride; her anonymity gradually fades till we come to know Helena, to find out about her still half-regretted (quite regrettable) first lover, her defunct career as an education journalist, her husband, James, and her three young children. The novel has some clearly autobiographical streaks in it as Gillott uses her experience to create a credible and sympathetic character and to express the larger feminist issues which were to become well publicized in the next decade: the frustrated creativity of the woman who interrupts her career for the sake of her children; the difficulty of retaining a sense of identity within marriage; the problem of accepting the nature of one's sexuality. Helena loves her children and her husband but feels ambivalent about her maternity and sexuality, even her menstruation: her femininity seems to her to involve her in uncontrollable forces, a situation she resents. Gillott shows concern in several novels with the conflict between the desire

for freedom and the necessary acceptance of one's nature and its inevitable limitations and restrictions.

The resolution of these themes in Helena's new acceptance of herself and of her love for her husband is a credible outcome. However, here Gillott's time schedule (the novel takes place within a single day) seems to trip her up; while one accepts that this is the proper resolution to which the novel has been moving, one doubts that such a transformation would be so abrupt. In other words, the conclusion is too hasty, and in this and other ways *Salvage*, like all her other novels, is flawed by a lack of critical rereading and revision. Nevertheless, it has an intensity which makes it one of the more interesting novels of a type which was to become popular in the late 1960s and the 1970s. As such, it was well reviewed. The *Times Literary Supplement*'s reviewer, while commenting that "the solution is too pat," went on to say that "Miss Gillott writes with assurance and sometimes startling perception."

Helena is like her author in her advantages and successes. She is intelligent, attractive and energetic, married, a mother—a fairly predictable kind of central character for a first novel by a woman. Garbie, the central character of *War Baby* (1971), is a far more unusual and difficult creation. She is ungainly, plain, almost simple, and totally lacking in any ordinary sense of self-protection. Herself illegitimate, she never marries, and the child she is carrying throughout the novel is about to be aborted as the book ends. The author's concern with the underprivileged and their relationship with the privileged is expressed through Garbie's thoughts and fears and through her relationship with her family. The product of a mismating between a foolish and careless working-class girl, Dotty, and the irresponsible upper-middle-class Rikki Pendleton, Garbie as a child is shunted between the dreary poverty of her aunt in Dagenham and the rural comfort of her uncle's home. The uncle, Jack Pendleton, is a Labour M.P., and Gillott uses this character and his private and political actions and opinions to embody the ineffectuality and moral ambivalence of the "haves" who, while wishing to do right by the "have nots," are incapable of accepting them as independent fellow human beings. The Pendletons *are* kind to Garbie, but their children scornfully christen her "the garbage girl"; none of them can accept her uncouthness and crudity; all of them expect her gratitude.

Gillott expands her theme of privilege onto the international level through the involvement of Jack Pendleton in African politics; his attitude (and, it is implied, the attitude of the British Foreign

Office) is again well-meaning but paternalistic, and therefore finally destructive. Garbie too becomes involved in African politics: her loneliness has led her into a relationship with Freddie, an extreme left-wing activist in his sixties, through whose influence she comes to take an active part in marches and demonstrations. This larger political element gives the novel a breadth which is lacking in the rather claustrophobic atmosphere of *Salvage*. It is worked out with conviction and political intelligence, though it is not always handled with the clarity and sureness necessary to make it fully effective.

Like its predecessor, *War Baby* has a dual time scheme and Garbie's story is handled by a series of flashbacks: the present time of the novel is Garbie's stay in the hospital where she is suffering from acute back pain. This pain turns out to be caused by pregnancy: the fetus is pressing against a spinal nerve. (The author suffered in a similar way when pregnant with her first son). The novel ends without any note of false optimism, for the hospital authorities and Jack Pendleton's wife manage between them to exert enough pressure on Garbie to make her assent to aborting the child she was looking forward to with secret delight.

War Baby is in many ways more ambitious and more objective than *Salvage*. It examines English society with a sharply critical eye and makes few sentimental concessions to the reader's comfort. If it lacks some of the power of its predecessor, it is largely because of this objectivity. Neither writer nor reader will identify in any way with either Garbie or her uncle, nor is one allowed to follow fully their mental processes. The blindness and essential callousness of the privileged is revealed through the reader's intellectual acceptance of a just accusation, rather than through an understanding of Garbie's feelings. Though the reviews of this novel were somewhat wary, they were agreed on the power of its irony.

The analysis of English society continues in *A True Romance* (1975). The Percivals had by this time moved to Somerset, where they were involved in running a small farm, work which Gillott loved and which expressed her economic and political convictions. Anthony Howard, former editor of the *New Statesman*, wrote in a brief memoir of Gillott that, "It was a period [the early 1970s] when the Left still believed in 'growth'—and every time we published an article extolling the Gross National Product as the Key to Britain's future, there would arrive an effective environmental riposte from deep in the heart of Somerset."

A True Romance is an effective environmental riposte: Gillott has pushed Britain a little into the future, a future of increased shortages and unrest. The only characters who act rationally in the novel are the group of young people establishing a small agricultural commune on some land belonging to the central character, Olivia, and her husband Leo. The only one of these young people who is developed at length is Olivia's daughter, Chloe, who shares with her author not only strong views of the importance of living off the direct results of one's labor, but also her return to Christianity.

For Jacky Gillott, this new religious life was directly connected with her artistic creativity. Writing about prayer, she discussed various kinds of imagination and especially "imagination of a more transcendental kind, into which things drift of their own inexplicable accord—the imagination to which one can only passively be open. Here, perhaps, God expresses himself. Personally I cannot otherwise account for certain marvellous images which present themselves to me, not images of God but in writing a novel particularly images I could not consciously have dreamed up myself." Christianity, in this novel, is welcomed by Chloe as essentially antiromantic, as a belief which leads to the loving acceptance of one's human needs, flaws, and limitations: this acceptance is seen as totally at odds with the technological dream of omnipotence and universal control and the ensuing unrealistic demands for ease and comfort.

It is this acceptance of faulty humanity which Chloe's mother, Olivia, lacks, which in fact she fights against. Olivia is a romantic novelist, one who creates a world where the totally feminine meets the totally masculine in a final, impossibly perfect happiness. At the age of forty-eight, she preserves her mask of feminine beauty with scrupulous anxiety. Above all, the essential fiction for her, one which must be preserved at all costs, is the love between her and her own mother (whose funeral begins the novel).

The somewhat melodramatic denouement of the novel involves Olivia's discovery of the illegitimate son whom she has cut almost completely from her life and memory. This discovery leads to destruction: the destruction of her house by fire, the destruction of her beauty by a violent assault, the destruction of her ideal image of her mother. This ruthless surgery, however, is healing, and it frees her to turn the current of her energies from ideals to realities: to her children and her own survival.

A noticeable difficulty in this novel, however, is that in denouncing an idealistic and romantic view of life, it creates its own romantic ideals. As the *New*

Statesman reviewer points out, its "best parts deal with the realities of the English landscape and the various animals whose behaviour Miss Gillott records with loving accuracy." The view of the small agricultural commune is utopian; within a few weeks it produces food that is adequate and excellent. Its young members work hard, but they neither suffer nor quarrel. They seem incredibly good humored, incredibly fortunate. And there is no real discussion of how they can achieve economic independence of the consumer society. They have a weaver—but where are the sheep to produce the wool? These may seem minor considerations, but in fact this kind of carelessness is damaging to a novel whose major theme is the urgent need for a return to a more realistic view of human nature and human society.

Gillott's next novel, *Crying Out Loud* (1976), is again influenced by her love for country life. The novel, which received favorable though not enthusiastic reviews, is dedicated to Sylvia Plath, who wrote:

> It is more natural to me lying down.
> Then the sky and I are in open conversation.
> And I shall be useful when I lie down finally;
> And the trees may touch me for once, and the
> > leaves have time for me.

The whole novel is colored by the pain of its central character, Maggie, whose family responsibilities have uprooted her from a happy rural life and left her with a house in the suburbs and an unsatisfactory career in television commercials. This novel returns to the claustrophobic family atmosphere of *Salvage*: it is concerned with Maggie's relationships with her husband and two sons (that is, a woman with three males); these relationships embody the central theme of aggression, as well as the difference between male and female aggression. Maggie's sons, full of rivalry and hostility toward each other, continually contemplate a world of hideous violence, both fictional and actual, on television.

As for their father, Maggie takes a Lawrentian view of the wound which disabled her journalist husband when he was covering the Vietnam War: as D. H. Lawrence sees Clifford Chatterley's crippled impotence as a kind of poetic retribution for his assent to World War I, so Maggie feels that her husband is suffering from his assent to, from his pleasure in, violence: " 'But you wanted to go. You wanted to be involved. The idea excited you. You thought it was someone else's war. An assignment, that's all, just something you could go and have a

look at then come home as easily as if you'd been covering a horse show. But nobody can just go and look and walk away. You didn't even walk away. You were carried away. And you're scarred by it. Not just here. . . .' And she touched his thigh gently." Maggie's views on male and female aggression are clarified in a bedtime story of Adam and Eve. In Maggie's version, while the fruit of the Tree of Knowledge makes the female "the mother of all living things," it makes the male hostile toward the rest of creation: "he swore aloud in his anger that if he could not be a part of the forest he would destroy it. He would visit his own curse upon it. He would destroy its bees and streams and birds and build his own jungle, a finer place than this." This aggression is especially fierce toward the female: "He will bring you sorrow and suffering. He will punish you always," says "The Master" to the Eve figure.

Maggie's unhappiness in her London life and her continual sense of the cruelty of a male dominated world are made more agonizing by her anxiety and guilt over her sensitive and partially deaf elder son: he is deaf presumably because of the antibodies in the bloodstream of his Rh negative mother. She feels guilty because of this and because of the former pregnancy (presumably aborted) which increased his risk in the womb. The mounting tensions and conflicts eventually lead to an unresolved and wretched finale in which the elder son leaves his brother possibly drowning and returns home to find his mother in a gas-filled room with her wrists slashed. His rescue attempt seems likely to end in both their deaths, and the novel ends with the father hearing the anguished cry for help.

Crying Out Loud is well titled, for Maggie seems to be doing just that for herself and her author. Gillott suffered from severe, eventually fatal, depressions: "From time to time a great black owl of depression comes to roost on my back. I can't do anything about it. Only wait until it chooses to flap away again." *Crying Out Loud* is clearly drawn from these painful experiences; this gives it much of its strength and coherence, but it also creates a noticeable imbalance, for Maggie is never viewed objectively, nor are her views ever seriously challenged. She is as poisoned with hostility as any other character in the novel, but whereas others are seen as themselves partly responsible for this poison, the implication is that Maggie is merely the victim of it; the author lacks the distance from her central character which might enable one to accept her view of her life and the world.

Crying Out Loud was followed by a book about the animals near Gillott's beloved Somerset home,

Providence Place–Animals in a Landscape (1978). This book was soon succeeded by her fifth and last novel, *The Head Case*, which is her most ambitious, original, and complex work (and accordingly received reviews ranging from the dismissive to the laudatory). In it, she uses the most heterogeneous and apparently impossible materials—including Celtic myth, Egyptian myth, coeducation, Marian cults, *The Magic Flute, The Tempest*—and succeeds in weaving these threads into a coherent if startling fabric. The exuberant and comic tone which unites all this material communicates the same intensity of the author's concern for serious issues: her concern for more loving and less aggressive relationships between the sexes (and in particular the proper acknowledgment by both sexes of the power of the female); and, similarly, her concern for more loving and less aggressive relationships between human beings and the rest of creation (and in particular the replacement of nuclear technology by the power of wind, sea, and, especially, sun).

The novel unites these themes in a movement, confusing at first but gradually becoming clearer as the book progresses, towards a final universal reacceptance of the sun goddess as supreme deity. This goddess, who combines the power of the sun with the power of the female, reclaims her natural place from the usurping warrior god, the supreme male, who is seen as the Urizenic ruler of a world obsessed with technological advancement, material comfort, and conquest. Thus the world's great age begins anew: "The seasons, benignly restored to their balance, brought forth great yields of maize, oats, wheat and barley.... The beasts thrived on their generous pasture, and the sun was reconsecrated by the northern barbarians who had once dreamt of constructing tall white temples to *Samholdanach*, descendent of Lugh, which, being translated, means polytechnician Smith and sorcerer.... The barbarians laughed aloud to think they had ever entertained such follies in their minds. Those chief among the perpetrators of the nuclear dream were discredited as false priests, and bound over to dig their gardens in perpetuity."

This great renewal is brought about on the mythological level by the sacrificial death of the central character, Reggie Montis, and on the practical level by the sacrificial death of his wife, Dorothy. Reggie at the beginning of the novel has left Dorothy and the civil service to become a schoolmaster at a boys' preparatory school at Tidmouth on the Dorset coast. He is constipated and conventional; his wife accuses him of being "an unimaginative man," and one theme of the novel is the growth of Reggie's imagination, which Gillott equates with the power of sharing the feelings of other people. Reggie's imagination grows partly through his contact with the inhabitants of Tidmouth; the beautiful, maimed Stephanie and her loving sister, Anna; the Mariolatrous Father Starkey; Reggie's landlady, Bella Pike; and in particular her granddaughter, Phoebe Orlebar, who at age twelve is the size of a five-year-old. When Dorothy meets Phoebe and becomes interested in the problems of PRG's (Persons of Restricted Growth), she realizes that she can use the PRG organization to gain publicity for her antinuclear campaign. Gillott has an unusual talent for the invention of public life as well as of private life, as was shown in *War Baby*. The benefit of her years as a journalist is clearly seen in the description of the Trafalgar Square rally of PRG's, where Dorothy announces that she has inhaled plutonium oxide "to demonstrate to the entire nation . . . the appalling danger . . . of the future that is planned for us. The non-future." As she gradually becomes ill she tours the country with this message, appears on television, and is finally pushed out of an upper-floor window "by a man who had shown a close interest in her movements over the last two months." The publicity resulting from the inquest on her death is said to be crucial "in alerting the public to the madness of their leaders."

While the practical significance of Dorothy's self-sacrifice is evident enough, Reginald's self-sacrifice, significant on a purely mythical level, is a more difficult matter. His imagination develops throughout the novel not only through personal contacts, but also through Mozart and Shakespeare and, above all, through his interest in archaeology. Gillott wrote this novel partly out of an interest in early British history which arose when her husband, John Percival, was doing research for a television series on the Iron Age. Reggie teaches prehistory and is especially interested in the total cultural break between Iron Age cultures and those it superseded. He is thus immensely excited to discover a Bronze Age site on the coast; it is clearly not a settlement, and he becomes puzzled and eventually obsessed by its significance, especially when in his excavations he finds bones which indicate the sacrifice through decapitation of a woman.

Listening to *The Magic Flute*, he has a sudden flash of enlightenment: just as Emanuel Schikaneder (Mozart's librettist) is said to have reversed the qualities of the Queen of the Night and Sarastro, so also have the Iron Age and the northern invasions wiped out all traces of the old religions which centered on a sun goddess and replaced her with a single stern male figure. His Bronze Age site he now sees as a sacred place of this religion defended fiercely against the invaders who, at their conquest, slew and decapitated the priestess. *The Head Case* is full of references to migraines (which plagued its author), to severed heads and dismembered gods, while Reggie is clearly being prepared for an important role—he undergoes, like Mozart's Tamino, ordeals by fire and water. Thus, when he is killed in a street accident, it comes as no surprise that his head is severed and lands at the feet of Phoebe Orlebar (the appropriately named incarnation of the sun goddess). Dorothy and Reggie die on the same afternoon: their pituitary glands are used to cure Phoebe's dwarfism, so that by the end of the novel when the proper union between earth and sun is restored, this incarnation of the sun can grow "as tall and straight and golden as the corn that flourished in the fields."

While this summary may indicate how audaciously and even wittily Gillott has mixed her themes, it cannot suggest the comic sense which makes this mixture palatable, which *almost* manages to make tolerable the jocular references to the posthumous conversations of Reggie with Shakespeare and Mozart ("Will" and "Wolfgang") in the final paragraph. (There is for instance a totally ridiculous, totally credible dog show.) Nor can any brief discussion cover all the interweavings of allusion and discussion. The nature of freedom and the significance of belief, for instance, are brought up almost casually and tied in loosely with a school performance of *The Tempest*, in which Reggie takes the part of Prospero who must liberate, while Phoebe is the Ariel who cannot be liberated. And the feminism of this novel is not only at the divine level: Dorothy has come to the point of making her side of the bed only, and the staff of Reggie's prep school is appalled and terrified by the idea of girls in the classrooms and women in their staff room.

This richness of themes and allusions is handled dexterously, and this last novel shows that Gillott had the potential for becoming a remarkable and original novelist. It was still largely a matter of potential, however: like all her novels, this one would have benefited enormously from a scrupulously critical reading of her drafts and from a disciplined reworking of her materials. Here her English is often coarse and stale, her background details vague and uncertain; and her allusions are

Dust jacket for Gillott's last novel, published the year before her suicide

confused and confusing. Reggie is equated (through his performance) with Prospero, but then suddenly is a Tamino figure, pursued by a serpent and undergoing ordeals. The possible parallel with Sarastro is never explored. The welter of myths in the last part of the novel is breathless and scrambled. But the mixture of comedy and earnestness, as well as the writer's generous exuberance, makes the reader feel a sense of loss, of promise wasted, in the knowledge that this was her last novel; she had one last book published, a collection of short stories called *Intimate Relations* (1980). Five days before her forty-first birthday in her Somerset home she took a massive overdose of aspirin and paracetemol: the verdict at the inquest was that she "took her own life while depressed."

Gillott has been quoted as saying "I am not an intellectual. I arrive at things by mental grope, by receiving and transmitting images while others prefer or are capable of a more logical account." The images she arrives at are often remarkable: one remembers, for instance, her treatment of anorexia nervosa in *A True Romance*, the cannibal rabbit in *Crying Out Loud*, the performance of *The Tempest* in *The Head Case*. Yet perhaps she was in too much haste to dismiss her intellect. As a novelist of ideas—and she was deeply concerned with political, religious, and economic ideas—she had an obligation to these ideas, an obligation to consider more fully their implications. As it is, the novels are full of contradictions; full, too, of minor inaccuracies, minor infelicities. The nine years of "keeping" which Horace and Pope recommend might be excessive; but another nine months of consideration and correction might have enabled Jacky Gillott to achieve the excellent novel which was certainly within her capacities.

Periodical Publications:
"Is There Anybody There," *Listener*, 20 June 1975, pp. 483-544;
"The Strongest Influence in My Life," *Listener*, 19 August 1976, pp. 208-209.

References:
Liz Forgan, "The Divine Comedy," *Guardian*, 7 April 1979, p. 4;
Anthony Howard, "Langham Diary," *Listener*, 25 September 1980.

Giles Gordon
(23 May 1940-   )

Randall Stevenson
University of Edinburgh

BOOKS: *Landscape any date* (Edinburgh: Macdonald, 1963);
Two and Two Make One (Preston, Lancashire, U.K.: Akros, 1966);
Two Elegies (London: Turret Books, 1968);
Eight Poems for Gareth (Frensham, Surrey, U.K.: Sceptre, 1970);
Pictures from an exhibition (New York: Dial, 1970; London: Allison & Busby, 1970);
Between Appointments (Farnham, Surrey, U.K.: Sceptre, 1971);
The Umbrella Man (London: Allison & Busby, 1971);
Twelve Poems for Callum (Preston, Lancashire, U.K.: Akros, 1972);
About a marriage (New York: Stein & Day, 1972; London: Allison & Busby, 1972);
One man, two women (London: Sheep, 1974);
Girl with red hair (London: Hutchinson, 1974);

Walter and the Balloon, by Gordon and Margaret Gordon (London: Heinemann, 1974);
Farewell, fond dreams (London: Hutchinson, 1975);
100 Scenes from married life (London: Hutchinson, 1976);
Enemies: a novel about friendship (Hassocks, Sussex, U.K.: Harvester Press, 1977);
The Oban Poems (Knotting, Bedfordshire, U.K.: Sceptre, 1977);
The Illusionist (Hassocks, Sussex, U.K.: Harvester Press, 1978);
Ambrose's Vision: Sketches towards the creation of a cathedral (Hassocks, Sussex, U.K.: Harvester Press, 1980).

Though his novels have never enjoyed large sales or much extended critical attention beyond reviews, Giles Gordon's position among contemporary British novelists is nevertheless an interesting and unusual one. He deserves attention particularly for the clever and intriguing experimental fiction which makes up a large portion of his work. He has been referred to as "the only true inheritor of the late B. S. Johnson's mantle," and, like Johnson, Gordon exhibits an unusual enthusiasm for innovation at a time when such experimental fiction has not been much in vogue among British writers. During the dozen years which have followed the publication (in 1970) of his first collection of short stories, he has established a reputation as one of the few British novelists committed to technical originality in his own fiction, and one fully aware of the experiments that have taken place abroad.

The son of a distinguished architect, Alexander Esme, and Betsy Balmont McCurrey Gordon, Giles Alexander Esme Gordon was born in Edinburgh, Scotland, on 23 May 1940. He recalls having had few close friends in his early years and turning to the printed word to compensate for a slightly lonely childhood spent in quiet, middle-class areas of Edinburgh. He was educated at Edinburgh Academy, where he showed promise in both English and art. Though his school was one of the most respected in Edinburgh, Gordon later questioned the distinctly Anglified nature of its teaching: he remembers first encountering the work of Robert Burns during these school years, and finding it unintelligible because it was written in a Scots Scots language and tradition for which his Edinburgh background and education had not prepared him. Gordon later recorded feeling unease, even guilt, about his Scottishness. Just as his experience of an isolated childhood may have dictated the later concern of his fiction with the separate existence of the self and the problematic nature of human relationships, so his experience of an education whose principles and values were not altogether those of the nation in which he grew up may also have contrib-

uted to the sense of uncertainty and disconnection in much of his fiction. More directly, the nature of his early experience may have encouraged his permanent departure from Scotland at the age of twenty-two. After leaving school in 1957, he studied book design and typography briefly at Edinburgh College of Art and was then employed by the Edinburgh publishers Oliver and Boyd as a trainee from 1959 until 1962. He considered at the time that his departure for England in that year was only a temporary one, but the better opportunities and greater financial rewards offered by publishing houses in London contributed to his decision to remain there. He has lived in London ever since, working in several capacities, mostly as an editor, for a number of publishers, before becoming editorial director of Victor Gollancz in 1967.

Before leaving Scotland, Gordon founded (in 1961) and later helped to edit *New Saltire*, at the time the only literary magazine in Scotland. He later published under his own imprint pamphlets of poetry, including work by Hugh MacDiarmid and Ian Crichton Smith. Shortly after arriving in London, Gordon also began to publish his poems: the first collection of these, *Landscape any date*, appeared in 1963 and was followed by two other collections during the 1960s. During 1964 and 1965, he contributed to the *Scotsman* newspaper, a weekly London column about books and authors, and also began to publish his own short stories in various journals.

The first collection of these was *Pictures from an exhibition* (1970), in which are to be found many of Gordon's subsequently recurrent concerns. The "pictures from an exhibition" of the volume's title are short, partly objective, partly impressionistic and subjective accounts of various works of art: usually paintings, but sometimes photographs as well. Several of these pieces experiment with unusual, partly mimetic typographical layouts, often approximating a kind of concrete poetry, or perhaps "concrete prose." Though the pictures from an exhibition make up only a part of the collection, a similar interest in unusual, innovative techniques declares itself throughout. Underlying his experimentation is Gordon's recurrent concern with the nature and status of the imaginative "reality" created in fiction; with the feasibility of turning the visible, experienced world into words; and with the resulting relationship of word to world. "Construction," a story which seems to describe strange activities on a peculiar building, is typical of the collection in the way it flaunts its status as fiction, presenting events logically disconnected from each other and from any possibility of existence in the

real world: there are continual reminders that the story is itself a construction—an artifact, artificial and unreal. Throughout *Pictures from an exhibition*, the reader's expectation of a plausible fictional world is teased and undermined, and he is forced to consider that the events and people described have only a verbal existence. As in "The Scorpion," in which an author deliberately chooses to interest himself in the word "scorpion," dispassionately ignoring the threat of a scorpion, the dissociation of word and object, and the nature of writing and fiction, often become the subject of the fiction itself. Several pieces, such as "Balls Balance" and "Thirteen," fantastically dissociated from everyday reality and employing words as much as objects for their meanings, draw particular attention to themselves as linguistic artifacts rather than conventionally plausible stories, and participate in the sort of experimentation with typographical layout of the pictures from an exhibition.

Gordon has explained that he is "intrigued and fascinated by words, by sentences, paragraphs, pages as sounds, shapes, rhythms as well as senses"; he also quotes with approval a reviewer who remarked of fiction in general that "the only reality it posits is that of its own pages. There is no 'real world,' no specific context to which it refers, and it is subversive precisely because it denies the validity, or stability, of any context. In other words, it is itself. A novel is a novel is a novel." *Pictures from an exhibition* is an early example of Gordon's creation of fictions which do not directly invite the reader to enter an imagined world, but draw his attention instead to the raw materials and processes of construction involved in the creation of such fictional worlds. The major strength of the collection is that such potentially austere and self-reflexive concerns are often relieved by a witty, colloquial style of familiarly direct address to the reader. As John Mellors later remarked in a *Listener* review of some of his short stories, "Gordon is one of the few 'experimental' writers to preserve a sense of humour," and it is partly this sense of humor which helps to create a deceptively but attractively simple, commonsense tone for complex, introspective fictions. Gordon also shows in pieces such as "The Window" a particular talent for discovering apt images through which to present his phenomenological preoccupations.

Gordon's first novel, *The Umbrella Man* (1971), is a strange, slightly fantastic story of the relationship between the eponymous umbrella man, Felix, and an affectionate but insouciant woman, Delia. Felix remarks, "I had always, as far back as I could remember anyway, stared at people through glass, in the bus, in the train, in cinemas," and he first (and later frequently) sees Delia separated from him behind the window of her house. As in the earlier short story, "The Window," the image is appropriate to the theme of desired contact with a visible other, along with her enforced inaccessibility. Felix has an isolated existence, seeking but hopelessly failing to establish relationships and increasingly focusing his desires upon the woman he has seen behind the glass, with whom he believes there exists a mysterious connection. After several disturbing experiences, including the gruesome disposal of the corpse of Delia's baby, accidentally killed, he meets her and does establish a relationship, though one consummated only after she has returned from a holiday in Greece during which she has written him excruciatingly frank letters about her sexual activities.

Any such account of the novel does little to indicate its actual nature, for the occurrences it presents are disturbing not so much in themselves, but as a result of their manipulation of the reader's credulity and the frequent disruption of expectations. Of one episode in the novel a character remarks, "It had, in its entirety . . . an impossible dream-like quality. Where was the clear-cut monotony of reality?" This judgment and question could be aptly directed upon the novel as a whole. The strangeness of *The Umbrella Man* is a result partly of the oddity of the story it tells, but largely of the unusual methods employed by its author, extending the talent for technical experiment evident in his early short stories. The narrative of *The Umbrella Man* is presented from three separate but confusingly intermingling points of view: the first-person narratives of Felix and Delia themselves and an objective third-person narrative voice. Transitions from one perspective to another are not always easily recognized, particularly in the early pages of the novel. Not only is it difficult to establish who is narrating each section, it is (partly as a result) also difficult to assess the veracity of each account. As in the short stories, the distinction between what is subjective or imagined and what is objective or actual is one which becomes thoroughly blurred. The reader is obliged to wonder how much of the novel's action exists only in the imaginations of its characters, one of whom asks "Do all the people . . . outside this door even exist? Are they figments of my imagination, or are they real?" Does Felix really, for example, drop the corpse of Delia's baby down the funnel of a railway engine as it passes beneath a bridge? Do poppies really sprout from barren soil,

bloom, and wither all in a single day, or is this hallucination, magic, or fantasy? The novel cleverly raises, frustrates, and plays with such questions, often presenting improbable or incredible events only to make them seem largely natural a few pages later, or sometimes vice versa.

Not all of the mysteries and uncertainties of the novel are ever fully resolved, though the function of its confusions is clarified by the ingenuity of its conclusion. *The Umbrella Man* ends with the consummation of the relationship it has presented—final sections introduce a new first-person-plural narrative voice, the "we" of Felix and Delia. Such a conclusion exemplifies the operation and appropriateness of the strategy throughout: the novel concerns the difficulty of achieving a relationship between two disparate individuals, and this is enacted by the narrative's confusing alternation between conflicting, constantly interchanging perspectives, finally unified. The intelligence with which this technique is employed and sustained is impressive, especially in a first novel, though there are moments when cleverness strays toward sterility and tedium. For example, the repetitive presentation from several different points of view of successive descriptions of the same event, though undoubtedly in accord with the strategy of the novel, nevertheless sometimes seems distracting and superfluous.

Pictures from an exhibition and *The Umbrella Man* represent one of the two major directions in Gordon's writing—his commitment to experiment with the techniques and structures of narrative. His second novel, *About a marriage* (1972), introduces the other direction: a tendency toward autobiography, with an accompanying realistic style meticulously attentive to the details of everyday domestic life. The novel concerns Edward, "a young man with literary aspirations" who, like Gordon, has left Scotland and come to live and work in London. It is principally the story of his developing relationship with and eventual marriage to Ann, an artist and book illustrator. Gordon's wife, Margaret Anna Eastoe, whom he married in March 1964, is also an artist and illustrator of children's books; further details suggest that *About a marriage* may be a fictionalized autobiography. For example, Edward and Ann's children are born on the same dates (August 1968 and May 1970) as Gordon's sons, Callum and Gareth.

The story is told in Edward's first-person narrative and only at one moment flirts with the experimentation which characterizes Gordon's earlier work. Edward remarks the effect on his writing of a particularly troubled series of events: "Sometimes I really ceased to know whether something I had written was reportage or invention." There follows a fanciful, unrealistic section of writing, clearly Edward's fantasy rather than his usual straightforward, realistic presentation of the developing affair with Ann and of their initially difficult marriage.

Though straightforward by comparison with earlier work, this novel is nevertheless cleverly structured: every chapter begins with Edward's account of each of a series of weekly visits made to a local park with his two children and is followed by a retrospection upon an earlier stage of his relationship with Ann. By the final chapter, the series of reflections on the past has advanced to coincide with the present of Edward's visits to the park. Toward the end of the novel, Ann remarks to Edward, "You want to know me from the beginning again," and his narrative is clearly his attempt to do so—to associate the past development of their mutuality with the marriage which now exists. On his visits to the park, Edward repeatedly meets a slightly mysterious young mother to whom he is attracted; it turns out she too is called Ann, and the identity of her name with his wife's highlights Edward's rediscovery of Ann in view of his reflections on the history of their relationship. Like *The Umbrella Man*—though much more straightforward—*About a marriage* concerns the mystery and difficulty of reaching another person, communicating with her, and accommodating her needs and nature to one's own. The novel ends with Edward's acceptance of the satisfactory conclusion of this process: his reflections integrate past and present and result in the realization of his now happy marriage.

The principal strength of *About a marriage* is the closeness and intimacy with which Gordon presents through Edward's reflections the day-to-day banalities of an evolving relationship and marriage: tinned meals and lovemaking in a one-room apartment; Ann's fears of miscarriage; Edward's concern for her and for his side of their marriage; his simple experiences with his children in the park. Few of these events would be conventionally considered dramatic or significant enough to merit close attention in a novel. It is undoubtedly unusual—and potentially intriguing—to find such an extended account of the intimate details of developing relationship, marriage, and daily family life, but such a strength in *About a marriage* at least risks being a shortcoming. Though his autobiographical reflections are obviously significant for Edward, and perhaps for Gordon, they may be so specifically personal as to lack wider significance for their audi-

ence. The novelty and interest of *About a marriage* are genuine, and it is an engagingly intimate and tender narrative, but because this appeal is partly based on the unremarkable nature of the lives envisaged, the novel sometimes fails wholly to sustain the reader's attention.

Girl with red hair (1974) is an emphatic return to Gordon's experimental idiom. It is his most unconventional novel and the one which demonstrates most clearly the influence of the French writers of the *nouveau roman*, principally Michel Butor and Alain Robbe-Grillet, for whom Gordon has declared great admiration. Of the latter he remarks, "To me . . . he's probably the most influential and intriguing twentieth century fiction writer." *Girl with red hair* has several features obviously in common with the *nouveau roman*: like Robbe-Grillet's *Les Gommes* (1953), it is loosely a detective story, although one which, with its constant undermining of certainty about whether the events presented are "real" or wholly fictional, almost parodies the detective genre's concern with the discovery of the truth about some event or experience. Like *The Umbrella Man*, *Girl with red hair* often presents successively several different descriptions of the same event from alternative perspectives, and, like Robbe-Grillet's novel, concentrates on description of objects and the inanimate almost to the exclusion of attention to character or plot. In fact, the novel has no clear story or plot, or at any rate none that the reader can follow with any confidence. A murder may or may not have been committed; there are a number of possibly genuine suspects; the central persona of the novel may be connected with the possible murder either as investigator, suspect, or witness to events he may or may not have seen—or because he is imagining all or some of the events which the reader encounters. Even more perplexing, however, the central persona is identified as neither "I" nor "he," but as "you": *Girl with red hair* is written entirely in the second person, a technique which is most unusual, perhaps unique, in English literature, though Michel Butor's *La Modification* (1957) has attempted it in French.

The result of Gordon's employment of such strategies is an interesting but difficult novel: some acknowledgment of its difficulty appears in a further bizarre feature, the inclusion at the end of an index of characters and the pages on which they figure. This is actually helpful in sorting out some of the complexities of the novel. But perhaps part of the point of *Girl with red hair* is that not all of its complexities are intended to be reducible to coherence and simplicity. This aspect is best explained by one of Gordon's own comments about experimental fiction: "If in terms of its own originality—whatever uniqueness it possesses—the reader of a book has difficulty immediately in interpreting its territory, why shouldn't this be regarded as a challenge?" *Girl with red hair* is a novel whose difficulty is a deliberate part of its nature and subject. Like the *nouveau roman*, it is as much an act of criticism as of creation: it is an examination of the nature of fiction and a challenge to the reader's tacit assumption that novels present identifiable characters and coherence of developing plot and action. The continual use of "you" helps to direct the problems of the novel at the reader, urging him to reexamine the nature of his activity in reading, and to respond to this novel's demonstration of possible pleasures and perplexities other than those offered by conventional fiction.

Perhaps *Girl with red hair* succeeds too well as a challenging puzzle: the mysterious uncertainties of the *nouveau roman* are an engrossing entrapment of the reader, whereas Gordon's opaque involutions can be enervating and gratuitously impenetrable. But although he may be less dexterous than his mentors, *Girl with red hair* does deserve to be recognized as a rare, provocative attempt to extend into English literature some of the energy for experiment and innovation of the *nouveau roman*. As Valentine Cunningham pointed out in a *Times Literary Supplement* article, Gordon is one of few "serious anglicizers of French modes."

Farewell, fond dreams (1975) is a further collection of Gordon's short fictions, most of which had previously appeared in various journals. The material is similar in character to his first collection, *Pictures from an exhibition*. Several more pictures from an exhibition are included here, though these no longer concentrate on graphic art but now encompass films, dance, theater, and even newspapers. *Farewell, fond dreams*, however, also shows Gordon's development into new areas, particularly "faction"—stories which intermingle actual historical or contemporary events with imaginative embellishments of them. With Alex Hamilton, Gordon had edited *Factions*, an anthology of such material, in the previous year. *Farewell, fond dreams* contains "An attempt to make entertainment out of the war in Vietnam," a long piece which, as its title suggests, intersperses accounts of actual events in Vietnam with a humorous, imaginary correspondence between facetiously named political leaders of Britain and the United States. This faction, and much of the rest of *Farewell, fond dreams*, demonstrates Gordon's continued and developing interest in the relationships between the imaginary and the real; novel and life; word and world.

Reviewers of Gordon's short stories recognized the puzzling nature of the fiction which resulted from his examination of these relationships. Robert Nye acknowledged an uncertainty in approaching Gordon, adding that "His work is pitched against certainties." But several critics also shared Nye's further view that "Mr. Gordon is one of the liveliest, wittiest, and most perplexing young writers": though considered puzzling and sometimes difficult to read, Gordon has also often been seen as amusing, entertaining, and dexterous in undertaking his experiments. Christopher Ricks pointed to "a certain surrealistic expertise"; and Angus Wilson, finding Gordon "wonderfully entertaining," referred particularly to his "courage to use the language with such wit."

The fragmented, episodic structure of Gordon's next work, *100 scenes from married life* (1976), allows it to be described with only partial accuracy as a novel. It returns to the realistic idiom of *About a marriage*, continuing in a series of short passages the story of the marriage between Edward and Ann, now older and more settled. These accounts of their life together are interspersed with some humorously imagined vignettes of more famous relationships—Mr. and Mrs. Casanova and Romeo and Juliet. Wittily bathetic in themselves, these brief interludes also provide an ironic and oblique commentary on the experiences of Edward and Ann. As in *About a marriage*, a strong autobiographical streak seems to inform *100 scenes from married life*: Gordon's third child, his daughter Harriet, was born in February 1974, and Edward and Ann now also have a third infant. The resemblance between Edward and his author extends to their apparently sharing the same London telephone number. Unlike *About a marriage, 100 scenes from married life* is mostly related in the third person, but there are scenes in which Edward narrates, and it is perhaps a significant further indication of the partly autobiographical nature of the work that its pace and tension seem to increase in these sections. This is especially true of the novel's most engrossing episode, a brilliant and moving account of an unusually dramatic episode in family life, the sudden grave illness of a child. The rest of the novel shares the same simultaneous strength and weakness of *About a marriage*: it can be both unusually intriguing and often very moving, yet also potentially dull, to find the ordinary domestic life of a family—parents' visits at Christmas; days of office work for Edward; marital relations—rendered in such careful and tender detail. The risk of tedium is partly deflected by the inclusion of the amusing interludes; but a further problem is that it is disappointing to find, in a novel which ostensibly celebrates the maturing of a balanced relationship, that the narrative concentrates largely on Edward and is weighted by the predominance of his perspective. Ann is independently envisaged only briefly and in a way which subordinates her autonomy to her husband's point of view.

Continuing his interest in marriage, Gordon in his next work, *Enemies: a novel about friendship* (1977), presents and assesses the relationships within and between two families. Tom and his wife, Angela, inhabit a remote, unspecified European country, unaware of the threat of revolution their au pair has discovered to exist there. They are visited for a holiday by Tom's old friend, Frank, and his wife, Marjorie, who resumes an earlier affair with Tom. The examination of the relationships which exist and develop between these four adults relies on intimate accounts of the thoughts of each, and of the tensions which arise between them during hot, leisurely days of walks and encounters, and evenings spent enjoying with their children huge outdoor dinners in the twilight of Tom's splendid

garden. The families seem sequestered in their own languid world until, after the last night of the holiday, it is discovered that this garden has been wholly but mysteriously destroyed. This may possibly be the first gesture of the anticipated revolution, but the occurrence cannot be explained by any of the characters, and the novel concludes without elucidating it.

Enemies: a novel about friendship can be seen as an attempt by Gordon to synthesize the two previous (apparently almost opposite) strains in his fiction: toward experimentation on the one hand, and toward a realistically detailed and broadly psychological anatomy of human relationships on the other. Until its conclusion, the novel belongs largely to the latter category (though the mysterious nature of Tom's occupation, the isolation of the couples in a strange country, and some of the unspoken tensions which exist in their relationships contribute some of the dreamlike atmosphere of *The Umbrella Man*). With the cryptic disappearance of the garden, a much greater sense of oddity is suddenly introduced. The event can be partially rationalized as symbolic of the disappearance of innocence from the relationships the novel pre-

Dust jacket for Gordon's 1977 novel, which examines the relationships of four adults on holiday in a politically unstable country

sents, and of the discovery suggested by the title that at the heart of such human contacts there lurks the destructive enigma that friend and enemy are neither altogether antithetical nor dissociable categories. Or perhaps the mystery of the vanishing garden, like the mysteries of *Girl with red hair*, is deliberately irreducible: merely concurrent rather than necessarily analogous with the final mystery of the relationships between people. Once again, however, Gordon risks failure in seeking a strength for his fiction: for all its intriguing and powerful mystery, the unexplained suddenness of the garden episode at the end of the novel comes close to appearing a gratuitous and occult attempt to extend the significance of the fairly ordinary lives of the characters previously presented. The conclusion may seem disproportionately and arbitrarily attached to what has gone before; though this is jarringly effective, it is jarring nonetheless.

Reviewers responded to the risks and challenges involved in Gordon's strategies. Norman Shrapnel remarked in the *Guardian* "Giles Gordon has styled his theme in the boldest imaginable way. He mines for hidden meanings and teases out nuances." Shrapnel also pointed to one of the strengths earlier critics had praised in Gordon's short stories by adding that *Enemies* often has a strongly comic effect. Peter Ackroyd approved Gordon's methods to the extent of considering that the novel vindicated not only Gordon's technique, but fictional experimentation in general. He remarked in the *Spectator* that "Giles Gordon . . . has demonstrated that 'modern' fiction needn't be silly or laughable, that it can be written with the same expertise and considerably more subtly than the straight novel."

The themes of *The Illusionist* (1978), another collection of short stories, often resemble those of the material in *Pictures from an exhibition* and *Farewell, fond dreams*. Once again there is a concern with the diversity of subjective perspectives; with the nature of the relationship between illusion and reality; and concomitantly, with the nature of fiction and its connection with the real world. Such preoccupations sometimes emerge, as before, in strange fantasies such as the title story, "The Illusionist," about a magician who does not merely pretend to saw people in half; or "The jealous one," about a gunslinging cat; or "Letter to a Spanish painter," about a logically impossible yet apparently real correspondence with the surrealist Dali. Such ingenious, disturbing fantasies owe a debt, even more clearly than did Gordon's earlier work, both to Jorge Luis Borges's fiction of elaborate puzzles and

to Franz Kafka's talent for making inexplicable occurrences and alarming distortions in experience seem matter-of-fact and everyday. As in earlier collections, Gordon shows a careful precision in presenting the bizarre and fantastic: "Maestro," for example, is a meticulously elaborate account of mental breakdown occasioned by the horrifying complexity of a piece of classical music. There are also stories, such as "The sea," which further exhibit his talent for presenting weird occurrences or states of mind in colloquial language of apparent common sense. Robbe-Grillet's influence is still discernible in stories such as "Nineteen policemen searching the Solent shore," a complicated juggling of pattern and perspective.

Although Gordon's interest in the nature of fiction, illusion, and imagination informs *The Illusionist* as it did earlier works, the fantasies, tricky stories, and odd situations which result are now on the whole more carefully worked out and more engagingly written. Many of the pieces continue to depend upon ideas and reflexive cerebration about fiction itself, but such material is now less rawly presented and is elaborated more fully and deeply. Interestingly, there is also a clearer connection in this collection between Gordon's investigation of how the mind—source of imagination and illusion—can validly encounter the world beyond itself, and his anxiety about how the individual can reach other people. More clearly than before, behind much of the speculation of these stories there lies the lonely conviction that the mind is doomed by its nature and operation to be divorced from the world it envisages beyond itself, as well as from the other intelligences who inhabit that world. Of a view of London it is remarked, "there are eight million of us, more or less, in this city and none of us can know even by sight let alone in any more intimate way the rest of us. And each of us feels and is and has his separate, individual being."

This claustrophobic conviction that there is little possibility of release from the hermetic isolation of the self is responsible for the character of much of Gordon's work even beyond *The Illusionist*. It is a preoccupation which has perhaps persisted since Gordon first found in his reading some compensation for the loneliness of an isolating Scottish childhood, and which has come to affect variously *both* the experimental and the more conventional aspects of his writing. The two apparently disparate directions taken by Gordon's fiction are better appreciated if it is recognized that underlying each there is something of his concern with the mind's problematic attempt to reach beyond itself. His ex-

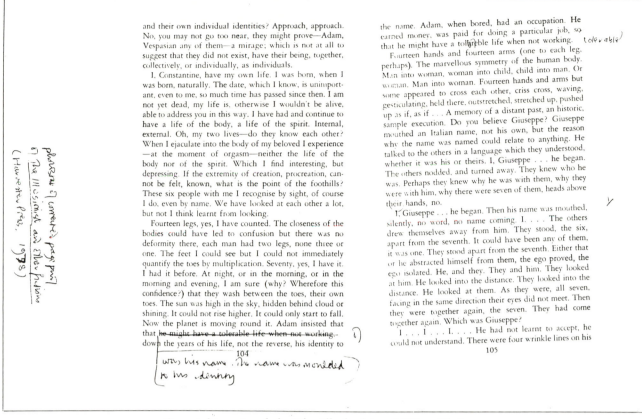

Corrected page proofs for The Illusionist and Other Fictions

perimental stories and novels, forming the greater part of his work, examine and challenge the way the mind employs fictions and illusions in encountering and assimilating experienced reality: the two semiautobiographical novels about marriage are concerned with the complex and difficult attempt to overcome the isolation of the self through human relationship and love. As Gordon remarks of his work, "There is a world out there, beyond the window. There is a world in my head. There is a world I try to pin down on paper. Three separate worlds that should bear some relation to one another." His comment encourages the view that his novels are various uses of the world pinned down on paper to examine the window which separates the mind and the world. The two more conventionally realistic novels, *About a marriage* and *100 scenes from married life*, analyze the nature and possibility of relationships with people beyond the glass, while his experiments explicitly assess the nature and extent of its translucence.

Although such a recognition of the underlying unity of Gordon's concerns enhances the appreciation of his fiction, it does not altogether exonerate

him from charges which might be legitimately advanced against both its experimental and its semiautobiographical phases. For all their intelligence and skill, each mode exhibits possible limitations in its author's imagination. The experimental work makes storytelling and imagination the subject rather than the process of fiction to an extent which can seem repetitive or sterile. It makes imagination the object of minute curiosity, rather than employing it as a powerful agent in transforming and assimilating experience: there is something self-indulgent and wearisomely introspective in fiction largely concerned with itself at the expense of responsibility for the world in which it is written. And *About a marriage* and *100 scenes from married life* seem so closely autobiographical that they might likewise be considered illustrative of an unhealthy predominance of self-consciousness and of Gordon's incapacity to achieve an imaginative transformation of his own experience into significant fiction.

There is justice in such charges, which have often been made by critics and reviewers of Gordon's work who do not share the largely favorable view of it suggested by Robert Nye, Peter Ackroyd;

and others whose remarks are quoted above. However, some of the critical doubts about the nature of Gordon's work are ones which might apply equally to any author with his interests or his commitment to taking risks, breaking new ground, and extending the scope of the novel's subject matter and self-awareness. Even if his work is not always wholly successful or appealing, it nevertheless deserves to be admired for the energy and originality of its experimentation, by no means all of which derives from the example of other writers such as Robbe-Grillet and the authors of the *nouveau roman*. In *Girl with red hair*, at least, the influence is clearly a strong one; but *Enemies: a novel about friendship* and *The Umbrella Man* show Gordon's capability for initiative and experimentation of a character wholly his own, and, particularly in the case of the latter, a powerful, technically adept novel results from his unusual balance of subjective narrative perspectives. Likewise, *100 scenes from married life* and *About a marriage,* perhaps actually by means of their auto-biographical character, are strikingly unusual attempts to enter into the banal, undramatic continuity of domestic family life—an area whose unpromising monotony has rarely encouraged its development as fiction. Peculiarly moving, surprising works result, discovering significant emotions in the ordinary current of quotidian existence, and often creating a feeling for the fascination of everyday life in all its deceptive simplicity.

Perhaps the greatest potential in Gordon's work lies in the possibility that he may incorporate the ingenuity of his experimental fiction with his more conventional talent for the anatomy of human relationships. Experiments reminding the reader that fiction is fiction are probably worthwhile, but there is a limit to how often they can be interestingly repeated, unless the insights they offer about the processes involved are reintegrated into imaginative writing itself. In this respect, *Enemies* is perhaps Gordon's most promising novel to date, as it contains the energetic fantasy and innovative vitality of his experimental fiction, as well as a more conventionally representational account of the couples' relationships. Unfortunately, as suggested above, *Enemies* is less than wholly successful in integrating these potentially disparate aspects. This is a shortcoming which also partly affects Gordon's most recent novel, *Ambrose's Vision: Sketches towards the creation of a cathedral* (1980). Significantly, Gordon chooses as one of his epigraphs a quotation from John Gower: "I undertoke/ . . . to make a boke/ Which stant between ernest and game." Like

Enemies, Ambrose's Vision seems not a synthesis of Gordon's two fictional modes, but a demonstration of a continued and unresolved double allegiance to them; on the one hand to an earnestness in treating the world beyond the book, examining in this novel the nature of human creativity and the monuments which result from it; and on the other to a playful exercise of virtuosity in creating a series of stylistically sophisticated, tenuously connected fantasies ("sketches" or "visions" of the bizarre developments in the career of a man apparently obsessed with building a cathedral). The two aspects seem to coexist rather than cohere, and the result is a rather unsatisfactory novel; one that is admirable for its fluent style and unusual imagination, but at times is simply uninteresting, trivial, or indulgent in the way these strengths are employed. Despite the dubious success of *Enemies* and *Ambrose's Vision*, however, it is possible that they show Gordon moving toward an ideal amalgam of his various talents. In his earlier career he seems to exercise alternately in separate

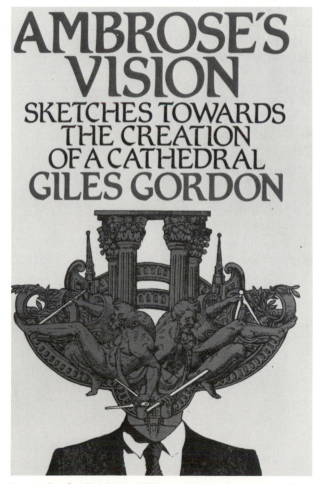

Dust jacket for Gordon's 1980 novel, an examination of the nature of creativity

works his faculties for earnestness and for game whereas the two most recent novels at least attempt to stand between the two in a single work. Gordon's greatest success may be still to come, and may follow from a more thoroughgoing and successful strategy of not only standing between the two aspects of his strength as a novelist, but of integrating them into works in which wit, ingenuity, technical dexterity, and playfulness are synthesized with his earnestness and insight in assessing relationships and their effects on the individual, the major theme of his more conventional fiction. At this stage in Gordon's career, it is possible only to suggest that if his talent for experiment can be employed not only for itself, but in further refining and developing the imaginative scope of his novels, he should continue and improve his position as one of the more interestingly diverse and intelligent of contemporary British novelists, and one of the few genuine innovators presently at work in the genre.

Gordon continues to live with his wife and three children in northwest London. In 1972, he gave up his work as a publisher and has since been director of Anthony Sheil Associates, a firm of literary agents responsible for the interests of many leading authors. During this time he has also continued his frequent contributions to various magazines, his occasional literary journalism, and his work as an editor, particularly of anthologies of short stories and of experimental writing. From 1965 to 1966 he was C. Day Lewis Fellow in Writing at King's College, University of London, and he was a member of the Arts Council Literature Panel from 1966 to 1970. He has been a member of the Society of Authors since 1971, and of the Writers' Guild of Great Britain since 1974. In 1980 he spent six months escaping everyday reality by traveling widely in Israel, India, and Nepal.

Other:

Factions, edited by Gordon and Alex Hamilton (London: Joseph, 1974);

Beyond the words: eleven writers in search of a new fiction, edited and with an introduction by Gordon (London: Hutchinson, 1975);

You Always Remember the First Time, edited by Gordon, Michael Bakewell, and B. S. Johnson (London: Quartet, 1975);

Members of the Jury, edited by Gordon and Dulan Barber (London: Wildwood House, 1976);

Prevailing Spirits: A Book of Scottish Ghost Stories, edited by Gordon (London: Hamilton, 1976);

A Book of Contemporary Nightmares, edited by Gordon (London: Joseph, 1977);

"The Thrie Estaitis: Scotch, Scots, Scottish," in *Jock Tamson's Bairns*, edited by Trevor Royle (London: Hamilton, 1977);

Modern Scottish Short Stories, edited by Gordon (London: Hamilton, 1978).

Contributors

Geoffrey Aggeler..*University of Utah*
Elizabeth Allen...*London, England*
Virginia Briggs..*University of Delaware*
Thomas O. Calhoun ....*University of Delaware*
Catherine Wells Cole..*Leatherhead, Surrey*
Peter Conradi ....*Kingston Polytechnic*
Thomas J. Cousineau ....*Washington College*
Patricia Craig ....*London, England*
Frank Crotzer..*University of Delaware*
Cathleen Donnelly ....*University of Delaware*
John Fletcher..*University of East Anglia*
Melvin J. Friedman ....*University of Wisconsin–Milwaukee*
Colin Greenland ....*North East London Polytechnic*
Kim D. Heine ....*Pennsylvania Institute of Technology*
G. M. Hyde...*University of East Anglia*
Fleda Brown Jackson ....*University of Arkansas*
Georgia L. Lambert..*London, England*
Morton P. Levitt..*Temple University*
Marla Levy ....*University of Delaware*
Patrick Lyons...*University of Glasgow*
David W. Madden..*California State University, Sacramento*
Priscilla Martin ....*University of East Anglia*
Barbara C. Millard..*La Salle College*
Rosemarie Mroz ....*University of Delaware*
Caryn McTighe Musil...*La Salle College*
S. J. Newman ....*University of Liverpool*
George O'Brien ....*Vassar College*
Malcolm Page..*Simon Fraser University*
Theresa M. Peter ....*University of Delaware*
Ellen Pifer ....*University of Delaware*
Lorna Sage ....*University of East Anglia*
Gerda Seaman..*California State University, Chico*
Sibyl L. Severance..*Pennsylvania State University*
Thomas J. Starr ....*University of Delaware*
Gerald Steel ....*King's College, London*
Randall Stevenson..*University of Edinburgh*
June Sturrock...*Simon Fraser University*
Sarah Turvey...............................*Roehampton Institute of Higher Education, London*
Gerard Werson ....*London, England*
T. Winnifrith ....*University of Warwick*